THE ESSENTIAL GUIDE TO MASTERING MADCAP FLARE

A Self-Teaching Assistant in Developing and Implementing Flare Projects

THE ESSENTIAL GUIDE TO MASTERING MADCAP FLARE

A Self-Teaching Assistant in Developing and Implementing Flare Projects

First Edition

C. T. Jones

Trademarks:

Central, Flare, and Mimic are all trademarks of MadCap Software. Other product names mentioned in this book may be trademarks or registered trademarks of their respective companies and the sole property of their respective owners and should be treated as such. Use of a term in this book should not be regarded as affecting the validity of any trademark or service mark.

Except for screen captures, this book was developed using MadCap Flare — 2021, MadCap Software Inc. Screen captures were created using Snagit 2022 (64-bit), TechSmith Corporation.

*This book is dedicated to my grandkids
Ivory-James and Carilena*

PREFACE

This book, by design, is for those beginning with Flare but want to get a running start. The book is a comprehensive coverage of the various tasks you'll encounter in developing and implementing Flare projects. You'll get an introduction to the primary UI components — including Editors, Windows, and Menus; as well as a guide to using the many tools and features designed to enhance the outputs and to make your job easier along the way.

Much consideration went into the content and the design of this book. From my own experiences of starting with Flare, I know the difficulty of quickly getting your arms around the many different tasks associated with Flare projects. There seem to be endless ways of doing each job, and there is no fixed sequence of doing things. While there is no lack of good Flare documentation — just knowing where to start, what to do next, and in what order can be a bit of a challenge.

My first goal was to determine everyday tasks that you would eventually need to perform. The next item would be to briefly present each task by describing the basic concept, the essential elements and offering application tips. The idea was to gather the topics that would be essential in helping you get right to work and become productive with Flare.

Finally, how you should approach this book is closely linked to its design. Not every task is covered — however, you will likely find the topics you want to focus on initially. You can read the book from cover to cover if you like, but that is unnecessary. If you are new to Flare, the tutorial at the start of each chapter is a great place to begin. As your project calls for a particular task, turn to the appropriate topic to find a quick introduction, followed by a step-by-step procedure. Using the Table of Contents, you can quickly find a particular task; and the Appendices offers other practical information. With the Glossary and Index, you can soon become familiar with Flare-specific and related terminology.

ABOUT THE AUTHOR

I received my Bachelor of Science in Electrical Engineering from Howard University and have made a career primarily as a Control Systems Engineer and Technical Instructor in the Automation Industry. I have also worked extensively as a Technical Writer in Software and IT Industries.

Early in my engineering career, I became profoundly aware of the challenging position of professional workers and their constant balancing act of performing daily tasks while keeping abreast of new and emerging technologies used in their work. This awareness and empathy led to my first book, creating a Technical Training Center, and the awakening of my great passion for adult education and learning.

Born of this new found passion was a dogged intent to learn to present complex technical topics in a method that anyone would understand. Eventually, a book design and development process would unfold, placing user tasks, presentation, quick learning, and retention at the center of my book development focus. This approach, reflected in my subsequent books, would give students and practicing users a straightforward self-teaching guide to the tools and technologies essential in their work.

My genuine passion for adult learning would evolve into technical writing and eventually working as a Technical Author. Several books later, including *"The Essential Guide to Mastering MadCap Flare,"* I still enjoy helping professionals learn the tools and technologies they need to carry out their work.

For several years now, I have been a freelance technical author. In this role, I have assisted companies with developing software products, training courses, tutorial course-ware, and user documentation.

– C.T. Jones –

ABOUT THIS BOOK

This book is organized to assist you in quickly getting to work with Flare! Key tasks like importing content, creating CSS and table stylesheets, creating and applying page layouts, defining variables and snippets, and using Flare editors are presented in a practical sequence. Each chapter contains a brief tutorial of Flare concepts that pertain to subsequent tasks. For easy viewing and understanding, each task is presented in a 2-page spread — on the left, a task is described under headings **Basic Concept**, **Essential Elements**, and **Application Tips**—on the right, the task is presented in a step-by-step format.

CHAPTER 1 — GETTING STARTED WITH FLARE

Chapter 1 introduces some essential elements of the Flare User Interface, including the primary menu operations and some essential tools. You are introduced to basic editors and how to configure some of the visual, operational, and workspace preferences for your convenience. Flare has many tools that, with a basic introduction, you'll be off to a new experience and in no time ready to work with projects.

CHAPTER 2 — CREATING THE FLARE PROJECT

Chapter 2 outlines ways to create a new project, using factory and custom templates or using one of many content import options, like MS Word or Adobe FrameMaker. You are introduced to the processes for importing content, starting with pre-import tasks that help produce a smooth and successful import and minimize post-import tasks of cleanup and managing and organizing newly created topics.

CHAPTER 3 — STYLESHEETS, MEDIUMS, AND MEDIA QUERIES

Chapter 3 introduces basic principles of working with Flare stylesheets, mediums, and media queries. Stylesheets will be at the core of all your Flare work and reflected in each of your target outputs. Understanding how to develop a robust stylesheet for use by a few users or a large team will be essential to creating a consistent and stylized appearance in all of your online and printed outputs.

CHAPTER 4 — TABLE STYLESHEETS AND STANDARD TABLE STYLES

Like most Flare operations, there are many ways to create, edit, and manage the appearance of tables. Chapter 4 examines how you can set table appearances using "standard" CSS tags or the Table Stylesheet Editor — a vital tool for consistently defining the appearance and position of every table in your document. Whether using CSS or table stylesheets, you can define every table characteristic.

CHAPTER 5 — FLARE VARIABLES AND SNIPPETS

Chapter 5 introduces basic concepts for developing and using variables and snippets. You will learn to use the Variables Editor to create single- and multi-definition variables and how to access and insert these user variables and Flare system and heading variables in your project. Also, you learn how with snippets, you can avoid rewriting short chunks of content that repeat throughout your project.

CHAPTER 6 — PAGE LAYOUTS AND TEMPLATE PAGES

Chapter 6 introduces the topics of page layouts and template pages. As these two elements lay the essential foundation for the design and flow of your printed and online pages, the work of page layouts and template pages are as important as developing a robust and flexible stylesheet.

CHAPTER 7 — WORKING WITH FLARE TOPICS

Chapter 7 introduces topics. Once you have imported your source content, topics will represent the primary way in which you interact with text content. Working with topics is quite extensive, and coverage in this book is only an introduction to some of the many Flare tools that allow the insertion of various elements and affect the behavior of portions of your content.

CHAPTER 8 — WORKING WITH FLARE TOC OUTLINES

Chapter 8 introduces the Flare TOC outline. The TOC file is either created manually or generated automatically based on the chapter and topic structure of an imported book or document. You'll learn in this chapter how the Flare TOC file ultimately serves as the outline from which the sequential order of your print target is created or as the tree-structured arrangement of books and pages in an online output with a side- or tripane-navigation.

CHAPTER 9 — DEVELOPING AND IMPLEMENTING FLARE PROJECTS

Chapter 9 pulls together the things you will have learned about working to develop and implement a project — it presents a systems approach to the work. We'll look at some of the many tools used to enhance a project and examine a project that can support a few writers managing a few documents or multiple writers working with several documents. Finally, a basic introduction to using GIT as a tool for your project's source control is presented.

CHAPTER 10 — WORKING WITH PRINT AND ONLINE TARGETS

Chapter 10 introduces the two most commonly used targets — the PDF print-based and the HTML5 online. You'll learn to create the target, specify its parameters, build and generate the output, and, where necessary, publish the output to a destination where others can access it. At this point, you'll be well on your way to confidently working with these and other target types.

CHAPTER 11 — BASIC DESIGN PRINCIPLES AND GUIDELINES

Chapter 11 presents some basic page layout and content design guidelines and practices. A goal is to employ these practices to develop aesthetically pleasing content and enhance the clarity of meaning through structure and presentation. Page layout considerations include design elements like grids, white space, borders, and rules. Similarly, content development considers design elements like structured content elements, development of titles, summaries, section headings, topic sentences, and paragraphs, ordered and unordered lists, topic symmetry, and parallelism.

CHAPTER 12 — BASIC GUIDELINES FOR MOVING TO ONLINE

Chapter 12 introduces basic design practices and considerations for moving content online. The intent is to assist you in developing content that is well organized, easily consumed, enhances user experience, adapts to the user device, and all in an aesthetically pleasing presentation. Also presented are the side, top, and tripane navigation methods and Flare online content elements like template pages, breadcrumbs, responsive layouts, drop-down text, expanding text, concept topics, and related topics.

CONTENTS

    © The Essential Guide to Mastering MadCap Flare

CHAPTER 1

GETTING STARTED WITH FLARE

FLARE MAIN MENU OPERATIONS

Flare main menus include *File*, *Home*, *Insert*, *View*, *Project*, *Analysis*, *Review*, *Tools*, *Table*, *Window*, and *Help*. This section briefly introduces the operations and principal uses of each menu.

THE FILE MENU

The Flare **File** menu supports various ways to create, open, and save new and existing Flare projects and files. Creating projects can involve using one of several wizards that guide you through the content import process from different source editors. The result will be the creation of a project containing topic files, image files, and other files generated during the import.

THE HOME MENU

The Flare **Home** menu contains standard editor-like tools such as a **Clipboard** toolset and the **Font** and **Paragraph** toolsets, which support formatting and alignment for text and paragraphs. These inline formatting tools, of course, are not the preferred editing methods.

The **Home** menu also has a **Styles** toolset that supports styles access from a **Style** drop-down pane and **Style Window** for style editing and creation; a **Formatting Window** for visually inspecting and, in some cases, editing paragraph styles and properties. A **Create Style Class** window supports the creation of new style selectors using an ad hoc method based on selected text. The **Responsive Layout** pane lets you create single-row grids in your content that support responsive outputs in which the structure of the content shifts, depending on the screen display size.

Finally, the **Home** menu contains **Find and Replace** tools that support whole project searches for text and elements; and a **Properties** toolset for viewing properties associated with any selected item.

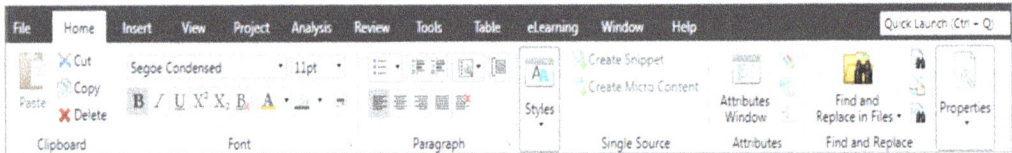

Figure 1-1. Flare Home Menu.

THE INSERT MENU

The **Insert** menu operations provide primary support tools for inserting various elements into Flare topics. You can insert images and multimedia objects like Flash or QuickTime movies, YouTube videos, PowerPoint slide shows, or insert direct screen capture using a screen capture utility from the **Multimedia** toolset. The **Links** toolset allows the insertion of hyperlinks, cross-references, and bookmarks. You can insert tables using the **Insert Table** dialog or the Rows-Columns drop-down palette.

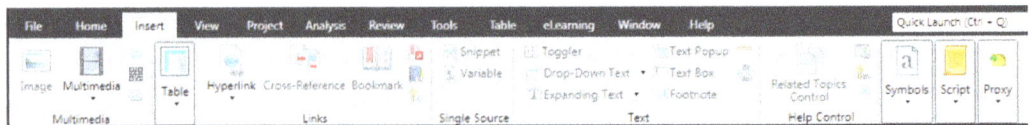

Figure 1-2. Flare Insert Menu.

THE VIEW MENU

The **View** menu provides a central place where you can display key Flare elements — like the Content Explorer, Project Organizer, Flare Start Page, Build, Message, File List, and Concept Windows; and panes like Page Frame Contents and MadCap Central Pane. These windows, which you can open according to your work preference and as needed, are not toggled off from the View menu. Each window must be closed from within the window. You can also save your workspace, including any open windows, so that you can recall it later.

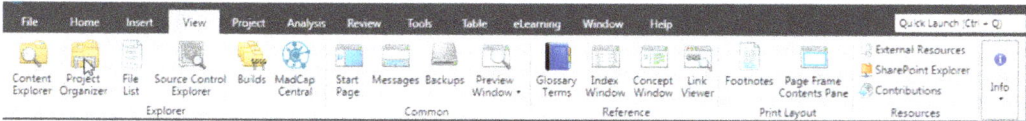

Figure 1-3. Flare View Menu

THE PROJECT MENU

The **Project** menu operations provide a central place to create a new file of any Flare supported file type. You can create a topic, page layout, snippet, or stylesheet; or import new source content using applications like Word, FrameMaker, Excel, or an existing Flare project. The Project menu also contains a toolset for building, viewing, and publishing the Primary or select targets, zipping and exporting the project, and viewing and setting general project properties.

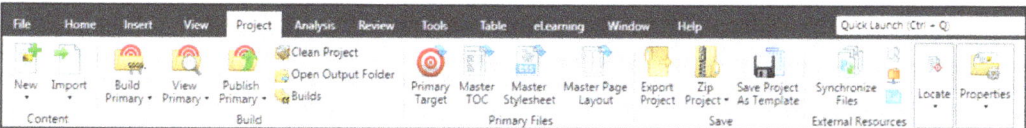

Figure 1-4. Flare Project Menu.

THE ANALYSIS MENU

The **Analysis** menu provides quick access to project analysis and reporting tools — tools that assist you in determining the relative health and status of your project. Easily find broken links, Undefined Items in your projects, such as images and topics, as well as Used Items like variables, conditional tags, and bookmarks. In addition to finding problems, tools like the Suggestions menu allow you to specify many items and auto-suggestions for which Flare can assist you while developing your project.

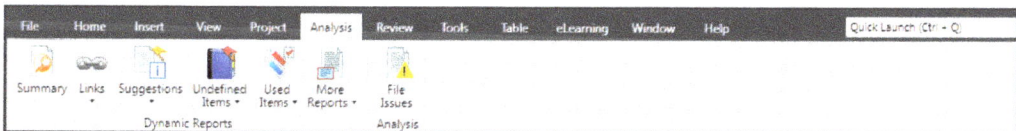

Figure 1-5. Flare Analysis Menu.

THE REVIEW MENU

The **Review** menu provides standard tools for tracking and reviewing changes, with tools to *show/hide changes*, *accept/reject changes* or *accept all; changes/reject all changes*; as well as tools for inserting and deleting content annotations. Tools are also available for managing a content review process, with the ability to *send for review*, *import review package*, and *open review packages*. Finally, the menu offers a Review Options dialog, with several tabs for setting various parameters and rules for Review, including the Flare application for the Interface, Language, Source Control, Spelling, and others.

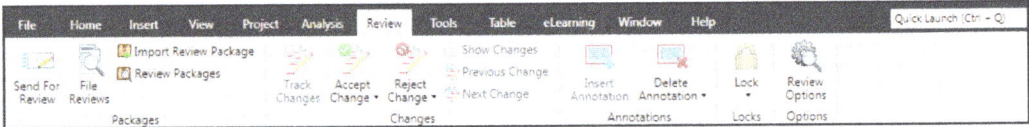

Figure 1-6. Flare Review Menu.

THE TOOLS MENU

The **Tools** menu provides several topic and project support tools, including the following:

a. A user-edited dictionary of commonly misspelled words.

b. A Spell Checker with several options for including content for spell-check.

c. A Thesaurus and Text Analyzer.

d. A Hyphenation Window for defining hyphenation rules.

e. A tool for managing templates files and folders.

f. A Cross-Reference Update tool for refreshing cross-references.

g. A tool for launching other installed MadCap applications.

h. Tools for macro record and playback and file management.

Figure 1-7. Flare Tools Menu.

THE SOURCE CONTROL MENU

The **Source Control** menu displays only if the open project is bound to a Source Control server like the GitLab server. Several tools are available to assist you with interacting with the project files that are local to your device and those on a remote server. You can view the **Pending Changes** list of files to which you have made recent changes. You can then **Commit All** or **Commit** one or more selected files in the list. To commit is to accept the changes that you have made and thereby "commit" them to the local repository (on your machine). After files are committed to the local storage, you can **Push** them to the remote repository (server).

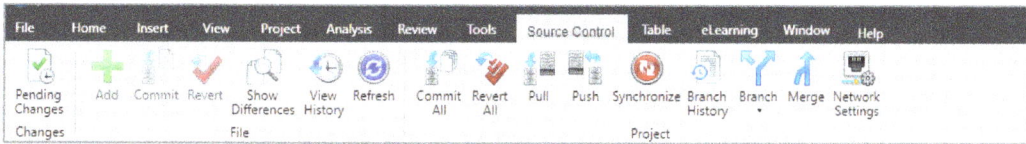

Figure 1-8. Flare Source Control Menu-Git Repository.

THE TABLE MENU

The **Table** menu supports several table operations, such as insert a new table to a topic, delete an existing table, and table operations like inserting rows and columns and merging and splitting table cells. This menu also supports converting selected text to a table, converting a table to text, applying a table stylesheet to an existing table, and inserting a caption above or below a table.

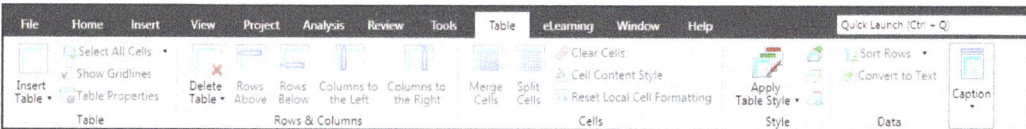

Figure 1-9. Flare Table Menu.

THE WINDOW MENU

The **Window** menu has a variety of tools designed to assist you with opening, pinning, docking, and closing, as well as saving the current desktop arrangement of your open project windows and panes. Some tools allow you to reload and reset the layout to the factory default.

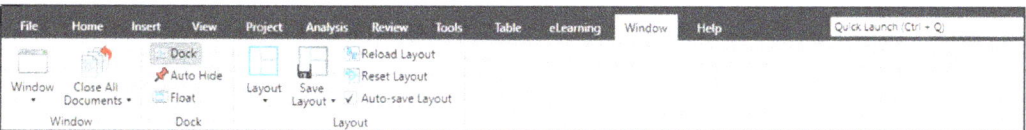

Figure 1-10. Flare Window Menu.

THE ELEARNING MENU

The **eLearning** menu provides a powerful set of tools for developing eLearning content elements and outputs. From this menu, you can access tools and elements for entering questions, including multiple choice and multiple response, as well as tools to create test and manage test results. This powerful feature lets you incorporate eLearning in your projects or export for integration in external applications.

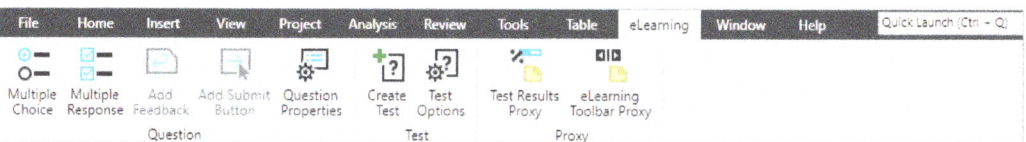

Figure 1-11. Flare eLearning Menu.

KEY FLARE EDITORS, WINDOWS, AND PANES

An essential part of quickly getting to know Flare is learning the basic operations and uses of several key Flare windows and editors. This section briefly introduces you to the Content Explorer, the Project Organizer, and a few other Flare tools that you will soon get to know well.

THE FLARE CONTENT EXPLORER

The *Content Explorer* is a primary Flare UI element. This folder structure is where you would place various content components of your project, like topic and snippet files, micro-content, image and multimedia files, and different content resources files like Stylesheets, Page Layouts, Table Stylesheets, and Template Pages. These latter files all enhance the appearance and arrangement of your online and print-based outputs. By default, this is where Flare places imported content or new content elements.

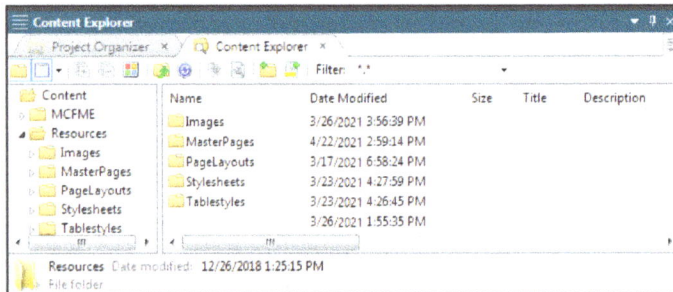

Figure 1-12. Flare Content Explorer.

THE FLARE PROJECT ORGANIZER

The *Project Organizer* is a primary Flare Explorer-like UI folder component, which organizes the non-content resources associated with your entire project. This folder structure provides access to supplemental content components, and tools to assist in the production, control, management, publishing, and maintenance of online and print outputs. Some of the items include TOC files, Variable files, Output Targets, Skin files, Reports, Index and Glossary tools, and Conditional Text files.

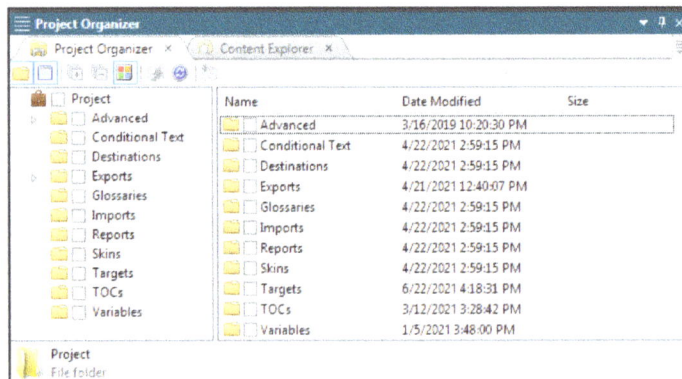

Figure 1-13. Flare Project Organizer.

Table 1-1. Other Flare Windows, Editors, and Panes

Flare Element	Brief Description
Page Layout Editor	Use this Flare editor to define page layouts for the different divisions of a book or document. Page layouts define page specifications and control how content is arranged and flowed onto the pages of each section of a book or document.
Table Stylesheet Editor	Use this Flare editor to define a set of styles to collectively control the appearance and positioning of tables, which you can apply to existing or new tables.
Topic Editor	Use this Flare editor to create, format, and edit your content, whether for online or print output. The Topic Editor's XML Editor view provides a WYSIWYG view as in Word or FrameMaker; the Text Editor view shows the HTML code of the same topic.
TOC Editor	Use this Flare editor to manually create tables of content (TOC) by adding and editing TOC entries and creating links to topics, movies, external files, other TOCs, browse sequences, or other Help systems.
Variables Editor	Use this editor to create and edit the definitions of variables (non-formatted data), like Product Name, Software Version, and Release Date, or any values that may change frequently. Variable sets (files) contain single or multi-definition variables.
Auto-Index Editor	Use this editor, associated with the Flare auto-indexing feature, to add index phrases and entries to an auto-index file. When you build the output, Flare scans the project topics and, based on the auto-index file, adds words it finds to the generated index and creates the required links to topics in which the word is found.
Alias Editor	Use this Flare editor to create and assign topic identifiers in a context-sensitive help system. You will subsequently map each identifier to a specific UI element like a dialog or window. Each identifier links the UI element to a particular topic that is called and displayed by the application code when the user focuses on that UI element.
Skin Editor	Use this editor to create skins that use TSide Navigation, Top Navigation or Tripane Navigation in online outputs. The user-friendly interface for editing skins consists of several tabs, displaying settings relevant to the selected skin type and using a fill-in-the-blanks approach for each configurable skin component.
Build Window	Use this window to build targets. It shows the **Status**, **Build Progress**, and **Compile Status** for one or more targets. You may simultaneously build multiple targets, and when a build is done, you may **View Output**, **Open Build Log**, or **Rebuild Target**.
Cascading Stylesheet Editor	Use this Flare CSS editor in the **Simplified View** or **Advanced View** to view, add, and modify CSS style selectors and style properties.
Source Control Explorer	A Flare explorer-like tool in which added, modified, or deleted (**Pending Changes**) project files, are listed and can be managed — for example, you may Commit, Revert, Push, or Pull files between a local and remote repository.

FLARE HELP OPERATIONS

The **Help** menu provides access to Flare's Online Help tools and Context-Sensitive Help (CSH). You would also access Flare PDF books, Videos tutorials, and Help Community from this menu.

Figure 1-14. Flare Help Toolbar.

ONLINE HELP

The *Online Help* system, the official online website for Flare, is opened from the main toolbar by clicking the **Open Help** button. This portal is where complete online help information and search access for Flare users reside. This is also the place I come when working and need to quickly find an answer to a specific Flare question. There are several ways to find what you're looking for, including the navigation menu and the quick access buttons to frequently used topics, for example, the Getting Started Guide, Getting Started Video, or Getting Started Tutorial. I find that the Search Bar works best for me.

DYNAMIC HELP

The *Dynamic Help* system is the Flare equivalent of Context-Sensitive Help (CSH). Dynamic Help, which you can trigger from the main toolbar, opens in an inline window alongside any other open windows. This instance of Help is a handy tool as you are initially starting with Flare. As you navigate between open windows and panes or open new windows, utilities, or dialogs, the Dynamic Help opens to the main help topic associated with the window or tool currently in focus. From that point, you can drill down as necessary. The topic remains open until another interface element comes into focus.

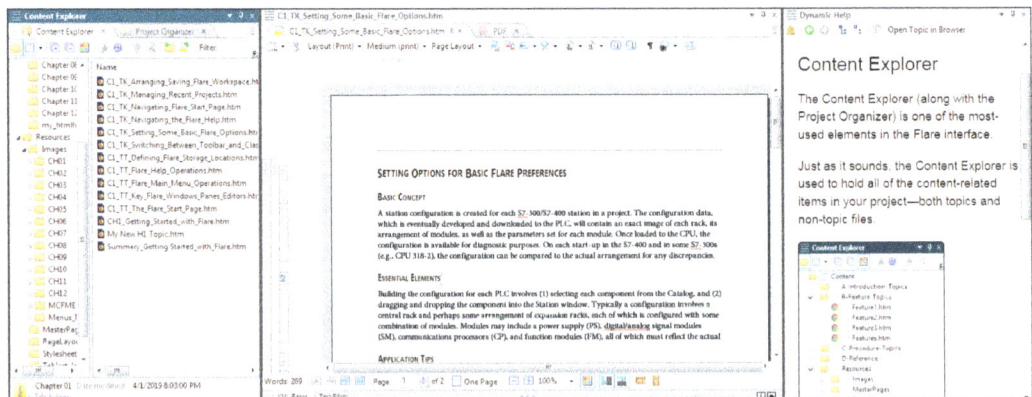

Figure 1-15. Flare Dynamic Help System Turned On.

You can undock the window to resize it for better viewing, or click on the window title bar and select **Standard Tabs** (Top). In this fashion, any windows you open are displayed in a tabbed view adjacent to the Dynamic Help window, allowing easier viewing.

The **View** menu is an excellent place to take Flare's Dynamic Help for a spin. Use the toolbar to click on some explorer-type windows like Content Explorer, Project Organizer, and SharePoint Explorer.

PDF GUIDES

The Flare PDFs Help option offers access to an extensive library of PDF Documents, User Guides, for example, for Images, Tables, Targets, and Cheat Sheets, which are brief 1-2 page documents on particular topics. Using PDFs may be an option for you — or perhaps an additional option if you learn by absorbing the details. I, for example, like to learn by doing and then by delving deeper into the written details when I'm looking for specific answers. In this way, I simultaneously learn how to navigate and perform certain operations, and at the same time, get deep-level answers to questions.

Each Flare feature has many aspects, and it seems that there is a myriad of ways to do things. If, for example, you want to learn all about Table Stylesheets, Page Layouts, or Styles, you can watch the appropriate video. Still, to get the in-depth details, you can reach for the associated PDFs, which are excellent in this regard!

VIDEOS

If you have more of a visual learning style, then perhaps the Flare video and webinar recordings library will assist you in getting to know Flare better or learn specific topics. A variety of videos are available, from those that provide a quick introduction to getting started to those that offer a series of videos that to allow you to go deeper with specific subjects. If this is one of your learning styles, the *Getting Started* video is an excellent place to start!

KEY LOCATIONS FOR FLARE PROJECT USAGE

Before starting with your Flare import and other related tasks, it's a good practice to have considered or already have created the folders to be used by your project. For example, you will need to decide where users will store Flare projects and your target outputs. To avoid long paths, consider creating your folder structure from a root directory.

- Create a default folder for Flare Projects — for example, C:\FlareProjects

- Create a folder for Flare Target Outputs — for example, C:\FlareOutputs

- Create a folder for Flare File and Project Templates — for example, C:\MyFlareTemplates

> **NOTE:** A point to consider here is whether you want the locations for the target outputs and project templates to be included inside or outside the project folder.

DEFAULT PROJECT PATH

The Flare default project location is your **Documents > My Projects** folder. This location is where Flare places each newly created project unless you specify otherwise. The Project folder field is automatically populated with the default path when you attempt to create a new project. At this time, you can keep this project path or designate a new location for storing the project.

Once specified, the new location becomes the new default location until changed. You should define the project folder locally instead of a remote and close to a root folder on your PC. This latter approach avoids the problem of long paths in some operating systems.

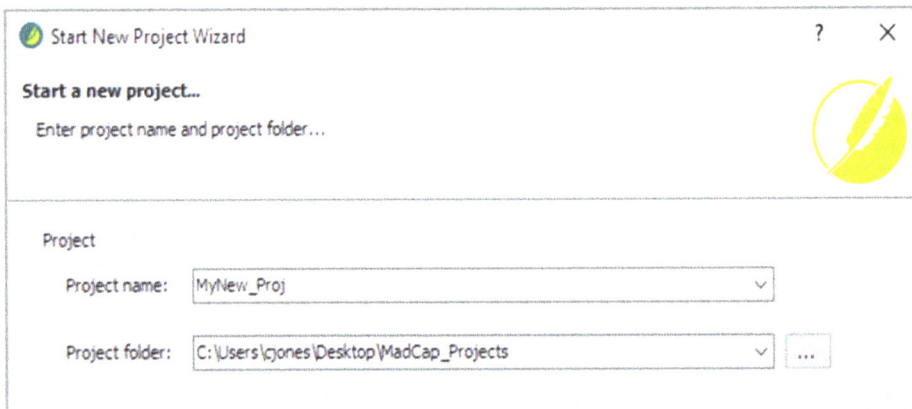

Figure 1-16. Specifying the New Project Path.

DEFAULT OUTPUT PATH

The default Output folder is where Flare places each generated output target unless you specify another location. You designate the **Output Folder** on the **General** tab of the target file. If you leave this parameter set for the default, the folder will be located in your current Flare project folder and named Output. When generated, Flare places the output of each target in the Output folder, inside a subfolder having a name based on the target file name.

For example, if the target file has the name MCME_PDF, Flare places the PDF output file in a sub-folder named MCME_PDF, located in the designated Output folder (Flare_Outputs). The use of an additional subfolder considers that Flare will place other targets in this Output folder. In this example, the target file, designated on the **General** tab, is named MCME.

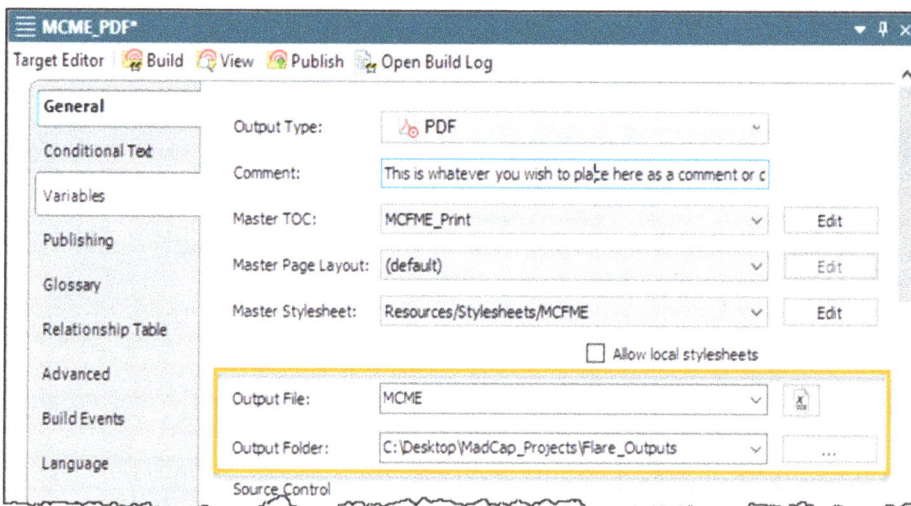

Figure 1-17. Specifying the Output Path.

EXTERNAL RESOURCES

The use of External Resources folders is a way of working with and maintaining access to files that are outside of your project. Typically this feature provides access to files that you expect will change over time and that you want to have synchronized with your projects. This scenario is typical with files like splash pages, UI images, logos, or PDFs that you offer as downloads.

You may specify External Resources folders for any local or network files to which you have access. The folders will be available to all of your Flare projects. Once you identify the folders, files can be copied to your project and mapped to be synchronized and updated whenever changes occur.

TEMPLATE FOLDERS

When it comes to saving certain of your files as templates, you will have the option to specify a template folder that you have already created. This location can be a local or remote drive or even a SharePoint or cloud drive. You need only make a single template folder to manage your template files, as Flare will generate appropriate sub-folders. A new template folder is created from the **Tool** menu, using **Tools** > **Manage Templates**.

When you save an existing file as a template, such as a topic file, variable file, or page layout file, and select your designated template folder, Flare generates a subfolder inside this folder, based on the file type. Topic templates, for example, are placed in a subfolder called **Content**; page layout templates are placed in a subfolder called **PageLayouts**, and Variables are placed in a subfolder called **VariableSets**. Your templates are then accessible to users when they create new files from templates.

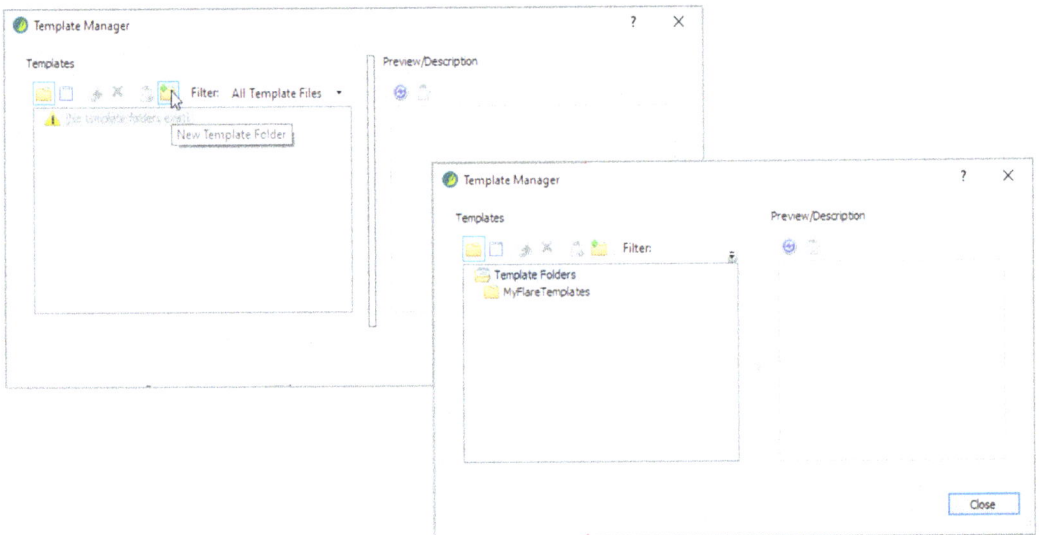

Figure 1-18. Template Manager—Add Template Folder.

SUMMARY ON GETTING STARTED WITH FLARE

In your initial work of preparing to move to Flare, proper planning is essential for good organization and project outcome. Such planning considers file and folder naming conventions, storage locations, and organizational structure for projects, templates, targets, and outputs. Your planning for these and other items will enhance your complete project work. In addition to these preliminary tasks, familiarity with Flare features, editors, and tools make the transition much more manageable.

Topics covered in this chapter have presented an introductory overview of crucial menu operations, windows, panes, and editors that you will encounter in your day-to-day work with Flare. Once you have become somewhat familiar with navigating in Flare and performed some of the tasks outlined in this chapter, you'll be prepared to proceed to creating your project and developing content.

CHECKLIST: GETTING STARTED WITH FLARE

- *As you get started, spend time navigating the main menus and exploring the various windows, panes, dialogs, and editors. Flare has many tools that will take time getting to know.*

- *If you're working primarily with existing projects, you may use the **File** menu **Open** command or click the toolbar button to browse and examine Flare folders, files, and projects.*

- *As you will be developing Flare projects, a first step is to create the folder where you want Flare to place new projects. The default project folder is "MadCap_Projects."*

- *You may also wish to create a separate folder to store Flare templates you make, including topic templates, project templates, and any other file templates. When you create a new template, the folder will be accessible for storage. Other users will also be able to access the folder when they wish to apply a custom template to a file or project they are creating.*

- *Use **File** > **Options** to open the dialog to specify global application preferences for your Flare work environment.*

- *Use the **View** menu to open windows with which you will most likely use. Move the windows around and arrange them using tabbed and accordion layouts to suit your working preference.*

- *Use the **Window** ribbon to practice naming, saving, and reloading as many layouts as desired.*

- *Explore Flare's **Dynamic Help** as well as **Online Help**. There are a variety of resources and options for learning about Flare in a way that best suits your style of learning.*

ARRANGING, SAVING, AND RELOADING THE FLARE WORKSPACE

BASIC CONCEPT

You can arrange your Flare workspace in many ways to best suit your preference and working convenience. There are many ways to place the windows and panes to your liking. You can undock windows and panes, resize and reposition them as desired, and save as many arrangements as you need, and recall them later.

ESSENTIAL ELEMENTS

The left-side of the workspace is where Flare usually places the **Content Explorer**, **Project Organizer**, the **Source Control Explorer**, and other explorer-type windows. These windows can be placed in a fixed arrangement using **Accordion Tabs** stacked at the bottom of the left side of the workspace area or as **Standard Tabs** across the top or bottom of the area. The right side of the workspace is where Flare places editors like the **XML Editor** and **Page Layout Editor**. These editors with the open files can also be placed in a fixed arrangement using **Standard Tabs** across the workspace top or bottom.

In addition to the fixed arrangements in which you can configure your workspace areas, you can also **Float** and **Dock** windows and panes. With windows undocked, you can then resize and reposition them as desired and leave them floating or re-dock when done. You can save arrangements, by name, to recall later once you have achieved the preferred layout, even with undocked windows.

APPLICATION TIPS

When working in the Topic Editor, use the **View** menu to disable the **Status Bar**, **Info Bar**, or both to get more working areas. It is also much easier to work with Flare using dual monitors.

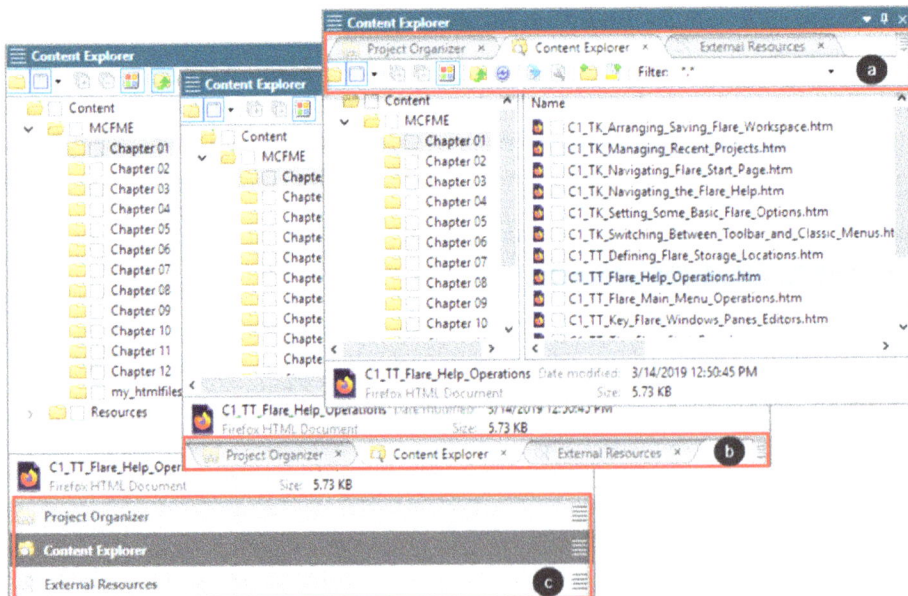

Figure 1-19. Fixed Window Arrangements **a)** Standard Tabs Top, **b)** Standard Tabs Bottom, and **c)** Accordion.

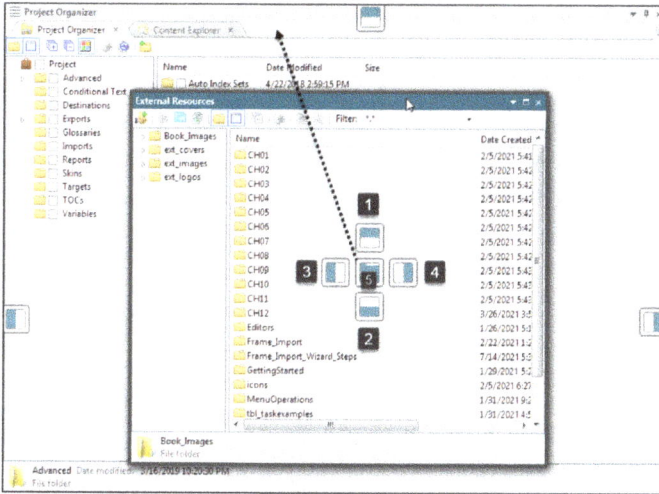

Figure 1-20. Placing Un-Docked External Resources folder as a Tabbed Position.

QUICK STEPS: ARRANGING, SAVING, AND RELOADING THE FLARE WORKSPACE

STEP	ACTION
1	Use the **View** menu to display a specific window that you want to open if it is not already open. For example, **View** > **Start Page** , **View** > **External Resources Window**, or **View** > **Source Control Explorer**.
2	To undock a window or tab, use the right-click on the window or tab title bar or click the drop-down arrow on the top right corner of the title bar and select **Float**. You can click and drag the window or tab title bar.
3	To re-position floating or un-docked window, click and grab the window title bar and then drag and drop the window, onto one of the animated position indicator icons. Do one of the following: **a)** To reposition the window in accordion style at the top of the current frame, drop the window onto the position indicator referenced by the number **1**, in Figure 1-20. **b)** To reposition the window in accordion style at the bottom of the current frame, drop the window onto the position indicator referenced by the number **2**, in Figure 1-20. The result is seen in c) of Figure 1-19. **c)** To reposition the window as a panel on the left-side of the current frame, drop the window onto the position indicator referenced by the number **3**, in Figure 1-20. **d)** To reposition the window as a panel on the right-side of the current frame, drop the window onto the position indicator referenced by the number **4**, Figure 1-20.
4	In this example, the **External Resources** Window was dropped onto the tab position indicator, referenced by the number **5**, in Figure 1-20. The result is shown in a) of Figure 1-19.
5	From the **Window** ribbon, udo any of the following: **a)** use the **Save Layout** drop-down arrow to save the current layout file. **b)** use the **Reload Layout** drop-down arrow to reload the last loaded layout. **c)** enable **Auto-save Layout** to automatically save your layout on closing Flare.

NAVIGATING THE FLARE USER INTERFACE

BASIC CONCEPT

The Flare User Interface comprises several file explorers, editors, various tools, and utilities that assist you with your project development. With time, yet before very long, you will be navigating the UI with ease. The first hurdle of UI navigation is knowing where things are and the purpose of each element. Of course, the next step would be learning to use each explorer, editor, window, and tool. As each new UI element is introduced, in this book, how to navigate the element is covered first.

ESSENTIAL ELEMENTS

As you get started with Flare, you'll likely spend a great deal of time working with the **File** ribbon — especially if you are importing content. You can initiate Import Wizards and add new files to the project from this menu. Your first work will likely be with the **Stylesheet Editor** as you develop and refine your stylesheet. Once you import content or begin creating new content, you will frequently use the **Home**, **Insert**, and **Table** ribbons in working with topics. For most writers, the operations on each ribbon should be familiar. They include many toolsets you commonly work with to edit text and tables and insert elements like cross-references, images, and hyperlinks into the content.

APPLICATION TIPS

How you initially interact with Flare will largely depend on whether your work is with a team or project where Flare is already implemented. In either case, however, you will still want to, as quickly as possible, become familiar with the essential UI menus and operations. These key components will undoubtedly include the **Content Explorer**, **Project Organizer**, **Stylesheet Editor**, the **XML Editor**, and the **Target Editor** print and online parameters.

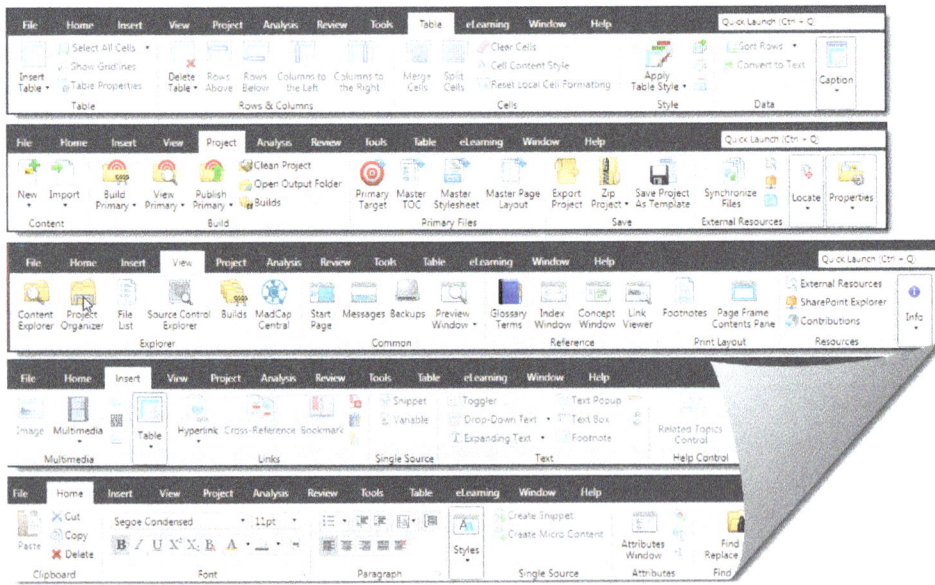

Figure 1-21. Flare UI Ribbons —Home, Insert, View, Project, and Table.

QUICK STEPS: QUICK TOUR ON NAVIGATING THE FLARE USER INTERFACE

STEP	ACTION
1	**File**: Use this ribbon to create, open, and save files and projects, to add Flare file types to the project and to initiate the various import wizards.
2	**Home**: This is where you'll be most of the time when working on topics. From here, you can use the **Edit** and **Styles** tools and initiate a **Find** and **Replace** operation.
3	**Insert**: This ribbon , like the **Home** strip is often used when working on topics. You can insert many element types, like images, variables, snippets, tables, cross-references, related topics, concept topics, drop-down text, expanding text, text popups, topic popups, and many other online output elements.
4	**View**: Use this ribbon when you just want to tour the Flare UI elements, or to directly open any of the Flare windows, explorers, and other tools for creating elements like glossaries and indexes. To have more viewing area, consider disabling the **Status Bar** and the **Info Bar**.
5	**Project**: Although there are other options, use this ribbon to create any of the Flare files, to initiate import from various sources, to build and publish the **Primary target**, and open the **Primary TOC** or **Primary Stylesheet**. From here, you can also zip and export projects.
6	**Analysis**: Use this ribbon to analyze problem issues with your project. You can create reports of **Used Items**, **Undefined Items**, and you can generate a variety of reports that you define.
7	**Review**: Use this ribbon to work with tracking changes and to send and receive review packages to SMEs.
8	**Tools**: Use this ribbon to access some of the many Flare tools like edit dictionary, spell check, text analysis, hyphenation, manage templates, update cross-references, and record and playback macros.
9	**Tables**: This ribbon , like the **Insert** ribbon, is often used when working on topics. You can insert tables and perform many other table operations, like delete, table, add rows and columns, insert rows and columns, merge and split table cells, create and edit table stylesheets, and convert tables to text.
10	**eLearning**: Use this ribbon to access the various tools and elements for entering questions, including multiple choice and multiple response, creating and managing test, and building eLearning courses.
11	**Window**: Use this ribbon to access open documents and windows, close all documents, save and reload your UI layouts.

CREATING AND DESIGNATING A TEMPLATE FOLDER

BASIC CONCEPT

To create custom templates of some of your files for use among a writing team, you will first need to designate one or more template folders, where custom templates can be stored. The template folder can be an existing folder that you select or make a new folder. Although Flare generates appropriate sub-folders inside the designated template folder, you can create as many template folders as required.

ESSENTIAL ELEMENTS

When designating custom templates folders, you can locate the folder on a local or network drive or a SharePoint server. When you save a file or project as a template and select your custom template folder, Flare adds the appropriate template subfolder based on the element type. When you create topic templates, Flare places them in a subfolder called "**Content**," it places Page Layout files in a sub-folder called "**PageLayouts**," and it puts Projects in a subfolder named "**Projects**."

Using templates offers a means of ensuring consistency in the appearance of files created by different team members. Users will have access to Factory Template files, from which you can create new files, and they will also have access to the custom templates you have made.

APPLICATION TIPS

Since a template folder must be designated in Flare for custom templates to be created and main-tained, it is best to specify it before creating new templates. You can create your template folder using the external file system or make a new template folder from within Flare. Until the folder is des-ignated, Flare will not be aware of the folder as a template folder.

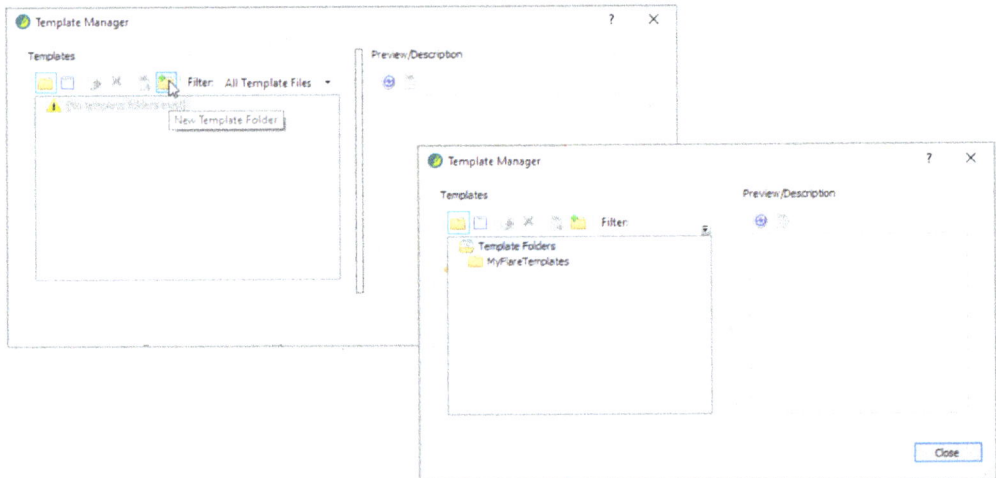

Figure 1-22. Template Manager—Add Template Folder.

QUICK STEPS: CREATING AND DESIGNATING A TEMPLATE FOLDER

STEP	ACTION
1	Select the **Tools** ribbon.
2	Click **Manage Templates** to open the Templates Manager.
3	Click the **New Template Folder** button to select or create a new template folder.
4	**Continue with Step 5** to select an existing folder, or **Continue with Step 9** to make a new folder.
5	**Select Existing Folder to designate as a custom template folder:**
6	From the **Select Folder** window, locate and select a folder to designate as the custom template folder.
7	Click **OK** to save the selection.
8	Click **Close** to close the **Template Manager** dialog.
9	**Make a New Folder to designate as a custom template folder:**
10	From the **Select Folder** window, click **Make New Folder** button to create a new custom template folder.
11	Name the new folder, for example, **CustomTemplates**.
12	Click **OK** to save the new folder.
13	Click **Close** to close the **Template Manager** dialog.

SETTING OPTIONS FOR SOME BASIC FLARE PREFERENCES

BASIC CONCEPT

Before getting started with Flare, you can define some basic preferences that apply globally to the application. In ways that you can determine, these preferences will affect how you work with various elements in the application and enable Flare to enhance your work experience in some precise ways. You will make these determinations through the setting you make and the options you allow.

ESSENTIAL ELEMENTS

Flare global settings and preferences are made from the **File** menu, using the **Options** dialogs. A few of the categories for defining settings are given here. On the **General** tab, you can affect the saving and the opening and closing of documents and the overall appearance of dialogs, menus, and backgrounds on the **Interface** tab.

Using the **Source Control** tab, you can enable **Bind Detection** and select one or more source control applications. As this operation can be time-consuming, it is best to choose only the **Source Control Provider** in use. The **XML Editor** tab lets you specify certain default behaviors for some commonplace operations, like pasting text from another application, cutting table columns and rows, and converting a table to text.

You can choose the default or a custom location from the **Spelling** tab for placing the global dictionary and any spelling options to employ while editing. Finally, the **Auto-Suggestion** tab is where you instruct Flare on what content to examine and make usage suggestions, such as variables, snippets, and other reusable elements.

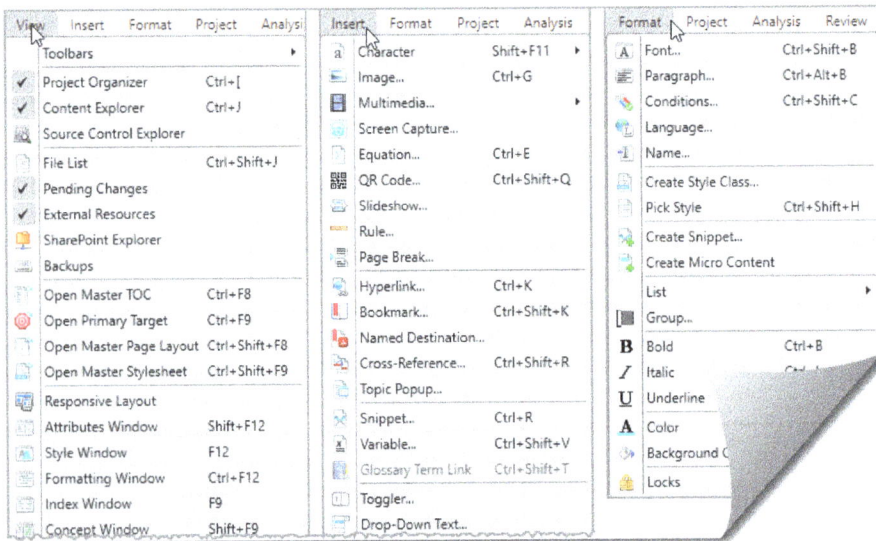

Figure 1-23. Classic Menu drop-down for View, Insert, and Format, when Options Interface Set for Tool Strip.

Figure 1-24. View Menu, when Options Interface Set for Ribbon.

Figure 1-25. Insert Menu, when Options Interface Set for Ribbon.

QUICK STEPS: SETTING OPTIONS FOR SOME BASIC FLARE PREFERENCES

STEP	ACTION
1	Select **File** > **Options**.
2	On the **General** tab consider the following settings:
	a) Enable the **Auto-Reload Documents** if you want all of the last open documents to be re-opened each time you re-open Flare.
	b) Enable the **Auto-save Documents** option and specify a duration in minutes to always automatically save your files while editing.
	c) Enable **Prefer Local Help** to access the locally installed Flare Help System if you are unable to access the Online Help because of a slow connection, lack of Internet service, or you are currently behind a firewall. To be available, the local Help System must have been installed during initial installation.
3	On the **Interface** tab, use the **Ribbon** option to display the menu commands as tabbed ribbons across the workspace top, or the **Tool Strip** option to use the classic drop-down menu display.
	Use the **Active Theme** drop-down to choose one of the themes that represent a combination of colors to use throughout the application.
4	On the **Source Control** tab, enable **Bind Detection** and enable any of the source control applications that you will use in the project. And, if applicable, select the mode of communications protocol to enable transfers between the Flare project and **MadCap Central**.
5	On the **Project Analysis** tab, enable any or all of the **Advance Scan Options** you wish to have Flare scan in your project. Enabling these options will allow you to later produce reports of Flare recommendations items such as variables, snippets, and new styles to eliminate repeated local formatting.
6	On the **Auto Suggestion** tab, if desired, **Enable Auto Suggestion** to enable the entire feature, and **Enable Snippet Auto Suggestion**, and set suggestion limitations. You can also decide whether you want Flare to create and save specific files.

NAVIGATING THE FLARE HELP SYSTEM

BASIC CONCEPT

The Flare Help System consists of several options that allow you to choose what best suits your learning preference. The primary containers in which the Help is divided include Flare's **Online Help** and **Dynamic Help**. Also from the **Help** ribbon is a collection of other Help operations and tools. Finally, you can employ a local installation of the Flare Help System for when online access is unavailable.

ESSENTIAL ELEMENTS

From the **Help** ribbon, you have access to Flare's **Online Help** system, which opens in a separate window, with a navigation tree that allows you to manually select areas of interest and topics. The tree is divided into sections that let you select and drill down through many functional work areas. The **Dynamic Help** button provides Flare's Context-Sensitive Help (CSH), which opens in a docked Window Pane to the right edge of the work area.

As you navigate the different areas of the UI, for example, the **Project Organizer** or **Content Explorer**, help topics starting with an overview are presented for the element in focus. You can learn all you need to know about the component as you scroll the window. The topic covers toolbar menus and buttons, key features, what you can do, and where applicable, complete details for setting parameters in dialogs. In addition to the main help system elements, there is access to tutorial-like **PDF Guides** and **Videos** on specific topics and access to the Flare **Help Community** of User Groups and Forums.

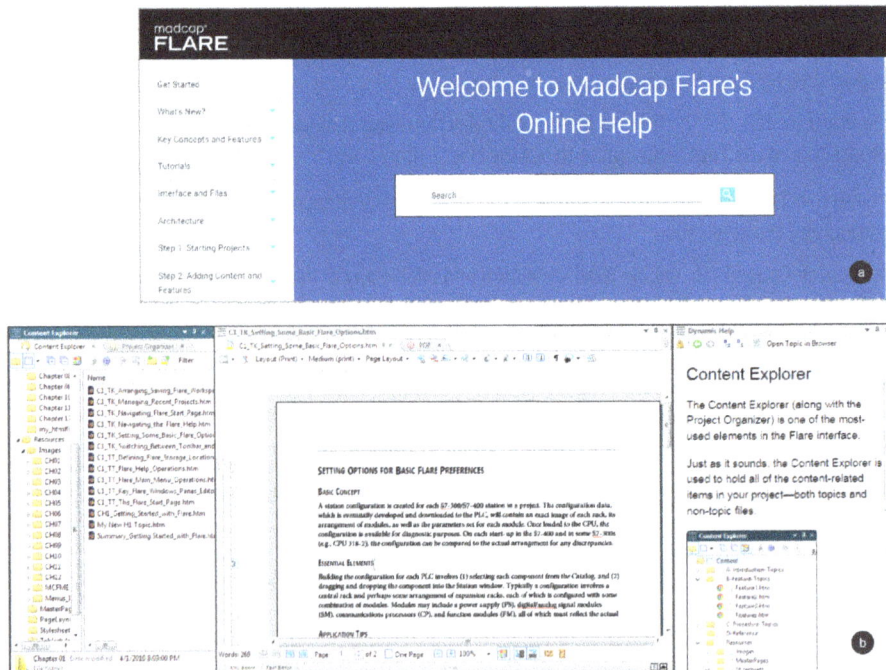

Figure 1-26. **a)** Flare Online Help System, and **b)** Flare Dynamic Help System Turned On.

QUICK STEPS: NAVIGATING THE FLARE HELP SYSTEM

STEP	ACTION
—	**To use Flare's Online Help**
1	You must have an Internet connection.
2	Click **Help** ribbon > **Open Help**. The Flare Online Help System opens in a separate browser window. From this window you have complete access to Flare Help and Search Systems.
—	**To use Dynamic Help**
1	You must have an Internet connection.
2	Open to any Flare window, pane, or dialog you want to use — for example the **Content Explorer**, the **Project Organizer**, the **XML Editor**, or the **Build Window Pane**.
3	Click the **Help** > **Dynamic Help** on the main ribbon. The Dynamic Help window opens to the right of any open window, and contains the associated context-sensitive help topic.
—	**To use Flare's Help Ribbon Tools**
1	You must have an Internet connection.
2	Click the **Help** ribbon and click on one of the following items as needed:
	a) Help Topic — Use this option as an alternative to opening the **Dynamic Help** pane. When this option is clicked, the CSH topic opens as a tabbed page in the workspace window, for the topic in focus.
	b) PDF Guides — These guides, which provide comprehensive details, can be very useful when you need to thoroughly understand a particular topic. For example **Table Stylesheets**, or **Page Layouts**.
	c) Videos — Videos, like the PDF, although much shorter, are quite useful when you want a quick understanding and overview of a specific topic. This visual tutorial will normally provide fast answers.
	d) Help Community — This option provides several ways you can get answers. You can join national or local user groups and forums that can provide ongoing community and support with Flare.
	e) Report a Bug — Use this option to report an issue you find occurring in the application. Your issue should be raised as it is important to you and possibly others. Your report, along with the reports of others, can impact how the issue is queued for resolution.
—	**To use locally installed Help** (Use this option when there is no Internet availability, the installation is behind a firewall, or you are experiencing a very slow connection).
1	Confirm whether the Flare Help System has been installed locally. If you are unable to connect with the Online Help, Flare automatically detects and switches to the installed Local Help system.
2	To install the Local Help system, if it was not previously included, use the Windows Control Panel :
	a) Open **Control Panel** > select **Programs** > **Programs and Features** > **Uninstall or Change Program**
	b) Choose **MadCap Flare** > **Uninstall/Change**
	c) Continue with the install dialog and select **Modify**
	d) Under **Select features** > enable **Local Documentation**
	e) Disable all other features that are not required

CHAPTER 2

CREATING THE FLARE PROJECT

INTRODUCING FLARE NEW PROJECT WIZARDS

Creating the Flare project is the first step if you are starting with Flare. You can start the new project with sample content if you use a Flare template or from existing content if you create the project based on a user Custom template or an existing Flare project. The new project can also be made from existing content, like MS Word or Adobe FrameMaker, when one of many Flare *import wizards* is used to import. Your choice of import wizard depend on the source application used to create that content.

Table 2-1. Flare File Menu New Project Wizards

New Project Wizard	Example Description
New Project	Use this wizard to create a new project by selecting from a set of Flare Templates designed to guide you through creating a project designed for Print, Online, or both Print and Online. You also get to specify the online navigation type as Top, Side, or Tri-pane. A set of several topics is provided as a project framework to get you started. The new project can be created from a **Factory Template** or user **Custom Template**, from an **Existing Project**, or from one of many Flare supported **Import Options** for existing source content, which can be imported.
Source Control	Use this wizard to download a project from a source control repository. For example, a new team member joins the team and needs the central project that the team uses. The project is downloaded from the remote repository that resides on a remote server.
MS Word Documents	Use this wizard to create a new project by importing source content originally created using Microsoft Word. Word files can also be imported to an existing project using the Word Import Wizard accessed from the **Project** menu.
HTML File Set	Use this wizard to create a new project by importing a specified group of HTML files. An HTML File Set can also be imported to either a new or an existing project, using the HTML File Set Import Wizard accessed from the **Project** menu.
Confluence Pages	Use this wizard to create a new project by importing Confluence Pages as source content. Confluence files can also be imported from a local or cloud server to a new or existing project, using the Confluence Import Wizard on the **Project** menu.
FrameMaker Documents	Use this wizard to create a new project by importing source content originally created using Adobe FrameMaker. FrameMaker files can also be imported to an existing project using the FrameMaker Import Wizard accessed from the **Project** menu.
RoboHelp Project	Use this wizard to create a new project by importing a RoboHelp project (**.MPJ** or **.XPJ**) file. You will have the option to convert all of the imported topic files to XHTML.
HTML Help File (.CHM)	Use this wizard to create a new project by importing a compiled Windows HTML Help (**.CHM**) file. You will have the option to convert all of the imported topic files to XHTML.
HTML Help Project	Use this wizard to create a new project by importing an entire HTML Help project (**.HHP** file). You will have the option to convert all of the imported topic files to XHTML.

PROJECT PRE-IMPORT TASKS

The following topics briefly outline some tasks for preparing your content for import to a new Flare project. These tasks are essential irrespective of the source editor files you are importing and can produce better post-import results. It is important to ensure that your content uses defined heading, paragraph, and character styles throughout, and as much as possible be free of inline formatting. Take as much time as needed to perform these tasks, and save hours or even days of post-import activities.

REVIEW AND KNOW YOUR CONTENT

Getting to know your source documents — how they're structured, how well the content of each subheading stands on its own as a chunk of useful information, will pay tremendous dividends. One of the best ways to make good decisions about what to do during the Flare import and after you start working with Flare is to know your documents well and how you can improve each before starting the import. During the import, one crucial task will be to specify one or more content heading levels like ChapterTitle, H1, and H2, which Flare will use to break your content into topics.

After a close review, you'll find that the heading levels you should specify may differ slightly for each book type. Many documents will likely break into topics that stand well on their own if the headings ChapterTitle, H1, and H2 are specified. Content under H3 and H4 is often short and does not stand alone as a topic. Finally, some books, like a Release Notes document, are best broken into topics based on the ChapterTitle heading alone — for example, New Features, Resolved Issues, and Known Issues.

- Examine each book differently to see how it is arranged.

- Find long sections that may cover more than a single topic and can be divided.

- Determine sections that stand well as a unit and is limited to a single chunk of information.

SHORTEN CHAPTER AND SECTION HEADINGS

Revisit chapter and section headings from each of your books or documents, and, where necessary, shorten and rename the headings. This task is essential since topic file names result from the headings found in the source content. Take this final opportunity to ensure your content has concise and informative titles, naming and grammatical consistency, and, as much as possible, employs active titles. For the most part, active titles should denote work that readers will accomplish — as opposed to titles that reflect system functions or operations. The idea is that users learn by doing.

- Use content minimization techniques.

- Use active headings that represent work-related tasks.

- Be brief and concise — consider language localization.

- Ensure that titles at the same level are grammatically consistent.

- Minimize titles, headings, images, and body content wherever possible.

- Use short concise topic headings for better menus and topic file names.

MINIMIZE OUTLINE DEPTH

This task is concerned with minimizing the number of HTML topics that result from your imported content. If time permits, this task is well worth the effort. Review each book chapter and the sections to see whether any H2 headings can become H1 headings. Look closely at H2 content to ensure that only a single significant discussion is covered.

- Where possible, eliminate headings greater than H3.

- In any case, try to limit headings to H1, H2, and H3.

- Consider whether some H2 headings could move to H1.

- Short topics covered in H3 or H4 can often be placed in a bullet list.

- Consider H3 and H4 content for Flare drop-down text in online outputs.

MINIMIZE CROSS-REFERENCE USE

As book documents are linear, writers are more likely to rely on and often overuse cross-references — both internal to the document and external. This overuse can lead to an annoyance to readers, having to bounce forward and backward through a document. A step towards moving online will be to minimize or, if possible, eliminate cross-references. Once you move your content online, using related and concept topics methods reduces the need for cross-references.

- Minimize or eliminate cross-references (internal/external) where possible.

- Eliminate references by placing figures and tables following the related text.

- Consider placing essential external references in a single location — like at the chapter start.

LIMIT PER-TOPIC USE OF IMAGES

As much as possible, limit each topic to a single image. If a single topic contains more than one concept, each concept within the topic is preceded with a sub-heading, for example, using a drop-down. You can then extend the guideline to include a single image per subheading. Although this is a guideline and not a rigid requirement, working with this practice in mind will help minimize the overuse of images and promote a clean-looking book or document and a more concise topic.

MERGE MULTI-SCREENSHOT IMAGES

Check your document for cases where multiple images are in a single frame. Someone may have used this approach to show side-by-side images for comparison or show a "Case A" and a "Case B." During import, Flare gives the option to "Flatten" these images to make a single image. To maintain the quality of your images, it may be worth your time, before the import, to consider using your image capture tool to merge these two images at 100 percent.

ELIMINATE PARAGRAPH TAG AND CHARACTER TAG OVERRIDES

Local formatting, sometimes called overrides, results from using the local formatting toolbar tools in your source editor to style your content. The more appropriate way to style your content is to apply styles from your stylesheet (CSS). This task is reasonably necessary and maybe one of the essential pre-import tasks you will perform. By eliminating overrides and using defined styles, you minimize the number of useless tags created in Flare. Eliminating overrides beforehand also produces a cleaner stylesheet created in Flare and cleaner-looking topics.

- Use available tools to eliminate overrides.

- Apply styles consistently throughout the document in your source editor.

- As much as possible, eliminate overrides — especially in headings like H1 through H6.

SET ADOBE DISTILLER SETTINGS FOR IMPORT

This task is mainly related to a FrameMaker import. If you are importing from FrameMaker, you will want to set the Adobe Distiller Settings before importing to Flare. Since Flare uses Distiller to convert images from FrameMaker, the correct settings are essential to ensure the best quality and a sharper result in the images imported into Flare.

- Set all Down Sampling fields to Off/None to prevent pixel reduction.

- Save Distiller Job Options after setting.

- Select the saved Distiller Job Options before closing.

ENSURE IMPORT OF DESIRED STYLES AND IMAGES

FrameMaker and Word styles available during the Flare import are based on the styles found in the source documents. Only the styles present in the imported document can be maintained and stored in the generated Flare stylesheet (CSS).

One way to ensure that you import any of the styles not currently used in the source content you are importing is to type each of the unused style names at the end of a document slated for import and apply the associated style to each of those names. These styles will then be imported and become part of the stylesheet (.css), available after completing the import.

- Create a list of unused style names at the document end and assign the associated style names.

- FrameMaker reference page images are not imported — if needed, move these images to some other place in your book before the import.

THE FLARE IMPORT PROCESS — AN OVERVIEW

This overview is an outline of the general tasks related to importing content to Flare, using one of the Flare New project Wizards — for example, the FrameMaker or Word Import Wizard. The main tasks for both these wizards are practically the same; but specific selections and conversion options, differ slightly for each import wizard.

START IMPORT WIZARD

Depending on your source editor, for example, Adobe FrameMaker or Microsoft Word, select **File > New Project >** then select the appropriate Import Wizard. Your first task will be to point to your source content files.

SPECIFY SOURCE FILES

At this step, the wizard prompts you to inform Flare of the source files you wish to import. From your PC, open the appropriate folder and specify the desired source files. For example, in the case of FrameMaker, you may select one or more document files (.fm) or the FrameMaker book file (.book), but you should not choose both. For Word imports, you may select as many individual files as desired.

SPECIFY NEW TOPIC STYLES

In this step, you tell Flare the headings — for example, **ChapterTitle**, **H1**, and **H2** to use as break-points for dividing the source into HTML topic files. Based on this information, Flare will scan the source files you specify and create a new topic each time it sees one of the selected topic headings.

Remember, the headings you choose should result in topics that you feel can stand well on their own. The more headings you specify, the more topics are created and that you must later manage. With some books, you may decide that the **ChapterTitle** is the only topic breakpoint you should specify. In such cases, the import would result in each topic being a complete chapter. This division level might be desirable, for example, with Release Notes or other documents, where you want the entire chapter to remain intact.

SPECIFY CONVERSION OPTIONS

This task allows you to choose from a list of options that will affect how objects such as text content and images will import; and how topic files are created and named. For the most part, the default settings produce satisfactory results. Better image results, for example, are obtained if you disable the option to **Preserve Image Sizes**. Also, be aware that if you instruct Flare to break long topics into segments, you can use the **File-name Length** setting to give Flare the maximum number of characters to use for naming automatically created topic files.

SELECT STYLESHEET/PRESERVE OR DISCARD SOURCE STYLES

In this step, if desired, you can point to an existing stylesheet that you want to have applied to the imported content and to maintain as the associated stylesheet in the imported project. You may also specify whether you want to "Preserve the Imported styles (for example, FrameMaker), or Discard Word Styles (Word import). If the styles are preserved, they can be mapped to Flare styles.

MAP PARAGRAPH STYLES

This step is where you map the Paragraph Styles of your source content to the Flare Paragraph Styles. Here, you are essentially assigning each imported paragraph style as a child class (style) under a Flare CSS parent style. All style tags that are not headings, for example, *bodytext, bulletitem, headertext, footertext,* and *cellbody,* should be mapped to the paragraph parent style, which is **<p>**.

Although your heading styles H1, H2, H3, H4, and so on, are also paragraph styles, they are, by default, mapped to the corresponding Flare parent heading style during the import. For example, your **H1** style is mapped to the Flare **<h1>** parent style; your **H2** style is mapped to the Flare **<h2>** parent style, and so on. You can review these mappings later in the imported stylesheet file.

Table 2-2. Example: Frame-to-Flare Paragraph Mapping

FrameMaker Paragraph Style	Flare Paragraph Style
Heading1 > H1	H1.Heading1
ChapterTitle > H1	H1.ChapterTitle
Heading2 > H2	H2.Heading2
bodytext > p	p.bodytext

MAP CHARACTER STYLES

This wizard step is for mapping the Character Styles from your content to the Character Styles in Flare. As with the mapping of Paragraph styles, here again, you are mapping to a Flare parent. For example, your **bold** style tag maps to the Flare **<b>** parent, your **italics** style tag to the Flare **<i>** parent, your subscript style to the Flare **<sub>** parent, and your superscript parent to Flare **<sup>** parent.

Your character styles for which there are no standard or associated style in Flare are all mapped to the Flare "span" parent style. The *span style* is another name for character style or styles that are used to affect the appearance of character-level content — for example, a single word, or a single sentence in a paragraph, as opposed to the entire paragraph.

Table 2-3. Example: Frame-to-Flare Character Styles Mapping

FrameMaker Character Style	Flare Character Style
bold > span	span.bold
italics > span	span.italics
subscript > span	span.subscript
superscript > span	span.superscript
hyperlink > span	span.hyperlink

MAP CROSS-REFERENCE STYLES

With this step, you map your Cross-Reference Styles to the Flare Cross-Reference styles. Since there are no standard Cross-Reference styles, Flare maps each of your imported cross-reference styles to the parent style <**MadCapXref**>, thereby creating child classes. Each child is assigned the name ""**MadCapXRef.whateverthenamewas,**" as shown in the following table.

Table 2-4. Example: Frame-to-Flare Cross-Reference Styles Mapping

FrameMaker Cross-Reference Styles	Flare Cross-Reference Styles
Appendix # and Title > MadCapXref	MadCapXref.Appendix # and Title
Chapter Title and Page > MadCapXref	MadCapXref.Chapter Title and Page
Heading and Page > MadCapXref	MadCapXref.Heading and Page
Figure # > MadCapXref	MadCapXref.Figure #
Table # > MadCapXref	MadCapXref.Table #

ACCEPT/REJECT IMPORTED FILES

In this final step, you simply scan and review the imported topics. Click on the **Type** column to sort by file type, then use the **Page Down** button to scroll through and select and view your HTML topics and images in the view pane before finally clicking the **Accept** button.

WHAT FLARE DOES WITH YOUR IMPORTED CONTENT

An essential part in getting to know Flare, especially if you've done an import of source content, is to learn what Flare has done post-import with the various components of your content. This section reviews what happened with each element and where it has been placed in your project.

HTML TOPIC AND IMAGE FILES

If you imported source content to Flare and used an import wizard, you told Flare the source files you wanted to import and specified heading levels you wanted Flare to use as breakpoints to create new HTML topics. For example, you may have selected a FrameMaker book (.book) file as the source, and you may have told Flare to use **BookTitle**, **ChapterTitle**, **H1**, and **H2** styles as breakpoints for dividing the source into individual HTML topic files.

A new HTML topic is created in the new project each time Flare encounters one of the headings that you specified as a topic breakpoint. Flare saves both the generated topics and imported image files in a subfolder named after the imported book file.

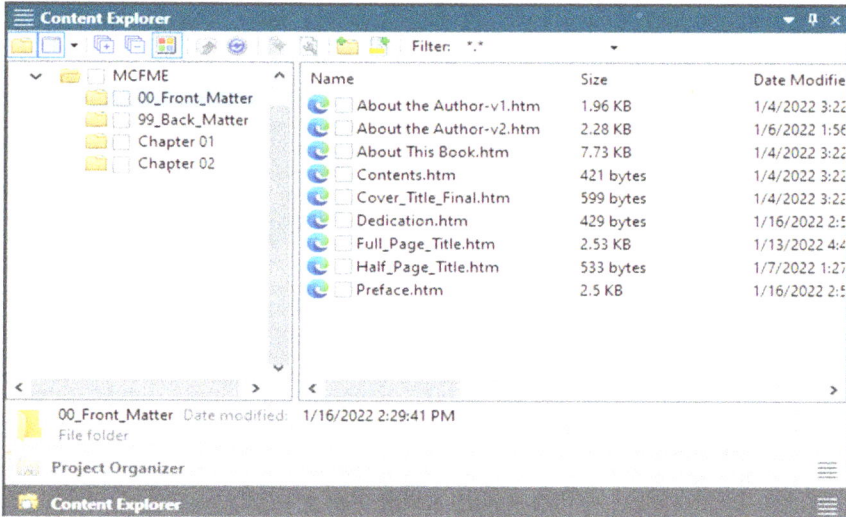

Figure 2-1. FrameMaker Imported Content to Flare HTML Topics.

MAPPED PARAGRAPH STYLES

Although your heading styles, for example, H1, H2, H3, H4, and so on, are also paragraph styles, during the import, they are, by default, mapped to the corresponding Flare parent heading style. For example, Flare maps your **H1** style to its <**h1**> parent style, maps your **H2** style to its <**h2**> parent style, maps your **H3** style to its <**h3**> parent style, and so on. You can review these mappings later in the imported stylesheet file.

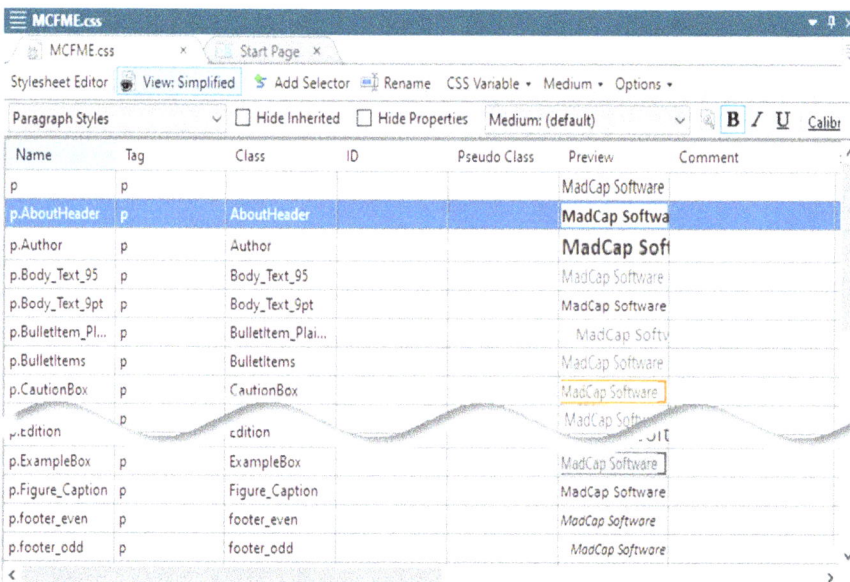

Figure 2-2. Imported Paragraph Styles to Flare Paragraph Styles.

MAPPED CHARACTER STYLES

Your character styles for which there are no standard or associated styles in Flare are all mapped to the Flare **span** parent style. The span style is another name for character styles or styles that are used to affect the appearance of character-level content — for example, a single word or single sentence in a paragraph, as opposed to an entire paragraph.

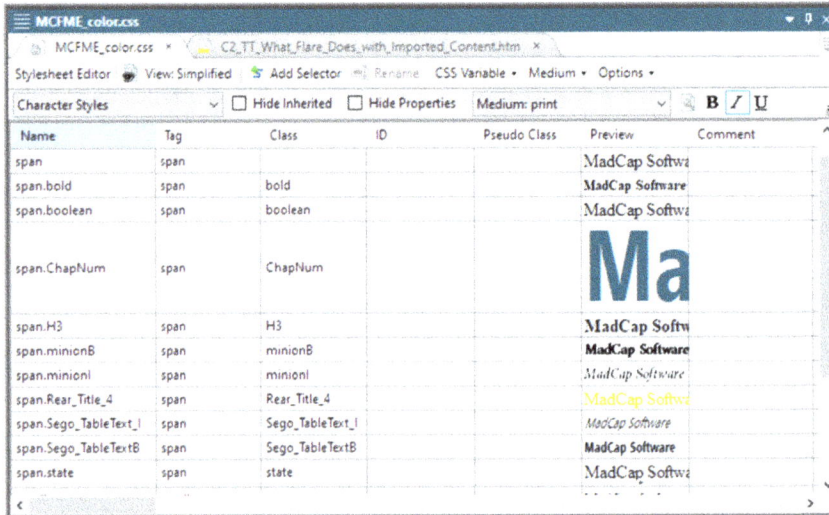

Figure 2-3. Imported Character Styles to Flare Character (Span) Styles.

MAPPED CROSS-REFERENCE STYLES

Since there are no standard Cross-Reference styles, Flare mapped all of your imported cross-reference styles to the Flare cross-reference style parent of "**MadCapXRef**." In short, each of your cross-reference styles will now appear as a child class under this parent. Each of your pre-import styles will have its original name but prefixed with the parent name "**MadCapXRef**" and separated by a period.

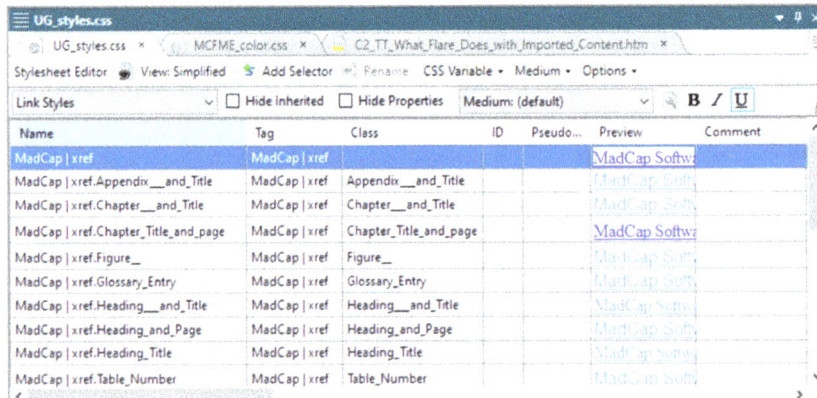

Figure 2-4. Imported Cross-Reference Styles to Flare Cross-Reference Styles.

PAGE LAYOUT FILES

If Flare finds an equivalent Page Layout file in your source content during import, the wizard places the converted input in the **Content Explorer > Content > Resources > Page Layouts**. For example, if your import was from FrameMaker, the wizard converted the FrameMaker equivalent pages to Flare Page Layout files — one for each imported FM file. Each file, in most cases, would only include Left Page and Right Page types. You may want to create new page layout files for each book section.

TOC FILE

When you import a document or book, such as a FrameMaker book (.fm.book), Flare generates a TOC file based on the book chapters and sections converted to Flare topics. The TOC structure comes directly from the heading levels (for example, H1, H2, and H3) found in the content. In the Flare TOC, your imported chapters become TOC books, and converted topics become TOC pages.

This TOC, very likely with some minor changes that you make, will be specified as one of the key parameters when configuring your Target file. Flare places the TOC file generated from your import in the folder **Project Organizer > Project > TOCs**.

VARIABLES FILE

If your source content, such as Word or FrameMaker, contained variables during import, Flare places the converted input in the Flare **Project Organizer > Project > Variables** folder. The imported variables are placed in a single variables file whose filename is based on the folder name assigned to the imported content. You can modify this name as you see fit.

CONDITIONAL TEXT FILE

Some source content editors allow you to create and apply conditional text phrases to parts of your content to determine whether designated content should be included or excluded from the output. Flare captures these conditional text phrases and stores them in a Flare Conditional Text file as part of the import process. Although you may keep the imported file, you can create additional Conditional Text files in Flare. Flare stores the imported conditional text phrases in a Conditional Text file in the folder **Project Organizer > Project > Conditional Text**.

FLARE IMPORT PARAMETERS FILE

During the import, you specified several options and parameters that gave Flare instructions on how to handle your source content. These instructions provided the name and location of the Source Files, the Topic Headings to use as breakpoints for creating HTML topics, and the mapping of your source Paragraph Styles, Character Styles, and Cross-Reference Styles to corresponding Flare styles.

Flare keeps all of your import decisions in an import file that is named based on the name of your source content. The file can be recalled later or at any time so that you can re-import your source files without having to re-enter each of the previously specified parameters. After an initial import and during a re-import, you can modify some of the parameters you set initially. For each of your imports, Flare stores import files in **Project Organizer > Project > Imports**.

PROJECT POST-IMPORT TASKS

If you carefully performed the recommended pre-import tasks, much of your imported content will look as you expect it to, although some items may need tweaking. Since you may still be new to Flare and unfamiliar with some techniques, the following topics outline some basic post-import cleanup tasks that will move your content closer to the final appearance that you want.

APPLYING STYLES TO IMPORTED CONTENT

All Paragraph, Heading, Character, and Cross-Reference styles that you may have imported, are now in your new stylesheet, located in the Stylesheet subfolder of the Resources folder. If a style used in one of the imported topics is no longer in the new stylesheet, then that content to which the specific style was applied may not look as expected. You can apply a new style to the content, as follows:

1. If you have generated an initial output, for example, a PDF, and some content looks incorrectly formatted, page through the content to find the topic where the content appears.

2. From the Content Explorer, locate the HTML topic and double-click to open the file.

3. Click the Tag Bar icon to toggle the tag bars ON if the tag bars are not currently displayed.

4. For Headings, click inside the heading > use the Style pane and select the style to apply.

5. For Paragraphs, click anywhere inside paragraph > use the Style pane and select style to apply.

6. For Character (span) Styles, select the text > use the Style pane and choose the style to apply.

> **TIP:** Styles listed in the drop-down, are based on how you have selected content — for example, clicking anywhere in a paragraph lists <p> styles only; selecting text list <span> styles only.

APPLYING STYLE TO IMPORTED TABLES NOT APPEARING CORRECT

Tables that you import may not look as expected but should reflect the imported table stylesheet if one was applied before the import. If, however, some tables do not look correct, you can apply the appropriate imported table stylesheet or any of your newly created table stylesheets.

1. If you have an initial output, for example, a PDF, page through the content to find a topic where a table appears to be incorrectly formatted.

2. From the Content Explorer, locate the topic containing the table.

3. Click anywhere in the table and the HTML tag bars should appear to the left of the topic page.

4. Click the Tag Bar icon if tag bars are not displayed (See buttons for structure bars).

5. Click the **Table** tag, right-click > select **Table Style**, and select appropriate Table style.

6. If necessary, use table column bars to resize column widths or row tag bars to resize.

APPLYING PAGE BREAKS FOR SPECIFIC PARAGRAPHS AND PAGES

After the import, there may be cases where you'd like the page break for a specific heading to occur on the next page or, in some cases, to not be pushed to the next page. You can easily manage this situation by opening the topic where the occurrence appears and minor tweaks to the topic heading.

1. Locate the topic in the Content Explorer. Use the **Filter** drop-down to select **Topic Files.**

2. Double-click on the topic to open it in the XML (Topic) Editor.

3. Click to place the cursor anywhere inside the heading you want to affect.

4. Right-click and select **Paragraph** to open, then open the Paragraph Properties dialog.

5. Select the **Breaks** tab, and under **Page Break**, specify one of the following:

    a. Click the drop-down **Before** > and select **Always**, to push the heading to the next page.

    b. Click the drop-down **Before** > and select **Avoid**, to prevent the heading from being pushed to the next page and to default to the previous page.

6. Click **OK.**

> **TIP:** Instead of using the method described above, you can choose to use the following:
> 1) First, find the topic that would appear just before the topic in question, then 2) Use **Insert** > **Page Break** after the very last paragraph or page element of that previous topic. This method avoids the local formatting that you would have used to override the heading paragraph style in the previous method.

RE-SIZING AND RE-POSITIONING IMAGES

After importing your source content and reviewing your resulting topics, you may find that some images need re-sizing or re-positioning or are just inconsistent in various ways. For example, some may be left-justified, some right-justified, and others are centered.

In your Flare-created stylesheet (CSS) file, you can find the inherited parent style <img> for styling images. Whatever properties you define for the parent style will be inherited by all of your images, for example, left-justified. You may also choose to create style classes to manage styling for your images. In **Simplified View** or **Advanced View**, the parent style <img> is found using the Style Category drop-down to select **Image Styles**. From the stylesheet, you can do one of the following:

a. Modify the <img> parent style to set the Alignment property to left, center, or right; or

b. Create <img> child classes, for cxample **img.left**, **img.center**, and **img.right** to use in styling your images to align left, center or right respectively. You can also set the **Padding** properties for the image top, bottom, left, and right.

ENHANCING THE CONTENT EXPLORER FOLDER STRUCTURE

The Flare Content Explorer is the primary container for project content and content resources. Inside the Content Explorer, Flare uses a default structure of specific sub-folders for storing different types of content. Although Flare will automatically place certain items in these default sub-folders, there are no rigid restrictions, and you can place items wherever you like and you can create new folders. In this discussion, I will offer a few suggestions as to how you might enhance the default folder structure.

THE DEFAULT FOLDERS

The default structure of the Content Explorer includes folders that will contain the main content elements of your project. This content includes HTML topic files, multimedia files, and various content resources like Images, Micro Content, Page Layouts, Snippets, Template Pages, and Stylesheets. These resources are directly tied to the project for styling, arranging the flow, and producing online and print outputs.

When imported to Flare, text content files that are converted to HTML topic files, and image files are all placed at the top level of the Content folder. With some imports, Flare places both the topic and image files in a subfolder whose name is based on the imported file name. You may consider adding an Images and TemplatePages folder.

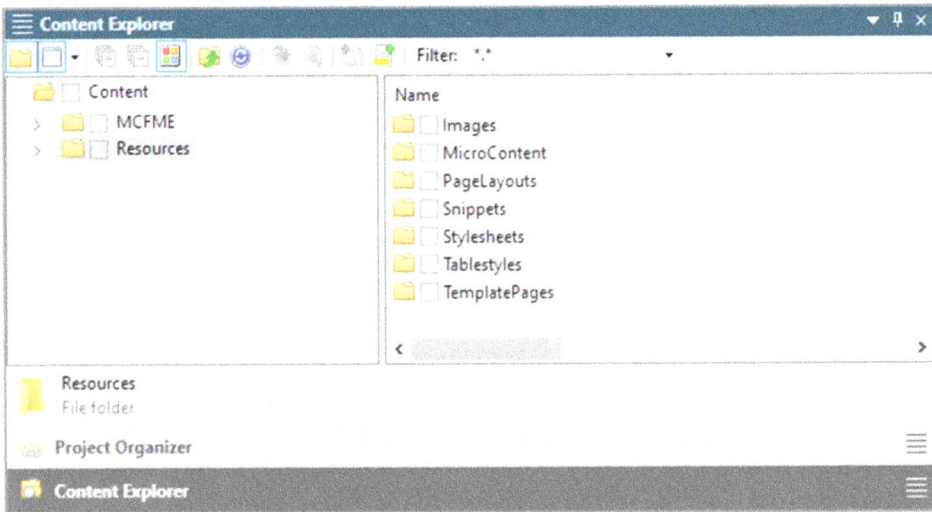

Figure 2-5. Content Explorer—Default Folders.

TOP-LEVEL CONTENT GROUP FOLDERS

Potential top-level folders might be **Product Family**, **Client**, **Business Location,** or other top-level grouping. For each top-level folder, you may have several sub-folders, for example, **Product-A, Product-B**, and **Product-C**; or **Client-A**, **Client-B**, and **Client-C**. This type of structure may result in a single large Flare project.

The next level of folders in this type of hierarchy might be the individual books, documents, or other content groupings that would belong to a product, client, or business location. **Product-A**, for example, may have several books or documents of different types. The same would be true for **Product B** as well. So, the second level of folder groups would, for example, be **Book-1**, **Book-2**, **Book-3**, and so on. This level of grouping would repeat for each product, client, or business location.

Chapters or some other division would then segment each book or document. So, the **Product-A** sub-folder contains book sub-folders, and finally, each book would have chapter sub-folders, for example, **CH01**, **CH02**, and **CH03**, as shown in the following image. In a training course, you might use the sub-folders **Unit-1**, **Unit-2**, **Unit-3**, and so on.

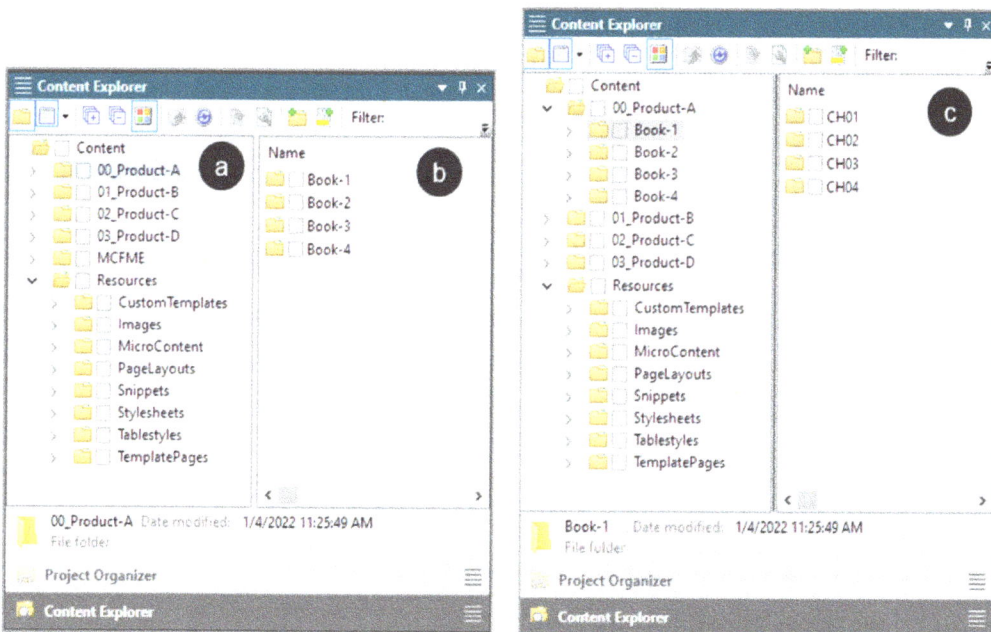

Figure 2-6. Content Explorer a) Product Family Folders b) Product Books and c) Book Chapters.

IMAGE FOLDERS

The **Images** folder is one of the default sub-folders generated in the **Resources** folder when creating a project from a template or an import. In some cases, you may need to make the **Images** subfolder. As images generally belong to a book, document, or Web site, perhaps you can decide whether to place an **Images** subfolder inside of each book folder or let the images subfolder remain under **Resources**. In such a case, you may still want to make an images subfolder for each book. If there is only one book you could create image subfolders for each chapter.

You may also find it necessary to place an additional top-level or global images folder for sharing images other than those of books or documents. You might also consider recreating an **Images** sub-folder under each book chapter for chapter images.

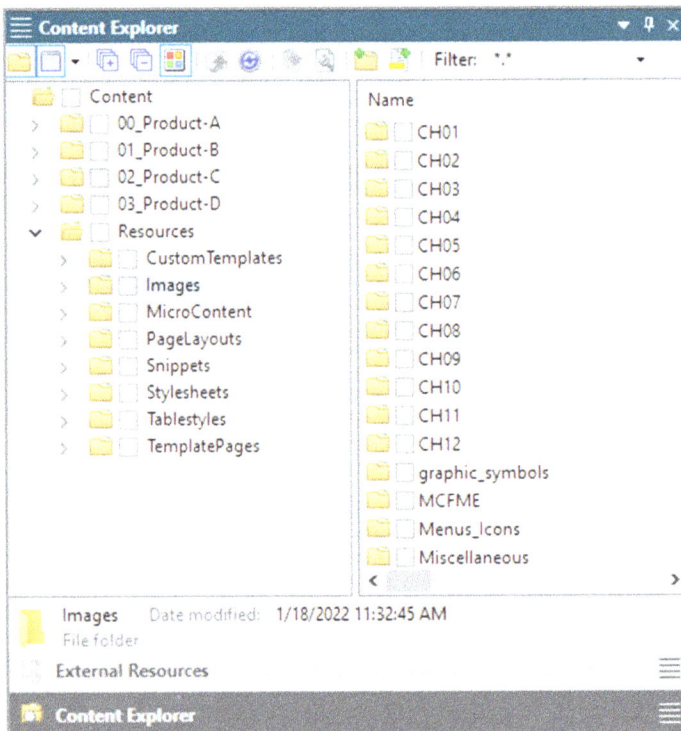

Figure 2-7. Content Explorer Resources—Image Folders.

CUSTOM TEMPLATE FOLDERS

Throughout a project, a team of writers will likely use the option of creating new projects and files and will use templates from the Flare **Factory Templates** folder. It is also very likely that you will want to create custom templates with time or even early in a project, from which writers can create new files and projects. By creating a **Custom Templates** folder to contain your templates, writers can point to this folder when creating new template files or new files or projects from templates.

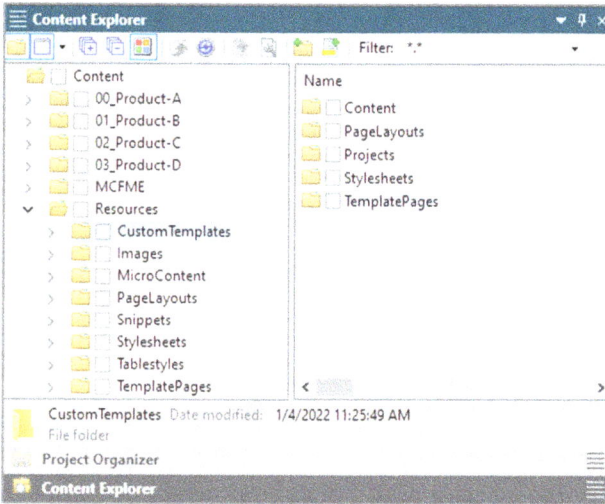

Figure 2-8. Content Explorer Resources — Custom Template Folders.

EXTERNAL RESOURCES FOLDERS

External Resources folders are folders you have identified in Flare, and users can view them by selecting **View > External Resources**. You may specify, as External Resources folders, any local or network files to which you have access. The folders will be available to all of your Flare projects. Once you identify the folders and files, they can be copied to your project and mapped to be synchronized and updated whenever changes occur.

When defining external resources folders, consider naming folders to coincide with the target folders. For example, as shown here, each external resources folder contains image files with a corresponding folder of the same name in the Contents folder.

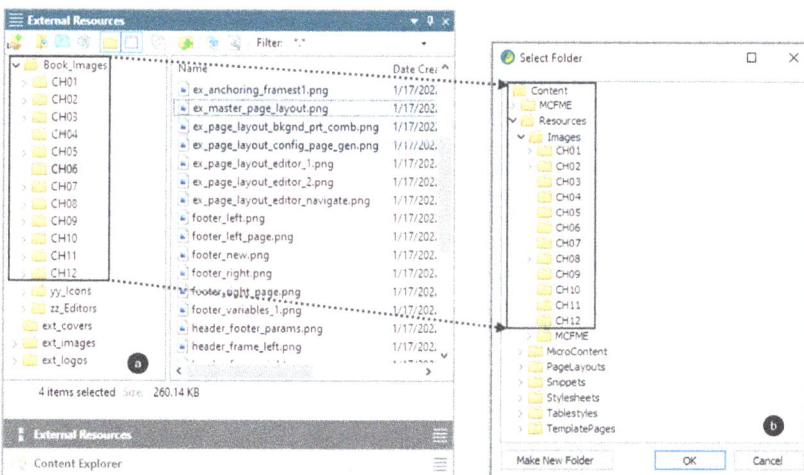

Figure 2-9. **a)** External Resources Folders, and **b)** Content Explorer Folders.

ENHANCING THE PROJECT ORGANIZER FOLDER STRUCTURE

The Flare Project Organizer is one of two primary containers for storing project files. These folder structures have a default structure of specific sub-folders for the different types of content. Whereas some of these default sub-folders must be used or are even best used, there are cases where you can place items wherever you like. In this discussion, a few recommendations for enhancements are given.

THE DEFAULT FOLDERS

The Project Organizer is an Explorer-like UI component containing folders that organize and store non-content resources associated with the project. This UI component also provides access to files and tools that assist in the production, control, management, and maintenance of online and print outputs. These resources include items like TOC, Variables, Target, Skin, Import, and Conditional Text files. Tools are also available for creating Reports, Indexes and Glossaries, and Context Sensitive Help.

If you import content to Flare, imported items may include Variables, TOCs, Import parameters, Condition Tags, and possibly Page Layout files depending on the source editor. Flare places each of these items into the associated Project Organizer subfolder. You may add sub-folders, as required, to any of the Project Organizer root folders.

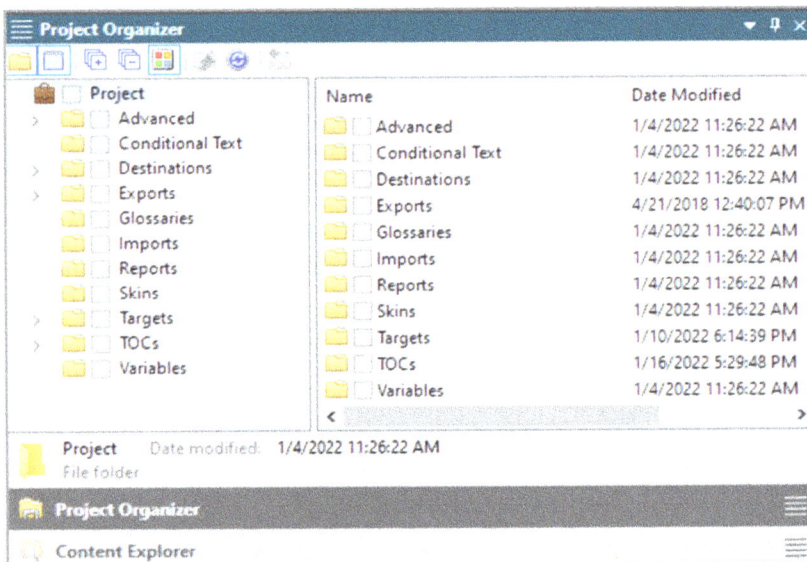

Figure 2-10. Project Organizer — Default Folders.

TARGET FOLDERS

Generally, you will have at least a single target file for each book or document and each HTML5 or other output type. However, there are cases when you may want to have multiple target files for a given book or document or other output types — this might be the case if you have one or more instances of a target to drive variations of a given output. Each variation would, naturally, have a unique name.

You might change one or more parameters or variables for each instance and perhaps condition tags to control the inclusion or exclusion of topics or TOC entries. Instead of the parameter modifications you might need to make for each target instance, you might consider creating a unique target for each instance. In this latter approach, the target parameters may, for the most part, remain unchanged for each new build or release of the output.

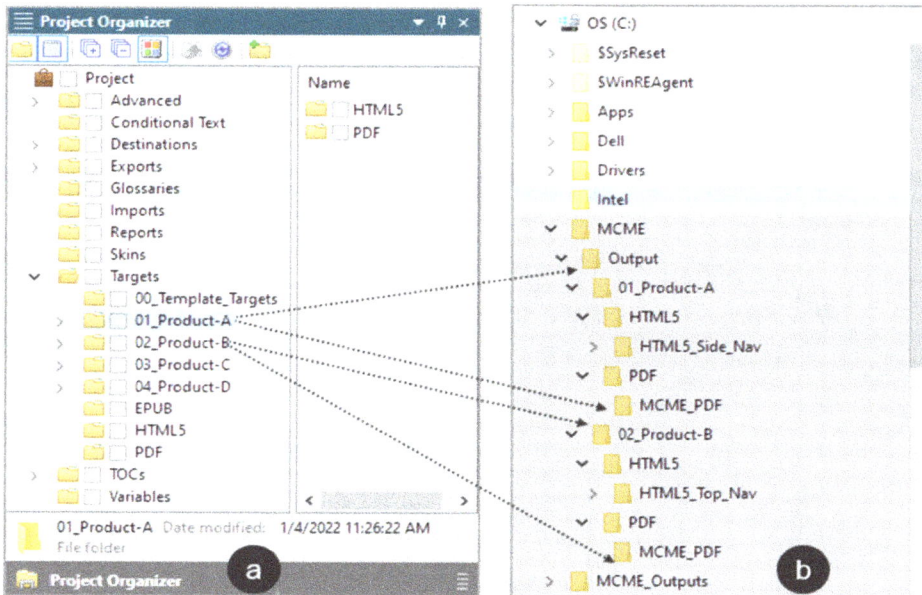

Figure 2-11. a) Project Organizer — Product Target Folders. B) Output Folder — Product Output Folders.

You can add subfolders to the root **Targets** folder, as required, to match your target folder structure requirements. The image above suggests a folder structure. In this proposed folder organization, I created a root target folder for each product, for example, **Product-A**, and **Product B**, **Product-C**, and **Product-D**. A subfolder was created in each of these product folders to place your **PDF** and **HTML5** target files. There may be multiple PDF and HTML5 targets for each product. Each target would have a unique name.

Imagine that you specify **MCME** as the **Output Folder** on each target file. This specification tells Flare that you want all your output files placed in this folder. When you build a target for a given product, for example, for **Product-A**, Flare creates the **MCME** folder you specified as the **Output Folder**, and inside it, Flare places the default folder named **Output**.

Flare creates a sub-folder structure identical to your **Targets** folder in this default **Output** folder. In this case, Flare creates the **Product-A** folder and the **PDF** or **HTML5** subfolder, inside the Output folder, based on the target type (PDF, HTML5) that you build. When Flare generates the output, it places it in a subfolder based on the name of the output file and then puts that folder in the appropriate **PDF** or **HTML5** subfolder. If there were multiple PDF or HTML outputs for **Product-A**, all subsequent PDFs would be placed in the **PDF** subfolder and all the subsequent HTML5 outputs in the **HTML5** subfolder. Each output file would be in a subfolder based on the file's name.

TOC FOLDERS

The **TOCs** folder is a default sub-folder generated in the **Project** folder of the **Project Organizer**. However, you can add subfolders to match your TOC organization requirements.

In this example, the TOC folder organization is similar to how the **Content Explorer** and the **Project Organizer** were structured. I have created a subfolder for the TOCs for **Product-A**, **Product-B**, **Product-C**, and **Product-D**. Within these folders, you may want to make subfolders for **Online TOCs**, and **Print TOCs**. There are many other possibilities for organizing your TOCs since you can have many TOCs in a project based on how you will use them. For example, you may decide to create a chapter for each chapter of a book.

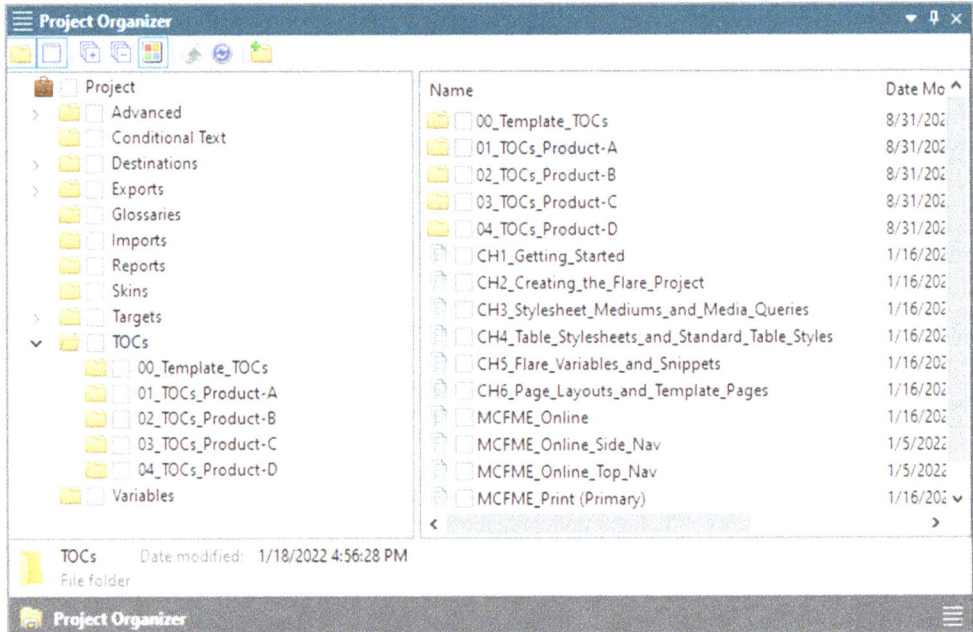

Figure 2-12. Project Organizer — Product TOC Folders.

SUMMARY ON CREATING THE FLARE PROJECT

Whether a small or large project, a single writer, or a team of several, specific tasks performed upfront will ensure getting off to a good initial start in preparing your move to Flare. These preliminary tasks are vital when your work involves migrating a volume of legacy content to Flare. Your work will have started well before working in Flare, preparing your content and work environment.

If you are importing the original project content, then pre-import tasks, and the post-import work involving project clean-up after the import, will be well worth the time. If done with a keen eye for detail and consideration for print and online outputs, these tasks will pay considerable dividends in quickly producing the desired results.

Once you've imported your content and become somewhat familiar with navigating in Flare, you can proceed with your Flare project work. While there are no set rules or fixed order of doing things in Flare, you may find it worthwhile to first focus on creating a new stylesheet, firming up your imported stylesheet, and developing your page layout files. Before starting an import, consider the import-related guidelines listed below. The remainder of this chapter presents some examples of related tasks.

CHECKLIST: CREATING THE FLARE PROJECT

- *If you are starting with Flare the first step will be to create a new project from the **File** menu and **New Project** sub-menu.*

- *The Flare "New project Wizard." allows you to quickly make your project from a Flare template designed to develop projects for online output, print output, or print and online (including eLearning and other HTML5 options). You can also use a user-created project template or an existing project for a quick start to your actual project work.*

- *The new Flare project can also start with a user-created project template or an existing project. Use of a custom template or existing project can mean a quick start to your actual project work.*

- *When importing source content, you can re-import your files as often as required, using the import file generated during and after your initial import. You can even backup and restart an import of your source content before ever completing the import process. When using an import wizard, you can back up to the point you wish to make changes before proceeding forward again.*

- *If you have many books or documents to import — for example, FrameMaker or Word books that have all used the same styles, consider importing one book first and then refining the imported styles. Later you can reference that stylesheet during your subsequent imports.*

- *If you had a robust stylesheet in FrameMaker or Word, consider preserving the stylesheet during the import and enhancing the stylesheet later as required.*

- *Once you've completed an import, review the imported files — you may find that some files are not needed. For example, Flare may create a page layout file for every FrameMaker chapter — these files will likely not be helpful, and you may want to create new page layout files.*

- *Review the imported Conditional Text and Variables files in the Project Organizer. These files may be helpful or may become part of Variable and Conditional Text files that you later create.*

CREATING A PROJECT USING THE NEW PROJECT WIZARD

BASIC CONCEPT

Like most tasks in Flare, there are many ways to create a new project. However, the most flexible means is very likely using the **New Project Wizard**. When using this wizard, you will have the option to indicate how Flare will gather the initial project content. The new project can be created from a **Factory Template** or user-defined **Custom Template**, from an **Existing Project**, or directly from any one of the many Flare supported **Import Options** for the source content.

ESSENTIAL ELEMENTS

Creating a project from a **Factory Template** project offers unique advantages if you are getting started with Flare. You can create your project with actual examples of online or print elements that give you a starting point from which to build. The factory templates, for example, are designed to assist you in developing **Print**, **Online**, **Tutorial**, or **Print and Online** projects. For example, you can choose a template to assist you in developing PDF User Guides, HTML5 websites or Knowledge bases, PDF brochures, or a combination of these.

Starting the new project with the source as **Custom Template** or **New From Existing** can also offer significant advantages. This approach can give users a running start with their actual work if many of the project elements already exist and reside in the custom project template or an existing project. For example, the template can contain the desired file and folder structure, the stylesheet, table stylesheets, template topics, page layout files, variables, essential images, and many other valuable elements.

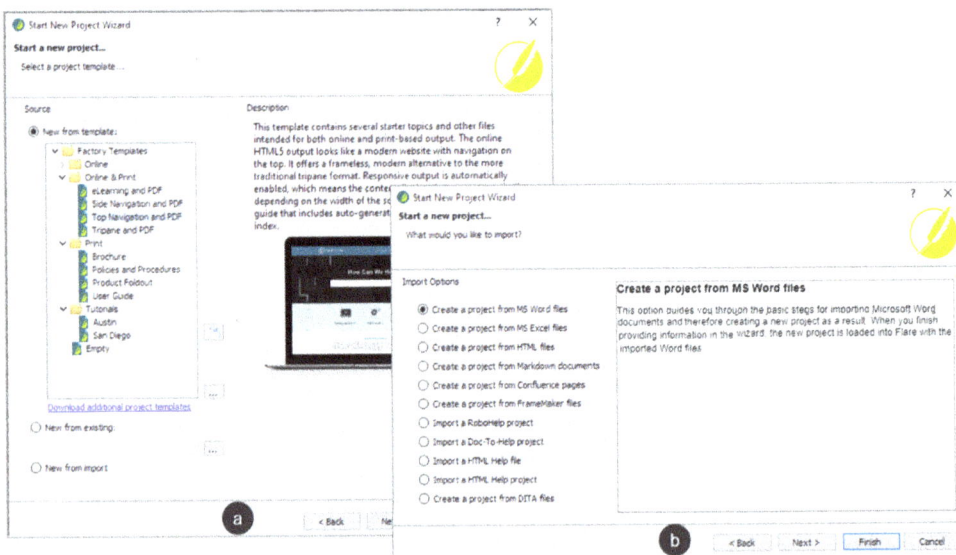

Figure 2-13. Flare New Project from — a) Factory Template, b) Existing Project, and c) Flare Import Option.

> **NOTE:** See *"Creating a Project Using the Word land FrameMaker Import Wizards."*

QUICK STEPS: CREATING A PROJECT USING THE NEW PROJECT WIZARD

STEP	ACTION
1	Click > **File** > **New Project** > **New Project**. The **Start New Project Wizard** dialog opens.
2	Enter a **Project Name** and specify a **Project Folder** or use the default project folder.
3	Choose the **Language** to use in this new project, and click **Next** to advance the wizard.
—	**To Create a New Project from a Factory Template:**
4	**a)** Under **Source**, select the **New from Template** option.
	b) Expand the **Factory Templates** sub-folders to view the available templates for **Online** only, **Online & Print**, **Print** only, and **Tutorials** projects.
	c) Select the project template to use for the new project and click **Next** to advance the wizard.
	d) Click the **Available Targets** drop-down to see the target types that will be created in the new project.
	e) Click **Finish** to generate the new project and store it in the defined location.
—	**To Create a New Project from a Custom Template:**
4	**a)** Under **Source**, select the **New from Template** option.
	b) Expand the **Custom Templates** sub-folders to view the available template projects.
	c) Select the project template to use for the new project and click **Next** to advance the wizard.
	d) Click the **Available Targets** drop-down to view the target types that will be created in the new project.
	e) Click **Finish** to generate the new project and store it in the defined location.
—	**To Create a New Project from an Existing Project:**
4	**a)** Under **Source**, select the **New from Existing** option.
	b) Click the **Browse** button ⎣ ⋯ ⎤ to locate and select the project file to use to create new project.
	c) Click **Next** to advance the wizard to the next screen.
	e) Click the **Available Targets** drop-down and choose the **Primary Target** to use for the project.
	f) Click **Finish** to generate the new project and store it in the defined location. The new project will contain all of the elements of the existing project that was used.
—	**To Create a New Project from one of the Flare Supported Import Options:**
4	**a)** Under **Source**, select the **New from Import** option.
	b) Under **Import Options**, choose one of the import options based on the type of documents you wish to import. For example, **MS Word**, **FrameMaker**, or **Confluence**. The appropriate Import Wizard is opened.
	c) Select the source files you wish to import.
	d) Advance through the wizard pages to specify a Project Name, Project Folder, and Language, then to define Paragraph, Character, and Cross-Reference Style Mapping, and finally specify the Import Options.
	e) Click **Finish** to generate the new project import conversion based on your selected input choices.
	f) Click **Accept** after you have reviewed the import results and are satisfied.

CREATING A NEW PROJECT FROM A PROJECT TEMPLATE

BASIC CONCEPT

When you are ready to create a new project, you can have a head start by creating the project using a template. Like other Flare elements that you create, you will have the choice of creating the project from a Flare Factory Template, or from a user-defined Custom Template.

Whether you choose a Factory Template or a Custom Template, the newly created project will initially contain the same content and project resource elements that are in the template. Regardless of which you choose, there are many are advantages to starting with a template.

ESSENTIAL ELEMENTS

Creating a project from a **Factory Template** project offers unique advantages if you are getting started with Flare. You can create your project with actual examples of online or print elements that give you a starting point from which to build. The factory templates, for example, are designed to assist you in developing **Print**, **Online**, **Tutorial**, or **Print and Online** projects. For example, you can choose a template to assist you in developing PDF User Guides, HTML5 websites or Knowledge bases, PDF brochures, or a combination of these.

Starting the new project with the source as a **Custom Template** can also offer significant advantages. This approach can give users a running start with their actual work if many of the project elements are already created and reside in the custom project template. For example, the template can contain the desired file and folder structure, the stylesheet, table stylesheets, template topics, page layout files, variables, essential images, and many other valuable elements.

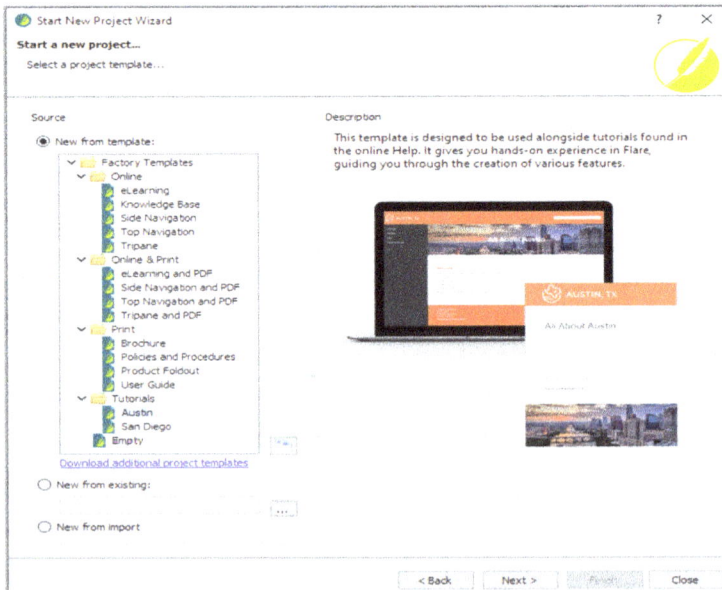

Figure 2-14. Creating a New Project from a Project Template.

QUICK STEPS: CREATING A NEW PROJECT FROM A PROJECT TEMPLATE

STEP	ACTION
1	Start Flare, if it is not already open; otherwise close all open files or the open project.
2	Click > **File** > **New Project**. The **Start New Project Wizard** dialog opens.
3	Enter a **Project Name**.
4	Specify a **Project Folder** or use the default project folder.
5	Click **Next** to advance the wizard to the next screen.
6	Select the **Source** option for **New from Template**, and do one of the following: **a)** Expand the **Factory Templates** sub-folders to view the factory templates available for **Online** only, **Online & Print**, **Print** only, and **Tutorials** projects. **b)** Expand **Custom Templates** (or other user-defined folders) template folders to view project templates.
7	Select the project template to use for the new project.
8	Click **Next** to advance the wizard to the next screen.
9	Click the **Available Targets** drop-down to view the target types that will be created in the new project.
10	Click **Finish** to generate the new project and store it in the defined location.

CREATING A PROJECT USING THE WORD IMPORT WIZARD

BASIC CONCEPT

Users can use the **New Project Wizard** for **MS Word Documents** to import Word files to an existing project, or as in this task, to create a new project. Often, after a project is createdt, you can use the i import additional source files using the wizard. Use of the wizard is straightforward, and guides you through a series of dialogs where your choices provide Flare with details on converting your content from Word to Flare.

ESSENTIAL ELEMENTS

The **Word Import Wizard** has three major parameter sets. First is **General** settings, where you specify a **Project Name** and **Project Folder**, use **Add Files** to choose files to import, and the **Output Type** drop-down to select the primary output type. The second parameter set lets you define style usage in the conversion. Although optional, the **Associate Stylesheet** drop-down enables you to choose an existing stylesheet to apply to the import content. If you choose this option, you can then use the mapping drop-down fields to map the Word styles to specific styles in the stylesheet.

Use the **Start New Topics On** check-boxes to tell Flare which styles encountered during the import to use as break-points to create new topics. Under **Style Mapping**, you can **Discard Word Styles** or keep them. If not discarded, Flare retains the styles and appends each style name to the appropriate Flare — for example, "**p.Caption.**" Flare also saves the imported content formatting, and your topics will look as they did before the import. Otherwise, Flare discard source style names and formatting.

Finally, an **Options** section lets you define optional settings to influence how Flare should handle elements like **Styles**, **Topics**, **Tables**, **Lists**, **Equations**, **Page Layouts**, and **Page Breaks** in the import. The default settings of these options generally produce satisfactory initial results, that you may change.

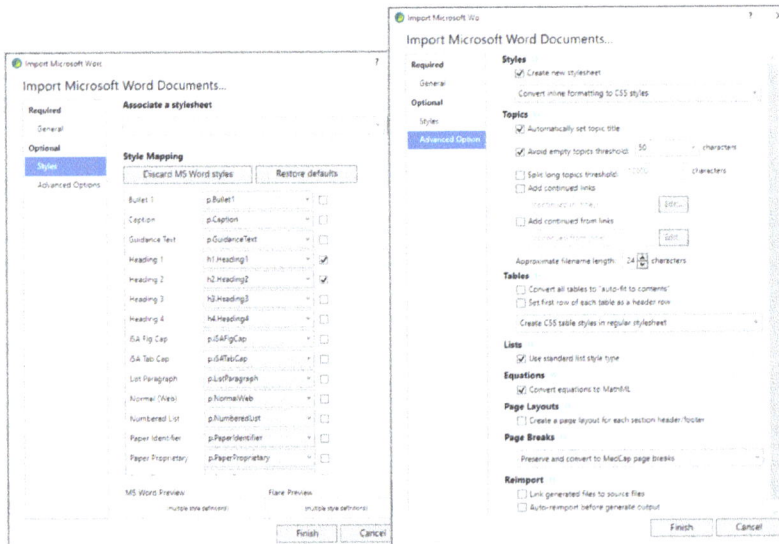

Figure 2-15. Word Import Wizard — a) Specify Stylesheet and Style Mapping and b) Select Conversion Options.

QUICK STEPS: CREATING A PROJECT USING THE WORD IMPORT WIZARD

STEP	ACTION
1	Click > **File** > **New Project** > **New Project**. The **Start New Project Wizard** dialog opens.
2	Enter a **Project Name** and specify a **Project Folder** or use the default project folder.
3	Use the **Output Type** drop-down to choose a Primary Output type for this project. For example, **HTML5**.
4	Click **Add Files** to open the Explorer to choose one or more Word files as the content to import.
5	Click **Next**, when done, to advance the wizard to the next screen.
6	**Associate Stylesheet:** (Optional) Click the **Browse** button ⋯ to locate and select an existing stylesheet (CSS) you wish to associate with the imported content. If you choose this option, under **Style Mapping** the CSS styles from the stylesheet are listed under the **Paragraph** or **Character** drop-down fields, so that you can map each Word style to a style in the CSS.
7	**Optional:** Under **Style Mapping**, do the following if you wish to modify the default style mapping: ■ Click the **Discard MS Word Styles** button, if you wish to keep the Word inline formatting and map it to Flare styles. The Word style names are not retained. ■ Click the **Restore Defaults** button, if at any point you click the **Discard MS Word Styles** button, but change your mind and want to restore the original Word styles. ■ **Paragraph:** Under **MS Word Style** on left, select any one or more Paragraph styles and map them to a Flare parent style. For example, select a paragraph style on the left (on the top) and then select <**p**> as the Flare parent style on the right (on the bottom). ■ **Character:** Under **MS Word Style** on left, select any one or more Character styles and map them to a Flare parent style. For example, select a character style on the left (on the top) and then select <**p**> as the Flare parent style on the right (on the bottom). ■ **Start New Topic On:** Enable the check box adjacent to each style to indicate the styles Flare should use as break-points at which to create new topics. During the content scan Flare creates a new topic each time one of these styles is encountered.
8	**Optional:** Click **Advanced Options** to enable the check-boxes according to your preferences of how Flare should handle **Styles**, **Topics**, **Tables**, **Lists**, **Equations**, **Page Layouts**, **Page Breaks**, and **Re-Importing**.
9	Click **Finish** to generate the new project import conversion, based on your selected input choices. All of the converted files are listed in a window.
10	Click on the **Type** column to sort by file type, then scroll through and view each imported HTML topic.
11	Click **Accept** after you have reviewed the import results and are satisfied.

> **NOTE:** See *"Re-Importing Source Files Using a Flare Import File."*

CREATING A PROJECT USING THE FRAMEMAKER IMPORT WIZARD

BASIC CONCEPT

Users can use the **New Project Wizard** for **FrameMaker Documents** to import FrameMaker files to an existing project, or as in this task, to create a new project. In many cases, after you have created a project, subsequent uses of an import wizard will be to import additional source files. The use of the wizard is reasonably straightforward — it guides you through a series of dialogs where your choices will provide Flare with details on converting your content from FrameMaker to Flare.

ESSENTIAL ELEMENTS

The **FrameMaker Import Wizard** has three major parameter sets. First is **General** settings, where you specify a **Project Name** and **Project Folder**, identify **Source Files** to import, and the project **Language**. The second parameter set lets you define the style usage in the conversion — **New Topic Styles**, for example, tells Flare which styles encountered during the import to use as break-points to create new topics. **Style Mapping** lets you associate the styles of each style category, in your content, as a class under a Flare parent style.

Although optional, **Associate Stylesheet** lets you choose an existing stylesheet to apply to the imported content. You can map the FrameMaker styles to the current CSS styles in the stylesheet by selecting this option. There is also an opportunity to **Preserve FrameMaker Styles** or discard them. If you pre-serve the styles, Flare retains the formatting properties of your source content, and your topics will look as they did before the import. Otherwise, the original style properties of the content are lost.

Finally, an **Options** section lets you define several optional settings that influence how objects like files and images convert and import. In general, the default settings of these options produce satisfactory initial results, but you can change them if necessary.

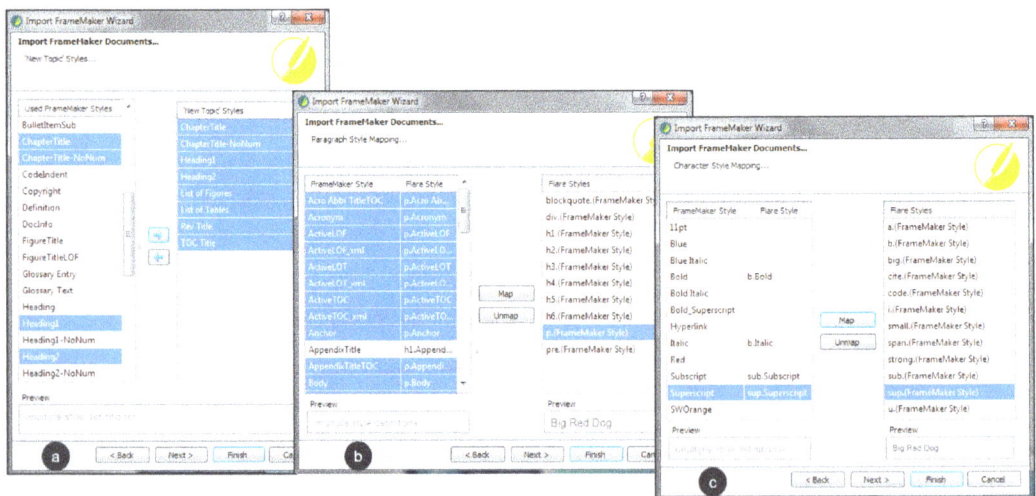

Figure 2-16. FrameMaker Import a) New Topic Styles, b) Map Paragraph Styles, and c) Map Character Styles.

QUICK STEPS: CREATING A NEW PROJECT USING THE FRAMEMAKER IMPORT WIZARD

STEP	ACTION
1	Click > **File** > **New Project** > **New Project**. The **Start New Project Wizard** dialog opens.
2	Enter a **Project Name** and specify a **Project Folder** or use the default project folder.
3	Choose the **Language** to use in this new project.
4	Click **Next** to advance the wizard to the next screen.
5	Follow screen instructions to select source files (.FM or .BK , or .MIF) to import. Click **Next** when done.
6	**New Topic Styles:** Under **Used FrameMaker Style** on left, choose the styles Flare should use as break-points at which to create new topics. During the content scan Flare creates a new topic each time one of these styles is encountered.
7	Click **Next** to advance the wizard.
8	**Associate Stylesheet:** Click the **Stylesheet....** button to locate and select a stylesheet you wish to associate with the imported content.
9	**Paragraph Style Mapping:** Under **Paragraph Styles** on the left, select one or more Paragraph styles and then select <**p**> as the parent style to which the style (s) should be mapped on the right.
	Although heading styles are also <**p**> paragraph styles. Map your heading H1 styles to Flare H1, your heading 2 styles to Flare H2, your heading H3 styles to Flare H3, and so on.
	Click **Next** to advance the wizard.
10	**Character Style Mapping:** Under **FrameMaker Style** on the left, select a Character style and then select the appropriate Flare parent to which the style should be mapped on the right.
	For example, map your "**bold**" to Flare parent <**b**>, your "**italics**" to parent <**i**>, your "**subscript**" to the parent <**sub**>, and your "**superscript**" to the Flare parent <**sup**>. Select all other remaining character styles you wish to keep, then select <**span**> as the parent style to which these styles should be mapped.
11	Click **Next** to advance the wizard .
12	**Cross-Reference Style Mapping:** Under **FrameMaker Style** on left, select all of the Cross-Reference and map them to a Flare parent Cross-Reference parent style "**MadCap|xref**." In the resulting stylesheet in Flare, your styles will be named "**MadCapXref.what-the-FrameMaker-namewas**."
13	Click **Next** to advance the wizard.
14	Click **Finish** to generate the new project import conversion based on your selected input choices. All of the converted files are listed in a window.
15	Click on the **Type** column to sort by file type, then scroll through and view each imported HTML topic.
16	Click **Accept** after you have reviewed the import results and are satisfied

NOTE: See *Re-Importing Source Files Using a Flare Import File."*

RE-IMPORTING FRAMEMAKER SOURCE FILES USING A FLARE IMPORT FILE

BASIC CONCEPT

After initially importing files to your project, or in some cases before completing the import, you can use the Flare import file to re-import if you are not satisfied with the initial results. You can modify any previously set options or parameters during the re-import process. You can repeat the process until you are satisfied. You can accept and generate the output when you are happy with the results. By default, Flare places the import file in the **Project Organizer** > **Project** > **Imports**.

ESSENTIAL ELEMENTS

The re-import is much the same as the original process — a difference is that all of the original saved data is available in the re-import. You can modify any of the original data and leave some parts unchanged. For example, you may add or remove **Source Files** and add or remove **New Topic Styles**. Reducing the number of new topic styles minimizes the number of topics that Flare creates. As you advance to each wizard tab, Flare saves your new selections. You can back up and make changes at any point.

On the **Options** (**Optional** with Word import) tab, you may have made several choices, which you may keep or change. With both Word and FrameMaker imports, you may have specified an existing stylesheet to use, which you may modify. When it comes to Style Mapping, you will have the option to **Preserve FrameMaker Styles** or keep or **Discard Word Styles**. Choosing to keep or discard the import styles will affect whether your imported content will have its original appearance after the import.

When you complete your updates to the import parameters, you can click the **Re-Import** button at the page top of the **Import Editor** tab to trigger the import process.

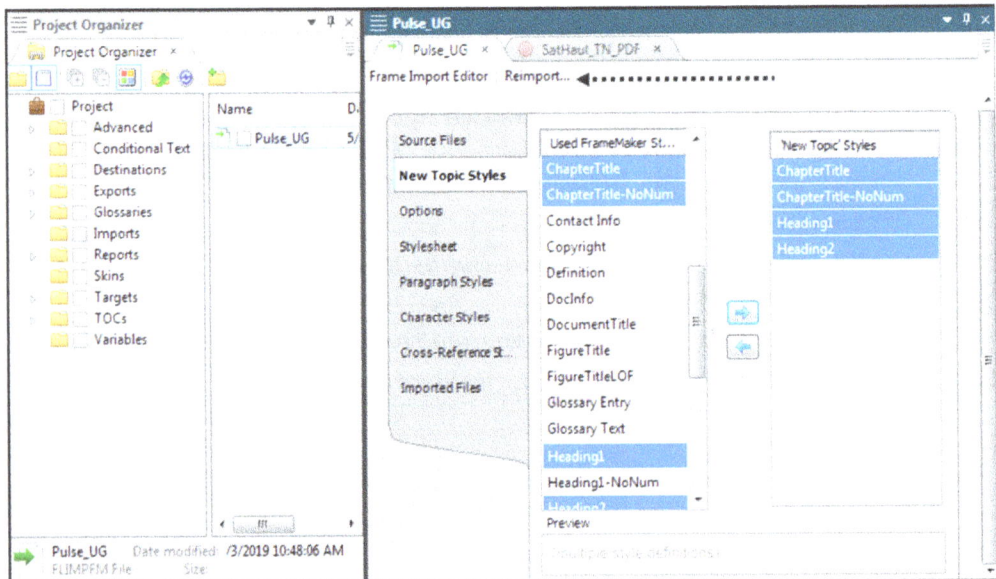

Figure 2-17. Flare Re-Import — New Topic Styles Selections Dialog.

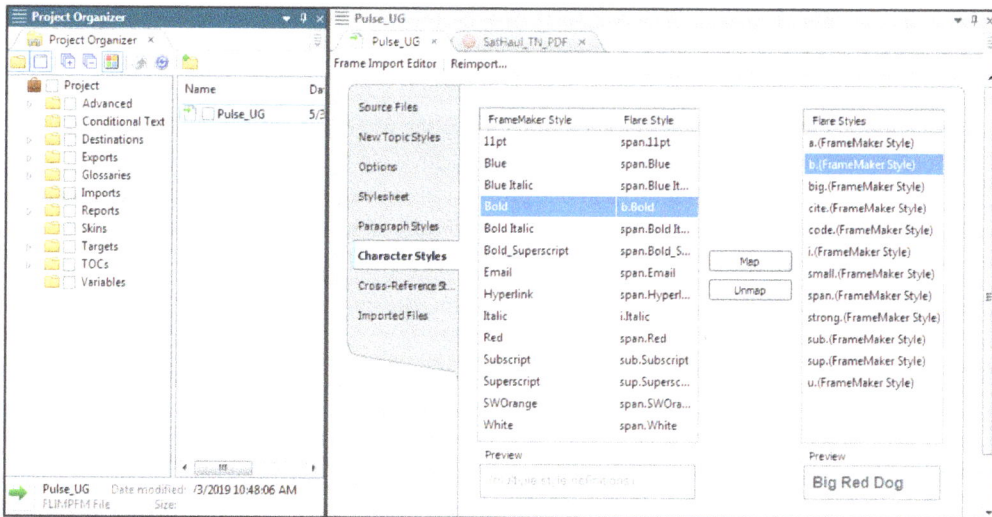

Figure 2-18. Flare Re-Import — Character Styles Mapping Dialog.

QUICK STEPS: RE-IMPORTING FRAMEMAKER SOURCE FILES USING A FLARE IMPORT FILE

STEP	ACTION
1	Select the **Project Organizer**.
2	Click on the **Imports** folder.
3	Locate and double-click on the Import file you wish to use. The file opens to the **Frame Import Editor**.
4	Click the **Source Files** tab, and add or remove any files from the listed files as required.
5	Click the **New Topic Styles** tab, and add or remove styles as required. Recall that the more styles you add, the more topics Flare creates. Also, use heading styles where the content can stand alone as topics.
6	Click the **Options** tab, and modify previous settings as required.
7	Click the **Paragraph Styles** tab, and modify the previous mapping of the FrameMaker paragraph styles to Flare paragraph parents, for example **<p>**, **<h1>**, **<h2>**, and so on.
8	Click the **Character Styles** tab, and modify the previous mapping of the FrameMaker character or span styles to Flare character parent styles.
9	Click the **Re-Import** button at the FrameMaker Editor top. The new project import conversion is re-generated based on your selected input choices. All of the converted files are listed in a window.
10	Click on the **Type** column to sort by file type, then scroll through and view each imported HTML topic.
11	Click **Accept** after you have reviewed the import results and are satisfied.

> **NOTE: Confirm Over-write Documents**: If some documents have been modified since they were imported, Flare gives you an opportunity to select whether to over-write the file or not with the re-imported file.

IMPORTING A FLARE PROJECT TO AN EXISTING PROJECT

BASIC CONCEPT

The need to import one or more Flare projects into an existing project might occur after deciding to work with one core project instead of several smaller projects. This approach might be a solution to manage a set of common shared resources in one project where you produce several documents or other outputs on a periodic release schedule. When you import each of the original projects to an existing project, Flare imports the entire contents unless you make specific exclusions.

ESSENTIAL ELEMENTS

A Flare project (.FLPRJ) file is imported into an existing project from the **Project** ribbon by selecting **Project > Import > Flare Project**. This operation opens the **Import Flare Project Wizard**. After choosing the project you wish to import, you will be allowed to enable or disable specific options that include or exclude files from the import. By setting the parameters for **Include Files**, you can determine topic file inclusion using the extensions (**HTML**, **htm**) and whether to **Auto-Include Linked Files**. Linked files are those linked to files you will be importing.

By setting the parameters for **Exclude Files**, you can determine file exclusions using specific Flare file extensions — for example, snippet (*.**flsnp**), topic (*.**html**, *.**htm**), page layout (*.**flpgl**), template pages (*.**flmsp**), and stylesheet (*.**css**) files. You can also determine file exclusions using **Import Conditions**, whereby you set **Condition Tags** that can include or exclude tagged files.

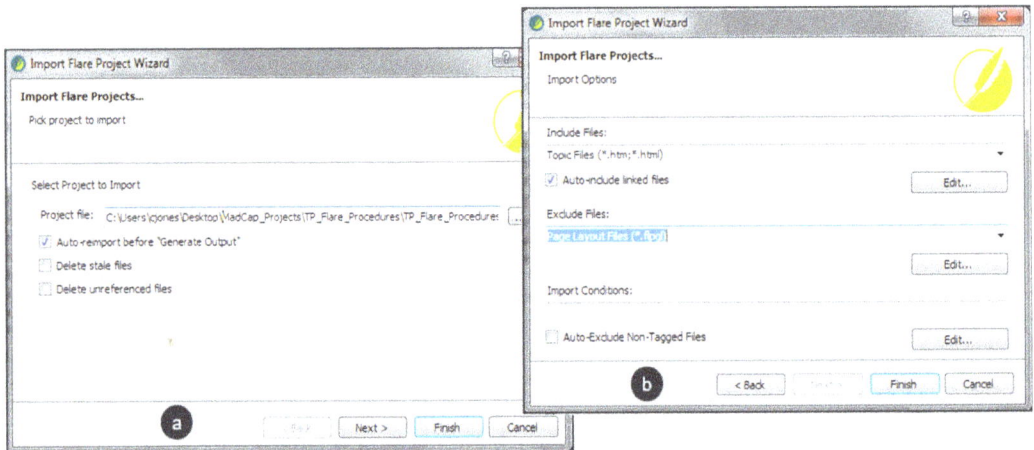

Figure 2-19. a) Select Project to Import to Existing Project b) Select Import Options to Include or Exclude Files.

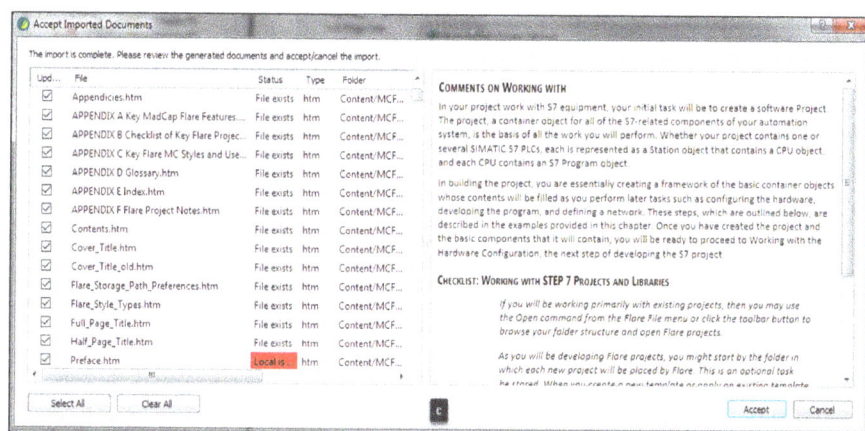

Figure 2-20. Review Files from Fare Project Import and Accept or Cancel Import.

QUICK STEPS: IMPORTING A FLARE PROJECT TO AN EXISTING PROJECT

STEP	ACTION
1	Click the **Project** ribbon, then click the **Import** drop-down and select **Flare Project**.
2	Click the **Browse** button adjacent to the **Project File** field and locate a Flare project (FLPRJ) file to import.
3	Use the three options below to enable options as follows:
	a) Enable **Auto-re-import before "Generate Output,"** to enable the option to automatically re-import imported documents before you build a target. This option is on the General tab of the target file.
	b) **Delete stale files** to delete files from your project that have been deleted from the source project.
	c) Enable **Delete unreferenced files** to be able to select which files can be re-imported later.
4	Click **Next** to advance the wizard. The **Import Options** dialog opens.
5	Use the **Include Files** drop-down to select the files to import from the project.
6	Disable the **Auto-include linked files** option to exclude from the import, files that are linked to topics or files that will be imported. The links will be removed.
	Click **Edit** to open the **Import File Filter** dialog and follow instructions to Add patterns for files to exclude from the import.
7	Use the **Exclude Files** drop-down to select the files to exclude from the import.
	Use the **Edit** button to open the **Conditional Text** dialog. From the available Condition Tag Sets select **Condition Tags** and specify whether to **Include** or **Exclude** tagged elements in the content.
8	Enable **Auto-Exclude Non-Tagged Files** option to ensure all topics non-tagged topics are not imported.
9	Click **Finish** to advance the wizard and open the **Accept Imported Documents** dialog. By default, all of the files designated for import have the **Updated** column check box enabled.
	Remove the check box for any file you do not want to be updated prior to completing the import.
10	Click **Accept** after you have reviewed the import results and are satisfied, otherwise **Cancel**.

COPYING EXTERNAL RESOURCES FILES TO THE PROJECT

BASIC CONCEPT

External Resources folders are a way of working with and maintaining access to files outside of your project. Typically this feature provides access to files that you expect will change over time, and you want Flare to synchronize the changes with your projects. This scenario is typical with files like splash pages, UI and logo images, or PDFs that you offer as downloads. This procedure initially copies files from designated External Resources folders to your project.

ESSENTIAL ELEMENTS

Flare will not list any folders and files unless you have previously identified them as external resources when you attempt to open the **External Resources** folders. You can tell Flare which folders to use as external resources from the **Project** ribbon > **External Resources**. In such a case, you will have to identify the folder before copying any files to the project. You must locate a folder from the identified **External Resources** folder and select files you wish to copy to the project. Flare prompts you to specify a destination folder to which the files will be copied or to **Make a New Folder** in the project.

APPLICATION TIPS

Consider using external folder names and project folder names that coincide when defining external resources folders. Each external resources folder contains image files that have a corresponding folder of the same name in the **Content > Resources > Images (CH01-CH12)** folder. See Figure 2-22.

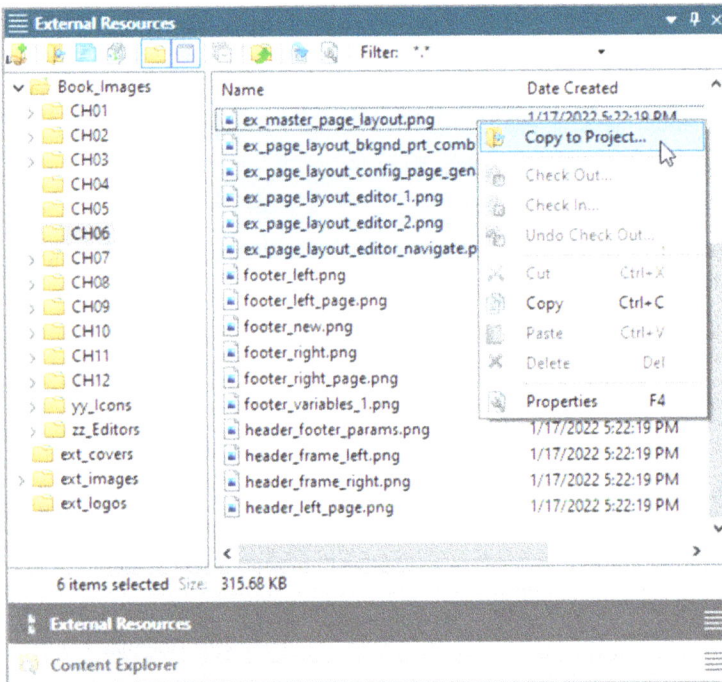

Figure 2-21. Copy Files from Flare External Resources Folders.

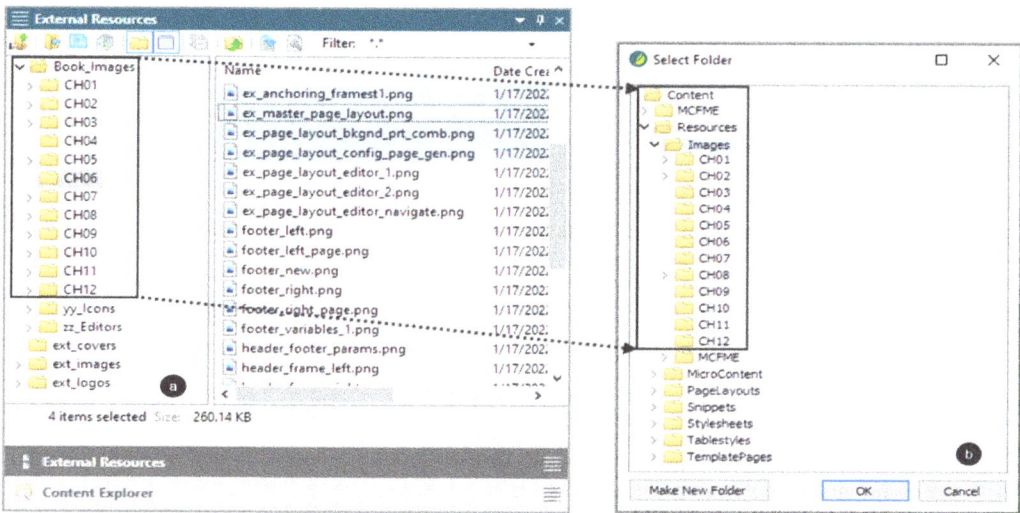

Figure 2-22. Example of Target Folders in Project.

QUICK STEPS: COPYING EXTERNAL RESOURCES FILES TO THE PROJECT

STEP	ACTION
—	**To identify External Resources folders in Flare:**
1	Click the **Project** ribbon.
2	Click the button 📁 to **Add a new external resources folder**. Do the following if no folders are listed:
3	Select the folder you wish to add to your project as an **External Resources** folder.
4	Click **OK** to add the folder.
5	Repeat the previous steps from Step 3 to add additional folders.
—	**To copy External Resources files to the project:**
1	Click the **Project** ribbon.
2	Click **External Resources** to open the window, if not already open.
3	Select the folder that contains files you wish to copy to the project.
4	Right-click and select **Copy to Project**
5	From the **Select Folder** window, choose a destination folder, or click **Make New Folder** button to create a new target folder.
6	Enable the option to **Keep file(s) synchronized**, to establish a connection between the copy of the files in the project and the original files in the mapped external resources folder.
7	Click **OK** to copy the files to the project.

CREATING A GLOBAL PROJECT STRUCTURE

BASIC CONCEPT

As described here, the "Global Project Structure" involves a parent project and two or more child projects. In this scenario, the child projects have individual responsibilities and produce different outputs, but all share a collection of identical resources maintained on the parent project. Each child project would periodically import the shared resources to ensure synchronization.

You can apply this global project model to a team of writers that collectively develop the documents associated with one or more product families. Each product family has a suite of documents developed and maintained from one of the child projects and is released regularly by one or more writers.

ESSENTIAL ELEMENTS

The global project serves mainly as a repository for the resource files shared among the child projects. These shared resources would be identical for all child projects and include files like template topics and topic templates, stylesheets, table stylesheets, variables, page layouts, template pages, condition tag sets, images, glossaries, and others.

Whereas each child project might be developed and maintained by a different team member, the global project might be updated and maintained by a designated team member or team lead.

APPLICATION TIPS

An alternative to a global project structure, in the scenario given above is a single project that manages multiple product families and the associated document suites. A set of common or "Shared Resources" would be developed for all writers. A source control application would provide backup and version control management. You would produce all of the targets from this single project.

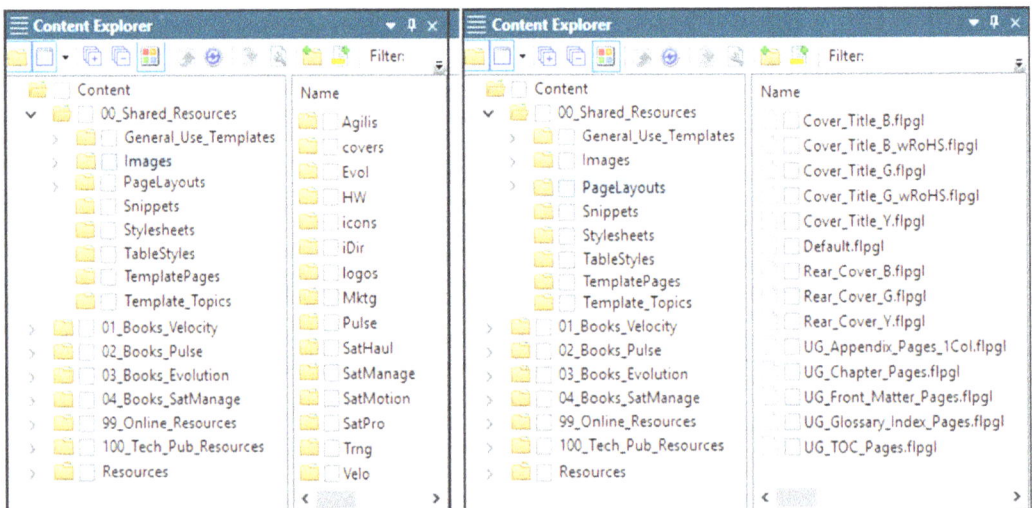

Figure 2-23. Global Project Shared Resources Folder — a) Images Subfolder b) Page Layouts Subfolder.

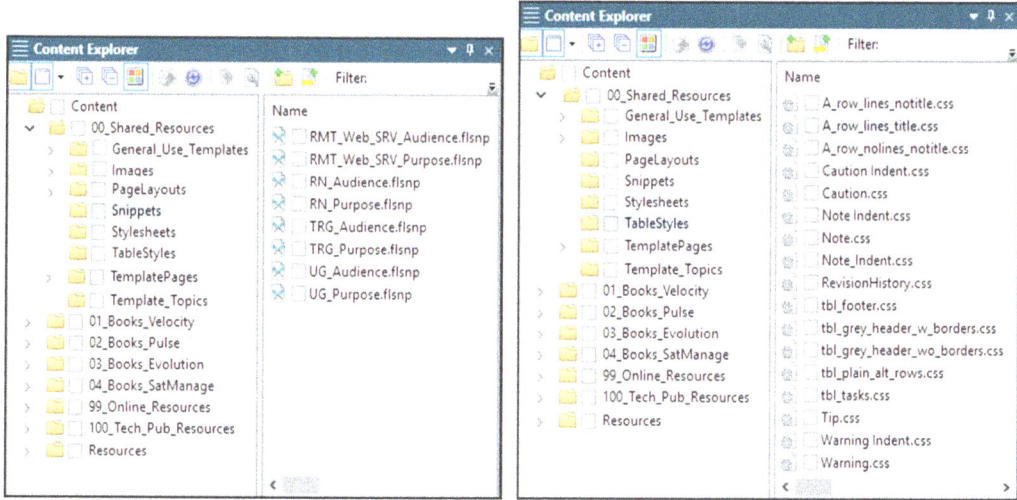

Figure 2-24. c) Snippets Subfolder d) Table Stylesheets Subfolder.

QUICK STEPS: CREATING A GLOBAL PROJECT STRUCTURE

STEP	ACTION
1	Develop a comprehensive and robust **Stylesheet** for both print and online outputs.
2	Create one or more document front and rear covers for each product suite.
3	Create a set of **Page Layout** files for the common sections of the documents in each product family. Examples include, Title and Cover Pages, Front Matter Pages, Chapter Pages, Glossary and Index Pages.
4	Create a common set of Document **Variables** for use across the product and document families.
5	Create a set of common **Snippets** that can be used across the product and document families.
6	Create a set of common **Table Stylesheets** that can be used across the product and document families.
7	Create a set of common **Template Pages** that can be used in online outputs across the product families.
8	Create a set of common **Template Topics** that can be used across the product and document families. These topics, like a generated TOC proxy topic can be placed in the TOC outline of any document.
9	Create a **CustomTemplates** folder and a set of custom templates for use across document families.
10	Create a set of common **Images** that can be used in online and outputs across the product families.
11	Create a set of **Conditional Tag Sets** that can be used in online and outputs across the product families.
12	Create a plan whereby each writer can **Import** and synchronize with the **Shared Resources** folder.

CHAPTER 3

STYLESHEETS, MEDIUMS, AND MEDIA QUERIES

KEY STYLE TERMINOLOGY AND CONCEPTS

An essential part of working with styles and stylesheets is understanding some key style terms and concepts. Terminology like HTML Elements, CSS, Selectors, and others may sound foreign but they are fundamental in understanding style use and application. This understanding will also simplify creating new styles and viewing how you apply styles to content in the Topic XML and Text Editor views.

HTML ELEMENTS

An *HTML element* is one of several individual components that can make up an HTML page or document. Components like Title, Headings, Body, Paragraphs, and Images. Each of these elements is enclosed in an identifying Start and End Tag starting with a document root. For example, a paragraph has the start <p> tag and the end </p> tag. HTML tags are either "block-level elements," like the <p> tag, which always have a line break after the end tag; or "inline elements," like the <span> tag, which can be placed next to each other and do not have a line break after the closing tag. You can view these tags in your topics if the structure bars are enabled or in the Text Editor view.

Table 3-1. HTML Elements from Basic Elements Category

HTML Element	Start	End	Examples
Root	<html>	</html>	<html>all page elements go between these two tags</html>
Head	<head>	</head>	<head>information about the page is placed here</head>
Page Title	<title>	</title>	<title>the page title is inserted between these two tags</title>
Body	<body>	</body>	<body>elements inserted here are considered body</body>
Heading (h1-h6)	<h1>	</h1>	<h1>This is an H1 section heading</h1>
Paragraph	<p>	</p>	<p>This is a paragraph</p>
Link	<a>	</a>	<a>href="www.address.com"</a> ; href is destination argument
Image	<img>	</img>	<img>src="Myphoto.jpg" alt="My Photo"</img>
Span	<span>	</span>	<span>an inline container for selected content</span>
Div	<div>	</div>	<div>container of grouped elements inside these tags</div>

CASCADING STYLE SHEETS (CSS)

A *Cascading Style Sheets* or *CSS* is the language used to style the HTML elements in a document. This CSS styling describes how HTML elements, like the previously introduced elements for <p>, <h1> through <h6>, <img>, <span> and others, will display or behave. Several CSS styles are already defined in your stylesheet and may be viewed in the Stylesheet Editor. Pre-defined styles for these HTML elements are essentially parent styles or primary styles. You can use these parent styles, but it is best to create child styles under parents. You can also modify parent styles but not create new ones.

ELEMENT ATTRIBUTE

An *Element Attribute* is a modifier that changes the default functionality of an HTML element by providing additional information. Each attribute is generally declared in a name="value" pair that directly follows the opening tag. While most attributes are arbitrary, for some elements, an attribute is required for the element to function correctly. The link tag <a>, for example, always uses the **href** attribute, as in **<a>href="www.destination.com"</a>**, to define the URL to a linked page. Similarly, the image tag <img> uses the **src** attribute to define the image path, as shown in the previous table.

PROPERTIES AND VALUES

A *property* is a characteristic of an HTML element. Each element has many properties for use in styling in a CSS rule. Text properties, for example, include font-family, font-size, font-variant, and font-weight. A *value* is the exact setting defined for a property. Each property has valid values from which you may specify a value. Example values for the properties given here are Segoe Condensed, 14 pts, small-caps, and bold, respectively. These properties, for which you can specify values, ultimately affect the appearance and behavior of the HTML element.

STYLE SELECTOR

In CSS, a *style selector* targets HTML elements that we want to apply formatting to in our HTML pages and documents. Generally, we think of style tags as what we use to physically apply formatting to headings, paragraphs, lists, or other parts of our content. These tags, however, are basic selectors — but in CSS, we can also create advanced selectors. With an advanced selector, you do not always have to physically select the content for the style properties defined in the selector to be applied. Advanced selectors are more complex tags and affect the styling or behavior of specific parts of our content.

In short, advanced selectors allow you to target, with fine-grained precision, specific elements in the content to be affected. Advanced selectors contain a pattern or rule (criteria) that, when matched, the defined properties are applied to all elements in your content that match the rule.

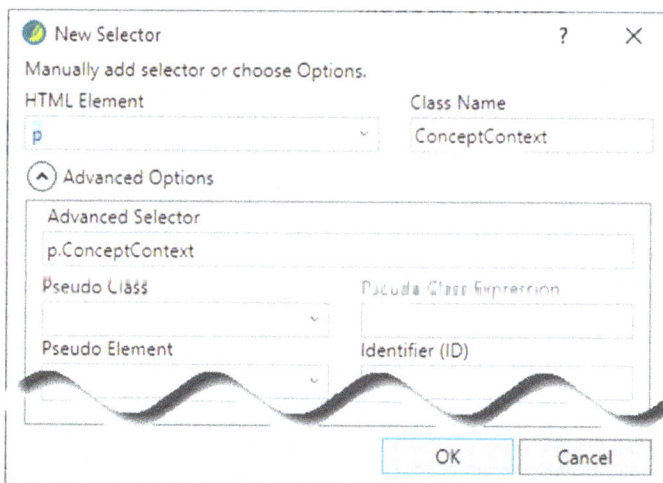

Figure 3-1. Add Selector Dialog.

STYLE CLASS

In CSS, a *class* (or *style class*) is the most common type of child that can be created under a parent style — parent styles like <p>, <h1>, <h2>, <div>, and <img>. For example, under the parent style <p> you might want to create child classes "body," "footer," and "header." Each style class you create inherits all of the properties of the HTML parent. When you override specific properties in a class, you give it its unique style. Creating child classes offer flexibility in styling different parts of your content.

In the stylesheet Simplified View, each style class is displayed in a row under its parent, prefixed with the parent tag, and separated by a period — for example, **p.bodytext**, or **h1.heading1**.

GENERIC CLASS

A *generic class* is not a child to any specific HTML parent, and as such, can be applied to styles associated with any parent — hence generic. For example, you might assign to a generic class the property of "centered," "blue," "bold," or "red" that can be applied to any content, regardless of the parent style. The generic class eliminates the need to create several styles to achieve the same effect — for example, "center justify" can be applied to styles with different parents. If, for example, you create a generic class called ".center," it can be applied to center align elements associated with <p>, <h1>, <img>, <div> or any parent style.

In the **Simplified View**, generic classes are displayed at the bottom of the stylesheet, and only with a preceding period, but not under a parent, as they have no parent. When the Styles Category is set for **All Styles**, generic classes are listed under **Generic Classes** in the **Advanced View**.

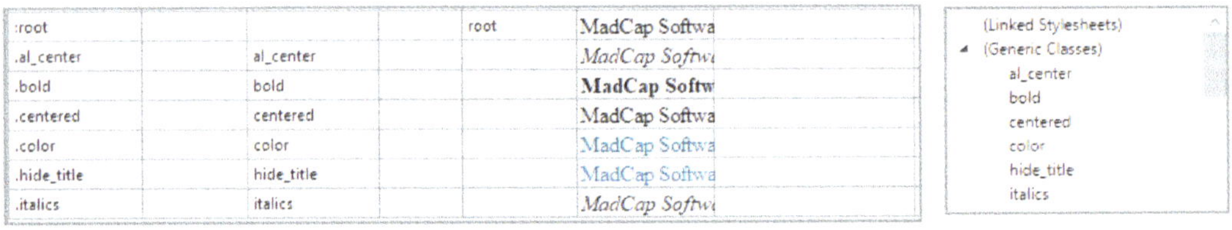

:root			root	MadCap Softwa		(Linked Stylesheets)
.al_center	al_center			*MadCap Softw*		▲ (Generic Classes)
.bold	bold			**MadCap Softw**		al_center
.centered	centered			MadCap Softwa		bold
.color	color			MadCap Softwa		centered
.hide_title	hide_title			MadCap Softwa		color
.italics	italics			*MadCap Softw*		hide_title
						italics

Figure 3-2. Generic Classes a) listed in Stylesheet Simplified View and b) listed in Stylesheet Advanced View.

PSEUDO-CLASS

A CSS *pseudo-class* (style) added to a selector specifies a state of an element or a relation to the element. In CSS, the pseudo-class takes the form **selector:pseudo_class { property: value; }**, with a colon in between the selector name and the pseudo name. With links, for example, pseudo-classes can be defined to target links not yet visited as **a:link{color:blue;}**, links already visited as **a:visited{color:purple;}**, and links that the user mouses over as **a:hover{color:green;}**. These may be the most common pseudo-class types you will encounter; however, there are several categories of pseudo-class.

A pseudo-class that targets a relation, for example, might target the relative position in the element. You might want to make the first list item <li> of an unordered list <ul> blue and the last list item red. In this case, the pseudo-classes **:first-child** and **:last-child** respectively would satisfy these criteria. In the Simplified View, as shown in the table, pseudo-classes follow the selector, preceded by a colon.

Table 3-2. Partial List of HTML Pseudo-Classes

Pseudo Class	Example	Example Description
:link	**a:link**	Selects all unvisited links
:visited	**a:visited**	Selects all visited links
:hover	**a:hover**	Selects link that currently has mouse over
:focus	**input:focus**	Selects the <input> element that currently has focus
:first-child	**p:first-child**	Selects every <p> element that is the first child of its parent
:last-child	**p:last-of-type**	Selects every <p> element that is the last <p> element of its parent
:nth-child(n)	**p:nth-child(2)**	Selects every <p> element that is the second child of its parent

PSEUDO-ELEMENT

A CSS *pseudo-element* is a keyword added to a selector to style a specific part of a targeted HTML element. For example, **::first-line** can be used to change the font of the first line of a paragraph; or **p::first-letter**, to style the first letter of every paragraph. A pseudo-element is slightly different from a pseudo-class. Pseudo-classes match elements that exist, and a pseudo-element targets "virtual" elements that may change depending on the actual HTML. For example, a pseudo-element can insert content before or after specific content if the rule matches.

In CSS, a pseudo-element selector applies styles to specific parts of your content in scenarios with no specific HTML element to select. For example, rather than putting the first letter of each paragraph in an element of its own, you can style them all using the pseudo-element **p::first-letter**. The style would be applied to the first letter of every paragraph.

In the stylesheet Simplified View, each pseudo-element is generally displayed in a row and preceded by a double colon — for example, **::before**, **::after**, **::first-line**, and **::first-letter**.

IDENTIFIER

An *Identifier (ID)* is added to a selector to identify a single element as being unique. Whereas an HTML element like <p> can have many classes, it can have only one identifier. Furthermore, you can only apply an ID to a single element on an HTML page. For example, <div id="sidebar"> would apply the "sidebar" style to the div that references it. The ID attribute also provides a document-wide unique identifier for an element.

When an identifier is given a name in the **Identifier (ID)** field of the New Selector dialog, the ID name is prefixed by a hashtag in the **Advanced Selector** field — for example, **#unique**.

INTRODUCING STYLESHEET MEDIUMS AND MEDIA QUERIES

A *medium* is a group of style settings in a stylesheet, generally applying to a specific use or output type. A CSS stylesheet may contain multiple mediums. For example, you might define one medium for online outputs and another for print outputs. Flare automatically generates the Default, Print, Tablet, and Mobile Mediums when you create a stylesheet. The style medium is specified on the **Advanced** tab when you configure a target file for a specific output.

THE DEFAULT MEDIUM

The *Default Medium* is always used unless another medium is specified. All other mediums in the stylesheet inherit new selectors created in the default medium. Also, specific style settings as modified in the default medium are inherited in the different mediums, unless that same setting in these other mediums was already explicitly specified. On the other hand, a style property modified in any other medium does not affect that property in the default medium.

> **NOTE:** New styles are best created in the Default Medium as they are inherited by the other mediums. Conversely, styles created in a medium other than the default are not inherited in the Default Medium.

THE PRINT MEDIUM

The *Print Medium* is intended for use with print-based outputs and is, therefore, generally specified with PDF and Word target files. A print medium is generated whenever you create a new stylesheet, but you may make additional print mediums if necessary. Like all mediums other than the Default Medium, the Print Medium is added to the project from the Stylesheet Editor using the **Add New Medium** command. It is initially a replica of the default medium.

MEDIA QUERIES

A *media query* is an alternative group of stylesheet settings automatically applied under certain conditions, like viewing the output on a particular screen size or device type. Queries are defined with specific criteria — such as maximum screen width, display orientation, or resolution. When the specified criteria are met, the appropriate media query is applied to the output. Flare provides a Tablet Media Query and a Mobile Media Query for use with smaller screens like smartphones.

INTRODUCING THE FLARE STYLESHEET EDITOR

The Flare Stylesheet Editor is used to create and modify CSS styles in regular stylesheets. You can generally find these stylesheet files in the Content Explorer — **Resources** > **Stylesheets**. Double-clicking on a stylesheet (.css) file opens the file in the Stylesheet Editor, which has two presentations for rendering and editing stylesheet selectors.

The *Simplified View* presents styles in a spreadsheet-like representation. When focused on a selector, you can use the editor toolbar to modify a minimum set of style properties. You can also double-click on a selector to open a simple dialog to edit the selector properties. The *Advanced View* is a tripane view of the stylesheet that provides full access to CSS styles and style properties.

THE SIMPLIFIED VIEW

In the stylesheet Simplified View, relevant CSS properties display in the column heads across the top of the stylesheet; and each style is listed alphabetically on a row (name and tag in the first two columns), forming a grid-like interface. Finally, each style element has its property values listed across the element row under the appropriate property column.

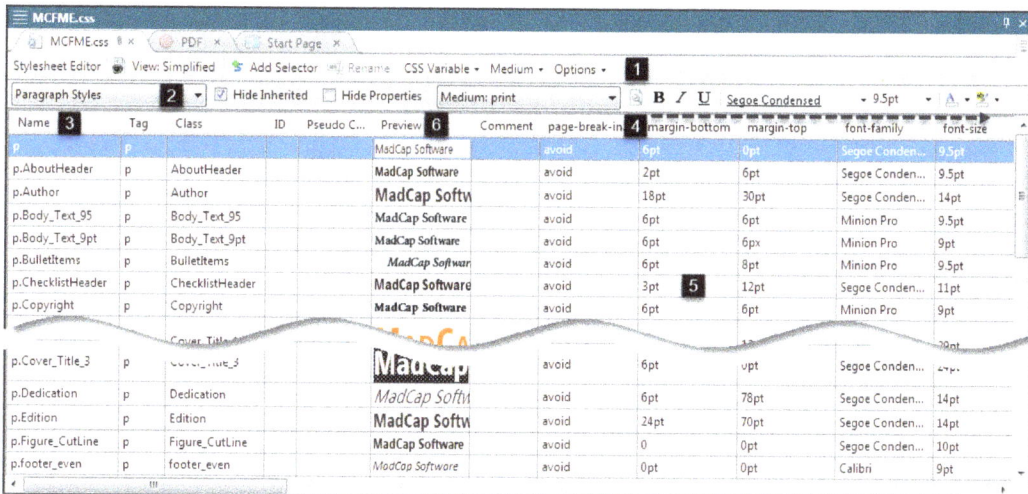

Figure 3-3. Flare Stylesheet Editor — Simplified View.

Table 3-3. Stylesheet Editor—Simplified View

Page Area	Brief Description
1	The **Toolbar Area:** You can **a)** switch to Advanced View, **b)** Add New Selector, **c)** switch stylesheet Medium, **d)** change properties view and other functions.
2	The **Style Category:** You can use the drop-down arrow to choose which CSS style category you wish to display and work with. For example, **Paragraph Styles** or **List Styles**.
3	The **Selector (Styles) Area:** Individual selectors (styles) are listed in alphabetical order in the first column of the grid, under the **Name** column head.
4	The **Style Properties:** You can choose which property of the currently selected style (selector) for which you wish to set values. Style properties names are listed in the top header row of the grid.
5	The **Property Values:** Each style class and its property values are listed across the selector row. You can type directly in a value field to modify the single value; double-click on the row to open the dialog associated with the style. Use the toolbar editor buttons at the right side of the toolbar, to simultaneously modify several values associated with the selected style class.
6	The **Style Preview:** Use this column and the associated row to preview the currently selected style as you modify the associated property values.

THE ADVANCED VIEW

The Flare stylesheet Advanced View displays individual HTML parent styles in a tri-pane view. Parent styles, like h1, h2, p, and span, are listed in the left-side pane. In this view, you can use the left-pane drop-down arrow to choose which parent Style Category to list, or you can choose to list All Styles, in which case all parent styles are listed. Child classes are listed immediately under their associated parent style, which can be expanded or collapsed.

Focusing on a specific parent style causes its property groups to be listed in the right-side pane. You can choose from the toolbar whether to list properties alphabetically or by property group. A *property group* is a related collection of CSS properties associated with a particular style class in CSS.

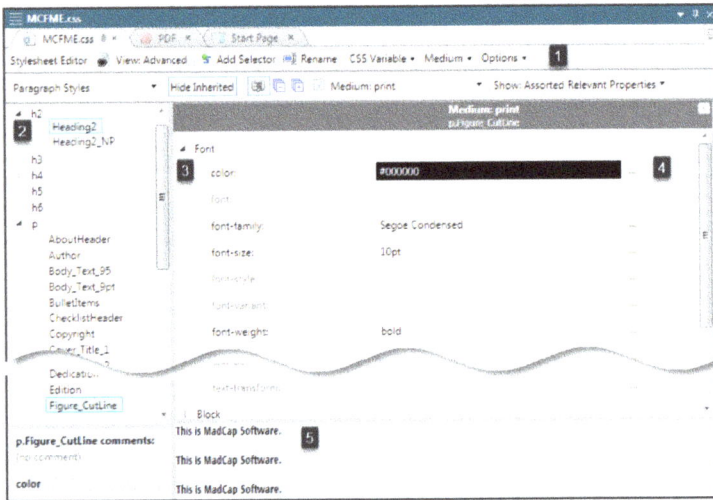

Figure 3-4. Flare Stylesheet Editor — Advanced View.

Table 3-4. Stylesheet Editor—Advanced View

Page Area	Brief Description
1	The **Toolbar Area:** You can **a)** switch to Simplified View, **b)** Add New Selector, **c)** switch between stylesheet mediums, **d)** change properties view, and other functions.
2	The **Style Category/Style Selector Area:** You can use the drop-down arrow to choose which CSS style category you wish to display and work with. For example, **Paragraph Styles** or **List Styles**.
3	The **Style Property Area:** You can choose the property of the currently selected style for which you wish to set values. Style properties are listed along the left side of the pane. A property group can be expanded or collapsed. Expand a property group to find the property you wish to modify.
4	The **Property Value Area:** With a property group expanded, you can choose the value you wish to modify for the currently selected style. Click on the field edit icon (**...**) to the right of the property.
5	The **Style Preview Area:** Use this pane to preview the currently selected style as you modify the associated property values.

INTRODUCING FLARE CSS STYLE CATEGORIES

When operating in the Flare Stylesheet Editor **Simplified View** or **Advanced View**, you can use the Styles Category drop-down to list all styles or limit the list by selecting a specific style category.

When working in the Topic Editor, the style categories, as shown in the table, are listed and can be accessed from the **Home** menu, using the **Styles Window** or the **Styles Pane** drop-down. In a given instance, the styles listed are context-sensitive and based on how you have selected content or placed your cursor. For example, focusing the cursor inside a paragraph causes <p> styles to be listed. Selecting specific content, like a word or sentence, causes <span> styles to be listed in the Styles Window.

Table 3-5. Flare Style Categories

Style Category	Brief Description
Auto-Numbered Styles	Includes style classes that support numerical or alphabetical numbering. For example, **FigureCaption**, **TableCaption**, or **ChapterNumber**.
Topic Styles	Includes the HTML styles and classes that can be applied to affect an entire topic.
Paragraph Styles	Style classes applied to an entire paragraph — for example, **p.body** or **p.copyright**.
Footnote Styles	Apply these styles to footnotes in your topic content. Your Flare stylesheet inherits several Footnote Styles, and you may add new style selectors.
Heading Styles	Apply these styles to headings that are placed above other content, as in topics — for example, **H1.heading1**, **H2.heading2**, and **H3.heading3**.
Character Styles	Apply these styles to a selected part of a paragraph as opposed to an entire paragraph—for example, **i.italics**, **span.bold**, or **span.superscript**.
Table Styles	Apply these styles to table elements, like caption, header, table body, footer, cell, row, and table column.
List Styles	Apply these styles to create formatted lists — for example a numbered list, such as a sequence of steps in a procedure; or an unordered lists, such as a bullet list.
Link Styles	Apply these styles to content that represent links, like cross-references, related topics, hyperlinks, or other such links, including external links.
Image Styles	Apply these styles format the images in a project.
Dynamic Effects Styles	Apply these styles to create Dynamic HTML effects like for menus, toggles, popup windows, drop-down text, and expanding text.
Reusable Content Styles	Apply these styles to reusable content like snippets, variables, headers and footers.
Generated Content Styles	Apply these styles to Flare generated content, such as a generated TOC, a generated Index, or a generated Glossary.
Controls/Form Styles	Styles that are applied to content that contains controls such as buttons and forms.

TYPICAL STYLES AND STYLE SETTINGS

If you have imported your content, you will likely have a head start with producing many of the styles needed in your project. However, you will still have to decide whether to keep the imported stylesheet or create a new one. A well-planned and robust set of styles will help to ensure that writers can easily style their documents and create aesthetically pleasing documents.

In your project, you will want to have suitable **Paragraph**, **Heading**, **Character**, **Table**, **List**, **Link**, and **Image** styles. A sample portion of a stylesheet is shown, with properties, in the table below. For the most part, these are styles and properties easily created in the **Simplified View** of the Stylesheet Editor. To complete your stylesheet, make sure to take advantage of the many inherited styles and properties.

Table 3-6. A Partial List of Typical Print Styles and Style Properties

Style Name	Font Family	Size	Variant	Bef-Aft	Line Hgt	Align
Copyright	MinionPro	10 pt		6 pt - 6 pt	12 pt	left
BodyText	MinionPro	10 pt		6 pt - 6 pt	12 pt	left
BulletLevel1	MinionPro	10 pt		6 pt - 6 pt	12 pt	left
BulletLevel2	MinionPro	10 pt		6 pt - 6 pt	12 pt	left
NumericList	MinionPro	10 pt		6 pt - 6 pt	12 pt	left
LowerAlphaList	MinionPro	10 pt		6 pt - 6 pt	12 pt	left
UpperAlphaList	MinionPro	10 pt		6 pt - 6 pt	12 pt	left
FrntMatterHead	Segoe Condensed	16 pt	Small Cap	0 pt - 3 pt	0 pt	left
AppendixTitle	Segoe Condensed	64 pt	Small Cap	0 pt - 36 pt	0 pt	left
ChapterTitle	Segoe Condensed	64 pt	Small Cap	0 pt -36 pt	0 pt	left
Heading1	Segoe Condensed	14 pt	Small Cap	8 pt - 3 pt	0 pt	left
Heading2	Segoe Condensed	12 pt	Small Cap	6 pt - 3 pt	0 pt	left
Heading3	Segoe Condensed	10 pt		6 pt - 3 pt	0 pt	left
CaptionFigure	Segoe Condensed	10 pt		0 pt - 14 pt	0 pt	center
CaptionTable	Segoe Condensed	10 pt		14 pt - 0 pt	0 pt	center
Gloss_Letter	Segoe Condensed	12 pt		16 pt-12 pt	0 pt	center
Gloss_Entry	MinionPro	9.5 pt		0 pt - 6 pt	11 pt	left
Gloss_Text	MinionPro	9.5 pt		0 pt - 6 pt	11 pt	left

SUMMARY ON STYLESHEETS, MEDIUMS, AND MEDIA QUERIES

Whether creating your project based on a Flare or a custom project template or based on an import, for example, from Word or FrameMaker, the stylesheet component will be an essential element. The cascading stylesheet (CSS), along with the page layout files for print targets and template pages for online targets, will have the most significant visible impact on the appearance of your outputs.

Time spent on creating a robust CSS will be time well spent. Improving your stylesheet, one style category at a time, is an opportunity to ensure that the styles are suited to your needs — for example, Heading, List, Paragraph, Character, Auto-Numbering, Cross-Reference, and Image Styles. Remember also to take advantage of Flare-inherited styles. In the end, your stylesheet will produce the appearance and the behavior you wish to achieve in your target outputs. Before starting with topics and other project work, consider the style-related guidance outlined below and the style-related tasks that follow.

CHECKLIST: WORKING WITH CASCADING STYLESHEETS AND STYLES

- *If you imported a robust stylesheet from FrameMaker or Word, consider preserving the stylesheet during the import and enhancing the stylesheet as required — primarily for online.*

- *Consider creating "generic styles" to minimize the number of styles needed. Generic styles, for example, ".center," ".bold," ".italic," ".right," and ".blue" can be applied to other parent styles.*

- *Although a CSS can contain multiple mediums, for example, the Default Medium, typically used with online targets, and a Print Medium, typically used for print targets, you may want to consider creating a separate stylesheet for your online and offline targets.*

- *Consider creating styles in the Default Medium as Flare automatically creates them in the Print Medium. Flare does not replicate, in the Default Medium, styles you create in the Print Medium.*

- *Remember — style property changes made in the Default Medium are applied to the same style property in the Print Medium unless the Print style property was already explicitly modified.*

- *When you explicitly modify a property in the Print Medium, its label appears dark gray, indicating the property has been set, which overrides changes to the property in the Default Medium.*

- *If a change you have made does not appear to take effect, be aware that when switching between the default and print mediums, Flare always returns to or opens to the last medium used.*

- *Consider using the **Simplified View** to make basic property changes to a style, for example, "font," "size," or "color," or when simultaneously editing a basic property for multiple style tags.*

- *Remember that while you can set basic style properties like "font," "size," "color," and paragraph properties from the Topic Editor ribbon, this would be "local formatting."*

- *As the Print Medium inherits styles from a stylesheet's Default Medium, to delete a style from the Print Medium, you must first delete it from the Default Medium.*

- *After completing an import, you may find you can delete some styles you no longer need. An example includes styles that affect the appearance of each TOC level (H1-H6) or styles you may have had to set the appearance of Index keywords. Your stylesheet inherits styles for this purpose.*

ADDING A NEW STYLESHEET

BASIC CONCEPT

In Flare, each stylesheet supports multiple mediums and media queries, where each medium, for example, **Default** and **Print**, are automatically created and generally intended to serve different purposes. While you will likely find a single stylesheet that will serve most, if not all, of your needs, you may create as many stylesheets as you deem necessary.

ESSENTIAL ELEMENTS

When you create a new stylesheet, you will use a factory template or a user-defined template to base the new stylesheet. You can also copy a stylesheet similar to what you want to create and modify the stylesheet to fit your additional needs.

APPLICATION TIPS

Consider creating selector classes for those inherited HTML parent tags you wish to use in your new stylesheet. Some examples may include heading styles (h1, h2, and h3), list styles (ol, ul), and image styles (img). Remember that although you cannot create new parent styles, you can modify a parent to suit your needs and that the properties of the parent are all inherited by child classes.

Knowing of this inheritance, you may want to define in the parent a limited set of properties that you want to be inherited by any of the style classes you may create. You can then define each child class with those properties that make it unique.

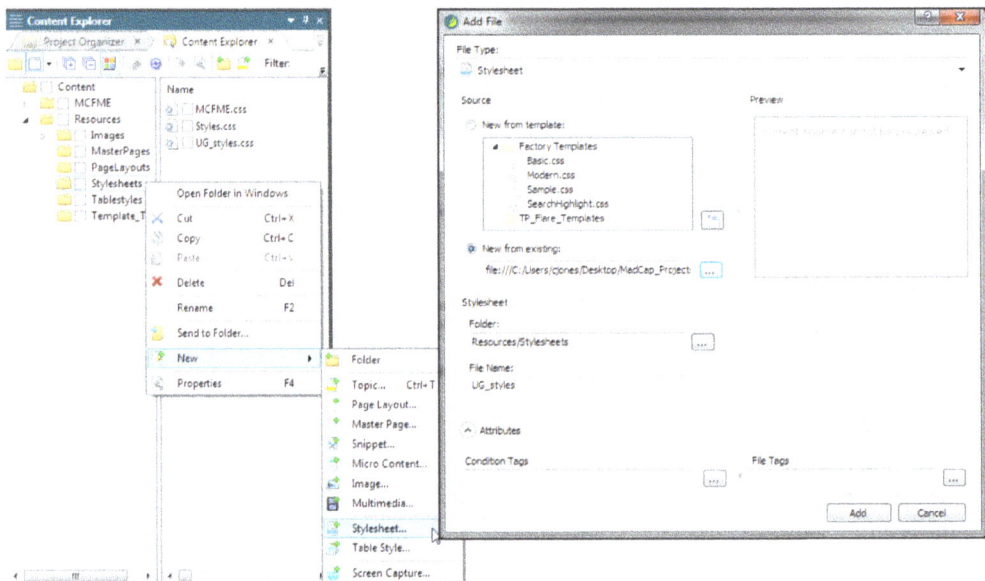

Figure 3-5. New Stylesheet Option Selected — Add File Dialog with Stylesheet Option Set.

QUICK STEPS: ADDING A NEW STYLESHEET

STEP	ACTION
1	Select the **Stylesheet** folder, in the **Resources** subfolder of the **Content Explorer**, or find and select the folder in which you wish to add the new stylesheet.
2	Right Click > **New** > **Stylesheet**. The **Add File** dialog opens.
3	Ensure that the **File Type** is set for **Stylesheet**.
4	**To create the new stylesheet use one of the following:** **a) From Templates**: Set the **Source** for **New From Template**, choose the **Basic** template from the **Factory Templates** folder or choose a template from a user-defined custom templates folder. **b) From Existing**: Set the **Source** for **New From Existing**, and use the browse button ⌐…⌐ to locate an existing stylesheet file upon which to bvase the new stylesheet.
5	Under **Stylesheet**, use the **Folder** field and choose the default folder **Resources/Stylesheets**, or browse and choose another folder in which to store the file.
6	Use the **File Name** field to specify the name for the new stylesheet file.
7	Click **Add** to save your new stylesheet.

NAVIGATING THE STYLESHEET EDITOR IN SIMPLIFIED VIEW

BASIC CONCEPT

In Flare, the CSS Editor **Simplified View** is a more straightforward way of looking at the stylesheet, its parent styles, child classes, and properties — somewhat simpler than viewing the same in the **Advanced View**. What is essential, is that the familiar grid-like format allows you to easily and quickly learn to view, modify, and add styles as necessary. While there are some limitations to this view, it is often a faster way of making style modifications. Finally, this view, called the Simplified View, should not lead you to infer difficulty using the Advanced View.

ESSENTIAL ELEMENTS

The **Simplified View** uses a grid-like or spreadsheet-like presentation that shows parent styles in the left-most column, with their subordinate child classes listed immediately below. The styles Flare lists in the present view are based on the current selection of the **Style Category** drop-down. The associated property value fields on the same row are to the right of each parent or child style. You can write directly to these fields. Also, the toolbar in the Simplified View has a collection of command options and view settings. On the far right is a set of standard properties that can be set directly from the toolbar for the selected style selector.

APPLICATION TIPS

When you are using the toolbar properties **Bold**, **Italics**, **Underline**, **Font**, **Font**, **Size**, and **Color**, at the right end of the toolbar, you can simultaneously modify the properties of one or more selected classes that will share one or more of the same properties.

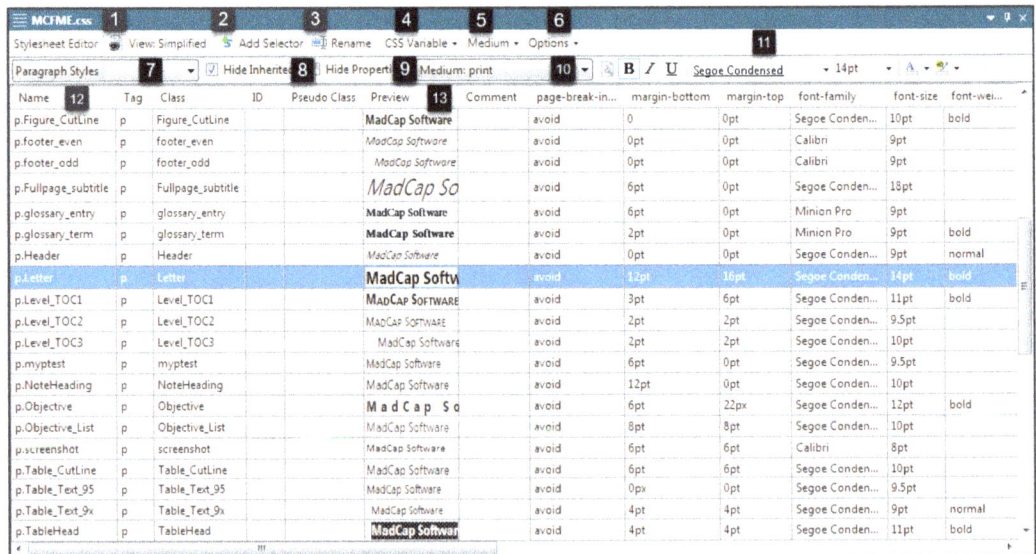

Figure 3-6. Navigating the Stylesheet Editor in Simplified View.

QUICK STEPS: NAVIGATING THE STYLESHEET EDITOR IN SIMPLIFIED VIEW

STEP	ACTION
1	If not already in **Simplified View**, click the **View: Advanced** button to switch to **Simplified View**.
2	Use the **Add Selector** button to create a new class as a child class to the parent style currently in focus.
3	Click the **Rename** button to modify the name of the currently selected style.
4	Use the **CSS Variable** drop-down to create a new CSS local or global variable.
5	Use the **Medium** drop-down (on upper ribbon) to **Add New Medium** or **Delete Medium** you select.
6	Use the **Options** drop-down arrow to select from a list of tools to manage stylesheets and styles — for example, select **Import Styles**, to open other stylesheet from which you wish to import selected styles; select **Manage Font Sets**, to ; select **Stylesheet Links**, to specify other stylesheets you want linked to your project; and, select **Disable Styles** to de-activate specific styles from use in your project.
7	Use the style category drop-down arrow to select a style category you currently wish to work with — for example **Paragraph Styles**, **Auto-Number Styles**, **Heading Styles** or **Character Styles**.
8	Click **Hide Inherited** to reduce the number of listed styles by hiding all of the styles inherited by the stylesheet when the stylesheet was created or imported. New stylesheets inherit from the factory.
9	Click **Hide Properties** to reduce the number of style properties listed across the stylesheet Editor top, by hiding all of the properties that are inherited by the stylesheet when the stylesheet was created.
10	Use the **Medium** drop-down (lower ribbon) to select a medium, if not selected — for example **Print** or **Default**, based on the medium you wish to edit. On each opening, Flare opens the last medium used.
11	This toolbar area contains standard editing tools that include font properties of bold, italics, underline, font family, font size, and font color. These properties can be set, from the toolbar, for the selected class.
12	This left-most column lists each parent style — for example **h1**, **h2** or **p** style, which appear with their child classes listed in the immediately following rows. The Property Values associated with each class (selector) are displayed to the right, on the same row.
13	As you modify each property value for a given style, the resulting appearance due to your changes are reflected in the **Preview** display field.

EDITING IN SIMPLIFIED VIEW USING THE STYLE TOOLBAR AND GRID

BASIC CONCEPT

The **Simplified View** includes toolbar commands and a limited set of standard font properties, including **bold, italics, underline, font family, font size, font color**, and **background color**. These tools and properties are part of the Stylesheet Editor. They offer a shortcut method for assigning the properties to selected styles directly, using the grid cells or in conjunction with the toolbar.

ESSENTIAL ELEMENTS

You can use the stylesheet toolbar properties and the individual grid cells to change a style selector currently in focus. A first step is, from the toolbar, to select the style category that contains the selector you wish to modify and then to focus on a chosen style or a grid cell (property) for a given style.

When the desired style category is in view and a style selected, the associated properties are in the adjacent cells on the same row. The property names are above the first listed selector across the grid top. To modify any property value of a selected style, you can type a numeric or text value directly in the cell or set the property value on the toolbar. You can also set a single property value, for example, "color" for multiple styles, by selecting the styles and then setting the property value on the toolbar.

APPLICATION TIPS

There are a couple of options when it comes to editing in the **Simplified View**. The option covered here is the most efficient when you wish to modify or set at least one of the toolbar properties **bold, italics, underline, font family, font size, font color**, or **background color**. Other available methods will include these items as well as additional items.

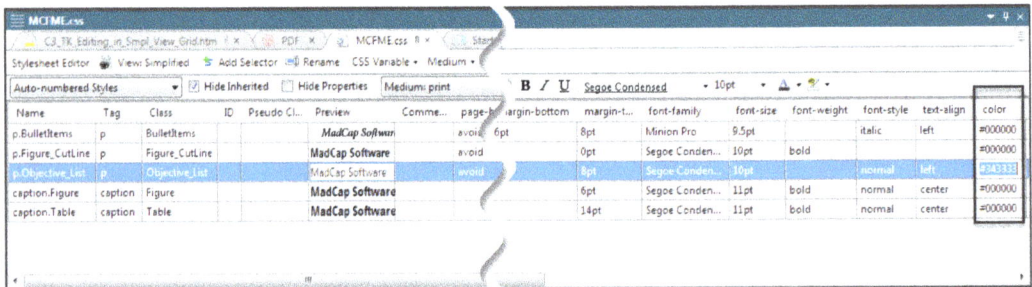

Figure 3-7. Stylesheet Simplified View — Editing a Single Selector in Stylesheet Grid.

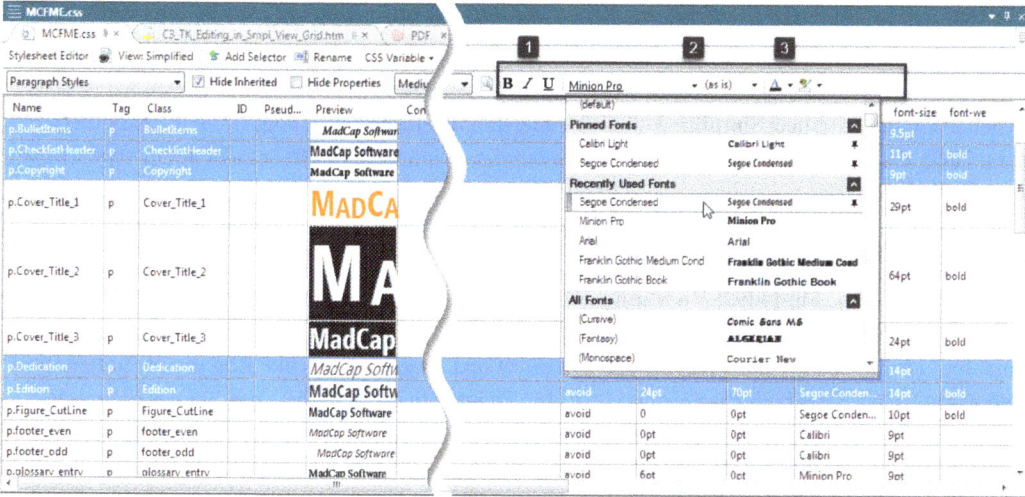

Figure 3-8. Stylesheet Simplified View — Editing Multiple Selectors Simultaneously Using Toolbar and Grid.

Quick Steps: Editing in Simplified View Using the Style Toolbar and Grid

STEP	ACTION
1	If not already in **Simplified View**, click the **View: Advanced** button to switch to **Simplified View**.
2	From the toolbar, select the Style Category drop-down and select the category of style you wish to edit.
3	Find and select a style selector you wish to modify.
4	To modify a single font property for a selected style, click directly in the grid cell, for example, **Font Size**, and type the desired value; or for the basic font properties set the property from the toolbar. See **Note**.
5	To modify a single font property, simultaneously for several styles, first use the **CTRL** key to select each of the styles, for example, **H1**, **H2**, **H3**, and **H4**, and then from the toolbar set the specific property, for example **Font Color**. You can also use **Copy/Paste**, to insert the same property value.
6	Click the **Save** button to save your work.

> **NOTE:** You can type the numeric or text value directly into the appropriate grid cell, for any style property you wish to modify. You can also use the toolbar to modify one of the basic style properties. Finally, if you are not familiar with specific units for a property, then you might choose to use the property dialogs.

EDITING IN SIMPLIFIED VIEW USING THE PROPERTIES DIALOGS

BASIC CONCEPT

When using the stylesheet **Simplified View**, a collection of **Properties** dialogs is the primary method for initially defining and modifying style properties. Once you have created new styles or style classes, you can double-click on a style you wish to edit to open the dialogs.

ESSENTIAL ELEMENTS

When editing in the **Simplified View** using the **Properties** dialog, you may use any or all of the tabs to define the style properties. Most styles, however, can be well-defined using the **Font** tab to specify basic font characteristics; the **Paragraph** tab, to select text characteristics like **Alignment**, **Indentation**, **Before** and **After** paragraph spacing, and text **Line Height** (the spacing between lines). Some style definitions may also require using the **Auto-number** tab, which you can use to create styles with automatic sequential numbering embedded.

APPLICATION TIPS

The use of the Auto-number tab is described in two other tasks in this section.

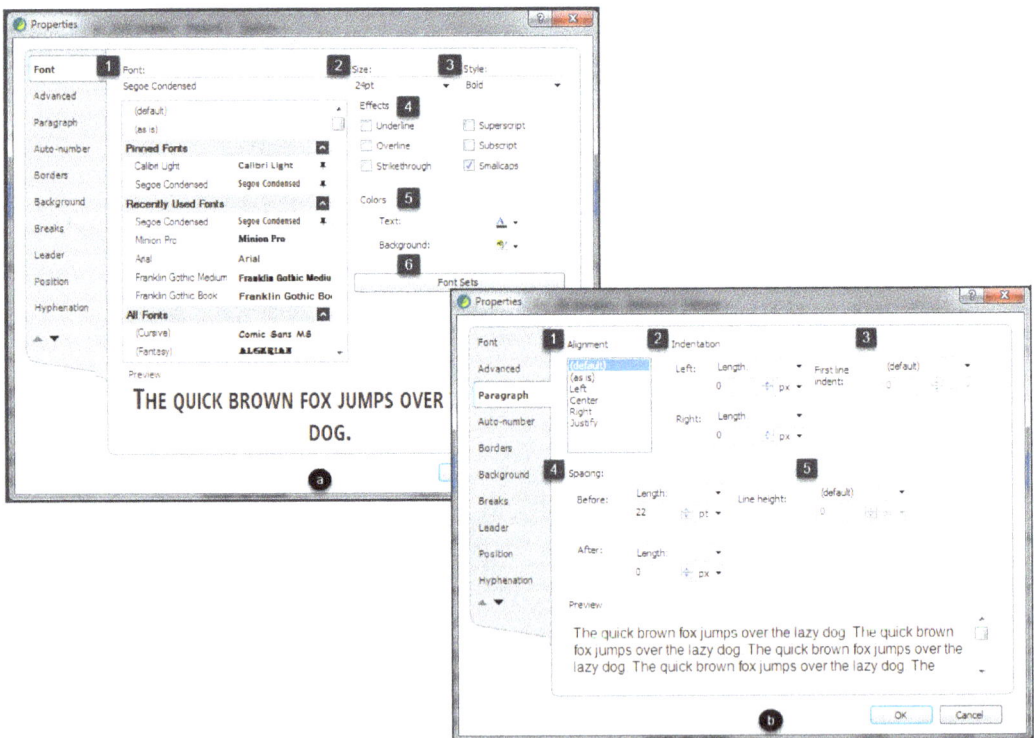

Figure 3-9. Stylesheet Simplified View a) **Font** Properties Tab; and b) **Paragraph** Properties Tab.

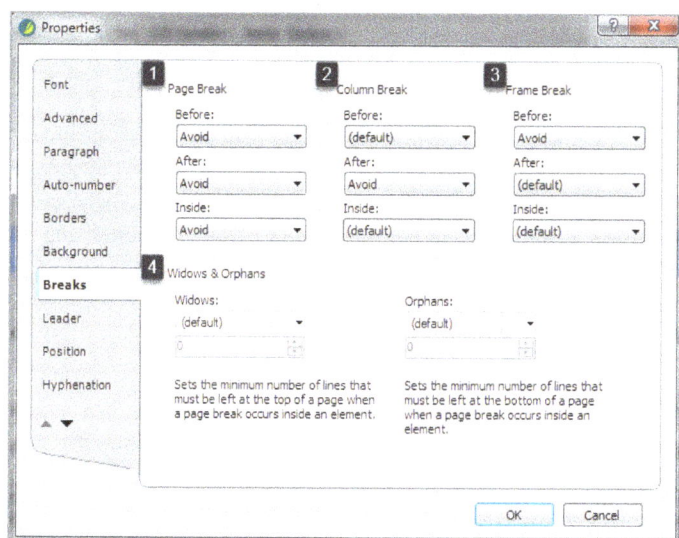

Figure 3-10. Stylesheet Simplified View — Breaks Properties Tab.

QUICK STEPS: EDITING IN SIMPLIFIED VIEW USING THE PROPERTIES DIALOG

STEP	ACTION
1	With the stylesheet open to the **Simplified** view, use the **Medium** drop-down, on the lower toolbar, and select the desired stylesheet medium you wish to edit — for example **Print**. The styles are listed.
2	At the left end of the Stylesheet Editor toolbar, use the drop-down and select the category of the style you wish to edit — for example **Paragraph**. The paragraph styles are listed.
3	Find and double-click on the style you wish to modify. The style **Properties** dialog opens. In this task example, the **Font**, **Advanced**, and the **Breaks** tab are used.
4	Select the **Font** tab, to specify the **Font** (Family), **Size**, **Effects**, **Color** (Text Color and Background Color).
5	Select the **Paragraph** tab, to specify the text **Alignment** (Left, Center, Right, Justify); to specify the text **Indentation** (Left, Right, and First Line Indent), using units of measure **px**, **pt**, or other; to specify **Spacing** (Before and After), using units of measure **px**, **pt**, or other; and finally; to specify the **Line Height** (typically 2-3 points greater than Font **Size**.
6	Select the **Breaks** tab, to specify the behavior of the style with respect to a **Page Break**, **Column Break**, and **Frame Break**. For each of the break types, use the appropriate drop-downs to set the behavior of the style. For the most part the defaults will work.
7	Click **OK** to save your style modifications.

NAVIGATING THE STYLESHEET EDITOR IN ADVANCED VIEW

BASIC CONCEPT

In Flare, the CSS Editor **Advanced View** is a more comprehensive way of looking at the stylesheet, its parent styles, child classes, and properties. This task is intended to give you a quick view of navigating the CSS Editor advanced view. By spending some time just getting to know what's involved, where things are, and how they're used, you can get a jump start on getting to work. While you're starting and perhaps have not yet created any styles, you can view some of the Flare inherited styles as you become familiar with the stylesheet editor.

ESSENTIAL ELEMENTS

The multi-pane structure in the **Advanced View** uses the left-pane to list parent styles and their child classes, based on the currently selected Style Category; the right-pane lists the properties and property value fields, based on the currently selected option for displaying the properties. You can choose to **Show: Assorted Relevant Properties, Show: Set (Locally) Properties, Show: Set Properties**, or **Show: All Properties**. The bottom pane gives an instant preview of your changes as you make them.

APPLICATION TIPS

When working in the **Advanced View**, ensure you have selected the **Medium** you intend to edit, for example, **Print** or **Default**. And, for your convenience, use the **Show** drop-down to choose the best display option for listing the properties of the style you are working with — for example, **Show: Assorted Relevant Properties, Show: Set (Locally) Properties, Show: Set Properties**, or **Show: All Properties**.

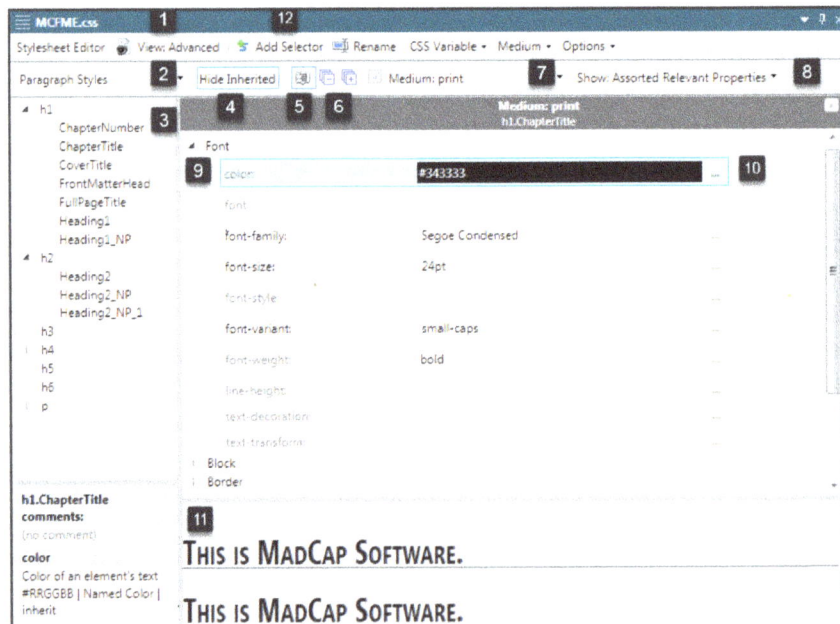

Figure 3-11. Navigating the Stylesheet Editor in Advanced View.

QUICK STEPS: NAVIGATING THE STYLESHEET EDITOR IN ADVANCED VIEW

STEP	ACTION
1	If not already in Advanced View, click the **View: Simplified** button to switch to **Advanced View**.
2	Use the style category drop-down arrow to select a style category you wish to work with — for example **Paragraph**, **Table**, **List,** or **Image** styles.
3	In the left-side pane, each parent style — for example the **h1**, **h2**, or **p** appears with their child classes listed below. When working with styles, it is best that you create child classes to establish the different appearances you want to achieve for the style. The child will inherit basic properties from the parent.
4	Click **Hide Inherited** to reduce the number of listed styles by hiding all of the styles inherited by the stylesheet when the stylesheet was created or imported. New stylesheets inherit from the factory.
5	For the currently selected style, click **Alphabetical View** or **Property Groups View** to togglebetween the modes in which the properties can be viewed. Item 9 in the image is displaying the property group.
6	Click **Collapse All** (- icon) to hide the properties of the currently listed property groups — for example **Font**, **Block**, and **Border**; click **Expand All** (+ icon) to show the properties of all the property groups.
7	Use the lower **Medium** drop-down to select the desired medium, if not selected — for example **Print** or **Default**, based on the medium you wish to edit. On each opening, Flare opens the last used medium.
8	For the currently selected style, use the **Show** drop-down arrow to show properties that are best suited to see while setting this style — for example **All Properties** (least likely), **Assorted Relevant Properties** (most likely), or the **Properties Set In this Stylesheet** (sometimes).
9	This column is a view of the properties of the currently selected parent style or child class. Depending on the current toolbar choice, the list may be in an **Alphabetical View** or a **Property Groups View**.
10	Each property displayed on the left has a property value field displayed to the right, on the same row. You may click inside the field or on the edit icon (**...**) to modify or specify a new property value.
11	As you modify each property value for a given style, the resulting appearance due to your changes, are reflected in the **Preview** display field.

EDITING A STYLE IN ADVANCED VIEW

BASIC CONCEPT

The **Advanced View**, offers a more comprehensive presentation of styles and style properties. The presentation is also a bit more flexible in terms of arranging the view to suit your preference and in viewing and in modifying the appropriate style properties. This view is advanced but not complex.

ESSENTIAL ELEMENTS

In the **Advanced View**, like with the **Simplified View**, a first step is to verify that you have displayed the correct **Medium**. You can then select the style category that contains the selector you wish to modify, and finally, find and select the parent style to the child style you want to change. These last two steps are both done in the left-pane.

With the desired styles in view and a style selected, the associated properties are listed by **Property Group** in the right pane, with each property value field just to the right of the property name. The property names are listed directly under the group name; for example, listed under the Font group are **color**, **font**, **font-family**, **font-size**, **font-style**, **font-variant**, **font-weight**, and others. To modify any property value of a selected style, you can type the numeric or text value directly in the value field, or click the field edit icon (**...**), just to the right of the property value field.

APPLICATION TIPS

A couple of important items to remember when you are becoming familiar with the Advanced View, are using the toolbar option to show properties as **Property Groups**, and setting the **Show** drop-down option to list only the **Assorted Relevant Properties**.

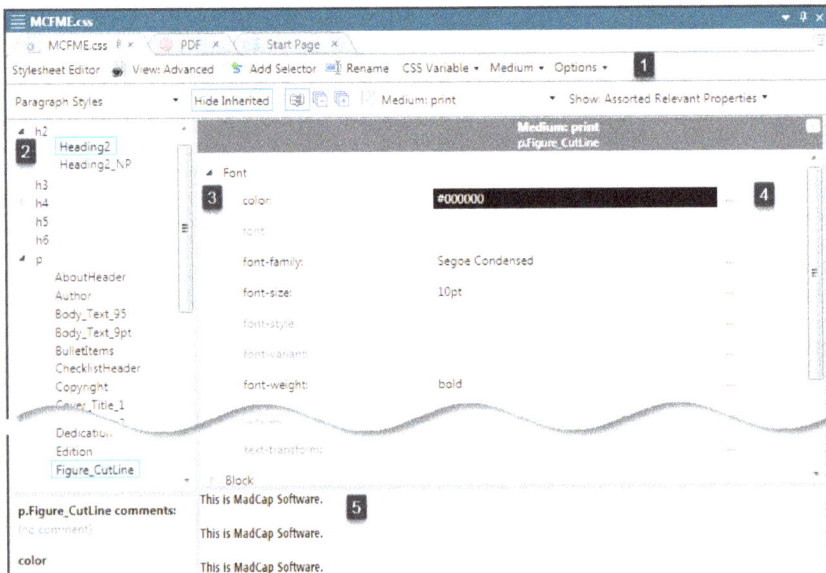

Figure 3-12. Editing a style in the Stylesheet Editor Advanced View.

QUICK STEPS: EDITING A STYLE IN ADVANCED VIEW

STEP	ACTION
1	If not already in Advanced View, click the **View: Simplified** button to switch to **Advanced View**.
2	From the toolbar, select the Style Category drop-down and select the category of style you wish to edit.
3	On the lower part of the toolbar, use the first toggle button 🔲 to list the properties in the **Property Groups View**, instead of the **Alphabetical View**. This view places properties associated with the style into logical groupings that may be easier to work with initially.
4	Use the **Medium** drop-down to select the desired medium, if not selected — for example **Print** or **Default**, based on the medium you wish to edit. Flare always opens the last used medium.
5	For the selected style, use the **Show** drop-down to only list the **Assorted Relevant Properties**.
6	In the left pane, find the parent style of the selector you wish to modify.
7	Click on the expand button to the left of the parent style, to view its child selectors.
8	Find and select a style selector you wish to modify. All of the properties for the selector are listed in the right-side pane. The properties are listed in **Property Groups**, and only **Assorted Relevant Properties** are listed as were specified in Step 3 and Step 5. You can modify any of the property value fields.
9	Click inside field to modify the value directly or, if applicable, use the drop-down to choose a value.
10	View the impact of your changes in the Preview pane in the lower part of the window.
11	Click the **Save** button to save your work.

> **NOTE:** Recall that the **Print Medium** and its styles, are inherited from the **Default Medium**. Whether the Print Medium was derived from an imported stylesheet, or was newly created, it will contain inherited styles and properties. Once you make modifications to a Print Medium specific style property, that value will override any value that was inherited from the Default Medium. From then on, the modified property name is shown in black lettering, to indicate that it now overrides the property in the Default Medium.

CREATING A NEW STYLE SELECTOR

BASIC CONCEPT

When we refer to a style in Flare, we are often referring to a selector in its most basic form. The properties defined in a basic style selector are explicitly applied to the content when you use the style. We can also create advanced selectors whose defined properties target specific content parts. When Flare encounters those content elements in the HTML document, it is a match between the content and the selector's definition or rule. So, when you add a new style in Flare, you can add either a basic selector or an advanced selector.

ESSENTIAL ELEMENTS

As you complete the fields in the Add Selector dialog, you will either create a basic or advanced selector. You create a simple selector if you specify the **HTML Element** and **Class Name** only. For example, under the parent style <p> you might create child classes **p.bodytext**, **p.footer**, and **p.header**.

If, in addition to the **Class**, you specify a **Pseudo Class**, you are defining a pseudo-class Selector. With some pseudo-class types you select, you can choose a **Pseudo-Expression** to complete the selector. You can specify a pseudo-element selector if you choose a **Pseudo-Element** in addition to the **Class**. Finally, if you specify an **Identifier (ID)** and the **Class**, you are creating an identifier selector. You can style any or all parts of your content that match the selector criteria by setting these parameters.

APPLICATION TIPS

A new selector can be as simple as a child class to a parent, or as complex, as you need it to be, by defining specific criteria that causes the properties described in the style, to be applied only to the parts of your content that match the requirements specified by the selector.

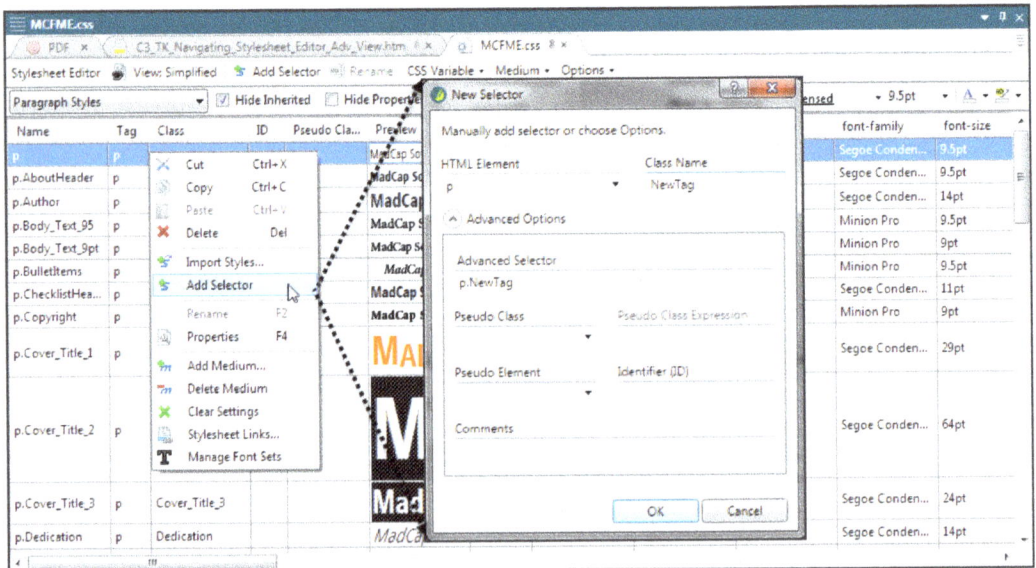

Figure 3-13. Add New Selector Using Right Click in Simplified View.

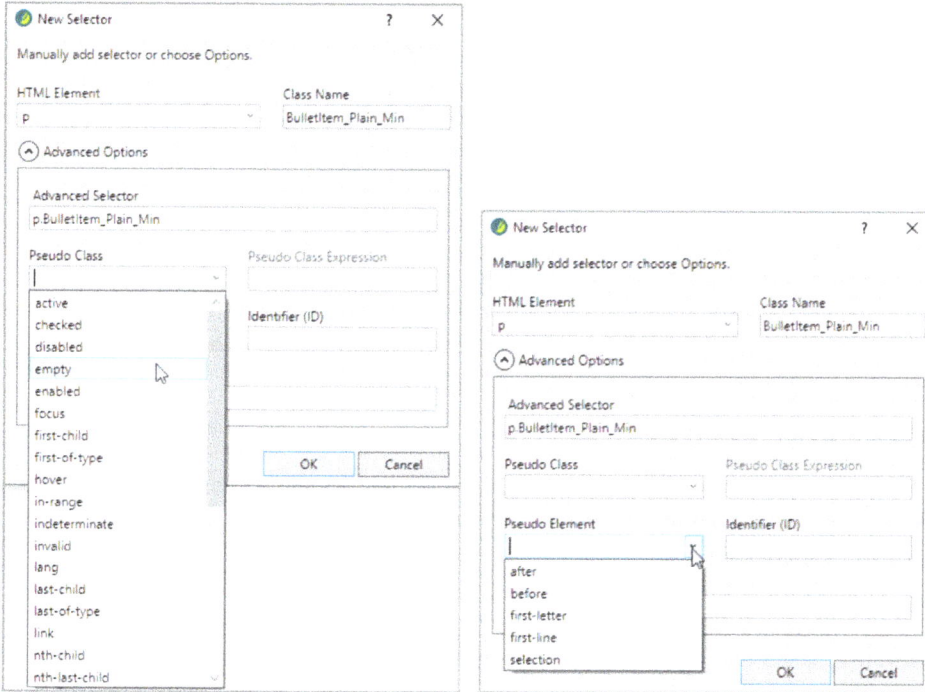

Figure 3-14. a) Add New Pseudo-Class Selector, and b) Add New Pseudo-Element Selector.

QUICK STEPS: CREATING A NEW STYLE SELECTOR

STEP	ACTION
1	Open your stylesheet in the Stylesheet Editor to the **Simplified View** or **Advanced View**, as you prefer.
2	Use the Style Category drop-down selector to show **All Styles**.
3	Select a parent style, for example <p>, <h1>, <h2>, or <div>, for which you are creating the selector.
4	On the toolbar, click the **Add Selector** button; or right-click on the parent and select **Add Selector**.
5	Use the **Class Name** field to enter the name of your new class selector.
6	Click **OK** to save a basic selector, or continue to Step 8, Step 9, or Step 10, to add an **Advanced Selector**; otherwise continue with Step 7 to complete the basic selector.
7	Now, in the stylesheet, define the properties to be applied by your Basic Selector.
8	To continue to create a Pseudo-Class Selector, use the drop-down to select a **Pseudo-Class**, then enter a **Pseudo-Expression**, if applicable. Only certain Pseudo-Classes support expressions.
9	To continue to create a Pseudo-Element Selector, use the drop-down to select a **Pseudo Element**.
10	To continue to create an Identifier Selector, enter an **Identifier (ID)**. The properties you define for the selector, will be applied to the single element that has that has been assigned the unique identifier.
11	In the stylesheet, define the properties to be assigned by the Pseudo-Class or Pseudo-Element Selector.
12	Click the **Save** button to save your work.

CREATING A GENERIC STYLE CLASS

BASIC CONCEPT

A *generic class* stands alone and is not a child of any HTML parent — as such, you can apply it to styles associated with any parent. The generic class .center, for example, can center align content associated with <p>, <h1>, <img>, or any parent style. Likewise, the generic style ".**italics**" could italicize content having those same parent styles.

Generic classes are uniquely convenient since, from time to time, you will need to apply a particular property to different parts of your content you have already used styles of other parents. Creating generic styles avoids creating a different style to achieve the same effect on styles with different parents. It also eliminates the temptation to use local formatting from the toolbar.

ESSENTIAL ELEMENTS

Generally, when you create a new style selector, the parent **HTML Element** and the **Class Name** are specified. Since a generic class has no parent, only the **Class Name** is specified. The only other step in creating a generic class is to define a specific property to the style.

APPLICATION TIPS

Generic styles are generally applied to already well-formed child classes of different parent styles — styles that already have unique properties. As such, you would typically define a generic style with just a single property that can be applied to other classes — for example, **Alignment** (left, center, or right), **Font Color** (red, black, or blue), or **Background Color**.

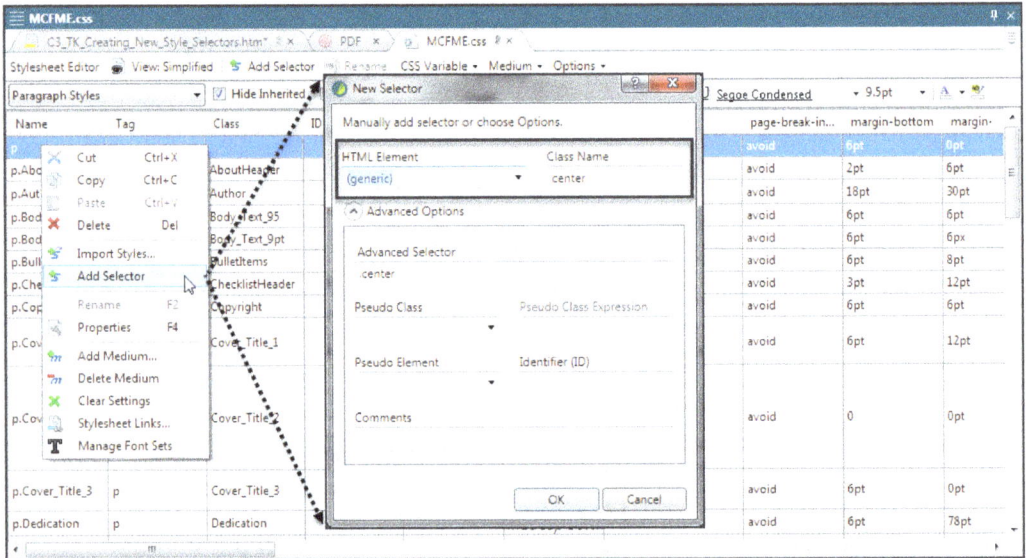

Figure 3-15. Add a Generic Class in Simplified View.

QUICK STEPS: CREATING A GENERIC STYLE CLASS

STEP	ACTION
1	Open the Stylesheet Editor to the **Simplified View** or to the **Advanced View**.
2	Use the Style Category drop-down selector to show **All Styles**.
3	Click the **Add Selector** button. The **New Selector** dialog opens.
4	Clear all text from the **HTML Element** field to blank; or you can also use the **HTML Element** drop-down to select **Generic**.
5	Use the **Class Name** field to enter the name of your new generic class selector.
6	Click **OK** to save the new generic selector.
7	In the Stylesheet Editor **Simplified View**, use the Style Category drop-down and select **All Styles**,
8	Find and select the row of the new generic class, listed as **.Center** (typically at bottom of stylesheet).
9	With the style row selected, scroll across, looking at the property names in the header row until finding the property **text-align**.
10	Double-click in the property cell (intersection of style and property) and enter "center " as the value.
11	Click the **Save** button to save your work.

> **NOTE:** If you choose to enter the property value for the new generic class in the **Advanced View** of the Stylesheet Editor. Use the **Style Category** drop-down and select **All Styles**, the new **.center** class will be listed under **Generic Classes**.

CREATING A NEW STYLE CLASS AD HOC

BASIC CONCEPT

In Flare, you can create new styles ad-hoc by basing the unique style on another style from your stylesheet. Consider using this feature when it is difficult to make the exact class you need or when you need a variation of an existing style, and you intend to use it frequently. However, you don't want to use local formatting each time you need this variation. You can get assistance by clicking on a similar style in an open topic and tweaking it using the local formatting toolbar. You can then create the style from your editing and tweak the style later in the stylesheet.

ESSENTIAL ELEMENTS

To create the new style, you can start by opening a topic that has a style similar style to what you want to make. For example, you may have a heading1 class that always starts after a page break, yet in some cases, you don't want the page break, and you also want to underline the heading variation. So, you would create a new style to modify the **Page Break** and add the underline property. As you base the new style on an existing class, it will inherit all other properties from the original parent. Flare lists the inherited properties with their current value in the bottom-left pane of the **Create Style** dialog. You can use the adjacent check box to enable or disable any inherited property.

Determining the parent style of the new style depends on how you place your cursor or select content. For a paragraph <p> or other block-level parents like h1, h2, and h3, or an ordered or unordered list, you would click anywhere inside the block element. You indicate a span <**span**> or character style by selecting the content. Either way, after showing the starting content, you can use the **Home** menu's **Font** and **Paragraph** tool-sets to supply additional styling you want. After completing the style or getting a good start, use the **Create Style Class** button to add the style to your stylesheet.

APPLICATION TIPS

Before finalizing the **Create Class** operation, you can open the **Styles Window** from the **Home** menu to verify that you have correctly indicated the parent style you want to inherit in the content.

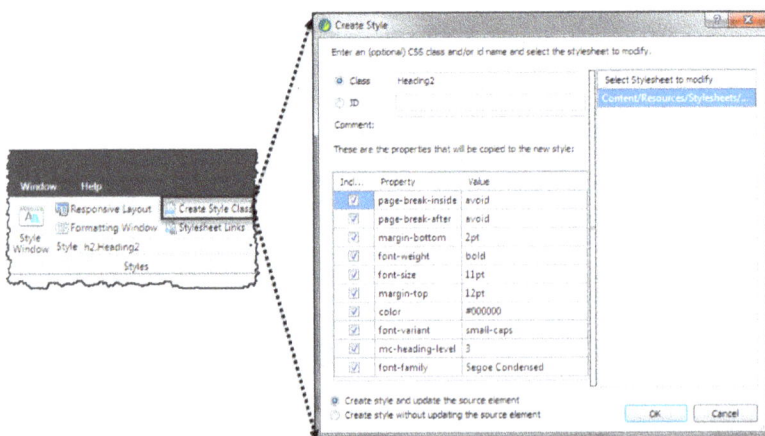

Figure 3-16. Add New Style Class Ad Hoc — Using Toolbar Create Style Class Button.

QUICK STEPS: CREATING A NEW STYLE CLASS AD HOC

STEP	ACTION
1	Open your XML Editor to any content file from which you wish to start the creation of a new class.
2	Find the content that has the parent style from which you wish to start creating a variation of the style. Use the following example methods to indicate the parent: **a)** For block-level content like H1, h2, or h3 click anywhere inside the heading. **b)** For an ordered or un-ordered list, click anywhere inside the element. **c)** For character-level <span> content, select the element.
3	Use the **Home** menu **Font** and **Paragraph** toolsets to edit the content as required to reflect any variations to the style that you want.
4	With the content still indicated, on the **Home** menu click **Style Window** or **F12**. The **Styles** window opens. The **Current Style and Local Formatting** (with any formatting you may have entered) are shown. Use this window to determine whether you have indicated the intended parent style, for example <**p**> or <**span**>, based on how you selected content.
5	Click the **Create Style** button. The Create Style dialog opens, with properties of the content style listed in the bottom-left pane of the dialog.
6	Click in the **Class** field and enter a name, without spaces, for the new style.
7	Use the check boxes adjacent to each of the listed properties, to **Enable** (include) or **Disable** (exclude) a property from the new style.
8	Select one of the following options: **a)** Choose **Create style and update source element**, to apply the new style to the selected source content. **b)** Choose **Create style without updating source element**, to not apply new style to the source content.
9	Click **OK** to save the new class.

> **NOTE:** You can now open the stylesheet to the appropriate medium or the **Style Window** on the **Home** menu, to continue adding properties or editing the new style.

USING AUTO-NUMBERING TO CREATE NUMERIC STYLES

BASIC CONCEPT

Writers of technical documents primarily use the Flare Auto-Numbering feature to create styles that imbed some form of sequential numbering to various content elements. This type of formatting is also typical, with styles applied to chapter and section headings and images, charts, and table captions.

ESSENTIAL ELEMENTS

When using the styles Properties dialog to create a style, you embed the sequential numbering properties using the **AutoNumber Commands** option of the Auto-Number tab. When you select **Show AutoNumber Commands**, Flare lists each command's description and syntax.

Auto-numbering commands can also combine a text string to appear in the style format with the auto-number. An example might be **F:Figure {chapnum}-{Cn+}**, where the prefix "Figure" always appears before an image number. The text is formatted using the **Format Commands** option, which supports basic formatting like family, size, color, background, bold, and italic. These properties each have a start and end delimiter that syntactically encloses the text. A text string, for example, is made bold by enclosing the string with the start delimiter {b} and end delimiter {/b}.

APPLICATION TIPS

This task only used the **Auto-Number** tab to define the Auto-numbering properties in the style's format. You must use the remaining **Properties** tabs, for example, **Font**, **Advanced**, and **Breaks**, to specify any other properties.

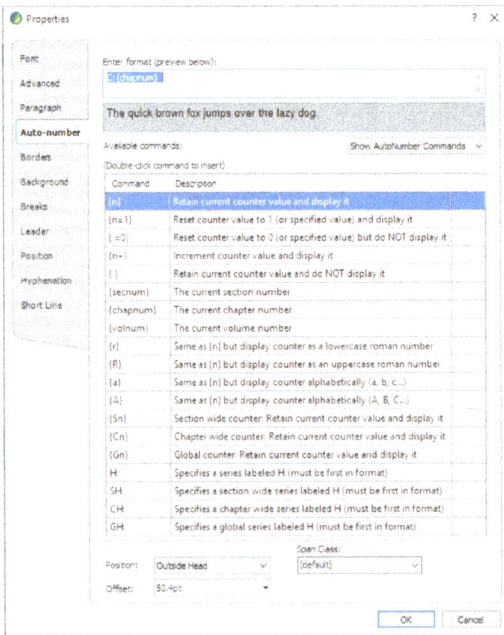

Figure 3-17. Using Auto-Numbering Dialog — AutoNumber Commands.

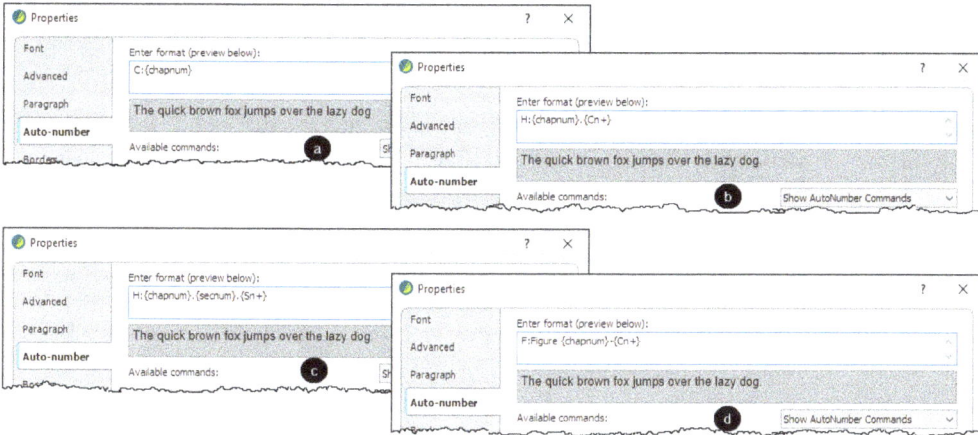

Figure 3-18. Auto-Number Styles a) Chapter Number b) Heading 1, c) Heading 2 d) Figure Number.

QUICK STEPS: USING AUTO-NUMBERING TO CREATE NUMERIC STYLES

STEP	ACTION
1	Open your stylesheet in the Stylesheet Editor to the **Simplified View** or **Advanced View**, as you prefer.
2	Under the paragraph parent, click **Add New Selector** > **HTML Element** > **p** > **Class** > **Caution**.
3	Click **OK** to save the new selector.
4	In the Stylesheet Editor double-click on the **Caution** selector to open the **Properties** dialog. **Note:** As you are creating a new class, after completing the **Auto-number** properties you will need to define the other properties for the style, for example, using the **Font**, **Advanced**, and **Break** tabs.
5	From the **Properties** dialog, select the **Auto-number** tab.
6	Use the **Available Commands** drop-down to select the **Show AutoNumber Commands** option. The auto-number commands and the required syntax for each is listed.
7	Use the **Enter Format** field, and enter **CH:Chapter {chapnum}**, according to syntax, to enter a Chapter Number auto-number format.
8	Follow the steps (**Step 2** through **Step 7**) to create each of the styles **H1**, **H2**, **H3**, and **FigureCaption**.
	a) Use the **Enter Format** field, and enter **H:{chapnum}.{Cn+}**, according to syntax , to enter the auto-number format for a Heading 1 style.
	b) Use the **Enter Format** field, and enter **H:{chapnum}.{secnum}.{Sn+}**, according to syntax , to enter the auto-number format for a Heading 2 style.
	c) Use the **Enter Format** field, and enter **H:{chapnum}.{secnum}.{Sn}.{n+}**, according to syntax , to enter the auto-number format for a Heading 3 style.
	d) Use the **Enter Format** field, and enter **F:Figure {chapnum}-{Cn+}.**, according to syntax, to enter the auto-number format for a Figure Caption style.
9	Click **OK** to save the new selector, and click the **Save** button to save your work.

Using Auto-Numbering to Create Non-Numeric Styles

Basic Concept

Generally, you would use the Flare auto-numbering feature to create styles that embed sequential numbering to chapter and section headings, charts, images, and tables. You can also use auto-numbering to embed a non-numeric text string with basic text formatting in a style class. This feature helps create certain style classes, often used in technical documents.

Essential Elements

In Flare, non-numeric formatting is created from the **Properties** dialog using the **Format Commands** option, of the **Auto-Number** tab. These commands support the insertion of a fixed text string, like "**NOTE**," to appear embedded in the style. You can format the string using basic text (font) formatting properties like **family**, **size**, **color**, **background**, **bold**, **italic**, **underline**, **subscript**, and **superscript**. Each has a start and end delimiter used to enclose and format text.

Application Tips

This task illustrates how the **Auto-Number** tab defines an auto-number format for a given selector. To specify additional style properties, you must use the **Font**, **Advanced**, **Breaks**, and other tabs. You can remove a format by removing both the start and end syntax delimiters.

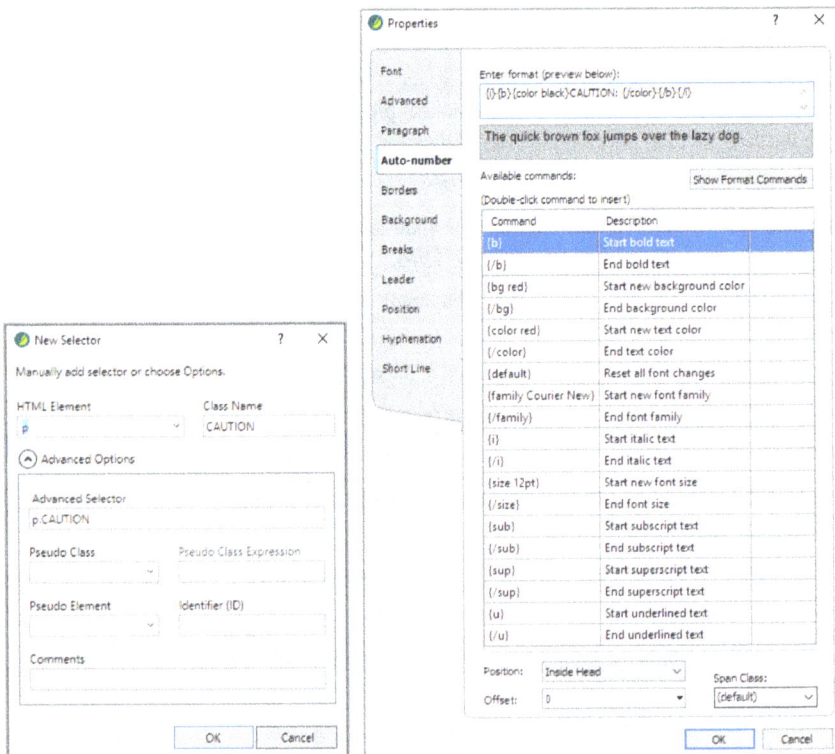

Figure 3-19. a) Add New Selector for Caution Style, and b) AutoNumber Feature — Using Format Commands.

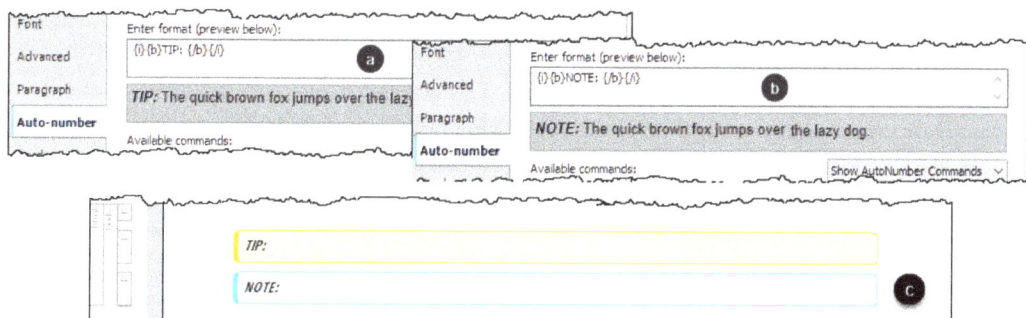

Figure 3-20. Auto-Number Commands for a) Tip and b) Note Format c) Tip and Note Styles.

QUICK STEPS: USING AUTO-NUMBERING TO CREATE NON-NUMERIC STYLES

STEP	ACTION
1	Open your stylesheet in the Stylesheet Editor to the **Simplified View** or **Advanced View**, as you prefer.
2	Under the paragraph parent, click **Add New Selector** > **HTML Element** > **p** > **Class** > enter **Note**.
3	Click **OK** to save the new selector.
4	In the Stylesheet Editor double-click on the **Note** selector to open the **Properties** dialog.
5	From the **Properties** dialog, select the **Font** tab and specify the **Font**, **Size**, **Style**, and **Color**. For example choose Segoe Condensed, 9.5, Regular, and #000000
6	Select the **Paragraph** tab and specify the **Before** (8 pt) and **After** (6 pt) paragraph spacing.
7	Select the **AutoNumber** tab, and use the **Available Commands** drop-down to select the **Show Format Commands** option. The format commands and the required syntax for each are listed.
8	Use the **Enter Format (preview below)** field, to enter **{i}{b}CAUTION:{/b}{/i}**, according to syntax. In this example, the text CAUTION is formatted using italics and bold. The format opened first is closed last.
9	Select the **Borders** tab, then use the **Padding** drop-down arrow, just to the right of the fields, to simultaneously set the **Left**, **Right**, **Top**, and **Bottom** fields at **5 pt** (points).
10	Use the **Border Radius** drop-down arrow, just to the right of the fields, to simultaneously set the **Top-Left**, **Top-Right**, **Bottom-Left**, and **Bottom-Right** fields at **6 px** (pixels), to create rounded corners.
11	Use the **Borders** drop-down arrow, to the right of the fields, and the following Step, to simultaneously define the **Left**, **Right**, **Top**, and **Bottom** borders.
13	Use the top-left field (**Length**) to choose the length option; use the top-right field to set the Line Color to **#00bfff**; use the bottom-left field to define the Line Width as **2 px**; and use the bottom-right field to set the Line Type as **solid**. Now, modify the **Left** border Line Width to **6 px**.
13	Select the **Background** tab, and the use the **Color** drop-down, select **More Colors** and specify **#F0FFFF**.
14	Select the **Breaks** tab, and under **Page Break**, select > **Inside** > **Avoid**.
15	Click **OK** to save the new selector.
16	Repeat **Step 2** through **Step 9**, to create similar styles for **Tip**, **Caution**, and **Warning**.

IMPORTING SELECTED STYLES FROM OTHER STYLESHEET

BASIC CONCEPT

In your Flare project work, you will very likely work with different stylesheets that you have created or that are Flare Factory stylesheets. From time to time, you may find that you would like to have certain styles in your current stylesheet that you have encountered or used in other stylesheets. You do not have to re-create these styles, but you can import them directly to your current project and stylesheet.

ESSENTIAL ELEMENTS

With your destination stylesheet opened in the Stylesheet Editor, you can access styles from other projects and stylesheets for import. The **Import Styles** option is accessed using the **Options** drop-down selector on the Stylesheet Editor. With the **Import Styles** dialog open, the **Library Folders** list the folders and stylesheets to which you have immediate access; however, you can use the browse button to access additional projects and folders. You can modify imported styles as required

APPLICATION TIPS

The **Library Folders** will display **Project Stylesheets**, **Factory Stylesheets**, and **Custom Templates**, folders from which you can select available stylesheets from which to import.

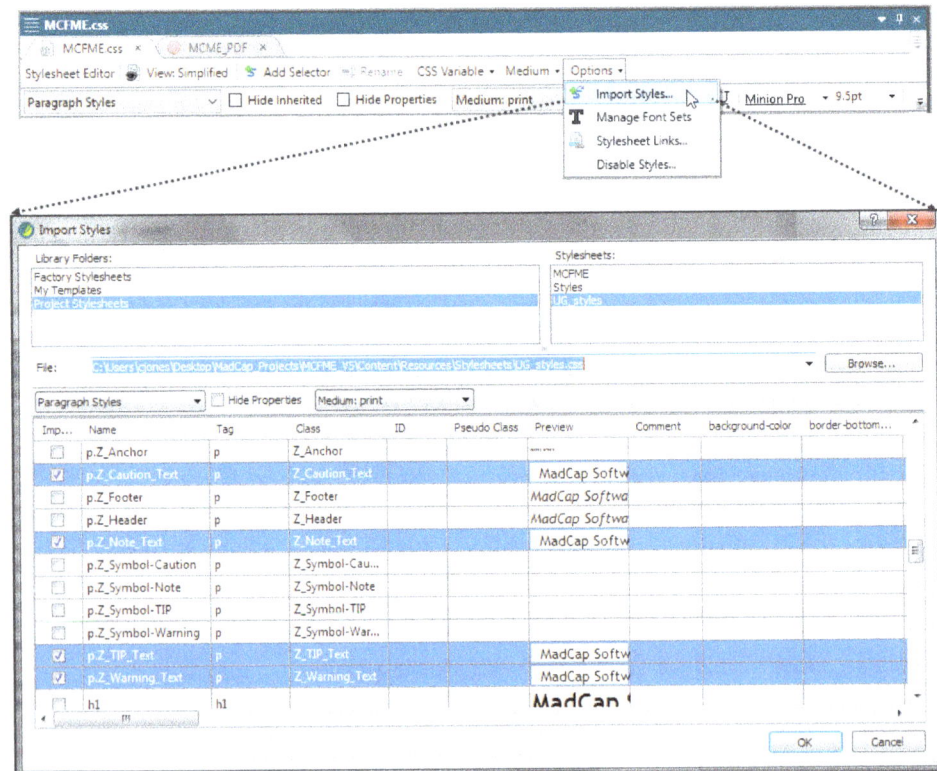

Figure 3-21. Flare Import Styles Dialog.

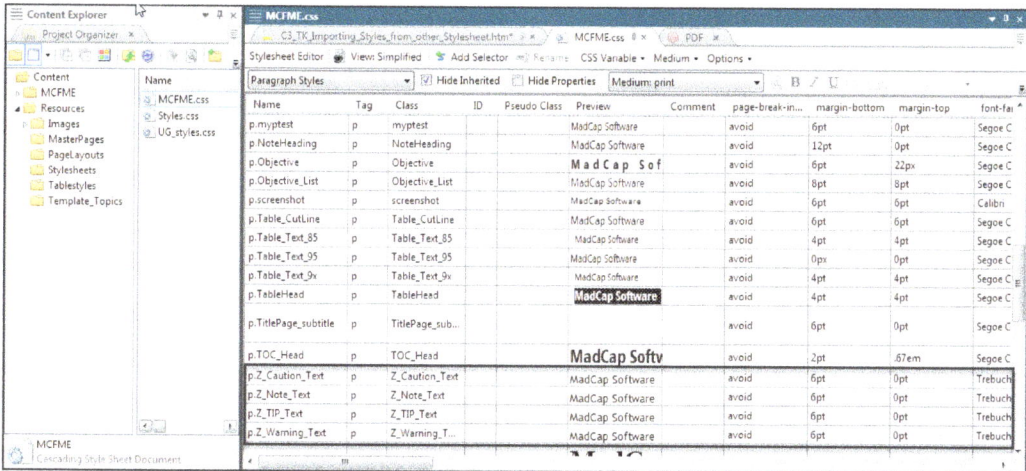

Figure 3-22. Imported Styles in Target Stylesheet.

QUICK STEPS: IMPORTING SELECTED STYLES FROM OTHER STYLESHEET

STEP	ACTION
1	Open your stylesheet in the Stylesheet Editor to the **Simplified View** or **Advanced View**, as you prefer.
2	On the Stylesheet Editor toolbar, click the **Options** drop-down and select **Import Styles**.
3	Under **Library Folders**, choose the folder that contains stylesheets from which you want to import styles.
4	Click **Project Stylesheets** to access the stylesheets found in the current project; or use the **Browse** button to search for other stylesheets. Stylesheets in each folder are listed in the right pane under **Stylesheets**.
5	In the top right pane, under **Stylesheets**, select the stylesheet from which you want to import. The styles of the selected stylesheet are listed in the bottom pane of the **Import Styles** dialog.
6	Across the top of the bottom pane, use the Styles Category drop-down to list **All Styles** or select a category, like **Paragraph Styles**.
7	Use the **Medium** drop-down to select the style medium from which you want to import, for example, **Print**.
8	In the bottom pane, use the adjacent check boxes to select styles you want to import to your stylesheet.
9	Click **OK** to initiate the import. The imported styles will be placed in your stylesheet according to the parent style category.
10	Click the **Save** button to save your work.

Chapter 4

Table Stylesheets and Standard Table Styles

INTRODUCING TABLE STYLESHEET AND STANDARD TABLE STYLES

In Flare, there are two ways to use styles to affect the look of tables in your project. First, you can use standard CSS table styles like td, th, tr, and the others listed in Table 4-1. A second option is to create custom table stylesheets. With table stylesheets, you can create tables with varying looks and patterns that you can apply in a single action to tables throughout your print or online content.

STANDARD CSS TABLE STYLES

Like other styles in your stylesheet, *CSS table styles*, are discrete styles — style tags, for example, the table caption, header row, rows, columns, table cells, and footer row. The Flare stylesheet inherits each of these parent table styles. Since these are parent styles, you can define child classes under each of these parents to suit your specific needs for styling the entire table or the individual table components.

Table 4-1. CSS Standard Table Styles

Parent Styles	Brief Description
table	Use this parent or one of its child classes to apply the defined style properties to the entire table, including a caption, rows, header and footer, if applicable, and table formatting.
caption	Use this parent or one of its child classes to apply the defined style properties to a table caption — a short table description you place at the table top or bottom.
thead	Use this parent or one of its child classes to apply the defined style properties to the first row in the table. A header row is much like any other table row, but it is optional. The header tag can contain multiple rows but must include at least one row <**tr**> tag representing a single row.
tr	Use this parent or one of its child classes to apply the defined style properties to a single table row included within the **tbody**, **thead**, and **tfoot** tags.
col	Use this parent or one of its child classes to define and group attributes that apply to table columns. The <**col**> elements are empty and serve only as a support for attributes. They may appear inside or outside an explicit column group <**colgroup**> element.
tbody	Use this parent or one of its child classes to apply the defined style properties to the body rows of a table — that is, including all table rows, except a table header row or table footer row. This style tag must include at least one row <(**tr**> tag, representing a single row.
tfoot	Use this parent or one of its child classes to apply the defined style properties to a footer row (the very last row in the table). Although the footer row is like any other table row, it is optional and commonly used to provide special footnotes about the table and its content. This style tag must include at least one row <**tr**> tag, representing a single row.
th	Use this parent or one of its child classes to apply the defined style properties to an individual header cell, similar to the <**td**> tag.
td	Use this parent or one of its child classes to apply properties to an individual table cell (data).
colgroup	Use this parent or one of its child classes to group columns together. You can specify the number of columns in the group by using the element's <**span**> tag or by the <**col**> element, which represents one or multiple columns.

> **NOTE:** Each of the styles listed in "CSS Standard Table Styles" on the previous page, are parent styles, for which you may define your own child classes. For example, **table.classA** and **table.classB**; or for example, **tfoot.classA** and **tfoot.classB**.

FLARE TABLE STYLESHEETS

Like a regular stylesheet used to format all of your text consistently, a Flare Table Stylesheet lets you create tables with a consistent look throughout your print and online outputs. You can use the Table Stylesheet Editor to create as many different table stylesheets as required while adding plain or patterned design elements. Even if you have imported many tables during an import, you can create and apply the new table styles to each of the existing tables using a single click.

Using five dialogs to configure consistent settings, you can quickly design sharp-looking tables from the Table Stylesheet Editor. These dialogs include the *General Settings*, defining properties that affect the entire table, and *Header Settings*, *Row Settings*, *Column Settings*, and *Footer Settings*. In addition to the Table Stylesheets, Flare also supports standard CSS table styles designed to format individual table components, including the table caption, header, footer, column, row, cell, and the entire table.

Whereas you can achieve appearances similar to that of table stylesheets, using standard CSS table styles, the Table Stylesheet Editor makes creating fancy or complex tables a bit easier.By default, Flare places table stylesheets files that you create in the **Content Explorer > Resources > Tablestyles**.

> **TIP:** A point to remember when creating table stylesheets in the Table Stylesheet Editor, is that you can create your table stylesheets using the **Default Medium** or **Print Medium**, however remember that the properties created in the default medium are copied to the print medium. You can then modify each medium to satisfy your online and online outputs respectively.

INTRODUCING THE FLARE TABLE STYLESHEET EDITOR

The Table Stylesheet Editor has five dialog tabs that allow you to quickly design table stylesheets with consistent settings for creating sharp-looking tables. These tabs include the General Settings, which define properties that affect the entire table, and *Header Settings*, *Row Settings*, *Column Settings*, and *Footer Settings*.

When using the table stylesheet editor, you can use some or all of these dialog tabs, depending on the look you are trying to achieve. For example, a particular table stylesheet may not require a header or a footer, or both Row and Column dialogs might be specified. It may also only need the inner border lines for rows and columns and not the outer borders. All of these design choices are easily made by simply specifying only the parameters you need.

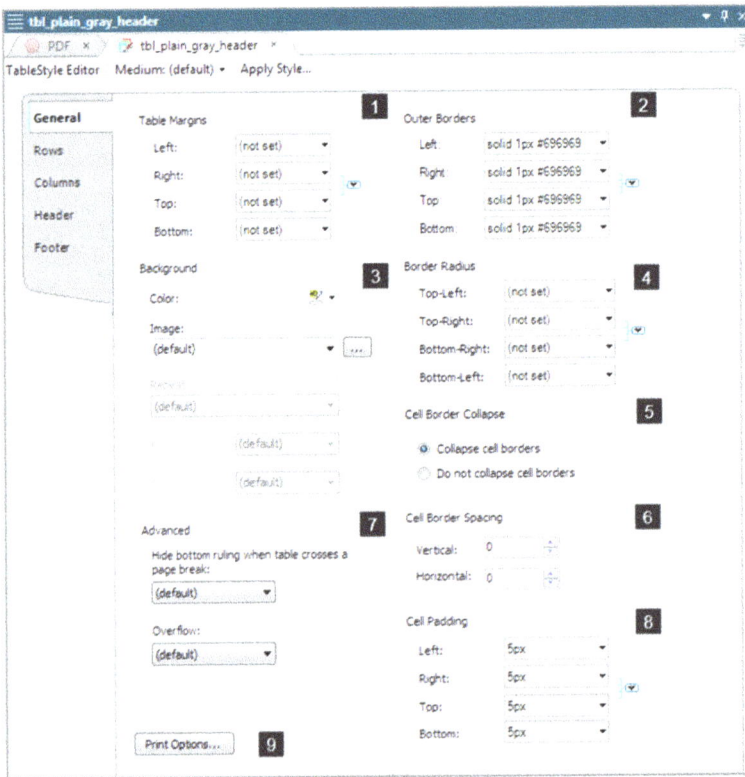

Figure 4-1. Table Stylesheet Editor — General Styles Dialog.

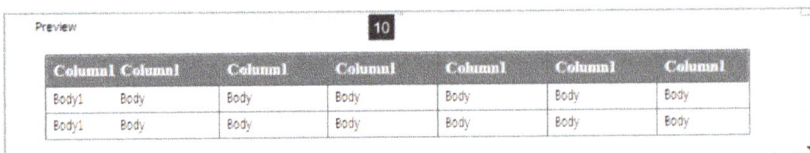

Figure 4-2. Table Stylesheet Editor — Each Table Editor Tab Presents a Preview Pane.

TABLE STYLESHEET GENERAL PROPERTIES

When creating a new stylesheet, the **General** tab is the best place to start. Here you define the parameters listed and described in Table 4-2. Affecting items like margins, borders, rounded corners, cell padding, background color, and page break control, the **General** properties tab applies to the entire table. Although these properties affect the table as a whole, some of the properties may be overridden by the same property set on the **Row** or **Column Styles** tab.

Table 4-2. Table Stylesheet – General Properties

Property Group	Brief Description
Table Margins	Specify the distance that should be maintained from the table borders to the left and right margins and on top and bottom sides, from the nearest paragraph or other content.
Outer Borders	Specify the type, color, and thickness of outer table borders. Border lines, for example, can be solid, double, dashed, or dotted, and thickness is in points, pixels, or other units.
Color	Specify a color that will be in the background of every cell of the entire table.
Image/Repeat	Specify an image to insert in the table background, and specify if the image should repeat (or not repeat) in the background of every cell of the entire table. If repeat is selected, specify the number of times to repeat, and the start position on the x-axis and y-axis.
Border Radius	Specify the measurement length, in pixels, points, inches, or another selected unit, to create rounded corners at the table top left and right corners, bottom left and right corners, or all corners. For example, specify the length in pixels at 12 px for all corners.
Cell Border Collapse	If the table is to have rounded corners, select **Do Not Collapse Borders**, and under the **Advanced** parameters, set **Overflow** to **Hidden**, to hide edges that may overflow.
Cell Border Spacing	Use the Horizontal and Vertical parameters respectively, to specify the spacing by which to increase or decrease horizontally or vertically adjacent cell borders.
Cell Padding	Specify the distance to be maintained between cell content and the cell top, bottom, left, and right side borders. Content, for example, includes text or images.
Advanced	If you set the **Border Radius** parameters to create rounded corners, then under the **Advanced** parameter group, set **Overflow** to **Hidden** to hide edges that may overflow.
Print Options	This **Print Options** dialog and the specified settings, as opposed to those on the Row tab, affect the printing of the entire table concerning Page, Column, and Frame Breaks.

NOTE: Notice that no Font styles or other such characteristics are specified here. Only general table features that you wish to apply to the entire table should be defined here. If **Cell Padding**, for example, is set here, then there is no need to specify it elsewhere.

TABLE STYLESHEET HEADER AND FOOTER PROPERTIES

When designing a new table stylesheet, the parameters found on the **Header Styles** tab and the **Footer** Styles tab are pretty much the same. While most table stylesheets will likely require a header, most will probably not require a footer. In some cases however, you will use both the **Header Styles** and the **Footer Styles** tabs. If not required in the table stylesheet, you can skip either of these dialogs.

When defining the parameters for a header or a footer, you will use a different tab, but the parameters that apply to both table headers and footers, are listed and described in Table 4-3.

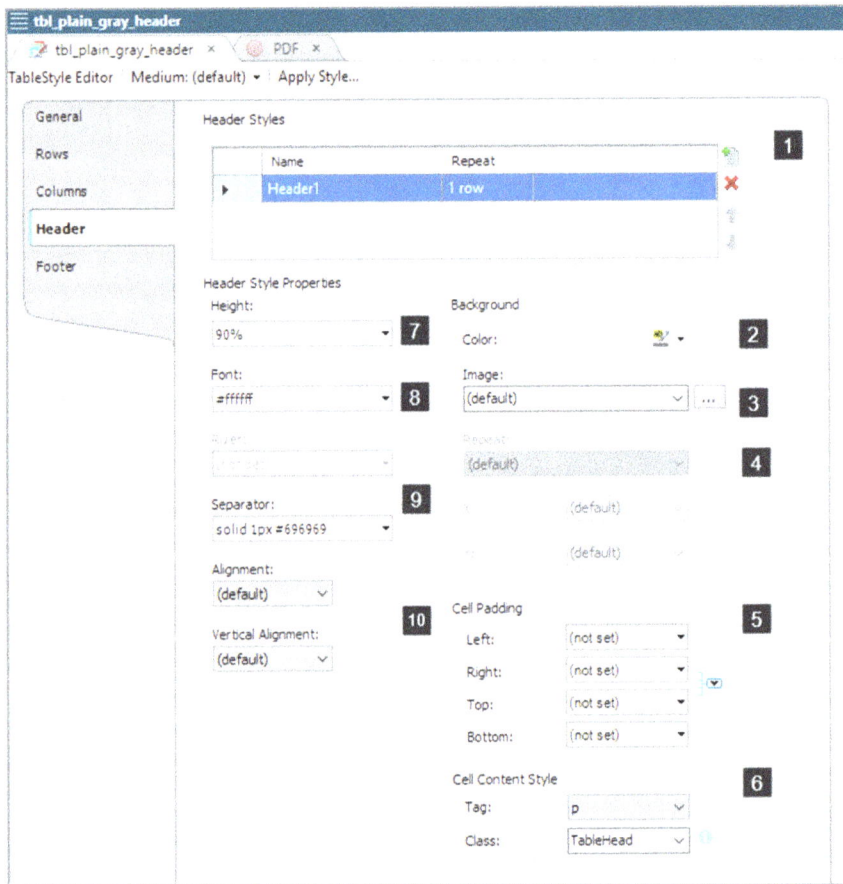

Figure 4-3. Table Stylesheet — Header Properties Dialog (Identical Footer Properties Dialog).

Table 4-3. Table Stylesheet – Header and Footer Properties

Property Group	Brief Description
Name	The default Header row has the Name **Header1**; however, you can use the Add Header Row (+) icon to insert additional header rows. Click slowly on **Name** to rename a Header Row.
Type/Repeat	Use the **Type** drop-down and select **Pattern** if the row is part of a pattern of one or more rows; then click in the **Repeat** field and use the increment button to specify the number of times the row should repeat. For example, 1 row or 2 rows.
Color	Specify the **Background Color** for the currently selected Header row using the **Color Palette** or the **Pick Screen Color** tool.
Image	If desired, select a **Background Image** to insert in the currently selected Header row.
Repeat	If the image is to repeat, use the **Repeat** field to select one of the repeat options, then specify desired X-alignment (Left, Right, Center) or Y-alignment (Top, Middle, Bottom).
Cell Padding	Specify the distance to maintain between cell content and the cell top, bottom, left, and right side borders. Content, for example, may include text or images.
Cell Content Style	Use the **Tag** drop-down arrow and the **Class** drop-down arrow to specify the default style parent and class to use for content placed in the table header. For example select <**p**> for the paragraph parent and "**TableHead**" as the class.
Height	Specify **Header Row Height**, in your choice of measurement units, for example, **1-inch**.
Font	Select a pattern definition under **Header Styles**, then use the drop-down to set **Font Weight**, **Style**, **Color**, and **Size** properties. **Note**: May not be needed if **Cell Content Style** is specified.
Ruler	Specify line color, type, and thickness of the inside line (Rule) between Header Rows when multiple rows are in a header definition. The line type, for example, may be specified as solid, dotted, or dashed; specify the thickness in your choice of units — for example, pixels, points, or inches. **Note**: Ruler is only enabled when **Repeat >1**.
Separator	Specify the line color, type, and thickness of the *Separator between Header Patterns*, placed at the end of the last header row in the first pattern and the start header row of the following pattern. The line type, for example, may be specified as solid, dotted, or dashed; specify the thickness in your choice of units — for example, pixels, points, or inches.
Alignment	Specify the horizontal alignment of the Header Row content as left, right, or center justified.
Vertical Alignment	Specify the vertical alignment of the Header content at the top, middle, or bottom of the cell.

> **TIP:** When defining a header, think of each line item as a single definition that can repeat one or more rows. So, for example, a single header definition may have a repetition of 1-row; then, a second definition may have a repetition of 2-rows, giving the table a total of 3-header rows.

TABLE STYLESHEET ROW PROPERTIES

After creating a new table stylesheet and specifying Header properties, you might define either the **Row** or **Column Styles**. Although we examine the **Row Styles** here, after closely considering the table stylesheet requirements, you may decide that only Row or Column styles need to be defined, but not both. That might be the case in some tables, for example, where aside from the header row, the row and column properties are essentially the same — like when there are two or more columns and only a single row.

Row table properties are listed and described in Table 4-4. As a note of learning, the row parameters described here, are similar to those defined later for the column.

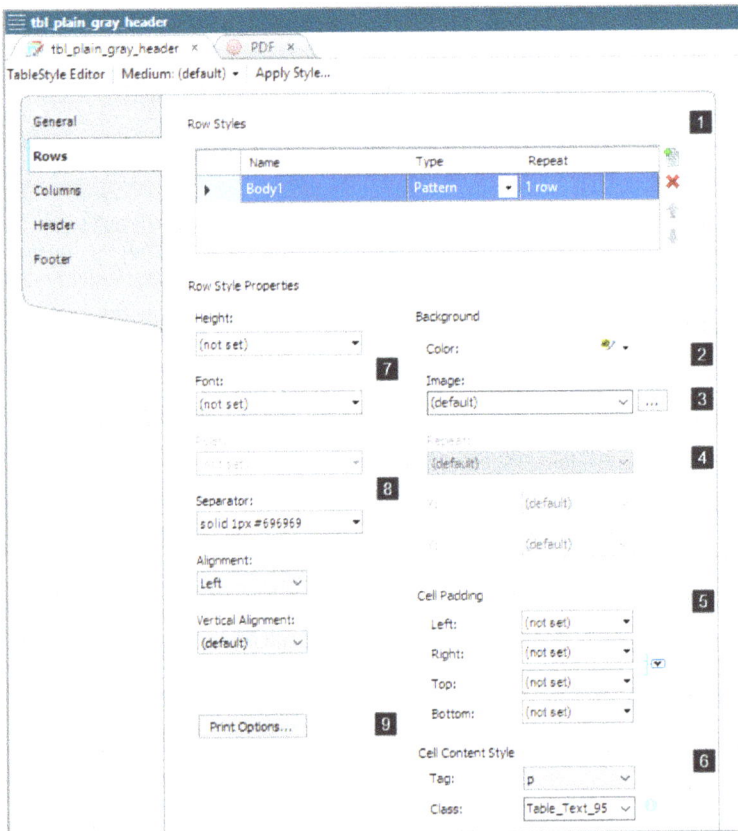

Figure 4-4. Table Stylesheet — Row Styles Dialog.

> **NOTE:** As you specify the desired **Row Styles**, a preview of the current pattern definition is shown to the right in the **Preview** pane.

Table 4-4. Table Stylesheet – Row Properties

Property Group	Brief Description
Name	The default row has the Name **Body1;** however, you can use the Add Header Row (+) icon to insert additional header rows. Click slowly on the **Name** to rename a Row.
Type/Repeat	Use the **Type** drop-down and select **Pattern** if the row is part of a pattern of one or more rows; then click in the **Repeat** field and use the increment button to specify the number of times the row should repeat. For example, 1 row, or 2 row.
Color	Specify **Background Color** for the current Row, with **Color Palette** or **Pick Screen Color** tool.
Image	If desired, select a **Background Image** to insert in the currently selected Row.
Repeat	If the image is to repeat, use **Repeat** to select one of the repeat options, then specify the desired X-alignment (Left, Right, Center) or Y-alignment (Top, Middle, Bottom).
Cell Padding	Specify the distance to maintain between cell content and the cell top, bottom, left, and right side borders. Content for example, includes text or images.
Cell Content Style	Use the **Tag** drop-down arrow and the **Class** drop-down arrow to specify the default style parent and class to use for content placed in the table rows. For example select <**p**> for the paragraph parent and "**TableText**" as the class. See **TIP** below.
Height	Specify the actual **Row Height**, in your choice of measurement units, for example, **1-inch**.
Font	Select a pattern definition under **Row Styles** > then use the drop-down to set **Font Weight**, **Style**, **Color**, and **Size** properties. **Note**: May not be needed if **Cell Content Style** is specified.
Ruler	Specify the line color, type, and thickness of the *inside line (Rule) between Rows*, within a pattern. The line type, for example, may be specified as solid, dotted, or dashed; specify the thickness in your choice of units — for example, pixels, points, or inches. **Note**: Ruler is only enabled when the row **Type** is set for **Pattern** and **Repeat >1**.
Separator	Specify the line color, type, and thickness of the *Separator between Row Patterns*, placed after the last row in the pattern and the first row of the following pattern. The line type, for example, may be specified as solid, dotted, or dashed; specify the thickness in your choice of units — for example, pixels, points, or inches.
Alignment	Specify the horizontal alignment of the Row content as left, right, or center justified.
Vertical Alignment	Specify the vertical alignment of the Row content at the top, middle, or bottom of cell.
Print Options	This **Print Options** dialog and the specified settings, as opposed to those on the **General** tab, affect the printing of table Rows concerning Page, Column, and Frame Breaks.

TIP: If a **Cell Content Style** is set on the "**Column Styles**" tab, you do not need to set it on "**Row**" tab.

TABLE STYLESHEET COLUMN PROPERTIES

After creating a new Table Stylesheet and specifying the General and Header properties, you would consider defining the Row or Column styles. Although we examine the **Column Styles** here, after closely evaluating the requirements of the table stylesheet, you may decide that either the Column or Row properties need to be defined, but not both.

A case when only the Column properties need to be specified might be a table, for example, where the content in each column is different in some way. For example, the text or background color of each column is different. You would specify the appropriate Column properties in such a case, but you could skip the corresponding properties in the Row dialog.

Column properties are listed and described in Table 4-5.

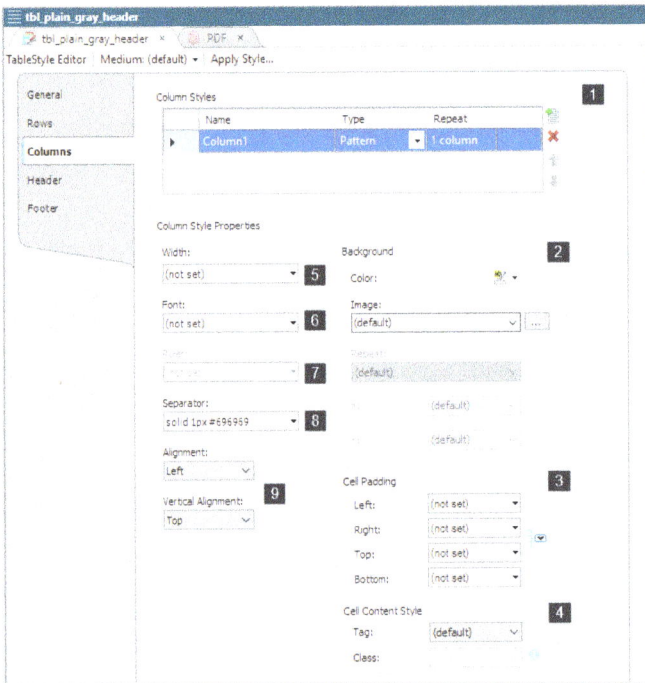

Figure 4-5. Table Stylesheet — Column Styles Dialog.

> **NOTE:** As you specify the desired **Column Styles**, the editor previews the current pattern definition to the right in the **Preview** pane.

Table 4-5. Table Stylesheet – Column Properties

Property Group	Brief Description
Name	The default row has the Name **Column1**; however, you can use the Add Column (+) icon to insert additional columns. Click slowly on the name to rename a column.
Type/Repeat	Use the **Type** to select **Pattern** if the column is part of a pattern of one or more columns; then click the **Repeat** field and use the increment button to specify the number of times the column entry should repeat. For example, 1 column or 2 columns.
Color	Specify a **Background Color** for the currently selected Column using the **Color Palette** or the **Pick Screen Color** tool.
Image	If desired, select a **Background Image** to insert in the currently selected Column.
Repeat	If the image is to repeat, use **Repeat** to select one of the repeat options, then specify the desired X-alignment (Left, Right, Center) or Y-alignment (Top, Middle, Bottom).
Cell Padding	Allows you to specify the distance maintained between the cell content and the cell top, bottom, left, and right side borders. Content, for example, includes text or images.
Cell Content Style	Use the **Tag** drop-down arrow and the **Class** drop-down arrow to specify the default style parent and class to use for content placed in the table columns. For example select <**p**> for the paragraph parent and "**TableText**" as the class. See **TIP** below.
Width	Specify the **Column Width**, in your choice of measurement units, for example, **2-inch**.
Font	Select a pattern definition under **Column Styles** > then use the drop-down to set **Font Weight**, **Style**, **Color**, and **Size** properties. **Note**: May not need if you set **Cell Content Style**.
Ruler	Specify line color, type, and thickness of the *inside line (rule) between Columns*, within a pattern. The line type, for example, may be specified as solid, dotted, or dashed; specify the thickness in your choice of units — for example, pixels, points, or inches. **Note**: Ruler is only enabled when the column **Type** is set for **Pattern** and **Repeat >1**.
Separator	Specify the line color, type, and thickness of the *Separator between Column Patterns*, placed after the last column in the pattern and the first column of the following pattern. The line type, for example, may be specified as solid, dotted, or dashed; specify the thickness in your choice of units — for example, pixels, points, or inches.
Alignment	Specify the horizontal alignment of the Column content as left, right, or center justified.
Vertical Alignment	Specify vertical alignment of the Column content at the top, middle, or bottom of the cell.

> **TIP:** If you set a **Cell Content Style** on the "**Row Styles**" tab, you need not set it on the "Columns" tab.

SUMMARY ON TABLE STYLESHEETS AND STANDARD TABLE STYLES

Just as you would use the regular stylesheet to format standard body text consistently, the Flare CSS also supports discrete formatting styles for individual table components, including the caption, header, footer, column, row, cell, and table body. Flare also supports a Table Stylesheet Editor that allows you to quickly design and create sharp-looking tables using five dialogs to configure settings that produce a consistent look in tables throughout your output.

Table stylesheet tabs include General settings, where you define properties that affect the entire table and header settings, Row settings, Column settings, and Footer settings. Using the Table Stylesheet Editor, you can create as many table stylesheets as required while adding plain or patterned design elements. Even if you have imported many tables during an import, you can create and apply the new table styles to each of the existing tables using a single click.

The following checklist offers some tips and guidelines for working with table styles and stylesheets.

CHECKLIST: TABLE STYLESHEETS AND STANDARD TABLE STYLES

- *You can use standard CSS table styles or table stylesheets to style your table, but using both is not recommended. The use of both types of table styles can interfere with certain Flare-generated content elements. Read more on this subject in Flare Help.*

- *Use the **General** parameters tab to specify settings that will affect the entire table, for instance, the outer borders, table margins, cell padding, or perhaps a table background image.*

- *Use the **Rows** parameters tab to specify settings that affect table rows only. You do not need to set a **Cell Content Style** in this dialog if you have set it in the **Columns** dialog.*

- *Use the **Columns** parameters tab to specify settings that will affect table columns only. You do need to set a **Cell Content Style** in this dialog if you have set it in the **Rows** dialog.*

- *Consider creating a table stylesheet for often used **Tip**, **Note**, **Caution**, and **Warning** elements.*

- *To better control the exact placement of content in your page layout footers, consider creating and placing a table stylesheet in the footer of your page layout files. This table will give you better control over your footer content's left, right, and center alignment.*

- *You may create a table first and then apply the table stylesheet, or you can apply a stylesheet when creating the table.*

- *Consider using the Flare "mc-repeat" and "mc-continuation" properties to control the repeat of table titles on tables that continue to the next page.*

- *A point to remember when creating table stylesheets in the Table Stylesheet Editor is that you can create your table stylesheets using either the **Default Medium** or **Print Medium.***

ADDING A NEW TABLE STYLESHEET

BASIC CONCEPT

In Flare, each table stylesheet is designed with specific purpose and characteristics that will provide a consistent appearance throughout your document and entire project. Like with standard CSS table styles, you can create your table stylesheets using both the Default Medium and Print Medium. Using both mediums allow you to assign different characteristics, for example type faces, sizes, colors and backgrounds. Different table stylesheets, means that each can be designed with an intended purpose.

ESSENTIAL ELEMENTS

When you create a new table stylesheet, you will have the choice of using a factory template or a user - defined template, upon which to base the new stylesheet. You can also make a copy of a table similar to what you want to create, and modify the characteristics later. To help in your decision, you can view the factory templates in the **Preview** pane, to decide on the suitability.

APPLICATION TIPS

Although you can create as many table stylesheets as needed, it is best to minimize the actual number that you create. The more table stylesheets you create, the more difficult it may become to manage a consistent use of each, throughout your documents.

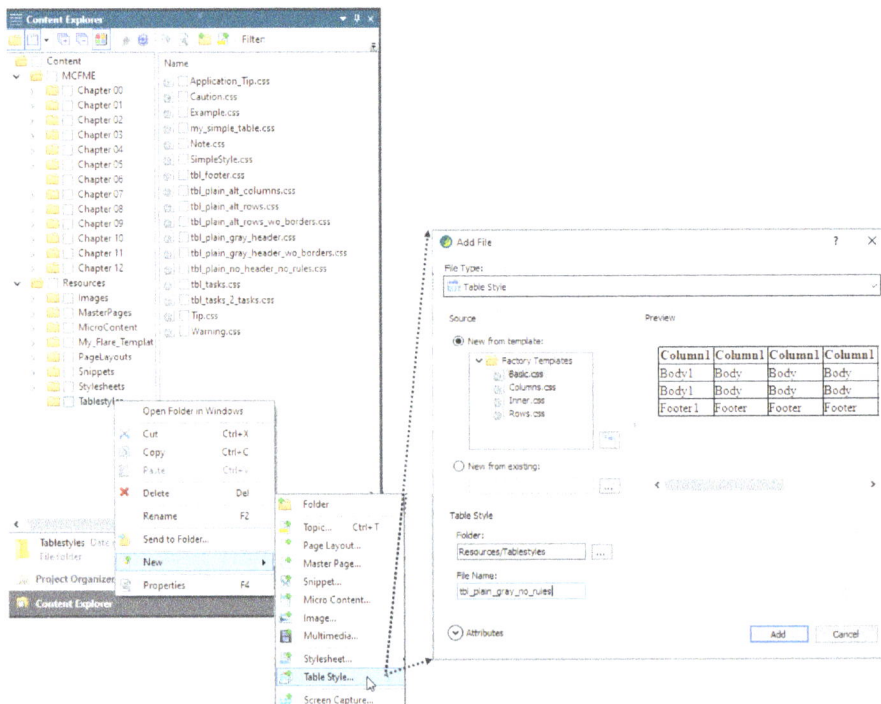

Figure 4-6. New Table Style Option Selected — Add File Dialog with Table Style Option Set.

QUICK STEPS: ADDING A NEW TABLE STYLESHEET

STEP	ACTION
1	Select the **TableStyles** folder, in the **Resources** subfolder of the **Content Explorer**, or find and select the folder in which you wish to add the new table stylesheet.
2	Right Click > **New** > **Table Style**. The **Add File** dialog opens.
3	Ensure that the **File Type** is set for **Table Style**.
4	**To create the new table stylesheet use one of the following:** **a) From Templates**: Set the **Source** for **New From Template**, then choose a template from the **Factory Templates** folder or choose a template from a user-defined **Custom Templates** folder. **b) From Existing**: Set the **Source** for **New From Existing**, and use the browse button ⌐···⌐ to locate the existing table stylesheet file.
5	Under **Table Style**, use the **Folder** field and choose the default folder **Resources/Tablestyles**, or browse and choose another folder in which to store the file.
6	Use the **File Name** field to specify a name for the new table stylesheet file.
7	Click > **Add** to save the new table stylesheet file.

CREATING A SIMPLE TABLE STYLESHEET

BASIC CONCEPT

You can create a simple table stylesheet using minimum parameters from the **General**, **Header**, and **Rows** tabs of the Table Stylesheet Editor. This task briefly describes those basic parameters needed to create a simple table quickly. It also illustrates that you can create a well-formed table using very few parameters and enhance it by defining additional characteristics or adding patterns.

ESSENTIAL ELEMENTS

Using the **General** tab, you can define essential characteristics for the entire table, including 1) **Margins**, to create a fixed spacing between the table borders and the page margin, 2) **Outer Borders**, which define the width and color of the exterior borders, 3) the **Background**, which allows a background **Color** and **Image** to be defined, and 4) **Padding**, to define a fixed spacing between cell text and the table borders.

Using the **Rows** tab, you define the essential characteristics for the table rows, including 1) a **Separator** between rows, 2) the text **Alignment**, and finally, you can specify 3) the **Cell Content Style**, which specifies the style used to define the text appearance in rows.

APPLICATION TIPS

When creating a new table stylesheet, always consider starting with an existing table stylesheet similar to the stylesheet you intend to make. **Copy**, **Paste**, and then rename the existing stylesheet. Then open the newly created stylesheet and modify the properties dialogs to achieve the desired result.

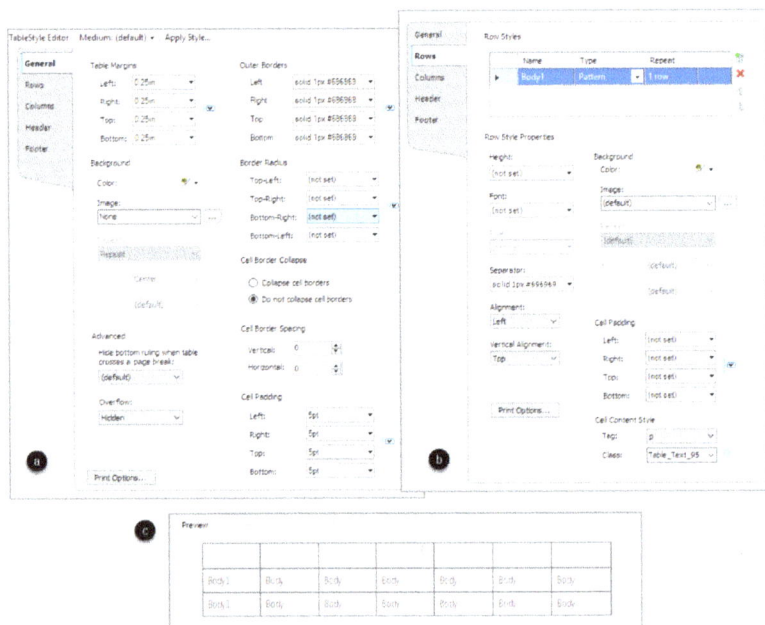

Figure 4-7. Simple Table Stylesheet a) General Tab Settings b) Rows Tab Settings, and c) Preview Pane.

QUICK STEPS: CREATING A SIMPLE TABLE STYLESHEET

STEP	ACTION
1	Add your new table stylesheet using the procedure "**Adding a New Table Stylesheet**. "
	Double-click on the table stylesheet, in the **Tablestyles** subfolder, to open it in the Table Styles Editor.
2	Click the **General** tab, to set parameters that will affect the entire table.
3	Use the **Table Margins** single drop-down arrow, just to the right of the fields, to simultaneously set the **Left**, **Right**, **Top**, and **Bottom** table margins — for example, **0.25 in**.
4	Use the **Outer Borders** drop-down, to the right of the fields, to open the multi-parameter field and simultaneously set the **Left**, **Right**, **Top**, and **Bottom** borders: in the top-left field select **Length**, and in the top-right field specify a Line Color — for example, **#696969**; use the bottom-left and middle fields to set a Line Width — for example, **1 px**, and use the bottom-right field to set the Line Type — as **solid**.
5	Use the **Cell Padding** single drop-down arrow, just to the right of the fields, to simultaneously set the **Left**, **Right**, **Top**, and **Bottom** padding for the field; or use the individual fields to set the padding values.
6	Click the **Rows** tab, to define parameters that will affect the rows of the new table.
7	Use the default **Name** of **Body1** for the row, or click slowly on the name to modify it.
8	Under **Row Style Properties**, use the **Separator** drop-down to open the multi-parameter field, then use the bottom left field to specify a Line Width of **1 px**, the top right field to specify a Line Color of **#696969**, and the bottom right field to specify the Line Type as **solid**.
9	Use the **Alignment** field to specify the horizontal alignment of cell data as **Left**, **Center**, **Right**, or **Justify**; and use **Vertical Alignment** field to specify the vertical alignment as **Top**, **Middle**, or **Bottom**.
10	Use the **Cell Content Style** field to specify, from your stylesheet, a style to use in the table row cells.
11	Click the **Header** tab, to set parameters that affect the table header.
12	Use the default **Name** of **Header1** for the header row, or click slowly on the name to modify it.
13	Under **Header Style Properties**, use the **Separator** drop-down to open the multi-parameter field to define a rule separator between the bottom header row and the table body: in the top-left field select **Length**, and in the top-right field specify a Line Color — for example, **#808080**; then use the bottom-left and middle fields to specify a Line Width — for example, **2 px**, and use bottom-right field to specify the Line Type — for example, **double**.
14	Use the **Alignment** field to specify the horizontal alignment of cell data as **Left**, **Center**, **Right**, or **Justify**; and use **Vertical Alignment** fields to specify the vertical alignment as **Top**, **Middle**, or **Bottom**.
15	Use **Cell Content Style** field to specify a style from your stylesheet, to use in the Header row cells.

CREATING A TABLE STYLESHEET WITH ALTERNATING ROW PATTERN

BASIC CONCEPT

An alternating row pattern is a good solution and an enhancement over a homogenous table of identical rows and columns. A table of patterned columns is especially suitable when the data in the alternating columns are somehow distinguished. In this way, the alternating pattern enhances and differentiates the data in each pattern. The result is that it is easier to focus on a single row of data or even compare or contrast rows than looking at an entire table of data.

ESSENTIAL ELEMENTS

A row pattern is created by defining individual row items consisting of one or more rows in a pattern. Each row item entry can be given a **Name**, for example, **Rows1** and **Rows2**, or Pattern1 and **Pattern2**. Each item has the **Type** defined as **Pattern** as opposed to **Custom**. The **Repeat** parameter specifies the number of rows in a pattern — for example, a **Repeat** of **2 rows**. Each pattern is assigned a Background **Color** that distinguishes it from the alternate pattern.

APPLICATION TIPS

When deciding whether an alternating row pattern is suitable, consider whether the data in each row pattern can also be viewed as a separate data set or has some characteristic that differentiates it from the adjacent pattern.

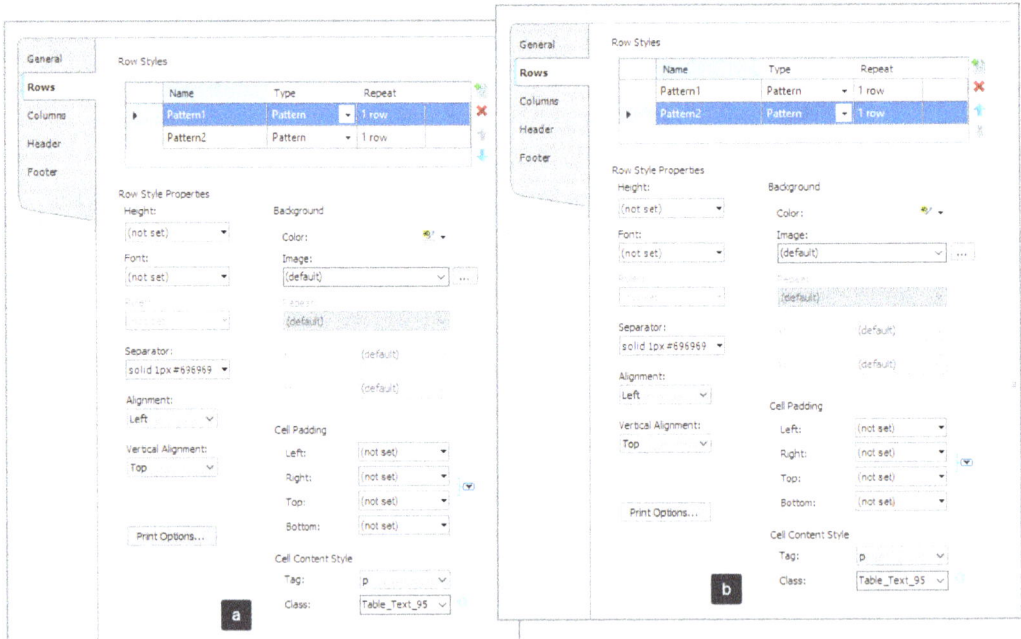

Figure 4-8. a) Parameter Settings for Row 1 Pattern, and b) Parameter Settings for Row 2 Pattern.

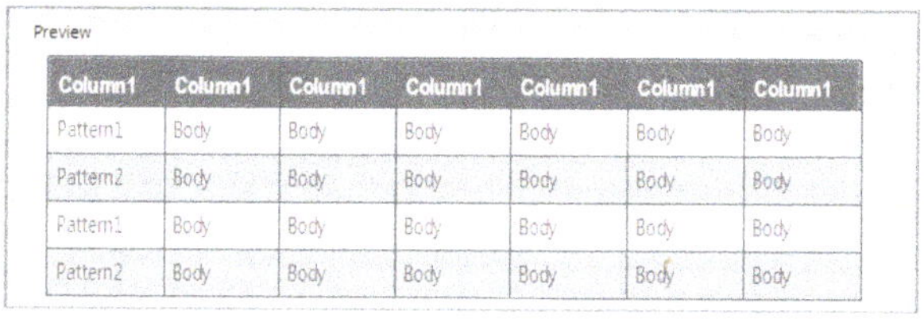

Figure 4-9. Stylesheet Preview — Alternating Row Pattern.

QUICK STEPS: CREATING A TABLE STYLESHEET WITH ALTERNATING ROW PATTERN

STEP	ACTION
1	Add a new table stylesheet named Alternating_Row_Pattern, using the procedure "**Adding a New Table Stylesheet**. "
2	Open your new table stylesheet, from the **Tablestyles** subfolder.
	Click the **General** tab, to set parameters that will affect the entire table.
	Use the **Table Margins** single drop-down arrow, just to the right of the fields, to simultaneously set the **Left**, **Right**, **Top**, and **Bottom** table margins — for example, **0.25 in**.
	Use the **Outer Borders** drop-down, to the right of the fields, to open the multi-parameter field and simultaneously set the **Left**, **Right**, **Top**, and **Bottom** borders: in the top-left field select **Length**, and in the top-right field specify a Line Color — for example, **#696969**; use the bottom-left and middle fields to set a Line Width — for example, **1 px**, and use the bottom-right field to set the Line Type — as **solid**.
	Use the **Cell Padding** single drop-down arrow, just to the right of the fields, to simultaneously set the **Left**, **Right**, **Top**, and **Bottom** padding for the field; or use the individual fields to set the padding values.
3	Click the **Rows** tab, to define parameters that will affect the alternating rows pattern. Two entries will be entered to create the alternating row pattern. Both entries will have a **Repeat** of **1-row**.
4	Use default **Name** of **Body1** for the first row item; or click the name slowly to rename it to **Pattern1**.
5	Use the **Pattern** drop-down under the **Type** field and select **Pattern** as the type of entry.
6	Under the **Repeat** field, use the increment/decrement button to select a **1- row** repeat.
7	Under **Row Style Properties**, use the **Color** drop-down to select a white **Background** color #FFFFFF.
8	Use the **Separator** drop-down arrow to open the multi-parameter field, to define a rule separator between the row patterns: in the top-left field select **Length**, and in the top-right field specify a Line Color — for example, **#696969**; then use the bottom-left and middle fields to specify a Line Width — for example, **1 px**, and use bottom-right field to specify the Line Type — for example, **solid**.
9	Use the **Alignment** field to specify the horizontal alignment of cell data as **Left**, **Center**, **Right**, or **Justify**; and use the **Vertical Alignment** field to specify the vertical alignment as **Top**, **Middle**, or **Bottom**.
10	Use the **Cell Content Style** field to specify, from your stylesheet, a style to use in the table row cells.
11	To the right of the **Row Styles** parameter group, click the **New item** button 🖺 to add a new row item.
12	Use the default **Name** of the second row item; or click slowly on the name to rename it to **Pattern2**.
13	Complete the procedure for the second row item by repeating the procedure from **Step 5**. On this item, specify a **Repeat** of **1-row** in Step 3, and a gray **Background** color **#DCDCDC**, in Step 7.

CREATING A TABLE STYLESHEET WITH ALTERNATING COLUMN PATTERN

BASIC CONCEPT

An alternating column pattern is a good solution and an enhancement over a homogenous table of identical columns and rows. A table of patterned columns is especially suitable when the data in the alternating columns are somehow distinguished. In this way, the alternating pattern enhances and differentiates the data in each pattern. The result is that it is easier to focus on a single column of data or even compare or contrast columns instead of looking at an entire table of data.

ESSENTIAL ELEMENTS

A column pattern is created by defining individual column items that consist of one or more columns in a pattern. Each column item entry can be given a **Name**, for example, **Columns1** and **Columns2**, or **Pattern1** and **Pattern2**. Each item has the **Type** defined as **Pattern** as opposed to **Custom**. The **Repeat** parameter specifies the number of columns in a pattern — for example, a **Repeat** of **2 columns**. Each pattern is assigned a Background **Color** that distinguishes it from the alternate pattern.

APPLICATION TIPS

When deciding whether an alternating column pattern is suitable, consider whether the data in each column pattern can also be viewed as a separate data set or has some characteristic that differentiates it from the adjacent pattern.

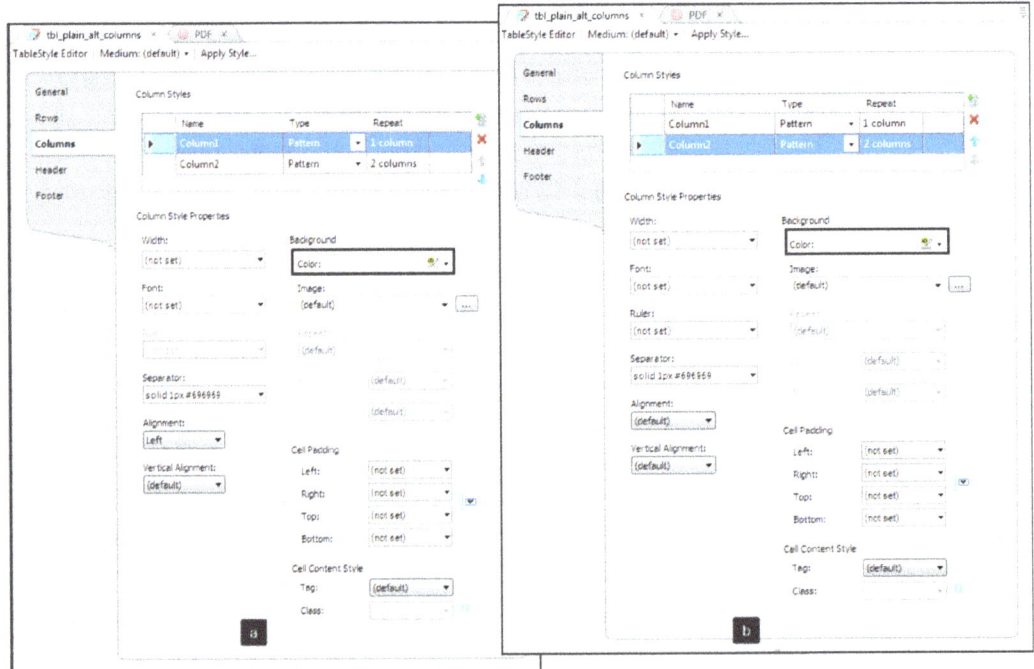

Figure 4-10. a) Parameter Settings for Column 1 Pattern, and b) Parameter Settings for Column 2 Pattern.

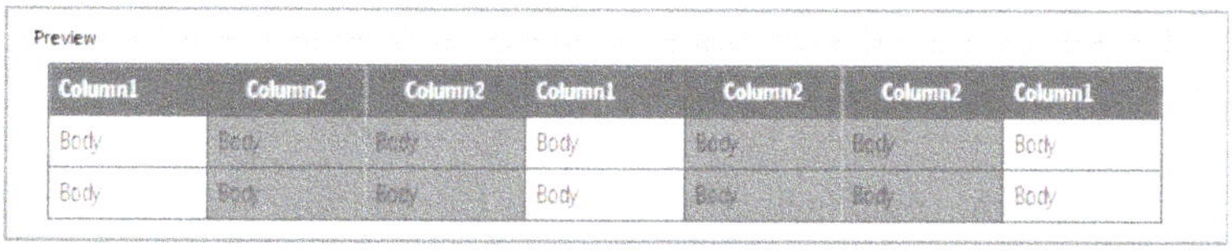

Figure 4-11. Stylesheet Preview — Alternating Column 1 Column 2 Pattern.

QUICK STEPS: CREATING A TABLE STYLESHEET WITH ALTERNATING COLUMN PATTERN

STEP	ACTION
1	Add a new table stylesheet named Alternating_Column_Pattern, using the procedure "**Adding a New Table Stylesheet**."
2	Open your new table stylesheet, from the **Tablestyles** subfolder.
3	Click the **General** tab, to set parameters that will affect the entire table.
4	Use the **Table Margins** single drop-down arrow, just to the right of the fields, to simultaneously set the **Left**, **Right**, **Top**, and **Bottom** table margins — for example, **0.25 in**.
5	Use the **Outer Borders** drop-down, to the right of the fields, to open the multi-parameter field and simultaneously set the **Left**, **Right**, **Top**, and **Bottom** borders: in the top-left field select **Length**, and in the top-right field specify a Line Color — for example, **#696969**; use the bottom-left and middle fields to set a Line Width — for example, **1 px**, and use the bottom-right field to set the Line Type — as **solid**.
6	Use the **Cell Padding** single drop-down arrow, just to the right of the fields, to simultaneously set the **Left**, **Right**, **Top**, and **Bottom** padding for the field; or use the individual fields to set the padding values.
7	Click the **Column** tab, to define parameters for the alternating columns pattern. Two entries will be entered to create the alternating column pattern. Column-1 will have a **Repeat** of **1-column**, and column-2 will have a **Repeat** of **2-column**.
8	Use default **Name** of **Column1** for the first column item; or click name slowly to rename it to **Pattern1**.
9	Use the **Pattern** drop-down under the **Type** field and select **Pattern** as the type of entry.
10	Under the **Repeat** field, use the increment/decrement button to select a **1-column** repeat.
11	Under **Column Style Properties**, use the **Color** drop-down to select a white **Background** color #FFFFFF.
12	Use the **Separator** drop-down arrow to open the multi-parameter field, to define a rule separator between the column patterns: In the top-left field select **Length**, and in the top-right field specify a Line Color — for example, **#696969**; then use the bottom-left and middle fields to specify a Line Width — for example, **1 px**, and use the bottom-right field to specify the Line Type — for example, **solid**.
13	Use the **Alignment** field to the horizontal alignment of cell data as **Left**, **Center**, **Right**, or **Justify**; and use the **Vertical Alignment** fields to specify the vertical alignment as **Top**, **Middle**, or **Bottom**.
14	Use the **Cell Content Style** field to specify, from your stylesheet, a style to use in the column cells.
15	To the right of the **Column Styles** parameter group, click **New item** button 🗒 to add a new column item.
16	Use the default **Name** of the second column item; or the name slowly to rename it to **Pattern2**.
17	Complete the procedure for the second column item by repeating the procedure from **Step 5**. On this item, specify a **Repeat** of **2-column** in Step 3, and a gray **Background** color **#A9A9A9**, in Step 7.

CREATING TABLE STYLESHEETS FOR TIP, NOTE, CAUTION, AND WARNING STYLES

BASIC CONCEPT

Earlier in this book, we created styles for the commonly used **Tip**, **Note**, **Caution**, and **Warning** text using the standard Paragraph class, and the Auto-Number property. Here in this example, each of these same styles are created using a table stylesheet, for each of the objects, that uses a paragraph style tag, that uses the Auto-Number Format Commands.

ESSENTIAL ELEMENTS

Each table stylesheets, including **Tip**, **Note**, **Caution**, and **Warning**, use an image representing the stylesheet purpose. In the end, each table stylesheet has a single row and two columns — where column 1 contains the image and column 2 contains a paragraph style that defines the appearance of the Note, Tip, Caution, or Warning text entry. You will need to create these styles in your CSS.

Although there is a single row in the table, only the columns are specified, since each column has different properties. In each table stylesheet, the text label, for example, "*NOTE,*" and the bold formatting, are done using the **Auto-Numbering Format Commands**. You do not need to configure properties on the table stylesheet **Header**, **Row**, and **Footer** tabs.

Table 4-6. HTML Elements from Basic Elements Category

Style Class	Font	Size	Line Color	Bkgnd. Color	Auto-Format
p.NoteText	Segoe	9.5 pt	#4682B4	#F5F5F5	{b}{i}NOTE: {/i}{/b}
p.TipTextText	Segoe	9.5 pt	#696969	#F5F5F5	{b}{i}TIP: {/i}{/b}
p.CautionText	Segoe	9.5 pt	#FFD700	#F5F5F5	{b}{i}CAUTION: {/i}{/b}
p.WarningText	Segoe	9.5 pt	#FF0000	#F5F5F5	{b}{i}WARNING: {/i}{/b}

APPLICATION TIPS

Where possible, consider creating styles that have identical properties in both the Default and Print Mediums. This approach allows common styles to be used and thereby minimize double maintenance.

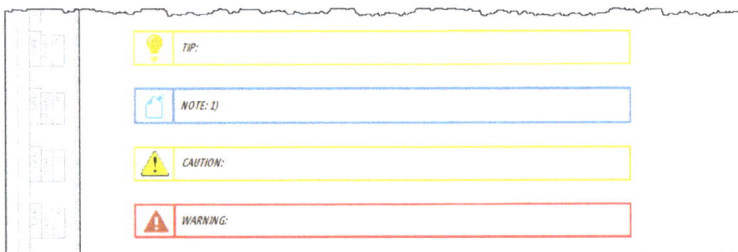

Figure 4-12. Table Stylesheet for Tip, Note, Caution, Warning, and Example Text.

QUICK STEPS: CREATING TABLE STYLESHEETS FOR TIP, NOTE, CAUTION, AND WARNING STYLES

STEP	ACTION
1	Create your new table stylesheet "**Note.css**", using the procedure "**Creating a New Table Stylesheet.** "
2	Open your new table stylesheet, **Note.css**, from the **Tablestyles** subfolder.
3	Click the **General** tab, to set parameters that affect the entire table.
4	Use the **Table Margins** drop-down arrow, just to the right of the fields, to simultaneously set the **Left**, **Right**, **Top**, and **Bottom** table margins; or use the individual fields to set **Top** and **Bottom** at **12 pt**.
5	Use the **Outer Borders** drop-down arrow, to the right of the fields, to simultaneously define the **Left**, **Right**, **Top**, and **Bottom** table borders. Use the top-left field and select the **Length** parameter; use the top-right field to set the Line Color to **#696969**; use the bottom-left and center fields to define the Line Width as **1 px**; and use the bottom-right field to set the Line Type as **solid**.
6	Use the **Cell Padding** drop-down, just to the right of the fields, to simultaneously set the **Left**, **Right**, **Top**, and **Bottom** padding — for example, **6 pt**; or use individual fields to set the padding values.
7	Click the **Columns** tab, to define parameters that will affect the Columns of the Notes table.
8	Use the default **Name** of **Column1** for the first column, or slowly click on the name field to modify it.
9	Use the **Pattern** drop-down under the **Type** field and select **Pattern** as the type of entry for **Column1**.
10	Under the **Repeat** field, use the increment/decrement button to select a **1 column** repeat.
11	Use the **Width** field to specify a width and desired unit of measurement, for example, **0.5** inches.
12	Under **Background**, use the **Color** drop-down and choose a background color if desired; and click the browse button ⌷ just right of the **Image** field to find and select an image to represent the Note object.
13	Under **Column Style Properties**, use the **Separator** drop-down to define the characteristics of the column separator line: in the top-left field select **Length**, and in the top-right field specify a Line Color — for example, **#696969**; then use the bottom-left and middle fields to specify a Line Width — for example, **1 px**, and use bottom-right field to specify the Line Type — for example, **solid**.
14	Use the **Alignment** field to specify a the horizontal alignment of the column as **Center**; and the **Vertical Alignment** field to specify the vertical alignment of the column as **Middle**.
15	**Complete the following steps for Column 2**.
16	To the right of the **Column Styles** parameter group, click the **New item** button 🗒 to add a new column.
17	Use the default **Name** of the second column item; or click slowly on the name to change it to **Column2**.
18	Use the **Width** field to specify a width and desired unit of measurement, for example, **5.25** inches.
19	Under **Background**, use the **Color** drop-down to choose a color, if desired, for example #DCDCDC.
20	Use the **Alignment** field to specify the horizontal alignment of the Note text as **Left**; and use **Vertical Alignment** field to specify the vertical alignment as **Top**, **Middle**, or **Bottom**.
21	Use the **Cell Content Style** field to specify, from your stylesheet, a style to use for the Note text.

INSERTING A NEW TABLE USING INSERT TABLE BUTTON

BASIC CONCEPT

A new table can be created and directly inserted into your contents from the Flare **Table** ribbon or from the **Insert** ribbon. From the **Insert Table** dialogs, you first define the table components such as the number of rows and columns, and then you would specify a CSS Style or a table stylesheet to assign the unique characteristics and appearance of the table.

ESSENTIAL ELEMENTS

The new table is defined using the **Insert Table** dialog, consisting of the **General** and **Borders** tab. You specify the **Table Size** on the **General** tab as the **Number of rows, columns, header**, and **footer** rows; Using the **Table Caption** parameters, you enter the caption **Text**, position, and **Repeat** and **Continuation** behavior. Using **Autofit Behavior**, you determine if the table content should be **Autofit to contents, Autofit to window**, or **Fixed column width**. Finally, you specify the **Table Style** using a table stylesheet or a CSS **Style Class**. On the **Borders** tab, you define the border characteristics of the table.

APPLICATION TIPS

Inherited CSS Table style properties **mc-caption-repeat** and **mc-caption-continuation** can be defined in your stylesheet and act as default values for the table caption behavior regarding whether Flare should repeat the caption on every page. You can specify **mc-caption-repeat** as "**true**" or "**false**," and you can define a default continuation string for **mc-caption-continuation** — for example, "**(Cont.)**".

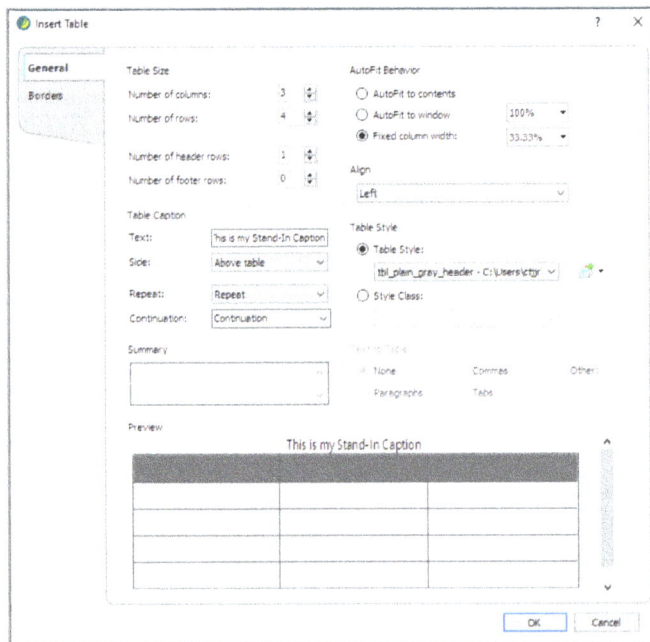

Figure 4-13. Insert Table Dialog — Using Insert Table button.

QUICK STEPS: INSERTING A NEW TABLE USING INSERT TABLE BUTTON

STEP	ACTION
1	From the **Insert** menu click the **Table** button; or from the **Table** menu, click the **Insert Table** button.
2	Click the **General** tab, to set basic parameters and characteristics of the entire table.
3	Specify the **Number of columns**, **Number of rows**, **Number of header rows**, and **Number of footer rows** you want the table to have.
4	Under **Autofit Behavior**, select **Autofit to contents**, if you want column widths to adjust in size based on the content; select **Autofit to window**, if you want the table size to auto-adjust to the output window size; and select **Fixed column width**, if you want column widths based on your specified width.
5	Under **Table Caption**, use the **Text** field to enter a table caption. Enter a temporary caption if not sure.
6	In the **Side** field, specify whether the table caption should appear **Above table**, or **Below table**.
7	In the **Repeat** field, choose **Repeat** if you want the table caption to be repeated on every page if the table continues to the next page; otherwise, choose **Don't Repeat**.
8	If you choose to repeat the table caption, use the **Continuation** field to enter a text string that follows the table caption — for example "(**Continuation**)" or "(**Cont.**)". See **Application Tips** on previous page.
9	Use the **Align** drop-down to specify whether the table should align **Left**, **Right**, or **Center**.
10	Choose **Table Style** and use the drop-down if you want to assign a table stylesheet for the new table.
11	Choose **Style Class** to assign a CSS **Table** style class to the table — for example, **Table.mytblclass2**.
12	Click the **Border** tab to set characteristics of the table border.
13	Use the **Outer Borders** drop-down arrow, to the right of the fields, to open the multi-parameter field and simultaneously define the **Left**, **Right**, **Top**, and **Bottom** table borders: in the top-left field select **Length**, and in the top-right field specify a Line Color — for example, **#696969**; then use the bottom-left and middle fields to specify a Line Width — for example, **1 px**, and use bottom-right field to specify the Line Type — for example, **solid**. You may also use individual fields to define the border parameters.
14	When **Collapse cell borders** is enabled, the row and cell borders are joined to form a single border, but are otherwise detached. This parameter must be disabled if creating rounded top or bottom edges.
15	Use the **Vertical** parameter of **Cell Border Spacing**, to increase the spacing between vertically adjacent cell borders, and the **Horizontal** parameter to increase spacing between horizontally adjacent borders.
16	Click **OK** to complete and insert the new table.

INSERTING A NEW TABLE USING ROW-COLUMN DROP-DOWN PALETTE

BASIC CONCEPT

In addition to using the **Insert Table** button on either the **Insert** menu or **Table** menu, you can also use the drop-down arrow shown on both buttons. This method of inserting a new table may offer a quicker way of inserting a table, but it may be a slower method, depending on your intentions. The table is inserted with only the requested number of rows and columns and without any styling. You must either use the standard table styles or apply a specific table stylesheet to add styling.

ESSENTIAL ELEMENTS

A row-column palette or grid is presented with this method when you click the drop-down arrow. The grid remains displayed until you move your cursor across the grid horizontally to indicate the number of columns and vertically downward to indicate the number of rows. When you click the grid on the final row or column is the table inserted with the selected rows and columns. The table is without a header, footer, or any styling.

APPLICATION TIPS

This method of table insertion may be more appropriate in those cases where you intend to style the table using CSS table styles as opposed to table stylesheets. If this is your intention, then remember that mixing both standard CSS table styles and table stylesheets is not recommended.

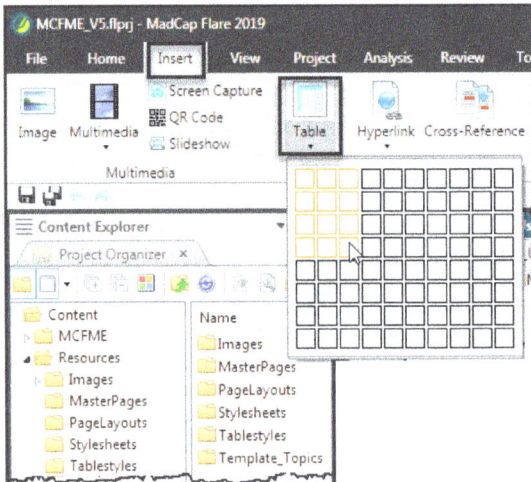

Figure 4-14. Insert Table Using Row-Column Palette from a) Insert Menu or b) Table Menu.

Figure 4-15. Table Inserted Using Row-Columns Drop-Down Palette.

QUICK STEPS: INSERTING A NEW TABLE USING ROW-COLUMN DROP-DOWN PALETTE

STEP	ACTION
1	Open the topic in which you want to insert a the new table.
2	From the **Insert** menu, click the **Table** drop-down arrow; or from the **Table** menu, click the **Insert Table** drop-down arrow.
3	Move your cursor across the grid horizontally, to indicate the desired number of columns; and move your cursor vertically downward, to indicate the desired number of rows.
4	Click the mouse when you have indicated the number of rows and columns. The table is inserted.
5	Click the **Show Tags** drop down arrow on the Editor ribbon, and select the **Block Structure Bars** if not already displayed; click the **Span Structure Bars** if not displayed.
6	The inserted table has no table header, caption, footer, or any styling; to add any of these elements, right-click anywhere in the table and select **Table Properties**.
7	Use the **General** tab to add a header, additional rows or columns, a table caption. After these elements are added, you may choose to apply a table stylesheet or save the changes and then continue to apply your discrete table style classes. Use the **Borders** table to modify the table exterior border properties.
8	If you wish to apply a table stylesheet to the new table, click the **Table Styles** drop-down arrow, to select a stored table stylesheet; or continue with the following steps if you wish to apply standard table styles.

Use the following steps to apply standard CSS styles to the individual table components:

With table tags shown on the block structure, you can select individual table components. This method requires that you have created child classes for each of the table component parent styles. **See Tip**.

a) To apply a style to the entire table, click the table (**table**) tag bar and use the **Style** pane drop-down to select your table style class — for example, (**table.class-1**); or continue.

b) To apply a style to the table header, click the table header (**thead**) tag bar and use the **Style** pane drop-down to select your table header style class — for example, (**thead.class-1**); or continue.

c) To apply a style to the table body, click the table body (**tbody**) tag bar and use the **Style** pane drop-down to select your table body style class — for example, (**tbody.class-1**); or continue.

d) To apply a style to a table row, click a table row (**tr**) tag bar and use the **Style** pane drop-down to select your table row style class — for example, (**tr.class-1**); or continue.

e) To apply a style to a table column, click a table column (**col**) span bar and use the **Style** pane drop-down to select your table column style class — for example, (**col.class-1**); or continue.

f) To apply a style to a table footer, click a table footer (**tfoot**) tag bar and use the **Style** pane drop-down to select your table footer style class — for example, (**tfoot.class-1**); or continue.

g) To apply a style to a table cell, click a table cell (**td**) tag bar and use the **Style** pane drop-down to select your table cell style class — for example, (**td.class**); or continue.

> **TIP:** Table parent styles <**table**>, <**tbody**>, <**thead**>, <**tcaption**>, <**tr**>, <**col**>, and <**tfoot**> are inherited in your stylesheet. It is recommended that you create child classes for each parent style instead of using the parent for styling. Creating child classes always give you greater styling flexibility.

RE-POSITIONING TABLE ROWS AND COLUMNS

BASIC CONCEPT

After having created a table, you will often determine that certain table rows or columns would be more effective if moved to a different position in the table. Moving table rows and columns in Flare is quite simple, and there are a few options.

ESSENTIAL ELEMENTS

When it comes to re-positioning table rows or columns, you have the option of using a drag-and-drop method or a **Copy** and **Paste** method. Before using the drag-and-drop method, use the **Show Tags** drop-down to enable the **Block Structure Bars** for when moving rows; and enable the **Span Structure Bars** for when moving columns. This last step is not needed if structure bars are visible.

APPLICATION TIPS

You can also use the alternate method shown on the following page to re-position columns. In the case of columns, you would fully select one or more columns to re-position.

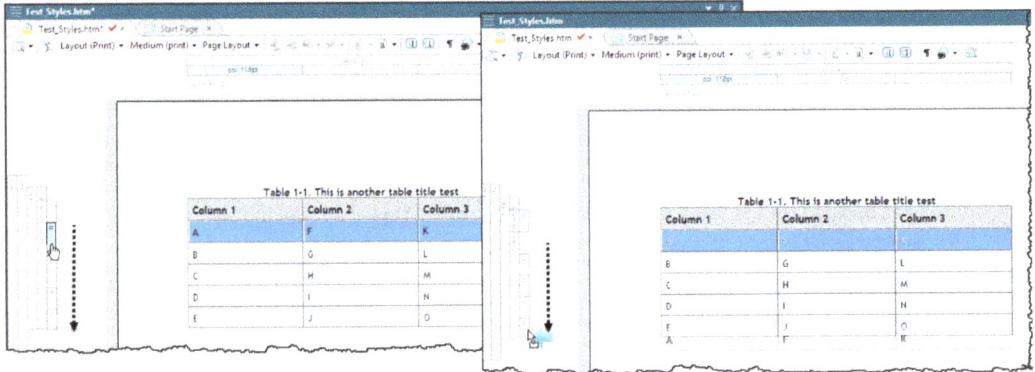

Figure 4-16. Re-Positioning Table Rows a) Click-and -Drag b) Drop at New Position.

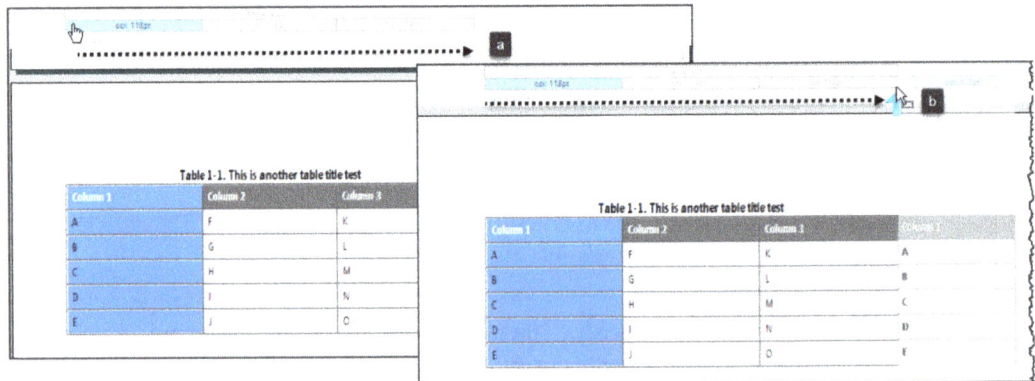

Figure 4-17. Re-Positioning Table Columns a) Click-and -Drag b) Drop at New Position.

QUICK STEPS: RE-POSITIONING TABLE ROWS AND COLUMNS

STEP	ACTION
	Use the following steps to re-position table rows:
1	Open the topic file that contains a table in which you want to re-position table rows.
2	Click the **Show Tags** button on the Editor ribbon, and select the **Block Structure Bars** if not already visible.
3	Position the table in view, so that the structure bars are seen to the left-side of the topic in the Editor.
4	Click on the **tr** tag (table row) to select the table row you want to re-position.
5	Drag the row until reaching the position you want it inserted — a blue arrow appears at row boundaries. Drop the row in the new desired position. Repeat the process if the row is dropped in the wrong position.
6	Click the **Save** button to save your topic.
	Use the following steps to re-position table columns:
1	Open the topic file that contains a table in which you want to re-position table columns.
2	Click the **Show Tags** button on the Editor ribbon, and select the **Span Structure Bars** if not already visible.
3	Position the table in view, so that the span structure bars are seen at the top-side of the topic in the Editor. You should see the table structure bars with the table bar on top with columns show underneath.
4	Click on a specific **col** tag (table column) to select the table column you want to re-position.
5	Drag the column until reaching the position you want it inserted — a blue arrow appears at column boundaries. Drop column in new position. Repeat process if the column is dropped in the wrong position.
6	Click the **Save** button to save your topic.
	Alternate Method (when re-positioning rows or columns with data):
1	Use your mouse to fully select one or more rows or columns you want to re-position.
2	Right-click, and **Cut** the selected rows or columns.
3	**a)** For rows, select a row (entire row) above which or below which you want to insert the cut rows.
	b) Right-click and select **Paste Above** or **Paste Below**, depending on where you want to insert the rows.
3	**a)** For columns, select a column (entire column) above or below which you want to insert the cut columns.
	b) Right-click and select **Paste Above** or **Paste Below**, depending on where you want to insert columns.

INSERTING NEW TABLE ROWS AND COLUMNS

BASIC CONCEPT

At any point after having created a table, you can always insert one or more new rows to the table or one or more new columns to the table. Inserting table rows and columns in Flare is quite simple, and once again, there are a few options.

ESSENTIAL ELEMENTS

When it comes to inserting new table columns and rows, you have the option of using **Table** ribbon commands, or you can use the right-click commands. Both **Table** ribbon and right-click commands allow you to insert a column to the left or the right of a given column, and you can insert a new row above or below a given row. Finally, you have the option of inserting a single row or column only, or you can insert multiple rows or columns.

To insert a single row or column, you click in the row or column to provide location reference; or to insert multiple rows or multiple columns, you will use the click and drag method to select one or more rows or columns as a reference.

APPLICATION TIPS

If you click anywhere in a row, you are at the same time clicking inside a column. You can then use the right-click to insert a new row Above or Below, and you have the option to insert a new column to the Right or the Left. The right-click menu has two **Insert** command groups — look to the lower **Insert** command group on the menu.

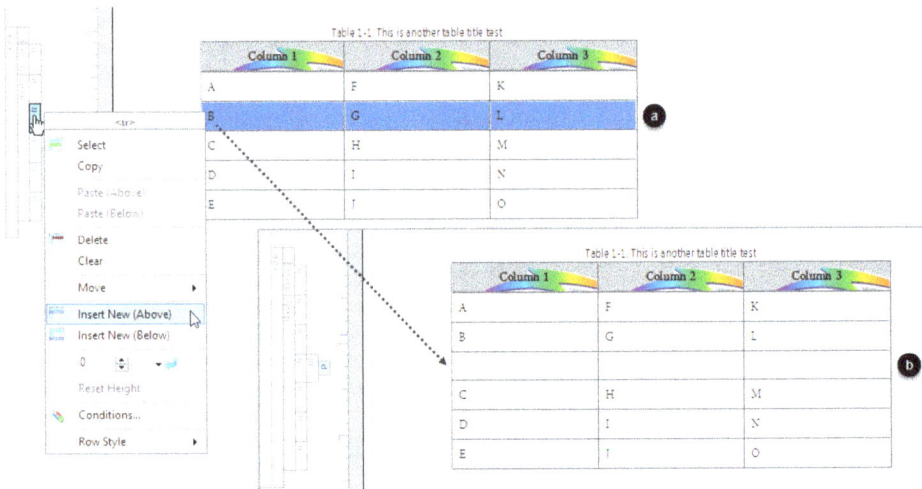

Figure 4-18. a) Before Inserting a New Table Row b) After Inserting New table Row.

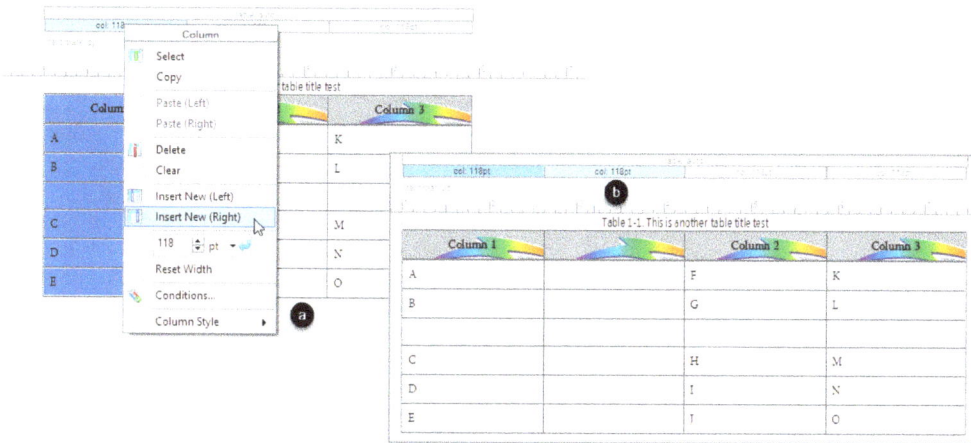

Figure 4-19. a) Before Inserting a New Table Column b) After Inserting New Table Column.

Quick Steps: Inserting New Table Rows and Columns

STEP	ACTION
	Use one of the following steps to insert a single table row:
1	With the topic or snippet open to the table click inside any row where you want to insert a new row(s) and do one of the following:
2	Right-click and select **Insert** > **Rows Above** or **Insert** > **Rows Below**.
3	From the **Table** ribbon, select **Rows Above** or **Rows Below**.
	Use one of the following steps to insert n-rows (for example 3-rows):
1	Click inside the table at the point where you want to insert two or more new table rows.
2	Click and drag to select the number of rows you want to insert.
3	Right-click and select **Insert** > **Rows Above** or **Insert** > **Rows Below**.
4	From the **Table** ribbon, select **Rows Above** or **Rows Below**.
	Use one of the following steps to insert a single table column:
1	With the topic or snippet open to the table click inside any column where you want to insert a new column(s) and do one of the following:
2	Right-click and select **Insert** > **Columns to the Left** or **Insert** > **Columns to the Right**.
3	From the **Table** ribbon, select **Columns to the Left** or **Columns to the Right**.
	Use one of the following steps to insert n-columns (for example 3-columns):
1	Click inside the table at the point where you want to insert two or more new table columns.
2	Click and drag to select the number of columns you want to insert.
3	Right-click and select **Insert** > **Columns to the Left** or **Insert** > **Columns to the Right**.
4	From the **Table** ribbon, select **Columns to the Left** or **Columns to the Right**.

APPLYING A TABLE STYLESHEET TO A SINGLE TABLE OR MULTIPLE TABLES

BASIC CONCEPT

A table stylesheet, after it has been modified, it can then be applied to existing tables. You can apply an edited table stylesheet to a single table in any topic or file, or you can apply the edited table stylesheet to multiple tables that exist in topics throughout your project.

ESSENTIAL ELEMENTS

You can update existing tables throughout your document or project, one at a time or simultaneously after identifying the folders and topics in which you wish to update the tables. A single table can be updated from within the topic, by clicking anywhere inside the table or selecting the table tag bar and then using the right-click and context sensitive command to **Apply Table Style**. As you simultaneously apply a table stylesheet to multiple tables, you will also have the option to **Overwrite existing table styles**, **Remove print table styles**, and to **Remove Local formatting**.

APPLICATION TIPS

When applying the edited table stylesheet to multiple tables, only select those topics in which you wish to apply the table stylesheet. The table stylesheet will be applied to all tables in the topics you select. If there are a few tables that are not the one that you are applying, you will need to go to those topics and reapply the appropriate table stylesheet.

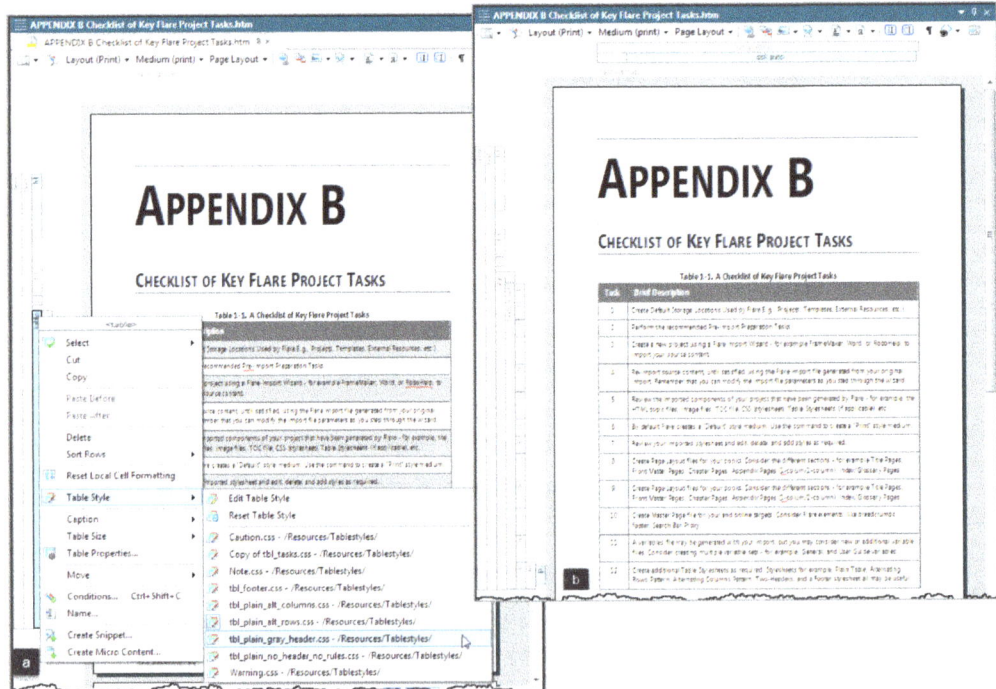

Figure 4-20. Applying Table Stylesheet a) Before Stylesheet Applied, and b) After New Stylesheet Applied.

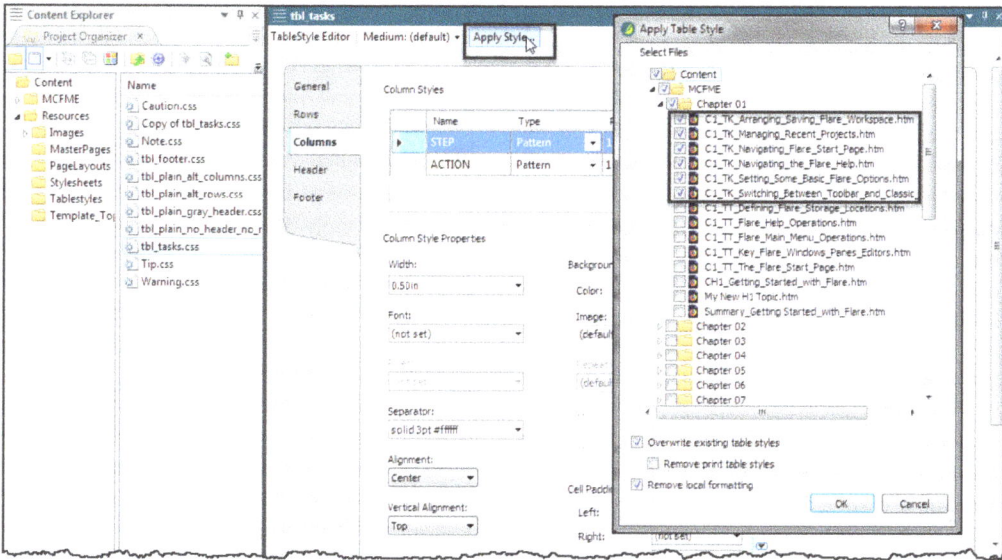

Figure 4-21. Selecting Topics to Apply Updated Table Stylesheet.

QUICK STEPS: APPLYING A TABLE STYLESHEET TO A SINGLE TABLE OR MULTIPLE TABLES

STEP	ACTION
1	Open the topic file that contains a table to which you wish to apply an edited table stylesheet.
2	Click **Show Tags** button on the Editor ribbon, and select the **Block Structure Bars** if not already visible.
	Use the following steps to apply a table stylesheet to single table:
3	Right-click on the table tag bar, for the table you wish to apply a table stylesheet, select **Table Style**, and then select the specific table stylesheet; or click anywhere in the table and right-click and select **Table Style** and select the desired table stylesheet.
4	**Use the following steps to apply a table stylesheet to multiple tables:**
5	Open in the TableStyle Editor, the table stylesheet you wish to apply to tables in multiple topics.
6	Click **Apply Style** on the **TableStyle Editor** ribbon. The **Apply Table Style** dialog opens.
7	Open your **Content** folder to browse and select files that include target tables to apply the table style.
8	Open specific sub-folders and use the check boxes to select sub-folders or topics to target tables. **Note:** Selecting a subfolder will result in all tables contained in the folder having the stylesheet applied.
9	Select **Overwrite existing table styles**, to overwrite existing table stylesheets (other than the one you are applying). With this option enabled, you may also select the option to **Remove print table styles**.
10	Select **Remove print table styles** to remove previously applied print table styles, on applying stylesheet.
11	Select **Remove local formatting**, to remove previously applied local formatting, on applying stylesheet.
12	Click **OK** to apply the table stylesheet to the selected tables.
13	Click the **Save All** button to save your work.

APPLYING STANDARD TABLE STYLES TO TABLE CONTENT

BASIC CONCEPT

In Flare, standard CSS styles are one of the two ways in which you can apply predefined styles to your tables and more specifically to the various components of a table. Whereas with table stylesheets, you simultaneously apply all of the styles that have been predefined for the individual table components, when you apply the table style. With the CSS table styles you must apply discrete style classes, like **td**, **th**, and **tr**, and the others directly to the component you wish to style.

ESSENTIAL ELEMENTS

Newly created stylesheets or imported stylesheets will both, by default, have standard table style tags for styling individual table components. Style tags for the table caption, header row, rows, columns, table cells, footer rows, and even for the entire table body, are all included. Each of these inherited CSS styles are, in fact, parent styles, similar to other inherited parent styles. As such, you can define child classes under each of these to suit your specific requirements for styling individual table components. Once having created these child classes, you can apply styles to the individual components of a table.

APPLICATION TIPS

In Flare, it is recommended against using both standard CSS table styles and table stylesheets in your topics. It is best that you choose one or the other as to avoid possible conflicts. This guideline is especially applicable in if you are also using Flare proxies.

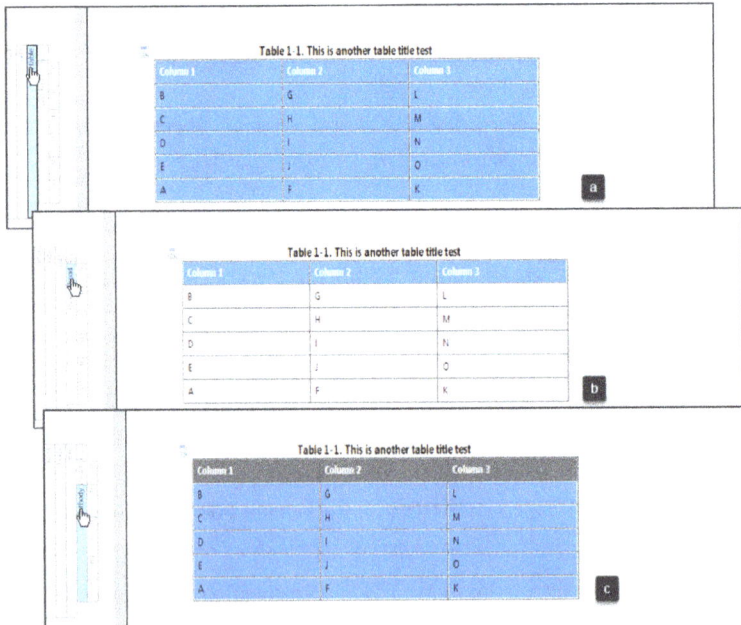

Figure 4-22. Applying Standard Table Styles a) <table> b) <theader>, and c) <tbody>.

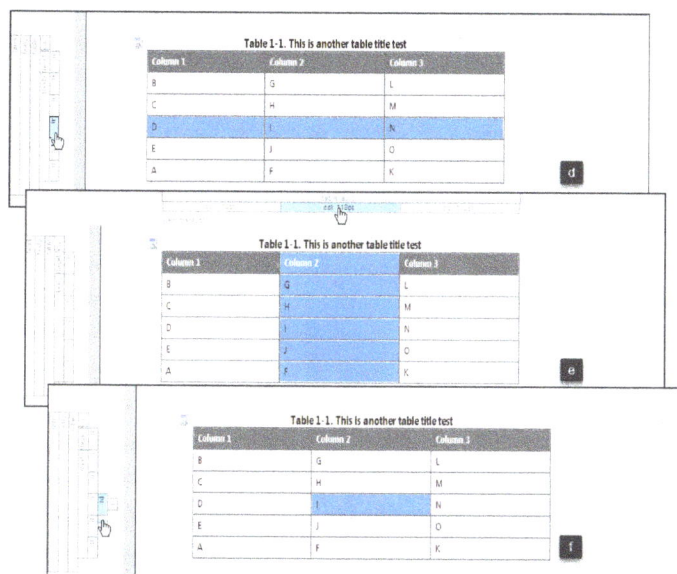

Figure 4-23. Applying Standard Table Styles a) <tr> b) <col>, and c) <td>.

QUICK STEPS: APPLYING STANDARD TABLE STYLES TO TABLE CONTENT

STEP	ACTION
1	Open the XML Editor to the topic and table where you want to apply standard CSS table styles.
2	Click **Show Tags** button on the Editor ribbon, and select **Block Structure Bars** if not visible on topic left.
3	Click **Show Tags** button on the Editor ribbon, and select **Span Structure Bars** if not visible on topic top.
4	Click on the **Table** tag (entire table) for the table for which you want to apply a style to the entire table.
5	Click on the **Header** tag (table header) of the table where you want to apply a style to the header only.
6	Click on the table **Body** tag (entire table body) where you want to apply a style to the entire table body.
7	Click on a table **tr** tag (entire row) for a selected row, where you want to apply a style to the entire row.
8	Under the **Span Structure Bars** click on a **col** (entire table column), for which you want to apply a style to the entire table column.
9	Click inside a table cell and then click the table **td** tag (table cell data) for the selected cell, for which you want to apply a style. When using the <td> tag to apply style to a specific cell, you may want to use **F8** (repeat last command) as required to apply the style to several cells.
10	Click the **Save** button to save your work when done.

> **TIP:** Table parent styles <**table**>, <**tbody**>, <**thead**>, <**tcaption**>, <**tr**>, <**col**>, and <**tfoot**> are inherited in your stylesheet. It is recommended that you create child classes for each parent style instead of using the parent for styling. Creating child classes always give you more flexibility in styling your content.

SPLITTING AND MERGING TABLE CELLS

BASIC CONCEPT

Merging table cells in Flare is just what you might expect — the result of combining two or more cells of adjacent columns is a single cell totaling the width of the merged cells; the result of joining two or more cells of adjacent rows is a single cell of the height of the merged cells. On the other hand, splitting table cells is likely more capable in Flare than with similar features to which you may be familiar. A very flexible tool for merging and splitting cells lets you create complex tables that would otherwise be difficult to produce.

ESSENTIAL ELEMENTS

You can merge any two or more adjacent cells using the **Table** ribbon option, or the right-click option to **Merge Cells**. Splitting cells is also possible using either the Table ribbon or the right-click option to **Split Cells**. You would split cells using the **Split Cells** dialog. The operation can be as simple as dividing a single cell into multiple rows or columns or splitting multiple cells that extend over two or more rows or columns. This operation gives you the option to merge before dividing the cells.

Using the **Split Cells** dialog results in a new table within the existing table — a table where you specify the number of columns or rows and header and footer rows. The result can be very simple or quite complex. When you choose to split multiple cells that may include multiple rows or columns, Flare gives you the option of merging the cells before performing the split.

APPLICATION TIPS

The **Split Cells** dialog is a powerful tool that can go beyond simple cell splitting and merging to design very complex tables. This tool is worth learning about to see how you might further employ it in working with complicated tables.

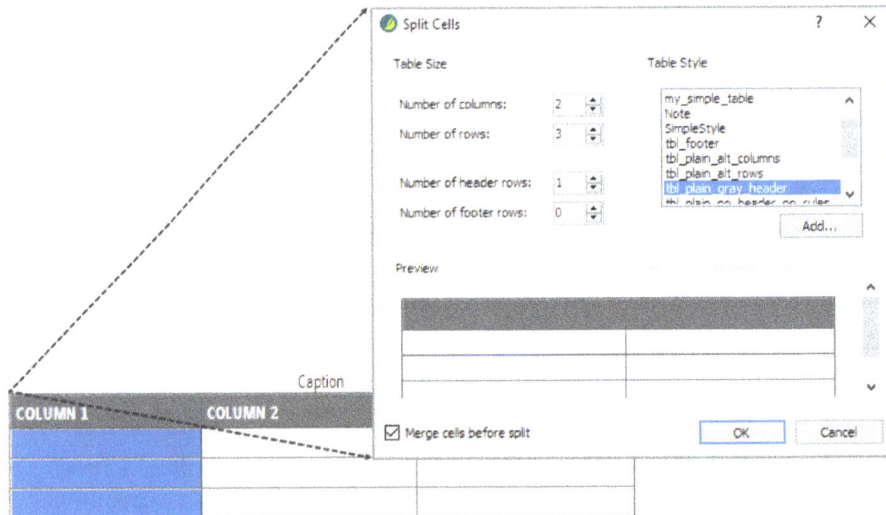

Figure 4-24. Split Table Cells Dialog.

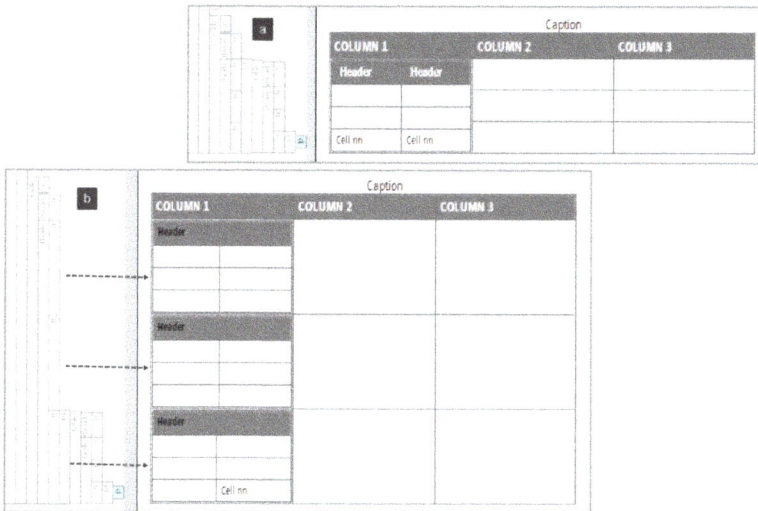

Figure 4-25. Splitting Table Cells a) Merge Cells Check-Box Selected b) Merge Cells not Selected Before Split.

QUICK STEPS: SPLITTING AND MERGING TABLE CELLS

STEP	ACTION
	Use the following steps to merge two or more row cells or column cells:
1	Open the topic or snippet that contains the table where you want to merge table cells.
2	Select two or more adjacent row cells or two or more adjacent column cells, then right-click and select **Merge Cells**. After merging 2-row cells, the merged result is a cell height of the combined rows; after merging 2-column cells, the merged result is a cell the width of the combined columns.
	Use the following steps to split a table cell (s):
1	Open the content file that contains the table where you want to split table cells. You can split a single cell.
2	Enter the **Number of columns**, into which the cell should be split. If you specify two or more columns, click the check box to **Merge cells before split**, if applicable. See **Note**.
3	Enter the **Number of rows**, to specify the rows into which the cell should be split. If you specify two or more rows, click the check box to **Merge cells before split**, if desired. See **Note**.
4	If applicable, enter the **Number of header rows**, that the resulting table should have.
5	If applicable, enter the **Number of footer rows**, that the resulting table should have.
6	From the **Table Style** pane, select a table stylesheet to apply to the table you specified.
7	Click the **Add** button to open the dialog if you want to add a new table stylesheet.

NOTE: In part **a)** of the Figure above, note that when the 3-cells selected to be split, are not merged prior to the split, the result is that the specified table is created in each of the existing cells. When the cells are merged prior to the split, as in part **b)**, the table is created only once, in the single resulting merged cell.

CHAPTER 5

FLARE VARIABLES AND SNIPPETS

INTRODUCING FLARE VARIABLES FILE

A *variable* is a symbolic name associated with one or more stored pieces of content referred to as a value, and each value is called a *definition*. You would typically use variables where a piece of content commonly appears throughout a single document or across several documents and changes from time to time — like "ProductName." When you insert a variable, as a placeholder, instead of the actual content, you can later change the value in one place instead of in multiple places. You can generally find variable files in the **Project Organizer** > **Project** > **Variables**.

Flare supports *Heading Variables*, *System Variables*, and *User Variables*. Heading Variables and System Variables are inherited and generally available in Flare, while User Variables are those that users create. User variables, created using the Variables Editor, and all other variables are inserted into your content files using the **Insert** > **Variable** option from the **Insert** menu or the right-click.

HEADING VARIABLES

Heading Variables are built-in with Flare and already available for inserting into your content. Using this variable set, you can display the headings of your content in the header or footer frames of Page Layout files. Heading variables are most useful in print-based output, but with limitations, you may also use them in online outputs. Using Heading variables (Level1-Level6), as listed in the dialog below, you can display the first occurrence of the corresponding heading level (h1-h6) in your document.

Glossary and Index headings can also be inserted and displayed in your output if you have a Glossary Proxy topic and Index Proxy topic in your content. Using the appropriate variables, inserted in page layout header frames, you can display the *FirstGlossaryPageTerm* and *LastGlossaryPageTerm* and the *FirstIndexTerm* and the *LastIndexTerm* on the alternating even and odd page headers of the glossary and index respectively. Flare does support Glossary and Index heading variables in online outputs.

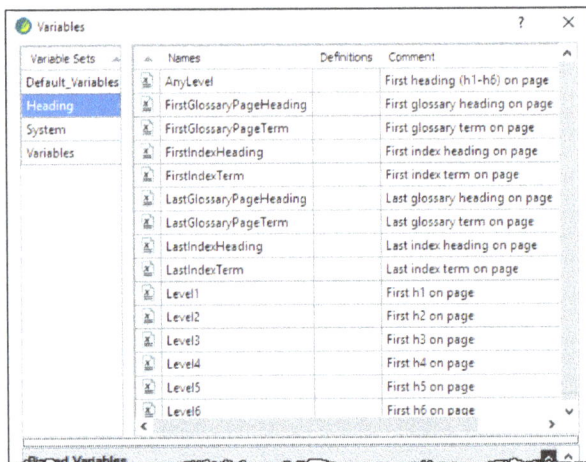

Figure 5-1. Headings Variables.

> **NOTE:** Heading variables, except glossary and index, can be used online in topics and snippets.

SYSTEM VARIABLES

Flare System variables are a built-in variable set you can use to display elements in your content that use auto-numbering — elements like Chapter, Section, and Volume Numbers. Users can insert these variables in page layout header or footer frames for Adobe PDF, Microsoft XPS, and XHTML outputs. *Date* and *Time* System Variables support windows long and short formats for displaying dates and times. *PageCount* and *PageNumber* variables, typically inserted in print-based outputs, display the total page count or the page number in page layout headers or footers.

Finally, using linked Title, Header, and File variables, you can link tables of contents (TOCs) and Browse Sequences to content in a linked topic file. This linking ensures that TOC and Browse Sequence entries are always synchronized with the associated topics.

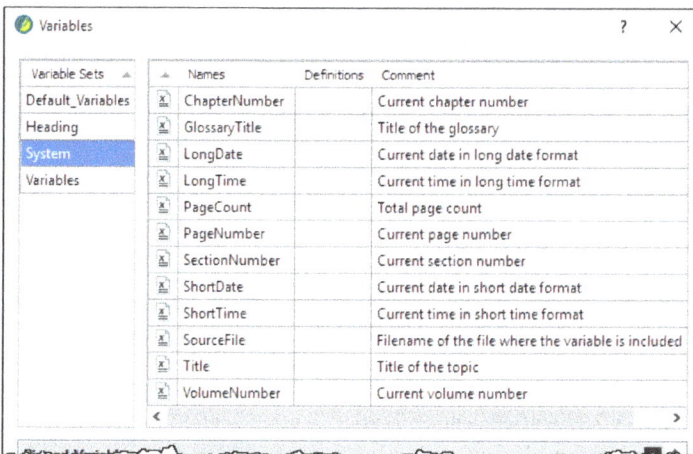

Figure 5-2. System Variables.

USER VARIABLES

As the term implies, user variables are variables that you can create and use throughout your content. As mentioned earlier, a value associated with a variable, in Flare, is called a definition. You may create two types of variables — **Single-Definition** and **Multi-Definition** variables. Depending on the variable use, you may need to define a single-definition or multiple-definitions for the variable.

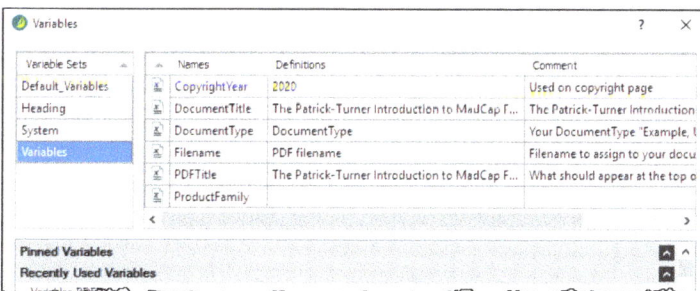

Figure 5-3. User Variables.

USER VARIABLES — SINGLE-DEFINITION

A *single-definition variable* is a variable that can only have a single defined value. A single-definition variable named ReleaseDate, for example, would represent a single date value as the release date.

Table 5-1. Single-Definition Variables

Variable	Definition	Comment
Author	Brilliant Training	Name of document author inserted in the PDF meta-data
Copyright_Year	2022	Current Copyright Year
Output_FileName	MCME	File name to be given to the generated target output file
Output_Folder	MCME	Folder designated for Flare generated target outputs
PDFTitle	Introduction to MadCap Flare	Title assigned to the output file and placed at the top of the TOC bookmarks
Release_Date	January 31, 2022	Scheduled Release Date

USER VARIABLES — MULTI-DEFINITION

A *multi-definition variable* is a variable that can have several defined values. When specifying the multi-definition variable at the target, you can only specify a single value. A multi-definition variable named DocumentTitle, for example, would define several document titles, but you would only select one title in the current instance of the target.

Table 5-2. Multi-Definition Variable

Variable	Definition	Comment
DocumentTitle	User Guide A	User Guide for clients in Group-A
	User Guide B	User Guide for clients in Group-B
	User Guide C	User Guide for clients in Group-C
DocumentType	User Guide	My Software User Guide
	Release Notes	My Software Release Notes
	Upgrade Procedure	My Software Upgrade Procedure
ProductFamily	X-1000	X-1000 Series
	X-2000	X-2000 Series
	X-3000	X-3000 Series

INTRODUCING THE FLARE VARIABLES EDITOR

In Flare, variables are created and contained in what is called a variable set. A variable set is a logical grouping of variables based on the purpose of the variables in the set. For example, you may create a variable set called Company that contains basic information like Name, Address, City State, Zip, Email, Phone, and Website. Another variable set, Document_Variables, might include variable data such as DocumentType, DocumentTitle, ProductFamily, and PDF_Title.

Using the Variables Editor, you can easily create variables that writers can employ across a single document or in all documents throughout the project. If you open the editor for the first time, you will see a variable file named **Default_Variables**, which you can open and view. The Default_Variables file is also called a variable set. You may create as many variable sets as needed to manage groupings of variables in your project, where each set may contain as many variables as required.

Name	Definition	Comment
CopyrightYear	2019	Used on copyright page
DocNumber	T0000nnn	Document Identifier Number
DocType_Abbrev	Document Type Shortname	Example: UG=User Guide; RN = Release Notes; TRG = Tech
DocType_Abbrev	APN	Application Note
DocType_Abbrev	ISM	Installation, Support & Maintenance Guide
DocType_Abbrev	WP	White Paper
DocType_Abbrev	SRG	System Reference Guide
DocType_Abbrev	SIG	Software Integration Guide
DocType_Abbrev	NUP	Network Upgrade Procedure
DocType_Abbrev	TB	Technical Bulletin
DocType_Abbrev	TN	Technical Note
DocType_Abbrev	RN	Release Notes
DocType_Abbrev	RG	Reference Guide
DocType_Abbrev	UG	User Guide
Abbrev	QSG	Guide
DocTyp...		Technica.
DocType_Abbrev	DLG	Design Limits Guide
DocType_Abbrev	UP	Upgrade Procedure (used for software only upgrade)
DocumentTitle	Your Document Title	Leave blank, or use iDiect Velocity/iDirect Evolution for TRG
DocumentTitle	Configuring Velocity Networks Using Pulse	
DocumentTitle	iBuilder	
DocumentTitle	iMonitor	
DocumentTitle	iDirect Velocity	Used for Release Notes or for Technical Reference Guide
DocumentTitle	iDirect Pulse Network Management System	Use for User Guide and Releasee Notes Document Title
DocumentTitle	Terminal Web User Interface	
DocumentTitle	Velocity Softare Integration Guide	

Figure 5-4. Flare Variables Editor.

Editor Toolbar Buttons and Icons

The command ribbon for the VariableSet Editor contains operations, as shown in the following table. Commands are available for adding new variable sets, new user variables, and Date-Time variables. Standard clipboard tools Copy, Cut, Paste, and Delete are available to assist with creating and defining variable set entries and definitions.

Table 5-3. Flare Variables Editor Toolbar Commands

Icon	Command	Brief Description
	Add Variable	Add a new variable to the variable set table.
	Add Date-Time Variable	Add a new Date-Time variable to the variable set table.
	Edit Variable Style	Open the Stylesheet Editor to edit the style of the selected variable.
	Add Variable Definition	Add a new definition to the variable currently in focus.
	Cut	Cut the selected element from the variable from the variables table.
	Copy	Copy the selected variable element to the clipboard.
	Paste	Paste the contents of the clipboard to the variable table.
	Delete	Delete the selected variable element from the variable file.
	Insert Variable	Insert a new variable to the variable set.
	Show/Hide	Toggle between show and hide the Evaluated Definition or the Flare syntax for the listed variables. The Evaluated Variable is the current value or actual text.

Introducing Flare Snippet File

In Flare a *snippet* can be a phrase, a sentence, one or two paragraphs, or even an entire topic. A snippet is a content chunk of any size, and you can insert it any number of times and places within the same or different topics. The use of snippets avoids the need to rewrite content repeated in several places in a project. Snippets can contain text, images, lists, a combination of these elements, or even other snippets. When you modify a snippet in one place, it changes wherever used. Snippets are located in the **Content Explorer > Content > Resources > Snippets**.

Flare has two types of snippets — block snippets and text snippets, where the type depends on how you insert the text. Flare also supports snippet variables and conditions that enhance the use of snippets. Snippet variables and snippet conditions add another layer of flexibility to the usage of snippets.

BLOCK SNIPPET

A *block snippet* is best suited for a content block, like a bullet or numbered lists, multiple paragraphs, or other blocks of content. When inserted on a blank line in a topic, you cannot add any other content to the block snippet. The block snippet, shown below, is a copyright block of several paragraphs, including the copyright year, owner, publisher, Website, Print Edition, and ISBN.

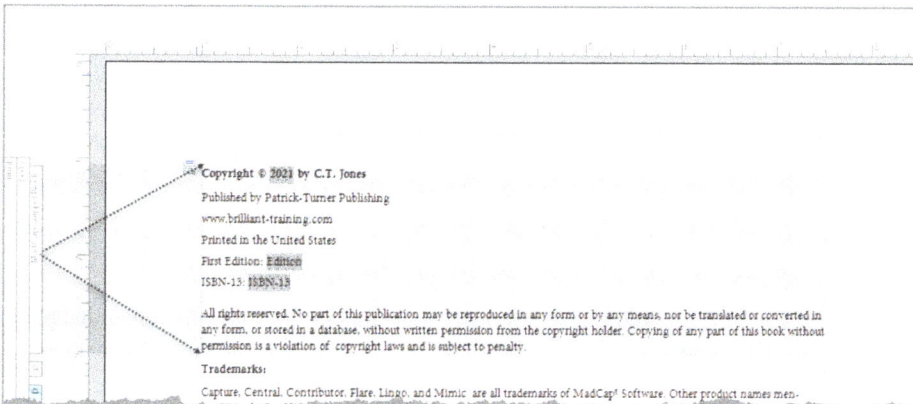

Figure 5-5. Image of a Block Snippet Highlighted when Selected.

TEXT SNIPPET

A *text snippet* can be inserted on a line with other content; however, you must place it before or after the existing content. A critical difference between the block and text snippets is that you can put a text snippet on a line with other content. If you need to place a text snippet on a new blank line containing additional text, that additional text must (can) be inserted first, and then the text snippet put either before or after that text. If you have turned markers on, a text snippet will display surrounded by brackets. A text snippet highlighted and enclosed in brackets is shown below.

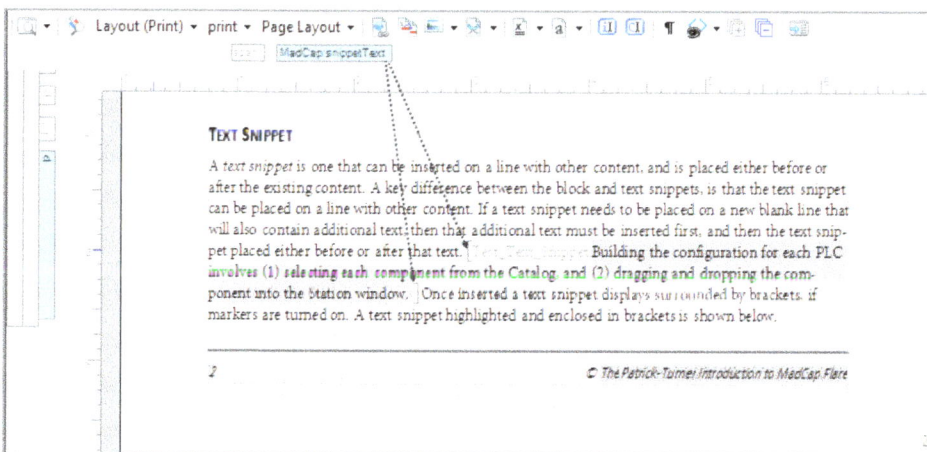

Figure 5-6. Image of a Text Snippet Shown in Brackets.

SNIPPET VARIABLE

A *snippet variable*, like standard variables, is created in the Variables Editor but used is in a snippet. You can modify the snippet variable definition directly at the snippet or the topic (in the Topic Properties). Variable definitions at the snippet override any definitions made in the Variables Editor at the topic or the target. A topic-level variable definition overrides the definitions set in the Variables Editor or defined on the Variables tab of the target file.

Using these override options, you can customize a snippet depending on its use. A snippet, for example, that appears multiple times in a topic, and the content is slightly different in each case, might be easily handled with a variable having multiple definitions. You could insert a different snippet definition at each snippet. A snippet that is used multiple times in a topic, each place having the same difference, might be handled by a topic-level variable definition. Regardless of the number of uses in a topic, the snippet content will be identical.

SNIPPET CONDITION

A *snippet condition* is a standard condition tag created in the Condition Tag Editor but intended to be applied to a specific part of a snippet to determine whether that part of the snippet should be included or excluded in the output. The use of a snippet condition lets you customize a snippet for use in multiple places, where the content is the same in most instances, but in a few cases, you want part of the content excluded. Like a snippet variable, you can apply or define the snippet condition at the snippet or the topic (in the Topic Properties).

When you apply the condition at the snippet, you can apply a different condition tag at each place the snippet is inserted in a topic or throughout the project. In this fashion, a single snippet used multiple times in a topic can be slightly customized for each use by applying the appropriate condition. Applying a condition to the topic means the same condition is applied to the snippet each time the snippet is used. A condition tag applied at the snippet takes priority over condition tags applied at the topic; a condition tag definition at the topic has priority over a condition tag defined at the target.

Summary on Working with Flare Variables and Snippets

Variables and snippets are not required; however, they provide efficiencies and flexibilities in print and online targets. These essential Flare elements are instrumental, for example, when working with small pieces of content that appear in multiple places in the same or different documents.

A snippet, just as it sounds, is a small segment of content. The snippet file can be as little as a phrase, a sentence, a single paragraph, or more. Content suitable for a snippet is generally the same in several places but may be slightly different in others. On the other hand, a variable is more like a value or short string of text — like a company name, street address, or date. You can define variables with a single definition (value), like today's date, or with multiple definitions as with an array. For example, the multi-definition variable might contain the titles of a collection of product user documents.

The following checklist outlines a few items to consider when working with variables and snippets, and some examples of related tasks follow in the remainder of this chapter.

Checklist: Working with Flare Variables and Snippets

- *If you imported content, and the import contained a variables file, it will be stored as a Variable file in the Project Organizer, along with the Flare Default_Variables set.*

- *When using the Flare Variables Editor, you can create as many variable files as needed, and each file can contain as many variables as required. Each file is called a variable set.*

- *You can create and use as many snippet files (snippets) as needed throughout your project.*

- *Consider a variables file for **General** information like company name, address, phone, web address, and other information. These are typically single-definition variables.*

- *Consider a variables file for **Document** information like **Document Type, Document Title, Document Revision, Filename, ReleaseDate,** and **PDFTitle**.*

- *A variables file can contain single definition variables or multi-definition variables. An example single definition variable might be **SoftwareVersion**; an example of a multi-definition variable might be **DocumentType**, which supports the definition of several document types; or **DocumentTitle**, which supports the definition of several titles.*

- *When defining multi-definition variables in a project, you can select only one definition for each variable when specifying the target parameters. A definition defined at the target generally overrides any initial definitions of the variable. Snippet variables have the highest precedence.*

- *Multi-definition variables also make it possible to create multiple targets, such as a target for each User Manual or Document Type. Each target can be preset and saved with the appropriate variables and other parameters. With this approach, you can build each target without always having to change all of the variables.*

- *In a multi-project/multi-writer environment, consider managing the Variable and Snippet files as part of the shared resources like Page Layouts, CSS, Table Stylesheets, Images, Template Pages, and Micro-Content. These elements can then be maintained, shared, and synchronized from a global project to ensure document consistencies and file integrity.*

NAVIGATING THE FLARE VARIABLES EDITOR

BASIC CONCEPT

The **Variable Editor** is the primary means of creating and editing variables in your project. The editor is mainly used to create and manage user-defined variables. Still, you can also add **System Date/Time** variable entries, of which you can format the output display and choose from several options for how the date/time is updated, for example, **Manual**, **On Build**, or **File Save**. The local toolbar ribbon across the editor top provides **Add**, **Delete**, **Copy**, and **Paste** variables tools.

ESSENTIAL ELEMENTS

The **Variables Editor** is a grid-like presentation that supports user-defined variables with single definitions or multiple definitions. Flare lists single-definition variables on a single row, and the variable's **Name**, **Definition**, and **Comment** in the adjacent columns to the right. You can directly edit each of these fields. Flare lists multi-definition variables in the same way but using multiple rows. Each definition following the first definition is listed on the rows directly beneath the initial variable entry and with the variable name repeated in the **Name** column.

APPLICATION TIPS

If you have multiple products or other book documents that already share a similar design or that you want to have a similar design, then consider a single Document Variable set, even if you intend to create other variable sets.

A single document variable set will ensure that you will not encounter a potential problem with different variable sets if you attempt to use variables in the document headers and footers of the shared page layout files.

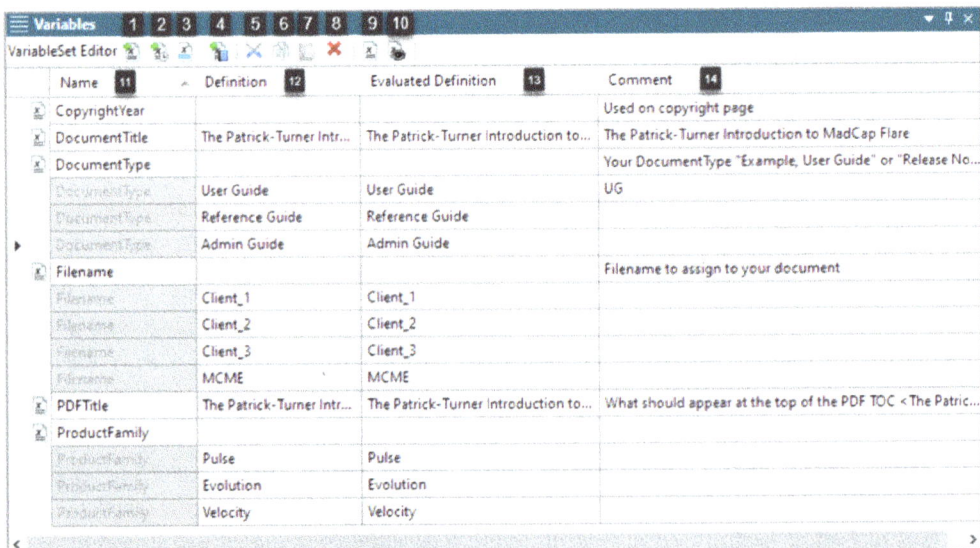

Figure 5-7. Navigating the Flare Variables Editor.

QUICK STEPS: NAVIGATING THE FLARE VARIABLES EDITOR

STEP	ACTION
1	From the **Project Organizer** > **Variables** subfolder.
2	Double-click on a file to open it in the Variables Editor.
3	Click the **Add Variable** button to add a new variable to the variables set.
4	Click the **Add Date Time Variable** button to add a new variable for date and time.
5	Click the **Edit Variable Style** button to open the CSS Editor and automatically create a style class specifically for the selected variable. The class is created under the **MadCap|variable** parent style.
6	Click the **Add Variable Definition** button to enter a new definition for the currently selected variable. The editor enters a new line under the variable name, to create an additional definition for the variable. To modify an existing definition, single or multidefinition, slowly click the **Definition** field until it turns blue.
7	Use the **Cut** button to cut the currently selected variable entry and place it on the clipboard.
8	Use the **Copy** button to copy the currently selected variable entry and place it on the clipboard.
9	Use the **Paste** button to copy the contents of the clipboard and paste it at the point of insertion.
10	Use the **Delete** button to delete the currently selected variable entry from the variable set.
11	For a variable entry, click in the **Definition** field and use the **Insert Variable** button 🖹 ▾ to select a variable as the definition. The variable syntax displays in the field, but the definition will appear in the output.
12	Click the **Show/Hide Variable Definition** button to toggle between showing and hiding the **Evaluated Definitions** column, to show the current value instead of the variable syntax for variables.
13	After clicking the **Add Variable** button, slowly click on the temporary **Name** (**NewVariable**) to enter a new name for the single-definition or multi-definition variable.
14	Double-click in a **Definition** field to enter an alphanumeric value for a single- or multi-definition variable.
15	The **Evaluated Definition** displays the current value of fixed definitions and variable definitions.
16	Click slowly or double-click in the **Comment** field to enter a comment for the the single- or multi-definition variable and definition (s), if applicable.

> **NOTE:** The stylesheet **Advanced View** is used to specify the specific properties you want to affect the unique appearance of the selected variable in the output. Once the style is created, it is automatically assigned to the variable in the output and does not need to be applied.

ADDING A NEW VARIABLE SET

BASIC CONCEPT

In Flare, you would generally create a variable set and the variables it contains for a specific purpose. You can create as many variable sets as needed to manage your requirements. Although you will likely find that a couple of variable sets will serve most needs, if not all, you may create as many as you deem necessary.

ESSENTIAL ELEMENTS

When you create a new variable set, you can use a factory template or a custom user-defined template to base the new variable set. You can also make the new variable set based on an existing variable set similar to what you want to create. You can then modify the variable set by adding new variables and definitions and changing existing ones.

APPLICATION TIPS

Although there are no limits to the number of variable sets you can create, there are advantages to limiting the number. The more variable sets you make, the more difficult it may become to manage their use throughout your documents. Using one variable set for your document variables can simplify matters. For example, when you wish to apply the same set of page layout files across multiple documents, you intend to use the heading variables from all of the documents in the headers and footers of the page layouts.

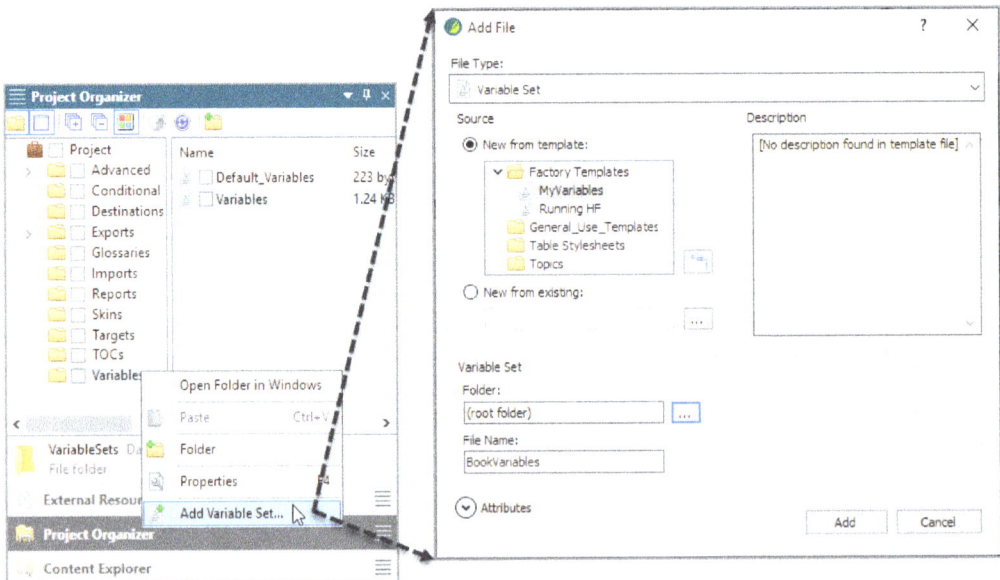

Figure 5-8. Add Variable Option Selected — Add File Dialog with Variable Set Option Selected.

QUICK STEPS: ADDING A NEW VARIABLE SET

STEP	ACTION
1	Select the **Variables** folder, in the **Project Organizer**, or select the subfolder in which you wish to add a new variable set. You may also create a subfolder in the root folder **Variables**.
2	Right cick > **Add Variable Set**. The **Add File** dialog opens.
3	Ensure that the **File Type** is set for **Variable Set**.
4	**To create the new variable set use one of the following:**
	a) From Templates: Set the **Source** for **New From Template**, then choose a template from the **Factory Templates** folder or choose a template from a user-defined **Custom Templates** folder.
	b) From Existing: Set the **Source** for **New From Existing**, and use the browse button ⌐···⌐ to locate an existing variable set from which you want to create the new variable set.
5	Under **Variable Set**, in the **Folder** field use the default **Root folder** (**Project/Variables**), or browse and choose a subfolder in the default folder in which to store the file.
6	Use the **File Name** field to specify a name for the new variable set file.
7	Click > **Add** to save the new variable set.

CREATING SINGLE-DEFINITION AND MULTI-DEFINITION VARIABLES

BASIC CONCEPT

Using the **Flare Variables Editor**, you can create variable sets, the equivalent of variable files, containing defined variables you can use throughout your content. Each variable in a variable set has a set definition or value. In practice, you can create two types of variables in Flare — single-definition and multi-definition variables. Depending on how you use a variable in the content, you may need to define variables with single definitions or multiple definitions.

ESSENTIAL ELEMENTS

The main tasks of defining variables in Flare are 1) creating **Variable Sets,** which are separate files you create to hold variables for a specific purpose; and 2) individual variables that you define with either a single-definition (value) or multiple definitions (values). If you need to manage variables for fundamentally different purposes in your project, then you should create a separate variable set for each purpose. If you want to have the variables in your output appear with a particular style, you can create a style class under the parent style **MadCap|variable** and edit the class properties.

APPLICATION TIPS

Variable definitions defined in the Variables Editor become the default definitions for variables wherever you use them in the project. These definitions, however, can be overridden by definitions made at the target level before the build. Target-level definitions become the values present in the output unless you specify other definitions for the variable, for example, at the snippet level or the topic level in individual topics. As multi-definition variables have more than one value, you would generally set a value at the target for the current instance of the target output.

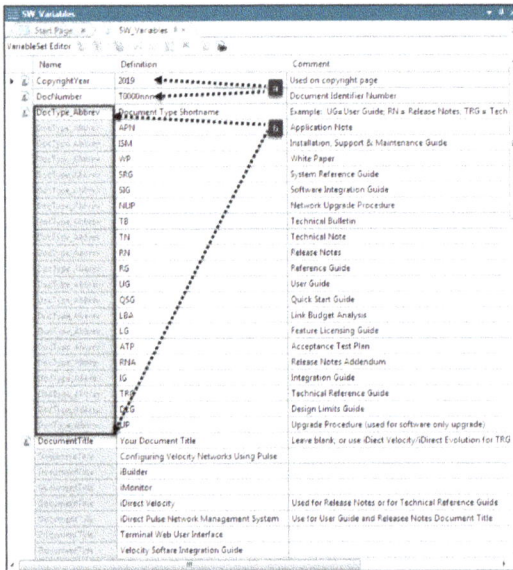

Figure 5-9. a) Single-Definition Variable b) Multi-Definition Variable.

QUICK STEPS: CREATING SINGLE-DEFINITION AND MULTI-DEFINITION VARIABLES

STEP	ACTION
—	**To Add, and Delete Single-Definition Variables:**
1	Click on any line to add a new variable to the variable set.
2	From the ribbon, click the **Add Variable** button; or right-click and select **Add Variable**. See **Note**.
3	In the **Name** field, click slowly on the default Name "**NewVariable**", to enter a name for the variable.
4	Click slowly or double-click in the adjacent **Definition** field of a variable to enter a value for the variable.
5	Optional: To remove a variable from the list of variables, click on the variable, and from the ribbon, click the **Delete** button; or right-click and select **Delete**.
—	**To Add, Insert, and Delete Definitions in Multi-Definition Variables:**
1	Click on the variable where you wish to add a new definition for the variable.
2	From the ribbon, click the **Add Definition** button; or right-click and select **Add Definition**. The definition is created, on the line following the initial variable entry, leaving the first Definition field blank. See **Note**.
3	Optional: To insert a new definition between two existing definitions, click on the definition, below which you want to insert a new definition., and then from the ribbon click the **Add Definition** button; or right-click and select **Add Definition**.
4	Optional: To insert a new definition above the first definition, click on the initial variable entry line, and from the ribbon click the **Add Definition** button; or right-click and select **Add Definition**.
5	Optional: To remove a definition from a list of multiple definitions, click on the definition, and from the ribbon click the **Delete** button; or right-click and select **Delete**.

> **NOTE: 1)** A new variable entry will eventually be sorted alphabetically, if immediately followed by a new variable entry, or if the file is closed and re-opened. Given this functionality, the initial position of a new variable entry does not matter.
>
> **NOTE: 2)** In a multi-definition variable, the first definition created is the default definition. You may leave this field empty if desired.

ADDING A NEW SNIPPET FILE

BASIC CONCEPT

As you work with your content, you may discover that certain small content segments repeatedly appear in your topics and perhaps throughout your project. This content may appear in the forms of a short document-related or company-related paragraph, a bullet list, company address, a tagged group, or other such items. These types of content may represent opportunities for snippets. As these items appear in different places and sometimes need changing, there is the risk they will become inconsistent in some places. You can achieve consistency and proper maintenance by creating snippets.

ESSENTIAL ELEMENTS

As you use snippets in multiple places, the content for each is generally unique and not candidates for templates. The factory template for creating a snippet does not contain any content. Creating a snippet from content that already exists is the best possible solution. If you use the factory template to create the file, you will need to open the file from the default folder and either write or paste the content.

APPLICATION TIPS

Consider having the snippet text you want to use before creating the new snippet. You can either type the text or paste the text to the new file when the file opens. Also, consider variables you want to insert in the text and whether they are already created in the Variables Editor.

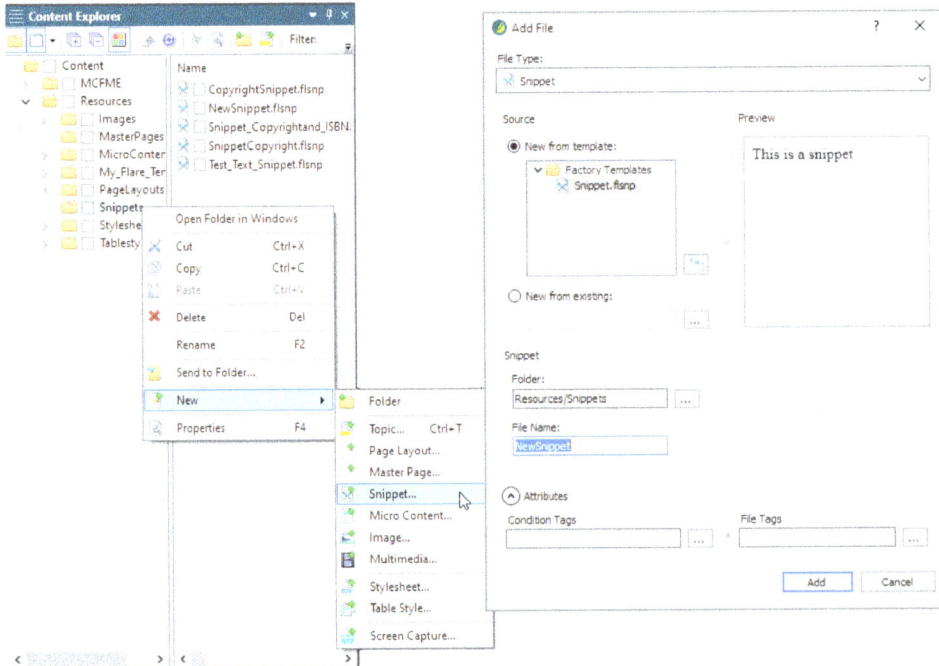

Figure 5-10. New Snippet Option Selected — Add File Dialog with Snippet Option Set.

QUICK STEPS: ADDING A NEW SNIPPET FILE

STEP	ACTION
1	Either write the snippet text or copy the text that you want to use in your new snippet file.
2	Select the **Snippets** folder, in the **Resources** subfolder of the **Content Explorer**, or find and select the folder in which you wish to add the new snippet file.
3	Right click and select **New** > **Snippet**. The **Add File** dialog opens.
4	Ensure that the **File Type** is set for **Snippet**.
5	**To create the new snippet file use one of the following:** **a) From Templates**: Set the **Source** for **New From Template**, then choose a template from the **Factory Templates** folder or choose a template from a user-defined **Custom Templates** folder. **b) From Existing**: Set the **Source** for **New From Existing**, and use the browse button ⋯ to locate the existing variable set.
6	Under **Snippet**, in the **Folder** field use the default folder **Resources/Snippets**, or browse and choose another folder in which to store the snippet file.
7	Use the **File Name** field to specify a name for the new snippet file.
8	Click **Add** to create the new snippet file. The file is opened in the **XML Editor**.
9	If applicable, enter or paste the text you wish to insert in the new snippet file.
10	Click the **Save** button to save your work.

CREATING A SNIPPET FILE FROM EXISTING CONTENT

BASIC CONCEPT

In some cases, you will discover existing content that would serve as a snippet, as it is repeated in several topics and documents throughout your project. You can directly convert this content into snippets. The standard steps of creating a snippet file and then entering or pasting the text content into a snippet are not required in these cases.

ESSENTIAL ELEMENTS

You can easily convert existing content directly to snippets using **Create** > **Snippet** from the **Home** ribbon. In the **Create Snippet** dialog, you only need to specify a name for the **Snippet File**, a **Project Folder** to store the file or use the default folder, and finally, tell Flare if you want to **Replace Source Content with the New Snippet**.

APPLICATION TIPS

You can find potential snippets throughout your project content if you look for them. The Flare method of creating the snippet from existing content is particularly suited for these cases.

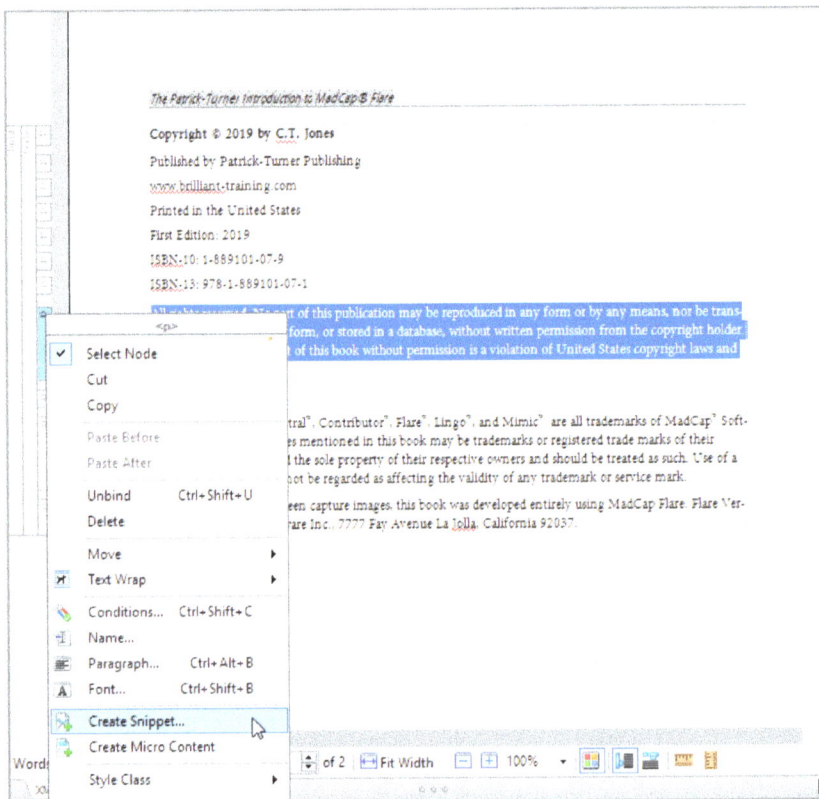

Figure 5-11. Selecting Topic Content to Create as New Snippet.

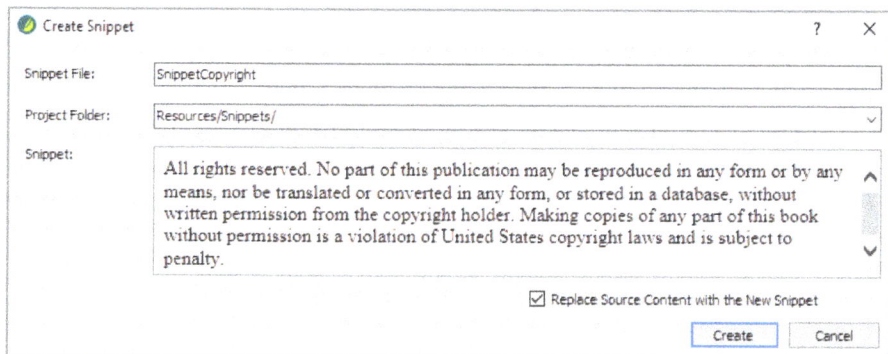

Figure 5-12. Preview of Snippet Content.

QUICK STEPS: CREATING A SNIPPET FILE FROM EXISTING CONTENT

STEP	ACTION
1	Open the topic that contains content you want to use to create a new snippet.
2	Select the content that you want to create as a new snippet.
3	From the **Home** ribbon, select **Create Snippet**. The **Create Snippet** dialog opens.
4	Use the **Snippet File** field to enter a name for the new snippet file.
5	Use the default **Project Folder** of **Content/Resources/Snippets**, or specify a different folder.
6	Click the check box **Replace Source Content with the New Snippet**. to replace the selected content with the new snippet.
7	Click **Create** to save the new snippet file.
8	To edit the snippet after it is inserted, locate the file in the place it was stored — for example, **Content Explorer** > **Content > Resources > Snippets**, and double-click on the Snippet file to open it in the Topic Editor. You can then modify the Snippet content.

SPECIFYING SNIPPET VARIABLE DEFINITIONS AT SNIPPET-LEVEL

BASIC CONCEPT

A snippet's content is generally the same wherever used; however, the content is slightly different in some instances — often by a single word or short phrase. For example, this slight difference might be with the product name or a product family and may occur in the same or another topic. You can manage this slight variation by specifying a snippet variable definition at the snippet level. A snippet-level definition happens at the snippet and therefore overrides a definition of the same variable used again in the same topic, at the project level (Variables Editor), at the target level, or different topics.

ESSENTIAL ELEMENTS

You can enter a snippet variable definition using a right-click on the snippet and selecting the **Snippet Variables** option. You would first choose the appropriate **Variable Set** from the **Snippet Variable** dialog. Then, you may select a predefined single-definition of the variable, choose from a list of definitions in a multi-definition variable, or enter a new definition directly.

Given the priority of defining the variable definition at the snippet, the definition applies to the specific snippet occurrence in the content. The same snippet could have a unique definition each time you use the snippet in the same topic or another topic.

APPLICATION TIPS

When creating a variable set for use with snippets, consider using a name like "SnippetVariables." You might even make a different variable set for each snippet that uses variables. When the **Snippet Variable** window opens, you can quickly identify the correct variable set, as shown in the second image.

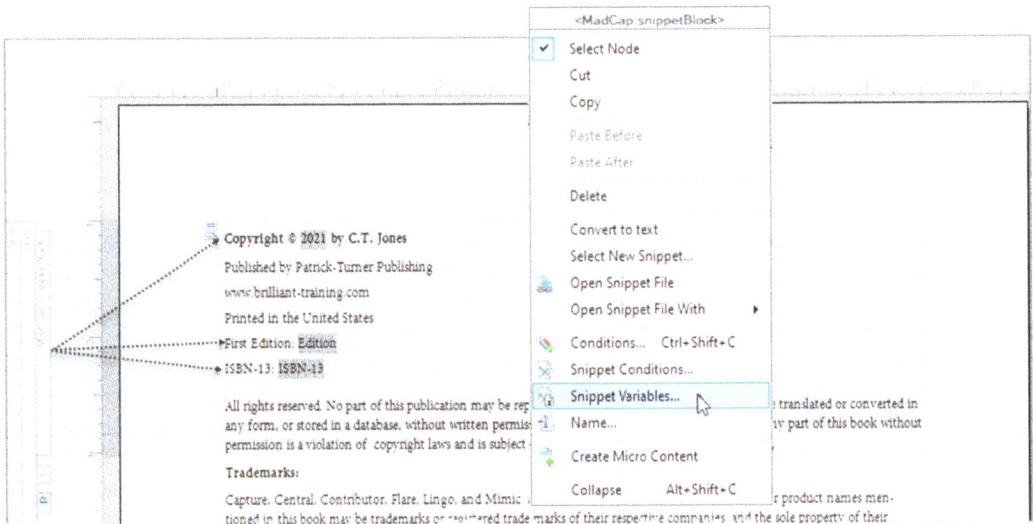

Figure 5-13. Snippet Variable Definitions at Snippet Level — Before Definition Override.

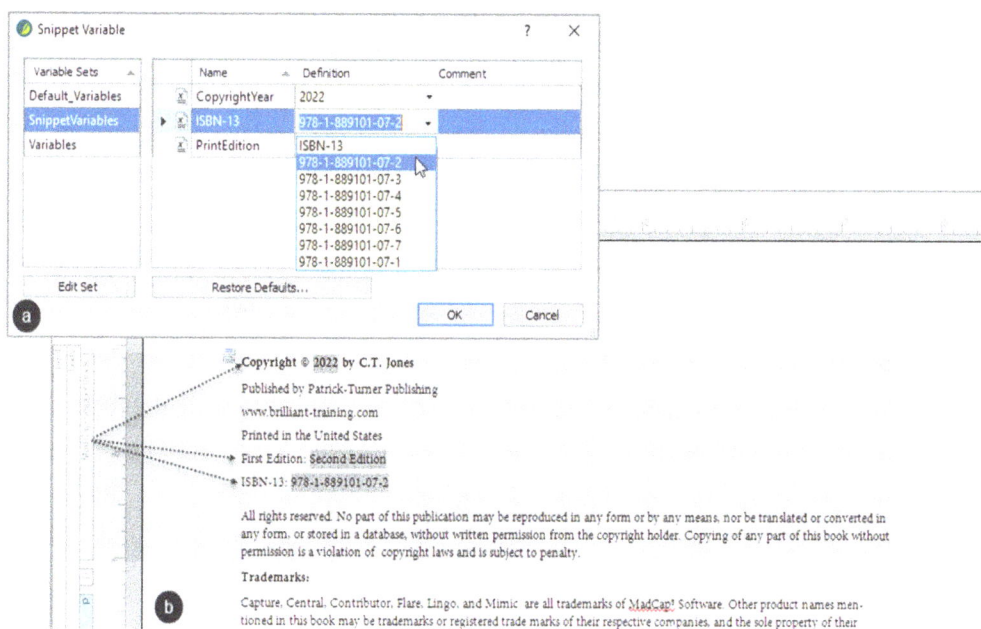

Figure 5-14. Snippet Variable Definitions Dialog — and Snippet After Definition Override.

QUICK STEPS: SPECIFYING SNIPPET VARIABLE DEFINITIONS AT SNIPPET-LEVEL

STEP	ACTION
1	Open the topic in which you want to modify the snippet variable definitions at the snippet-level.
2	Use the **Show Block Structure Bars** icon to **Show/Hide** the tag bars along the left edge of the topic.
3	Use the **Show Span Structure Bars** icon to **Show/Hide** the span bars along the top edge of the topic.
4	Click on the snippet, if visible, or click the **MadCap:snippetBlock** tag bar (for block snippets) or on the **MadCap:snippetText** span bar (for text snippet) to select the snippet.
5	Right-click and select **Snippet Variables**. The **Snippet Variable** window opens.
6	Choose from the list of **Variables Sets**, the set that contains the variable definitions you wish to use.
7	Do one of the following to specify a variable definition for the snippet: **a) Single-Definition Variable:** Click on the variable to select the default value or enter a value directly in the **Definition** to override the value. **b) Multi-Definition Variable:** Use the **Definition** drop-down arrow and select an override value you wish to use for the snippet. You may specify a value for each of the variables that the snippet contains.
8	Click **OK** to insert the variable definition.
9	Click the **Save** button to save your work.

SPECIFYING SNIPPET VARIABLE DEFINITIONS AT TOPIC-LEVEL

BASIC CONCEPT

A snippet's content is generally the same wherever used; however, the content is slightly different in some instances — often by a single word or short phrase. For example, this slight difference might be with a product name or a product family, and occur in the same or in another topic. You can manage this slight variation by specifying a snippet variable definition at the topic level. A topic-level definition happens at the topic and therefore overrides a definition of the same variable at the project level (in the Variables Editor), at the target level, or when you use the snippet in different topics.

ESSENTIAL ELEMENTS

You can enter a snippet variable definition at the topic level with a right-click to open the **Topic Properties** and select the **Snippet Variables** tab. From the **Snippet Variables** tab, you would first choose the appropriate **Variable Set**. Then, you may select a predefined single-definition of the variable, choose from a list of definitions in a multi-definition variable, or enter a new definition directly.

Given the priority of defining the variable definition at the topic, the definition applies throughout the topic for each use of that snippet. The same snippet could have a unique definition in another topic.

APPLICATION TIPS

When creating a variable set for use with snippets, consider using a name like "SnippetVariables." You might even make a different variable set for each snippet that uses variables. When the **Snippet Variable** window opens, you can quickly identify the correct variable set, as shown in the second image.

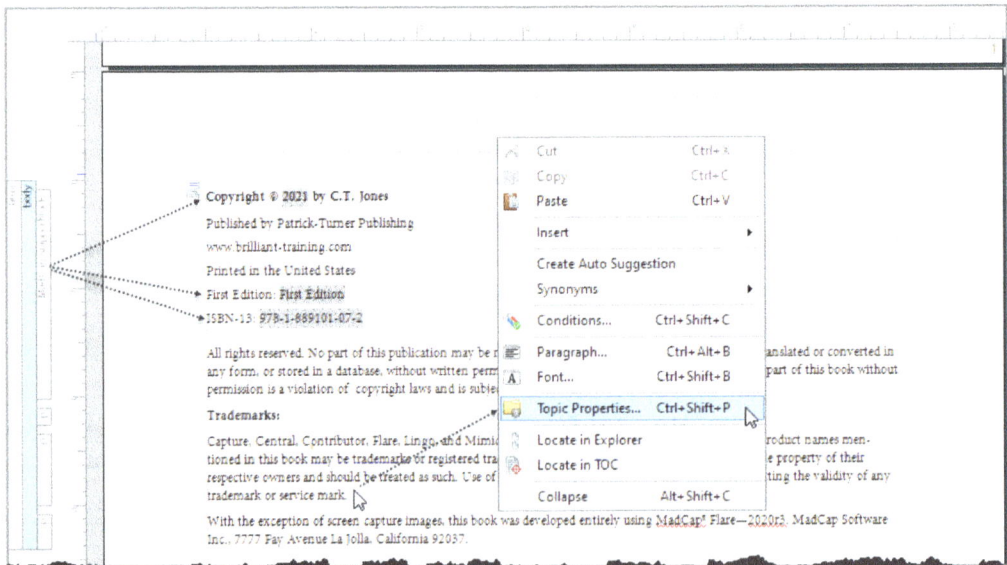

Figure 5-15. Snippet Variable Definition at the Topic Level.

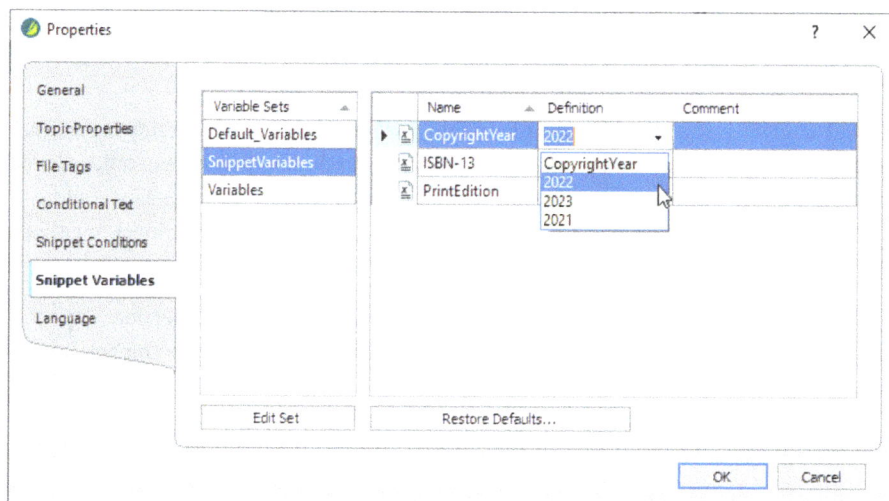

Figure 5-16. Snippet Variable Definitions at Topic level — Definition Selection and Override.

QUICK STEPS: SPECIFYING SNIPPET VARIABLE DEFINITIONS AT TOPIC-LEVEL

STEP	ACTION
1	Open the topic in which you want to modify the snippet variable definitions at the topic-level.
2	Click anywhere inside the topic, right-click and select **Topic Properties**.
3	Click the **Snippet Variables** tab.
4	Choose from the list of **Variables Sets**, the set that contains the variable definitions you wish to use.
5	Do one of the following to specify a variable definition for the snippet:
	a) Single-Definition Variable: Click on the variable to select the default value or enter a value directly in the **Definition** to override the value.
	b) Multi-Definition Variable: Use the **Definition** drop-down arrow and select an override value you wish to use for the snippet. You may specify a value for each of the variables that the snippet contains.
6	Click **OK** to insert the variable definition.
7	Click the **Save** button to save your work.

SPECIFYING SNIPPET CONDITION TAGS AT SNIPPET-LEVEL

BASIC CONCEPT

Generally, a snippet's content is the same wherever used, but it is slightly different in some instances. Often this difference is achieved by including additional content or excluding part of the standard snippet content — for example, by including or excluding an additional phrase or sentence. You could manage this slight snippet variation by using a snippet condition tag specified at the snippet to either add or remove some portion of content.

A snippet condition tag specified at the snippet is unique to the snippet instance. It overrides any other definition of the same condition tag at the target level, or another instance of the snippet, in the same or a different topic.

ESSENTIAL ELEMENTS

You can specify a snippet condition tag with a right-click on the snippet and select the **Snippet Conditions** option. From the **Snippet Conditions** dialog, choose the appropriate **Condition Tag Set**, specify a specific **Tag**, then select the **Action** to **Include** or **Exclude** the tagged content for this instance of the snippet. A condition tag specified at the snippet is unique to the snippet instance, and therefore you can apply a different tag for each snippet instance in the same topic.

Given the priority of a condition tag specified at the snippet, a snippet used multiple times in a topic can be slightly customized to include or exclude content by selecting a condition tag for each snippet.

APPLICATION TIPS

When you create condition tag sets for use with snippets, consider using file names like "SnippetConditions." You might even make a different tag set for each snippet that uses condition tags. When the **Snippet Conditions** window opens, you can quickly identify the correct tag set.

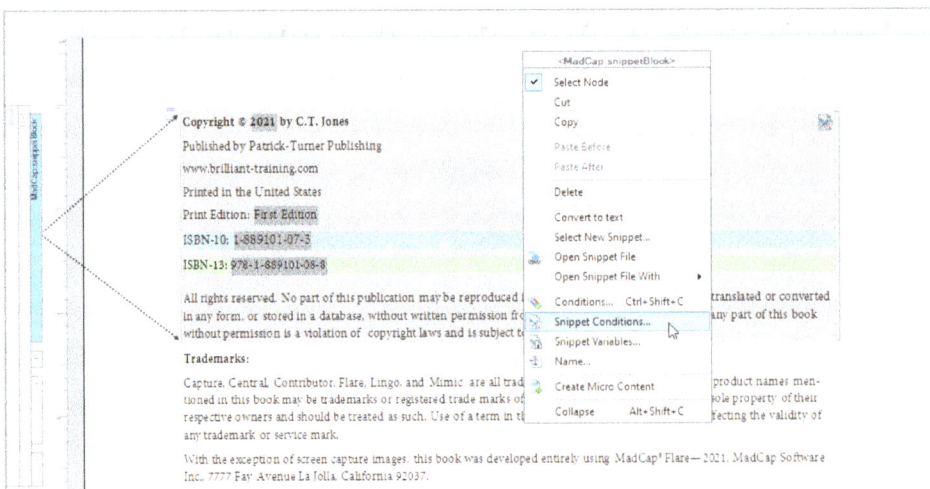

Figure 5-17. Set Snippet Condition Tags at Snippet-Level — ISBN-10 and ISBN-13 Before Condition Applied.

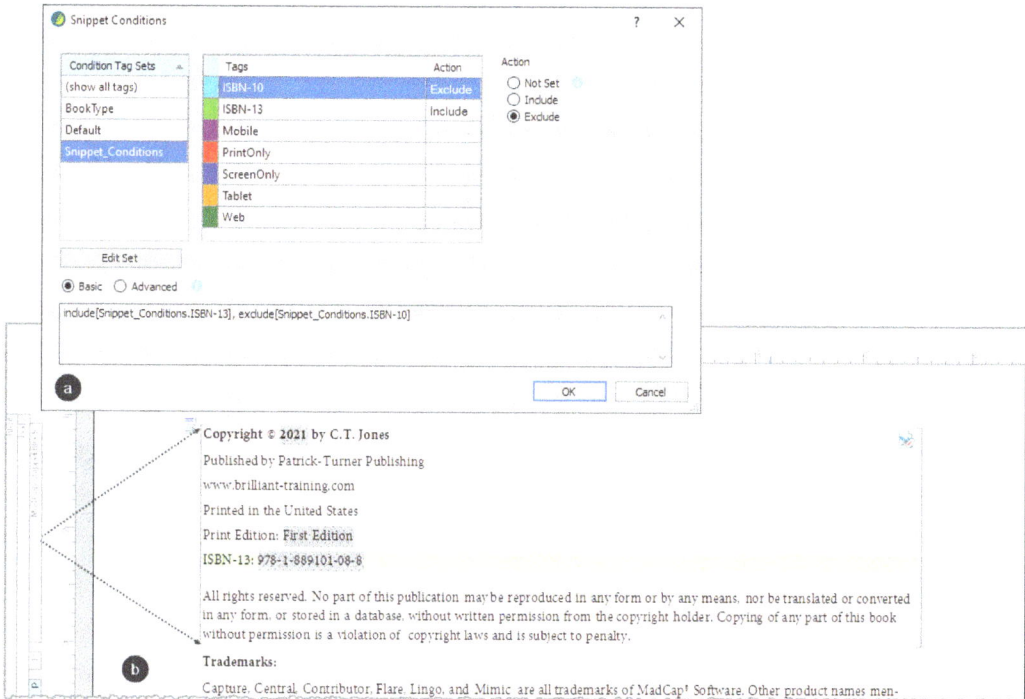

Figure 5-18. a) Set Snippet Condition Tags — b) Snippet with ISBN-13 only, after ISBN10 Tag Excluded.

QUICK STEPS: SPECIFYING SNIPPET CONDITIONAL TAGS AT SNIPPET-LEVEL

STEP	ACTION
1	Open the topic in which you want to specify a snippet condition tag at the snippet-level.
2	Use the **Show Block Structure Bars** icon to **Show/Hide** the tag bars along the left edge of the topic.
3	Use the **Show Span Structure Bars** icon to **Show/Hide** the span bars along the top edge of the topic.
4	Click on the snippet if visible, or click the **MadCap:snippetBlock** tag bar (for block snippets) or on the **MadCap:snippetText** span bar (for text snippet) to select the snippet.
5	Right-click and select **Snippet Conditions**. The **Snippet Conditions** window opens.
6	From the **Condition Tag Sets**, select the tag set from which you wish to specify a conditional tag.
7	From the listed **Tags** options, choose a specific tag.
8	From the **Action** options, choose the option to **Include** or **Exclude** content where the tag is applied, for this snippet; or leave the tag as **Not Set**, and the conditional tag will not be applied to the snippet.
9	Click **OK** to accept the snippet condition setting.
10	Click the **Save** button to save your work.

SPECIFYING SNIPPET CONDITION TAGS AT TOPIC-LEVEL

BASIC CONCEPT

Generally, a snippet's content is the same wherever used, but it is slightly different in some instances. Often this difference is achieved by including additional content or excluding part of the standard snippet content — for example, by including or excluding an additional phrase or sentence. You could manage this slight snippet variation by using a snippet condition tag specified at the topic to either add or remove some portion of content.

A snippet condition tag specified at the topic-level, essentially overrides any other definition of the same condition tag at the target level, or in another use of the snippet, in a different topic.

ESSENTIAL ELEMENTS

You can specify a snippet condition tag at the topic after selecting the snippet, with a right-click on the open topic and selecting the **Topic Properties** option. Choose the appropriate **Condition Tag Set** from the **Properties** dialog, specify a specific **Tag**, and choose the **Action** to **Include** or **Exclude** the tagged content for this snippet instance. A condition tag you select at the topic applies every time you use the snippet in the topic, regardless of the number of times you use the snippet.

APPLICATION TIPS

When you create condition tag sets for use with snippets, consider using file names like "SnippetConditions." You might even make a different tag set for each snippet that uses condition tags. When the **Snippet Conditions** window opens, you can quickly identify the correct tag set.

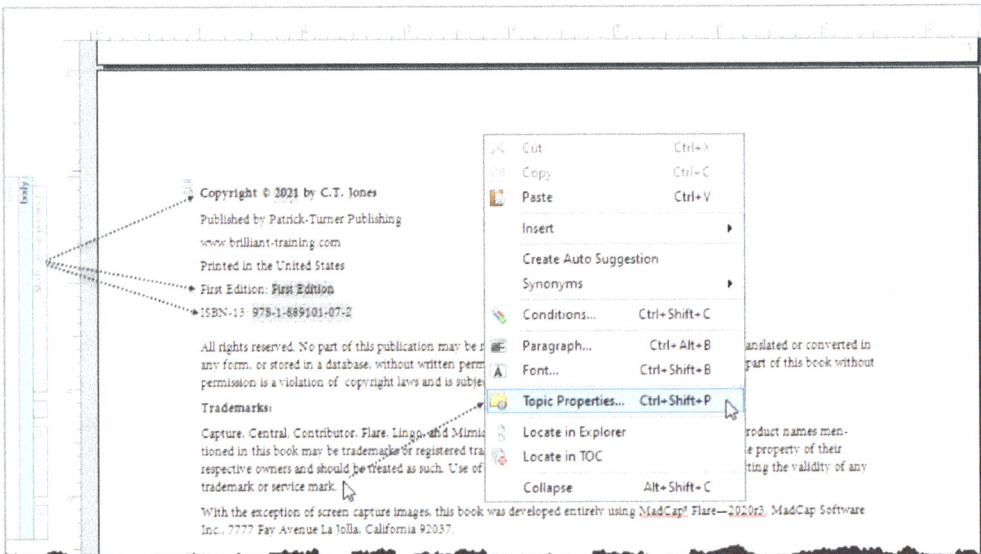

Figure 5-19. Specify Snippet Conditional Tags at Topic Level.

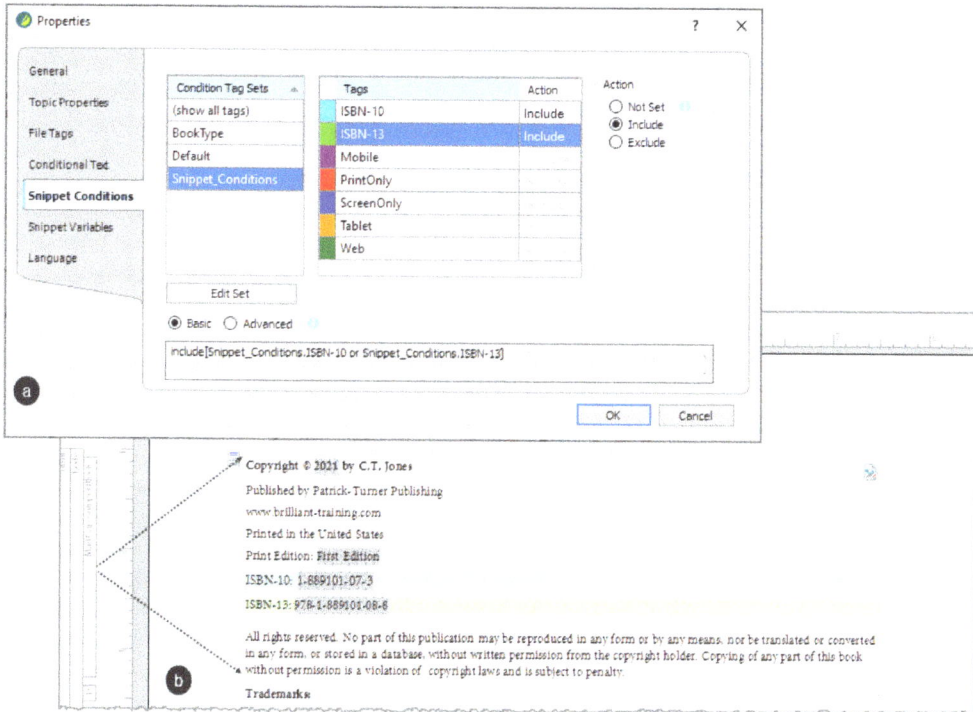

Figure 5-20. a) Specify Snippet Conditional Tags at Topic level — b) Snippet in Topic After Condition Applied.

QUICK STEPS: SPECIFYING SNIPPET CONDITIONAL TAGS AT TOPIC LEVEL

STEP	ACTION
1	Open the topic in which you want to modify snippet condition tags at the topic-level.
2	Click anywhere inside the topic and right-click and select **Topic Properties**.
3	Right-click and select **Topic Properties** to open the Topic Properties dialog.
	Click the **Snippet Conditions** tab.
4	From the **Condition Tag Sets**, select the tag set from which you wish to specify a condition tag.
5	From the listed **Tags** options, choose a specific tag.
6	From the **Action** options, choose the option to **Include** or **Exclude** content where the tag is applied, for this snippet; or leave the tag as **Not Set**, and the condition tag will not be applied to the snippet.
7	Click **OK** to accept the snippet condition setting.
8	Click the **Save** button to save your work.

CHAPTER 6

PAGE LAYOUT AND TEMPLATE PAGES

INTRODUCING FLARE PAGE LAYOUT FILES

In Flare, you would create a Page Layout file to define the physical layout and how content flows onto the pages of a section of a book or document or an entire document. In other words, you might create a separate page layout file for each of the major divisions of the document. For example, you could create different files for the Cover Title Pages, Front Matter Pages, Chapter Pages, Glossary Pages, Index Pages, and Appendix Pages. If all of the pages in the document have the same layout, you could use a single page layout file.

Flare Page Layout files are in the **Content Explorer > Content > Resources > PageLayouts**.

PAGE LAYOUT FILE REQUIREMENTS

Your initial work of determining how the sections of your document are differentiated will aid in deciding on page layout file requirements. From there, you can determine how many files are needed. Some documents, for example, a legal document, may have all pages the same legal size. And there is no real differentiation in different sections of the document and how content flows onto the pages. Textbooks or user guides are altogether different — there are generally clear divisions.

A textbook generally contains a Front Matter section, which includes the pages from the cover to just before the first chapter; a Chapter Pages section, which consists of the first page of each chapter and all of the left and right pages up to the chapter end; and perhaps Index and Glossary sections. In this scenario, you could create a different page layout file for the Front Matter, Chapter Pages, the Index, and Glossary. You could go a step further and choose to break off the Cover page and Copyright page from the Front Matter to create a file called CoverPages. Since an Index and Glossary may have a similar and layout (for example, 2-columns), you might create a single IndexGlossary file.

FLARE PAGE LAYOUT FILE TEMPLATES

When it comes to deciding on and creating your page layout files, you won't have to start from scratch, but you can start by using any of Flare's standard page layout file templates. As a starting baseline, these layout files have standard sizes that you can modify as required.

You can use page layout template files to control content arrangement and flow in a given section of your document, manual, or book. How you can use Flare page layout template files is briefly described in the following table.

Table 6-1. Flare Page Layout File Templates

Template Name	Brief Description
ChapterA4.flpgl	This file, designed to control the arrangement and flow of Chapter Pages, is based on the international standard A4 page size of 21 cm x 29.7 cm, and includes Title, Empty, First Left, First Right, Left, Right, Empty Left, and Empty Right page types.
ChapterLegal.flpgl	This file, designed to control the arrangement and flow of Chapter Pages of a legal document, is based on a standard legal size of 8.5 in x 14 in, and includes Title and Normal page types.

Table 6-1. Flare Page Layout File Templates (cont).

Template Name	Brief Description
ChapterLetter.flpgl	This file, designed to control the arrangement and flow of Chapter Pages, is based on the standard letter page size of 8.5 in x 11 in and includes a Title, Empty, First Left, First Right, Left, Right, Empty Left, and Empty Right page types.
ChapterResizable.flpgl	This re-sizable page layout file, designed for Chapter pages, is based on a standard letter page size of 8.5 in x 11 i. The file includes Title, Empty, First Left, First Right, Left, Right, Empty Left, and Empty Right page types. **See Note 1.**
Default.flpgl	Used by default wherever a page layout is required, and no other file is specified. Generally, you will want to create a page layout file to control the content flow for each section of your books or documents.
FrontMatterResizable.flpgl	This re-sizable page layout file, designed for the Front Matter pages of a document, is based on the standard letter page size of 8.5 in x 11 in. The file includes First Right, Left, Right, Empty Left, Empty Right, and Empty page types. See **Note 1**.
GlossaryResizable.flpgl	This re-sizable page layout template, designed for a book or manual Glossary pages, is based on a standard letter page size of 8.5 in x 11 in. The file includes First Right, Left, Right, Empty Left, Empty Right, and Empty page types. See **Note 1** and **Note 2**.
IndexResizable.flpgl	This re-sizable page layout template file, designed for Index pages of a document, is based on the standard letter page size of 8.5 in x 11 in and includes First Right, Left, Right, Empty Left, Empty Right, and Empty page types. See **Note 1** and **Note 2**.
NormalResizable.flpgl	Based on a standard letter size of 8.5 in x 11 in, this file is designed to control the arrangement and flow onto pages where all pages are the same. This re-sizable page layout template includes the Normal page type only. See **Note 1**.

NOTE: 1) The files with "Resizable" in the name have the frames of each page anchored to the page edges. Anchored frames maintain the same distance from the edges of the page, even if you later change the size of the page.

NOTE: 2) The GlossaryResizable and IndexResizable page layout files manage the contents of a Flare generated Glossary or Index files, respectively. However, these same files can serve as templates for creating page layout files for your own manually created Glossary and Index topics.

PAGE LAYOUT PAGE TYPES

Page Types represent one of the two main Page Layout File components that allow you to control how content is arranged and flowed onto the pages of your document. As mentioned earlier, the sections of your book, for example, Front Matter and Chapter Pages, will likely have different Page Layout files to accommodate the differences in the document divisions. Likewise, the different types of books and documents may require a different set of page types to manage the flow of content in each section, starting with the first page of the section and from one page to the next. Also, see Page Layout Frames.

Table 6-2. Flare Page Layout Page Types

Page Type	Brief Description
Title (T)	This page type and its arrangement is generally applied to the first page of your document or book — more specifically the cover title of a document. Also see **Normal** and **Empty** page types.
First (F)	This page type and its arrangement is generally applied to the first page of each chapter and in documents where there is no concern for left and right pages — typically all pages are the same after this page. See the **Normal** Page Type.
First Left (FL)	This page type and its arrangement, as defined, is generally unique and applied to the first page of each chapter in a document in which you want the chapter to start on the left page.
First Right (FR)	This page type and its arrangement, as defined, is generally unique and applied to the first page of each chapter in a document in which you want the chapter to start on the right page.
Left (L)	This page type and its arrangement, as defined, is applied to all of the pages that fall on the left side in a book or document. on the left side. Also see **Right** Page Type.
Right (R)	This page type and its arrangement, as defined, is applied to all of the pages that fall on the right side in a book or document. on the left side. Also see **Left** Page Type.
Normal (N)	This page type and its arrangement is generally applied to all pages in a book or document after the first page, and the remaining pages are in the document are all the same after the first page. This page type typically follows a First or Title page. Also see **Title** and **First** page types.
Empty (E)	This page type is applied to an empty page occurring in the book or document. This page type, which, as the name implies, is generally absent of any content, might be used immediately following a Title page, unless otherwise the Empty Left or Empty Right page type is used.
Empty Left (EL)	This page type, as defined, is applied to an empty page that falls on the left — typically needed when an empty page is required, when there is a First Right page type for a new Chapter. This page may have no more than a left page header and footer. Also see **First Right** Page Type.
Empty Right (ER)	This page type, as defined, is applied to an empty page that falls on the right — typically needed when an empty page is required, when there is a First Left page type for a new Chapter. This page may have no more than a right page header and footer. Also see **First Left** Page Type.

Page Layout Frames

Page Layout Frames represent the second of the two main Page Layout File components that govern how content is arranged and flowed onto the pages of your document or book. Each layout page can contain multiple frames, each of which you will select and position on the page based on the frame type and on how you wish to control the flow of specific content types. For example, frames manage header content, body content, footer content, and in some cases, images or decorations.

Suppose you are responsible for creating the page layout files. In that case, your task in working with page frames will involve selecting frame types, according to the usage shown in the table below, then inserting and arranging the frames onto the page as desired. Finally, you would specify the parameters of each frame. Typical frame parameters include size, borders or background, and how many columns.

Table 6-3. Page Layout Frames

Frame Type	Brief Description
Header Frame	A frame, generally placed at the page top of each page layout page, where you want the content repeated. Header content usually includes some combination of chapter or topic headings, page numbers, or other content.
Body Frame	A frame, generally placed on a page layout page to manage the arrangement and flow of the main body text on a page. You may place one or more Body Frames on a page layout page. Body frames will generally contain one or more columns.
Footer Frame	A frame, generally placed at the page bottom of each page layout page, where you want the content repeated. Footer content usually includes some combination of chapter or topic headings, page numbers, or other content.
Image Frame	A frame, generally placed on a page layout page, to manage the placement and flow of a single image on a page. You may insert one or more Image Frames on a page layout page.
Decoration Frame	A frame, generally placed on a page layout to manage placement of special content such as a block quote or other content for aesthetic purposes. The frame supports text, color, images, and a background and border. You may place multiple Decoration Frames on a page layout.

INTRODUCING THE FLARE PAGE LAYOUT EDITOR

Using the Page Layout Editor, you can create or modify the desired layout for a set of page types. If you open the editor to a newly created file, the file will contain a set of default page types, represented as thumbnail-size pages. Each thumbnail is labeled and presented in the right panel of the Page Layout Editor. This right panel is called the Page Overview Pane.

 If you have based your page layout file on a Flare page layout template like ChapterResizable, then it will already contain default page types such as First Right (FR), Left (L), Right (R), Empty Left (EL), and Empty Right (ER). Remember, you may have as many page layout files as required to manage the content flow onto the pages of the different sections of your book or document. With the file opened, the first task is defining specifications of each page — for example, Page Type, Page Size, and Margins. Then, for each page, you must insert the frames as needed and specify the parameters for each

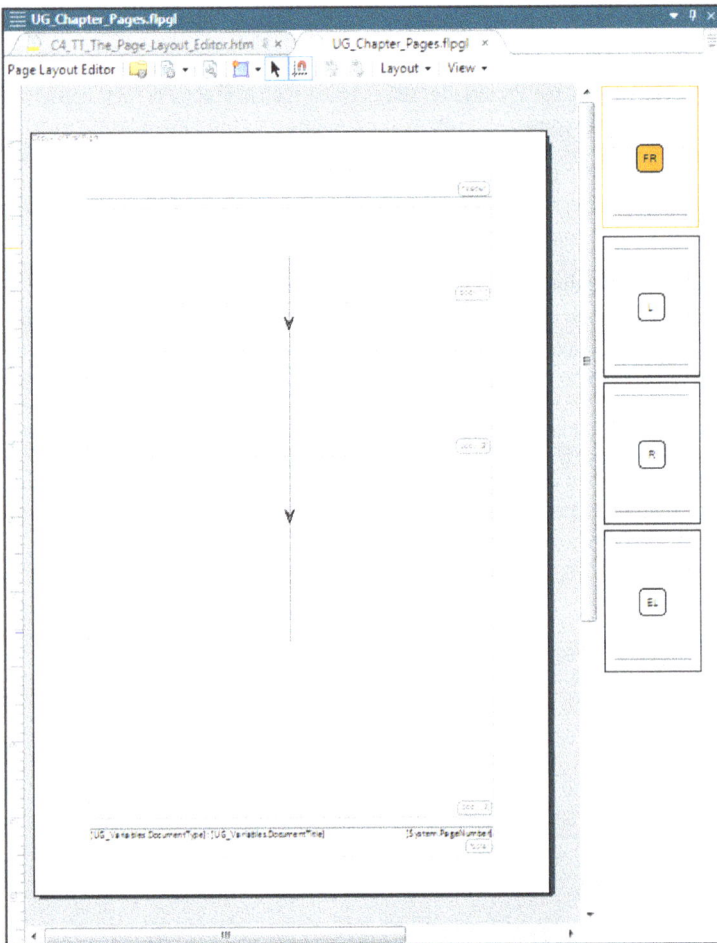

Figure 6-1. Flare Page Layout Editor — Page Overview Bar Enabled.

PAGE OVERVIEW PANE

As mentioned earlier, previously defined page types are presented in the overview pane. If you intend to use any of the existing page, you may need to modify the page parameters for those pages. After examining the page types and deciding which are necessary, you may need to add or remove some of the page types. After that, you are ready to define the parameters of each of the remaining pages.

Let's say, for example, the final page types include Title, First Right, Left, Right, and Empty Left, and that all of the page sizes will be the same. One by one, you can open each page type and specify the General properties — for example, Page Size, Margins, and Orientation; then Background properties, and finally, Print Marks properties.

KEY PAGE LAYOUT EDITOR PREFERENCES

Before getting started, consider defining some key editor preferences that make working on page layouts somewhat easier. These are primarily settings under the Layout Menu and the View Menu. First, consider switching on the Horizontal Rulers and Vertical Rulers. With these visual preferences set, you may wish to select the preferred units of measure you intend to work with — for example, Inches, Pixels, or Points. Initially, it may be best to set the page scaling to 100%. Later, you may choose to select **Fit to Width**, **Fit to Height**, or both. These settings present a full view of the current page.

DEFINING PAGE SPECIFICATIONS

You will likely begin by defining the page properties for each page in the Page Overview Pane when you get started. You can add or remove a page type as necessary. Selecting a page in the Overview Pane causes it to appear in the main editor window. You can then edit the page by adding frames.

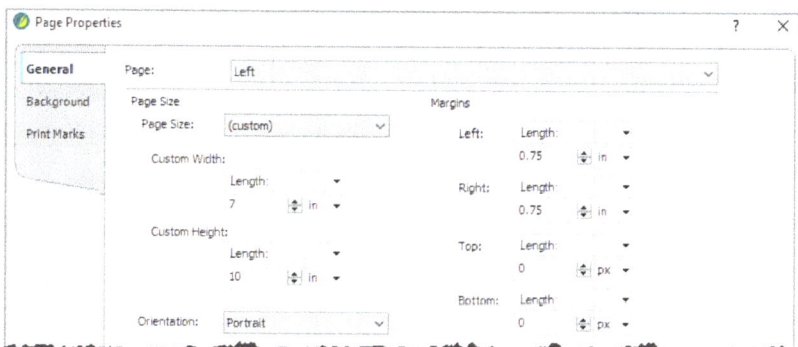

FRAME OPERATIONS

Once you have completed defining the Page Properties, you are ready to start working on the layout for each page type. Defining the page layout means placing frames onto the page in the desired arrangement and defining the parameters of each of the frames. Generally, unless a page is empty, a typical page will have a Header Frame, Footer Frame, and one or more Body Frames, depending on the page type. As you'll see later, whereas you can determine and enter what goes in Footer and Header frames, you do not insert content into Body Frames. Content is flowed onto each page and into Body frames.

PAGE LAYOUT EDITOR TOOLBAR

A starting place with the Page Layout Editor is to become familiar with the user interface and its basic operations. In general, tools are available to add new page types to the file, edit parameters of each page type, such as page dimensions, margins, and so forth, and tools for inserting new frames onto a page and editing the frame properties.

The **Layout** drop-down menu provides tools and operations to assist with working with page or frame objects, such as rotating and aligning objects. Finally, the View menu operations allow for the enabling or disabling of the visual aids. These aids include visual elements like margins, bleed lines, vertical and horizontal rulers, and tools to scale the display size in various ways that adjust the page display to enhance editing and tools for managing the overall view of the editor window.

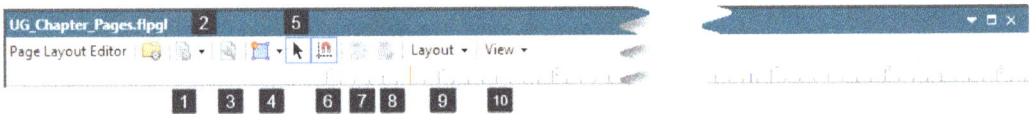

Table 6-4. Page Layout Editor Toolbar Buttons and Icons

Item	Toolbar Element	Brief Description
1	File Properties	View the **General**, **File Tags**, and **Conditional Text** properties for the page layout file.
2	Page Properties	Click button to display the **Page Properties** dialog for the selected page
2	Page Properties Drop-Down	Click drop-down arrow to display the Page commands
3	Frame Properties	Display the **Frame Properties** dialog for the selected frame
4	New Frame Drop-Down	Select Frame to insert frame on open page. Header and Footer frame selection is disabled if a Header or Footer Frame is already on the page.
5	Select Mode	Enable the **Select Mode** to allow object selections
6	Snap Frames Icon	Select snap-to-grid to enable snapping of frames to near-by positions.
7	Edit Frame	Enable editing of selected frame. Used with Header and Footer Frames.
8	Select Frame Template	Open Template Dialog for editing the selected Header or Footer Frame.
9	Layout	Click **Layout** command menu to access commands to affect the various positions, orientations, or alignments of page layout objects.
10	View	Click **View** command menu to access commands to affect the various visual aids for working with page layouts.

INTRODUCING FLARE TEMPLATE PAGE FILES

In Flare, a *template page* is another Flare component that lets you manage your topic content. Similar to page layout files used primarily with framing and flowing your content for print outputs, template pages are mainly used to manage the flow of content in your online outputs. Template pages, however, are also used in managing Word print outputs for defining specifications like page size and orientation and for applying content such as header and footer text.

Whereas page layout files use various page types and frame types to manage content flow onto print output pages, template page files use a variety of Flare proxy elements that assist in flowing specific content onto the pages of online outputs. Content elements placed on a template page cause the content to be repeated on every topic to which the template page is applied. For an online output, for example, you might use a template page to place features like search bars, breadcrumbs, topic toolbars, menus, mini-TOCs, or footer text to multiple topics, or even to all topics in the output.

FLARE TEMPLATE PAGE PROXY ELEMENTS

In Flare, a proxy is a placeholder you can use with print or online outputs and in which the placeholder is replaced for content when you build the output. You can insert proxies in topics or template pages. When used in a topic, the proxy content is output in the topic only; if you insert a proxy element in a template page, the proxy content appears in all topics where the template page is applied.

The items listed and described below represent Flare proxy elements that you can use to control how your online content is arranged and flowed onto the pages of your online outputs.

Table 6-5. Flare Proxy Elements Usable in Template Pages for Online Outputs

Proxy Element	Brief Description
Search Bar Proxy	Add this proxy as a placeholder in your template page to generate a search bar in the HTML5 output. The search bar appears in each topic to which the template page is applied.
Breadcrumbs Proxy	Add this proxy as a placeholder in your template page to display on each topic where the template page is applied the exact path taken, using the table of contents entries.
Menu Proxy	Add this proxy element to your template page to generate a topic TOC file menu in each topic to which the associated template page is applied.
Topic Toolbar Proxy	Add this proxy element placeholder in your template page to generate a topic toolbar in the HTML5 output on each topic to which the template page is applied. This element can be an alternative or additional toolbar option.
Mini-TOC Proxy	Add this proxy element to your template page to generate and place a small portion of your TOC or TOC headings in each topic where the template page is applied.
Body Proxy	Add this proxy as a placeholder to insert the content from your topics, when the HTML5 output is generated for each topic to which the associated template page has been applied.

EDITING A FLARE TEMPLATE PAGE

Flare template pages are typically located in the **Content Explorer** > **Resources** > **TemplatePages**. You may create as many template pages as you require, in this location or any other preferred location. When you double-click or use **File** > **Open** to open a template page, it is opened for editing in the same XML Editor in which topics are opened.

Since you can have multiple template pages, each of them may use any of the Flare proxy elements as required to produce a desired output. Multiple template pages might be used, for example, in an online business site, where one template page is used for a unique site home page arrangement, a second template page layout is applied to the first topic or landing page of three different segments of the site, all of which have a similar layout; and finally, a third template page is applied to all of the remaining topics.

Remember, you can create as many template pages as required to manage the different types of topic arrangements in your online output.

DEFINING THE TEMPLATE PAGE CONTENT

Some Flare proxies can be used for print outputs, some for online outputs, and some can be used in both print and online outputs. For example, the glossary and index proxies are mainly used in print outputs; the breadcrumbs, search bar and search results proxies are mainly used in online outputs; and finally, the mini-TOC proxy is often used in both print and online outputs. In actual practice, you may find that while some proxies are inserted directly into topics, others are inserted in a template page. Inserting the proxy onto a template page causes whatever is in the proxy placeholders to be output on every topic to which the template page is associated.

If you want every topic in your online output to include a header or footer that contains specific information, then that information is either inserted above or below the body proxy. To add header in your online outputs, the header content is inserted above the body proxy on the template page; footer content is added by inserting the content below the body proxy on the template page.

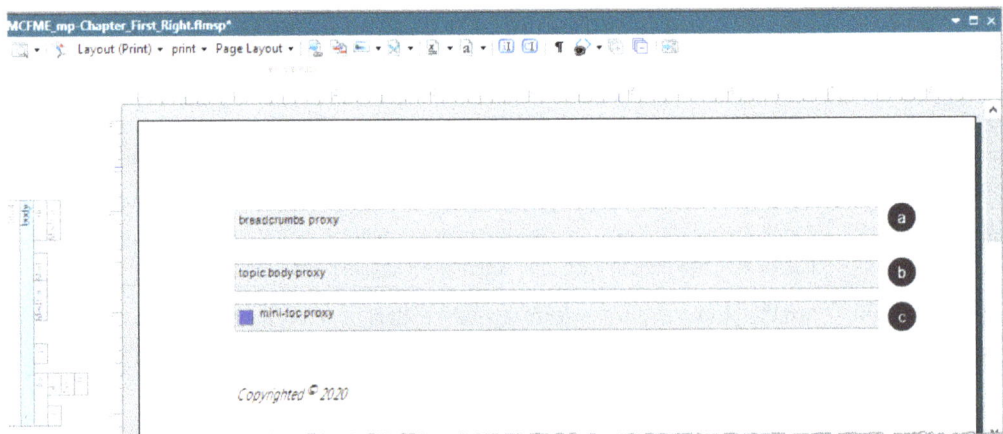

Figure 6-2. TemplatePage in XML Editor with: a) Breadcrumb Proxy, b) Topic Body Proxy, and c) Mini-TOC Proxy.

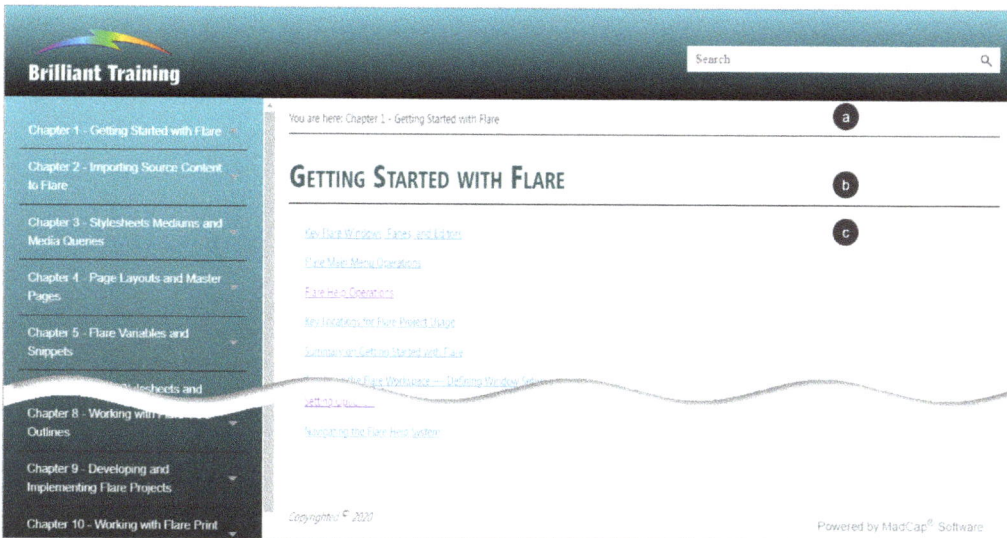

Figure 6-3. HTML5 Output with Proxy Content Inserted a) Breadcrumbs, b) Topic Body, and c) Mini-TOC.

APPLYING THE TEMPLATE PAGE

As the Flare template page lets you use proxy placeholders that allow certain elements to be placed on a single topic, multiple topics, or all topics, to satisfy your HTML online output, you may need multiple template page files. For example the arrangement on you main start or home page, as it may be quite different, may require it's own template page, called **MyHome.fmsp**. Then, there may be a group of topics that all have a similar arrangement and can share the same template page, **SectionLanding.flmsp**; and finally all of the remaining topics might share a third template page, called **Other_Topics.fmsp**.

- If there are elements on a template page that you want to appear on all of your topics, for example, breadcrumbs, topic body, and footer content for your online outputs — then you would associate that template page on the **Advanced** tab of the HTML target file. The template page elements would be automatically inserted in all topics unless overridden at the topic level.

- If there are elements on a template page that you want to appear on a selected group of topics only, for example, breadcrumbs, a mini-TOC, and topic body — then you would associate that template page on the **Topic Properties** dialog of each topic in the selected group.

- If there are elements on a template page that you want to appear on a single topic only, for example, for the initial start page of your HTML output — then you would open that single topic and associate that template page on the **Topic Properties** dialog.

> **TIP:** A template page assigned at the topic level will override a template page set at the target file.

SUMMARY ON PAGE LAYOUTS AND TEMPLATE PAGES

After the Flare stylesheet, page layout files and template page files have the most impact on the appearance of your print and online outputs. Page layout files use different page types and frame types to manage the flow and arrangement of content. On the other hand, template page files use Flare proxies to let you define the content you want to appear in one or multiple topics of your output. Template pages also manage how content is arranged and flows onto the pages of your online output.

Before starting with the development of your page layouts and template pages, consider the guidelines outlined below. The remainder of this chapter presents some examples of tasks related to page layouts and template pages.

CHECKLIST: PAGE LAYOUTS AND TEMPLATE PAGES

- *If you have imported content and are now anxious to see the desired appearance in your documents, after firming up some initial details with your stylesheet, you might create and apply your page layout files to your Print TOC. For online content, you might create and apply appropriate template pages to specific topics.*

- *Typical page layout files for most technical books will include Front Matter, Chapter Pages, Glossary, Appendix, and Index files. You might also have a Cover Title section, but instead, you could place a "CoverTitle" page in the Front Matter section.*

- *Generally speaking, you may need an Appendix page layout file for appendices with 1-column and another file for 2-column pages. Also, you may wish to use a single file for both the Glossary and Index, for example, if they both use 2-columns.*

- *When you import source content from FrameMaker, Flare creates a page layout file for each of the FrameMaker chapters — these files may not be beneficial and can be deleted. You may need to develop new page layout files.*

- *Consider creating and inserting a footer table stylesheet into the footer of your page layout files. The table allows better control of the left, right, and center alignment of footer content.*

- *When deciding on page types for each of your page layout files, consider the sections of your books or documents. For example, for the Chapter pages file, if the first page of each chapter will appear on the right and have a unique layout, you need a First Right. You will also need Left Page, Right Page (maybe with header and footer frames), and perhaps an Empty Left.*

- *Consider creating and using multiple Template Pages to apply to groups of topics where you want specific content elements to appear on each topic to which the template page is applied.*

- *Whether or not breadcrumbs or page footers appear on some or every online page is controlled by a template page file applied to the associated topics.*

- *Use Flare proxy elements like breadcrumbs, topic toolbar, or eLeaning toolbar on Template Pages to be applied to associated topics.*

NAVIGATING THE PAGE LAYOUT EDITOR

BASIC CONCEPT

The Page Layout Editor is the primary means of defining and working with page layout files in your project. First, you should understand the concept of page groupings and how the books or documents in your project are divided into major sections. Now with an understanding of the working areas of the Page Layout Editor, you're ready to take the next step. The Page Layout Editor has the main controls for adding or removing pages, editing page properties, and adding and editing page frames.

ESSENTIAL ELEMENTS

The Page Layout Editor has two main areas — the **Page Overview Bar**, which shows the file pages as thumbnails, and the page working area, which displays the selected page. **Page Properties** like **Size**, **Orientation**, and **Background**, of each page, can be opened and defined after double-clicking on the thumbnail. After defining page properties, you then use the working area to establish the page layout, by adding the desired frame types, like **Header**, **Body**, **Image**, and **Footer** in the desired arrangement. Finally, you would define the **Frame Properties** of each of the page frames. **Frame Properties** include **Size** and **Position**, **Columns**, **Background**, and **Borders**.

APPLICATION TIPS

Start by setting some key visual indicators to simplify your work in the Page Layout Editor. Use the **View** drop-down and select **Vertical Ruler** and **Horizontal Ruler**; select **Margins**, and if applicable, **Padding** and **Bleed**; Finally, click **Page Overview** if not currently displayed.

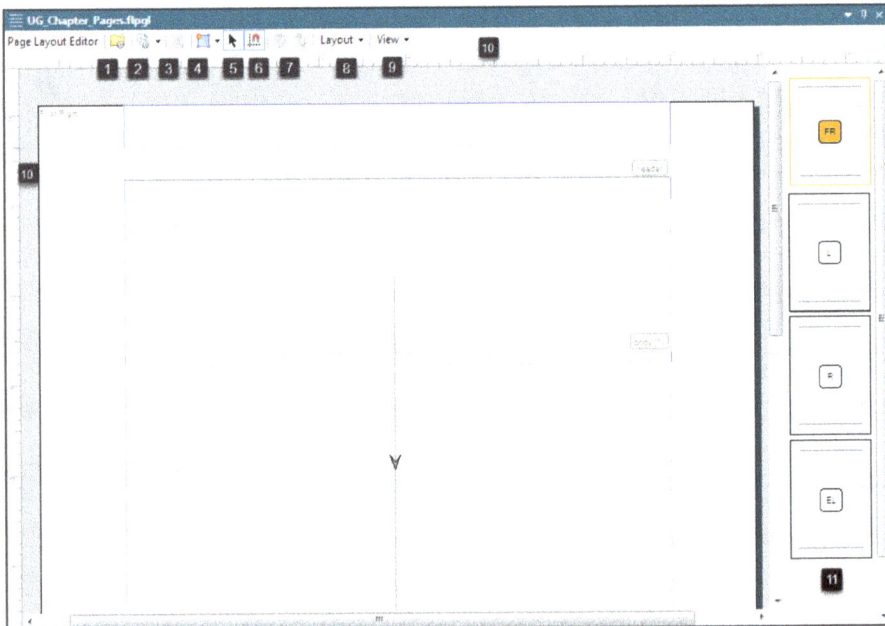

Figure 6-4. Navigating the Page Layout Editor.

QUICK STEPS: NAVIGATING THE PAGE LAYOUT EDITOR

STEP	ACTION
1	In the Content Explorer click on the **PageLayouts** subfolder.
2	Double-click on a page layout file, for example, **Default.flpgl**, to open the file in the **Page Layout Editor**.
3	Click the **File Properties** button to view the properties of the currently open page layout file.
4	Click the **Page Properties** button to view the properties of the page selected in the **Page Overview Bar**, or use the drop-down to select a page layout command, like **Copy Page**, **Add Page** or **Mirror Page**.
5	Click on a page frame (Body Frame, Header Frame, Footer Frame, or Image Frame), then click the **Display Page Item Properties** button to view the properties of the selected item.
6	Click the **New Frame Mode** button to draw a new frame on the page, or use the drop-down arrow to select a frame type to insert, for example, a Header Frame, Body Frame, Image Frame, or Footer Frame. If you select an Image Frame, the **Insert Image** dialog opens for you to choose an image to insert.
7	Click the **Select Mode** button to enable the element select mode, whereby you can select and manipulate a page element, for example, to **Align**, **Rotate**, or **Anchor** the element.
8	Click the horseshoe-like icon, on the Editor ribbon, to enable the **Snap-to-Frame** option, to appropriately snap and align an inserted frame to other page objects — for example, snap to the page margins.
9	Click on a page frame, and click the **Layout** drop-down arrow to select an operation by which to affect or manipulate the frame in focus. For example, **Rotate**, and **Vertically** or **Horizontally Align**.
10	Double-click on any page frame to edit the **Frame Properties**.
11	Click the **View** drop-down to toggle between Show/Hide for various page layout visual indicators, for example, **Page Overview Bar**, **Anchor Lines**, **Bleed Markers**, **Margins**, **Vertical** and **Horizontal Rule**.
12	When displayed, right-click on the **Vertical Rule** or **Horizontal Rule** to set the ruler units of measure.
13	Click on a page thumbnail, in the **Page Overview Bar**, to display the page in the center editing pane.
14	Double-click on a page thumbnail, in the **Page Overview Bar**, to edit the **Page Properties**, for example, **Page Size**, **Orientation**, , **Margins**., **Background**, and **Print Marks** for each of the pages.

CREATING A PAGE LAYOUT FILE FOR CHAPTER OR APPENDIX PAGES

BASIC CONCEPT

In many books, particularly technical books and documents like user guides and reference guides, the main body of the work is called "chapter pages." This document section is generally distinguished from other parts in that it has several chapters, each of which starts with a chapter title page, followed by a series of left-side and right-side pages. While not always, these technical books will often have an "appendix pages" section, which will generally have a layout and flow similar to that of chapter pages.

ESSENTIAL ELEMENTS

Flare provides four page layout templates from which you can choose to create a page layout file for chapter pages. You can select one of the standard page size files, which include **ChapterLetter** (8.5 in x 11 in), **ChapterLegal** (8.5 in x 14 in), and **ChapterA4** (21 cm x 29.7 cm), the A4 international standard. Alternatively, you can choose the **ChapterResizable** file and specify the size accordingly.

APPLICATION TIPS

Although Chapter Pages and Appendix Pages are both covered in this section, it is mainly because of similarities. However, you may choose to create separate page layout files for each. For an appendix, you can use the same template you used for the chapter pages; or once you have completed the chapter pages page layout, you can copy it and rename it accordingly for the appendix page layout file.

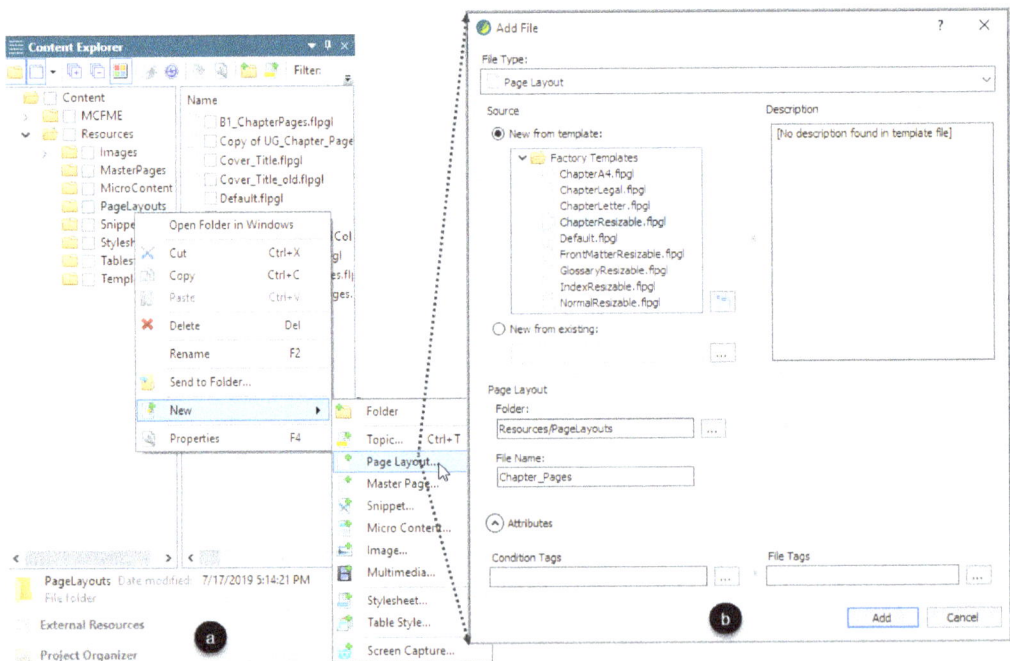

Figure 6-5. a) New Page Layout Option Selected from Right Click and b) Add File Dialog Set for Page Layout.

QUICK STEPS: CREATING A PAGE LAYOUT FILE FOR CHAPTER AND APPENDIX PAGES

STEP	ACTION
1	In the **Content Explorer**, select **Resources** > **PageLayouts** subfolder.
2	Right-click and select **New** > **Page Layout**. The **Add File** dialog opens.
3	Ensure that **File Type** is set for **Page Layouts**.
4	With the **Source** set for **New From Template**, and the **Factory Templates** folders open, choose the file **ChapterResizable** as the template to use to create the new page layout file. This template option has the flexibility of allowing the page size to be changed later without having to resize the page frames.
5	Under **Page Layout**, use the **Folder** field and use the default folder (**Resources/PageLayouts**), or browse and choose another folder in which to store the new page layout file.
6	Use the **File Name** field to specify the name for the new page layout file, for example, **ChapterPages**.
7	Click > **Add** to save the new page layout file.

CREATING A PAGE LAYOUT FILE FOR GLOSSARY AND INDEX PAGES

BASIC CONCEPT

Technical documents like software user guides and reference guides, and other technical books, such as horticulture or the stock market, will often have glossary and index pages. These sections may flow differently from different sections of the document and require their page layout files. Both sections will generally have a start or title page, followed by left-side and right-side pages. These sections are also similar in that the body content often flows onto a 1-column or a 2-column page.

ESSENTIAL ELEMENTS

Flare provides a page layout template file from which you can create the page layout for your glossary pages and a page layout template from which you can make the page layout for your index pages. As you start the page layout file, you select the template accordingly — **GlossaryResizable** for the glossary and **IndexResizable** for the Index.

APPLICATION TIPS

Glossary Pages and Index Pages are both covered in this section, mainly because of their similarities. As they are quite the same in almost all cases, you could create a Glossary-Index page layout file used for both, although there are advantages of keeping them separate. Since they are generally the same in layout and flow, for example, having a 1-column or 2-column format, you may decide to create the entire glossary page layout first and then copy it and rename it for the index page layout file.

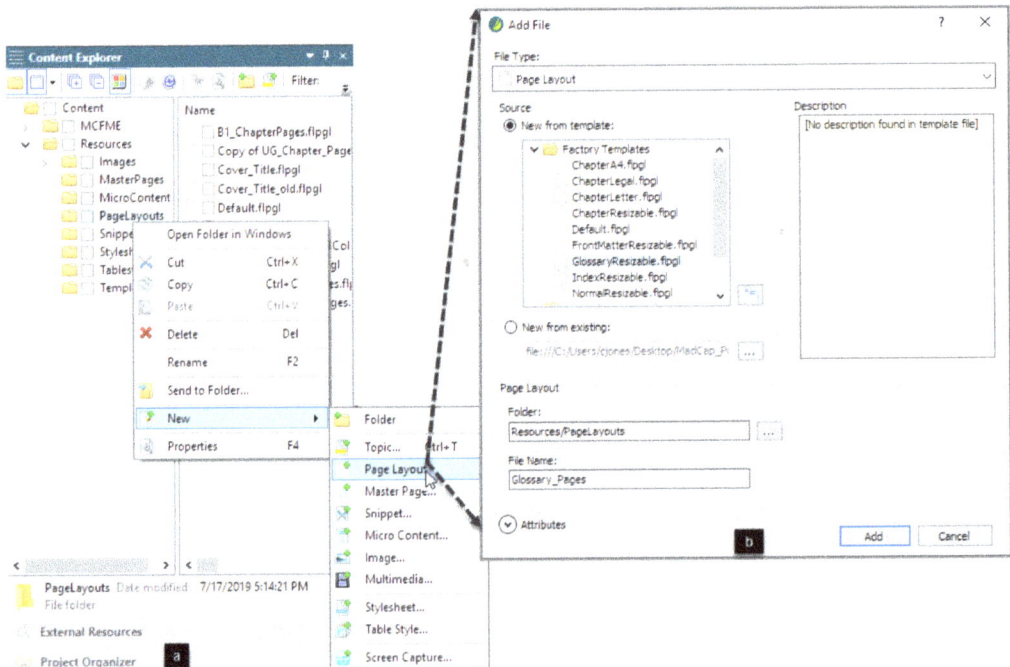

Figure 6-6. a) New Page Layout Option Selected from Right Click and b) Add File Dialog Set for Page Layout.

QUICK STEPS: CREATING A PAGE LAYOUT FILE FOR GLOSSARY AND INDEX PAGES

STEP	ACTION
1	In the **Content Explorer**, select **Resources** > **PageLayouts** subfolder.
2	Right-click and select **New** > **Page Layout**. The **Add File** dialog opens.
3	Ensure that **File Type** is set for **Page Layouts**.
4	With the **Source** set for **New From Template**, and the **Factory Templates** folders open, choose the file **GlossaryResizable**, as the template from which to create the page layout file for your glossary pages; or choose **IndexResizable**, as the template if your are creating the page layout file for your index pages.
5	Under **Page Layout**, use the **Folder** field and use the default folder (**Resources/PageLayouts**), or browse and choose another folder in which to store the new page layout file.
6	Use the **File Name** field to specify the name for the new page layout file, for example, **GlossaryPages**, or **IndexPages** if you are creating a page layout file for an index.
7	Click > **Add** to save the new page layout file.

ADDING AND REMOVING PAGES IN PAGE LAYOUT FILE

BASIC CONCEPT

As you develop page layout files, part of the task is in determining what page types are required in a given section of a book or document. For example, the page types needed in a Title and Copyright pages section would be different from the requirement of a Front Matter pages section, which in turn may be slightly different from a Chapter pages section. This decision mus be partly based on the decision of how each section is started, and on the general page-to-page flow of each of the sections.

New page layout files that you create, will generally be based on a Flare template or a file that you have previously created. In either case, the pages already included in the file may not exactly fit the needs of your new document — some page types may need to be added, while some may need to be removed.

ESSENTIAL ELEMENTS

The pages required when configuring a page layout file, must be based on the general landscape of the pages within a given section of a document. For example, a Cover Title and Copyright section may have the pages **Title**, **Left**, and **Empty**; a Chapter Pages section may have pages **First Right** or **First Left**, **Empty Left** or **Empty Right**, and **Left** and **Right**. Exactly which pages are needed, is a decision you will have to make for each book type and for each of the major sections of a book or document. In some cases, you may be working with a set of documents, that can share the same page layouts.

APPLICATION TIPS

In Flare, Page Types have default names like **Title**, **Empty Left**, **Empty Right**, **First Left**, **First Right**, and **Empty**. Although you can assign a name to each page type in a file, it may be less confusing and simpler to stick with the default names, as there will be no conflict among the different layout files.

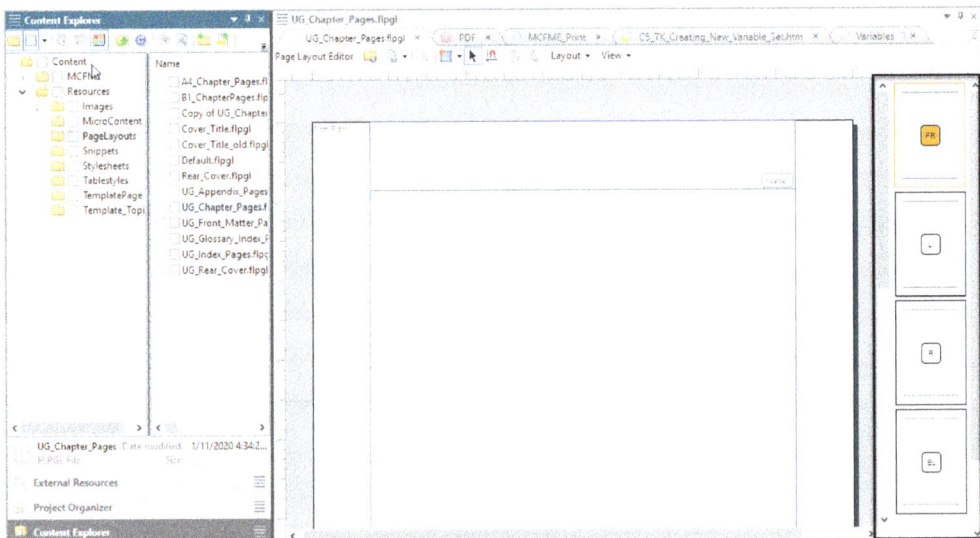

Figure 6-7. Adding Page Layout Page Types.

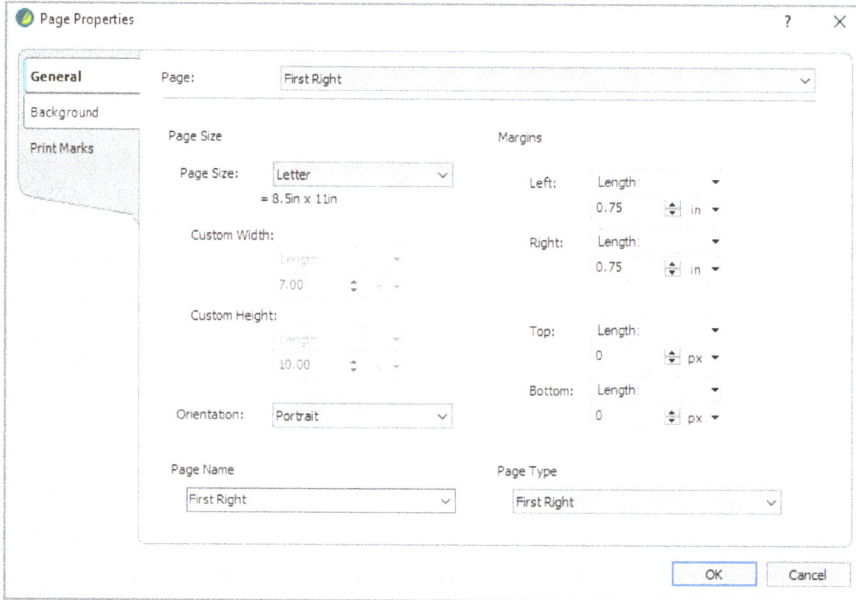

Figure 6-8. Adding Page Properties — General Tab Properties.

QUICK STEPS: ADDING AND REMOVING PAGES IN PAGE LAYOUT FILE

STEP	ACTION
1	Open the Page Layout Editor to the desired file. The page types are displayed in the Page Overview Bar.
2	To remove a page, click on the thumbnail in the Page Overview Bar (right-most pane), for example **Title**, **FL**, **FR**, **L**, **R**, **EL**, **ER**, **E**, or **N**, and right-click and select **Remove**.
3	To add a new page, right-click in the Page Overview Bar (right-most pane), and select **Add Page**; or click on the **Page Properties** drop-down and select **Add Page** > select **Page Type**, for example, **Title Page**, **First Page**, **First Left**, **First Right**, **Left**, or **Right**.
4	To remove a page type, select the thumbnail in the Page Overview Bar (right-most pane), right-click and select **Remove Page**; or click the **Page Properties** drop-down and select **Remove Page**.

TIP: For a group of user documents that all have the same major sections (and layout of each section), for example, Title and Copyright, Front Matter, Chapter Pages, Glossary, and Index, then a single set of page layout files (a file for each of the sections), may serve for all of the documents.

CONFIGURING PAGE LAYOUT PAGE PROPERTIES

BASIC CONCEPT

The page layout file for a given section of your book or document will generally include several pages. Each page is represented by a thumbnail image, on the Page Overview, with a letter abbreviation indicating the page type — for example, **FL** (First Left), **FR** (First Right), **L** (Left), **R** (Right), and **EL** (Empty Left). The first step is to configure the properties of each of the pages defined in the page layout file.

ESSENTIAL ELEMENTS

When configuring page layout pages, you will use three dialog tabs using the **Page Properties** dialog. The **General** tab, to specify the **Page Size**, **Margins**, **Page Name**, and **Page Type**; the **Background** tab, to establish a background Image and background **Color** (solid or gradient), if applicable for the page; and the **Print Marks** tab, to specify **Bleed** parameters for print jobs.

APPLICATION TIPS

In Flare, each Page in the page layout has a default name similar to the page type. So, the default names are **Title**, **Empty Left**, **Empty Right**, **First Left**, **First Right**, **Left**, **Right**, and **Empty**. Although you can assign a unique name to each page in the **Page Properties** file, it is less confusing and simpler to stick with the default names, as there will be no conflict among different layout files.

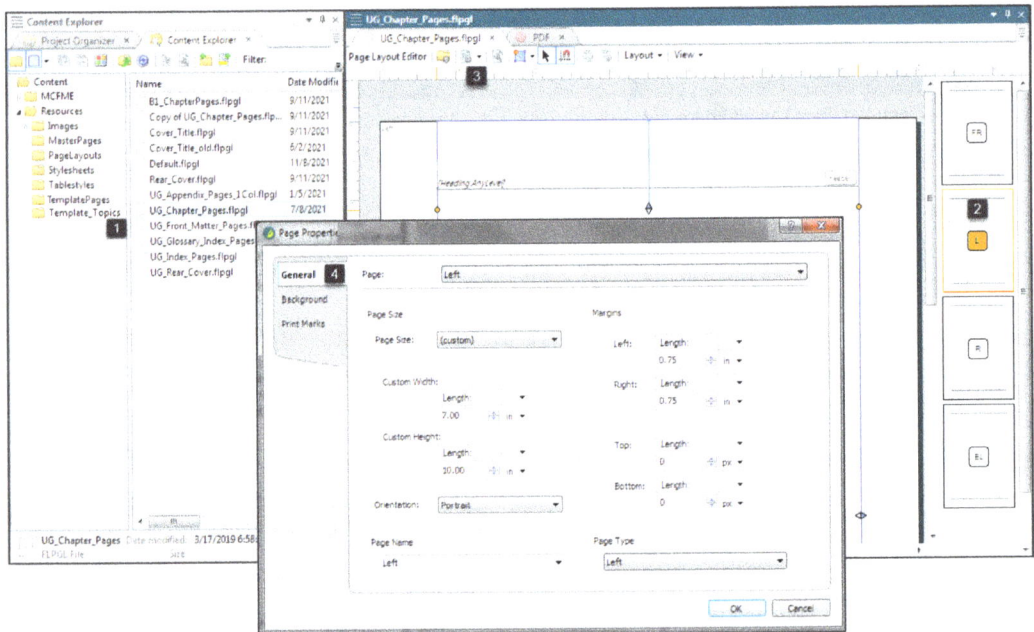

Figure 6-9. Configuring Page Layout Page Properties — General Settings.

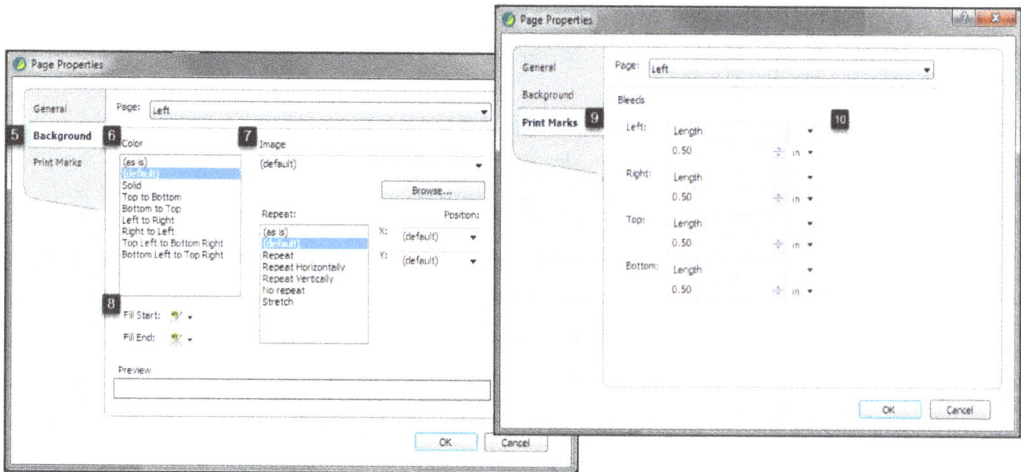

Figure 6-10. Configuring Page Layout Page Properties — a) Background Settings b) Print Settings.

QUICK STEPS: CONFIGURING PAGE LAYOUT PAGE PROPERTIES

STEP	ACTION
1	Open the Page Layout Editor to the desired file. The pages are displayed in the Page Overview Bar.
2	Double-click on the thumbnail of the page whose basic properties you wish to configure, for example, **Title**, **FR**, **L**, **R**, **EL**, **ER**, **E**, or **N**; or right-click on the thumbnail and select **Page Properties**.
3	Click the **General** tab, to specify the **Page Size** drop-down, **Orientation**, **Margins**, and **Page Name**.
4	a) Use the **Page Size** drop-down to select a standard size or choose **Custom** to specify a **Custom Width** and **Custom Height** in **inches**, **pixels**, or other unit.
	b) Select **Orientation** as **Portrait** or **Landscape**; use **Page Name** to enter a unique name for the page or use the default (same as Page Type).
	c) Use **Margins** to specify **Left**, **Right**, **Top**, and **Bottom** page margins (distance from content and page edge), in **inches**, **pixels**, or other unit.
5	Click the **Background** tab, to specify any page background **Color**, or **Image**, and image **Repeat** options.
6	Under **Color**, choose **Solid** or a gradient option (for example, **Top to Bottom** or **Bottom to Top**); then use **Fill Start** and **Fill End** drop-downs to select a start and end gradient color; if applicable, use the **Image** drop-down and select **None**, or use **Browse** to find and select an image to insert in the background. Use **Repeat** to select an option, use **X** to align the image horizontally and **Y** to align vertically.
7	Click the **Print Marks** tab, to specify print bleed parameters if applicable.
8	If applicable, under **Bleed**, use the **Left**, **Right**, **Top**, and **Bottom** to specify the bleed length in **inches**, **pixels**, or other unit of length.
9	Click **OK** to save your **Page Properties** modifications.
10	Repeat the procedure, from **Step 2**, to configure additional pages until properties are done for all pages.
11	Click the **Save** button to save your work.

ADDING PAGE LAYOUT HEADER AND FOOTER FRAMES

BASIC CONCEPT

Adding a header and footer frame to the pages in each of the sections of your document can be an essential page layout design element. The header and footer frames can display the content you want readers to see at the page top and page bottom as they turn each page. Once you place header and footer frames in the page layout, you can insert Flare system variables and user variables to display essential information in the left and right-page headers and footers. For example, you can display the system date and time, page numbers, book title, chapter or section headings, or custom text or images.

ESSENTIAL ELEMENTS

Before placing and configuring layout header or footer frames, the basic page properties, like the page size, orientation, and background for the given page, should already be defined. You must specify the frame parameters, **Size**, **Position**, and **Padding** for the header and footer frames on each page of your layout file. Generally, the frame size (**Width** and **Height**) are the same for the footer and header. The distance from the top is naturally greater for the footer, but the left position is typically the same.

APPLICATION TIPS

You can only place a single header frame and a single footer frame on a page. If a header or footer frame already exists, you cannot add a new one to the layout. You can only modify an existing header or footer frame. Also, you may add or remove a header frame or footer as required.

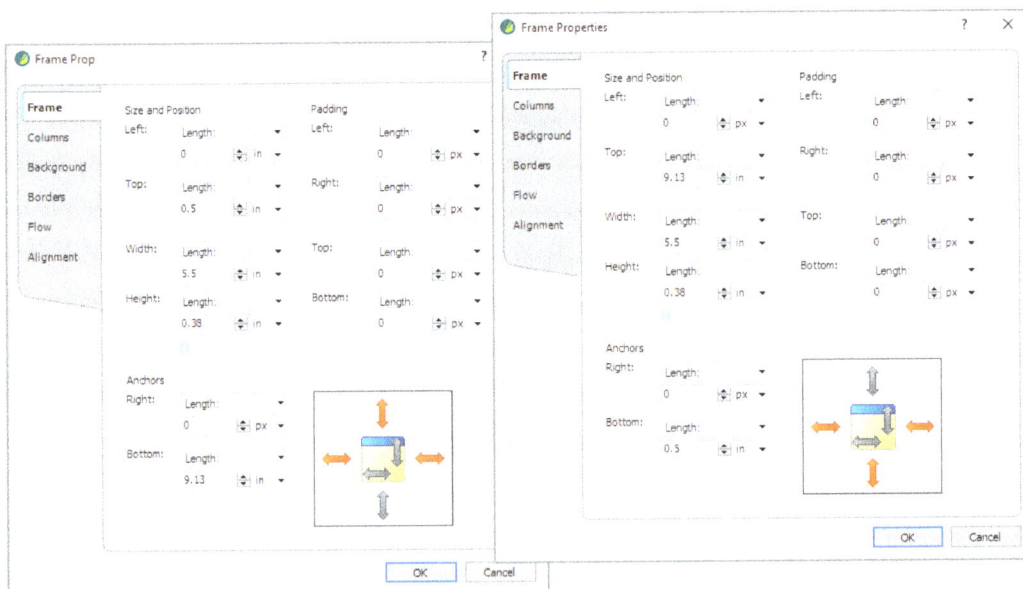

Figure 6-11. a) Header Frame Properties and b) Footer Frame Properties.

QUICK STEPS: ADDING PAGE LAYOUT HEADER AND FOOTER FRAMES

STEP	ACTION
1	Open the Page Layout Editor to the desired file. The page types are displayed in the Page Overview Bar.
2	First, ensure that the basic page properties like **Page Size** and **Orientation** are already defined for each of the pages in the open page layout file. See *Configuring Page Layout Page Properties*.
3	From the editor ribbon, click **View** to set a few preferences to enhance the editing window; for example, **View** > **Horizontal Ruler**; **Vertical Ruler**; page **Margins**; or **Fit to Height** to show the entire page.
4	Click the horseshoe-like icon, on the Editor ribbon, to enable the **Snap-Frame** option, to appropriately snap and align an inserted frame to other page objects — for example, snap to the page margins.
5	Right-click on the ruler edge and set desired units of measure to **inches**, **pixels**, **points**, or **centimeters**.
6	Select the thumbnail (**FR**, **L**, **R**, **EL**, **ER**, **E**, or **N**) of the page you wish to configure a header. The page opens in the page layout editing window.
7	(Skip step if a page header already exist). Click **New Frame Mode** drop-down and select **New Header Frame Mode**. Click and drag your cursor to create the header rectangle.
8	Click the **Frame** tab, to specify the body frame settings for **Size and Position**, **Padding**, and **Anchors**. Use the drop-down to the right of the value fields, to set unit of measure for each parameter.
9	Use **Left** to specify distance from the left margin; use **Top** to specify distance from top margin; specify the **Width** and **Height** of the frame. The height is the difference in length from the start measurement to the end measurement. The width and height can only be modified if anchored frames are disabled.
10	For more than 1-column, click **Columns** tab, to specify column **Count**, **Gap**, and a **Column Divider**.
11	Use **Count** field to specify number of columns; and use **Gap** to specify the distance between columns, in **inches**, **pixels**, or other unit. If applicable, use **Column Divider** to specify a separating rule **Style** (Solid, Double, Dashed, or Dotted); then specify the rule **Width**, **Margin Top**, **Margin Bottom**, and **Color**.
12	Click the **Background** tab, to specify frame background **Color**, **Image**, and image **Repeat** options.
13	Under **Color**, choose **Solid** or a gradient option (for example, **Top to Bottom** or **Bottom to Top**); then use **Fill Start** and **Fill End** drop-downs to select a start and end gradient color; if applicable, use the **Image** drop-down and select **None**, or use **Browse** to find and select an image to insert in the background. Use **Repeat** to select an option, use **X** to align the image horizontally and **Y** to align vertically.
14	Click the **Borders** tab, to specify frame borders if applicable.
15	Use the drop down fields **Left**, **Right**, **Top**, and **Bottom** to specify the line width in **inches**, **pixels**, or other unit of length, for the left, right, top, and bottom borders of the frame, respectively. **Note:** Use the left-half of the field group to specify line width, and second-half of the field group to specify line color.
16	Click **OK** to save your modifications to the **Frame Properties**.

> **TIP:** You can configure a border on any or all sides of a header or footer frame. To have the effect of a ruler that separates the header content from the body content, add a border of at least 1-px on the bottom edge of the header frame; to have the effect of a ruler that separates the footer content from the body content, then add a border of at least 1-px on the top edge of the footer frame.

ADDING PAGE LAYOUT BODY FRAMES

BASIC CONCEPT

Body frames are placed on a page layout to allow the flow of body content onto a page. In general, the available content for a given page fills one frame before moving on to the next frame, unless there is no more content or there is an explicit break command in one of your styles that issues a break command to move to the next frame. Styles can imbed a **Page Break**, **Frame Break**, or **Column Break**.

ESSENTIAL ELEMENTS

Depending on the page type, how you arrange your content, and how you want it to flow can help determine the number of body frames needed on a given page. For example, although not limited, Left and Right pages typically have a single body frame, so the body content for these pages will flow from start to end of the left page (frame) and continue to the right page (frame) and repeat until the end.

Let's say on a First Right chapter page, you have two chunks of content — 1) Chapter Number and Title, and 2) and a one-paragraph introduction followed by a mini-TOC. You could decide on a single body frame or two since you know the page area this content will require.

APPLICATION TIPS

If two body frames, body[1] and body[2], are used in the previous example, then the style class for Chapter Title would need a break command to **Frame Break** > **After** > **Always**, to push the mini-TOC and introductory paragraph to the next frame. Otherwise, a single body frame that is large enough would work as well. However, using the **Break** command in styles offers better control of flow.

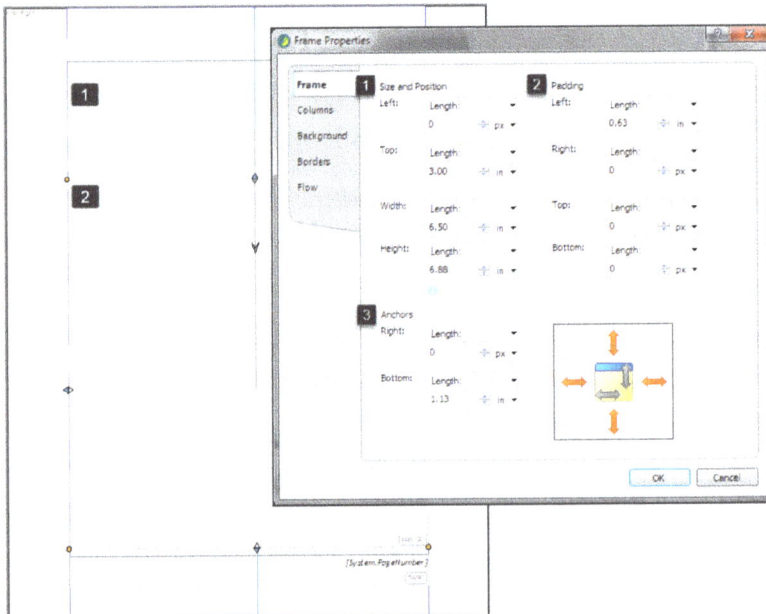

Figure 6-12. Page Layout Page with Body 1 and Body Frame 2.

QUICK STEPS: ADDING PAGE LAYOUT BODY FRAMES

STEP	ACTION
1	Open the Page Layout Editor to the desired file. The page types are displayed in the Page Overview Bar.
2	First, ensure that the basic page properties like **Page Size** and **Orientation** are already defined for each of the pages in the open page layout file. See *Configuring Page Layout Page Properties*.
3	From the editor ribbon, click **View** to set a few preferences to enhance the editing window; for example, **View** > **Horizontal Ruler**; **Vertical Ruler**; page **Margins**; or **Fit to Height** to show the entire page.
4	Click the horseshoe-like icon, on the Editor ribbon, to enable the **Snap-Frame** option, to appropriately snap and align an inserted frame to other page objects — for example, snap to the page margins.
5	Right-click on the ruler edge and set desired units of measure to **inches**, **pixels**, **points**, or **centimeters**.
6	Select the thumbnail (**FR**, **L**, **R**, **EL**, **ER**, **E**, or **N**) of the page you wish to configure a body frame. The page opens in the page layout editing window, and may have some number of frames already defined.
7	(Skip step if not adding a new body frame). Click **New Frame Mode** drop-down and select **New Body Frame Mode**. Click and drag your cursor to create the body frame rectangle.
8	Click the **Frame** tab, to specify the body frame settings for **Size and Position**, **Padding**, and **Anchors**. Use the drop-down to the right of the value fields, to set unit of measure for each parameter.
9	Use **Left** to specify distance from the left margin; use **Top** to specify distance from top margin; specify the **Width** and **Height** of the frame. The height is the difference in length from the start measurement to the end measurement. The width and height can only be modified if anchored frames are disabled.
10	For more than 1-column, click **Columns** tab, to specify column **Count**, **Gap**, and a **Column Divider**.
11	Use **Count** field to specify number of columns; and use **Gap** to specify the distance between columns, in **inches**, **pixels**, or other unit. If applicable, use **Column Divider** to specify a separating rule **Style** (Solid, Double, Dashed, or Dotted); then specify the rule **Width**, **Margin Top**, **Margin Bottom**, and **Color**.
12	Click the **Background** tab, to specify any frame background **Color**, **Image**, and image **Repeat** options.
13	Under **Color**, choose **Solid** or a gradient option (for example, **Top to Bottom** or **Bottom to Top**); then use **Fill Start** and **Fill End** drop-downs to select a start and end gradient color; if applicable, use the **Image** drop-down and select **None**, or use **Browse** to find and select an image to insert in the background. Use **Repeat** to select an option, use **X** to align the image horizontally and **Y** to align vertically.
14	Click the **Borders** tab, to specify frame borders if applicable.
15	Use the drop-down fields **Left**, **Right**, **Top**, and **Bottom** to specify the line width in **inches**, **pixels**, or other unit of length, for the left, right, top, and bottom borders of the frame, respectively. **Note:** Use the left-half of the field group to specify line width, the second-half of the field group to specify line color.
16	Click **OK** to save your **Page Properties** modifications.
17	Repeat the procedure from **Step 6**, to add and configure additional body frames.
18	Click the **Save** button to save your work.

INSERTING PAGE HEADER CONTENT

BASIC CONCEPT

Once you place header frames in page layout files, essential information can be inserted and displayed in the left-page and right-page headers. Without the header frames in place, you cannot insert content. When you place content in the page header of a given page type, that content will be repeated on every page of that type in the page layout file. If no content is inserted in the header frame, for example, the header of a First Right page, then no content is displayed on a page of the same type.

ESSENTIAL ELEMENTS

You can insert header content on pages wherever a header frame has been placed. You can also choose not to insert content in specific headers. For example, in a Chapter Pages layout file that has header frames installed on the First Right (FR), Left (L), Right (R), and Empty Left (EL), you may choose not to insert any content on the first page of each chapter. You may, however, decide to place content in the Left page header, Right page header, and on the Empty page header.

To add content to a header, you must select the page header and press F2 to enable editing. You can choose to align the content to the left, right, or center in each header. In addition to inserting whatever content you wish to appear in a left or right header, you can also insert variables from user-defined variable sets, **Heading** variable sets, and **System** variable sets.

APPLICATION TIPS

Consider aligning left-header content to the left and right header content to the right. In this way, the content will display at opposite ends of the left and right pages. You may also consider center aligning both the left and right header. In this way, the content displays opposite each other in the page center.

Also, consider creating a table stylesheet with no header or borders, 2-rows, and 2-columns. Insert the table into the header to gain more fields for content placement and better left/right alignment control.

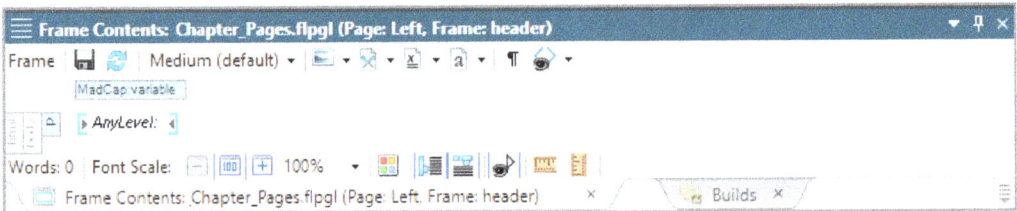

Figure 6-13. Left Page Header Frame.

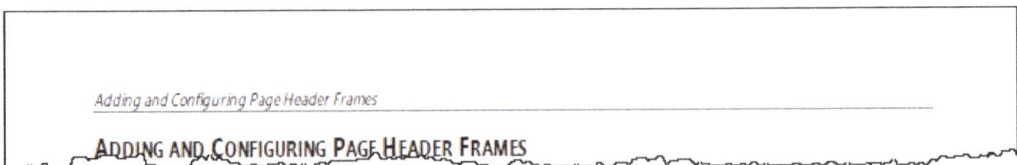

Figure 6-14. Left Page Header — Actual Page.

☰ **Frame Contents: Chapter_Pages.flpgl (Page: Right, Frame: header)***	▼ ⏻ ✕

Frame 💾 🔁 print ▾ 🖼 ▾ ⬚ ▾ 𝓍 ▾ a ▾ ¶ 👁 ▾ 🔳 🔳

> MadCap:variable

▸ *AnyLevel* ◂

Words: 0 ┆ Font Scale: ⊟ 🔢 ⊞ 100% ▾ ┆ 🔲 📊 🖼 📑 🔳 🔳

🔲 Frame Contents: Chapter_Pages.flpgl (Page: Right, Frame: header)* ✕ ⎜ 🔳 Builds ✕

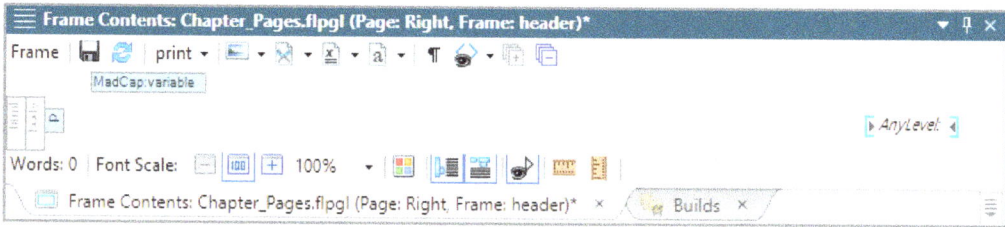

Figure 6-15. Right Page Header Frame.

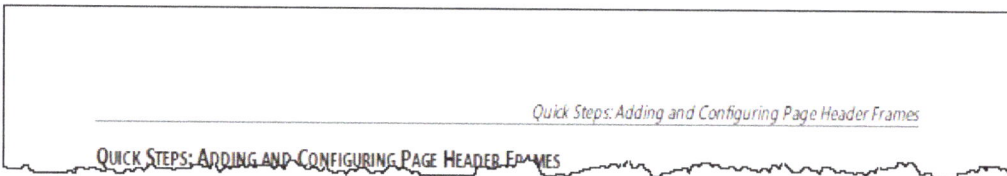

Quick Steps: Adding and Configuring Page Header Frames

QUICK STEPS: ADDING AND CONFIGURING PAGE HEADER FRAMES

Figure 6-16. Right Page Header — Actual Page.

QUICK STEPS: INSERTING PAGE HEADER CONTENT

STEP	ACTION
1	Open the Page Layout Editor to the desired file. The page types are displayed in the Page Overview Bar.
2	Select the thumbnail (**FR**, **L**, **R**, **EL**, **ER**, **E**, or **N**) of the page where you wish to insert header content. The page opens in the page layout editing window.
3	In the editing window, click the header (the frame is highlighted) and press **F2** to enable for editing.
4	The **Frame Contents** window is opened with the header, as a new pane at the workspace bottom. The file name and the page name appears in the window title bar. **Note**: See the command ribbon across the window top, and the visual indicator icons across the window bottom. You may need to open the window wider if the bottom ribbon is not visible. Move the cursor slowly toward the window title bar until the double arrow head icon appears for expanding the window.
5	If not already displayed, in the frame window, set the **Medium** drop-down to **Print**.
6	Click inside the **Frame Content** window at the position where you want to insert content. If there is a table inside the header then click inside the cell where you want to insert text, an image, or a variable.
7	If applicable, click the **Insert Image** button 🖼 ▾ to open the dialog and select an image to insert; or use the drop-down to select a **Recently Used Image** or a **Pinned Image**.
8	If applicable, click the **Insert Variable** button 𝓍 ▾ to open the dialog, and from the **Variables** window, select a **Variable Set** from which to choose a variable, then select a specific variable; or select a variable from **Recently Used Variables** or a **Pinned Variables**. Click **OK** to insert the variable.
9	With your cursor inserted anywhere in (or just in front of) the content, use the **Paragraph** tool on the **Home** ribbon, to align your text, image, or variable content **Left**, **Center**, **Right**, or **Justified**.
10	Click the **Save** button, in the **Frame Content** window, before leaving the window.

INSERTING PAGE FOOTER CONTENT

BASIC CONCEPT

Once you place footer frames in page layout files, essential information can be inserted and displayed in the left-page and right-page footers. Without the footer frames in place, you cannot insert content. When you place content in the page footer of a given page type, that content will be repeated on every page of that type in the page layout file. If no content is inserted in the footer frame, for example, an Empty Left, or First Right page, then no content is displayed in the output for those pages.

ESSENTIAL ELEMENTS

You can insert footer content on pages wherever you have placed a footer frame. You can also choose not to insert content in specific footers. For example, in a Chapter Pages layout file that has footer frames installed on the First Right (FR), Left (L), Right (R), and Empty Left (EL), you may choose not to insert any content on the first page of each chapter. You may, however, decide to place content in the Left page footer, Right page footer, and on the Empty page footer.

To add content to a footer, you must select the page footer and press F2 to enable editing. You can choose to align the content to the left, right, or center in each footer. In addition to inserting whatever content you wish to appear in left or right-footer, you can also insert variables from user-defined variable sets, **Heading** variable sets, and **System** variable sets.

APPLICATION TIPS

Consider aligning left-footer content to the left and right-footer content to the right. In this way, the content will display at opposite ends of the left and right pages. You may also consider center aligning both the left and right-footer. In this way, the content displays opposite each other in the page center.

Also, consider creating a table stylesheet with no header or borders, 2-rows, and 2-columns. Insert the table into the footer to gain more fields for content placement and better left/right alignment control.

Figure 6-17. Left Page Footer Frame.

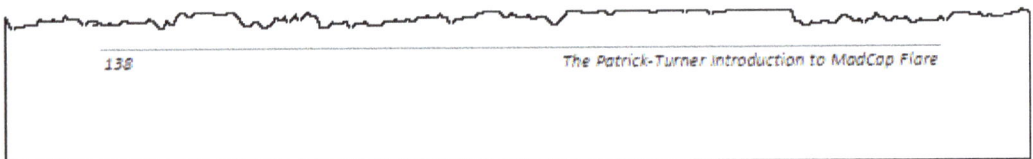

Figure 6-18. Left Page Footer — Actual Page.

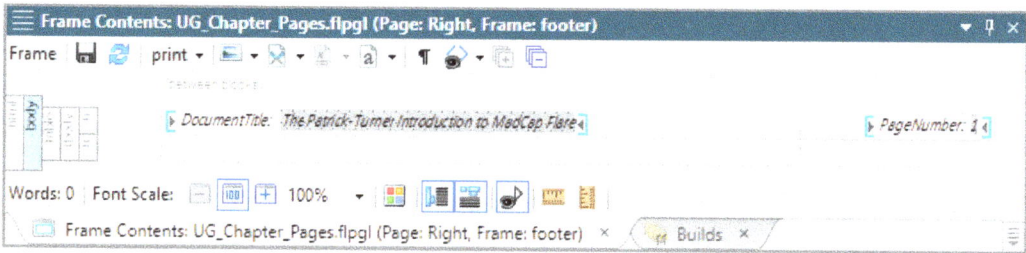

Figure 6-19. Right Page Footer Frame.

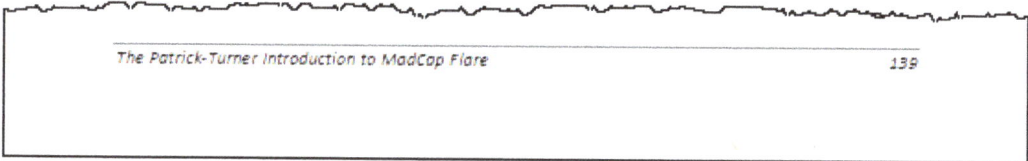

Figure 6-20. Right Page Footer Frame — Actual Page.

QUICK STEPS: INSERTING PAGE FOOTER CONTENT

STEP	ACTION
1	Open the Page Layout Editor to the desired file. The page types are displayed in the Page Overview Bar.
2	Select the thumbnail (**FR**, **L**, **R**, **EL**, **ER**, **E**, or **N**) of the page you wish to insert footer content. The page opens in the page layout editing window.
3	In the editing window, click the footer (the frame is highlighted) and press **F2** to enable for editing.
4	The **Frame Contents** window is opened with the footer, as a new tab at the workspace bottom. The file name and the page name appears in the window title bar.
	Note: See the command ribbon across the window top, and the visual indicator icons across the window bottom. You may need to open the window wider if the bottom ribbon is not visible. Move the cursor slowly toward the window title bar until the double arrow head icon appears for expanding the window.
5	If not already displayed, in the frame window, set the **Medium** drop-down to **Print**.
6	Click inside the **Frame Content** window at the position where you want to insert content. If there is a table inside the footer then click inside the cell where you want to insert text, an image, or a variable.
7	If applicable, click the **Insert Image** button ▼ to open the dialog and select an image to insert; or use the drop-down to select a **Recently Used Image** or a **Pinned Image**.
8	If applicable, click the **Insert Variable** button ▼ to open the dialog, and from the **Variables** window, select a **Variable Set** from which to choose a variable, then select a specific variable; or select a variable from **Recently Used Variables** or a **Pinned Variables**. Click **OK** to insert the variable.
9	With your cursor inserted anywhere in (or just in front of) the content, use the **Paragraph** tool on the **Home** ribbon, to align your text, image, or variable content **Left**, **Center**, **Right**, or **Justified**.
10	Click the **Save** button, in the **Frame Content** window, before leaving the window.

ANCHORING PAGE LAYOUT FRAMES

BASIC CONCEPT

In Flare, the frame anchoring option allows you to lock down the frames on a page layout to the page margins. In doing so, the page layout frames are automatically resized if the page size is enlarged or decreased at some later point.

ESSENTIAL ELEMENTS

When it comes to anchoring the frames in your page layout, there are three options — 1) leaving the frames un-anchored (disabled); in this case, the appearance of pages in the output will be based exactly on the set margins, and if the page size changes the output appearance may become unreadable 2) you can selectively lock the frame **Top**, **Bottom**, **Left**, and **Right** side anchors to the page margins, which locks the distance from the frame edge to the margin; or 3) you can set the inside anchors, using the horizontal and vertical arrows. These arrows center the frame horizontally and vertically on the page.

APPLICATION TIPS

Before anchoring page frames, ensure that the basic page properties like **Page Size**, **Orientation**, and **Margins** are already defined, for each of the pages, in the page layout file. Page width and height can only be modified if anchored frames are disabled.

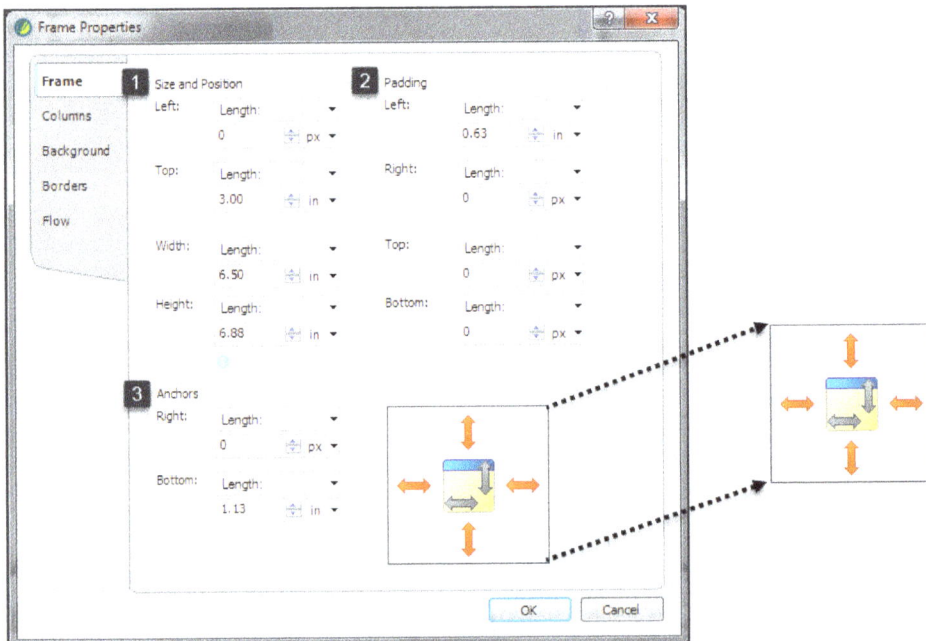

Figure 6-21. Anchoring Page Frames to Page Borders or to Page Center.

QUICK STEPS: ANCHORING PAGE LAYOUT FRAMES

STEP	ACTION
1	Open the Page Layout Editor to the desired file. The page types are displayed in the Page Overview Bar.
2	First, ensure that the basic page properties like **Page Size** and **Orientation** are already defined for each of the pages in the open page layout file. See *Configuring Page Layout Page Properties*.
3	Select the thumbnail (**FR**, **L**, **R**, **EL**, **ER**, **E**, or **N**) of the page where you want to enable anchoring options. The page opens in the page layout editing window.
4	Double-click on a **Frame** where you intend to specify settings for **Anchors** options.
5	Click on the **Frame** tab.
6	Click on the arrows outside of the box to anchor the frame to the **Top**, **Bottom**, **Left**, and **Right** sides of the frame. You can choose to enable or disable any of the outside anchors.
7	Click on the vertical or horizontal arrows inside of the box to anchor the frame by centering it vertically or horizontally on the page. You can also select both arrows. If you anchor horizontally, the left and right anchors are disabled; if you center the frame vertically, the top and bottom anchors are disabled.
8	The width and height can only be modified if anchored frames are disabled.
9	Click **OK** to save your modifications to the **Frame Properties**.
10	Repeat the procedure from **Step 4**, to anchor a different frame on the current page.
11	Repeat the procedure from **Step 2**, to select a new page where you want to anchor the frames.
12	Click the **Save** button to save your work.

> **NOTE:** Before applying the anchor settings, ensure that you have specified the settings for the frame size and position, using the fields **Left**, **Right**, **Top**, **Bottom**, **Width**, and **Height**.

ADDING A FLARE TEMPLATE PAGE FILE

BASIC CONCEPT

In Flare, the template page element serves both print and online outputs, but you will use it primarily in online outputs. While there is no limit on the number of template pages you may define and use in your project, a typical HTML5 output may have somewhere between one and three template pages. Once you have created one or more template page files, you can configure the placement and arrangement of various Flare proxies on the page to manage the flow of content in your online outputs.

ESSENTIAL ELEMENTS

To ensure the arrangement and flow you want for your project's various topics, you may need to create different template pages to cover the diverse needs in the online output.

A previously described online output scenario for a business site offers insight into how you can determine the template pages requirement. In this scenario, we use a total of three template pages. We might apply one template page to a unique home page arrangement; we could apply a second template page to three topics, each of which is a landing page of three different segments of the site, all of which have a similar layout. Finally, we could apply a third template page to the remaining topics.

APPLICATION TIPS

You can configure a template page to use a variety of Flare proxy elements that assist in flowing specific content onto the pages of online outputs. Elements you place on a template page are repeated on every topic the template page is applied. Some example proxy elements you might put in a template page include search bars, breadcrumbs, topic toolbars, menus, mini-TOCs.

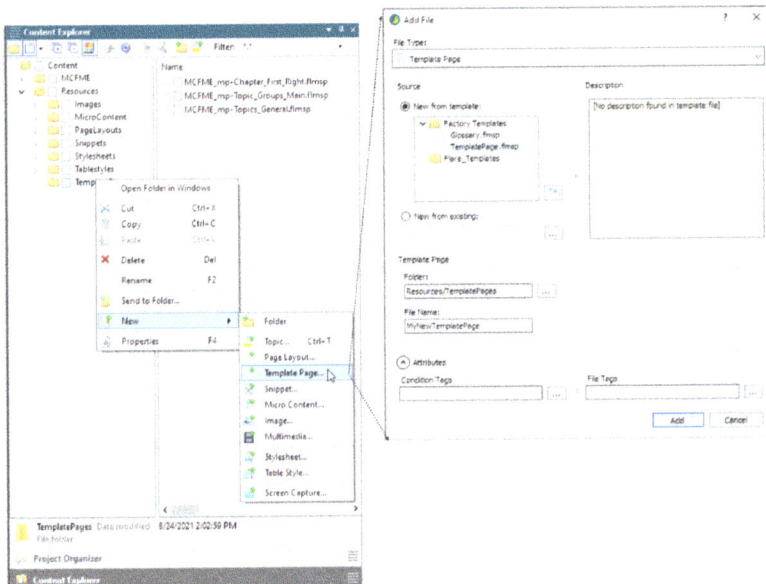

Figure 6-22. New Template Page Option Selected — Add File Dialog with Template Page Option Set.

QUICK STEPS: ADDING A FLARE TEMPLATE PAGE FILE

STEP	ACTION
1	Select the **TemplatePages** folder, in the **Resources** subfolder of the **Content Explorer**, or find and select the folder in which you wish to create the new template page file.
2	Right-click and select **New** > **Template Page**. The **Add File** dialog opens.
3	Ensure that the **File Type** is set for **Template Page**.
4	**To create the new template page use one of the following:** **a)** From Templates: Set the **Source** for **New From Template**, then select the **TemplatePage** template from the **Factory Templates** folder or choose a template from a user-defined **Custom Templates** folder. **b)** From Existing: Set the **Source** for **New From Existing**, and use the browse button ⌐…⌐ to locate the existing template page file.
5	Under **Template Page**, use the **Folder** field and choose the default folder (**Resources/TemplatePages**), or browse and choose another folder in which to store the new template page file.
6	Use the **File Name** field to specify a name for the new template page. For example, **MyHomePage.flmsp**.
7	Click > **Add** to save the new template page file.

> 💡 **TIP:** The template page that should be applied to most of your topics, should be entered in the **Template Page** field on the **Advanced** tab of the HTML5 target file. All other template pages can be applied to specific topics or groups of topics, using the **Topic Properties** for those topics.

CONFIGURING TEMPLATE PAGES TO ARRANGE AND FLOW ONLINE CONTENT

BASIC CONCEPT

Similar to page layouts that arrange and flow topic content into your print outputs, template pages support the arrangement and flow of content onto online output pages. In online outputs, project content is arranged and flowed onto pages based on the individual template pages, the content placeholders (proxies) they each contain, and topics to which the template pages are applied.

ESSENTIAL ELEMENTS

You can choose from various Flare content placeholder (proxy) elements to configure the flow of different content types onto pages of online outputs. Elements you place on a template page are repeated in the output on each topic to which you apply the template page. Typical proxy elements include the breadcrumbs proxy, topic body proxy, and mini-TOC proxy.

A topic's body content flows when you use a body proxy; the user menu navigation path flows and displays at the top of each topic when you use a breadcrumb proxy, and the headings of a topic can be listed when you use a mini-TOC proxy. For content you want to display in the header of each page, you must insert it on the template page just above the body proxy. Any content you wish to display in the footer of each page, you must insert on the template page just below the body proxy.

APPLICATION TIPS

Header content, inserted on a template page, above the body proxy, might include a company logo; and footer content, inserted on a template page below the body proxy, might consist of company name, address, and logo.

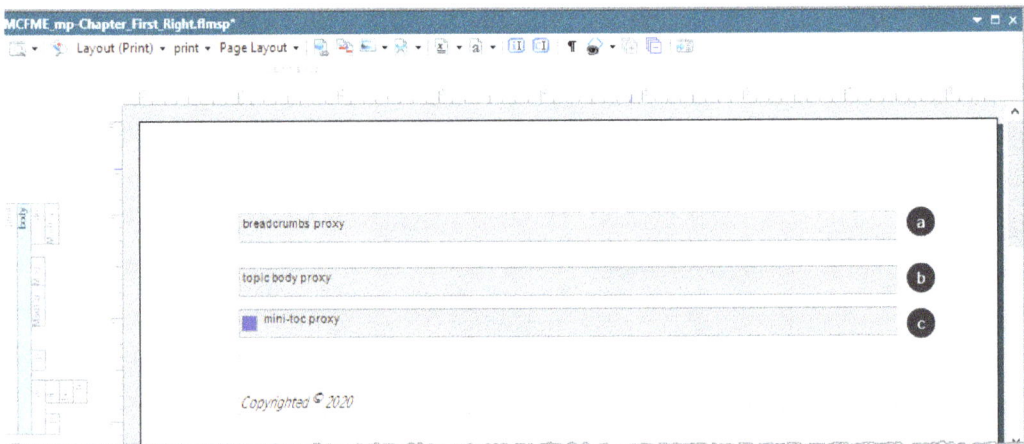

Figure 6-23. TemplatePage in XML Editor with a) Breadcrumb Proxy, b) Topic Body Proxy, and c) Mini-TOC Proxy.

QUICK STEPS: CONFIGURING TEMPLATE PAGES TO ARRANGE AND FLOW ONLINE CONTENT

STEP	ACTION
1	Open any of the template page files that you have created and want to insert proxies to flow content. You may have multiple template page files, each of which will be applied to a different group of topics.
2	Place the cursor at a point in the template page where you want to insert a proxy. As required, do any or all of the following: **a)** From the **Insert** ribbon, click the **Proxy** drop-down > **Insert Breadcrumbs Proxy**, to flow current user navigation trail through menus and topics and display at the top of each topic. **b)** From the **Insert** ribbon, click the **Proxy** drop-down > **Insert Body Proxy**, to flow the main content of each topic onto the page. **c)** From the **Insert** ribbon, click the **Proxy** drop-down > **Insert Mini-TOC Proxy**y, to flow topic header content into the mini-TOC. Edit the mini-TOC to determine the **TOC Depth** (headings to output in the TOC).
3	**To insert header content**: Use the keyboard up-arrow to move the cursor just above the body proxy that you inserted, and then type or insert any content you want to display as a header on each topic to which the template page is applied.
4	**To insert footer content**: Use the keyboard down-arrow to move the cursor just below the body proxy that you inserted, and then type or insert any content you want to display as a footer on each topic to which the template page is applied.

> **NOTE:** Remember that some proxies, for example the **Search Bar Proxy**, may not need to be inserted in a template page if the element is provided in the output skin.

CHAPTER 7

WORKING WITH FLARE TOPICS

INTRODUCING THE FLARE TOPIC EDITOR

Creating, formatting, and editing your project content will involve the Flare Topic editor, whether for online or print targets. There are two such topic editors, or more precisely, one editor with two presentations — an XML Editor View that provides a standard representation like that in Word or FrameMaker; and a Text Editor View that presents the HTML code view of the same topic.

XML EDITOR OVERVIEW

The *XML Editor* is the standard tool for entering your content in Flare, and is opened automatically whenever you open a topic, snippet, or template page. You can open a topic, template page or snippet in the XML editor with a right-click on the file and selecting **Open** or by double-clicking on the file in the Content Explorer. The file opens in the XML Editor window, on a tab labeled with the file name.

Like many other such editors, the XML Editor presents a WYSIWYG view for simple editing. You can quickly type and format your content using standard paragraph editing tools. After familiarizing your-self with the main editor tools, and the basic techniques for applying styles to content, working with topics in the XML Editor will be as user-friendly as with any other WYSIWYG editor.

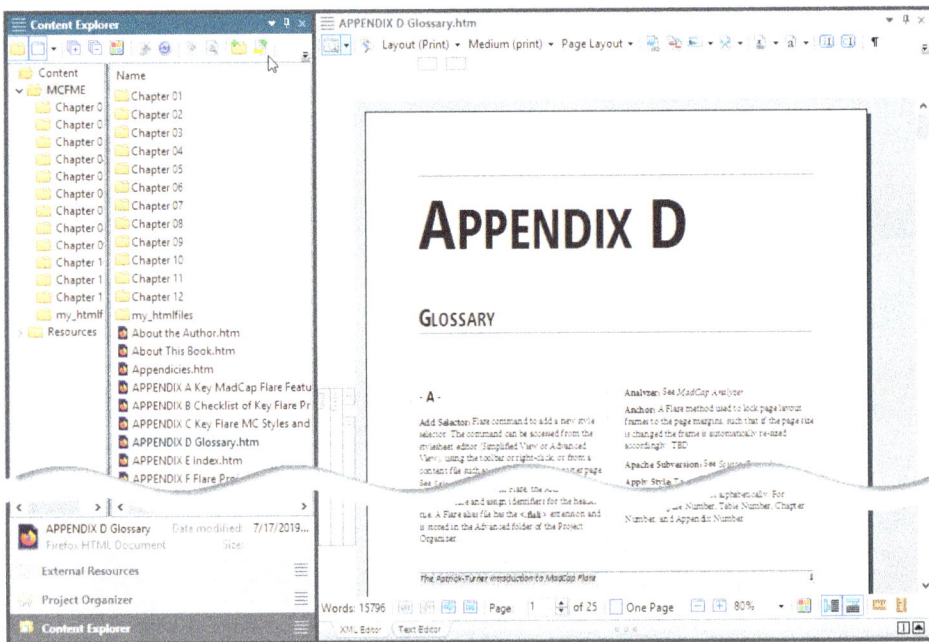

Figure 7-1. Flare Topic Editor — XML Editor View.

XML EDITOR MENU AND TOOLBAR

The first four items on the XML Editor are tools that enhance the viewing options for rendering the topic as you will eventually see it. There are tools for selecting your layout preferences, the stylesheet medium, and the page layout file and page type that the topic will use in the output. These latter tools allow you to view the topic as it will look in the output while you are still editing.

The second set of tools allows you to insert elements and objects into the topic, such as cross-references, variables, images, special characters, and snippets. Finally, the third set of tools allows you to Show/Hide the various visual aids displayed in a given topic. The image below shows Flare XML Editor toolbar buttons and icons, while the table provides a brief description of the most frequently used XML Editor operations.

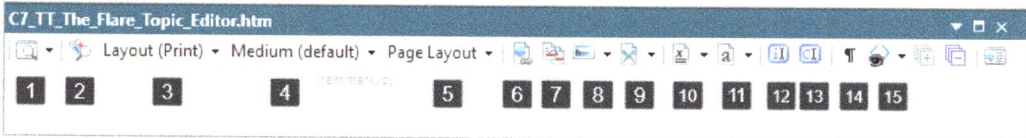

Table 7-1. Flare Topics XML Editor Toolbar Buttons and Commands

Item	Command	Brief Description
1	Preview Target	Click the button to preview the topic based on the primary target, or click the drop-down to select a target to preview the topic.
2	Select Conditional Expression	Set the conditional tags for inclusion or exclusion to form the expression that will determine how Flare will render this topic or specific content.
3	Layout	Select the appropriate **Layout** in which to render and view the open topic.
4	Medium	Select the appropriate stylesheet **Medium** to use in rendering the open topic.
5	Page Layout	Select the appropriate stylesheet **Medium** to use in rendering the open topic.
6	Insert Hyperlink	Open the **Insert Hyperlink** dialog to specify and insert a hyperlink in the text.
7	Insert Cross-Reference	Open **Insert Cross-Reference** dialog to specify and insert a cross-reference.
8	Insert Image	Open the **Insert Image** dialog to insert an image in at the insertion point.
9	Insert Snippet	Open the **Insert Snippet Link** dialog to insert a snippet into the text.
10	Insert Variable	Click the button to open the **Insert Variable** dialog or click the drop-down, to select and insert from the **Recently Used Variables** or **Pinned Variable**s list.
11	Insert Character	Click the button to open the **Insert Character** dialog or click the drop-down, to insert from the **Quick Character** dialog or the **Recently Used Characters**.
12	Toggle Index Entry	Toggle between manual **Index Entry Mode** on/off.
13	Toggle Concept Entry	Toggle between **Concept Entry Mode** on/off.
14	Show/Hide Spaces	Toggle between **Show/Hide** spaces and paragraph markers in text.
15	Show Tags	Use the Show Tags button to view the basic HTML elements tags inline, or use the enable/disable drop-down from various visual indicators.

TEXT EDITOR OVERVIEW

The Text Editor renders the HTML code view of the currently opened topic. Although this would not likely be the preferred method, experienced CSS and HTML users could certainly create and edit topics using the Text Editor. After some use, the Text Editor often becomes a useful way of troubleshooting specific problems or issues you may encounter with some topics presented in the XML Editor.

This view is also helpful when using the Find/Replace utility. As you become more familiar with HTML and CSS code, you too will likely find similar uses of the Text Editor view. With a topic open in the XML Editor, click the Text Editor tab to switch to the corresponding HTML code.

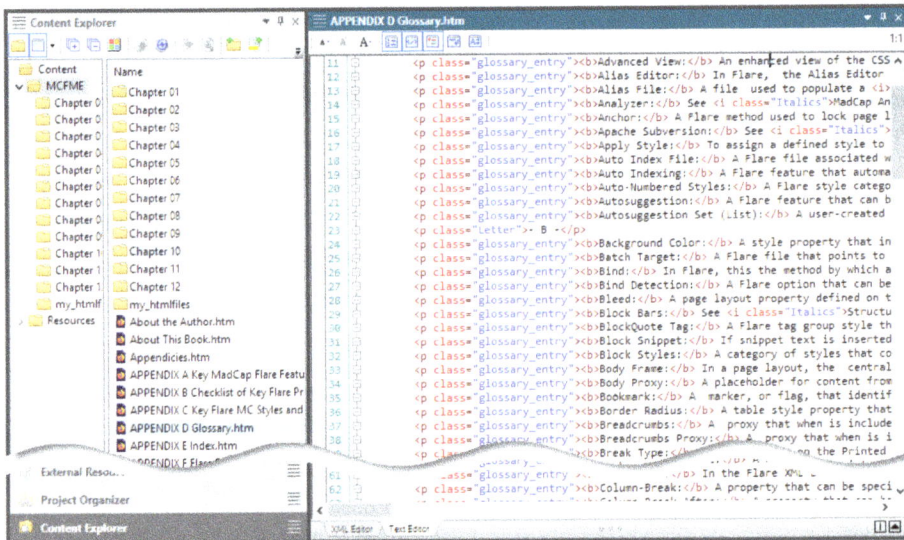

Figure 7-2. Flare Topic Editor—Text Editor View.

TEXT EDITOR MENU AND TOOLBAR

The tools on the Text Editor ribbon are only a few, and these are primarily intended to enhance the user viewing in this mode. First, there are the **Font Size** controls, whereby you can change the font size using three buttons. You can increase the size, decrease the size, and return to the default size. The Show/Hide **Syntax Colors** toggle lets you switch between showing and hiding the HTML-coded syntax for the various block elements and inline elements.

With the aid of highlighted syntax colors, for example, the HTML start and end syntax for each element, and the various highlighted parent and child classes, you'll soon understand the coding. Like most text editors, there is also a **Word Wrap** toggle that lets you get a complete view of long text blocks. You may initially start using the Text Editor in some of your **Find and Replace** searches, but soon you'll see how the Text Editor can sometimes be a vital debugging tool.

USING TOPIC TEMPLATES AND TEMPLATE TOPICS

When it comes to inserting new topics in your project, there are a couple of methods that you can use to simplify your work and minimize any duplication. These methods, which involve using topic templates and template topics, are presented in the following topics.

TOPIC TEMPLATES

Topic Templates, are pre-defined topic elements from which you can create new topics. The new topic will look like the template you based it on — and it will have the name you give it and be stored where you specify. Flare has several factory templates that you can use as the base for creating a new topic. You can also create custom templates that you can use to create other new topics. You can create a custom topic template from scratch or an existing topic that you save as a template.

Suppose you wanted each H1 topic to be created with a particular structure, for example, a paragraph and a bullet list. You could make the topic and save it as your H1 template. The topic would be available from your list of custom templates. In this way, each H1 topic, when created, would have the same structure. When a writer is ready to make a new H1 topic, they will use the option to develop the topic by selecting New from Template and then choosing the H1 Topic Template.

Table 7-2. Useful Flare Factory Topic Templates

Topic Template	Brief Description
TopicForIndex	Based on the Flare index proxy, a new topic based on this template, creates an index topic of terms, in your project, as specified in an Auto-Index file and generated by Flare.
TopicForGlossary	Based on the Flare glossary proxy, a new topic based on this template, creates a glossary topic of key terms as specified in the Glossary file and generated by Flare.
TopicForListOfImages	Based on the Flare List-Of-Proxy, a new topic based on this template, creates a topic that will generate an list of auto-numbered images found in your document.
TopicForListOfTables	Based on the Flare List-Of-Proxy, a new topic based on this template, creates a topic that will generate an list of auto-numbered tables found in your document.
TopicForTOC	Based on the Flare TOC Proxy, a new topic based on this template, creates a topic that generates a TOC of topics in your document with heading levels like H1, H2, and H3.

TEMPLATE TOPICS

Whereas you can create new topics from topic templates, Template Topics is a term that I use to refer to topics previously made for one document, but you can use it in one or more other documents. For this different use, a template topic is not copied or created again, but you would reference it in a TOC where you want to use it. As you develop new TOCs for other books, the HTML files for these Template Topics, if needed, can be dragged from the folder that you have designated for template topics and dropped directly into the new TOC. The following table lists some examples of template topics.

Table 7-3. Examples of Typical Template Topics

Topic Template	Brief Description
Cover Title	Use a cover title page topic template for a group of user documents or manuals that use the same cover design. You could use multi-definition variables to manage specific differences in titles and other cover information.
Copyright Topic	Use a copyright topic template that includes any snippets or variables required to differentiate among different books or documents.
Contents	Use a book TOC topic template that is placed in the front matter of a book. The topic uses a Flare TOC proxy to generate the Contents which is unique for each document.
List of Tables	Use a list-of-tables topic template placed in the front matter of each book. The topic uses a Flare List-Of-Tables proxy to generate a list of tables that is unique to each document.
List of Figures	use a list-of-figures topic template that is placed in the front matter of a book. The topic uses a Flare List-Of-Images proxy to generate a list of images unique to each document.
Glossary	A glossary topic that is placed in the back matter of a book. The topic only contains a Flare glossary proxy to generate a glossary that is unique for each document. In this case, the appropriate glossary file must be selected on the **Glossary** tab of the target file.
Appendix-A	Use an appendix topic template that has a list of industry acronyms and abbreviations.

SUMMARY ON WORKING WITH FLARE TOPICS

Topics are at the core of a Flare project, and as such, Flare offers many tools and utilities that support creating, editing, managing, analyzing, and reporting on topics. As in other chapters, brief tutorials have been presented at the beginning of this chapter to offer a quick overview of working with topics.

The remainder of this chapter presents several of the features, tools, and techniques used to develop and edit topics for print and online targets in your project. Furthermore, examples of tasks such as creating and naming topics, creating topic templates, creating topics from templates, and applying styles to topic content are presented. The following chapter on working with TOCs will continue with operations that support linking to topics both in print and in online modes.

The following checklist offers some tips and guidelines for working with topics in Flare. Some examples of topic-related tasks follow in the remainder of this chapter.

CHECKLIST: WORKING WITH FLARE TOPICS

- *Consider creating topic templates that users can use to generate topic types that you and your team members commonly use in your projects. For example, consider templates for a Cover Title topic, Chapter topic, H1 topic, H2 topic, and Appendix topic.*

- *Consider unique content design element templates for those books or documents with particular design elements you want others to use — for example, a Summary page or a Checklist page.*

- *Consider replacing any imported TOC topic file with a TOC proxy topic to generate a table of contents topic that writers can insert in the front matter section of their book or document.*

- *Use Flare topic templates of commonly used Flare proxies to create proxy topics like TOC proxy, List-of-Tables proxy, List-of-Figures proxy, and Index proxy.*

- *Consider creating topics using Flare proxies for online targets, including TOC proxy, Glossary proxy, List-of-proxy, Index proxy, and the Breadcrumbs proxy.*

- *Remember to use the **Preview Topic** button, located at the left-most position of the Topic Editor ribbon, to get a quick view of how the topic will render when built. Select the appropriate target.*

- *When testing topic changes, you can reduce the number of target builds by using the Preview Topic window to see what the topic will look like when rendered.*

- *Use the **Layout**, **Medium**, and **Page Layout** drop-downs to choose Print Layout or Web Layout, Print or Default medium, and the appropriate page layout file and page type for viewing how the output should appear. These tools provide a more accurate view, while editing, of what a topic will look like for print and online views (even for devices), like Mobile and Tablet.*

- *Many of the elements you insert in topics are available on the Insert ribbon — for example, special characters, tables, images, bookmarks, snippets, variables, cross-references, and page breaks.*

- *See "Basic Guidelines for Moving to Online," for more information on inserting items like popup text boxes, popup topics, drop-down text, and expanding text, used primarily for online outputs.*

NAVIGATING THE XML TOPIC EDITOR

BASIC CONCEPT

The XML Editor is the primary means of editing topics, snippets, and template pages in Flare. You will have a jump start on working with topics by knowing the layout, where things are, and how you will use them. The Topic Editor has two main toolbar ribbons, one across the editor's top and the other across the editor's bottom, for setting workspace visual preferences and editing topics. In addition to these tools, much of the topic work will involve the **Home**, **Insert**, and **Table** ribbons.

ESSENTIAL ELEMENTS

From the **Home** ribbon, you can apply styles from the **Style** drop-down pane or the **Style Window**, with ability to create or edit styles. You also have access to a **Find and Replace** tool that supports total project searches. You can insert different content from the **Insert** ribbon, such as images and screen captures, multimedia objects like movies, videos, slide shows, and link elements like **Cross-References**, **Hyperlinks**, and **Bookmarks**. Finally, from the **Table** ribbon, you can insert tables, add rows and columns, merge and split cells, apply table stylesheets, convert tables to text and text to tables.

APPLICATION TIPS

Start by setting some key visual indicators to simplify your work. Ensure that the appropriate stylesheet Medium is selected, for example, **Print** or **Default**; use the **Page Layout** drop-down and choose the proper **Page Layout** file and **Page** to view the topic. Use the **Show Tags** drop-down to select your view preferences — for example, **Show Block Structure Tags** and **Span Structure Tags**.

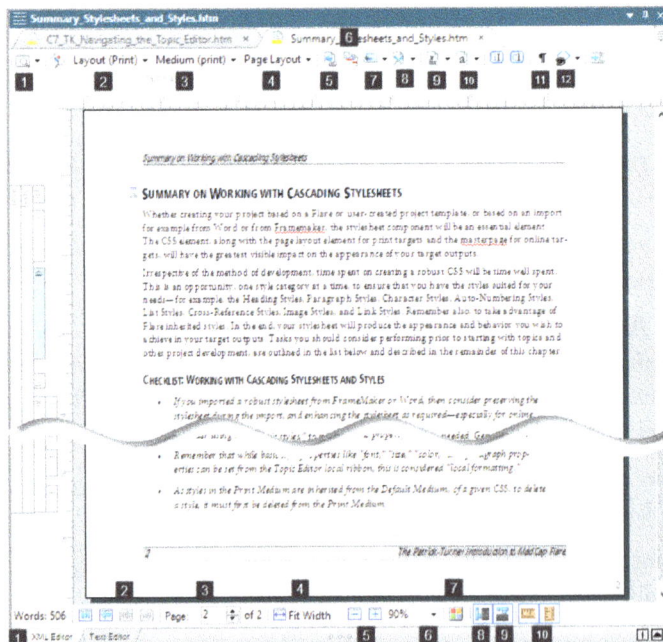

Figure 7-3. Navigating the Topic Editor Toolbar.

QUICK STEPS: NAVIGATING THE XML TOPIC EDITOR — TOP TOOLBAR

STEP	ACTION
0	From the **Content Explorer**, double-click on any topic file (***.html**) to open it in the Topic Editor.
1	Click the topic preview icon, at the ribbon left, to render the topic as it will appear in the Primary target; or use the drop-down and select the desired target to use to render the current topic as it will appear.
2	Click the **Layout** button to select layout mode — **Web**, **Tablet**, **Mobile** or **Print** in which you wish to view the current topic in the topic editor. The associated CSS Medium and Page Layout switch automatically.
3	Click the **Medium** button to select style medium to use — for example, **print**, **mobile**, **tablet**, or **Default**, when working on the current topic. Generally, Print medium for PDF or Word, and Default for online.
4	Click the **Page Layout** button to select the desired page layout file and the specific Page Type to use for working on the current topic. For example, ChapterPages > First Right for the chapter title page.
5	Use the **Insert Hyperlink** button to select and insert any one of several hyperlink options into the topic.
6	Use the **Insert Cross-Reference** button to select and insert to the topic, a Cross-Reference option.
7	Use the **Insert Image** button to find and insert an image or select from a list of recently pinned images.
8	Use the **Insert Snippet** button to insert any snippet or select from a list of recently pinned snippets.
9	Use the **Insert Variable** button to insert a variable from a variable set or from recently pinned variables.
10	Use the **Insert Character** button to insert any of the available normal text or special characters.
11	Click the **Paragraph Marker** button to toggle between **Show/Hide** paragraph markers and spaces.
12	Click the **Show Tags** icon, to toggle between **Show/Hide** all of the various Flare markers in the topic; or click the drop-down arrow to select any one of the markers to toggle between **Show/Hide**.

QUICK STEPS: NAVIGATING THE TOPIC EDITOR — BOTTOM TOOLBAR

STEP	ACTION
1	Click the **XML Editor** tab or the **Text Editor** tab to switch between the Topic Editor presentations.
2	Use page control buttons to **Go to First Page**, **Previous Page**, **Next Page**, or **Go to Last Page**.
3	Enter number in **Page** field to jump to a specified topic page number or use the increment/ decrement button to advance the page number forward or backward.
4	Click **Scale to 100%** button to choose from selections to scale the topic display from 1-100%; fit 1, 2, 4 or 8 pages in the window; or display 2-pages at 100%; or adjust the page to fit the current window size.
5	Use Zoom-Out. (**CTRL±**) and Zoom-In (**CTRL +=**) buttons to reduce or increase the topic display.
6	Use the **Set Scaling** drop-down to scale the topic page display size between **10%** and **300%**.
7	Use the **Conditional Indicators** button to **Show/Hide** any conditional text indicators in the topic.
8	Use the **Show Block Structure Bars** icon to **Show/Hide** the HTML tag bars along left edge of the topic.
9	Use the **Show Span Structure Bars** icon to **Show/Hide** the HTML span bars above the topic edge.
10	Use the **Horizontal** and **Vertical Ruler** buttons to toggle between **Show/Hide** display of the rulers.

CREATING A NEW TOPIC TEMPLATE

BASIC CONCEPT

Creating topic templates is one way of ensuring that as writers develop new topics in your project, they do so in a consistent manner that adheres to the composition of the chosen templates. Defining the desired structure may require developing a set of templates that writers will apply whenever creating different topic types. For example, you may need to create a template for chapter first page topics, H1 topics, and H2 topics. In each of these templates, you could insert any common elements needed in the topic type and guidelines for content structure based on the kind of template.

ESSENTIAL ELEMENTS

You may create as many topic templates as you need. To create a new topic template from an existing topic requires that you first open the file and then from the **File** ribbon, **Save as Template**. Flare will prompt you to identify your Template Folder. Flare prompts you to designate an existing folder or make a new custom template folder if a folder was not previously established. A Template Folder can be created beforehand, using the **Tools** ribbon, and selecting **Manage Templates**.

APPLICATION TIPS

When you create a new topic, you will use a factory template or a user-defined template upon which to base the new topic. If user-defined topic templates have not been defined, consider creating templates for any of your document pages that are created frequently or considered standard throughout your project. Examples may include the Chapter first page, H1, and H2 topics.

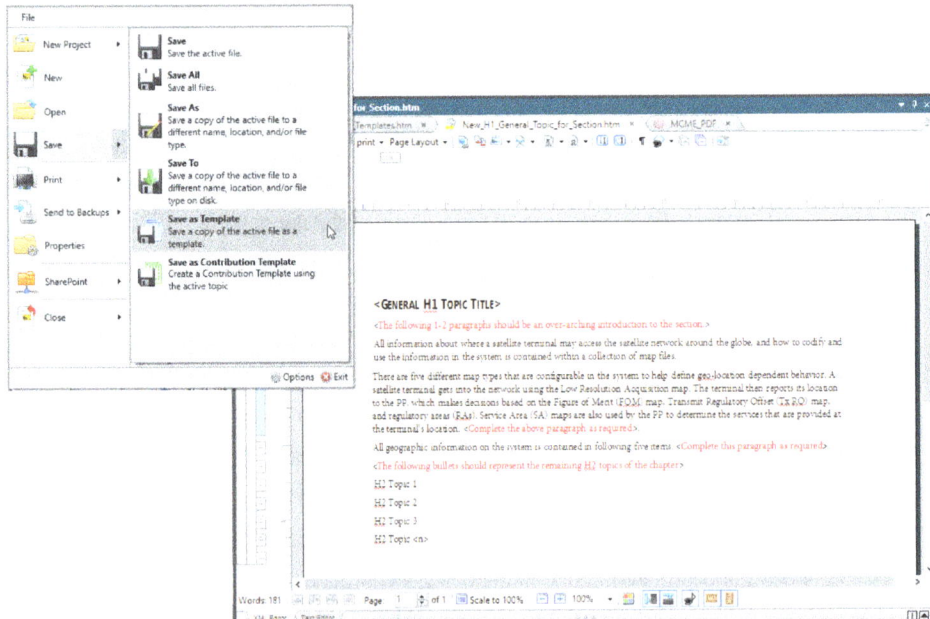

Figure 7-4. Saving an Existing Topic as a Template.

QUICK STEPS: CREATING A NEW TOPIC TEMPLATE

STEP	ACTION
1	In the XML Editor, open the topic file you wish to save as a new topic template file.
2	From the Flare ribbon, click **File** > **Save** > **Save as Template**. The **Save as Template** dialog opens.
3	If no template folders appear in the **Template Folder** pane, click the [icon] **Manage Templates** button. The Template Manager dialog opens.
4	Click the **New Template Folder** button [icon] to add a new template folder, like **CustomTemplates**.
5	Click **OK** to save the designated template folder.
6	Close the **Template Manager**.
7	With the file still open in the XML Editor, click **File** > **Save** > **Save as Template**.
8	Select the Template folder in which to place the new template.
9	Use the **Template Name**, or enter a new name in the field.
10	Click **OK** to save the template. The file is saved successfully and will be available in the template folder.

> **NOTE:** Flare creates the **Contents** subfolder in which to store topic templates. See .

ADDING A NEW TOPIC FILE

BASIC CONCEPT

In most Flare projects creating new topics is one of the most common tasks you perform. Although a common task, it is best to have a standard practice for making topics, especially as a team of writers. Using a template, whether a Factory Template or a user-defined template, helps adhere to a standard structure and method of creating new topics. Using a template, you can even provide general structural guidelines for developing the topic content.

ESSENTIAL ELEMENTS

As for creating a new topic file, there are several ways: 1) from the **File** menu, select **New** and in the **Add File** dialog **File Type** > **Topic**, 2) from the **Project** ribbon, click **New** > **Add Topic**, 3) from a TOC outline file, right-click and select **Add New Topic**, and 4) from the desired folder in the **Content Explorer**, right-click and select **New** > **Topic**. In each of these cases, you can choose to base the topic on a **Factory Template**, a user-defined **Custom Template**, or on an **Existing File**. A new topic based on a current topic will be identical to the existing topic but you can modify it as required.

APPLICATION TIPS

Although some users will be tempted to copy and paste topics, there are certain drawbacks to this method, of which you should be aware. When you copy a topic, all of its cross-references, links, and file path come along for the ride. These items, which can lead to hidden problems, can be remedied with additional work. With good practices, you can avoid this pitfall.

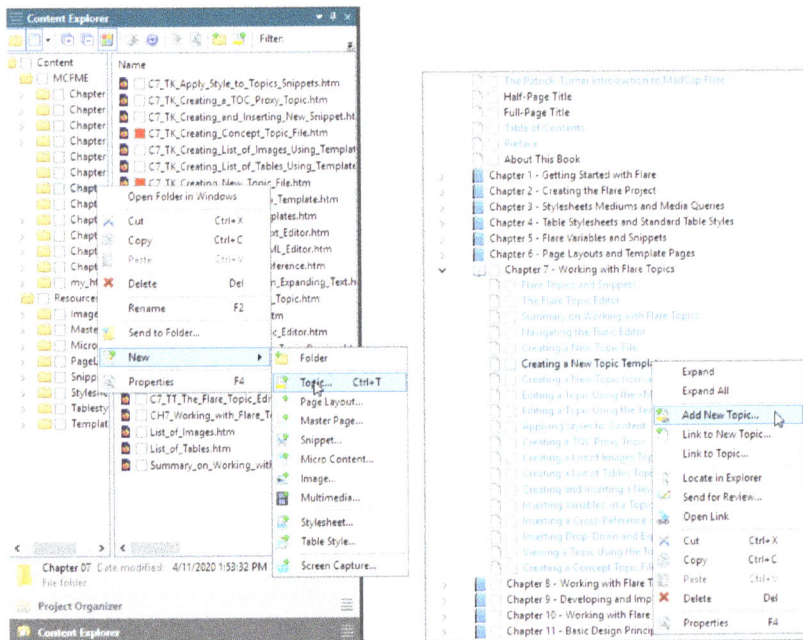

Figure 7-5. New Topic Option Selected — Add File Dialog with Topic Option Set.

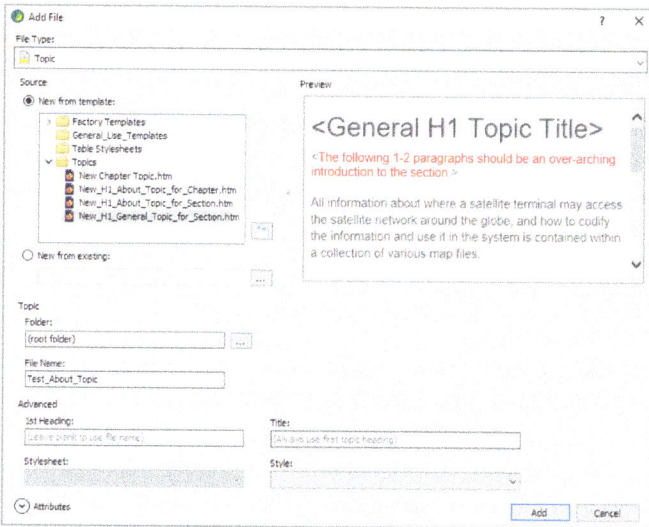

Figure 7-6. Add File Dialog-Topic File Selected.

QUICK STEPS: ADDING A NEW TOPIC FILE

STEP	ACTION
1	Select the subfolder, in the **Content Explorer**, or find and select the folder in which you want to create the new topic file.
2	Right-click and select **New** > **Topic**. The **Add File** dialog opens.
3	Ensure that the **File Type** is set for **Topic**.
4	**To create the new topic use one of the following:** **a) From Templates**: Set the **Source** for **New From Template**, then choose a template from the **Factory Templates** folder or choose a template from a user-defined **Custom Templates** folder. **b) From Existing**: Set the **Source** for **New From Existing**, and use the browse button ⌷ to locate an existing topic file.
5	Under **Topic**, use the **Folder** field and choose the default folder, or browse and choose another folder in which to store the new topic file.
6	Use the **File Name** field to specify a name for the new topic file. For example, **MyNewTopic.html**.
7	In the **1st Heading** field, enter the first heading you wish to appear in the topic. Leave this field blank to always use the file name as the first heading to appear in the new topic.
8	In the **Title** field, enter the title you wish to use for the topic in the **Topic Properties**, and to appear as the TOC outline entry. Leave the field blank to use the first topic heading to serve as the title of the topic, and as the TOC entry.
9	Click > **Add** to save the new topic file.

SETTING THE TOPIC LAYOUT PREFERENCE

BASIC CONCEPT

One of the first things to set in the XML Editor is the appropriate Layout preferences. How you set these preferences determines the appearance of the open topic. These settings, which include both the CSS **Medium** and the choice of the **Layout**, are essential for you to see while in the XML Editor, the rendering of the topic as it will appear when output for Web Layout or Print. Not setting a specific preference may result in the topic not appearing as expected.

ESSENTIAL ELEMENTS

On the XML Editor top toolbar, just to the left of the **Preview** topic button, are the controls for setting the topic layout preference. You can switch the layout preference between **Web Layout** (**Web**, **Tablet**, or **Mobile**) and **Print Layout**. If you change the Layout to Web, Flare automatically switches the Medium to the **Default Medium**. Flare renders the topic as it would be for the selected online output and using online styles. If you change the **Layout** to **Print**, Flare automatically switches the Medium to the **Print** medium, and Flare displays the topic as it would be for print output, using the print styles.

When you select the **Layout** as **Print**, you must also select the **Page Layout** drop-down and choose the appropriate page layout file and the Page Type that will eventually be applied to the page when you build the project. The layout file will present the topic in the XML Editor, as it will appear when the topic is built in the target and generated in the output.

APPLICATION TIPS

Preferences set for a given topic will expire upon closing the topic or the project — on re-opening the project, topics for which you previously set choices you will need to set again.

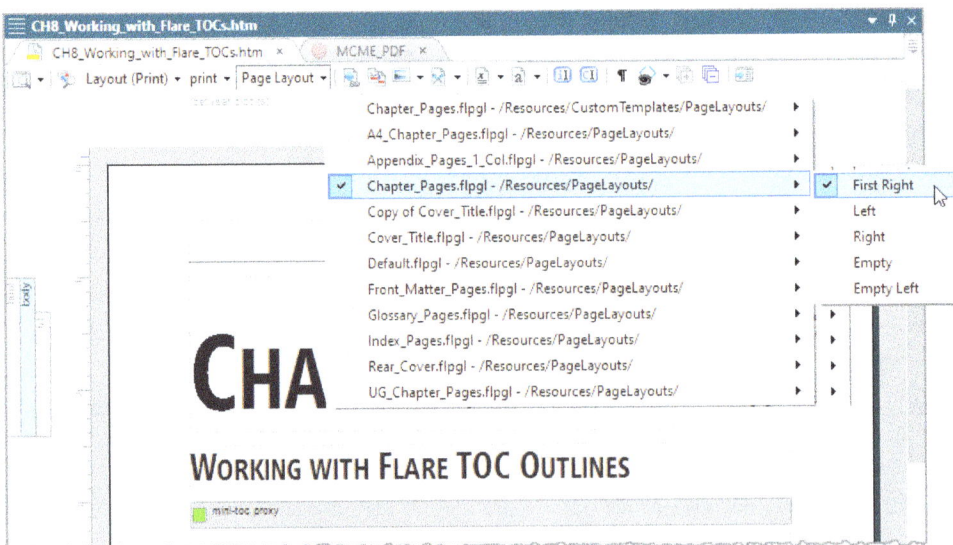

Figure 7-7. Setting the Topic Layout Preference Print Layout — ChapterPages Layout File — First Right Page.

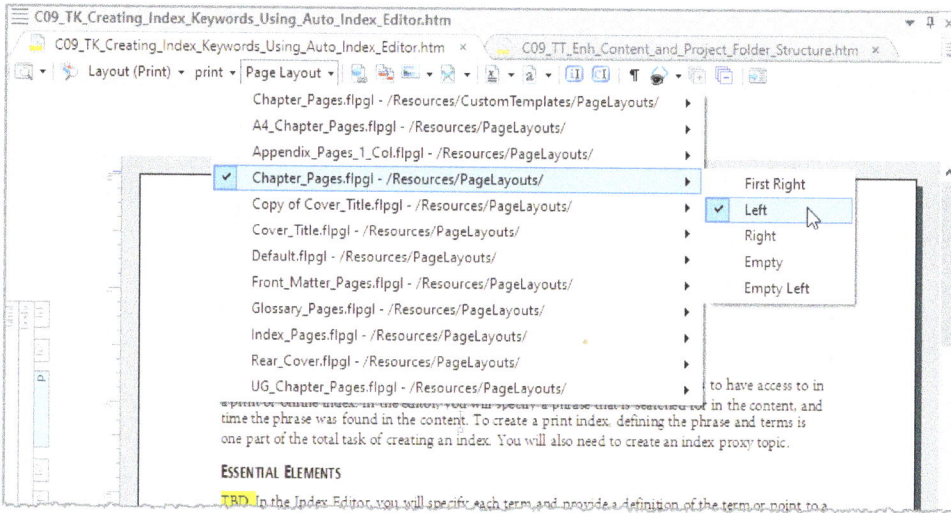

Figure 7-8. Setting the Topic Layout Preference Print Layout — Chapter Pages Layout File — Left Page.

QUICK STEPS: SETTING THE TOPIC LAYOUT PREFERENCE

STEP	ACTION
1	From the **Content Explorer**, open the topic you want to edit.
—	**Set a Layout Preference for Web Outputs** (Web Layout, Web Layout Tablet, Web Layout Mobile):
2	Use the **Layout** drop-down and choose one of the following as the appropriate selection for the topic:
	a) **Web Layout:** with this selection, the **Default Medium** is automatically set.
	b) **Web Layout Tablet:** with this selection, both the **Tablet** and **Mobile** Mediums are automatically set.
	c) **Web Layout Mobile:** with this selection, the **Mobile** Medium is automatically set.
—	**Set a Layout Preference for Print Outputs:**
2	Use the **Layout** drop-down and select the **Print Layout** as the appropriate layout for rendering the topic.
3	Use the **Page Layout** drop-down and choose the appropriate page layout file to be applied to the topic in the output — for example, **ChapterPages**; and choose the appropriate **Page** — for example, **Left**.

APPLYING STYLES TO TOPIC CONTENT

BASIC CONCEPT

Applying styles to content in Flare, for example, Topics, Snippets, or Micro-Content is quite similar as with other WYSIWYG editors; however, it is slightly different and offers several ways to access the styles available in your stylesheet. The **Style** drop-down pane provides access to Paragraph, Heading, Character, Table, List, Link, and other styles in your CSS stylesheet.

ESSENTIAL ELEMENTS

When applying styles in Flare, you must consider that you can view the topic for print as a PDF target or online as perhaps an HTML5 target. As you apply styles, you should also know whether the **Default** or **Print** medium is selected. In any case, you will have access to **Auto-Numbered**, **Paragraph**, **Span** or **Character**, **Heading**, **Image**, **List**, **Link**, and other style categories.

If there are tables in your topic, you will also be able to access and apply CSS table styles and table stylesheets in your topic. The styles that appear listed in the styles pane are context-sensitive and only appear based on how you select the content to which you want to apply a style.

APPLICATION TIPS

There are several interface options for selecting and applying style selectors; for example, you can access the **Style** pane and the **Style Window** on the **Home** ribbon. The guidelines in this task are based on using the **Style** drop-down pane.

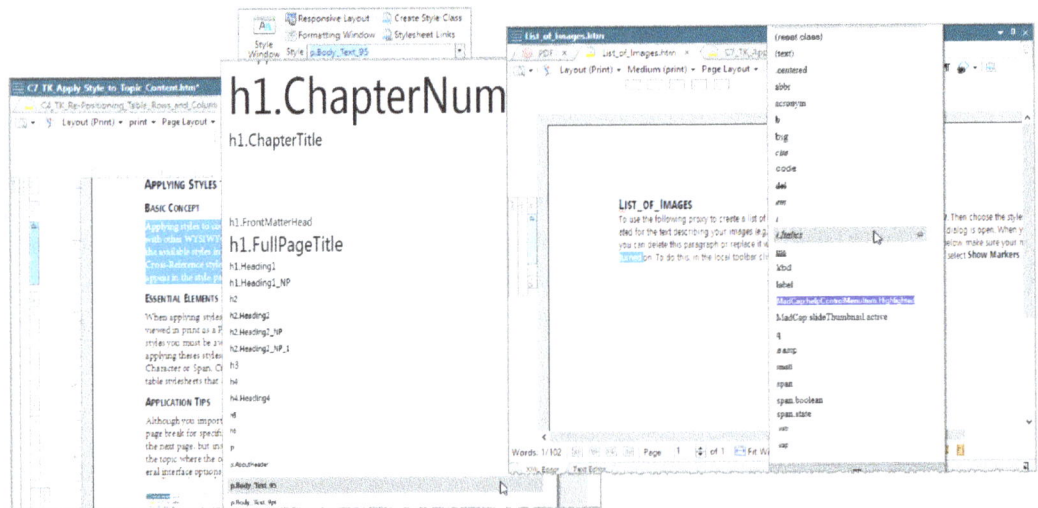

Figure 7-9. a) Style Pane with Paragraph Content Selected b) Style Pane with Character (Span) Content Selected .

QUICK STEPS: APPLYING STYLES TO TOPIC CONTENT

STEP	ACTION
—	**Use the following guidelines to apply styles to headings, paragraph, and span content:**
1	Open a topic file that contains content to which you want to apply styles to body content.
2	Click the **Show Tags** button on the Editor ribbon, and select **Block Structure Bars** if not already visible.
3	There are several interface options for selecting and applying style selectors. The following examples are based on using the **Style** drop-down pane on the **Home** ribbon.
4	**For Headings:** Click anywhere inside a heading paragraph, and use the **Style** drop-down to choose the desired style selector.
5	**For Paragraph or Image:** Click anywhere inside a standard paragraph, image or other block content, like lists, and use the **Style** drop-down to choose the desired style from the list of paragraph selectors.
6	**For Character (Span):** Select the portion of text to which you want to apply a character style, then use the **Style** drop-down to choose the desired character style selector from the listed character styles.
—	**Use the following guidelines to apply standard CSS styles to the individual table components:**
1	Open a topic file that contains content to which you want to apply standard CSS styles to table content.
2	Click the **Show Tags** button on the Editor ribbon, and select **Span Structure Bars** if not already visible.
3	With table tags shown on the block structure bar, you can select individual table elements. This method requires that you have created child classes for each of the table element parent styles. **See Tip**.
4	To apply a style to the entire table, click the table (**table**) tag bar and use the **Style** pane drop-down to select your table style class — for example, (**table.class-1**); or continue.
5	To apply a style to the table header, click the table header (**thead**) tag bar and use the **Style** pane drop-down to select your table header style class — for example, (**thead.class-1**); or continue.
6	To apply a style to the table body, click the table body (**tbody**) tag bar and use the **Style** pane drop-down to select your table body style class — for example, (**tbody.class-1**); or continue.
7	To apply a style to a table row, click a table row (**tr**) tag bar and use the **Style** pane drop-down to select your table row style class — for example, (**tr.class-1**); or continue.
8	To apply a style to a table column, click a table column (**col**) span bar and use the **Style** pane drop-down to select your table column style class — for example, (**col.class-1**); or continue.
9	To apply a style to a table footer, click a table footer (**tfoot**) tag bar and use the **Style** pane drop-down to select your table footer style class — for example, (**tfoot.class-1**); or continue.
10	To apply a style to a table cell, click inside the cell and then click the table data cell (**td**) tag bar and use the **Style** pane drop-down to select your table cell style class — for example, (**td.class**).

TIP: Table parent styles <**table**>, <**tbody**>, <**thead**>, <**tcaption**>, <**tr**>, <**col**>, and <**tfoot**> are inherited in your stylesheet. It is recommended that you create child classes for each parent style instead of using the parent for styling. Creating child classes always give you greater styling flexibility.

CREATING A TABLE OF CONTENTS TOPIC USING THE TOC TEMPLATE

BASIC CONCEPT

The topic template **TopicForTOC** is just one of several templates available in the Flare **Factory Templates** folder, which you can leverage. If you intend to insert a Table of Contents (TOC) topic that lists the chapters and sections of each chapter in the document, this template will allow you to create that topic quickly. There are also other methods, in Flare, of creating a TOC topic in the output.

ESSENTIAL ELEMENTS

Each proxy element in Flare is a content placeholder for a specific type of content. When you build the target containing the proxy topic, the appropriate content flows into the topic. Since Flare creates the Table of Contents topic from a template that contains the TOC Proxy, a Table of Contents of chapters and sections in your document flows into the TOC topic when you build the target.

Once Flare completes the build, the Table of Contents topic is generated in the output based on where you place the topic in the TOC outline. For example, you may have inserted the TOC topic item just following the title and copyright page.

APPLICATION TIPS

Although Flare embeds the TOC Proxy in the **TopicForTOC** template, you have the option of creating your topic to generate a Table of Contents. You would make the topic, insert a new line, and use **Insert > Proxy > TOC Proxy** from the main ribbon.

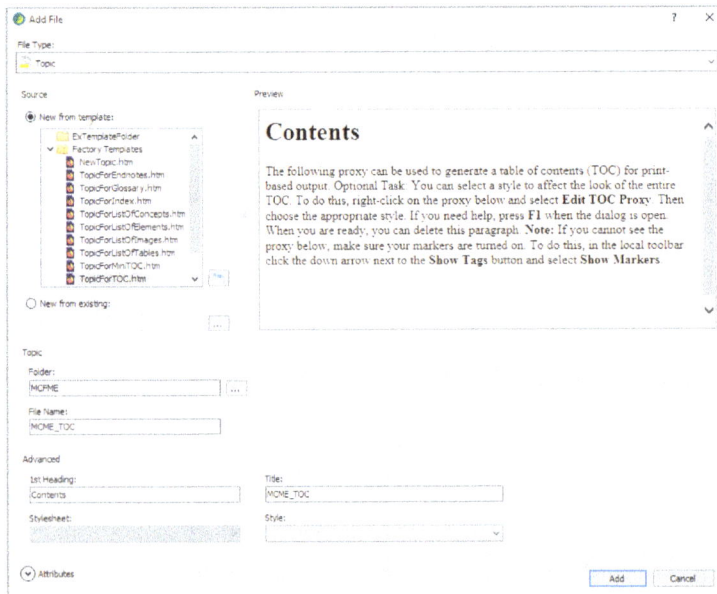

Figure 7-10. Add File Dialog — with TOC Proxy Topic Template Specified.

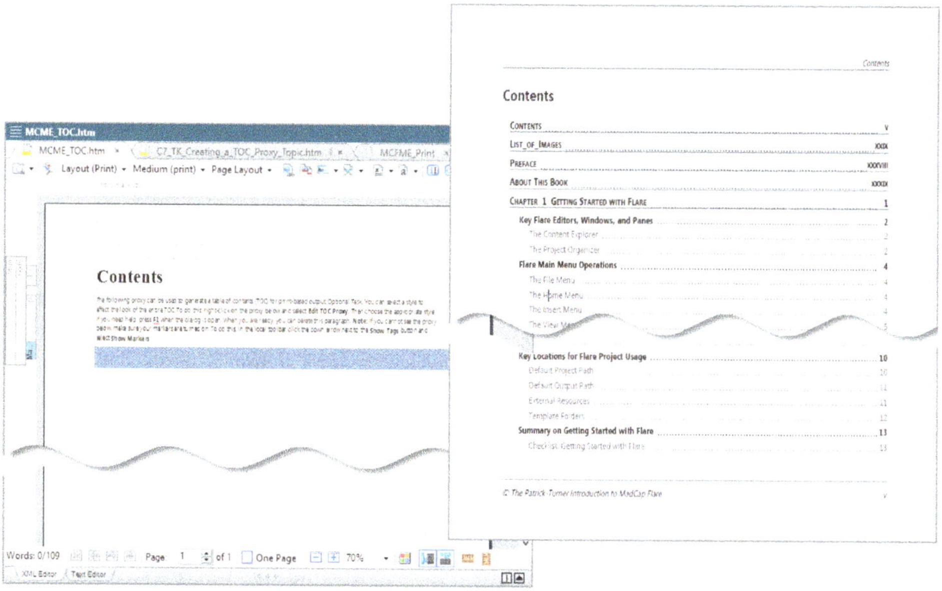

Figure 7-11. a) TOC Topic with TOC Proxy Inserted b) Table of Contents (TOC) Topic Generated in Output.

QUICK STEPS: CREATING A TABLE OF CONTENTS TOPIC USING A TOC TEMPLATE

STEP	ACTION
1	Click **File** >**New**, to create a new topic file that will use a standard Flare template.
2	In the **Add File** dialog, ensure that the **File Type** to create is set for **Topic**.
3	Under the **Source** pane, select **New From Template**.
4	From the **Factory Templates** folder, select the file **TopicForTOC**.
5	Under **Topic** > **Folder**, click the browse button ⋯ to find and select a folder to store the new topic.
6	Under **File Name**, type a name for the new HTML topic file — for example, **Contents**.
7	In the **Title** field, type the name you wish to display in the TOC.
8	Select the **Style** to apply to the topic heading - for example, **h1.FrontMatterHead**.
9	Click the **Add** button to create the topic.
10	Delete the default text from the topic.
11	Place the HTML file for this topic in your TOC outline file at the point you want the TOC to appear in the front of the document. You can drag and drop the file from the Content Explorer to an open TOC file.

> **TIP:** There is always more than one way to accomplish a task. Although you may not have as much control, you can tell Flare to auto-generate a TOC and insert it at the front of your document. On the **Advanced** tab of the target file, under **Output Options**, enable the option to **Generate TOC Proxy**.

CREATING A LIST OF IMAGES TOPIC USING LIST-OF-IMAGES TEMPLATE

BASIC CONCEPT

The template **TopicForListofImages** is one of several templates available in the Flare Factory Templates folder, which you can leverage. If you intend to insert a topic into your document that lists each of the images found in the document, you can use this template to create the topic quickly.

ESSENTIAL ELEMENTS

Since the **List of Images** topic is created from a Flare template that embeds the **List-Of Proxy**, a list of all of the specified tables found in the content flow into the **List of Images** topic when you build the target. Flare will generate the list based on the auto-number style applied to images in your content and that you specify in the proxy. Once Flare completes the build, the List of Images topic is generated in the output based on where you placed the topic in the TOC outline. For example, after the TOC.

APPLICATION TIPS

Although the **List-Of-Proxy** is embedded in the **TopicForListofImages** template, you can also create the topic without using the template. Create a new topic, insert a new line, and use **Insert > Proxy > List-Of-Proxy** from the main ribbon. Then, if applicable, edit the proxy to specify the parent tag and class used to auto-number images in your content.

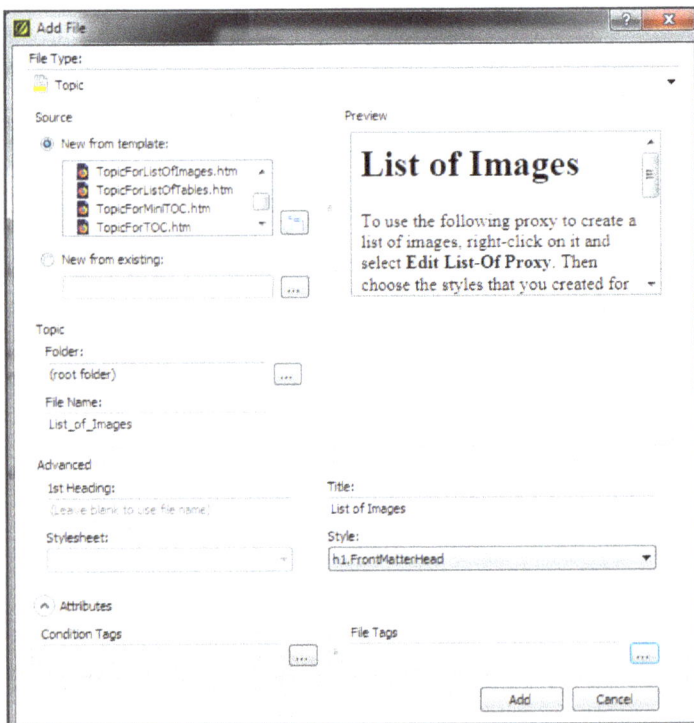

Figure 7-12. Add File Dialog — List-Of-Images Proxy Topic Template Specified.

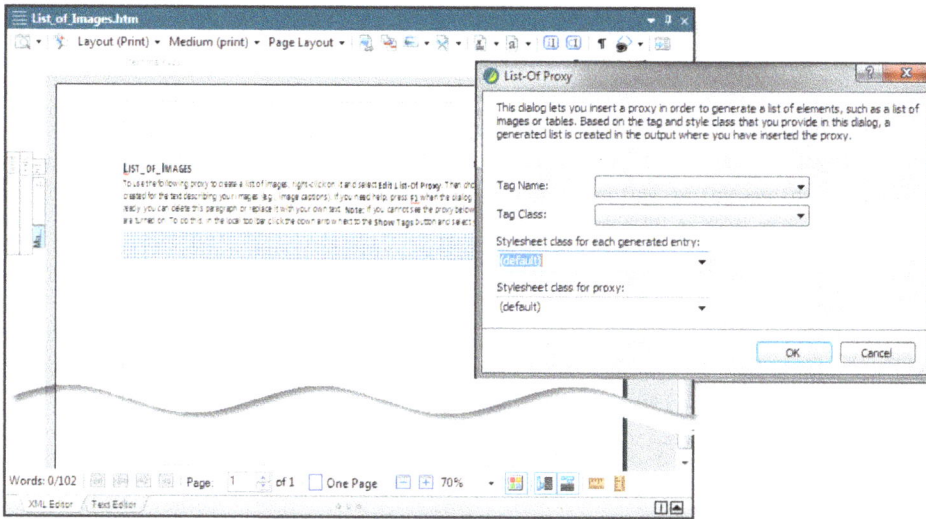

Figure 7-13. A List of Images Topic — Using List-Of-Proxy.

QUICK STEPS: CREATING A LIST OF IMAGES TOPIC USING LIST-OF-IMAGES TEMPLATE

STEP	ACTION
1	Click **File** >**New**, to create a new topic file that will use a standard Flare template.
2	In the **Add File** dialog, ensure that the **File Type** to create is set for **Topic**.
3	Under the **Source** pane, select **New From Template**.
4	From the **Factory Templates** folder, select the file **TopicForListOfTables**.
5	Under **Topic** > **Folder**, click the browse button [....] to find and select a folder to store the new topic.
6	Under **File Name**, type a name for the new HTML topic file — for example, **list_of_images**.
7	In the **Title** field, type the name you wish to display in the TOC.
8	Select the **Style** to apply to the topic heading - for example, **h1.FrontMatterHead**.
9	Click the **Add** button to create the topic.
10	Delete the default text from the topic or you can replace it with your own text, if text is required.
11	Right-click on the **List-Of-Proxy** tag that immediately follows the default text, and select **Edit List-Of-Proxy**. If proxy tag, is not visible, as shown in the figure above, click the **Show Tags** drop-down on the toolbar and select **Show Markers** to turn on the markers.
12	Use the **Tag Name** drop-down and select the parent tag — for example the paragraph tag <**p**>.
13	Use the **Tag Class** drop-down and choose the selector class used to style the image captions in your content — this will be the style selector that auto-numbers your tables, for example **Figure_Caption**.
14	Place the HTML file for this topic in your TOC file at the point you want it to appear in the document. You can drag and drop the file from the Content Explorer to an open TOC file.

CREATING A LIST OF TABLES TOPIC USING LIST-OF-TABLES TEMPLATE

BASIC CONCEPT

The template **TopicForListofTables** is one of several templates available in the Flare Factory Templates folder, which you can leverage. If you intend to insert a topic into your document that lists each of the tables found in the document, you can use this template to create the topic quickly.

ESSENTIAL ELEMENTS

Since the **List of Tables** topic is created from a Flare template that embeds the **List-Of Proxy**, a list of all of the specified tables found in the content flow into the **List of Tables** topic when you build the target. Flare will generate the list based on the auto-number style applied to tables in your content and that you specify in the proxy. Once Flare completes the build, the List of Tables topic is generated in the output based on where you placed the topic in the TOC outline. For example, after the TOC.

APPLICATION TIPS

Although the **List-Of-Proxy** is embedded in the **TopicForListofTables** template, you can also create the topic without using the template. Create a new topic, insert a new line, and use **Insert > Proxy > List-Of-Proxy** from the main ribbon. Then, if applicable, edit the proxy to specify the parent tag and class used to auto-number tables in your content.

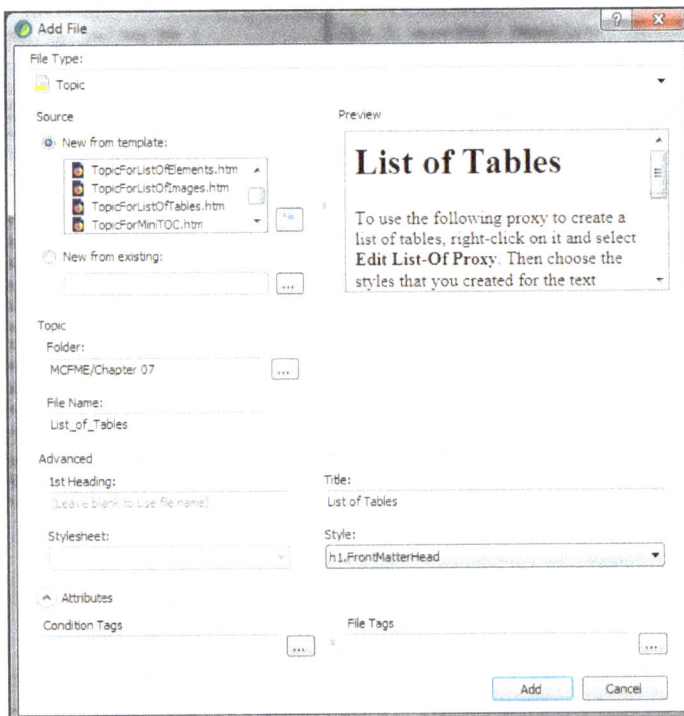

Figure 7-14. Add File Dialog — List-Of-Tables Proxy Topic Template Specified.

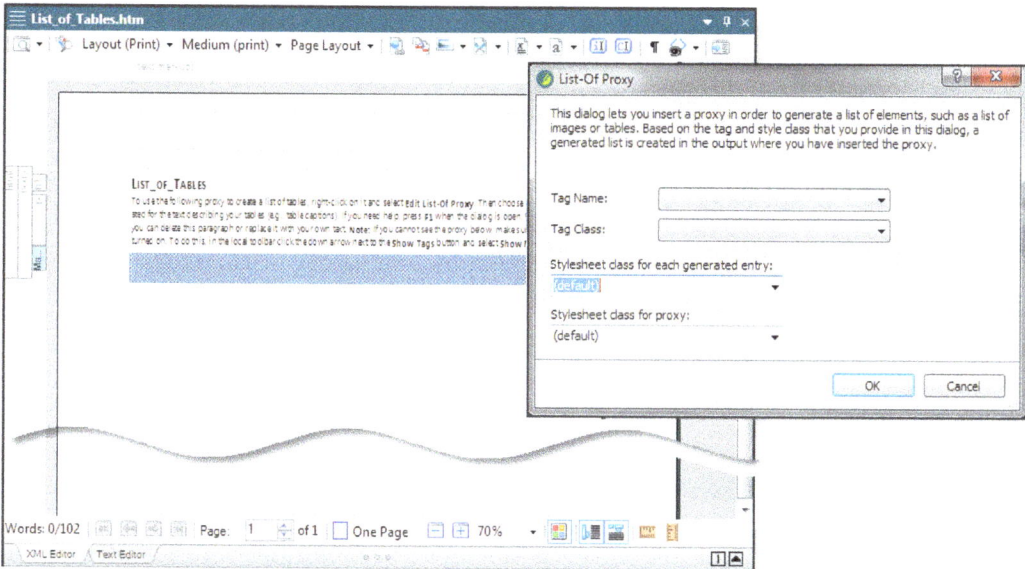

Figure 7-15. A List of Tables Topic — Using List-Of-Proxy.

QUICK STEPS: CREATING A LIST OF TABLES TOPIC USING LIST-OF-TABLES TEMPLATE

STEP	ACTION
1	Click **File** > **New**, to create a new topic file that will use a standard Flare template.
2	In the **Add File** dialog, ensure that the **File Type** to create is set for **Topic**.
3	Under the **Source** pane, select **New From Template**.
4	From the **Factory Templates** folder, select the file **TopicForListOfTables**.
5	Under **Topic** > **Folder**, click the browse button ⋯ to find and select a folder to store the new topic.
6	Under **File Name**, type a name for the new HTML topic file — for example, **list_of_tables**.
7	In the **Title** field, type the name you wish to display in the TOC.
8	Select the **Style** to apply to the topic heading — for example, **h1.FrontMatterHead**.
9	Click the **Add** button to create the topic.
10	Delete the default text from the topic or you can replace it with your own text, if text is required.
11	Right-click on the **List-Of-Proxy** tag that immediately follows the default text, and select **Edit List-Of-Proxy**. If the proxy tag is not visible, as shown in the figure above, click the the **Show Tags** drop-down on the toolbar and select **Show Markers** to turn on the markers.
12	Use the **Tag Name** drop-down and select the parent tag — for example the paragraph tag **<p>**.
13	Use the **Tag Class** drop-down and choose the selector class used to style the images in your content — this will be the style selector that auto-numbers your images, for example **Table_Caption**.
14	Place the HTML file for this topic in your TOC file at the point you want it to appear in the document. You can drag and drop the file from the Content Explorer to the open TOC file.

INSERTING A MINI-TOC PROXY IN AN EXISTING TOPIC

BASIC CONCEPT

In Flare, there are several proxy elements that you can insert directly into a topic as a placeholder for a specific type of content. Flare also provides several templates that already imbed one of these proxies — hence the proxy is included in topics you create from the template. There is a template, for example, that contains the glossary proxy, one that includes the index proxy, one that includes the TOC proxy, and another that includes the mini-TOC proxy. There are also other such templates.

While this latter method of incorporating proxies in templates has particular efficiencies, there may be some cases where you will prefer to insert the proxy in a topic that you are creating or already exists.

ESSENTIAL ELEMENTS

This task adds a mini-TOC proxy to a topic that already exists. There are benefits to taking this approach in some cases. In this case, a chapter's first-page topic has already been designed and created for each chapter. At some point, you decide to add a mini-TOC on each chapter's first page to list the first-level topics (or additional headings) found in the chapter. You can insert the mini-TOC proxy element in each chapter's first-page topic.

APPLICATION TIPS

If you place a mini-TOC below a Heading-1 in a topic with Heading-2 and Heading-3, and you enter a TOC Depth of 3, then the mini-TOC will display heading-2 and heading-3.

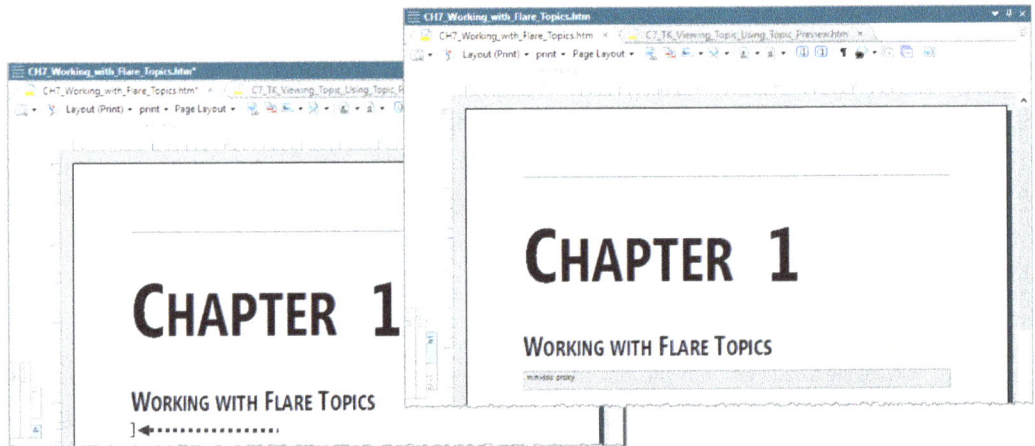

Figure 7-16. Existing Chapter First Page Topic, and b) Chapter First Page Topic with Mini-TOC Proxy Inserted.

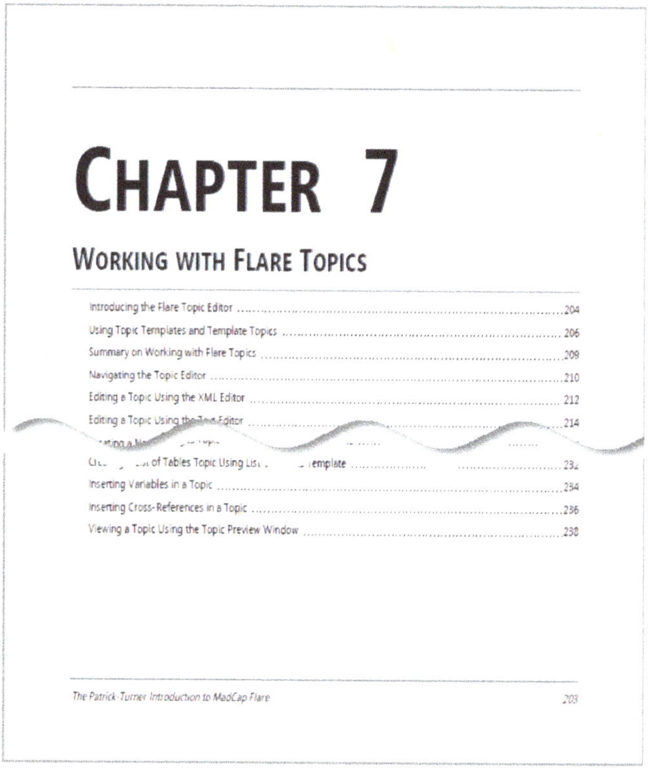

CHAPTER 7

WORKING WITH FLARE TOPICS

The Patrick-Turner Introduction to MadCap Flare   *203*

Figure 7-17. Chapter Topic Page after Mini-TOC Proxy Replaced by Mini-TOC Content.

QUICK STEPS: INSERTING A MINI-TOC PROXY IN AN EXISTING TOPIC

STEP	ACTION
1	Open the existing topic in which you want to insert a mini-TOC proxy.
2	Insert a new line at the position where you want to the mini-TOC to be placed. For example, create a new line, immediately following the chapter title, for placing the mini-TOC proxy.
3	Click in the position, and from the **Insert** ribbon, click **Insert > Proxy > Insert Mini-Toc Proxy**.
4	Right-click on the mini-TOC Proxy element and select **Edit Mini-TOC Proxy**.
5	Use the **TOC Depth** field to enter a number typically between 2-3, to indicate the number of heading levels to show in the mini-TOC. Based on the number you enter and the structure of the main TOC in your project, the number indicates the number of headings to show below the heading level of the current topic.

NOTE: If the mini-TOC is inserted below a Chapter Heading, and the TOC has heading level 1 and heading level-2, and you enter a TOC Depth of 2. The mini-TOC will display heading-1 only. See Figure 7-17.

INSERTING A GLOSSARY PROXY IN AN EXISTING TOPIC

BASIC CONCEPT

There are several proxy elements that you can insert directly into a topic as a placeholder to output a specific content type. Flare also provides several templates that already imbed one of the available content placeholders (proxies) — for example, there is a template that already contains the glossary proxy. In some cases, however, you may want to create the topic and insert the proxy or insert the proxy in a topic that you have previously created. If, for example, you have created a glossary topic and it has a first-page design that you wish to keep, then you can simply place the glossary proxy in this topic.

ESSENTIAL ELEMENTS

The glossary topic is easily created by inserting the glossary proxy on the first page of the topic you may have already created for the glossary topic. If you are not starting from an existing topic, make the topic, insert a new line, and use **Insert > Proxy > Insert Glossary Proxy** from the main ribbon. If applicable, right-click on the proxy and select **Edit Glossary Proxy** to **Generate Headings**. The headings referred to here, are those alphabetical letters that normally separate the sections of a glossary.

APPLICATION TIPS

The completion of a print or online index is a two-part task. The first part is creating the glossary topic, using the Flare glossary topic template or an existing topic in which you inserted the glossary proxy, or creating your topic and inserting the index proxy. The second part of the task involves using the Flare Glossary Editor in the development of the actual glossary content. See **Chapter 9**.

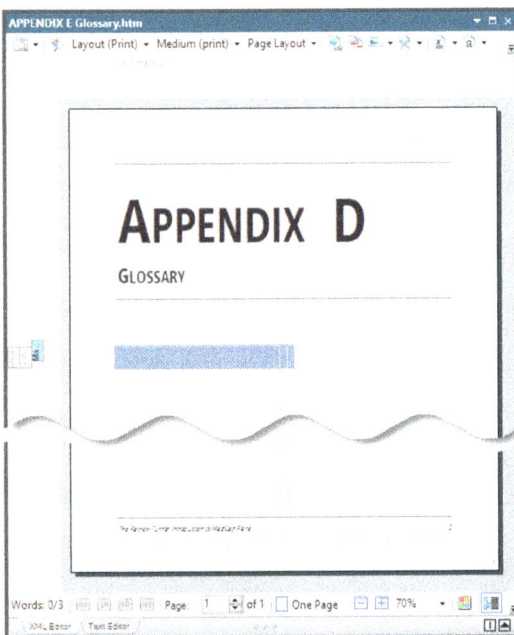

Figure 7-18. Glossary Proxy Topic.

QUICK STEPS: INSERTING A GLOSSARY PROXY IN AN EXISTING TOPIC

STEP	ACTION
1	Open the existing topic in which you want to insert the Flare glossary proxy.
2	Insert a new line at the position where you want the glossary to start with the letter-A. For example, in this glossary example that has 2-columns, the proxy is placed in the first column, on the line immediately after the Glossary title.
3	From the **Insert** ribbon, click > **Proxy > Insert Glossary Proxy**.
4	Right-click on the Glossary Proxy element and select **Edit Glossary Proxy**.
5	Use the **Generate Headings** drop-down to answer **Yes** or **No**, as to whether the alphabet headings that start each group of glossary terms should be included. For example, "**-A-**", "**-B-**", and "**-C-**". **See Note**.
6	Use the drop-down to select a **Stylesheet class for the proxy element**, which you have created; otherwise, leave this field blank.

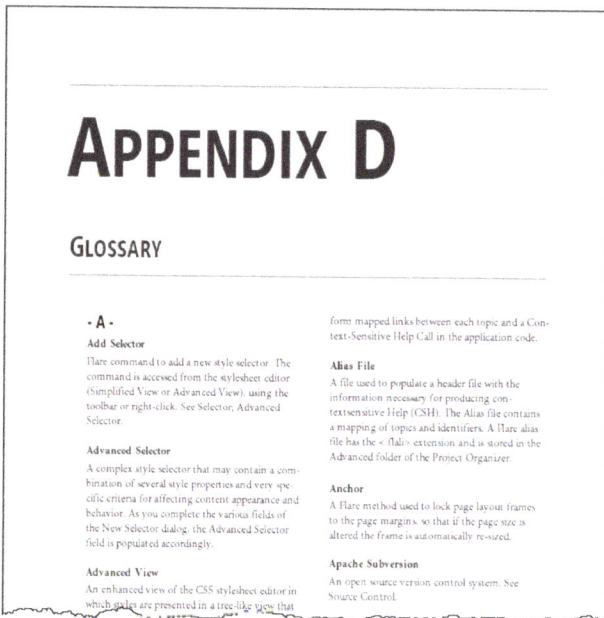

APPENDIX D

GLOSSARY

- A -

Add Selector

Flare command to add a new style selector. The command is accessed from the stylesheet editor (Simplified View or Advanced View), using the toolbar or right-click. See Selector; Advanced Selector.

Advanced Selector

A complex style selector that may contain a combination of several style properties and very specific criteria for affecting content appearance and behavior. As you complete the various fields of the New Selector dialog, the Advanced Selector field is populated accordingly.

Advanced View

An enhanced view of the CSS stylesheet editor in which styles are presented in a tree-like view that

form mapped links between each topic and a Context-Sensitive Help Call in the application code.

Alias File

A file used to populate a header file with the information necessary for producing context-sensitive Help (CSH). The Alias file contains a mapping of topics and identifiers. A Flare alias file has the <.flali> extension and is stored in the Advanced folder of the Project Organizer.

Anchor

A Flare method used to lock page layout frames to the page margins, so that if the page size is altered the frame is automatically re-sized.

Apache Subversion

An open source version control system. See Source Control.

Figure 7-19. Auto-Generated (Proxy) Glossary Output.

> **NOTE:** You can use specific MadCap styles and properties that are available for styling the glossary appearance, including the glossary headings, terms, definitions, and the glossary proxy container. Glossary headings particularly are styled using the selector **div.GlossaryPageHeading**, which you can edit.

INSERTING AN INDEX PROXY IN AN EXISTING TOPIC

BASIC CONCEPT

There are several proxy elements that you can insert directly into a topic as a placeholder to output a specific content type. Flare also provides several templates that already imbed one of the available content placeholders (proxies) — for example, there is a template that already contains the index proxy. In some cases, however, you may want to create the topic and insert the proxy or insert the proxy in a topic that you have previously created. If, for example, you have created an index topic and it has a first-page design that you wish to keep, then you can simply place the index proxy in this topic.

ESSENTIAL ELEMENTS

The index topic is easily created by inserting the index proxy on the first page of a topic you may have already created. If you are not starting from an existing topic, make the topic, insert a new line, and use **Insert > Proxy > Insert Index Proxy** from the main ribbon. If applicable, right-click on the proxy and select **Edit Index Proxy**, to specify whether to **Generate Headings**. The headings referred to here, are those alphabetical letters that normally separate the sections of an index.

APPLICATION TIPS

The completion of a print or online index is a two-part task. The first part is creating the index topic, using the Flare index topic template or an existing topic in which you inserted the index proxy, or creating your topic and inserting the index proxy. The second part of the task involves using the Flare Index Editor in the development of the actual index content. See **Chapter 9**.

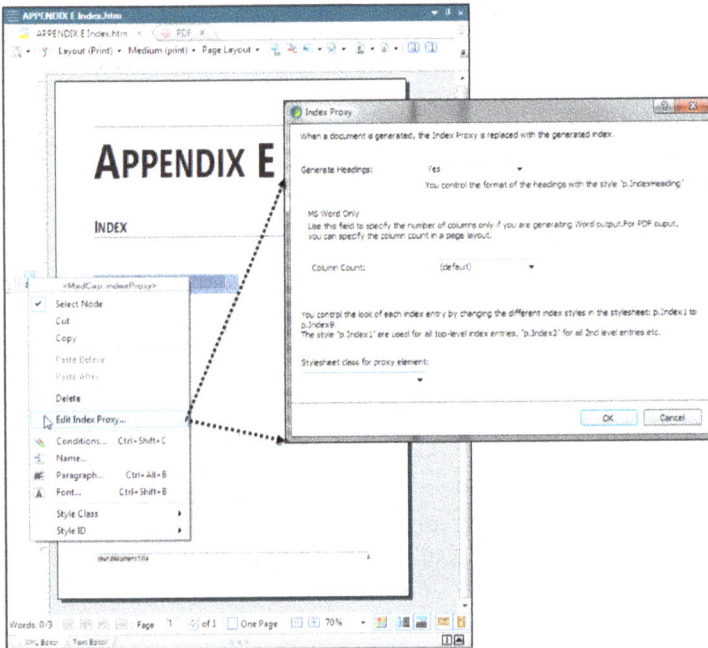

Figure 7-20. Index Proxy Topic Dialog.

QUICK STEPS: INSERTING AN INDEX PROXY IN AN EXISTING TOPIC

STEP	ACTION
1	Open the existing topic in which you want to insert the Flare index proxy.
2	Insert a new line at the position where you want the index to start with the letter -A. For example, in this index example that has 2-columns, the proxy is placed in the first column, on the line immediately after the Index title.
3	From the **Insert** ribbon, click **Proxy > Insert Index Proxy**.
4	Right-click on the Index Proxy element and select **Edit Index Proxy**.
5	Use the **Generate Headings** drop-down to answer **Yes** or **No**, as to whether the alphabet headings that start each group of index terms should be included. For example, "**-A-**", "**-B-**", and "**-C-**". **See Note**.
6	Use the drop-down to select a **Stylesheet class for the proxy element**, which you have created; otherwise, leave this field blank.

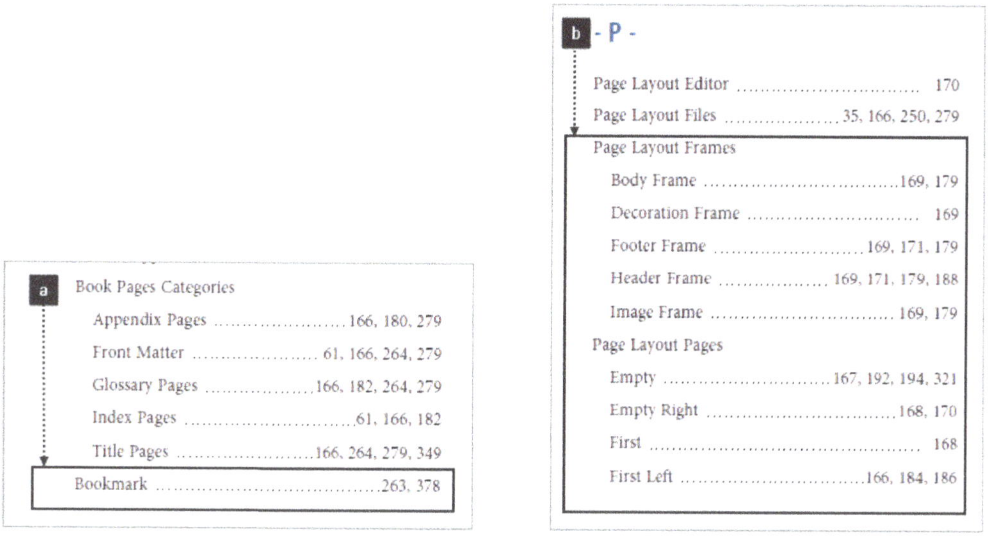

b - P -

```
Page Layout Editor ................................  170
Page Layout Files ..................35, 166, 250, 279
  Page Layout Frames
      Body Frame ................................169, 179
      Decoration Frame .............................  169
      Footer Frame ........................169, 171, 179
      Header Frame ............... 169, 171, 179, 188
      Image Frame ................................169, 179
  Page Layout Pages
      Empty .............................167, 192, 194, 321
      Empty Right ................................168, 170
      First ..............................................  168
      First Left ..............................166, 184, 186
```

a Book Pages Categories

```
      Appendix Pages ........................166, 180, 279
      Front Matter ..................... 61, 166, 264, 279
      Glossary Pages ..................166, 182, 264, 279
      Index Pages ..........................61, 166, 182
      Title Pages ........................166, 264, 279, 349
    Bookmark .....................................263, 378
```

Figure 7-21. Auto-Generated Index Showing a) Index Keyword; and b) Two Index Keywords with Sub-entries.

NOTE: You can use specific MadCap styles and properties that are available for styling the index appearance, including the index headings, keywords, and the index proxy container. Index headings particularly are styled using the style selector **p.IndexHeading**, which you can edit.

INSERTING CROSS-REFERENCES IN A TOPIC

BASIC CONCEPT

In Flare, you can insert cross-references throughout your content, with a target in the open topic or another topic in the project. While you can immediately use the **MadCap|Xref** style inherited in Flare, you can create and edit your cross-reference child classes under this default style. Cross-references are possible in both online and print outputs.

ESSENTIAL ELEMENTS

The **Insert Cross-Reference** dialog has two options under the **Link To** drop-down that accesses several cross-reference target options. You can choose **Topic In Project** to select any HTML topic accessible in the entire project or select **Place in document**. If you select **Place in document**, you can select a target from several options that drill down through the open topic. You can select from **Bookmarks**, **Headings**, **Paragraphs**, **Ordered** and **Unordered List Items**, specific **Styles**, and **Table Content**, for example, table caption or a specific row.

Using standard cross-reference Format Commands, you can create and edit a cross-reference to include page number information, the title of the topic, or even a file path.

APPLICATION TIPS

In addition to the **Insert > Cross-Reference** menu option, you also have access to the right-click **Quick-Cross-Reference** command option. This option provides a shortcut to **Bookmarks** in the current document, **Same Folder** topics, and other currently **Open Documents**.

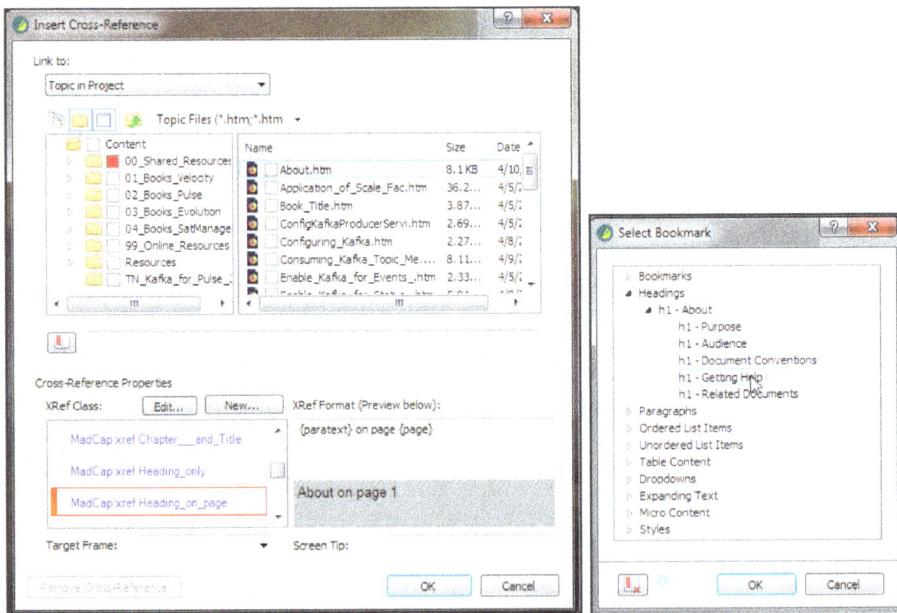

Figure 7-22. Insert Cross-Reference a) Target Topics in Project and b) Bookmarks, Headings, and Other Targets.

QUICK STEPS: INSERTING CROSS-REFERENCES IN A TOPIC

STEP	ACTION
1	Open the document in which you want to insert a cross-reference.
2	At the insertion point, use the right-click or the **Insert** ribbon, and select **Insert** > **Cross-Reference**.
3	Use the **Show/Hide** buttons on the dialog ribbon, to display the folders and files in the project.
4	Under **Link To**, select one of the following two options as the cross-reference target.

1) Topic in Project:

a) From the **Content** folder find the subfolder and locate a specific topic as the cross-reference target.

b) Select the target topic from the adjacent topic list pane.

c) In the **Cross-Reference Properties** dialog, select the appropriate cross-reference class from the list of cross-reference styles; or click the **New** button to create a new cross-reference selector class.

d) Click **OK** to insert the cross-reference.

2) Place in this document: Use one of the following steps for this option:

a) If applicable, click the **Bookmark** drop-down to select from a list of possible target bookmarks.

b) If applicable, click the **Headings** drop-down to select from a list of headings (for example, h1, h2, and h3) that are contained in the current topic and are possible targets of the cross-reference.

c) If applicable, click the **Paragraphs** drop-down to select from a list of paragraphs contained in the current topic and are possible targets of the cross-reference.

d) If applicable, click the **Ordered List Items** drop-down to select a list item as the target cross-reference.

e) If applicable, click **Unordered List Items** drop-down to select a list item as the target cross-reference.

f) If applicable, click the **Table Contents** drop-down to select any of the listed table elements, such as the table caption, table header, or even a specific table row as the specific target cross-reference.

g) If applicable, click the **Table Contents** drop-down to select any of the listed table elements, such as the table caption, table header, or even a specific table row as the specific target cross-reference.

h) If applicable, click the **Styles** drop-down to select any of the listed styled content elements, as the specific target cross-reference.

i) Click **OK** to insert the cross-reference.

INSERTING VARIABLES IN A TOPIC

BASIC CONCEPT

You can insert variables anywhere in your project, including the content of topics and snippets, in the page headers and footers of page layout files, and some Properties dialogs. While you can immediately insert System and Heading variables inherited in Flare, user variables you want to insert must have been created in the Variables Editor. You can determine what user variable sets are available by opening **Project Organizer > Project > Variables**.

ESSENTIAL ELEMENTS

You can insert any variable from any available **Variable Sets**, including **System**, **Heading**, and user-defined variable sets. A variable is inserted from the **Insert** ribbon or the right-click, using **Insert > Variable**. When you are editing page layout files, the local toolbar also contains the **Insert > Variable** option. One or more variables can be inserted on a line, separated by spacing or content. Whenever you click the **Insert Variables** button, you have access to the **Variable Sets**, including **System**, **Heading**, and User-Defined variables. There is also a quick selection from either the **Pinned Variables** or **Recently Used Variables**.

APPLICATION TIPS

If you create snippet variables in your project, consider placing them in a separate variable set file. With this approach, your snippet variables become easier to identify when inserting or modifying the snippet variable.

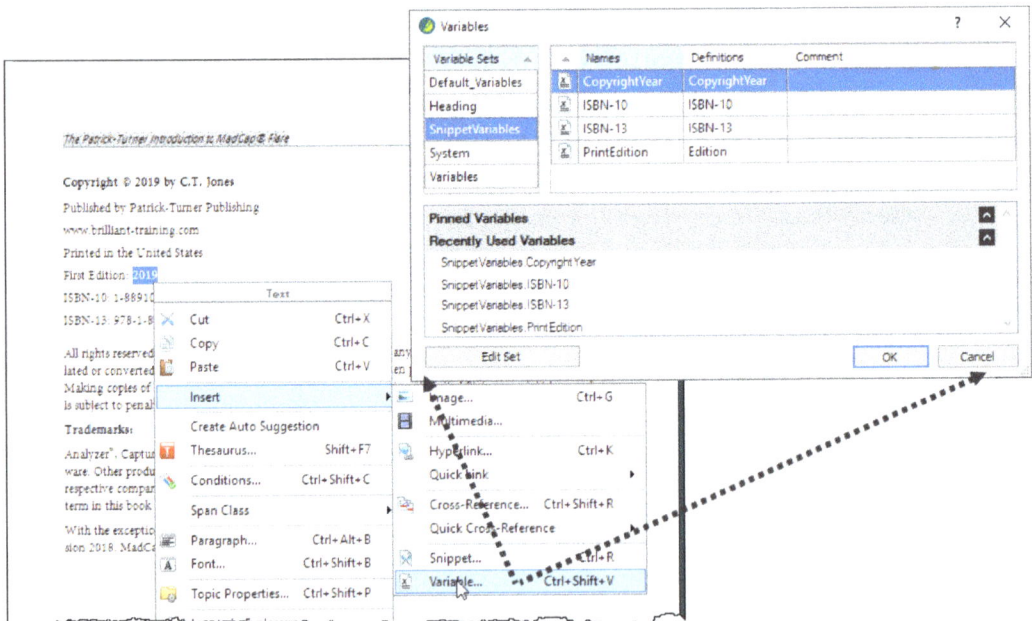

Figure 7-23. Insert Variable in Topic — Choose Variable Set and Select Variable.

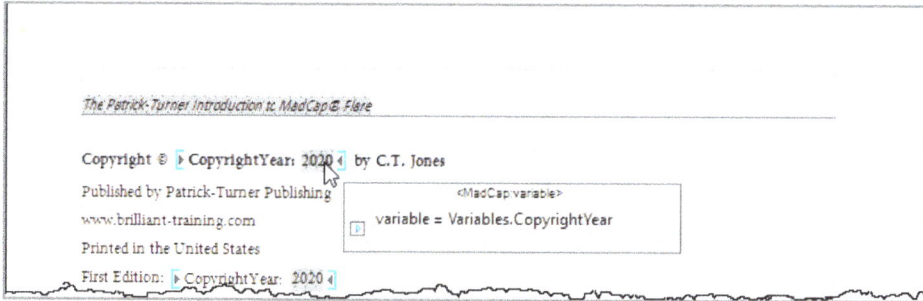

Figure 7-24. Topic Showing Inserted Variable for Copyright.

QUICK STEPS: INSERTING VARIABLES IN A TOPIC

STEP	ACTION
1	Open the document in which you want to insert a variable.
2	At the insertion point, use the right-click or the **Insert** ribbon, and select **Insert** > **Variable**. The **Variables** dialog opens.
3	From the variable listed under **Pinned Variables**, or under **Recently Used Variables**, click on a variable to make a quick selection of a variable to insert, or use the following: **a)** Click any of the **Variable Sets** (for example, **Heading**, **System**, or other), from which to select a variable. **b)** Click on a variable to insert, and then click **OK**.

NOTE: System and Heading variables are often inserted in page layout page headers or page footers.

INSERTING SNIPPETS IN A TOPIC

BASIC CONCEPT

If you have previously created snippets in your project, you can insert them anywhere in your content. Flare generally places snippets in the **Content Explorer** > **Content** > **Resources** > **Snippets**, but you may also put them in another folder. A snippet is inserted in a topic much like a variable, an image, or any other element, after positioning the cursor at the desired insertion point.

ESSENTIAL ELEMENTS

You can insert a snippet at any place in your content, for example, in topics and page layouts. The snippet is inserted from the **Insert** ribbon or the right-click, using **Insert** > **Snippet**. When editing page layout files, the local toolbar also contains the **Insert** > **Snippet** option. Whenever you click the **Insert Snippet** button, you have access to the **Snippets** folder, and there is also a quick selection from either **Pinned Snippets** or **Recently Used Snippets**.

APPLICATION TIPS

If you are creating snippet variables in your project, consider placing them in a file separate from any other of your variable sets. With this approach, your snippet variables become much easier to identify when modifying the snippet variable at the snippet.

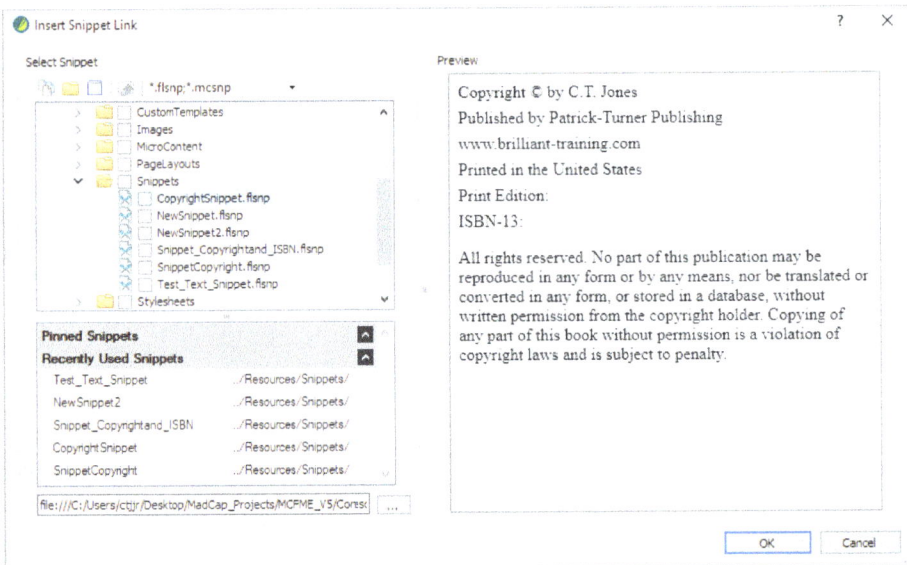

Figure 7-25. Insert Snippet Link Dialog.

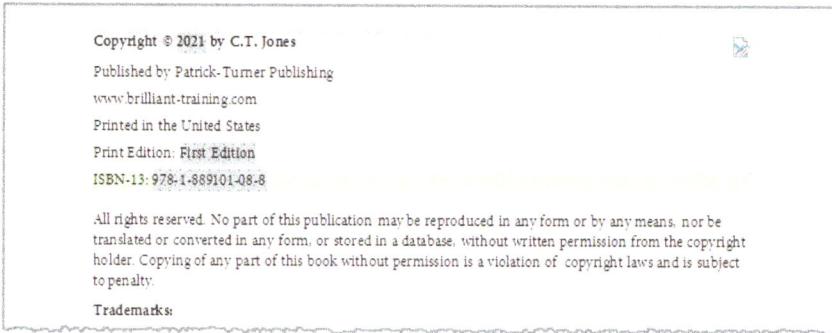

Figure 7-26. Inserted Snippet.

QUICK STEPS: INSERTING SNIPPETS IN A TOPIC

STEP	ACTION
1	Open the topic in which you want to insert a snippet file.
2	Click at the place in the topic where you want to insert the snippet. See **Note**.
3	From the **Insert** ribbon, click **Snippet**, or right-click and select **Insert** > **Snippet**. The **Insert Snippet Link** window opens, to files previously saved as snippets.
4	From the **Content Explorer** > **Snippets** > select the desired snippet file.
5	Click **OK** to insert the snippet.
6	Click the **Save** button to save your work.

NOTE: 1) Block Snippet: Insert a new line on which to insert the block snippet file.

NOTE: 2) Text Snippet: If you are inserting a text snippet that you want to be placed inline with other text, then that other text must be inserted on the line, prior to inserting the text snippet. The text snippet can then be inserted before or after the existing text. Otherwise, the text snippet becomes a block snippet and no other text can be placed inline with the snippet.

VIEWING A TOPIC USING THE PREVIEW WINDOW

BASIC CONCEPT

The **Preview Window** in Flare is an excellent tool for obtaining a view of your topic as it will be rendered in the output. Typically, you would work on topic edits, and at some point, you would build the output with the appropriate target file to see the results. This method can be slow depending on the size of your project and the number of topics compiled. The **Preview Window** lets you shortcut the compile and build process to see the results immediately.

ESSENTIAL ELEMENTS

With single-sourcing in Flare, each of your topics could be targeted for any number of outputs, for example, a PDF document or an HTML5 knowledge base or Web site. After choosing the associated target file, you can appropriately render each of these outputs in the **Preview Window**. Flare generates the topic using the **Primary Target** if you do not select a target and press the Preview button.

APPLICATION TIPS

You can also use a more direct method while editing to view a topic as it should appear. Select the appropriate **Layout, Medium**, and **Page Layout** on the XML Editor toolbar. For example, for print output of the chapter page, set the **Layout** to **Print**; select the **Print Medium**, select the **Page Layout** file as **Chapter Pages**, and **Page Type** as **First Right**. The topic will then appear as you expect it. Since a chapter pages layout file would also have **Left** and **Right** pages, you could set the Page Type for the **Left** or **Right** page for viewing most topics.

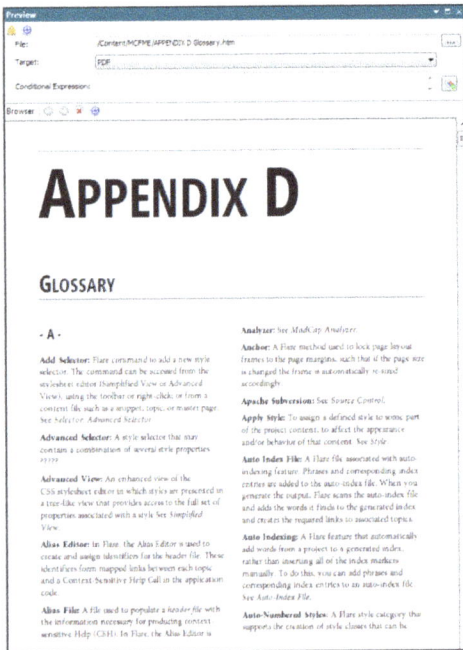

Figure 7-27. Topic Rendered Using Topic Preview Window.

QUICK STEPS: VIEWING A TOPIC USING THE PREVIEW WINDOW

STEP	ACTION
1	Open the desired topic.
2	After editting a topic, click the **Preview** button 🔍 ▾ to render the topic in the **Primary Target**; or click the drop-down arrow and select the desired target by which to render the topic in Preview mode.
3	With the topic displayed in the Preview window, you can use the **Target** drop-down to switch the target.
4	With the topic displayed in the Preview window, you can click in the **Conditional Expression** field and use the button 🪄 to view the impact of applying a conditional expression on tagged elements in the content.
5	Use the **Refresh** button 🔄 to update the preview output.
6	Close the **Preview** window when done.

> **NOTE:** While viewing a topic in the Preview window, you can click on any other open topic tab to display the topic in the **Preview** window.

CHAPTER 8

WORKING WITH FLARE TOC OUTLINES

INTRODUCING THE FLARE TOC

The Flare TOC file serves as an outline that defines the sequential order of your print output; or in some instances, as the basis of the navigation component in online output. For example, the TOC outline file is the basis of the tree structure in a PDF output and a side-navigation or tripane-navigation online output. In a top-navigation site, the TOC is the basis of the menu items. A TOC is generally generated automatically when content is imported, or manually using the TOC Editor.

Flare requires a designated TOC for each print and online output. By specifying a TOC in the target file, you tell Flare which topics to include in the output. Whether created automatically through an import or manually using the TOC Editor, Flare generally places TOC files in the **Project Organizer > Project > TOCs**.

PRINT TOC

A *print TOC*, is any TOC that you have designated for use in one of your print targets. You would designate a print TOC, for example, when defining the target parameters for a PDF output before building it. In operation, a print TOC serves as an outline that determines the sequential order in which the topics in your print target are output. Like other TOCs, a print TOC can be generated manually by dragging and dropping HTML or other files from the content Explorer to the TOC Editor; or automatically from an import or using the Auto-Generate feature to create TOC entries.

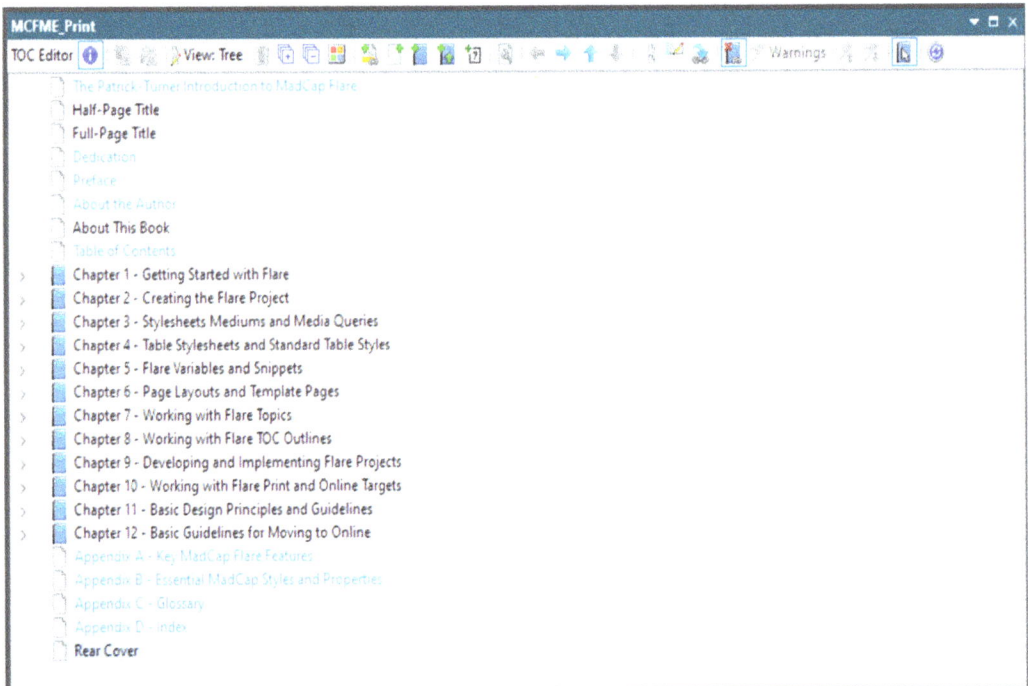

Figure 8-1. Typical Flare (Print) TOC File Opened in TOC Editor.

ONLINE TOC

An *online TOC*, is a TOC that you have designated for use in one of your online targets. You would specify an online TOC, for example, when defining the target parameters for an HTML output before building it. Although print and online outputs may look the same from an outward appearance, they have different behavior in operation. Whereas a print TOC serves as an outline for the sequential order when creating your print target, an online TOC serves as the navigation element (or tree) — for example, in an HTML output with side-navigation or tripane-navigation, or as the menu items in an HTML output with top-navigation.

Often, an online TOC is created directly from a print TOC, mainly by removing print-specific topics.

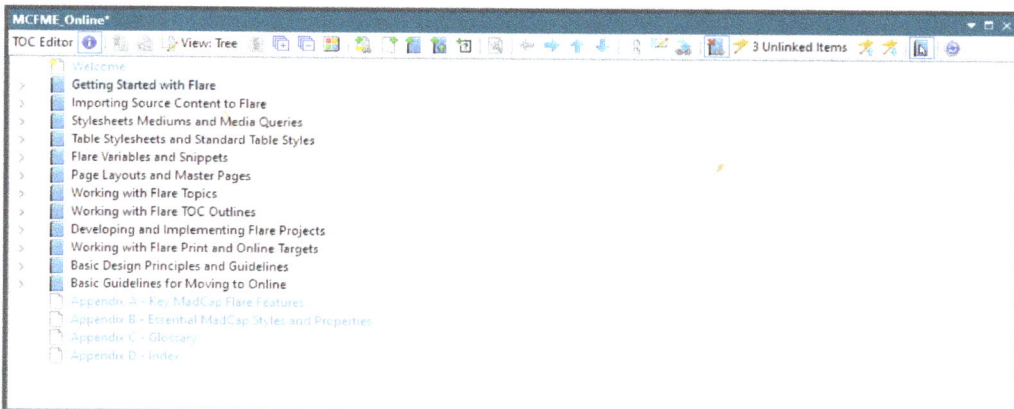

Figure 8-2. Typical Flare (Online) TOC File Opened in TOC Editor.

PRIMARY TOC

In a given project, you may eventually create many TOCs, to serve different purposes. In most projects, a print TOC is created and specified for each print output target, and an online TOC may be created and defined for each online output target. In a project with multiple targets, the *Primary TOC* is simply one that you designate as being primary. A Primary TOC can be specified at the Project level, using **Project** ribbon **Project Properties** > **Primary TOC**, or at the Target level, using **General** > **Primary TOC**.

If there are several TOCs, and you have not designated one as primary, Flare automatically designates the first TOC it finds in the project as the primary TOC. With a Primary TOC, you have the option of creating links to other TOCs that you want to include in the output. If a TOC is specified as the primary TOC both at the project and target levels, then one specified at the target takes precedence.

INTRODUCING THE FLARE TOC EDITOR

Working with the TOC Editor, you can create the TOCs required for print and online outputs. In this work, you define the behavior of the TOC in relationship to your content. You will establish how the TOC links to various types of content, the association of page layout files to TOC entries, and provide TOC details to ensure that auto-numbering in your content happens correctly.

The TOC Editor parameter dialogs include:

1. The **General** tab, lets you define TOC item appearance and links to various content types.

2. The **Printed Output** tab lets you define the association of your TOC items to page layout files.

3. The **Auto-Numbers** tab lets you define relationships between the TOC and your auto-numbered content.

4. The **Conditional Text** tab lets you manage the exclusion or inclusion of TOC items.

> **NOTE:** The Auto-generate tab and the Advanced tab are not covered in this discussion.

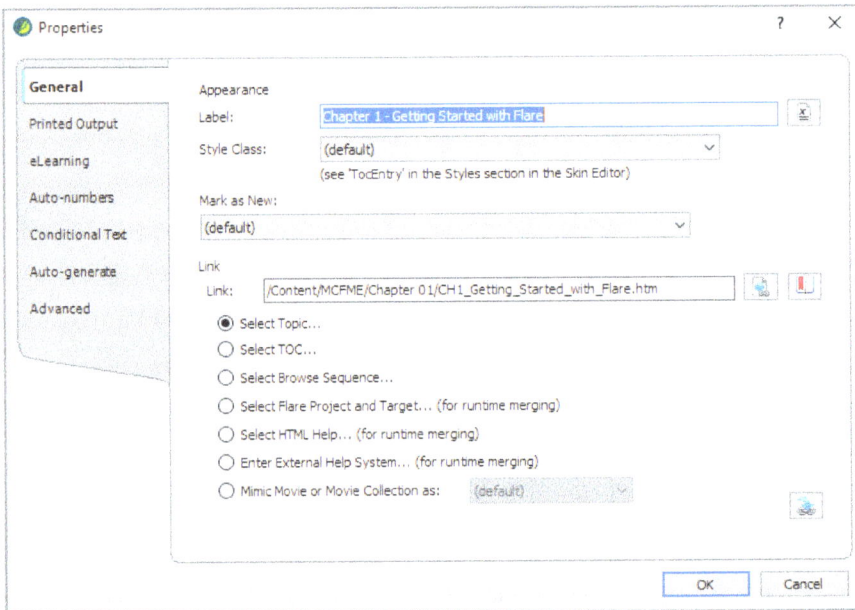

Figure 8-3. TOC Editor — General Properties Dialog.

FLARE TOC EDITOR GENERAL PROPERTIES

From the **General Properties** tab, you can affect the **Appearance** of the TOC by specifying the TOC **Label**, and if applicable, a **Style Class** defined in the stylesheet (a Skin file under TOC Entry). Identifying an item to link to the TOC item is the other primary use of this tab. You can link each TOC item to a single item only. The General Properties are briefly described in Table 8-1.

Table 8-1. TOC Editor – General Properties

Property Group	Brief Description
Label	Use this field to enter a name directly or insert a variable to define the name you want to appear for this TOC entry. You may also use the **Advanced** tab of the **TOC Properties** to have this label automatically set to the title of the linked file.
Style Class	(Optional) Suppose you have configured specific **TOC Entry** style class settings, for a supported online skin, for example, a Tripane-Skin. In that case, you can use the **Style Class** field to select a class to apply to the selected TOC item, or you can leave the default setting to use the parent style.
Mark as New	Use this option to mark a TOC entry as "new" (or not previously available) in the output.
Link	For each TOC item, you can specify from a list of things to link to — for example, a Topic, a Movie file, another TOC, Flare project, or HTML help (**.CHM**) system.

FLARE TOC EDITOR PRINTED OUTPUT PROPERTIES

The **Printed Output Properties** is where you use specific TOC entries to inform Flare of the different break-points in your content. Using these break-points, you can tell Flare how and when to apply the appropriate page layout files you have created to manage the flow of content in your print outputs.

After specifying a **Break Type** as **Chapter Break** or **Page Layout Break**, you can determine the appropriate **Page Layout file**, starting **Page Type**, and **Page Number** to apply to the selected TOC item. Once applied, upon building the target, the content is flowed onto the printed output using the pages of the layout file, until reaching the next TOC item, at which another page layout file is specified.

The Printed Output Properties are briefly described in Table 8-2.

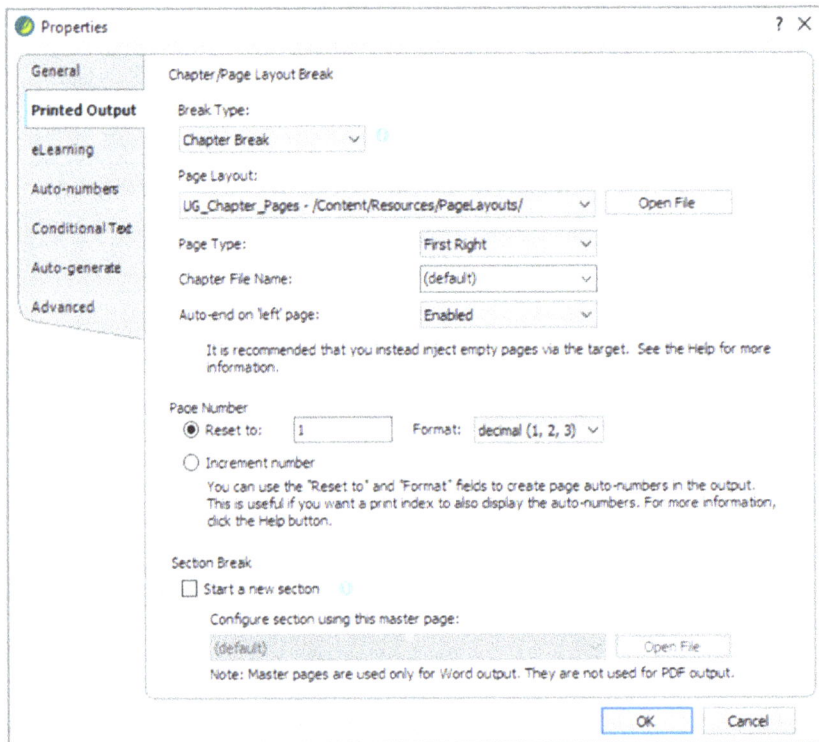

Figure 8-4. TOC Editor—Printed Output Properties Dialog.

Table 8-2. TOC Editor – Printed Output Properties

Property Group	Brief Description
Break Type	Use this drop-down option to select **Chapter Break**, **Page Layout Break**, or **None** as the type of break at this particular TOC entry.
	A **Chapter Break** indicates a TOC entry as a starting point in a part of the document for which you created a page layout file. After you specify a page layout file, the content flows onto subsequent pages until encountering a new breakpoint.
	A **Page Layout Break** indicates a TOC breakpoint at which the page layout switches from the normal flow but without causing a new chapter break. For example, a switch in page orientation from portrait to landscape.
	A setting of **None** prevents any breaks or changes in the page layout or page type.
Page Layout	Use the **Page Layout** drop-down to specify the page layout file to use starting at this breakpoint and until the next breakpoint in the TOC and content. You would typically use a different page layout file with each logical division of a book or document.
Page Type	Use this drop-down to select from the currently specified page layout file, a specific **Page Type** to be applied as the starting page for the current TOC item.
Chapter File Name	This optional entry, lets you specify a name you want the chapter to have.
Auto-end on "left page"	Enable this option if your content should be forced to end on a left page. This selection is typical if the major sections of your document generally start on a First Right page.
Page Number	Use this option to specify **Reset to** = '**1**' or some other number if you wish to set the starting page number for this TOC breakpoint.
	Use the default to **Increment number** to continue numbering from the previous layout.
	Use **Format** to specify the number format to use. See **Note 1**.
Section Break	Enable the **Start a new section**, option to mark Heading 1 TOC items in the content, where both Chapter and Section auto-numbering are used in the content. See **Note 2**.

NOTE: 1) Like most Flare tasks, there are alternate ways to create page numbers in your output. I prefer using **ChapterNumber/Page Number** variables in page layout footers. Still, if you select the '**Text**" option in the **Format** field, you can insert Auto-Number commands in the **Reset to** field to insert page numbers.

NOTE: 2) When you configure the **Printed Output** and **Auto-Numbers** tabs for sections in your content containing auto-numbering, the TOC item of the first Heading 1 section will have **Reset to** = '**1**' specified under **Section Number** on the **Auto-Number** tab. You then must enable the **Start a new section** option for all of the next Heading 1 sections in the same chapter.

FLARE TOC EDITOR AUTO-NUMBERS PROPERTIES

The **Auto-Numbers** dialog, in partial conjunction with the **Printed Output** dialog, is used to specify the information needed by Flare to ensure proper numbering in your content where you are using the {volnum}, {chapnum}, and {secnum} auto-numbering commands.

In this dialog, you can specify the starting number of a new chapter, volume, or section, depending on the TOC item. Furthermore, at different break-points, you can specify whether to continue with the previous number or increment the number. Finally, you can select the number **Format** in which each of these elements should be numbered — for example using **Decimal**, upper or lower case **Roman** or **Alpha**. The Auto-Numbers Properties are briefly described in Table 8-3.

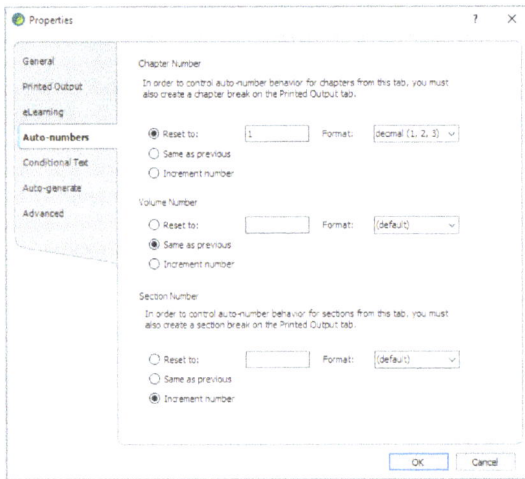

Figure 8-5. TOC Editor — Auto-Numbers Properties Dialog.

Table 8-3. TOC Editor – Auto-Numbers Properties

Property Group	Brief Description
Chapter Number	Use **Chapter Number**, to specify a starting number, a **Format** for numbering chapters, and whether to continue with the **Same as previous** chapter number or to **Increment number**.
Volume Number	Use **Volume Number**, to specify a starting number, a **Format** for numbering volumes, and whether to continue with the **Same as previous** volume number or to **Increment number**.
Section Number	Use **Section Number**, to specify a starting number, a **Format** for numbering sections, and whether to continue with the **Same as previous** section number or to **Increment number**.

FLARE TOC EDITOR CONDITIONAL TEXT PROPERTIES

Just as with other elements of your content, you can specify whether to include or exclude certain TOC items based on conditional tags that you assign. By assigning conditional tags, you can include or exclude a TOC item, depending on the instance of a given target. If excluded, neither the TOC item nor the linked item will appear in the output.

To tag a selected TOC item, select the **Conditional Tag Set**, then select the one or more **Condition Tags** that apply to the currently selected TOC item.

The Conditional Text Properties are briefly described in Table 8-3.

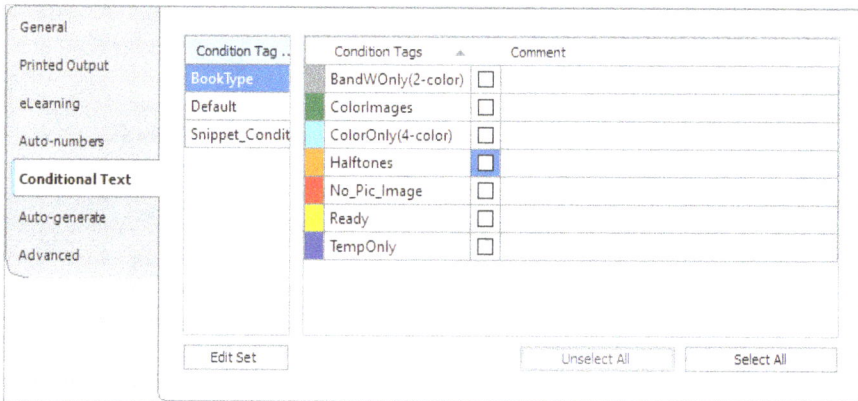

Figure 8-6. TOC Editor — Conditional Text Tab.

Table 8-4. TOC Editor – Conditional Text Properties

Property Group	Brief Description
Condition Tag Sets	The listed **Condition Tag Sets** represent those that have been defined in the project. Each set contains a collection of **Condition Tags** any of which can be assigned to a TOC item.
Condition Tags	A list of tags that have been defined in one of the **Condition Tag Sets**. Clicking on the tag set displays the **Condition Tags** it contains.
Edit Set	Clicking on the **Edit Set** button enables you to open the selected tag set. Once opened, you can edit the tag set as required.

A PAGE LAYOUT FILE AND TOC MAPPING EXAMPLE

The following table illustrates a basic mapping of Page Layout files to TOC item breakpoints.

Table 8-5. Ex. TOC and Applicable Page Layout Files (**B/T** = Break Type; **FR** = First Right; **L/R** = Left/Right)

Book Component	B/T	Layout File	Page
The Patric-Turner Introduction to MadCap Flare	Page/L	TitlePages	Title
Half Page Title	Page/L	FrontMatter	FR
Full Page Title	Page/L	FrontMatter	FR
Table of Contents	Page/L	FrontMatter	Right
Preface	Page/L	FrontMatter	Cont. L/R
About This Book	Page/L	FrontMatter	L/R
Chapter 1 - Getting Started with Flare	Chapter	ChapterPages	FR
Chapter 2 - Creating the Flare Project	Chapter	ChapterPages	FR
Chapter 3 - Stylesheets, Mediums, and Media Queries	Chapter	ChapterPages	FR
Chapter 4 - Table Stylesheets and Standard Table Styles	Chapter	ChapterPages	FR
Chapter 5 - Flare Variables and Snippets	Chapter	ChapterPages	FR
Chapter 6 - Page Layout and Template Pages	Chapter	ChapterPages	FR
Chapter 7 - Working with Flare Topics	Chapter	ChapterPages	FR
Chapter 8 - Working with Flare TOC Outlines	Chapter	ChapterPages	FR
Chapter 9 - Developing and Implementing Flare Projects	Chapter	ChapterPages	FR
Chapter 10 - Working with Print and Online Targets	Chapter	ChapterPages	FR
Chapter 11 - Basic Design Principles and Guidelines	Chapter	ChapterPages	FR
Chapter 12 - Basic Guidelines to Moving Online	Chapter	ChapterPages	FR
Appendix A - Key MadCap Flare Features	Chapter	ChapterPages	FR
Appendix B - Key MadCap Styles and Properties	Chapter	ChapterPages	FR
Appendix C - Glossary	Chapter	GlossaryPages	FR
Appendix D - Index	Chapter	IndexPages	FR

SUMMARY ON WORKING WITH FLARE TOC FILES

The Flare TOC file serves as an outline that determines the sequential order of your print output. The TOC outline also functions as a navigation element in the tree structure for a side-navigation or tri-pane-navigation online output or the menu items in a top-navigation output. The notable point here is that the TOC file described in this chapter is not the Table of Contents topic file generally placed in the front of a book or document.

The following checklist offers some tips and guidance for working with and developing TOC files in your project. Some examples of TOC-related tasks follow in the remainder of this chapter.

CHECKLIST: WORKING WITH FLARE TOC FILES

- *The Flare TOC file (.FLTOC), located in the **Project Organizer**, can be created manually or is generated based on a TOC outline from imported FrameMaker or Word files.*

- *A TOC for the project can be created by manually dragging HTML topic files from the **Content** folder and dropping them into the TOC Editor window at the desired position.*

- *TOC entries can be shifted up or down to the left (promoted) or to the right (demoted) in the TOC structure, using the directional arrows.*

- *If you use the drag-and-drop method to build a TOC, then the entry that appears in the TOC is the first heading found in the topic. You can modify this behavior in the Topic Properties dialog.*

- *Consider creating a TOC file for each chapter of a book you intend to use as source content online. Shorter TOCs work better in mini-TOC proxies or Menu proxies for top navigation.*

- *You can link TOC items to existing HTML topics located in the Content folder. This feature is accessed using the right-click when the TOC item (entry) is selected.*

- *Using a right-click option on the TOC, you can create a new topic and simultaneously link it to a new TOC item (entry) that you create in the process.*

- *TOC entries may link to HTML files in the Content folder, external links such as Web sites, or even files such as PDF books or movie files.*

- *Consider replacing an imported table of contents (TOC) file with a Flare TOC proxy topic that will generate a TOC topic file that you can insert in the front matter section of your document.*

- *Defining **TOC Properties** for **Page Breaks** and **Section Breaks**, work in conjunction with Page Layout files to ensure proper numbering of books or documents that use auto-numbering.*

NAVIGATING THE FLARE TOC EDITOR

BASIC CONCEPT

The TOC Editor is the primary means of creating and working with TOC outlines in your project. You will mainly use the editor to develop and manage the TOCs in your project, but you can also add new topics, create links to new or existing topics, and create links to other types of TOC items and other TOCs. The TOC Editor is also used to define the various break-points in your content and associate these items to your page layout files. Finally, using the TOC Editor, you can affect the behavior of your content that uses auto-numbered styles.

ESSENTIAL ELEMENTS

You can switch the view between the standard **Tree View** and the **Grid View** from the TOC Editor toolbar ribbon. Each TOC item is listed on a single row in the grid-view, configurable parameters in the adjacent columns. While in the **Grid View**, you can selectively show columns or hide them from the view. Also, from the toolbar ribbon, tools are available to apply conditional tags, create and link to new topics, and create new books and new items.

Once TOC entries are created and linked, available tools allow you to reposition entries by moving them up and down or to the left or right. Finally, you can show unlinked books and review any warnings of items that may need fixing in the TOC.

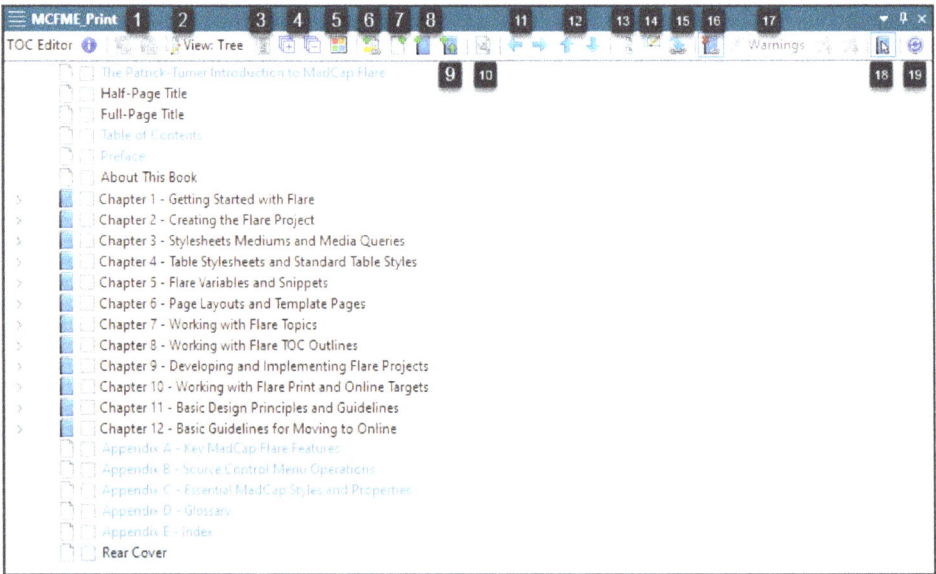

Figure 8-7. Flare TOC Editor.

QUICK STEPS: NAVIGATING AND SETTING TOC EDITOR

STEP	ACTION
1	Click **Project Folder** > **Project** > **TOCs**, and double-click on a desired TOC to open it in the TOC Editor.
2	By default, the TOC is in the **Tree** view. Click **View: Tree** to switch to the TOC **Grid** view or **View: Grid**. Click **View: Grid** to switch back to the Tree view.
3	When in the Grid view, click the **Show/Hide Columns** button, to enable/disable check boxes to select which columns to **Show/Hide**. In this mode you can configure the column width and background color.
4	Click the **Expand All/Collapse All** buttons, to expand or collapse all TOC entries, respectively.
5	Click **Show indicators for condition tags** button, to toggle **Show/Hide** condition tag indicators.
6	Click the button **Create a new topic and link to it**, to simultaneously create a new topic and link it to a new TOC entry.
7	Click the **New Item** button, to insert a new TOC item. The item can be linked to a topic, movie, or other item.
8	Click the **New Book** button, to insert a new TOC book.
9	Click the **New Top-Level Book** button, to insert a new TOC book, or left-most book item.
10	Use **F4** or click the **Display Properties** button to open the **Properties** dialog for the selected item.
11	Click **move-left/move-right** buttons, to move the TOC item to the left or the right respectively.
12	Click the **Up/Down** buttons, to move the TOC item up or down in the TOC respectively.
13	Click the **Locate file** button to find the selected file in the Content Explorer or the Project Organizer.
14	Click the **Send linked document** button, to package and send one or more selected topics to reviewers, using MadCap Central or an email.
15	Click the **Open linked file** button to open the file linked to the selected TOC item.
16	Click the **Show unlinked books** button, to show TOC books that are unlinked to a topic or other item.
17	Use next and previous warnings buttons to navigate through current Flare TOC warnings.
18	Click the toggle button **Displaying Topic Properties** or **Opening Topic** button to switch the operation of the double-click on a of TOC item.
19	Click the Refresh button to update the TOC outline with any changes you have made in TOC Titles.

ADDING A NEW FLARE TOC OUTLINE FILE

BASIC CONCEPT

In Flare, there is no limit on the number of TOCs you may create and use in your project. Most projects will typically have a TOC for each target, for example, a print TOC for each PDF output and an online TOC for each HTML5 output.

ESSENTIAL ELEMENTS

Creating a new TOC file is generally created from the **Project Organizer** in the TOC subfolder. Select **Project > TOCs >** right-click and select **Add Table of Contents** from the **Project Organizer**. When the **Add File** dialog opens, ensure that the **File Type** is set for TOC. When you create a new TOC outline file, you will choose to create the new file from a **New from Template** (factory or user-defined) or **New from Existing** TOC outline file.

Depending on the exact situation, you may decide to make a copy of an existing TOC similar to what you want to create and later modify the TOC entries and links. Once you create the file, you can use the various available methods to populate the TOC entries.

APPLICATION TIPS

Creating and using multiple TOCs can add certain flexibilities to your projects, especially where there are several documents in a single large project. With multiple documents, for example, each can have its target and its TOC, which allows simultaneous development by several individuals.

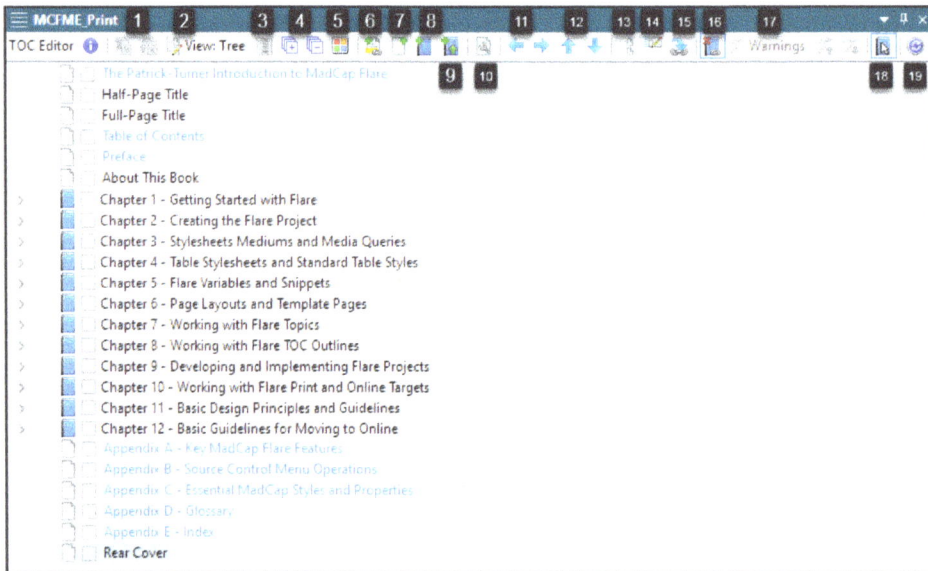

Figure 8-8. Add Table of Contents Option Selected — Add File Dialog with TOC Option Set.

QUICK STEPS: ADDING A NEW FLARE TOC OUTLINE FILE

STEP	ACTION
1	Select the **TOCs** folder, in the **Project Organizer**, or select a subfolder in which you wish to add the new TOC outline file. You can create a subfolder in the root folder **TOCs** if desired.
2	Right-click > **Add Table Of Contents**. The **Add File** dialog opens.
3	Ensure that the **File Type** is set for **TOC**.
4	**To create the new TOC Outline file use one of the following:**
	a) From Templates: Set the **Source** for **New From Template**, then choose the **MyTOC** template from the **Factory Templates** folder or choose a template from a user-defined **Custom Templates** folder.
	b) From Existing: Set the **Source** for **New From Existing**, and use the browse button ⌐⋯⌐ to locate an existing TOC outline.
5	Under **TOC**, in the **Folder** field use the default **Root folder** (**Project/TOCs**), or browse and choose a sub-folder in the default folder in which to store the new TOC outline file.
6	Use the **File Name** field to specify a name for the new TOC outline file.
7	Click > **Add** to save the new TOC outline.

CREATING AN ONLINE TOC FROM A PRINT TOC

BASIC CONCEPT

After having created a print TOC, it will very likely include many of the same topics you will want as part of your online content. With time spent reviewing the topics and the TOC entries, it should become more apparent which content items would be equally viable online. After determining what content is appropriate for online, creating the new online TOC is the next step.

ESSENTIAL ELEMENTS

Since much of your online content is the same as the print content, you can start by making a copy of the print TOC and renaming it to designate it as the online TOC. Next, identify and remove the TOC entries that are (**a**) intended for print outputs only; (**b**) items that can serve for both print and online outputs, but will need review and perhaps some editing or use of conditional tags for online and (**c**) items that can serve both for print and online outputs, but may require additional review to determine suitability for online. The items labeled 'b' in the image represent the main body of your content.

APPLICATION TIPS

Whereas you may find it a simple task to determine what topics from your print outputs you should include in your online work, the job of making that content more suitable for online presentation may take a bit longer. You will need to select the appropriate topics and edit them as required online. For additional assistance, see " *Basic Guidelines for Moving to Online.*"

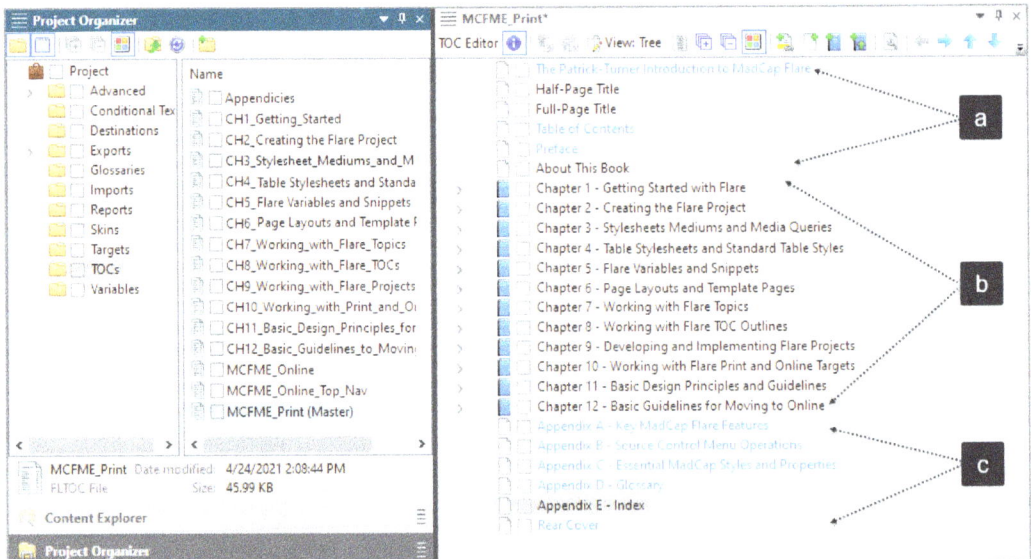

Figure 8-9. An Example Print TOC.

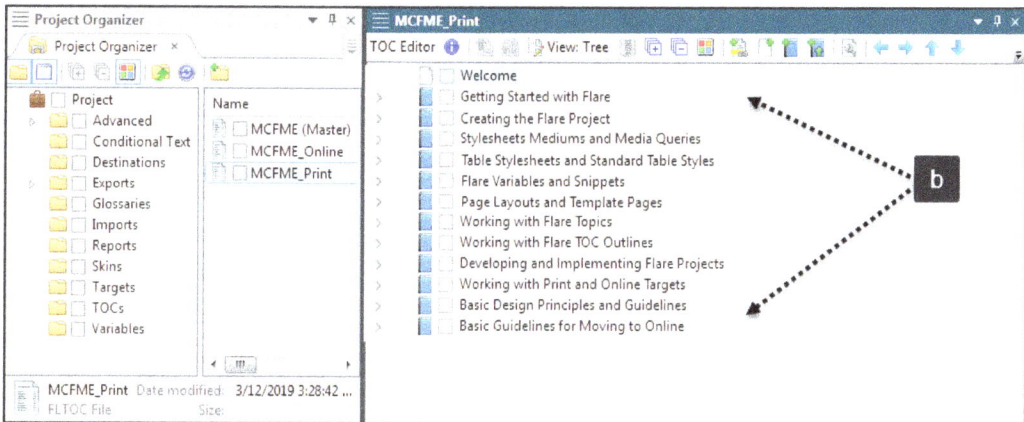

Figure 8-10. New Online TOC Created from a Print TOC.

QUICK STEPS: CREATING AN ONLINE TOC FROM A PRINT TOC

STEP	ACTION
1	From the **Project Organizer** > **TOC** subfolder, copy and paste your Print TOC file.
2	Rename the copied Print TOC file, perhaps using the same name and appending the word "**Online**."
3	Double-click on the newly created file to have it open in the TOC Editor.
4	Remove, from the TOC outline, all page or book entries from the Front Matter pages section, which are intended for Print Outputs only. See the TOC entries, pointed to by (**a**), in Figure 8-9.
5	After reviewing the topics for suitability, remove, from the TOC outline, all Back Matter page or book entries, which are intended for Print Outputs only. See the TOC entries, pointed to by (**c**), in Figure 8-9.
6	The remaining TOC entries represent items that would remain in the Online TOC. See Figure 8-10.
7	Additional TOC items and topics may need to be created specifically for online — for example, a Home page or a Welcome topic.
8	Click the **Save** button to save your work.

CREATING AND LINKING A NEW TOPIC IN THE TOC OUTLINE

BASIC CONCEPT

Another way of creating a new topic, is directly from the TOC outline. You might use this method when you are developing your TOC from scratch. It may also be helpful when you are already working with the TOC outline and determine that you need to insert a new topic. This method is efficient as, in one operation, you can simultaneously create a new topic, insert a new TOC entry and link the entry to the new topic.

ESSENTIAL ELEMENTS

The operation to create a new TOC entry and a new topic simultaneously is initiated from the TOC after clicking at the point where you wish to insert the new TOC entry. Using a right-click, select the option to **Link to New Topic**. When creating the topic, the entry you place in the **Title** field determines the label on the TOC entry. If the field is left blank, Flare uses the first heading found in the topic as the **Title**. You will enter a **File Name** for the new topic and use the **1st Heading** field under **Advanced** to specify a name for the first topic heading. Finally, use the **Style** drop-down to choose a style to apply to the first heading in the new topic.

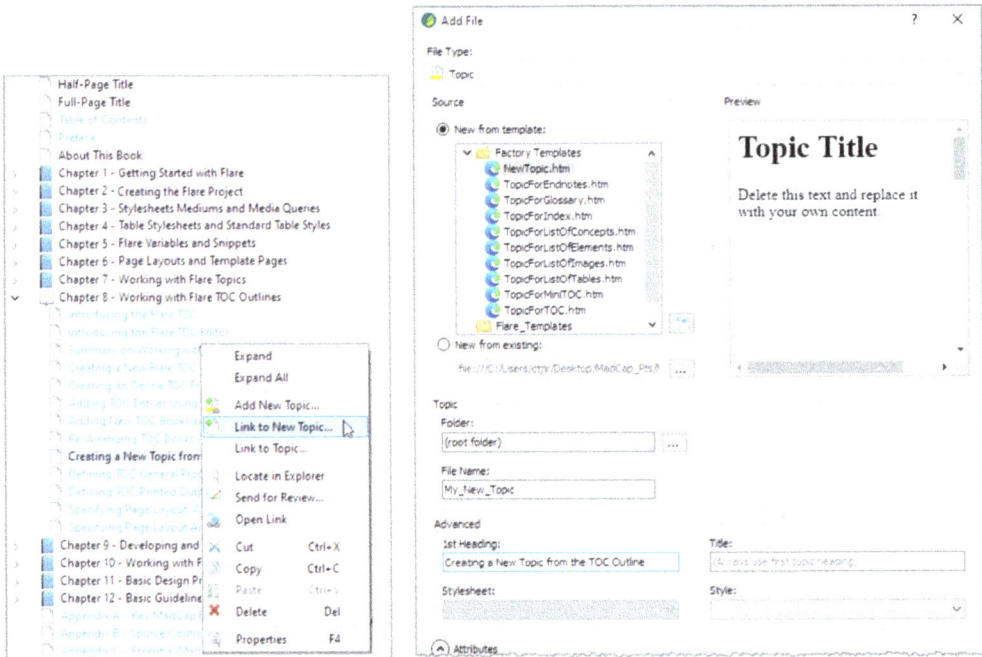

Figure 8-11. Creating a New Topic from the TOC Outline.

QUICK STEPS: CREATING AND LINKING A NEW TOPIC IN THE TOC OUTLINE

STEP	ACTION
1	From the TOC Outline, click the position where you want to create a new TOC entry and link it to a topic.
2	From the TOC toolbar ribbon click the **Create a new topic and link to it** button 🖼, or right-click and select **Link to New Topic**. The **Add File** dialog opens.
3	Ensure that the **File Type** is set for **Topic**.
—	**To create the new topic based on a template use the following:**
4	Set the **Source** for **New From Template**, then choose a template from the **Factory Template** folder or choose a template from a user-defined **Custom Templates** folder.
5	Continue with **Step 7**.
—	**To create the new topic based on an existing topic file use the following**:
6	Set the **Source** for **New From Existing**, and use the browse button ⌷ to locate the existing topic file.
7	Under **Topic**, use the **Folder** field and choose the default folder, or browse and choose another folder in which to store the new topic file.
8	Use the **File Name** field to specify a name for the new topic file. For example, **MyNewTopic**
9	In the **1st Heading** field, enter the first heading you want to appear in the new topic. Leave this field blank to if you want to use the file name as the first heading to appear in the new topic.
10	In the **Title** field, enter the title you want to use for the topic in the **Topic Properties**, and to appear as the TOC outline entry. Leave the field blank to use the first topic heading to serve as the title of the topic and as the TOC entry.
11	Use the **Style** drop-down and choose a style to apply to the first heading placed in the new topic.
12	Click **Add** to save the new topic file.

ADDING, LINKING, AND RE-ARRANGING TOC BOOKS AND ITEMS

BASIC CONCEPT

You can create TOCs from an import, using the drag-and-drop method, or automatically, using the heading levels of your content. Regardless of how you make the TOC, you can always edit or add to the TOC using the tools provided on the TOC Editor ribbon. TOC books, topics, and other items can be added, linked, and re-arranged in any way that suits your requirements.

ESSENTIAL ELEMENTS

Whether starting with an existing TOC or an open TOC file without any entries, you can add TOC items by dragging-and-dropping single or multiple topic files or entire sub-folders from the **Content Explorer** into the editor. Files placed into the editor create TOC entries that are already linked. You can also **Create a new book**, or **Create a new item**, and then later connect the new book or item to a specific topic or another type of item. From the TOC Editor local ribbon or the right-click, you can **Create a new topic and link to it** simultaneously from the TOC entry.

All newly added TOC entries can be re-arranged in the TOC using the **move-up/move-down** buttons and the **move-left/move-right** buttons.

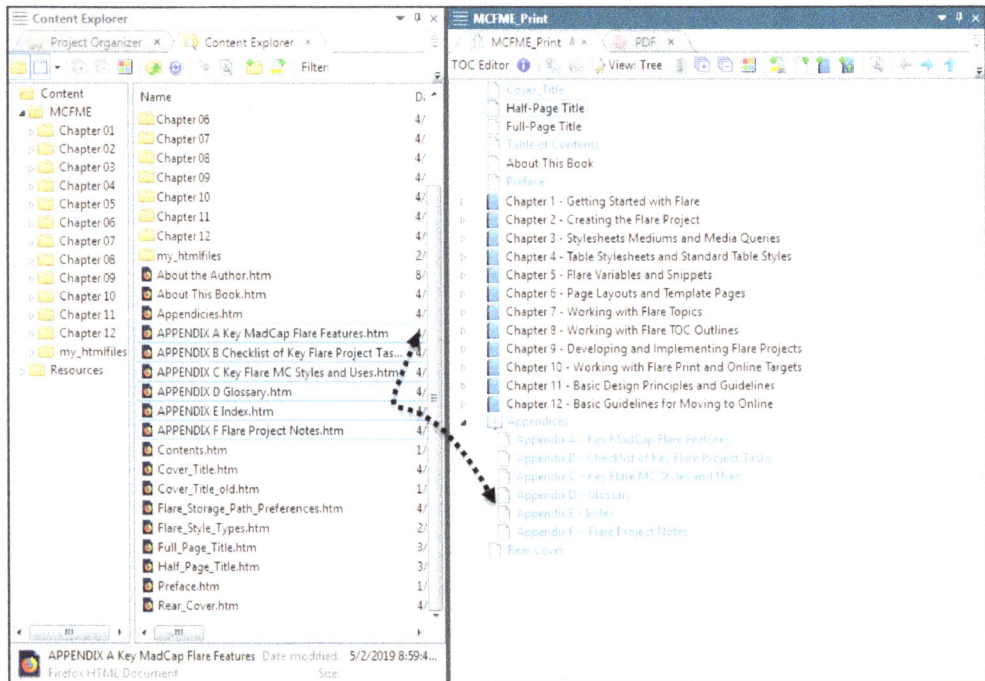

Figure 8-12. Dragging and Dropping Content to the TOC Editor as New TOC Items.

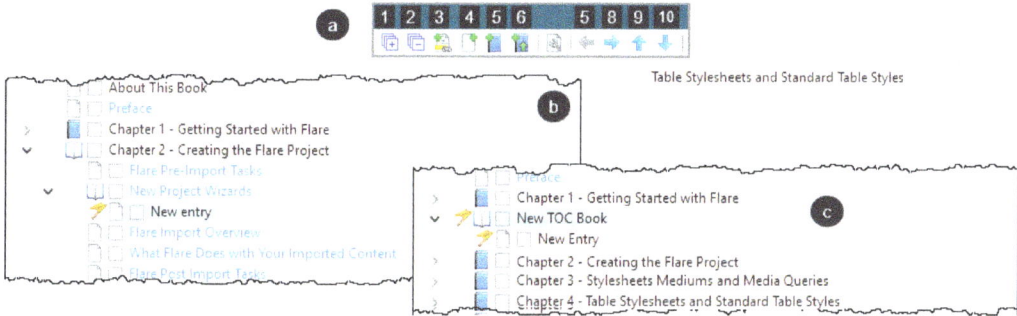

Figure 8-13. a) TOC Editor Tools for Adding and Rearranging TOC, b) Adding TOC Item, and c) Add ind TOC Book.

Quick Steps: Adding, Linking, and Re-Arranging TOC Books and Items

STEP	ACTION
—	**Add New TOC Folders and Topics Using Drag-and-Drop Method**
1	Select the **Project Organizer** > **TOC** folder, and open the TOC where you want to add items.
2	Open the **Content Explorer** to the folders and files you want to move to the TOC as new items.
3	Select a complete folder or use the **CTRL** key and select one or more individual files to move to the TOC.
4	Click and hold the mouse to drag the files to the TOC Editor. A large blue arrow will appear and move up and down to aid in positioning the collection of files where you want to insert them.
5	Drop the files at the desired position in the TOC.
—	**Add New TOC Items**
1	Click on a TOC book in which you want to add the new item.
2	Click the **New Item** button, to insert a new TOC item, for example topic, movie, other. The item is inserted at the bottom position of the book.
3	Use the **move-up/move-down** buttons, to move a TOC item up or down in the TOC.
4	Right-click and select **Link to New Topic**, to create a new topic, and link it to the new TOC item; or right-click and select **Link to Topic**, to open the Content Explorer to link the TOC item to an existing topic.
—	**Add New TOC Books (Books and Top-Level Books)**
1	Click the **New Book** button, to insert a TOC book. The book is inserted below the book you selected.
2	Use the **move-up/move-down** buttons, to move TOC books up or down in the TOC.
3	Click the **move-left/move-right** buttons, to move the TOC item to the left or right.
4	Expand and right-click on the book and select **Link to New Topic**, to create a new topic and link it to the book; or right-click and select **Link to Topic**, to open the Content Explorer to link the book to a topic.
5	Now, right-click on the new TOC item that was created inside the book and select **Link to New Topic**, to create a new topic and link it; or right-click and select **Link to Topic**, to open the Content Explorer to link the TOC item to an existing topic.

DEFINING GENERAL PROPERTIES OF TOC ITEM

BASIC CONCEPT

If your TOC was created using the drag-and-drop from the Content Explorer or is the result of an imported project, then you may not require the **General** tab that often. Most of your TOC items will already have the **Labels (names)** that you want to appear on the TOC, and they will likely have **Links** to specific topics or other types of items. These are the main functions you would perform using the **General** tab. Even if you create new topics from the TOC, you will have the opportunity to, at the same time, link the topic to the TOC item and specify the title.

ESSENTIAL ELEMENTS

You can type in a name you want to assign to the selected TOC item in the **Label** field, even if it already has a name. The **Style Class** is optional, but you can apply a style you have previously defined in the Tripane Navigation skin for specific TOC elements. Use **Mark as New** to indicate that the online TOC item is new and was not present before. You can specify a topic or a bookmark from the current project to be linked to the TOC item from the **Link** field. In addition to the latter link items, several other options are listed from which you can choose to link to the TOC entry.

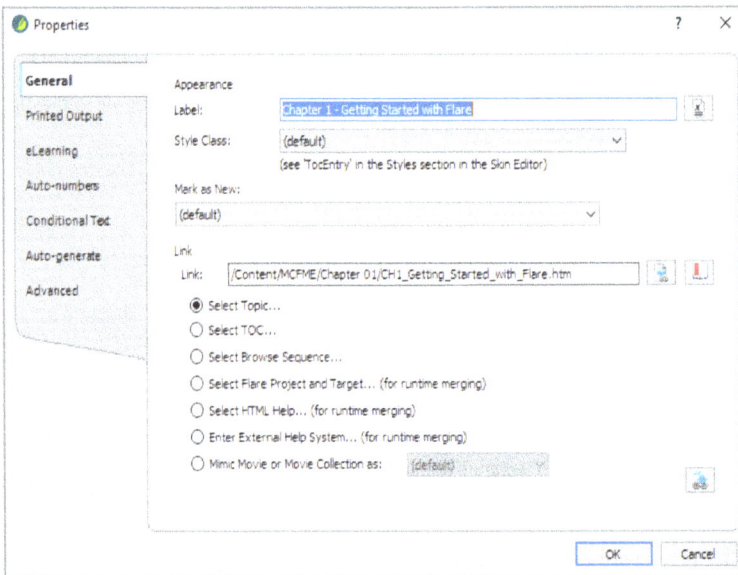

Figure 8-14. TOC General Properties Dialog.

QUICK STEPS: DEFINING GENERAL PROPERTIES OF TOC ITEM

STEP	ACTION
1	Open the TOC file in which you want to specify the **General** parameters.
2	Select a TOC item, right-click and select **Properties**. The Properties dialog opens.
3	Click the **General** tab.
4	The **Label** field displays the title given to the TOC item.
5	Use the **Style Class** field to select a style class you may have created under **TocEntry** in the Skin Editor. You may also leave the **default** entry to use the parent Toc Entry style. See **Note**.
6	Use the **Mark as New** drop-down and select '**Yes**' to display the TOC entry as "new" (as not previously available) in the output. By default the TOC entry is marked with an asterisk. If '**No**' is selected, the property values for the **TocEntry** style (defined under **Styles** tab on the Skin Editor) are overridden.
7	The **Link** field displays the path of the item currently linked to the TOC item. Click the button ![icon] **Select Link** to browse and select a new item to link to the TOC item; or click the button ![icon] **Select Bookmark** to open the dialog to select a bookmark to link to the TOC item.
8	Enable the **Select Topic** option, to open a dialog to browse and select a topic to link to the TOC entry.
9	Enable the **Select TOC** option, to open a dialog that lists the TOCs in your project. Browse and select the TOC to link to this entry.
10	Enable the **Browse Sequence** option, to open a dialog that lists the browse sequences in your project. Browse and select the browse sequence to link to this TOC entry.
11	Enable the **Select Flare Project and Target** option to open a dialog that lists the available Flare projects, from which you can select the project to link to this TOC entry.
12	Enable the **Select HTML Help** option to link to an HTML Help System (or **.CHM** file). When the dialog opens you will be able to find and select the file and enable/disable specific options, including linking to a specific topic in the Help system.
13	Enable the **Enter External Help System** option to link to an external help system. When the dialog opens you are able to: **a)** Enter the name of the Help System output file to which you want to establish the link. **b)** Enter the full path to a Help System output file, which will be copied to your Flare project when you compile the project.
14	Enable the option **Mimic Movie or Movie Collection as** to open the dialog to find and select any one of the individual Mimic movie or a movie collection file types to link to the entry.
15	Click **OK** to save your work.

> **NOTE:** The available styles depend on the type of skin. When a WebHelp output type, you can use the Toc Entry style on the **Styles** tab of the Skin Editor to change the look of individual entries in your TOC.

DEFINING PRINTED OUTPUT PROPERTIES OF TOC ITEM

BASIC CONCEPT

The **Printed Output** tab is key to mapping the TOC and its entries to your content to determine how Flare applies Page Layout files and Page Types to the parts of your print output. The **Printed Output** tab also plays a role in conjunction with the **Auto-Numbers** tab in ensuring that auto-numbering happens correctly for sections in your content by identifying the start of new sections.

ESSENTIAL ELEMENTS

The **Break Type** parameter group allows you to identify specific TOC items as a **Chapter Break** or a **Page Layout** break. These break types are generally at a point in your content where you specify a **Page Layout** file and a specific **Page Type** to be applied to start at the TOC item. These points in the TOC include items that mark the start of content like Title Pages, Front Matter Pages, Chapter Pages, and Glossary pages. A **Page Layout** break marks a point where there is a change in the normal page flow and requires that a specific **Page Type** be applied.

You must also select **Enabled** or **Disabled** to indicate whether the content starting at the TOC item should be set to **Auto-end on 'left' page**. For the **Page Number**, you would enable **Reset to** and then specify a start page number; or leave the default to Increment number from the last section.

APPLICATION TIPS

The **Section Break** is used in conjunction with the **Printed Output** tab to manage the behavior of auto-number sections in your content. You must enable the **Start a new section** option for all H1 sections after setting the first section set to start at '1' by setting **Reset to** = '1' on the **Printed Output** tab.

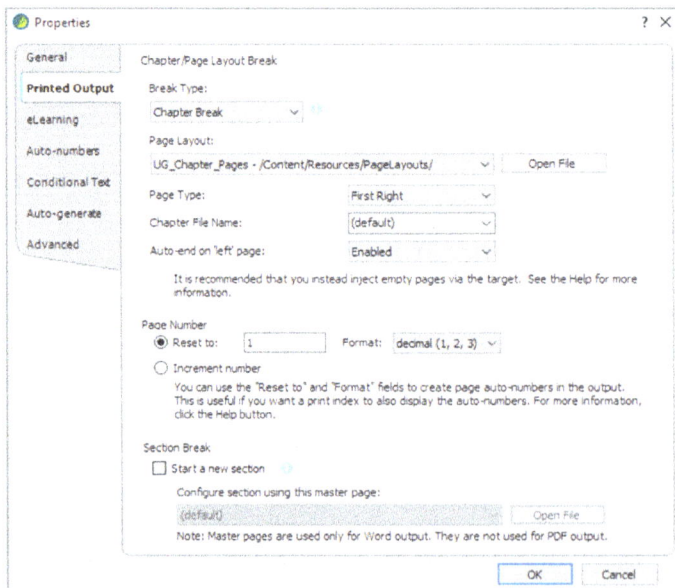

Figure 8-15. TOC Printed Output Properties Dialog.

QUICK STEPS: DEFINING PRINTED OUTPUT PROPERTIES OF TOC ITEM

STEP	ACTION
1	Open the TOC file in which you want to specify the **Printed Output** parameters for a TOC item.
2	Select a TOC item that is a **Chapter Break** or **Page Layout Break**, and right-click and select **Properties**.
3	Click the **Printed Output** tab.
4	Do one of the following: **a)** use the **Break Type** drop-down and select **Chapter Break**, if the item represents an actual chapter or other main breakpoint at which the page layout file changes, for example, for Front Matter pages. **b)** use the **Break Type** drop-down and select **Page Layout Break**, if the TOC item represents a point at which there is a page layout change that is different from the normal flow of pages, for example, a change from portrait to landscape. See **Note 1**.
5	Use the **Page Layout** drop-down to choose a page layout file to apply to the TOC item at this breakpoint.
6	Use the **Page Type** drop-down to choose, from the currently select page layout file, the page type to use at the start of this TOC breakpoint.
7	Use the **Auto-end on 'left' page** drop-down to choose **Enabled** if this section should end on an even page; or choose **Disabled**, if the section should be forced to end on the right page; or choose **as is**.
8	Under **Page Number**, select **Reset to** and enter a page number you want for the start of this breakpoint. If this is the beginning of a main breakpoint, you might set the page number to '**1**' or '**i**'; otherwise, **Reset to** should remain disabled, and **Increment number** is enabled by default. See **Note 2**.
9	Use the **Format** drop-down to choose the format for page numbers. For example, you might choose **Decimal** for Chapter pages, and you might choose lowercase **roman** for Front Matter pages.
10	Under **Section Break**, the **Start of a new section** option should remain disabled for the initial H1 sections in your content (H1-1) that uses use auto-numbering. See **Application Tips** on previous page.
11	Click on the **Auto-numbers** tab to configure the parameters if your content uses auto-numbering styles.

> **NOTE: 1)** It is important to note that the **Break Type** and the **Page Layout** file need only to be applied to the starting points (break-points) in your TOC and not to all of the TOC entries. Once the starting point of a breakpoint is specified along with the Page Layout file and **Page Type**, the pages defined in the layout file are appropriately applied to the subsequent pages in the section until reaching the end of that section.
>
> **NOTE: 2)** There are alternate ways to generate the page numbers. The instructions given here assume that you have inserted the **System.PageNumber** variable in your page layout files. You also have the option of inserting the page number starting at a TOC entry, by choosing '**Text**" as the option in the **Format** field and using Auto-Number format commands to specify the page number in the **Reset to** field.

DEFINING AUTO-NUMBERS PROPERTIES OF TOC ITEM

BASIC CONCEPT

You would use the **Auto-Numbers** tab in conjunction with the **Printed Output** tab to control the auto-numbered styles in your content. Using the **Auto-Numbers** tab, you can reset the start count for chapters, volumes, and new sections in your content that use auto-numbered styles. You can also determine the number format, which may vary depending on the content section. For example, Title and Front Matter pages might use roman numerals, while Chapter Pages might use decimal numbers.

ESSENTIAL ELEMENTS

The **Chapter Number**, **Volume Number**, and **Section Number** parameter groups let you link and synchronize your TOC with the auto-numbered styles used in your content. Each parameter group uses a 'Reset to' parameter to initiate a start count value in your content at a selected TOC breakpoint.

Flare, by default, enables the **Same as previous** option to maintain the last count, and the **Increment number** to increment the count from the previous count. The **Format** lets you specify the numbering as **Decimal**, upper or lowercase **Roman**, or **Alpha**. If a TOC entry starts a new section (level-1 heading) in the content, you should enable the **Start new section** option on the **Printed Output** tab.

APPLICATION TIPS

Although the **Section Number** grouping on the **Auto-Numbers** dialog also supports print outputs for Word and FrameMaker, this topic is only for PDF print outputs.

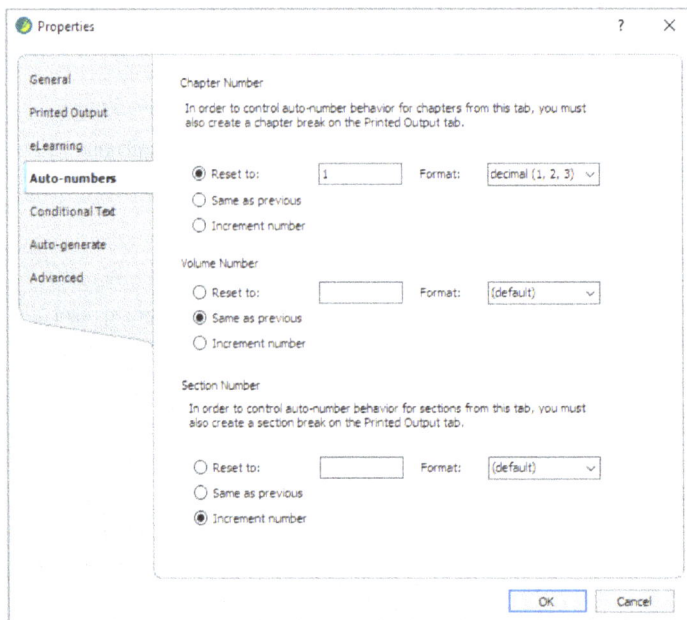

Figure 8-16. TOC Auto-Numbers Properties Dialog.

QUICK STEPS: DEFINING AUTO-NUMBERS PROPERTIES OF TOC ITEM

STEP	ACTION
1	Open the TOC file in which you want to specify the **Auto-Numbers** parameters for a TOC item.
2	Select a TOC item, right-click and select **Properties**. The Properties dialog opens.
3	Click the **Auto-Numbers** tab.
4	Under **Chapter Number**, select **Reset to** and enter '**1**' when the selected TOC item is a Chapter Break and is also a first chapter — even if this is the first of several appendix sections (chapters) and the number format is uppercase alphabets. Otherwise, **Reset to** should remain disabled. See **Note 1**.
5	Use the **Format** drop-down to choose the type of numbers to use for the chapter number. For example, you might choose **Decimal** for regular Chapter pages; and lowercase **Roman** for Front Matter pages; and you might choose uppercase **Alpha** for Appendix pages.
6	Under **Volume Number**, select **Reset to** and enter '**1**' when the selected TOC item is a Chapter Break and is also a first volume. Otherwise, **Reset to** should remain disabled. See **Note 2**.
7	Use the **Format** drop-down to choose the type of numbers to use for the volume number. For example, you might choose uppercase **Roman** numerals to distinguish from the chapter numbers.
8	Under **Section Number**, select **Reset to** and enter '**1**' when the TOC item is the first Heading 1 section in your auto-numbered content. Otherwise, **Reset to** should remain disabled, and the **Increment number** parameter is enabled. See **Note 3**.
9	Use the **Format** drop-down to choose the number type to use for the auto-number sections in the content.
10	Click **OK** to save your work.

NOTE: 1) Increment Number, for **Chapter Number**, is enabled by default for all TOC items designated as a chapter break other than where **Reset to** is set to '1', and automatically increments from '1' for each new chapter break, until reaching the last TOC item that you designate as a chapter break.

NOTE: 2) Same as previous, for **Volume Number**, by default is enabled and maintains the previous count (volume number) until a selected TOC item has the **Increment Number** option enabled.

NOTE: 3) The **Increment number** option, for **Section Number**, by default is enabled, but works in conjunction with the **Printed Output** tab when you enable the check box for **Start new section** for a selected TOC item. These TOC items are typically Heading 1 sections (**2-n**) other than the first Heading 1 section, which has **Reset to** ='**1**'. The section number is then incremented for each section after the first section.

SPECIFYING TOC PAGE LAYOUT AND AUTO-NUMBER CHAPTER BREAKS

BASIC CONCEPT

Flare must be told how the layout of your book will look and where the Chapter and Section breaks occur — you do this using page layout files. This process will affect the numbering of Chapters, Sections, and pages. This task assumes that a page layout file was created for each of the book's main sections, and the ChapterPages file will be applied to each of the book chapter topics in the TOC.

ESSENTIAL ELEMENTS

On the **Printed Output** tab, you would choose **Chapter Break** as the **Break Type** and apply the **ChapterPages** layout file and **First Right** page to each chapter in the book. For the first chapter only, you would enable the **Reset to** parameter, set the **Page Number** to '1', and select the **Format** for **Decimal**. The **Auto-end on the 'left' page** should be enabled. Flare then automatically applies the **Left** and **Right** pages of the page layout file in an alternating sequence until reaching the end of the chapter. If required, Flare inserts an **Empty Left** page to ensure that each chapter starts on the **First Right** page. For the first chapter only, you would enable the **Reset to** parameter on the **Auto-Numbers** tab and set the **Chapter Number** to '1.' The defaults settings may be left unchanged for chapters **2-n**.

APPLICATION TIPS

Even if you do not use auto-numbering in your content, you may still need to apply the page layout files to your TOC to achieve the look and flow specified in the layout files. You can also apply page numbering in the page layouts if you have done so, perhaps in the footers.

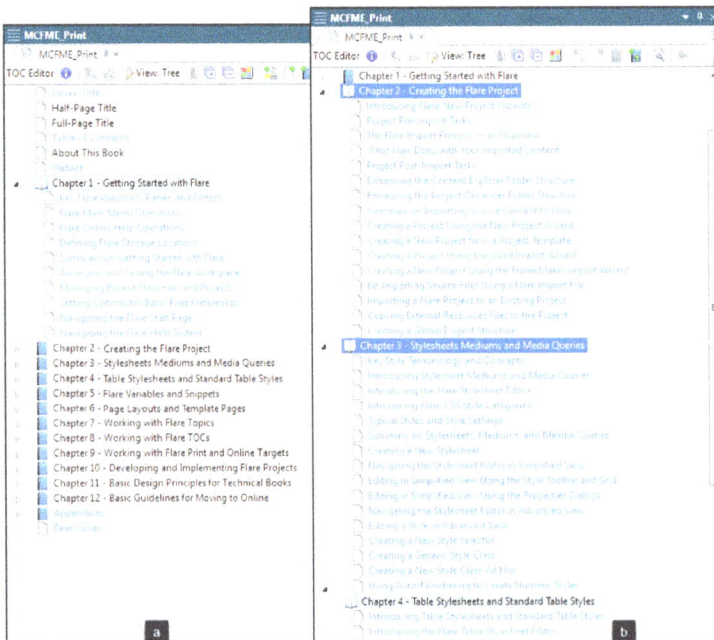

Figure 8-17. Specifying Chapter Breaks for a) Chapter 1, and b) Chapter 2-through Chapter (n)

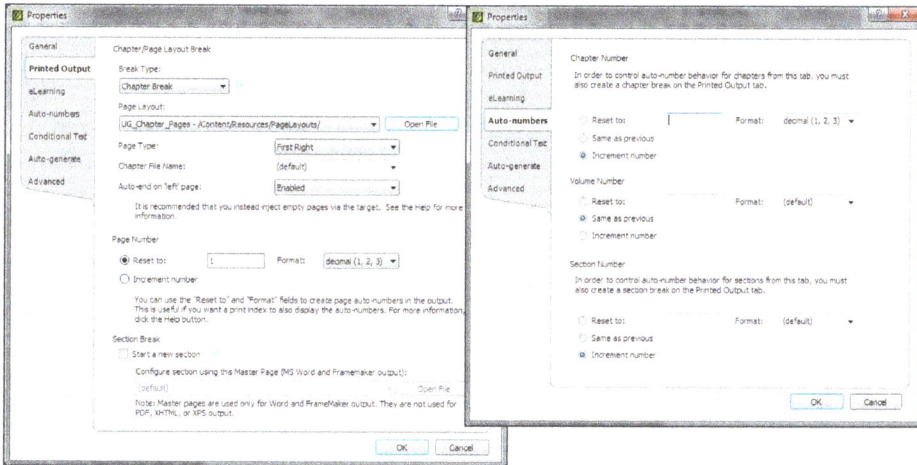

Figure 8-18. Specifying Chapter Page Layout and Auto-Numbers Properties.

QUICK STEPS: SPECIFYING PAGE LAYOUT AND AUTO-NUMBER CHAPTER BREAKS

STEP	ACTION
1	Open the desired TOC outline file you want to work with.
2	Click on the Open book icon for the first Chapter, while leaving all other chapter book icons closed.
3	Click on the First Chapter TOC item and right-click to open the **TOC Properties** dialog (or click **F4**).
4	Select the **Printed Output** tab, and under **Break Type** and select **Chapter Break**.
5	Click the **Page Layout** drop-down and select your **ChapterPages** page layout file.
6	Click the **Page Type** drop-down and select **First Right** (or the correct page for your book) as the page.
7	Use the **Auto end on "left page"** drop-down and select **Enabled** (if chapters start on Right Page).
8	Under **Page Number**, enable **Reset to** and enter "**1**". Use the **Format** drop-down and select **Decimal**.
9	Select the **Auto-numbers** tab, and under **Chapter Number** enable **Reset to** and enter "**1**" in the field. Use the **Format** drop-down and select **Decimal**. This step sets the first chapter number to start at "**1**."
10	Leave all the other defaults unchanged.
11	Expand the TOC book icons of the remaining chapters (**2** through **n**).
12	Hold down the **CTRL** key and select the TOC item for each remaining chapter. See part b of Figure 8-17.
13	With chapters **2** through **n** selected, right-click and select **TOC Properties** (or click **F4**) to open the dialog.
14	Select the **Printed Output** tab, and under **Break Type** and select **Chapter Break**.
15	Click the **Page Layout** drop-down and select your **ChapterPages** page layout file.
16	Click the **Page Type** drop-down and select **First Right** (or the correct page for your book) as the page.
17	Use the **Auto end on "left page"** drop-down and select **Enabled** (if chapters start on Right Page).
18	Under **Page Number**, ensure that **Reset to** is disabled. Use the **Format** drop-down and select **Decimal**.
19	On the **Auto-numbers** tab, leave the defaults unchanged.

SPECIFYING PAGE LAYOUT AUTO-NUMBER SECTION BREAKS

BASIC CONCEPT

With this task, you provide Flare information to ensure correct auto-numbering of the sections in your content. It informs Flare of the start of new sections in each chapter, starting with the first section of the chapter. For example, 1-1 in Chapter 1, 2-1 in Chapter 2, 3-1 in Chapter 3, and so on.

ESSENTIAL ELEMENTS

On the **Auto-numbers** tab, the first task is to set the starting section of each chapter to '**1**,' using the **Reset to** parameter. Based on the auto-numbering format used thus far in this example, the first sections would be numbered 1-1 for Chapter 1, 2-1 for Chapter 2, 3-1 for Chapter 3, and so on. After identifying the first section of each chapter, the second part of this task is on the **Printed Output** tab, under **Section Breaks**.

Here, you enable the **Start a new section** check box for each of the remaining level-1 sections in each chapter to tell Flare where each new section begins. The defaults settings on the Printed Output tab should be left unchanged. The remaining sections would be numbered 1-2, 1-3, and 1-4 for Chapter 1, 2-2, 2-3, and 2-4 for Chapter 2, and 3-2, 3-3, and 3-4 for Chapter 3, and so on.

APPLICATION TIPS

Suppose a Section-1 TOC item, for example, 1-1, 2-1, or 3-1, is a TOC book item that contains other topics. In that case, you should first expand the book to avoid applying settings intended for H1 only to those secondary topics.

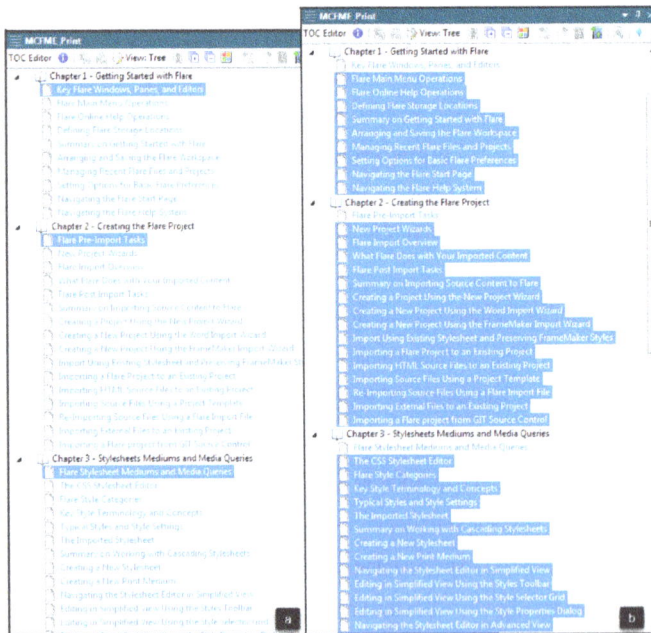

Figure 8-19. a) Section-1 in each Chapter; and b) Section-2-through (n) in each Chapter.

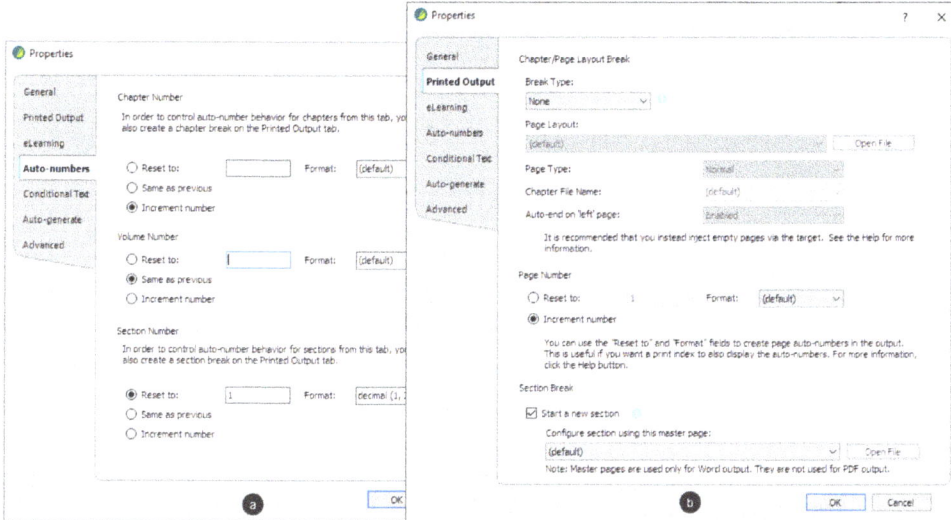

Figure 8-20. a) Reset Auto-Number Section-1 Each Chapter b) Specify Start a New Section 2-n Each Chapter.

QUICK STEPS: SPECIFYING PAGE LAYOUT AUTO-NUMBER SECTION BREAKS

STEP	ACTION
1	Open the desired TOC outline file you want to work with.
2	Click on the **Expand All** button to open all books and pages. Close all but the first-level (H1) books.
3	Hold down the **CTRL** key and select the TOC entry for section-1 (H1) of each chapter. See (a) Figure 8-19.
4	With section-1 TOC entries selected, right-click and select **TOC Properties** (or click **F4**) to open the dialog.
5	Select the **Auto-numbers** tab, and under **Section Number** enable **Reset to** and enter "**1**" in the field. Use **Decimal** as the **Format**. You have specified the first section of each chapter. See Figure 8-20.
6	Click the **OK** button to save the parameters for section-1 in all of the chapters.
7	With the books remaining expanded and only the top-level books open and selected, the parameters for the remaining H1 sections (**2** through **n**), can be specified as being a start of a new section.
8	Use the **CTRL** key and select each of the remaining H1 sections **(Section 2 through n)** in each chapter. You may find it easier to do one chapter at a time. See Figure 8-19.
9	With sections 2-n selected for the remaining chapters, right-click and select **TOC Properties** (or use **F4**).
10	Select the **Printed Output** tab, and under **Section Break** enable **Start a new section**. See Figure 8-20.
11	On the **Auto-numbers** tab, leave the defaults unchanged.

> **NOTE:** As seen in Figure 8-19. , the TOC outline in this example is flat, and only has H1 topics. If some H1 topics are books that contain H2 topics, then you cannot select all of the 2-n sections in a chapter as shown here. You will need to open those books and then use the CTRL key to selects the H1 topic only.

CHAPTER 9

DEVELOPING AND IMPLEMENTING FLARE PROJECTS

INCORPORATING KEY FLARE FILE TYPES

Although you may be just getting started with Flare, it will help to know the various Flare file types. You will come to know some of these files simply because of the typical project work — with others, knowing them in advance may lead you to explore their benefits and consider their use.

Table 9-1. Key Flare File Types

File Type	Extension	Brief Description and Usage
Alias File	.flali	A file created in the Flare Alias Editor and used to populate a *header file* with information necessary for producing context-sensitive Help. The Alias file is stored in the Project Organizer **Advanced** subfolder and contains a mapping of topics and the associated identifiers.
Auto-Index File	.flaix	A file created in the Auto-Index Editor and used with the auto-indexing feature. You can add index entries (terms) to the auto-index file. When you generate the target output, Flare scans the source content to find terms in the auto-index file and adds the words it finds to the auto-generated index contained in the Index Proxy topic you will have created.
Conditional Tag Set	.flcts	A file that contains a collection of related condition tags. When applied to specific content, styles, or other elements, Condition tags can determine whether those elements will be included or excluded from the output.
Destination File	.fldes	A file that specifies a location, such as a network drive, a website, or a SharePoint server, where Flare will place a target's built output files. Once you create a destination file, you can publish the built output files to the designated location for access by others.
File Tag Set	.flfts	A Flare file in which you can create a set of tags that users can apply to topics and other files to associate some information from the tag set. For example, you can create a tag set that consists of the team writers. You can then assign a writer's name from the tag set to any file. You might also create a file tag set of statuses, like *In Progress*, *Done*, and *Hold* You can then create reports to find files that have an assigned tag..
Glossary File	.flglo	A Flare XML file to which you may add glossary terms and definitions that may be used in online and print-based outputs. Flare adds words from the glossary file you created to the auto-generated glossary in the Glossary Proxy topic you created when you generate the target output.
Header File	.h	A simple text file that contains information for connecting dialogs, web pages, or windows of an application to associated Help topics in a project. You can create the **.h** file using the user-friendly Alias file Editor.
Import File	.flimp	A Flare file that saves each of the settings you specify during the process of importing source content. You can re-use the import file to re-import the source content as many times as needed while adjusting the import settings as required.

Table 9-1. Key Flare File Types (cont).

File Type	Extension	Brief Description and Usage
Template Page	.flmsp	A Flare file in which you define elements like breadcrumbs, menus, tool-bars, search bars, mini-TOCs, or footer text to enhance your online output. A template page can be applied to one or more topics in your online output but can also define page specifications in Word print outputs.
Page Layout	.flpgl	A Flare file you create using the Page Layout Editor to define print page specifications like page size, margins, registration marks, bleeds, and crop marks. With page layouts, you determine how content is flowed onto a page, using header, footer, body, image, and decoration frames. Page layouts are mainly applied to print outputs.
Skin File	.flskn	A file that stores behavior and appearance information for an online output window. Appearance elements include items like size, position, menu and UI navigation and controls, buttons, search panes, TOCs, and user interface and text appearance.
Snippet File	.flsnp	A Flare file that can replace a content chunk that appears in several places throughout a project. A snippet — for example, can be a phrase, a sentence, one or two paragraphs, or an entire topic. Creating a snippet eliminates the need to rewrite content used multiple times in a project.
Synonym File	.mcsyns	A Flare file you would create using the Synonym Editor contains a list of user-defined synonyms or words with the same or similar meaning. You can add a synonym file to a project to enhance user search results.
TOC File	.fltoc	The Flare TOC outline file contains the entries that determine what topics are used to create the print or online output. TOC entries either represent the menu items or the navigation menu of an online target or print PDF.
Variables File	.flvar	A Flare file that stores a defined set of single-definition and multi-definition variables that can be used throughout your content.

INTEGRATING SOURCE CONTROL WITH GIT/BITBUCKET

Whether in a single or multi-author environment, with a few or many documents, there are several benefits of employing a source control application like Git/BitBucket. Git is just one of several source control applications that integrate with Flare to support a secure authoring environment. In this environment, project storage and version management are handled on a remote server. Writers can check out and check in the latest updates as needed. Listed below are a few benefits of working with Git.

- Secures all project changes in a remote repository.

- Check out the latest project updates and check in the local repository updates to the server.

- Displays all file additions, deletions, and modifications in a Source Control Explorer.

- Ability to commit changes to a single file or multiple files to the local repository.

- Ability to revert a single file or multiple files to a previously committed version.

- Synchronize local and remote repositories in a single author or multi-author environment.

GETTING STARTED WITH GIT

Before getting started, you must determine if the Git application is already being used. Many software development and documentation teams use a Git server to handle version management and storage. All new Git users need to establish a server account with login credentials. If your documents are managed in separate projects, you will need to create a remote repository on the server for each project. After creating a repository, you would bind (connect) your project to the repository. You may also need to push the project to the repository. Writers that do not initially have the project locally will need to import it from the remote repository. The Flare documentation has complete instructions.

FLARE SOURCE CONTROL OPERATIONS

The **Source Control** menu, shown below, and described in the following table, displays only if the open project is bound to a Source Control server like Git. The operations on the menu will differ slightly depending on the application. The items on this menu are of the Git application.

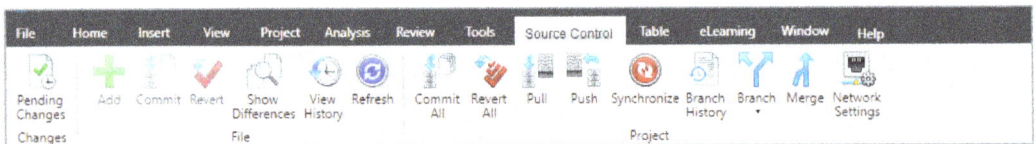

Figure 9-1. Flare Source Control Menu-Git Repository.

Several operations assist writers in interacting with project files local to their devices and on the remote server. By opening the **Source Control Explorer**, from the **View** menu, you can view the **Pending Changes** list of files with recent changes, including added and modified files. You can then **Commit** one or more selected files or **Commit All** of the files in the list. To commit is to accept the changes you have made and thereby "commit" them to the local repository (on your machine). After files are committed to the local storage, you can **Push** them to the remote repository on the server.

Suppose you are working in a team of writers, all working on the same project. In that case, they to will have committed changes to their respective local repositories and subsequently pushed those changes to the remote repository on the server. After committing your local changes, the **Synchronize** command pulls updates from the remote repository before pushing your updates to the server.

Table 9-2. Key Flare Menu Operations for Git Source Control

Menu Operation	Brief Description and Usage
Pending Changes	Use this operation to list source files that you have added, modified, or deleted in a project. The updates are pending check-in. The files in the **Pending Changes** list can be committed, reverted, pushed to, or synchronized with the remote repository.
Commit	This operation is used to save to the local repository, files selected in the Pending Changes list. From the Source Control menu you can use the **Commit** or **Commit All** option.
Commit All	This operation is used to save, to the local repository, all of the files in the Pending Changes list. From the Source Control menu you can use the **Commit** or **Commit All** option.
Revert	Use this operation to undo or discard the most recent modifications to one or more selected source files, and return the files to the previously committed version. See **Revert All**.
Revert All	Use this operation to undo or discard the most recent modifications to all of the files of the files in the Pending Changes list, and return them to the previously committed versions.
Pull	Use this operation to retrieve your source controlled project from the remote repository, along with updates from all other users, and download it to the local repository. See **Push**.
Push	Use this operation to send or upload the committed changes in your local repository to the remote repository of your source control application. See **Pull**.
Synchronize	Use this operation to synchronize the files you have committed to your local repository with any files that have also been committed by others and pushed to the remote repository. This option, which should be done after a **Commit**, first performs a **Pull** to update the local database, with committed files from the remote repository, and then a **Push** of any local commits to the remote repository. After the **Synchronize** operation, the files in the local and remote repositories are in synch and form a completely updated database.
* Repository	In a source control project, this is a logical container that holds the Flare project source file. References can be made to the "remote repository," which resides on the source control server; and the "local repository," which is the "working copy" of the project on your device.
* Local Repository	A local copy of your source control content that acts as working copy of your Flare project.
* Remote Repository	The remote copy of the source control content that is stored on a remote location, and to which users push their committed repositories of the project.

NOTE: * The repository terms are not Source Control operations, but are provided for reference only.

REVIEWING FLARE PROJECT TEAM TASKS

At some point, often early on, you will realize that there is an enormous number of tasks to be done in Flare — far too many for a single person, but enough to keep a collaborative team busy! This section hopefully introduces and assists in determining how a team might share these tasks. As much as possible, everyone should get involved — there's something for everyone!

While there is something in Flare for everyone, some tasks are best done by one or two team members working together as a small committee. Some jobs will require some up-front collaboration by all team members to make some crucial decisions. For example, tasks like naming conventions and overall structure for files and folders, and perhaps decisions on what variables and conditional phrases to use, all should have the team's input. Finally, there are some tasks and Flare skills that should involve the entire team — a few of these items are listed below:

- Know the naming conventions for files and folders.

- Use and apply the available styles, variables, and snippets.

- Apply the Page Layout properties to appropriate TOC entries.

- Create Topics from templates or existing topics.

- Familiarity with project Conditional Tags and how to apply to content.

- Specify Target settings for General, Variables, Conditional Text, Advanced, and PDF Options.

Table 9-3. Example Flare Project Tasks (**TL**=Team Lead, **TC**=Team Committee, **WT**=Whole Team)

Task	Assign	Brief Description
Define Project Structure	TC	Define a central project where everyone works; or a distributed project where writers use separate projects and a global project to share common resources like stylesheets, page layouts, snippets, and variables.
Create Default Storage Locations	TC	Create default storage locations used by Flare — for example, for projects, templates, and external resources.
Perform Recommended Pre-Import Preparations	WT	Perform recommended pre-import preparation tasks on specified documents, if importing will be done.
Import Legacy Documents	TL/WT*	Create one or several projects using a Flare Import Wizard — for example FrameMaker, Word, or RoboHelp, to import your legacy source content.
Review Imported Content Components	TL	Review imported content components that have been generated by Flare — for example, HTML, Image, TOC, and Stylesheet files; and, if applicable, Table Stylesheets. You can modify import file parameters as you step through the wizard or open later and re-import content.

Table 9-3. Example Flare Project Tasks (TL=Team Lead, TC=Team Committee, WT=Whole Team) (cont).

Task	Assign	Brief Description
Develop Cascading Style Sheet File	TL	Review your imported stylesheet, if applicable, and edit, delete, and add styles as required. Remember you may need both Print and Online (Default) Style Medium.
Develop Page Layout Files	TL	Create Page Layout Files for the sections of your books, as needed, for example — Cover Title Pages, Front Matter Pages, Chapter Pages, Appendix Pages (1-column/2-column), Index, and Glossary Pages.
Develop Variables Files and Snippet Files	TC	Create Variable Sets and Snippets as needed. Consider creating multiple variable sets — for example, General, and User Guide variables. And, consider using **Options** dialog > **Project Analysis** > **Advanced Scan Options** to **Collect Snippet** and **Variable Prospects**.
Develop Template Page Files	TL	Create one or more Template Page files for the parts of your online targets. Consider Flare elements, like breadcrumbs, header, body, footer.
Create Table Stylesheets and Standard Table Styles	TL	Create additional Table Stylesheets as required. Stylesheets for example, Plain Table, Alternating Rows Pattern, Alternating Columns Pattern, and Two-Headers stylesheet. Your CSS will inherit standard Table styles that you can modify and create style classes.
Determine and Create PDF Target Files	TC	Determine and create required PDF Target files. Consider a PDF target for each book or for each book type, if your have created differentiating variables that can be set at the target.
Determine and Create HTML Target Files	TC	Determine and create the required of HTML Target files. Consider an HTML target for each site you intend to create.
Review Flare Skin Templates	TC	Review Flare Skin Templates and decide on navigation type. Create a skin based on a template, and modify the skin parameters as needed.
Apply Page Layout Files to TOC Break Points	WT	If applicable, learn to apply Page Layout files to TOC Chapter and Page Layout breaks, on the TOC Printed Output and Auto-Numbers tab.
Define Conditional Tag Sets	TC	Determine Conditional Tag Sets, the tag names, and how they will be used and applied in your content for online and print targets.
Source Control Setup for Documents	TL/WT*	Work with IT/DevOps to determine application setup requirements, and with team members to setup accounts and import initial project.

> **NOTE:** * To perform an efficient and consistent job of importing legacy documents, and to achieve the desired outcome, requires up front preparation and that those responsible thoroughly understand the job. The import task might be accomplished more efficiently if performed by a selected individual.

ENHANCING PROJECT SEARCH RESULTS

Essential to any online help system is for users to find what they search for, and the results are helpful. If you have selected the MadCap Search Engine on the HTML5 target as your project search engine, there are two options for enhancements that can improve user search results.

SEARCH SYNONYMS

In Flare, you can use *synonyms* to enhance a user's search, mainly by ensuring that the user does not end up with a null search result. You can use the Flare Synonym Editor to create two types of synonyms — Directional Synonyms and Group Synonyms. Each of these synonym types produces different results. In both cases, the synonyms must be of a single word only. For example, you cannot create a synonym named "style sheet" for the word "stylesheet."

DIRECTIONAL SYNONYM

A *directional synonym* is a word that operates in one direction only when used in a search. For example, a search of the directional synonym "automobile" would find results that include the synonym "Honda. " A search for "Honda," on the other hand, would not find results for "automobile," since the synonym is in one direction only. You might choose the directional synonym method for terms you know are not in your project, yet users may use these terms to search for similar terms. In such cases, you would still produce results based on synonyms you have provided.

Table 9-4. Example: Directional Synonyms

Directional Synonym	Synonyms
automobile	Honda, Volkswagon, Chevy, Buick, Cadillac
target	HTML5, PDF, EPUB, Word

GROUP SYNONYMS

A *group synonym* is any one of a collection of words that all return the same search results. This method is helpful if you have several similar terms in your project, yet you want the search to produce the same results whenever users enter any of those terms. A user search using any of the words results in a list of topics where any synonym is found.

Table 9-5. Example: Synonym Group

Synonym Group	Synonyms
target	PDF=HTML5=EPUB=Word
animal	dog=cat=cow=chicken=bird

Summary on Developing and Implementing Flare Projects

Whether your Flare work involves content for just a few or a large number of books or documents, you will likely struggle with the question of whether to use a single project or multiple projects. There is no correct answer to this question, but you should rest easy in knowing that Flare can easily manage either decision. A single project to manage one or several documents or multiple projects, each of which handles one or more documents, can serve equally well. Regardless of the option you choose, you can always revert if you so desire. Without difficulty, you can merge several projects to create a single project or, if necessary, segment a single large project into multiple smaller ones.

In building a project, your completed tasks fill a container with content and supporting objects built and published as print or online outputs. Project content is created and formed as you work with regular stylesheets and table stylesheets, page layouts and template pages, variables and snippets, topics, TOCs, targets, skins, and a variety of other objects. The presentation and appearance of your content can be enhanced by Flare's many support features and tools. The following checklist outlines a few items to consider in developing and deploying your project. Some examples of project development-related tasks follow in the remainder of this chapter.

Checklist: Developing and Implementing Flare Projects

- *Before moving forward with the many details associated with Flare project development, make sure to spend adequate time firming up your CSS stylesheet.*

- *Consider creating a team among which the various project tasks can be divided and shared. Review the various projects and tasks and consider how team members will share them.*

- *Spend time planning for project-wide items like naming conventions for folder and file, folder and file structure, and using and naming condition tags.*

- *If multiple writers regularly develop documents for various products, consider creating and using shared resources, like stylesheets, table stylesheets, snippets, template pages, and page layouts.*

- *If creating multiple projects, consider creating a template from which writers can create new projects. Only the required objects need to be selected when users make a new project.*

- *Suppose you have resource files like images, videos, or other files that are occasionally modified. In that case, you can use the "Import External Resources" option to copy and synchronize these files with your project to ensure that the project and external resources files are updated.*

- *Like the inherited TOC level styles, TOC1-TOC9, your stylesheet also inherits styles for each Index keyword level, which you can modify. These styles include Index1 through Index9.*

- *Plan how you can use group and directional synonyms to enhance user online search results.*

- *Consider using a source control/versioning application like GIT, MadCap Central, Perforce, and Subversion to store and maintain backups and versions of your project files.*

- *If using the Auto-Index file in conjunction with an Index proxy topic, consider disabling the Ignore Case option to generate an index with a minimum of entries listed for each keyword.*

APPLYING PROJECT LEVEL PROPERTIES

BASIC CONCEPT

Settings made in the **Project Properties** represent project-wide settings in Flare, and become the default settings if the same settings are not provided elsewhere in the project. Furthermore, if no specific settings are made in the Project Properties and in no other place, for example, at the Target file or in the **Topic Properties**, then Flare uses its appropriate **Default** files instead. For example, the Flare default stylesheet and default page layout file.

ESSENTIAL ELEMENTS

The **General** tab of the Project Properties provides information about the project, like the **Name** and **Location** and when it was **Created** and **Modified**. You can modify the properties on the **Defaults**, **Language**, and **Source Control** tabs.

When the project contains more than one TOC file, Page Layout file, or Stylesheet, the **Defaults** tab lets you specify the most widely used of these elements as the **Primary TOC**, **Primary Page Layout** file, and **Primary Stylesheet**, respectively. Use the **Language** tab to set the language used in the project.

APPLICATION TIPS

Like those made on the **Defaults** tab, project-level settings can be overridden by settings made at the target-level, or the local level, like in the **Topic Properties** for a Snippet, or in the **TOC Properties**, with Page Layout files.

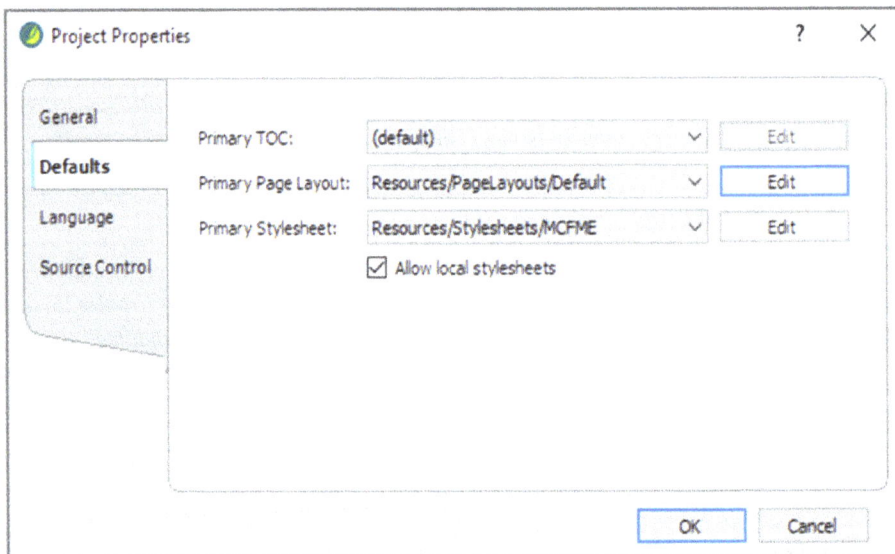

Figure 9-2. Applying Project Level Default Properties.

QUICK STEPS: APPLYING PROJECT LEVEL PROPERTIES

STEP	ACTION
1	Select the **Project** ribbon.
2	Click **Project Properties**.
3	Click the **Defaults** tab.
4	Select the **Primary TOC** in your project. If there are multiple TOCs in the project, one must be specified as the primary. If you have not chosen one as primary, Flare chooses the first TOC it finds in the project.
5	Select the **Primary Page Layout** file to be used in your project. Generally, if there are multiple page layout files, different page layout files are applied to different parts of your document. In cases like this, which is typical, it is best that a Primary Page Layout file not be specified.
6	Select the **Primary Stylesheet** to use as the project-wide stylesheet your project. When their are multiple stylesheets in the project, this stylesheet will be used in all cases, unless one is specified at the Target level or in the Topic Properties. See **Note** 1.
7	Click the **Language** tab and select the language to be used in this project. For example, **English**.
8	Click the **Source Control** tab to specify a source control provider and other project parameters. See **Note** 2.

> **NOTE: 1)** Project-level **Defaults** are overridden by settings made at the Target-level, and at the local-level, like in **Topic Properties**, at the Snippet-level, or in the TOC Properties, as with Page Layout files.
>
> **NOTE: 2)** Key information regarding the setup and requirements of your Source Control platform can be obtained from your IT or DevOps organization.

SAVING A PROJECT AS A PROJECT TEMPLATE

BASIC CONCEPT

Using a project template is one way of ensuring that as a writing team creates each new project, the project will have a structure consistent with the chosen template. The project template should contain the baseline content and resources that need to be part of each new project. Since the template will have a fixed structure and set of resources, each new project, based on the template, will have the intended file structure, naming conventions, storage locations, and the specific project content and resources. The base content of the project template is entirely up to your choosing.

ESSENTIAL ELEMENTS

To provide the baseline project structure that writers will apply whenever creating a new project, you must already have a project that has the desired file structure and resources. The **Save Project as Template Wizard** is used to create the project template. You would start the wizard from the **Project** ribbon, using **Save Project as Template**. After the wizard starts, you must identify a **Template Folder**. You must create a template folder first if one was not previously designated.

As you proceed through the wizard, the **Content Explorer** files are presented first, in a tree format, then the files of the **Project Organizer** are presented. An adjacent check box is just to the left of each folder, subfolder, and file. If you select the check-box for a file, Flare will include it in the new project. Flare will also include all the files contained in folders and subfolders if you mark the folders.

APPLICATION TIPS

Consider including elements such as, page layout files, stylesheets, table stylesheets, glossaries, template page files, target files, variables and snippet files, conditional text files, and target and skin files that you have already configured.

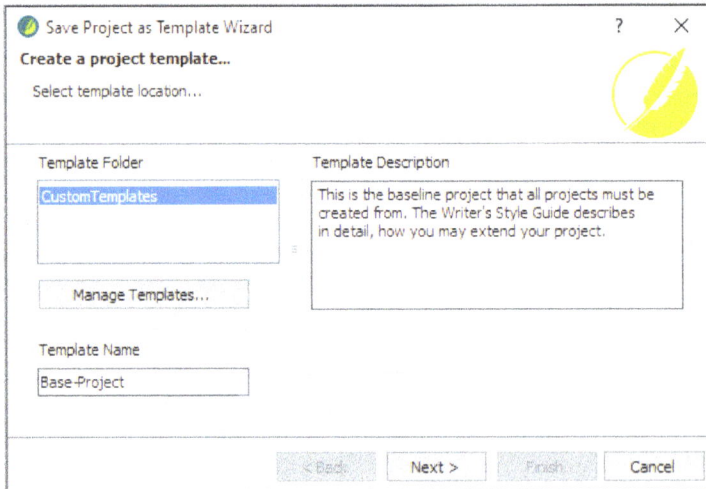

Figure 9-3. Save a Project as Project Template — Selecting the Desired Folders.

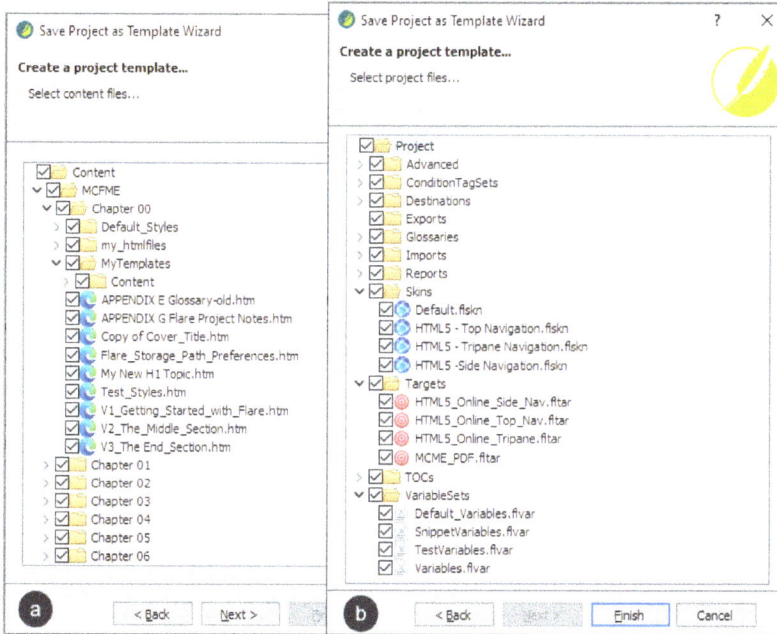

Figure 9-4. (a) Content Explorer Folders and Files, and (b) Project Organizer Folders and Files.

QUICK STEPS: SAVING A PROJECT AS A PROJECT TEMPLATE

STEP	ACTION
1	Open the Flare project file you want to save as a new project template file.
2	From the Flare **Project** ribbon, click **Save Project as Template**. The wizard dialog opens.
3	Use the **Template Name** field to enter a name for the project template.
4	Use the **Template Description** field to enter a descriptive comment of the project use.
5	Click **Next** to advance the wizard.
6	From the **Content Explorer**, use the drop-down arrows to expand the content folders and sub-folders and use the check boxes to mark each subfolder or file that should be saved to the new project template.
7	After setting sub-folders and files to Include from the **Content Explorer**, click **Next** to advance the wizard.
8	From the **Project Organizer**, use the drop-down arrows to expand the project folders and sub-folders and use the check boxes to mark each subfolder or file that should be saved to the new project template.
9	After selecting the sub-folders and files to include from the **Project Organizer**, click **Finish** on the wizard.
10	The project template is successfully saved with the assigned name, in the designated template folder.

CREATING CONDITION TAG SETS AND CONDITION TAGS

BASIC CONCEPT

In Flare, a *condition tag* is a single-sourcing control element that can be selectively applied to parts of your content or specific files to determine whether Flare should include or exclude the content or file from a particular output. A *condition tag set* is a logical grouping of condition tags or simply a container that holds a group of condition tags. Condition tag sets are created using the **ConditionTagSet Editor** and stored under the **Conditional Text** subfolder in the **Project Organizer**.

ESSENTIAL ELEMENTS

You can create as many condition tag sets as you like, and each tag set can contain as many condition tags as needed to serve the purpose. All of the condition tag sets and the tags they contain can be applied anywhere in your project content, in the same or different target outputs.

APPLICATION TIPS

You can use the **Show Tags** drop-down arrow to choose **Conditions**, to visualize condition tags that have been applied to various files and content elements in your project. Items to look for includ TOC items, selected text, topics, snippets, and others. You can also click on the **Show Indicators** icon on the XML Editor bottom toolbar.

The behavior of a condition tag to **Include** or **Exclude** content from the output is generally determined on the **Conditional Text** tab of the target file before you build the target.

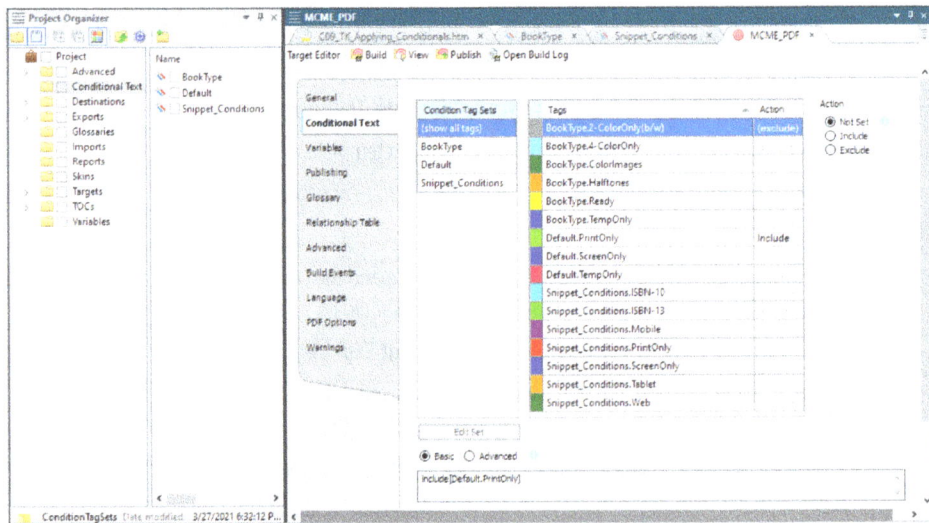

Figure 9-5. Create a Conditional Tag Element.

> **NOTE:** Use positive conditional names like **Release2.1**, **ColorImages**, **Black_and_White**, and **PrintOnly**; avoid using negated names. Use the lowline character to connect multi-word folder and file names.

QUICK STEPS: CREATING CONDITION TAG SETS AND CONDITION TAGS

STEP	ACTION
—	**To Create a Condition Tag Set**
1	Click on the **Project Organizer**.
2	Right-click on the **Conditional Text** folder > select **Add Condition Tag Set**.
3	Ensure that the **File Type** is set for **Condition Tag Set**.
4	**To create the new condition tag set use one of the following:**
	a) From Templates: Set the **Source** for **New From Template**, choose the **MyConditionTags** template from the **Factory Templates** folder or choose a template from a user-defined **Custom Templates** folder.
	b) From Existing: Set the **Source** for **New From Existing**, and use the browse button ⋯ to locate the existing Condition Tags file.
5	Under **Condition Tag Set**, use the **Folder** field and choose the default (root) folder, or browse and choose another folder in which to store the new condition tag set file.
6	Use the **File Name** field to specify a name for the new file. For example, **MyConditionTagSet.flcts**.
7	Click **Add** to create the Condition Tag Set file.
—	**To Create a Condition Tag**
1	Click on the **Project Organizer**.
2	Click on the **Conditional Text** folder.
3	Click the **Show Files** button, to reveal Conditional Tag Sets, if no files are visible in the right pane.
4	Under **Name**, double-click the Condition Tag Set file in which you want to add a new Condition Tag. The **Condition TagSet Editor** window opens.
5	On the Editor ribbon, click the **New Item** button, to insert a new **Condition Tag**.
6	In the **Condition Tag** field, click on the **NewTag** name and enter a name for the new Condition Tag.
7	Use the assigned **Background** indicator color for the tag, or use the drop-down and choose a new color.
8	Use the **Comment** field to describe the new Condition Tag.
9	Click the **Save** button to save your work.

APPLYING CONDITION TAGS

BASIC CONCEPT

To *apply condition tags* in your project, is similar to applying a style in your project — it is to assign the properties or behavior associated with the condition tag to the project element to which it is applied. The actual behavior of a condition tag is generally determined at the target file, when the condition tag is either set to be **Included** or **Excluded** from the output upon the target being built.

ESSENTIAL ELEMENTS

In Flare, you can apply a condition tag to any content or any file — for example, selected text, a sentence, a paragraph, a topic, all of the topics in a folder, TOC items, a table row, a table column, a table cell, or the entire table, and even a style. When a condition tag is applied, the indicator color shows if condition tag indicators are turned on.

For selected text, the text is shown highlighted using the tag color. The **MadCap:conditionalText** span tag is also shown using the color on the span bars; for a tagged paragraph, the text is highlighted using the tag color, and the same color highlights the tag bar. For files and folders, the adjacent tag indicator box will show the indicator color.

APPLICATION TIPS

A condition tag is applied to a style using the mc-conditions property, which you can set in your stylesheet. In the **Advanced view**, and with properties listed in the **Alphabetical View**, locate the **mc-conditions property**; otherwise, the property is listed with **Unclassified** properties in the **Grouped View**. You might use this feature, for example, to exclude the FigureCaption style in online outputs.

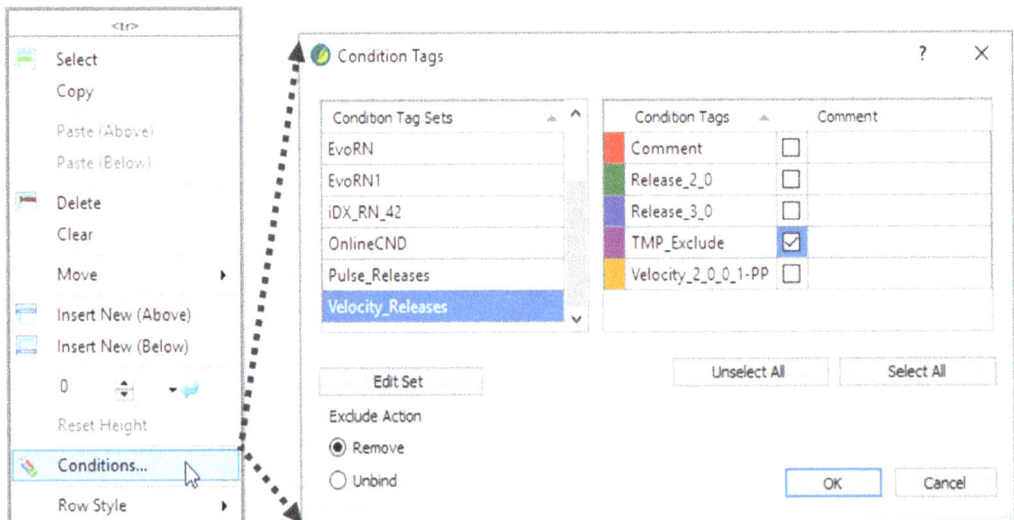

Figure 9-6. Apply Condition Tag from a Condition Tag Set.

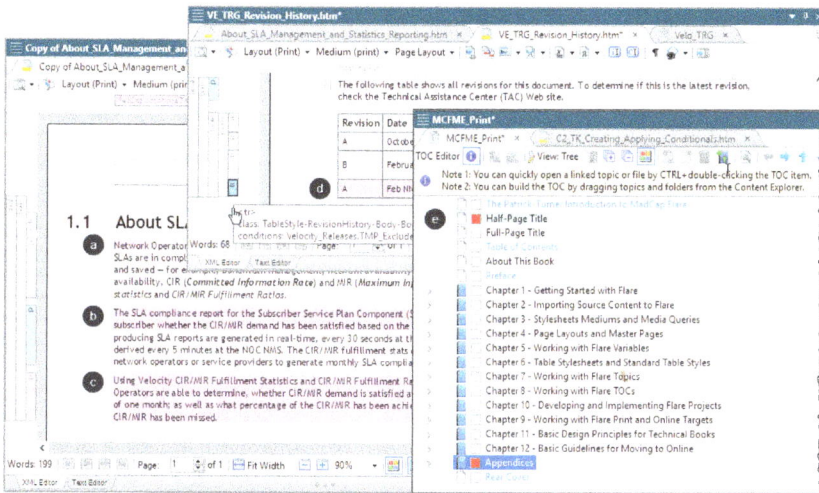

Figure 9-7. Apply Condition to a) word b) sentence or selection, c) paragraph, d) table, row, or column, e) TOC.

QUICK STEPS: APPLYING CONDITION TAGS

STEP	ACTION
—	**To Apply a Condition Tag to a Topic**
1	Open the topic to which you want to apply a condition tag.
2	Right-click select **Properties** > select the **Conditional Text** tab > select **Condition Tag Set** > and select a specific **Condition Tag** > and click **OK** to apply the condition tag.
—	**To Apply a Condition Tag to a File**
1	Open the folder in which the file is located in the **Content Explorer** or in the **Project Organizer**.
2	Select the file to which you want to apply a condition tag.
3	Right-click select **Properties** > select the **Conditional Text** tab > select the **Condition Tag Set** > and select a **Condition Tag** > and click **OK** to apply the condition tag.
—	**To Apply a Condition Tag to Selected Text** (word, sentence, or other span selection)
1	Select a word, sentence or other selected (span) text to which you want to apply a condition tag.
2	Right-click and select **Conditions** > select a **Condition Tag Set** > and select a tag from **Condition Tags**.
—	**To Apply a Condition Tag to a Paragraph**
1	Click anywhere inside the paragraph.
2	Right-click and select **Conditions** > select the **Condition Tag Set** > and select a specific **Condition Tag**.
3	Click **OK** to apply the condition tag.
—	**To Apply a Condition Tag to a TOC Item**
1	Open the TOC in which you want to apply a condition tag.
2	Right-click on the TOC item > select **Properties** > select the **Conditional Text** tab > select the **Condition Tag Set** > and select a specific **Condition Tag** > and click **OK** to apply the condition tag.

DEFINING THE APPEARANCE AND PLACEMENT OF TOC ITEMS

BASIC CONCEPT

If you have created a topic that generates a print TOC in your output, you can modify the appearance of the individual TOC entries and the entire container that holds the TOC. Your stylesheet contains inherited style selectors that you can use to perform this task. Also, in your stylesheet is an inherited style property that you can use to determine the hierarchy level of each TOC entry and whether a given heading level from your content appears in the TOC at all.

See *"Creating a Table of Contents Topic Using the TOC Template" on page 220.*

ESSENTIAL ELEMENTS

Using the inherited p-styles (**p.TOC1** through **p.TOC9**), you can modify properties like **Font, Size, Alignment,** and **Spacing** for TOC entries. These styles, listed under the **Generated Content** styles category of your stylesheet, have default settings that are mapped directly to the headings (h1-h6) in your content. For example, **p.TOC1** defines the appearance of level-1 headings in the TOC, **p.TOC2** defines the appearance of level-2 headings, and **p.TOC3** defines the appearance of level-3 headings, and so on.

Another inherited property is the **mc-heading-level,** which you can use to define the TOC indentation of each heading in your stylesheet. By default, the **mc-heading-level** is set to '1' for h1 styles, '2' for h2 styles, '3' for h3 styles, and so on. This mapping is, therefore, directly linked to the h1 through h6 styles in your content. An **mc-heading-level** of '1' indents the TOC entry to align to the left-most position in the TOC. An **mc-heading-level** of '2' aligns the TOC entry to the second-level of indentation from the left, and so on with each higher level. A TOC entry with an **mc-heading-level** of '0' will not appear in the TOC at all.

APPLICATION TIPS

You can also assign the **mc-heading-level** to styles other than the typical headings, if you want them to appear at specific levels in the TOC. For example, you may want to assign an mc-heading-level to the document title and each Front Matter and Back Matter Heading of your print content. You can also set the **mc-heading-level** property to '0' for headings that you do not want to appear in the TOC.

Name	Tag	Class	ID	Pse...	Preview	Comm...	color	dis...	font-family	font-si...		margin-bottom	margin-left	margin-right	margin-top
p.TOC1	p	TOC1			MADCAP SOFTWARE..		#000000	block	Segoe Conden...	10pt	0	6pt	0pt	0	6pt
p.TOC2	p	TOC2			MADCAP SOFTWARE		#000000	block	Segoe Conden...	9.5pt		4pt	10pt	0	6pt
p.TOC3	p	TOC3			MadCap Software		#000000	block	Segoe Conden...	9.5pt		4pt	10pt	0	4pt
p.TOC4	p	TOC4			MadCap Softwa		#696969	block	Segoe Conden...	9.5pt		4pt	20pt	0	4pt
p.TOC5	p	TOC5			MadCap			block	Minion Pro	9.5pt	0	6pt	40pt	0	6pt
p.TOC6	p	TOC6			MadC			block	Minion Pro	9.5pt		6pt	50pt	0	6pt
p.TOC7	p	TOC7			Ma			block	Minion Pro	9.5pt		6pt	60pt	0	6pt
p.TOC8	p	TOC8						block	Minion Pro	9.5pt		6pt	70pt	0	6pt
p.TOC9	p	TOC9					transp...	block	Minion Pro	9.5pt	0	6pt	80pt	0	6pt

Figure 9-8. Defining the Appearance of Generated TOC Heading Entries.

Name	Tag	Class	ID	Pseudo Cl...	Preview	Comment	border-botto...	...	mc-auto-num...	mc-auto-num...	mc-auto-num...	mc-heading-level
h1	h1				MadCap					0	inside-head	1
h1.AppendixTitle1	h1	AppendixTitle1			MADCAP	#808080		CH:Appendix (...	0		inside-head	1
h1.ChapterNumber	h1	ChapterNumber			MA					0	inside-head	1
h1.ChapterTitle	h1	ChapterTitle			MADCAP	#808080		CH:Chapter [c...	0		inside-head	1
h1.CoverTitle	h1	CoverTitle								0	inside-head	1
h1.FrontMatterHead	h1	FrontMatterHead			MadCap Sof					0	inside-head	1
h1.FullPageTitle	h1	FullPageTitle			MADCA					0	inside-head	0
h1.Heading1	h1	Heading1			MADCAP SOFTW					0	inside-head	3
h1.Heading1_NP	h1	Heading1_NP			MADCAP SOFTW					0	inside-head	3
h2	h2				MadCap Softwar					0	inside-head	4
h2.Heading2	h2	Heading2			MADCAP SOFTWAR					0	inside-head	4
h2.Heading2_NP	h2	Heading2_NP			MADCAP SOFTWAR					0	inside-head	4
h2.Heading2_NP_1	h2	Heading2_NP_1			MADCAP SOFTWAR					0	inside-head	3
h4	h4				MadCap Softwar					0	inside-head	0
h4.Heading4	h4	Heading4			MadCap Softwar					0	inside-head	5

Figure 9-9. Using mc-Heading Level Property to Specify the Placement of Generated TOC Heading Entries.

QUICK STEPS: DEFINING THE APPEARANCE AND PLACEMENT OF TOC ITEMS

STEP	ACTION
1	Open the desired stylesheet and use the **Medium** drop-down to select the **Print** medium.
2	If the Simplified View is not displayed, click the **View Advanced** button to switch the view.
3	Select the **Generated Styles** category, using the **Styles** drop-down on the bottom-left of the toolbar.
4	Scroll down and, under the **Name** column, find the TOC1, TOC2, TOC3, TOC4, TOC5, TOC6, TOC7, TOC8, and TOC9 selectors, under the **p**-parent. These selectors affect the appearance of the print TOC entries.
5	In the Simplified View, double-click on each of the following selectors to open the style **Properties** dialog: **a)** Use **p.TOC1** to set the styles of the level-1 headings — for example, Font, Size, and Paragraph Spacing. **b)** Use **p.TOC2** to set the styles of the level-2 headings — for example, Font, Size, and Paragraph Spacing. **c)** Use **p.TOC3** to set the styles of the level-3 headings — for example, Font, Size, and Paragraph Spacing.
6	Specify the **mc-heading level** property for each of the paragraph headings in your stylesheet for which you want to affect the placement in the TOC hierarchy. Valid entries are **0-9**, where '**1**' places the TOC entry in the left-most position, '**2**' places the TOC entry in the second position from the left, and '**0**' means headings with this setting will not appear in the TOC.

NOTE: You can also use the MadCap style selector **MadCap|tocProxy**, to affect the appearance of the print TOC container, including elements like the container background color, image, border, and others.

DEFINING THE APPEARANCE OF MINI-TOC ENTRIES

BASIC CONCEPT

When you have inserted a mini-TOC proxy in a topic and placed the topic in your TOC outline, the mini-TOC will appear in the topic when you build the target. You can define the appearance of the individual mini-TOC headings and the container that holds the mini-TOC. You can also specify the number of heading levels you want Flare to list in the mini-TOC.

See *"Inserting a Mini-TOC Proxy in an Existing Topic."*

ESSENTIAL ELEMENTS

Using the inherited styles (**p.MiniTOC1** through **p.MiniTOC9**), you can modify properties like **Font**, **Size**, **Alignment**, and **Paragraph Spacing** for the mini-TOC headings. These styles are under the **Generated Content** style category of your stylesheet. The style **p.MiniTOC1**, for example, defines the appearance of the first-level headings that appear in the mini-TOC, **p.MiniTOC2** defines the appearance of the second-level headings, and **p.MiniTOC3** defines the appearance of third-level headings.

The headings present in a mini-TOC are based on **TOC Depth**, and where the mini-TOC is inserted in the topic. There are a few options for affecting the **TOC Depth** — one method is to define it directly in the mini-TOC proxy, with a right-click on the proxy element and selecting **Edit Mini-TOC Proxy**. If you insert the mini-TOC after a Chapter heading, for example, and the TOC Depth is set to '3', then h1 and h2 headings in the topic are listed in the mini-TOC.

APPLICATION TIPS

You can also set the **TOC Depth** in the **mc-toc-depth** property in your stylesheet. And yet another method of affecting the TOC Depth is to enable the **Use TOC Depth** option on the **Advanced** tab of the target file. This method, which will use the absolute depth of your TOC, may result in a much longer mini-TOC if there are several levels of headings in your topic. The setting in the mini-TOC proxy takes priority if you have defined two or more of these options.

A further note is that the styles applied to headings in the mini-TOC always start with **p.MiniTOC1**. Hence, the appearance of the h2 headings, if it is the first heading, will be defined by **p.MiniTOC1**.

Name	Tag	Class	ID	Pse...	Preview	Comm...	color	dis...	font-family	font-si...		margin-bottom	margin-left	margin-right	margin-top
p.MiniTOC1	p	MiniTOC1			MadCap Software		#000000	block	Segoe Conden...	9.5pt	U	6pt	0pt	0	4pt
p.MiniTOC2	p	MiniTOC2			MadCap Software...			block	Segoe Conden...	9.5pt		6pt	6pt	0	6pt
p.MiniTOC3	p	MiniTOC3			MadCap Softwa			block	Segoe Conden...	9.5pt		6pt	20pt	0	6pt
p.MiniTOC4	p	MiniTOC4			MadCap S			block	Minion Pro	9.5pt		6pt	30pt	0	6pt
p.MiniTOC5	p	MiniTOC5			MadCap			block	Minion Pro	9.5pt	0	6pt	40pt	0	6pt
p.MiniTOC6	p	MiniTOC6			MadC			block	Minion Pro	9.5pt		6pt	50pt	0	6pt
p.MiniTOC7	p	MiniTOC7			Ma			block	Minion Pro	9.5pt		6pt	60pt	0	6pt
p.MiniTOC8	p	MiniTOC8						block	Minion Pro	9.5pt		6pt	70pt	0	6pt
p.MiniTOC9	p	MiniTOC9						block	Minion Pro	9.5pt	0	6pt	80pt	0	6pt

Figure 9-10. Defining the Appearance of Generated mini-TOC Heading Entries.

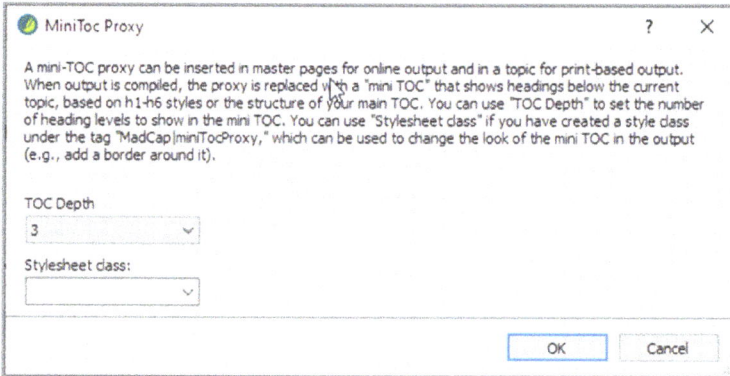

Figure 9-11. Editing miniTOC Proxy to Set TOC Depth.

QUICK STEPS: DEFINING THE APPEARANCE OF MINI-TOC ENTRIES

STEP	ACTION
—	**Use the following steps to set styles that determine the appearance of mini-TOC entries**
1	Open the desired stylesheet and use the **Medium** drop-down to select the **Print** medium.
2	If the Simplified View is not displayed, click the **View Advanced** button to switch to the view.
3	Select the **Generated Styles** category, using the **Styles** drop-down on the bottom-left of the toolbar.
4	Scroll down and, under the **Name** column, find MiniTOC1, MiniTOC2, MiniTOC3, MiniTOC4, MiniTOC5, and through MiniTOC9, under the **p**-parent. These selectors affect the appearance of mini-TOC entries.
5	In the Simplified View, double-click on each of the MiniTOC selectors to open the style **Properties**: **a)** Use **p.MiniTOC1** to set the styles of the level-1 headings — for example, **Font**, Size, and Spacing. **b)** Use **p.MiniTOC2** to set the styles of the level-2 headings — for example, Font, Size, and Spacing. **c)** Use **p.MiniTOC3** to set the styles of the level-3 headings — for example, Font, Size, and Spacing.
—	**Use the following steps to specify the depth of headings that should be listed in the mini-TOC**.
1	In the topic where the mini-TOC proxy is located, right-click on the proxy and select **Edit MiniTOC Proxy**.
2	Enter a value, typically 2-4, for the **TOC Depth**. A value of '**3**' will list up to two additional heading levels that appear in the topic following the heading after which the mini-TOC is placed. This option for determining the number of headings to include in the mini-TOC is closest to the mini-TOC element — as such, it has priority over any other method that might be used as well.

> **NOTE:** You can use the MadCap style selector **MadCap|miniTocProxy**, or a class that you have created under this parent style, to affect the appearance of the print mini-TOC container, including elements like the container background, image, border, and others.

CREATING INDEX KEYWORDS USING THE AUTO-INDEX EDITOR

BASIC CONCEPT

Using the Flare Index Editor is one method of defining terms you want users to have access to in a print or online index. In the editor, you specify a phrase Flare searches for in the content and an index term you want to appear in the index with a page number for each time Flare finds the phrase. To create a print index, defining the phrases and terms is one part of the complete task of creating an index. You will also need to make an index proxy topic.

ESSENTIAL ELEMENTS

In the Index Editor, you will do what results in the keywords that comprise the print output index. Using the Index Editor, you specify a **Phrase** for which Flare searches in the content. You also enter the **Index Term** or keyword you want Flare to insert in the Index for each **Phrase**. The **Index Term** is generally the same as the **Phrase**, but not always. Each time Flare finds the **Phrase** in the content, and the index term is recorded, followed by the page number. Carefully consider the use of the **Ignore Case** option. If most of your keywords or phrases are in your section titles and are capitalized, disabling the **Ignore Case** option can minimize the phrase occurrences in the content and index entries.

APPLICATION TIPS

To complete the generation of your index and produce an output in your documents, you'll also need to create an Index Proxy topic, as illustrated in the topic *"Inserting an Index Proxy in an Existing Topic"* and then insert that topic into the TOC outline.

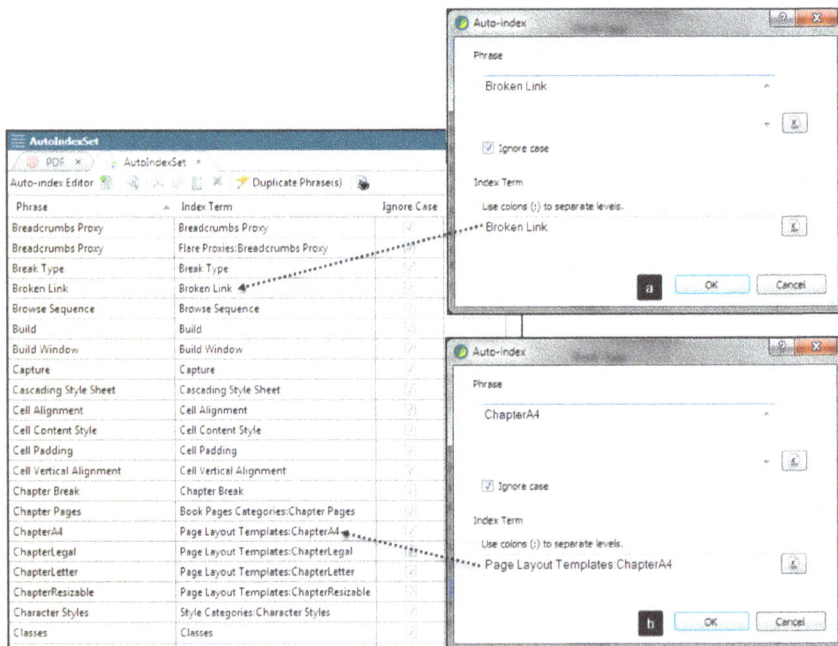

Figure 9-12. Auto-Index Editor Showing a) Index Entry/Term; and b) Index Entry/with Sub-levels.

QUICK STEPS: CREATING INDEX KEYWORDS USING THE AUTO-INDEX EDITOR

STEP	ACTION
1	From the **Project Organizer**, select **Advanced** > Auto Index Sets, to create a new auto index set.
	Right-click on the **AutoIndex Sets** folder and select **Add Auto-index Phrase Set** to create a new auto-index phrase file set. Create the file using a factory or user template or from an existing file.
2	With the file created, double-click on the file to open it in the **Auto-index Editor**.
3	Click on the **New Item** button to open the dialog to insert a new index entry.
4	Use one of the following methods to enter a single keyword entry or a keyword and a sub-level entry.
—	**To create a single keyword index entry use the following:**
5	In the **Phrase** field, enter a single index keyword phrase that Flare will search for in the content.
6	Enable the **Ignore Case** option if lowercase or uppercase instances of the keyword, when found, will be added to the index, along with the page number on which the term was found.
7	Use the **Index Term** field to enter what you want to appear in the index as the keyword entry. For example, for the **Phrase** 'TOC Editor," you might also enter '**TOC Editor**' in the **Index Term** field. Note: This entry, which will appear as the index term, does not have to be the same as the phrase.
8	Click **OK** to accept the new single keyword entry in the index file.
—	**To create an index keyword entry with a sub-level entry use the following:**
5	In the **Phrase** field, enter a single index keyword phrase that Flare will search for in the content.
6	Enable the **Ignore Case** option if lowercase or uppercase instances of the phrase, when found in the content, will be added to the index, along with the page number on which the term was found.
7	Use the **Index Term** field to enter what you want to appear in the index as the keyword entry, with the sub-level entry separated by a colon. For example, for the **Phrase**, you might enter '**Topic Toolbar Proxy**,' and for the **Index Term**, you might enter **Flare Proxies: Topic Toolbar Proxy**. See **Note**.
8	Click **OK** to accept the new single keyword entry in the index file.

> **NOTE:** Often, when there are sub-level entries, there may be multiple entries under a given keyword. For example, you may want to list all of the Flare proxies under the Index Term 'Flare Proxies.' The items Body Proxy, TOC Proxy, mini-TOC Proxy, and the others would be entered as sub-level keyword terms as follows: **Flare Proxies: Body Proxy**, **Flare Proxies: TOC Proxy**, and **Flare Proxies: mini-TOC Proxy**.

DEFINING THE APPEARANCE OF INDEX KEYWORDS

BASIC CONCEPT

Suppose you have created a topic that generates a print Index in your output. For such a case, you can modify the appearance of the individual Index keywords and the entire container that holds the Index. Your stylesheet contains inherited style selectors that you can use to perform this task.

ESSENTIAL ELEMENTS

Using styles (**p.Index1** through **p.Index9**) inherited in your stylesheet, you can modify properties like **Font**, **Size**, **Alignment**, and **Paragraph Spacing** for the subsequent levels of index keywords. The selector **p.Index1**, for example, defines the appearance of first-level keywords in the print index, the selector **p.Index2** defines the appearance of second-level keywords, and so on.

You can also modify the style **p.IndexHeading** to affect the appearance of the alphabetical letter at the beginning of each index section, and the property **mc-heading-format** to affect the letter format. You can also view and adjust all of these styles under your stylesheet's **Generated Content** style category.

APPLICATION TIPS

See *"Creating Index Keywords Using the Auto-Index Editor"* and see *"Inserting an Index Proxy in an Existing Topic."*

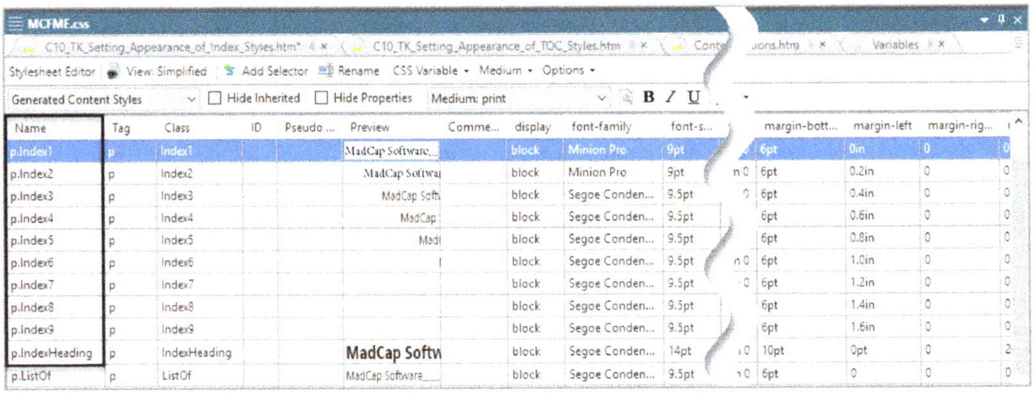

Figure 9-13. Defining the Appearance of Generated Index Heading Entries.

QUICK STEPS: DEFINING THE APPEARANCE OF INDEX KEYWORDS

STEP	ACTION
1	Open the desired stylesheet and use the **Medium** drop-down to select the **Print** medium.
2	If the **Simplified View** is not displayed, click the **View Advanced** button to switch the view.
3	Select the **Generated Styles** category, using the **Styles** drop-down on the bottom-left of the toolbar.
4	Scroll down and, under the **Name** column, find the selectors **Index1** through **Index9**, under the **p**-parent. These selectors affect the appearance of print Index entries.
5	Use **p.Index1** to set the styles of the level-1 keywords — for example, Font, Size, and Paragraph Spacing.
6	Use **p.Index2** to set the styles of the level-2 keywords — for example, Font, Size, and Paragraph Spacing.
7	Use **p.Index3** to set the styles of the level-3 keywords — for example, Font, Size, and Paragraph Spacing.
8	Use **p.IndexHeading** to set the appearance of the alphabetical headings that separate index sections. By default, the index headings format is defined in the **mc-heading-format** property as **{A}**, and the headings appear as: **A**, **B**, **C**, and **D**. If you modify the default to **{a}**, the headings will appear as: **a**, **b**, **c**, and **d**. You can also modify the default format to **-{A}-**, and headings will appear as: **-A-**, **-B-**, **-C-**, **-D-**.

> **NOTE:** You can also use the MadCap style selector **MadCap|IndexProxy**, to affect the appearance of the print Index container, including elements like the container background color, image, border, and others.

CREATING GLOSSARY TERMS USING THE GLOSSARY EDITOR

BASIC CONCEPT

Using the Flare Glossary Editor is one method of defining terms you want users to have access to in a print or online glossary. In the editor, you will specify each glossary term and provide a definition or point to a topic where a user can view the definition. To create a print glossary, defining the terms and definitions is one part of the total task. You will also need to make a glossary proxy topic.

ESSENTIAL ELEMENTS

In the Glossary Editor, you can specify each **Term,** and you have the option to either enter the **Text** for the definition or point to a specific **Topic** in which users can view the definition. Defining the terms and definitions is just one part of creating a print glossary. You will also need to make a glossary proxy topic. When you build the target, Flare generates the glossary in the output at the point at which you inserted the glossary proxy topic in the TOC outline.

APPLICATION TIPS

See how to create a Glossary Proxy topic, as described in *"Inserting a Glossary Proxy in an Existing Topic,"* and then insert that topic in the TOC outline.

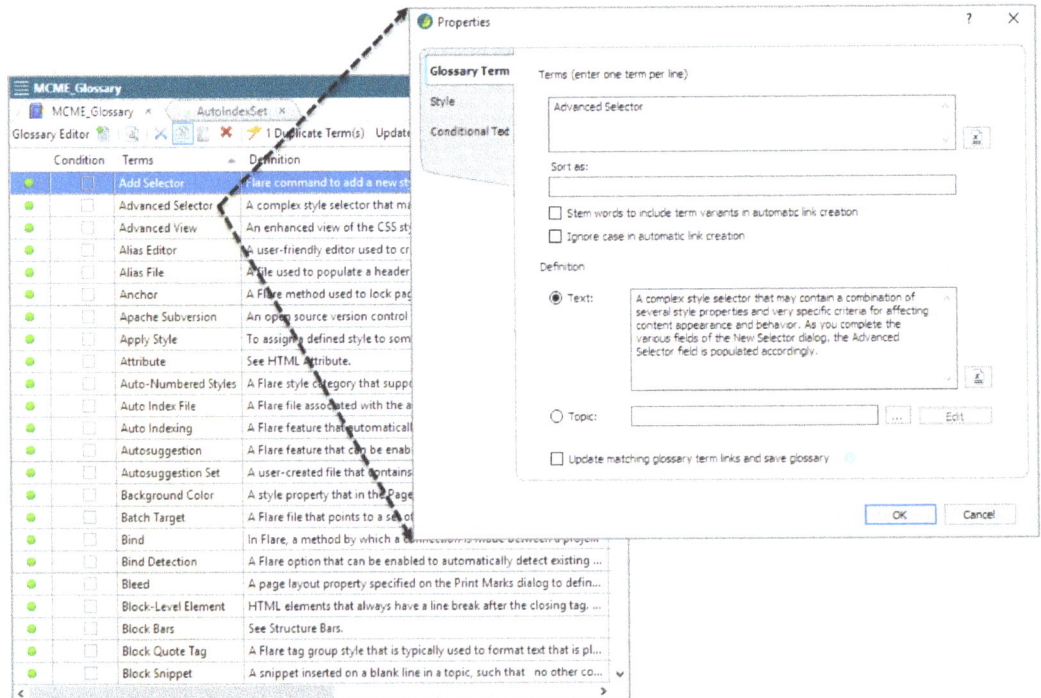

Figure 9-14. Glossary file Editor — Term and Definition Entry.

QUICK STEPS: CREATING GLOSSARY TERMS USING THE GLOSSARY EDITOR

STEP	ACTION
1	From the **Project Organizer**, right-click on the **Glossaries** folder and select **Add Glossary** to create a new glossary file.
2	Double-click on the file to open it in the **Glossary Editor**.
3	Click on the **New Item** button, or right-click and select the **New** option to open the dialog to insert a new glossary entry.
4	Select the **Glossary Term** tab.
5	In the **Terms** field, enter a single new term.
6	Under **Definition**, enable **Text** and enter a definition for the new term; or enable **Topic**, and specify a topic in which the definition is located.
7	Click **OK** to accept the new term entry in the glossary file.
8	Repeat the procedure, from step 3, to enter additional glossary terms.

DEFINING THE APPEARANCE OF GLOSSARY ELEMENTS

BASIC CONCEPT

When you have created a Glossary Proxy topic, entered glossary terms and definitions using the Glossary Editor, and placed the Glossary Proxy topic in your TOC outline, the glossary will appear in the output when you build the target. You can use glossary style selectors inherited in your stylesheet to define the appearance of individual elements in the glossary and the container that holds the glossary.

ESSENTIAL ELEMENTS

Using selectors inherited in your stylesheet, you can modify properties like **Font**, **Size**, **Paragraph Spacing**, and **Alignment** of the glossary elements. For example, define the appearance of glossary definitions using the style class **div.GlossaryPageDefinition**, and the appearance of the container that groups each term and definition using the class **div.GlossaryPageEntry**.

The appearance of the alphabetical headings between glossary sections is defined using the class **div.GlossaryPageHeading** and the appearance of print-output glossary terms are defined using the style class **div.GlossaryPageTerm**. Finally, you can define the appearance of glossary terms in an online output using the style class **a.GlossaryPageTerm**. You can also view and modify all of these styles under your stylesheet's **Generated Content** style category.

APPLICATION TIPS

See *"Creating Glossary Terms Using the Glossary Editor,"* and also see *"Inserting a Glossary Proxy in an Existing Topic."*

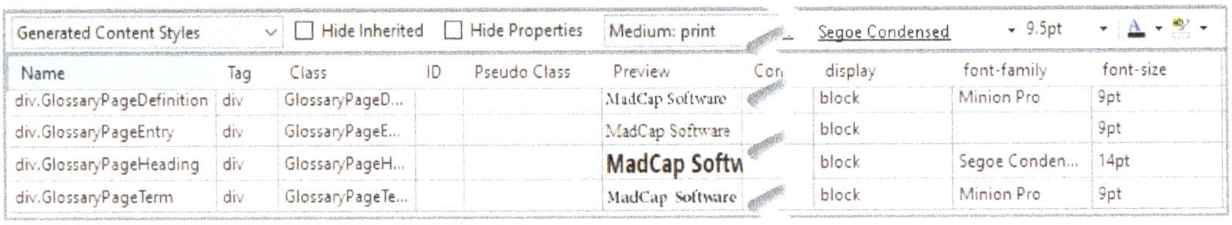

Generated Content Styles	☐ Hide Inherited	☐ Hide Properties	Medium: print	Segoe Condensed	▾ 9.5pt	▾ A ▾

Name	Tag	Class	ID	Pseudo Class	Preview	Con	display	font-family	font-size
div.GlossaryPageDefinition	div	GlossaryPageD...			MadCap Software		block	Minion Pro	9pt
div.GlossaryPageEntry	div	GlossaryPageE...			MadCap Software		block		9pt
div.GlossaryPageHeading	div	GlossaryPageH...			**MadCap Softw**		block	Segoe Conden...	14pt
div.GlossaryPageTerm	div	GlossaryPageTe...			MadCap Software		block	Minion Pro	9pt

Figure 9-15. Defining the Appearance of Generated Index Heading Entries.

QUICK STEPS: DEFINING THE APPEARANCE OF GLOSSARY ELEMENTS

STEP	ACTION
—	**Use the following steps to set styles that determine the appearance of glossary elements**
1	Open the desired stylesheet and use the **Medium** drop-down to select the **Print** medium.
2	If the Simplified View is not displayed, click the **View Advanced** button to switch the view.
3	Select the **Generated Styles** category, using the **Styles** drop-down on the bottom-left of the toolbar.
4	Scroll down and, under the **Name** column, find the glossary style selectors div.GlossaryPageHeading, div.GlossaryPageTerm, div.GlossaryPageDefinition, div.GlossaryPageEntry, and a.GlossaryPageTerm, under the **div**-parent.
5	In the **Simplified View**, double-click on each of the selectors in Steps 6-10 to open the style **Properties**:
6	Use **div.GlossaryPageHeading** to set the appearance of the alphabetical headings that separate the glossary sections.
7	Use **div.GlossaryPageTerm** to set the appearance of print-output glossary terms.
8	Use **div.GlossaryPageDefinition** to set the appearance of the glossary definitions.
9	Use **div.GlossaryPageEntry** to set appearance of the container that groups each term and definition.
10	Use **a.GlossaryPageTerm** to set the appearance of the link style for online-output glossary terms.
—	**Use the following steps to specify the appearance of the glossary container**
1	Click the **View Simplified** button to switch the Stylesheet Editor to the **Advanced View**.
2	On the lower-half of the toolbar, select the **All Styles** category, using the **Styles** drop-down button.
3	Scroll down and, in the left pane, find the glossary container selector **MadCap|GlossaryProxy**, or a class that you have created under this parent style, to set the properties of the glossary container.
4	Use the **Show** drop-down button and select **Assorted Relevant Properties**.
5	Click the button ⓐⓩ **Switch to Grouped View** to list the relevant properties as property groups.
6	Modify the container style properties as desired.

CREATING DIRECTIONAL AND GROUP SEARCH SYNONYMS

BASIC CONCEPT

An essential part of any Help System is a robust search engine that can always return beneficial results. Flare offers two search enhancements that help to ensure that users always obtain helpful search results. On the HTML5 target **Search** tab, you can choose from the **Search Engine** options of **MadCap Search**, **Google Search**, and **Elasticsearch**. Each of these methods has its pros and cons; however, the MadCap Search option is tailored to offer several advantages for Flare implementations.

ESSENTIAL ELEMENT

If you choose **MadCap Search,** you can enhance your search results by using the **Synonym Editor** to configure **Directional Synonyms, Group Synonyms,** or both. You would generally use directional synonyms to provide synonyms for words not found in your content, but users may search for these words. Since the synonym is in your content, the query will return results. You would use group synonyms when there are multiple terms in your content where you always want to return the same results. Since group synonyms are considered equal, they all will produce the same search results.

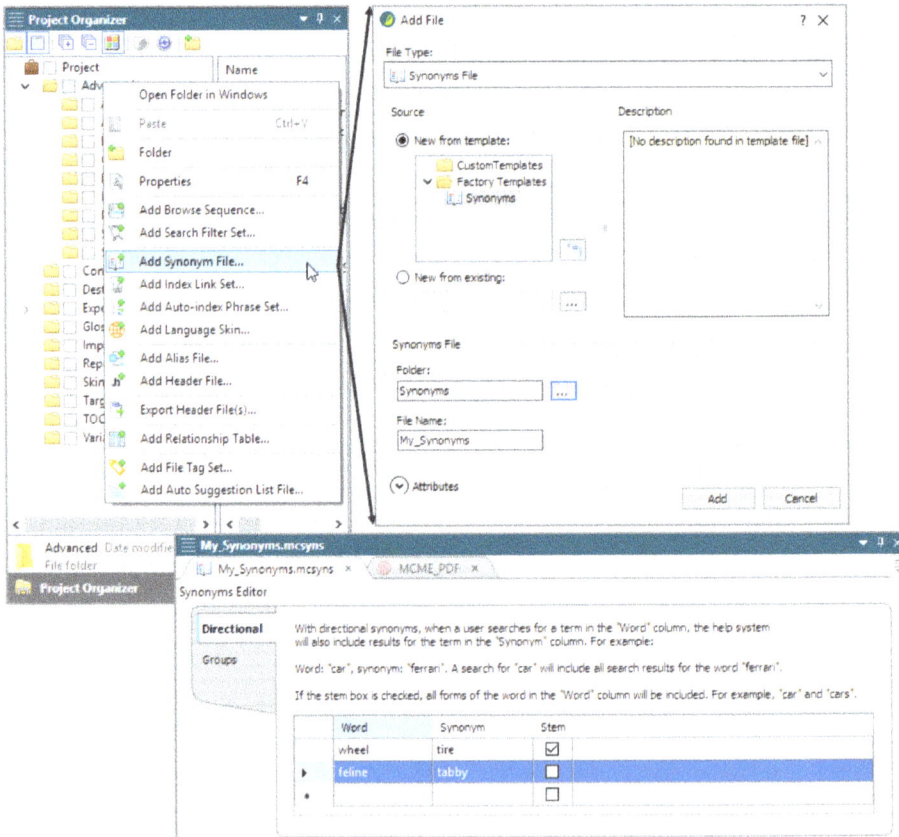

Figure 9-16. Add New Synonyms File.

QUICK STEPS: CREATING DIRECTIONAL AND GROUP SEARCH SYNONYMS

STEP	ACTION
1	Select the **TOCs** folder, in the **Project Organizer**, or select a subfolder in which you wish to create the new Synonym file. If you wish you can create a subfolder in the root folder **Synonyms**.
2	Right-click > **Add Synonym File**. The **Add File** dialog opens.
3	Ensure that the **File Type** is set for **Synonym File**.
—	**To create the new Synonym File based on a template use the following:**
4	Set **Source** for **New from template**, and choose the **Synonyms** template from the **Factory Templates** folder or choose a Synonym file template from a user-defined **Custom Templates** folder.
5	Continue with **Step 7**.
—	**To create the new Synonym File based on an existing file use the following**:
6	Set the **Source** for **New from existing**, and use the browse button [...] to find an existing synonym file.
7	Under **Synonym File**, in the **Folder** field use the default **Root folder** (**Project/Synonyms**), or browse and choose a subfolder in the default folder in which to store the new Synonym file.
8	Use the **File Name** field to specify a name for the new Synonym file.
9	Click **Add** to save the new Synonym file.
—	**To create a directional synonym file use the following:**
1	Click on the **Directional** tab, to enter directional synonyms.
2	Click in the **Word** field, and press **F2** key, then enter a word, for example, "**Wheel**," that is not in your content, but you want the same search results returned as if the user entered a synonym, like "**Tire**," which is in your content.
3	In the **Synonym** field, enter a word, for example, "**Tire**," that is in your content and for which you want to have the normal search results returned if the user searches for the term given in the **Word** field.
4	Select the **Stem** option to return all topics in the search where words are found containing the stem of the term entered in the **Word** field. For example, words that include the term plus 'ed', 'es', 'ing', or 's'.
—	**To create a group synonym file use the following:**
1	Click on the **Groups** tab, to enter a synonym group — a group of words that all will produce the same search results.
2	Click in the **Group** field, and press the **F2** key, then enter each word in the synonym group, with the equal sign in between each word. For example, **word1** = **word2** = **word3**, and so on.
3	Select the **Stem** option to return all topics in the search where words are found containing the stem of each of the group synonyms. For example, words that include the synonym plus 'ed' , 'es' , 'ing', or 's'.

BINDING A FLARE PROJECT TO GIT SOURCE CONTROL

BASIC CONCEPT

For each project you wish to manage under source control, you must create a separate remote repository on the server. The next step is to bind or connect each project to the repository and push it to the server if it is not already done. Once a project is bound and uploaded to a particular source control application, users can import or check out the project to their local machine.

ESSENTIAL ELEMENTS

In Flare, you would bind a project to the Git source control application from the **Project Properties** dialog on the **Source Control** tab. To bind the project is to connect it to the source control remote server and application. You must specify the **Source Control Provider**, your **Name**, and **Email** address from the **Source Control** tab. If the project is not already on the server, you have the option to push it to the server as part of the bind operation.

APPLICATION TIPS

For additional information on using Git, see *"Project Integration with Git Source Control,"* and see *"Importing a Flare Project From GIT Source Control."*

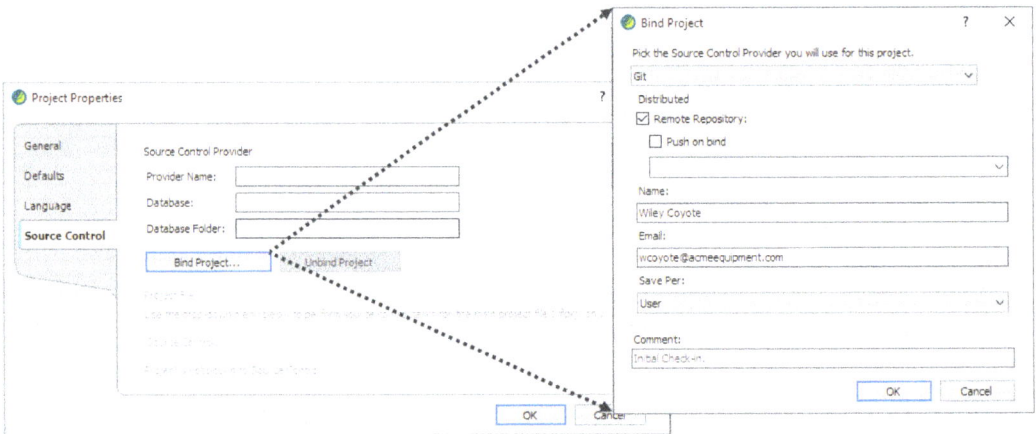

Figure 9-17. Bind Flare Project to Source Control Application.

QUICK STEPS: BINDING A FLARE PROJECT TO GIT SOURCE CONTROL

STEP	ACTION
1	Click **Project** > **Project Properties**. The Project Properties dialog opens.
2	Click the **Source Control** tab.
3	Click the **Bind Project** button. The **Bind Project** dialog opens.
4	Use the drop-down to select **Git** as the **Source Provider**.
5	Under **Distributed**, the **Remote Repository** is enabled by default.
6	Enable the **Push on bind** option if you wish to push the Flare project to the Git server for the first time.
7	Enter your **Name** and **Email** address. This access information must match your established account.
8	Save **Per User**.
9	Click **OK**. Flare adds the project files to source control, and does an initial check-in of your project to the Source Control remote repository if you enabled the **Push on Bind** option. Flare will display the **Source Control** menu on the ribbon.

IMPORTING A FLARE PROJECT FROM GIT SOURCE CONTROL

BASIC CONCEPT

Users can download or import a Flare project from Source Control after being initially bound and uploaded to the source control repository. An import by users places a working copy of the project on their local machine. Every user that needs to work on the project will need to import the project. Each user downloads the project to a folder designated during the import and, from then on, can check out the project, make updates, and check in when done with a working copy.

ESSENTIAL ELEMENTS

The import task assumes that the Flare project you wish to import was previously bound and uploaded to the Git server and that the project is not currently on your local device. The project is stored on the server in what is referred to as the remote repository. When you complete the import successfully, the project will be placed on your device in the local repository.

For you to import the project, you will need an established Git server account. If the Git server is already in operation, you should be able, with instructions, to create your account — otherwise, you may need assistance from your IT or DevOps team.

APPLICATION TIPS

For additional information on using Git, see *"Project Integration with Git Source Control,"* and see *"Binding a Flare Project to GIT Source Control."*

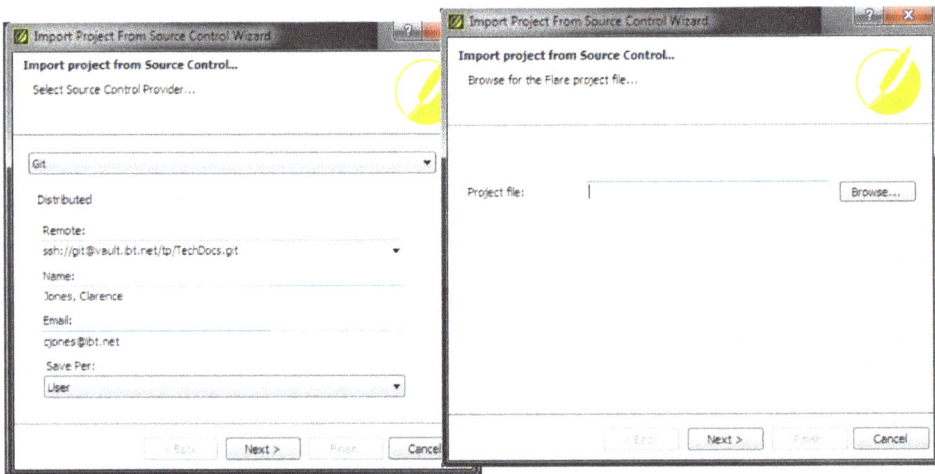

Figure 9-18. New Project Import — Using Source Control Import Wizard.

Quick Steps: Importing a Flare Project From GIT Source Control

STEP	ACTION
1	Click **File** > **New Project** > **Import from Source Control**.
2	Use the drop-down selector to choose the **Source Control Provider**.
3	Enter the Server in the **Remote** field.
4	Enter your **Name** and **Email** address.
5	Use **Save Per User**.
6	Click **Next**.
7	In the **Project File** field, click the **Browse** button to locate the project in the source control repository.
8	Click **Next**.
9	Enter the **Project Name**.
10	Choose the **Project Folder**.
11	Click **OK**. Flare performs the initial project pull to your local repository, in the folder you designated.

NOTE: With Git, you must fir set up the repository on the server and then you can connect or bind your project to the remote repository.

CHAPTER 10

WORKING WITH PRINT AND ONLINE TARGETS

INTRODUCING THE FLARE TARGET FILE

A *target file*, in Flare, is a file that contains all of the parameters you specify for building and generating a particular type of output — for example, a PDF print output or an HTML5 online output. You will generally create or find target files in the folder **Project Organizer > Project > Targets**. Using targets, you can produce any of several output types available in Flare. Other target examples include HTML Help and EPUB. The following table describes some of the main Flare target types.

After creating many of the essential components of your project, you will create the target file and specify the output type you wish to produce. You will then configure the target file dialogs to define the components you want to include and the behavior you want to trigger in the output. You can create as many targets as required in a single project, using as many different outputs types as necessary.

Table 10-1. Flare Target and Output Types

Target Type	Brief Description
HTML5	The HTML5 target is Flare recommended for creating online output. This target supports the HTML5 output specification developed by the World Wide Web Consortium (W3C) and the Web Hypertext Application Technology Working Group. HTML5 output is fully responsive and offers features unavailable in older WebHelp outputs. HTML5 output deployment can be web-based or desktop-deployed and consists of a file set that you must distribute to end-users.
Clean XHTML	Clean XHTML produces an output of HTML files, free of MadCap-specific tags and independent of other MadCap-generated files. A Clean XHMTL output is without skins, navigation, search, or other features and is only the single-sourced output from your content. This type of output supports the use of the output in many ways. For example, the output can be embedded in other software, like wikis, e-Learning systems, or other software applications.
EPUB	This target produces an EPUB output or book, an online format developed and maintained by the International Digital Publishing Forum (IDPF). EPUB output is generally electronically viewed on devices like tablets and phones, but it is structured much like a book or manual. The EPUB output is similar to print-based outputs and produced much the same as a PDF output.
PDF	The PDF target produces the widely used standard "Portable Document Format," or simply a PDF output; Adobe's open standard format for electronic document exchange.
Word	The Word target produces a Word output in the DOCX, DOC, PDF, or XPS formats.
Eclipse Help	Used by content developers who want to use Flare and their Flare project content to produce a plug-in for an Eclipse Help system. The output displayed in the Eclipse Help Viewer supports dynamic, searchable content that integrates as a plug-in to your Eclipse environment.
HTML Help	HTML Help is used to create Help systems for Windows 32-bit desktop applications and requires Internet Explorer on end-user systems. This older output type consists of a single ".**CHM**" file that is distributed to users. HTML Help is a good choice if you want users to deal with a single file only and store and open the output locally.

TARGET AS A SINGLE-SOURCING TOOL

A target file is an essential single-sourcing tool. In each specific instance, you determine the generated output based on the elements and parameters you choose for that target. In configuring a target, you specify the **Output Type** to define the output format you want to generate and a **Primary TOC** file to indicate which topics to use. You would then select a **Primary Stylesheet** to define the styles to use. From the **Conditional Text** tab, you specify what topics and other tagged components to include or exclude, or if applicable, what content displays depending on the device used. Finally, you select **Variables** definitions, which can output specific content depending on your selections.

In short, the target file gives you the control to create multiple instances of a given output, each using different content from the same source, based on the various parameters you select each time.

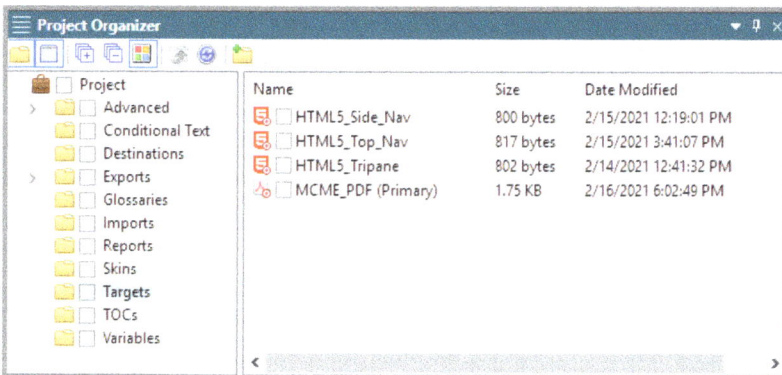

Figure 10-1. Target Files in Project Organizer.

THE FLARE HTML5 ONLINE TARGET

In Flare, the HTML5 target is the most commonly used and recommended online output option. The Target Editor tabs and parameters for working with the HTML5 target and the PDF target, for the most part, are the same. Slight differences in the HTML5 and PDF dialog parameters are noted.

The HTML5 output online format requires its own skin, where there are several options from which to choose. Side Navigation skins position the main navigation element to the left or right of the topic pane. Top Navigation lists menu items across the top, and topics display below in a pane. Both of these options support a flexible frameless output as in modern websites. Finally, the older Tripane Navigation uses three panes and places a toolbar and search bar on top, a navigation pane on the left, and the main topic pane to the right and just below the top pane.

When you use the HTML5 target, you can specify that no skin be used in the output. No skin, or a so-called frameless output, means no main menu or navigation element is generated. In such cases, you would need to use Flare proxies and other elements inserted into your content for navigation and generally to access your topics or other content. You will have the option of adding various links like cross-references and hyperlinks, topic pop-ups, image maps, and other elements. Flare proxies and skin components will allow you to insert short menus, toolbars, and search bars.

THE FLARE PDF AND WORD PRINT TARGETS

The PDF and Word targets are two often used print options. Most of the target dialogs and the associated parameters are the same for both of these print options. For example, the **General**, **Conditional Text**, **Variables**, and **Publishing Destination** dialogs are the same. Both of these print options have an Advanced options tab, which will be described. Although you can generate a PDF output directly, using a PDF target, an **Advanced** tab option of the Word target also lets you generate a PDF output while simultaneously building the Word output.

You can also set specific **PDF Options** in the Target Editor. These options let you specify how images, document properties, the initial view, and security are handled in the output. The parameters for these are not covered in the following topics, as they are commonly used and familiar to most writers using Adobe Acrobat.

INTRODUCING THE FLARE TARGET FILE EDITOR

The *Target Editor* is a graphical user interface that consists of several tabs for manually specifying the various parameters associated with a target output. Like with other Flare editors, you have the option of using the Flare Internal Text Editor as an alternative way of editing target files.

Later in this section, the Target Editor's tabs are reviewed, and the most commonly used parameters are described. Most parameters, once set, rarely need to be modified, but from time to time you may need to change the **Actions** on the **Conditional Text** tab or specific definitions on the **Variables** tab. For example, to generate a unique instance of the output, a conditional tag might need to be excluded or included, or you might modify one or more variable definitions. For a software release, you might change the Release Date, Software Version, and Document Revision.

> **NOTE:** Where a dialog is the same for the most part for PDF, Word, and HTML5, but has one or two additional Word or HTML5 parameters, then those parameters will be noted.

THE PRIMARY TARGET

When there are multiple targets in your project, you can specify one of them as the Primary Target. The *primary target* is simply one that you designate as the primary and is generally the one you use most often. After specifying a target as the primary, there are several **Project** menu buttons that you can use for quick and convenient access when managing and working with the Primary target. These buttons include **Build Primary**, **View Primary**, **Publish Primary**, and open **Primary Target**.

THE TARGET BUILD

A *target build*, is the process of compiling a defined target that will produce the desired output—for example, a PDF file. The collection of project items you specify, either directly or indirectly by completing the target dialogs, are the basis of the target build and the subsequent output. You can either use the **Build Primary** options on the **Project** menu or the **Build** button on a target file open in the **Target Editor** to build your target. If there are multiple targets, you may choose a batch target file created in the **Batch Target Editor** or use available command-line options.

The generated output, both the content and appearance, are based on elements you specified in the target — elements such as the TOC, a Cascading Style Sheet (CSS), Page Layout, or Template Page file, and variable definitions. Flare will store the output file in the folder you designated as the **Output** folder on the **General** tab of the target file.

THE TARGET PUBLISH

Once a target has been built, it can then be published. To publish a target is to place the generated output files in a location that others can access — that location is called a publishing destination. Flare supports several options for publishing your output files. One method is manually publishing the target by copying your output files directly from the project **Output** folder to a desired local or remote location. Another approach is to let Flare automatically push your files to the desired location, based on the information contained in a Publishing Destination file.

While a publishing destination is optional in most cases, it is specifically required to use Elasticsearch in your HTML5 output or generate a Clean XHMTL output for publishing to the SalesForce®, ZenDesk, or ServiceNow® platforms. A publishing destination is generally required when you want Flare to push the output files to the desired location. Destination files (.fldes), when created, are stored in the **Project Organizer > Project > Destinations**.

TARGET GENERAL PARAMETERS

The **General** parameters tab includes the parameters most commonly applied to the target. The tab has some parameters that are likely specified in most or all of your PDF targets and other parameters that support variables that may change for each of your PDF targets.

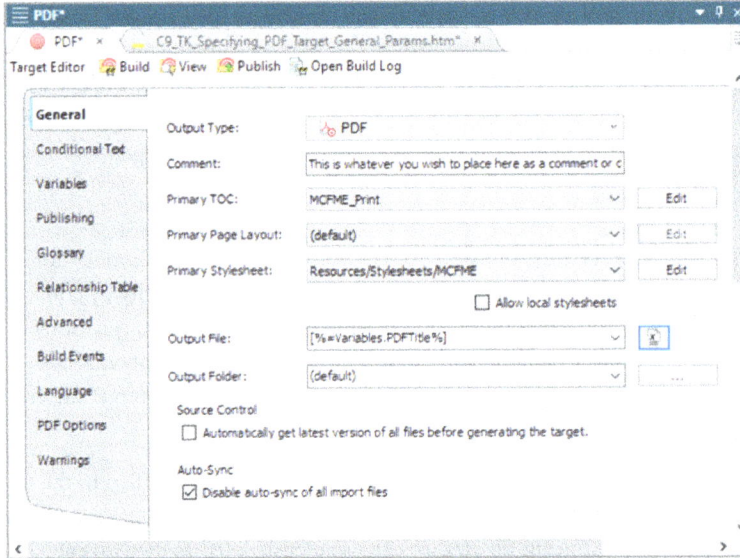

Figure 10-2. Target Editor — Target General Parameters Dialog.

Table 10-2. Target Editor–General Parameters

Parameter	Brief Description
Output Type	Specify the intended output type for this target, for example, **PDF** or **HTML5**.
Primary TOC	As a project can have several TOC files, which can be stitched together, you must specify the main TOC file to associate with the target. In most cases, a target will have a single associated TOC file, which would be the Primary TOC. **Note:** If a **Primary TOC** file is specified in the **Project Properties** file and a different one is specified in the Target file, the TOC specified at the target file will take precedence.
Primary Page Layout	Most documents will have different sections, each of which has a separate page layout file applied to the chapters and sections of the TOC file. In this case, the Primary Page Layout file need not be specified and can be left as Default. **NOTE:** If a **Primary Page Layout** file is specified in the **Project Properties** file and a different one in the Target file, the page layout specified at the target will take precedence.

Table 10-2. Target Editor–General Parameters (cont).

Parameter	Brief Description
Primary Stylesheet	As a project can have several stylesheets, you must specify the main stylesheet file to be applied when the target output is generated. **NOTE:** If a **Primary Stylesheet** file is specified in the **Project Properties** file and a different one specified in the Target file, the stylesheet specified at the target takes precedence.
Output File	Specify a file name you want Flare to assign to the PDF output. You can type a file name directly in the field or use the **Select Variable** icon, to open the available variables files to select a file name or variable containing the file name.
Output File	Specify the Word file format for the generated output as **.doc** or as **.docx**. Flare supports Word 2003 and later. **Note:** This parameter only appears on the **General** tab if the **Output Type** is set for **Word**.
Output Folder	Specify the folder where Flare should place the generated target output, or click the **Browse** button to find and select your designated output folder. This folder essentially becomes the top-level Output folder, as Flare will create appropriate sub-folders if your targets are in folders of their own in **Project Organizer** > **Targets**.
Source Control	Select this check-box if you want Flare to always get the latest files from the source control repository before building the target output. **Note:** Although it always appears, this parameter is only applicable when a source control application like Git is in use.
Auto-Sync (Disable)	Select check-box to disable Flare from synchronizing with all imported files before the build. Flare checks if any imported files have been externally updated and should be automatically updated if the check-box is not enabled.
Startup Topic	Specify an opening topic for this HTML5 output. Typically a splash page or a specific landing page that provides users with access to the online pages of your HTML5 output is specified. **Note:** This parameter only appears on the **General** tab if the **Output Type** is set for **HTML5**.
Browse Sequence	If applicable, specify the browse sequence used in this online output. This method, where supported, might be used to provide users with a pre-defined series of topics, like with a process flow that sequentially presents the task a user should perform. **Note:** This parameter only appears on the **General** tab if the **Output Type** is **HTML5**. The Browse Sequence must be enabled in the associated skin, for example, HTML Tripane.

TARGET CONDITIONAL TEXT PARAMETERS

Using the **Conditional Text** tab, you can control the inclusion or exclusion of specific items from the output, based on condition tags already applied in your content and by setting the **Action** parameter.

While the settings you define on this tab for a specific target may include certain content and exclude other content, you might define these same parameters quite differently for another target. In this fashion, you can draw from the same source files to create different outputs by using different targets and settings for the condition tags. On the **Conditional Text** dialog for HTML5 outputs, you can also use the **Display by Media Query** options to determine what content is displayed based on the device.

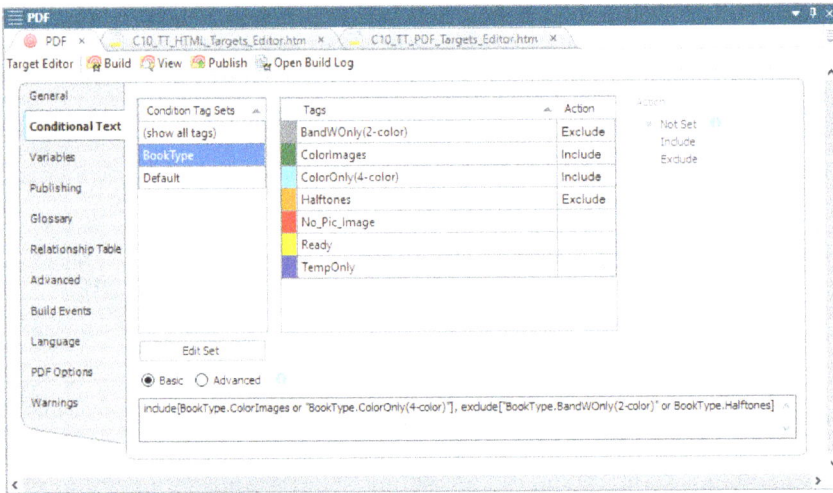

Figure 10-3. Target Editor — Conditional Text Parameters for PDF and Word Print Outputs.

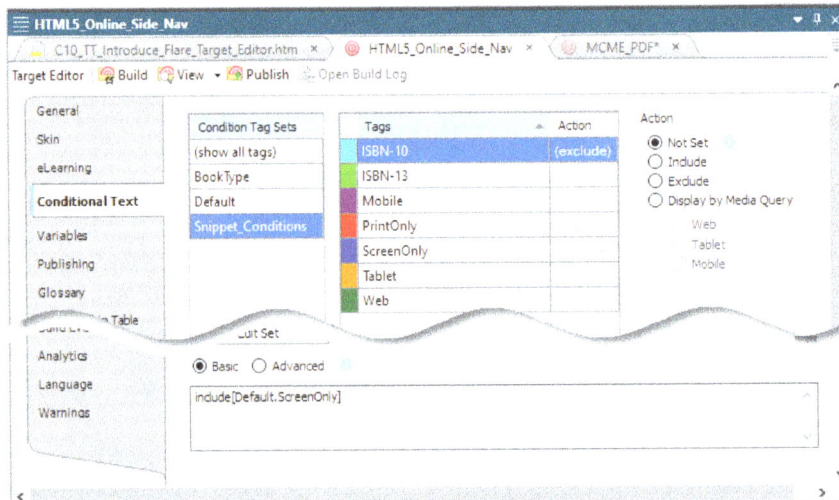

Figure 10-4. Target Editor — Conditional Text Parameters for HTML5 Online Outputs.

Table 10-3. Target Editor–Conditional Text Parameters

Parameter	Brief Description
Conditional Tag Sets	Upon selecting the **Conditional Text** tab, all of the conditional tag sets found in the project are listed, including the Default. You may specify tags from and of the listed sets.
Tags	Each Conditional Tag Set, when selected, lists the tags contained in the set. Click (**Show All Tags**) to list all tags from all sets simultaneously. Since each tag name is preceded by the tag set to which it belongs, you can use this display instead of switching between sets when specifying whether a tag should be included or excluded. See **Action Group (Radio Selectors)**.
Action	For each tag listed under **Tags**, the adjacent cell under the **Action** column reflects how a tagged item is treated when the target is built — for example, "**Included**" or "**Excluded**."
Action (Radio Selectors)	Use the **Action** radio selectors, to specify whether to **Include** or **Exclude** the selected tag in the build, or leave the tag as **Not Set**. You settings will define an expression. See **Note**.
Edit Set	Clicking **Edit Set** opens the **Condition Tag Set** Editor to the currently selected tag set. Tags in the set can then be modified, added, or deleted from the set.
Basic	This parameter is one of two modes where you may work with conditional tags applied to parts of your content that you wish to control whether the content is included in or excluded from the target output. As you use the **Action** column radio selectors **Include**, **Exclude**, and **Not Set**, Flare automatically builds condition tag expressions (See **Note**) in a read-only (Basic Mode only) display pane at the lower part of the dialog. In **Basic** mode, the condition tag expression is based alone on the **OR** operator.
Advanced	This parameter is the second of two modes in which you can create condition tag expressions (See **Note**) applied to the target output. Unlike the **Basic** mode, in which the conditional tag expressions are created automatically by Flare, the **Advanced** mode is more of a manual entry mode for more experienced users — users that are confident in using logic operators to form logic combinations. In the Advanced mode users can create expressions using logic operators **AND**, **OR**, **NOT**, and brackets to support additional logic combinations. These elements support combining conditional tags to form more complex expressions.

NOTE: A conditional tag expression is a logical combination of specific conditional tags applied to the target output upon build.

TARGET VARIABLES PARAMETERS

In Flare, variables that you have created, both single-definition and multi-definition, can be inserted anywhere throughout your project, such as in topics, snippets, and page layout footers and headers. Using the **Variables** tab, of the Target Editor, you can set a specific value for each variable that you have defined in your project. The value that you specify will be, for the current instance of the target output you are building and the value displayed in the generated output.

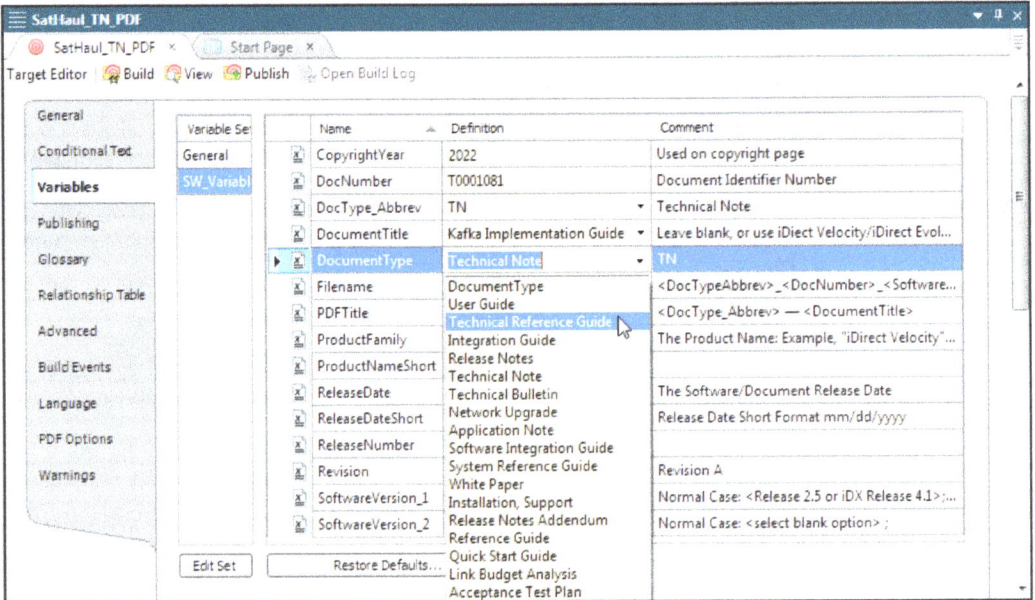

Figure 10-5. Target Editor — Variables Parameters Dialog — Inserting a Specific Variable Definition.

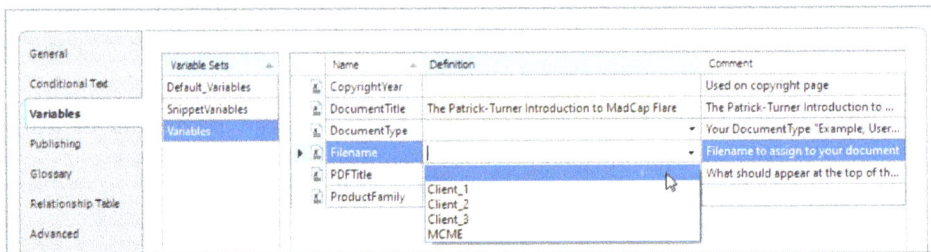

Figure 10-6. Target Editor — Variables Parameters Dialog — Inserting a Blank (Null) Variable Definition.

Table 10-4. Target Editor—Variables Parameters

Parameter	Brief Description
Variable Set	When the **Variable** tab is selected, all variable sets found in the project are listed, including the General (Default) variable set. A variable set may contain both single-definition and multi-definition variables.
Name	The **Name** column lists all variables contained in the currently selected variable set.
Definition	A **Definition** is a specific value assigned to a given variable. **1)** A single-definition variable has a single assigned value listed in the adjacent row of the **Definition** column. For example, **Copyright Year**, has a single defined value of "2022" and **Release Date**, which has a single defined value of "May 30, 2022." **2)** A multi-definition variable, for example, **DocumentTitle**, can have several values or definitions. The first of these values is in the adjacent row of the **Definition** column. The remaining values of a multi-definition variable are accessed using a drop-down arrow. **See Note**.
Edit Set	Clicking **Edit Set** at the dialog bottom opens the **Variable Set Editor** to the currently selected variable set. The variables and definitions can then be modified, added, or deleted.
Restore Defaults	Since you may enter a definition (value) directly to a variable field immediately before building the target, clicking **Restore Defaults** allows a return to the original definitions defined in the variables file.

NOTE: Before the build, you may directly specify a new definition (value) for variables with a single definition or multiple definitions. This entry may be a direct entry of the value in the target field or by clicking the adjacent **Edit Set** button to open and edit the variable file to make the addition.

NOTE: You can only select a single value for a multi-definition variable. The chosen definition applies to the current instance of the target output.

PDF TARGET ADVANCED OPTIONS

The **Advanced** tab, for PDF outputs, involves choices of whether you want Flare to generate and add certain content items to your output. Various options allow you to enable or disable the performance of specific operations by Flare. These options, in general, are not required and are simply a matter of choice. The following table may not describe all of the available options.

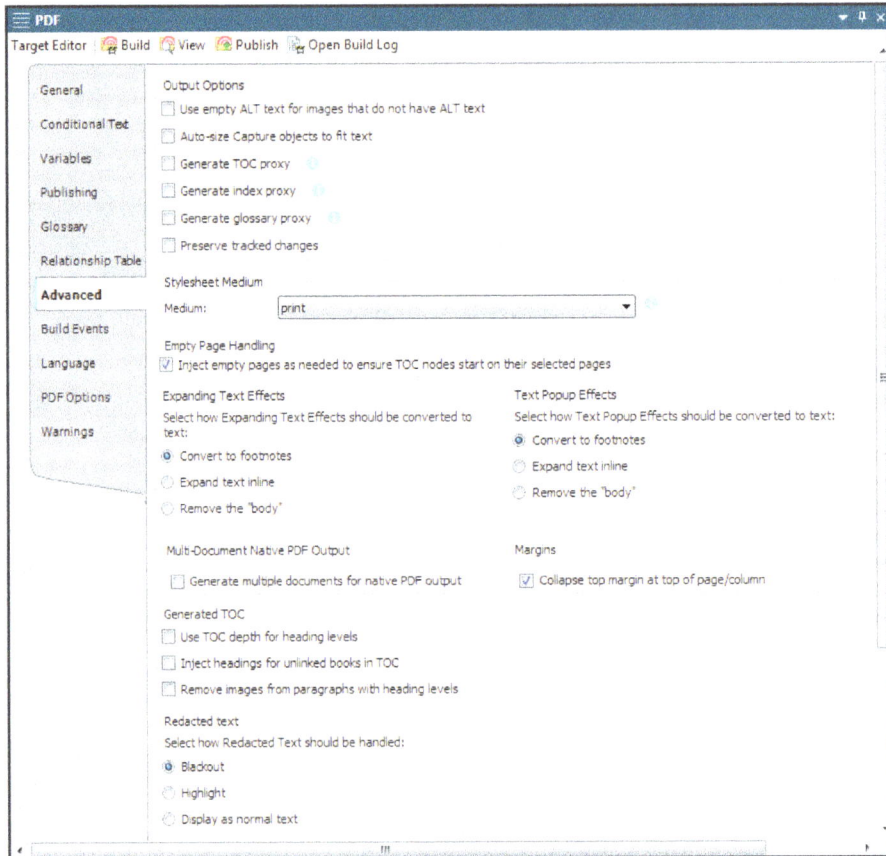

Figure 10-7. Target Editor — PDF Target Advanced Options Dialog.

Table 10-5. Target Editor – PDF Advanced Options

Dialog Parameter	Brief Description
Use Empty Alt Text for Images	Enable this option if you have not specified alternate text to use when a referenced image is missing. Flare will not insert any text about the missing image but instead a blank.
Auto Size Capture Objects to Fit	Enable this option so that when Flare generates the output, it automatically re-sizes call-out objects to fit the contained text as necessary.
Generate TOC Proxy	Select check-box if you have not created a TOC topic in your content and want Flare to generate and insert a TOC in the front part of your document.
Generate Index Proxy	Select check-box if you have not created an Index topic in your content and want Flare to generate and insert an Index in the back part of your document.
Generate Glossary Proxy	Select this check-box if you have not created a Glossary topic and you want Flare to generate and insert a glossary in the back part of your document.
Preserve Tracked Changes	Select this check-box if you are tracking changes in your Flare content and wish to show these tracked changes in your PDF or Word output.
Stylesheet (Medium)	On the **General** tab, you specified a **Primary Stylesheet** that Flare should use to generate the target; here, you select a stylesheet **Medium** that Flare should use when generating the target — for example, the **Print** medium.
Empty Page Handling	There may be no demands in your documents for pages to precisely land on the left or right side, and the injection of empty pages by Flare is not needed. In other cases, this option works in conjunction with those cases where you have created empty page types in your page layout files to ensure that Flare automatically injects blank pages to ensure your content lands as expected.
Expanded Text Effects/ Text Pop-up Effects	Use the radio selectors to specify what Flare should do with text that would usually be expanded text or presented in a pop-up window in the output.
Use TOC Depth for Heading Levels	If you have enabled the option for Flare to generate a TOC proxy, enabling this check-box will cause the heading levels in your document, for example, H1, H2 and H3, to be based on the depth of the associated item in the TOC.
Inject Headings for Unlinked TOC Books	Content headings not linked to topic files are generally not included in the generated TOC. Enabling this option causes Flare to include those headings.
Remove Images From Paragraphs with Heading Levels	Depending on the output type in which you may have included an image in headings, enabling this option may remove the image from the content heading, or the TOC, or both the content heading and the generated TOC.

HTML5 TARGET ADVANCED OPTIONS

The **Advanced** tab for HTML5 outputs offers many options from which to choose to tell Flare how to affect certain appearances and behaviors in the generated output. There are also choices of whether you want Flare to create and add certain items to your output. Finally, various options allow you to enable or disable the performance of specific operations by Flare.

These advanced options, in general, are not required and are simply a matter of choice. The following table may not describe all of the available options.

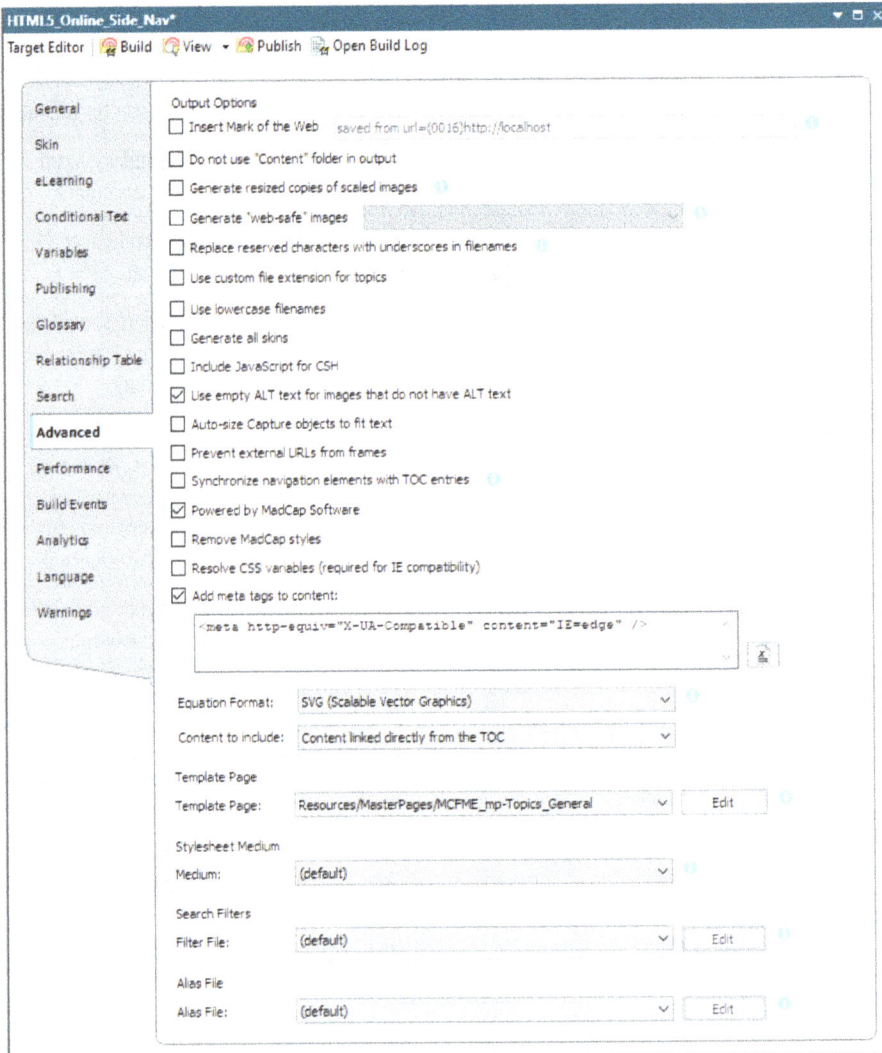

Figure 10-8. Target Editor — HTML5 Target Advanced Options Dialog.

Table 10-6. Target Editor – HTML5 Advanced Options

Dialog Parameter	Brief Description
Do not use Content folder in output	Enable this option to tell Flare not to create this folder when you build the online output. The folder, instead, is placed at the root of the **Output** folder.
Use custom file extensions	Enable this option to allow any custom file extension that you specify in the drop-down for topics that you have given this extension.
Use lowercase file names	Enable this option to tell Flare to convert all folder and file names to lower-case. This option is helpful with case-sensitive operating systems like UNIX.
Generate all skins	This option, set by default, tells Flare to generate every skin in the project; if disabled, Flare will only generate the skin specified on the HTML5 target.
Include JavaScript for CSH	With this option, enabled by default, Flare allows a URL or JavaScript to open your output. Having JavaScript files enabled in your output might cause security warnings when files are scanned. If security warnings are displayed, you may want to exclude JavaScript files from your output.
Use empty ALT text for images that do not have ALT text	Enable this option if you have not specified alternate text to use when a referenced image is missing. Flare will not insert any text about the missing image but instead a blank.
Prevent external URLs from frames	Enable this option to prevent anyone from loading an external website by appending an unknown and possibly malicious website in your normal URL.
Remove MadCap styles	You can enable this option if, for some reason, there are issues in your online output and you need to remove MadCap styles from the production.
Resolve CSS variables	If you expect your users to use the Internet Explorer (IE) browser, enabling this option ensures compatibility with CSS variables.
Add meta tags to content	Specify this option to add one or more custom meta tags to be enabled in your HTML target outputs.
Template Page	You may have created several template pages for different purposes or different HTML5 outputs in the project. You need to specify the primary file for use with most topics in the current HTML5 output.
Medium	You may have created several online mediums in your project for different purposes or different HTML5 outputs; in such cases, you need to specify the specific medium for use with the current HTML5 output.
Alias File	You may have created several Alias files in this project to be associated with CSH. Specify the specific Alias file for use with the current HTML5 output.

HTML5 TARGET SKIN PARAMETERS

From the HTML5 **Skin** parameters tab, you can specify a full skin to display your online output, or you can identify smaller individual skin components, to support user navigation in the output. You would use these skin components in conjunction with appropriate Flare proxies in those cases where you may have chosen to use a frameless (skinless) output.

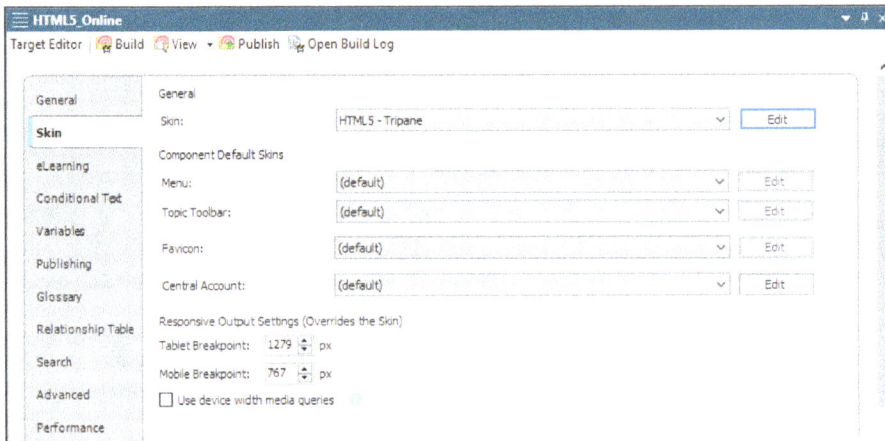

Figure 10-9. Target Editor — HTML5 Target Skin Parameters Dialog

Table 10-7. Target Editor – HTML5 Skin Parameters

Property	Brief Description
Skin	Specify the skin that Flare should use to display target output. Here you would specify **None** for a frameless output or a Flare skin that you have previously configured. Typical choices include **HTML5-Top Navigation**, **HTML5-Side Navigation**, or **HTML5 Tripane Navigation**.
Component Default Skins	Default skin component elements you may select include a **Menu**, **Topic Toolbar**, **Favicon**, and **Central Account**. Here, you would specify one or more skin components you have previously configured for use in your frameless output.
Tablet Breakpoint	Specify a breakpoint in pixels that you want to trigger a responsive output for tablet devices. This setting takes priority over any setting defined for tablet devices on the associated skin.
Mobile Break-point	Specify a breakpoint, in pixels, that you want to trigger a responsive output for mobile devices. This setting takes priority over any setting defined for mobile devices on the associated skin.

NOTE: Only Flare media queries, for example, Web, Tablet, and Mobile, are supported and controlled by the breakpoints specified in the target.

WORD TARGET ADVANCED OPTIONS

Several options on the **Advanced** tab involve choosing whether you want Flare to generate and add certain content items to your output. Various options allow you to enable or disable the performance of specific functional operations by Flare. Many of the options are not required; however, there are some defaults you may wish to include. While they may not be necessary, some parameters may represent best practices when generating your PDF output.

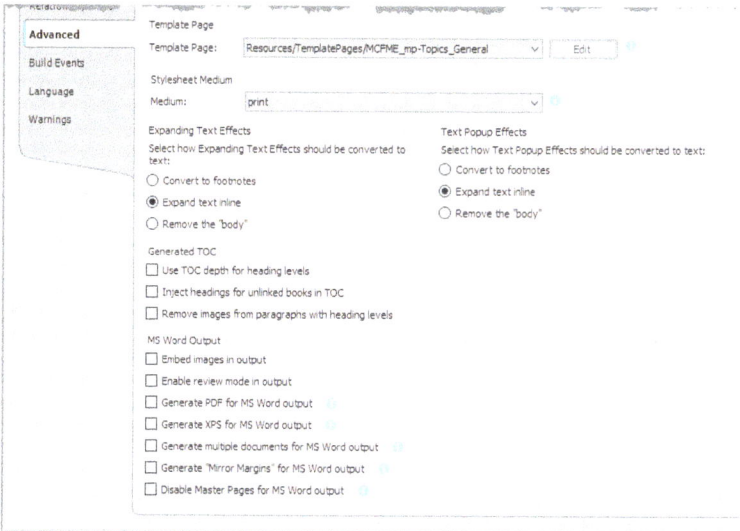

Figure 10-10. Target Editor — Word Target Advanced Parameters Dialog.

Table 10-8. Target Editor — Word Advanced Options

Dialog Parameter	Brief Description
Use Empty Alt Text for Images	Enable this option if you have not specified alternate text to use when a referenced image is missing. Flare will not insert any text about the missing image but instead a blank.
Auto Size Capture Objects to Fit	Enable this option so that when Flare generates the output, it automatically re-sizes callout objects to fit the contained text as necessary.
Generate TOC Proxy	Select this check-box only if you have not created a TOC topic and want Flare to generate and insert a TOC at the front section of your document.
Generate Index Proxy	Select check-box only if you have not created an Index topic and want Flare to generate and insert an Index in the back section of your document.
Generate Glossary Proxy	Select this check-box if you have not created a Glossary topic and you want Flare to generate and insert a glossary in the back of your document.
Generate Glossary Proxy	Select this check-box if you have not created a Glossary topic and you want Flare to generate and insert a glossary in the back of your document.

TARGET PUBLISHING PARAMETERS

Once you build a target output, it can then be published. To publish the target output files is to place the files in a location that others can access. Using the **Publishing** tab, you can specify, from a list of defined destination files, that determine where a built output can be published. Destination files (.fldes), are created and stored in **Project Organizer > Project > Destinations**.

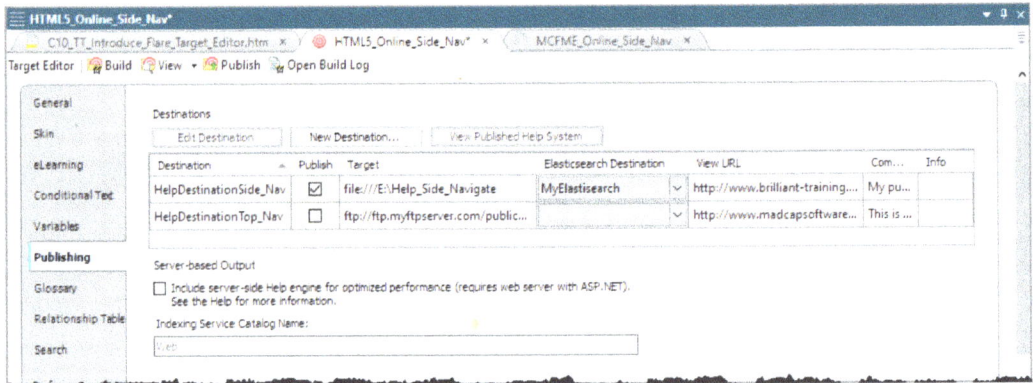

Figure 10-11. Target Editor—HTML5 Target Publishing Parameters Dialog

Table 10-9. Target Editor – Publishing Parameters

Property	Brief Description
Destination	The Publishing tab lists all of the destinations that have been defined in the project. destinations that are assigned to a target are checked; destinations that are not assigned to a target are unchecked. You may assign any number of destinations to a target.
Target	The Target field displays the target location specified in the destination file.
Elastisearch Destination	* If you have enabled the **Elasticsearch** option as the **Search Engine Type** on the **Search** tab of the HTML5 target, then the Elasticsearch drop-down will be displayed.
Server-based Output	Enable this option to take advantage of HTML advanced server-side features like automatic runtime project merging, server-side search, and searching of non-XHTML files. **Note:** While enabling **Server-based Output** causes this option to be built in your target, other steps must be performed on the HTML5 hosting server, to view and display the HTML5 server-based output. Those same steps are also necessary on your local machine to view and test the results.

NOTE: * To enable the **Elasticsearch** feature, you must select this option and configure the remaining parameters on the target **Search** . On the **Publishing** tab, you must specify the Elasticsearch Destination.

SUMMARY ON WORKING WITH PRINT AND ONLINE TARGETS

When it comes to Target files, you may define as many print and online targets as needed. At a minimum, you might define a target for each PDF and HTML5 output you produce. You can also create different targets for variations of the same book — for example, other formats and sizes, or to accommodate different audiences or companies. You can adjust the content of each target based on conditional tags, variables, and snippets in your content and how they are applied differently at build.

In defining the parameters of your targets, some parameters will generally stay the same while others are occasionally modified — perhaps based on a new release. Each new release, for example, will have a different date, software release version, and other parameters that may have associated variables.

The following checklist offers some tips and guidelines for working with print and online targets. Following, in the remainder of this chapter, are some examples of print and online target-related tasks.

CHECKLIST: WORKING WITH PRINT AND ONLINE TARGETS

* *Consider a central folder for target files that an entire team can use. This approach supports team access to all of the targets. A network drive, as opposed to local desktops, allows a single Flare output folder where all targets are generated and accessible.*

* *A target is a file whose parameters you configure to generate a specific print output (PDF or Word) or online (HTML5) output. You may configure as many different targets as required.*

* *Any **Responsive Output Settings** you adjust on the **Skin** tab of the target file will override any settings made on the **Setup** tab of the Tripane skin settings.*

* *When you have selected **MadCap Search Engine** on the HTML5 target, consider specifying the HTML5 target **Search Results**, including the **Advanced Search Options**, to enhance the results and minimize the impact of index terms, glossary terms, and micro-content on user searches.*

* *In a multi-project and multi-writer environment, consider managing the target files as part of shared resources like Page Layouts, CSS, Table Stylesheets, Snippets, Variables Images, Template Pages, and Micro-Content. These files can be maintained, shared, and synchronized from a global project to ensure document consistencies and file integrity.*

* *As an alternative approach to a global project in which a single project is responsible for the shared resources, consider developing all documents in a single large project, where shared resources are maintained in this project and preferably by an assigned individual.*

Specifying Target General Parameters

Basic Concept

The **General** parameters of any target file are the most basic of the settings for the target—they define the type of output and where Flare should place the generated result. Given that it is common to create a unique target file for each print or online output, once the parameters are specified, they rarely need to be changed for each output build.

Essential Elements

When specifying the **General** parameters, you must provide the **Output Type** generated by the target — for example, **PDF** or **HTML5**. Since there may be several TOCs in a project, you must tell Flare which to use as the **Primary TOC**. If there are multiple TOCs and you do not specify one, Flare uses the first one it finds in the project. Use the **Primary Page Layout** to select a page layout file to use if all topics in your project are the same and use the same page layout. You can leave the **default** option specified if there are multiple page layout files in the project, and you will apply those layout files to the different parts of the TOC outline. A **Primary Stylesheet** must also be defined as the stylesheet that most topics will use when more than one stylesheet. See **Note**.

You can directly enter the **Output File** name for the generated print or online output, or you can click the **Insert Variable** button to open the **Insert Variable** dialog. The **Output Folder** parameter lets you use the default output folder location or browse and select a specific folder to place the output. If applicable, enable the **Source Control** option to automatically pull the latest version of the files before building the target. Finally, you can Enable or Disable auto-sync of all imported files before the build.

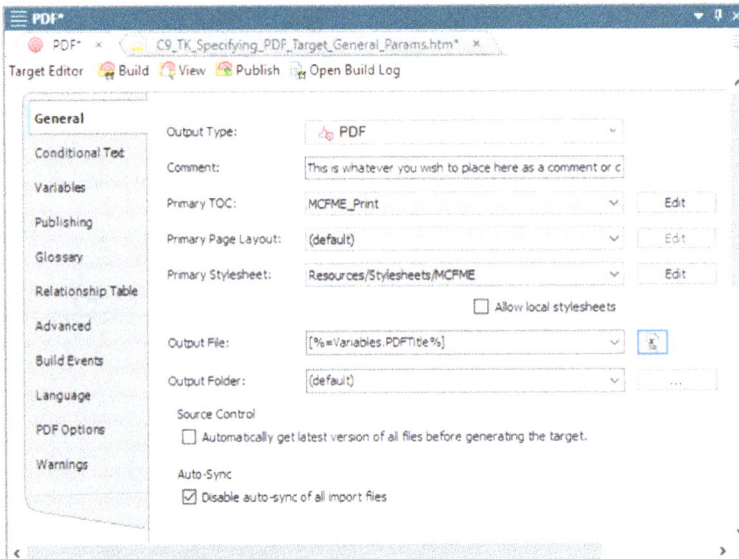

Figure 10-12. Target Editor — General Parameters Tab.

QUICK STEPS: SPECIFYING TARGET GENERAL PARAMETERS

STEP	ACTION
1	From **Project Organizer** > **Targets** folder, open the desired target file.
2	Click the **General** tab.
3	Use the **Output Type** drop-down to select the type of output for this target. For example, PDF or HTML5.
4	Use the **Primary TOC** drop-down to select the primary TOC or the TOC associated with this target.
5	Use the **Primary Page Layout** drop-down to select the page layout file to use if most or all topics in your project will use the same page layout file; or leave the **default** option specified if there are multiple page layout files in the project and those layout files will be applied to the different parts of the TOC outline.
6	Use the **Primary Stylesheet** drop-down to select the stylesheet used by most topics, in a project that has multiple stylesheets.
7	Enable the **Allow local stylesheets** option, to indicate that a stylesheet can be specified locally in the topic properties in order to override the primary stylesheet specified above.
8	In the **Output File** field use **Default** to allow Flare to assign the default name or do one of the following: **a)** Enter a name directly for the output file that will be generated upon build. **b)** Click the **Select Variable** button, just to the right of the filed, to open the **Variables** dialog and from one of the **Variable Sets**, select a variable name that has been created for the output file name. **c)** From the **Variables** dialog, choose one of the user **Variable Sets**, and click **Edit Set**, to open the **Variables Editor** to insert a new variable and definition for the Output File variable definition.
9	In the **Output Folder** field use **Default** to allow Flare to place the output file in the default folder or do one of the following: **a)** Use the drop-down and select one of the previously used output folder locations to place the file **b)** Use the Browse button, to the right of the field, and find and select a folder in which to place the generated output file.
10	Use the **Source Control** option, if applicable, to pull the latest version of the files prior to generating the target output.
11	Use the **Auto-Sync** option, if applicable, to prevent the automatic synchronization of all imported files upon each build of this target.

NOTE: For the HTML targets you can enter a **Startup Topic** as the first topic that is presented when users open your online output. You can also specify a **Browse Sequence** as the primary browse sequence you want initially displayed when there are more than one browse sequence in the project. If there is only one browse sequence it will automatically be displayed when the output is opened.

SPECIFYING TARGET CONDITIONAL TEXT PARAMETERS

BASIC CONCEPT

Conditional text refers to elements of your project content to which conditional tags have been applied. Until you define the behavior of the condition tags on the **Conditional Text** tab of the target file, there is no impact in the output on text or other elements to which condition tags have been applied. When you specify these parameters in the target file, you tell Flare whether the tagged content should be included or excluded in the output when you build the target.

ESSENTIAL ELEMENTS

Throughout the content, various parts of the content may have had condition tags applied. All of the **Condition Tag Set**s in the project are accessible on the **Conditional Text** Tab. Based on tags used in the content, you may specify tags from any or all of the **Condition Tag Sets** for a given instance of a target. To define **Tags**, you can click **Show All Tags** to list tags from all of the **Tag Sets**, choose a specific **Condition Tag Set**, select one of the Tags. Finally, select **Include**, **Exclude**, or **Not Set** to the far right under the **Actions** column. Repeat the process for the Tags that need to be defined.

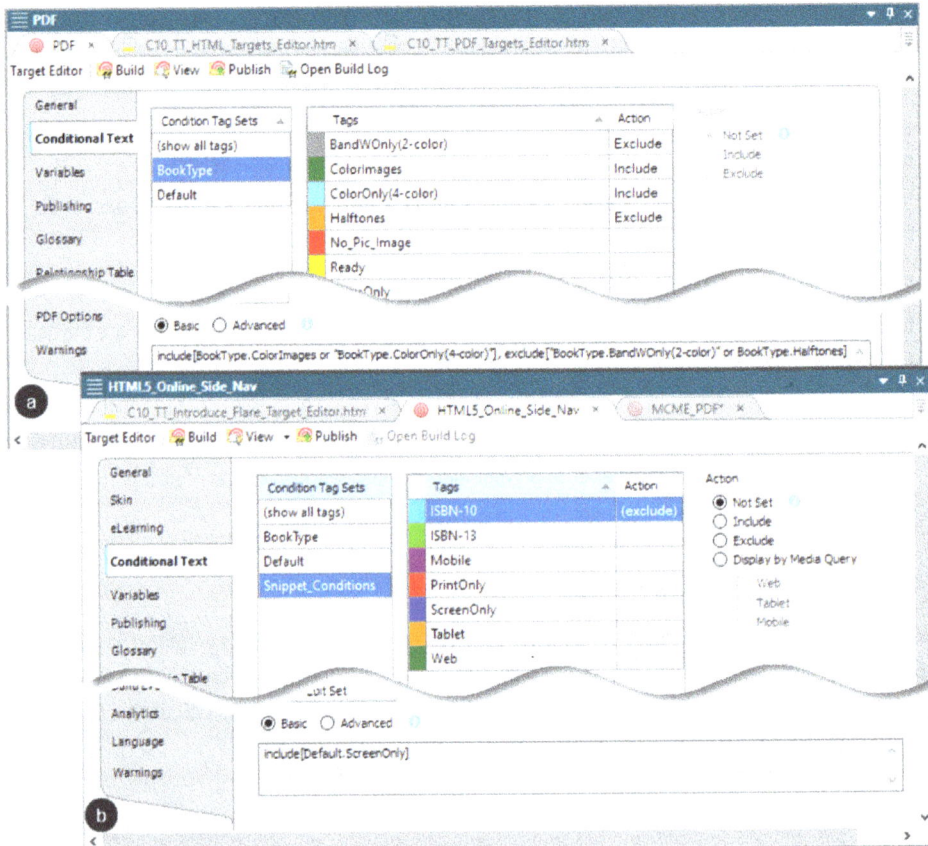

Figure 10-13. a) PDF Target — Conditional Text Dialog and b) HTML5 Target — Conditional Text Dialog

QUICK STEPS: SPECIFYING TARGET CONDITIONAL TEXT PARAMETERS

STEP	ACTION
1	From the **Project Organizer** > **Targets** folder, open the desired target file. For example, PDF or HTML5.
—	**To specify conditional tags for a PDF target:**
2	Click the **Conditional Text** tab.
3	Under the **Conditional Tag Sets**, -choose show all tags, to list all of the tags in all of the tag sets; or choose a specific condition tag set , where the tags you wish to use are contained.
4	Under the **Tags** column, select a tag for which you wish to specify a setting.
5	Under the **Action** column, and with the tag selected, specify whether to **Include** or **Exclude** content where this tag has been applied. Content in your project for which this tag has been applied, will be either included or excluded based on this action.
6	Continue with the same Condition Tag set, to specify the action of other tags, or repeat the steps from Step 3, to choose additional condition tags.
—	**To specify conditional tags for an HTML5 target:**
2	Click the **Conditional Text** tab.
3	Under the **Conditional Tag Sets**, -choose show all tags, to list all of the tags in all of the tag sets; or choose a specific condition tag set , where the tags you wish to use are contained.
4	Under the **Tags** column, select a tag for which you wish to specify a setting.
5	Under the **Action** column, and with the tag selected, do one of the following: **a)** Specify whether to **Include** or **Exclude** content where the selected tag has been applied; **b)** Select **Display by media query**, to indicate that the content to which the selected tag, for example **Web**, **Tablet**, or **Mobile**, has been applied, should be displayed based on the current media query in use.
6	If you selected **Display by media query**, then choose one of the following: **a) Web**, to display content to which a Web tag was applied, if the user is viewing a web-sized screen **b) Tablet**, to display content to which a Tablet tag was applied, if the user is viewing a tablet-sized screen **c) Mobile**, to display content to which a Mobile tag was applied, if the user is viewing a smart phone-sized screen
7	Continue with the same Condition Tag set, to specify the action of other tags, or repeat the steps from Step 3, to choose additional condition tags.

NOTE: Selecting all three media query check boxes has the same effect of choosing the **Include** option.

SPECIFYING TARGET VARIABLES — SINGLE AND MULTIPLE DEFINITIONS

BASIC CONCEPT

You and other writers may use the variables you define in a project throughout the entire project. Users can apply these variables differently for different targets or different instances of the same target. Variable sets in a project may contain variables defined with a single definition or with multiple definitions. Before each target build, you can specify the required values for each single and multi-definition variable applicable to the current instance of the target.

ESSENTIAL ELEMENTS

When you open a target file, the values displayed in each variable field are default values, defined in the variable set or the last values previously used. If a definition needs to be changed, you may directly specify a different value for a single-definition or multi-definition variable. You can make a direct value entry by entering the value in the target field or clicking the adjacent **Edit Set** button to open and edit the variable file to make the change or new addition. However, with multi-definition variables, you would typically use the adjacent drop-down arrow to choose one of the listed definitions instead of making a direct entry.

APPLICATION TIPS

You can only enter a single value at build time for a multi-definition variable. The value you enter will be used in the current instance of the target build and output. Generally, other definitions in a multi-definition variable are used for other similar targets. However, depending on how you have created the variable, the multiple definition values may also be used for different instances of the same target.

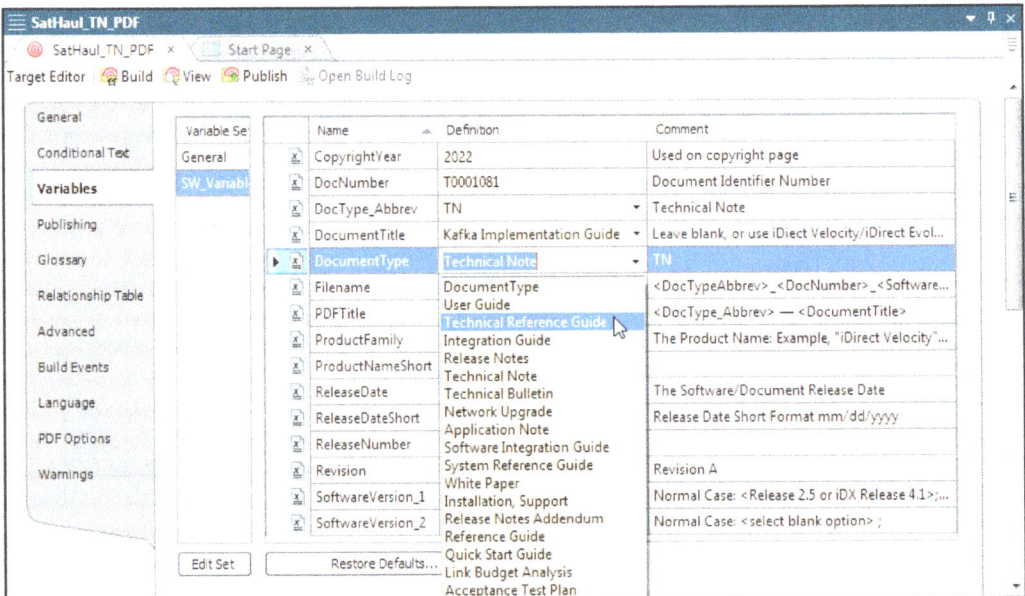

Figure 10-14. PDF Target Variables Dialog — Applying Single and Multiple Definitions Variables.

QUICK STEPS: SPECIFYING TARGET VARIABLES — SINGLE AND MULTIPLE DEFINITIONS

STEP	ACTION
1	From the **Project Organizer** > **Targets** folder, open the target file, where you want to assign definitions.
2	Click the **Variables** tab. The variable sets available in the project are listed.
3	Under **Variable Sets**, choose the specific variable set where you want to enter or modify variable definitions. Single-definition and multiple-definition variables are both listed under the **Name** column.
4	**To modify a single-definition variable at the target:** A single-definition variable has a single value displayed in the **Definition** field. Click in the **Definition** field and enter a value to assign to the variable for this instance of the target.
5	**To modify a multiple-definition variable at the target:** A multi-definition variable has a drop-down arrow ˅ to the right of the the first variable **Definition**. Use the drop-down to select a definition to assign to the variable for this instance of the target.
6	Click the **Save** button to save your changes to the target file.

ADDING AN OUTPUT PUBLISHING DESTINATION

BASIC CONCEPT

Once you have built your target and Flare has generated the output files, you can access these files in the **Output Folder** designated on the **General** tab of the target file. For others to access the output files, you must place the files in a publishing destination. A *publishing destination* is simply a local or remote directory that designates where you will put the output files for public access. There are several options for creating publishing destinations in Flare.

ESSENTIAL ELEMENTS

This task is to create the destination file in your project and then configure the destination **Type**. The destination **Type** dictates how the output files are moved to the destination. When getting your output files to the destination, you can manually copy and paste them to a local or remote location or specify that Flare will push the files to where you want them placed.

From the Project ribbon, you can select **New** > **Add Destination** or from **Project Organizer** > **Project** > **Destinations** > right-click > **Add Destination**. Flare immediately opens the file for editing. You can choose a destination **Type** that specifies how Flare will move your files to a specified destination. You can select from the options **File System**, **FTP** (secured or unsecured), **MadCap Central**, **Salesforce®**, **ServiceNow®**, or **Zendesk**.

APPLICATION TIPS

In most cases, a publishing destination is optional; however, you must provide one to use Elasticsearch in your HTML5 output or generate a Clean XHMTL output to be published to SalesForce®, ZenDesk, or ServiceNow®. See *"Specifying Target Publishing Parameters."*

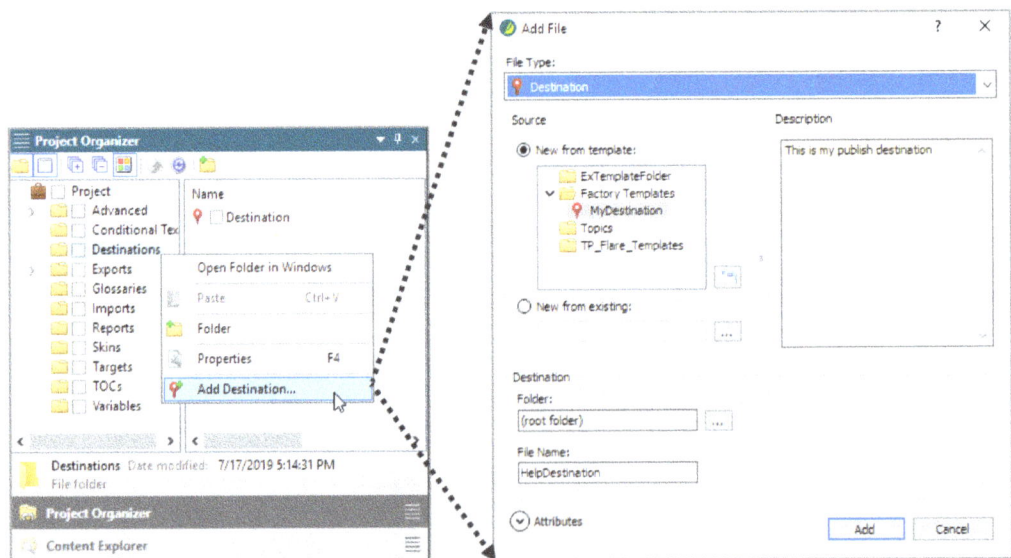

Figure 10-15. Add Destination — Add File Dialog with Destination Option Set.

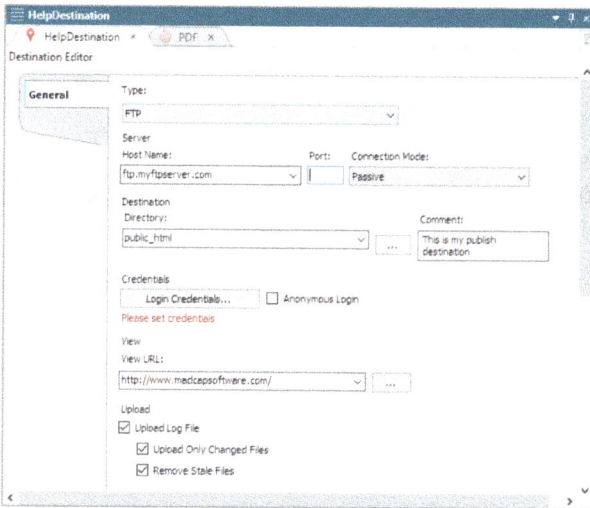

Figure 10-16. Add Publish Destination Parameters Dialog.

QUICK STEPS: ADDING AN OUTPUT PUBLISHING DESTINATION

STEP	ACTION
—	**To Create a Destination File:**
1	Click the **Project Organizer** > right-click on the **Destination** folder, and select **Add Destination**.
2	Ensure that the **File Type** is set for **Destination**.
3	**To create the new Destination file use one of the following:**
	a) From Templates: Set the **Source** for **New From Template**, then choose the **MyDestination** template from the **Factory Templates** folder or choose a template from a user-defined custom templates folder.
	b) From Existing: Set the **Source** for **New From Existing**, and use the browse button ⌐…⌐ to locate the existing Destination file from which to create the new file.
4	Under **Destination**, in the **Folder** field use the default **root folder** (**Project/Destination**), or browse and choose a subfolder in the default folder in which to store the file.
5	Use the **File Name** field to specify the name of the new Destination file.
6	Click **Add** to save your new Destination file. The new destination file opens in the Destination Editor.
—	**To Configure the Destination:**
1	Use the **Type** drop-down and select the destination type — for example, one of the following:
	a) choose **File System**, if the output files will be published to a local or remote file location
	b) choose **FTP**, if you want the output files sent to an FTP site using an unsecured connection
	c) choose **SFTP**, if you want the output files sent to an FTP site using a secured connection
	d) choose **MadCap Connect** for **Salesforce®**, **Zendesk**, or **ServiceNow®** as the destination option
2	Get assistance from your IT team to specify parameters for your **FTP**, **SFTP**, or **MadCap connect** choice.

SPECIFYING TARGET PUBLISHING PARAMETERS

BASIC CONCEPT

Once you have built your target and created one or more publishing destinations, you are ready to publish your output. Publish the output means manually placing the files in the destination or having Flare push the output files automatically to the designated destinations. One additional step before publishing the target is to specify the desired publishing parameters on the target file.

ESSENTIAL ELEMENTS

From the **Publishing** tab of the chosen target file, you can select and enable the **Publish** option for one or more destinations for where you would have the output files pushed. You may select as many destinations as necessary to provide access to others. From this tab, you also have an **Edit Destination** option for changes you may wish to make before publishing. Suppose you have chosen **Elasticsearch** as the **Search Engine Type** on the **Search** tab of the HTML5 target. In that case, Flare displays the **Elasticsearch Destination** drop-down for you to select the required elasticsearch destination.

APPLICATION TIPS

In most cases, a publishing destination is optional; however, you must provide one to use the Elasticsearch option in your HTML5 output or generate a Clean XHMTL output to be published to SalesForce®, ZenDesk, or ServiceNow®.

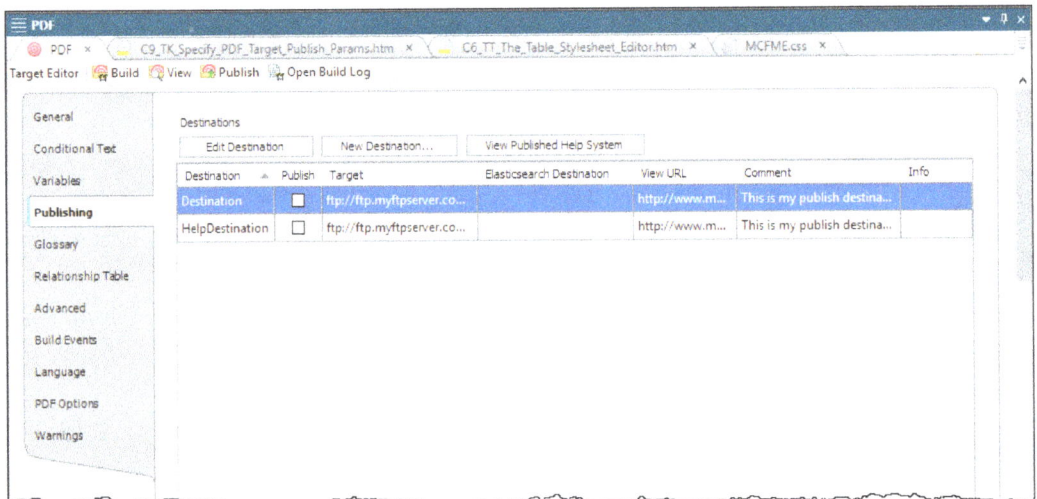

Figure 10-17. Target Editor — Publishing Parameters Tab.

QUICK STEPS: SPECIFYING TARGET PUBLISHING PARAMETERS

STEP	ACTION
1	From the **Project Organizer** > **Project** > **Targets** folder, open the target file, where you want to specify publishing parameters.
2	Click the **Publishing** tab. The destination files available in the project are listed under **Destinations**.
3	Use the **Publish** check-boxes to enable one or more associated destinations for publishing, when publishing is triggered.
4	With a destination selected, use the **Edit Destination** button to open and edit the destination file; or use the **View Published Help System** button to go to the listed URL to view the published output.
5	If you have chosen the **Elasticsearch** option as the **Search Engine Type** on the **Search** tab, you also need to use the Elasticsearch Destination drop-down to select a destination.
6	Click the **Save** button to save your changes to the target file.

> **NOTE:** *To enable the **Elasticsearch** feature, you will need to select this option and configure the remaining parameters on the **Search** tab of the HTML5 target.

USING THE TARGET EDITOR FOR SINGLE TARGET BUILD AND PUBLISH

BASIC CONCEPT

If your project has multiple print and online targets, you may want to consider creating and using a batch target file. A batch target file supports the ability to schedule and simultaneously build and publish several target files. Once you place targets in the batch file, you can selectively enable or disable whether specific targets should be built or published for a scheduled batch run.

ESSENTIAL ELEMENTS

Flare opens the Target Editor whenever you open any target file. You can manually trigger a **Build**, **View**, or **Publish** from the **Target Editor** ribbon for the open target file. You would build a target file after you have configured the necessary parameters on the various tabs and are ready to get the latest view of your output. In the early stages of working with your project and building the target, verifying items before building include the **Output Type**, **Primary TOC**, **Primary Stylesheet**, the **Output File** and **Output Folder**, and the **Variables** tab, that you have set the correct variable definitions. Before publishing a target, ensure that you have specified the required parameters on the **Publishing** tab.

You may start multiple builds or publish tasks from the Target Editor; however, the build or publish jobs will queue at some point when Flare is too busy.

APPLICATION TIPS

In addition to the Target Editor, you might also consider the Batch Target Editor if you have several target files that you might typically generate on somewhat of a release cycle. Using the Batch Target Editor, you can configure multiple targets to be built and published on a scheduled basis to automatically perform the batch target build and publish based on your specification. See *"Using the Batch Target Editor for Multi-Target Build and Publish."*

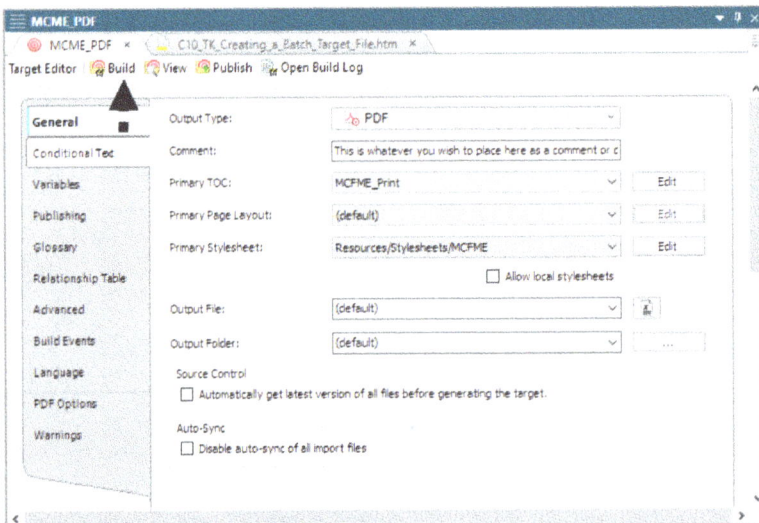

Figure 10-18. Build Single Target in Target Editor.

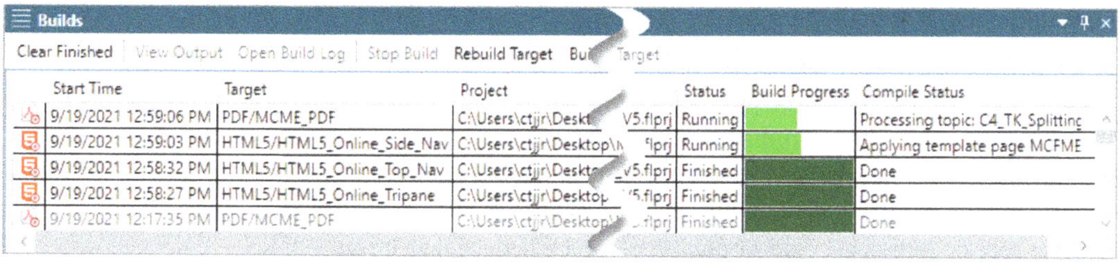

Figure 10-19. Target Build Window.

QUICK STEPS: USING THE TARGET EDITOR FOR SINGLE TARGET BUILD AND PUBLISH

STEP	ACTION
1	From the **Project Organizer** > **Project** > **Targets** folder, open the target file, where you want to trigger a build or publish of the target.
2	Modify parameters on any of the tabs that need changing prior to building or publishing.
3	Click the **Clear Finished** button to clear all of the previously built or published targets from the window.
4	Click the **Build** button to compile and build the output files for open target file and generate.
5	Click the **View** button to open and view the output file generated by the open target file.
6	Click the **Publish** button to push the generated output files to the locations specified in the destination files designated in the publish parameters specified on the **Publishing** tab of this target file.
7	Click the **Open Build Log*** button to view the log file that is generated each time the target is built. The log file contains a log of warnings, messages, and errors reported by the compiler during the target build.

> **NOTE:** ***** By default, the log file is stored at the root level of the output folder for that target. You can use the Flare Options dialog, **File** > **Options**, to specify where you would like the log file to be output.

USING THE BATCH TARGET EDITOR FOR MULTI-TARGET BUILD AND PUBLISH

BASIC CONCEPT

If your project has multiple print and online targets, you may want to consider creating and using a batch target file. A batch target file supports scheduling and simultaneously building and publishing several target files. Once you place targets in the batch file, you can selectively enable or disable whether specific targets are built or published for a scheduled batch run.

ESSENTIAL ELEMENTS

This task is to create the batch target file in your project and then configure the file behavior for how you want to carry out the target builds. When you make a new file, Flare immediately opens it for editing. Each of the targets is listed in a separate row, where each row displays the **Target Type**, a **Build** check-box, a **Publish** check-box, the **Last Built**, and the **Last Published** date. You can enable or disable a check-box for a target to indicate whether to build or publish in the next manually triggered or scheduled task. You can manually start a **Build and Publish**, a **Publish Only**, or a **Build Only** from the **Batch Target Editor** ribbon for the selected targets.

You can also create a scheduled task to perform the batch target build and publish. When you switch to the **Schedule** tab, Flare prompts you to complete a scheduled task. Flare then creates the job and automatically generates the required job header information. You will need to define the remaining scheduling details.

APPLICATION TIPS

The **Advanced Settings** schedule allows the scheduled task to be repeated within a given recurrence. For example, if set to occur **Daily**, you can also specify that the batch occurs every 12 hours for 1 Day.

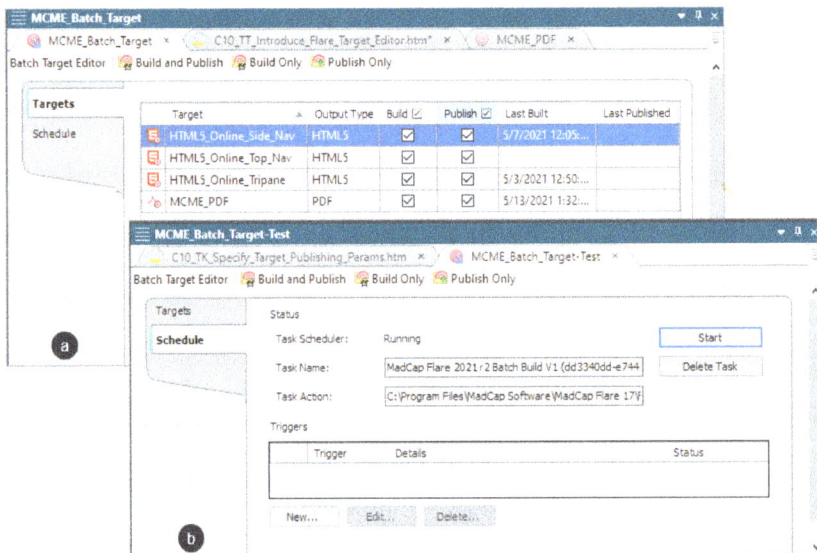

Figure 10-20. Batch Target Editor — a) Defining Target Parameters and b) Defining Schedule Parameters.

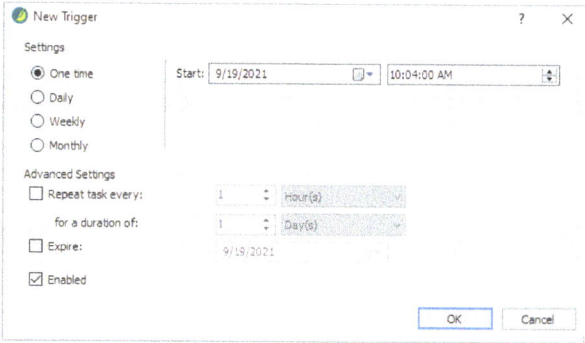

Figure 10-21. Target Batch File Configuration Dialog.

QUICK STEPS: USING THE BATCH TARGET EDITOR FOR MULTI-TARGET BUILD AND PUBLISH

STEP	ACTION
—	**To Create a Batch Target File:**
1	Click the **Project Organizer** > right-click on the **Targets** folder, and select **Add Batch Target**.
2	Ensure that the **File Type** is set for **Batch Target**.
3	**To create the new Batch Target file use one of the following:**
	a) From Templates: Set the **Source** for **New From Template**, then choose the **MyBatchTarget** template from the **Factory Templates** folder or choose a template from a user-defined **Custom Templates** folder.
	b) From Existing: Set the **Source** for **New From Existing**, and use the browse button [....] to locate the existing Batch Target file from which to create the new file.
4	Under **Batch Target**, in the **Folder** field use the default **Root folder** (**Project/Targets**), or browse and choose a subfolder in the default folder in which to store the file.
5	Use the **File Name** field to specify the name of the new Batch Target file.
6	Click **Add** to save your new Batch Target file. The new batch target file opens in the Batch Target Editor.
—	**To Configure the Batch Target:**
1	Use the **Build** and the **Publish** check-boxes to enable or disable the option.
2	Click the **Build Only** button to trigger build all of targets for which the **Build** check-box is enabled.
3	Click the **Publish Only** button to trigger publish all targets for which the **Publish** check-box is enabled.
4	Click the **Build and Publish** button to trigger a build and then publish for all targets for which the **Build** and **Publish** check-boxes are enabled.
—	**To Schedule a Batch Target Task:**
1	Click the **Schedule** tab, and if no scheduled task is available, you will be prompted to create the task.
2	Choose the task **Setting** as **One time**, **Daily**, **Weekly**, or **Monthly**, to define a recurrence schedule.
3	Use **Start** to specify a Start Time and Start Date to trigger the batch build and publish operation.
4	Use the **Advanced Settings** to define a **Repeat**, and **Expire**, and an **Enable** schedule option. The scheduled task is not triggered to run unless **Enable** is selected.

CHAPTER 11

BASIC DESIGN PRINCIPLES AND GUIDELINES

USING STRUCTURAL PAGE LAYOUT DESIGN ELEMENTS

Visually compelling content, whether for print or online, is no accident but is designed based on informed choices that you can make. Such decisions are essential for your page layout and content.

Aside from Front-Cover or Home-Page appeal, your page layout and content have the most significant impact on how readers consider, react to, or eventually interact with a book, document, or website. If the initial reaction is that the presentation is unattractive, you will not entice readers to explore any further. They expect each page to be appealing, logically organized, and easily navigated.

This section considers ways you can enhance the page layouts of your print or online content. You can creatively employ visual design elements like vertical and horizontal grids, rules, and borders to add aesthetic appeal to your page layouts. Later in this chapter, we consider the content similarly by introducing structural design elements and guidelines for developing your content. Page layout design elements can naturally contribute to the visual appeal of your content.

USING A GRID ARRANGEMENT

A *grid*, is usually a two-dimensional arrangement of intersecting straight or curved lines called grid lines. Although transparent, the grid serves as a framework for placing image or text blocks in a visually coherent theme.

Examples include a vertical grid of 2-columns, a horizontal grid of 4 -text blocks, or a combination grid of 4-horizontal text blocks, with a 1-vertical column to the left or right. Quick Start Guides, Brochures, Magazines, Annual Reports, and similar documents typically employ a 2- or 3-column grid. If suitably chosen and combined with other page design elements, like white space, grids can make books, documents, and online content more visually attractive and readable.

When it comes to online content, grid use can simplify the design of your responsive layouts. Page layout frames and the use of the Flare Responsive Layout tool can facilitate the layout of your desired grid structure. The following are some examples of grid layouts.

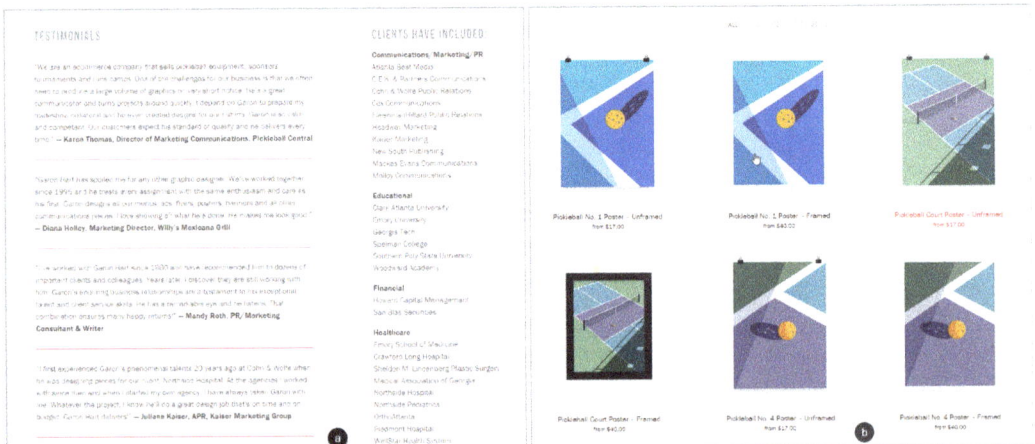

Figure 11-1. **a**) Combined 1 x 4 Grid with Rule Separation and **b**) 2 x 3 Grid of Images with Caption Separation.

USING RULES AND BORDERS

Rules and borders are also visual elements that, when used sparingly, can provide a unique accent to the appeal of your content. Horizontal rules used in your headers and footers, for example, form a boundary of the page top and bottom. Furthermore, you can use rules in conjunction with the grid structure to accent the vertical or horizontal separation between rows and columns, respectively. A rule with color, for example, can accent the separation of text or images in a grid.

Finally, although a page border might not always be an appealing element, a border used around a blockquote to provide a visual offset may be appropriate in some cases.

- Consider placing a rule between grid text or image elements.

- Consider placing a rule below header content and above footer content.

- Consider the use of a border around blockquote to offset from surrounding text.

USING AMPLE WHITE SPACE

In page layouts, *white space*, also referred to as *negative space*, includes areas of a page that are left unmarked — like margins, gutters, and spacing between columns. It also consists of the space between lines of type (leading or line-height) and between graphics, figures, or other objects on the page. The use of padding can ensure adequate spacing between text and objects. The balance between positive (or non-white) and negative spaces is key to page aesthetics and readability.

When it comes to page layout design considerations, providing ample white space will have more impact on your overall content than most others — yet, it is often overlooked or not considered at all. With inadequate white space or a page with too much information, it becomes difficult to read and risks not being read or viewed. You can avoid this problem by carefully using adequate margins, leading, a readable typeface, padding, and other spacing techniques. White space gives readers a place and time to breathe and consider what they have already read before moving on.

- Select an appropriate page size for your document.

- Draw attention to specific elements by leaving ample white space around the element.

- Specify page margins of 3/4 inches to 1 inch on both sides.

- Keep single column width to 5 inches or less for print (8 inches or less for online).

- Keep at least 3/8 inch horizontal spacing between multiple columns or grid elements.

- Limit columns to 3 or less.

USING PAGE HEADERS AND FOOTERS

Each page element is essential given that visual appeal, logical organization, and navigation are the first opportunities to engage a reader or a web visitor. Page layout headers and footers can be part of that first point of engagement — as readers encounter each page.

While headers and footers provide essential information, they are also part of the visual landscape — like the mile-markers on a highway, they can mark each page's content and tell the reader where they are. Headers mark the page top and the start of the page's information, while footers mark the page bottom and provide essential information like page numbers and other information. Together, headers and footers provide a visual boundary that can be informative and add visual balance and pause.

- Headers and Footers provide an offset space for placing helpful information.

- Provide visual boundaries and balance that offer a sense of uniformity and location.

BASIC GUIDELINES OF TYPOGRAPHY USAGE

Typography is the art of selecting and arranging type so that written text is legible and appealing. The process involves selecting typefaces, point sizes, line height or line spacing (leading), and adjusting letter-spacing (kerning) between pairs of letters. Using typography effectively is generally the art of experienced graphic designers — but, through following some basic guidelines, we amateurs can make good choices and decisions.

SELECTING A FONT

Effective typography starts with choosing an appropriate font or typeface — a small decision that impacts how audiences view, read, and react to your content. Some have said that typefaces have personalities—some convey a tone of seriousness, others humor, and yet others a certain technical quality. In the end, you should choose a typeface that complements and projects your message and not one that contradicts and competes with your message.

Deciding on a font starts with choosing between two categories of fonts — serif fonts and sans serif. In typography, *serif fonts* contain a small line or stroke attached to the end of a stroke in a letter or symbol. In French, "sans" means without, and hence, *sans-serif fonts* means fonts without serifs — like Arial and Calibri. Serif fonts like Times Roman and Book Antiqua are considered formal and typically used in newspapers, reports, and textbooks. San-serif fonts tend to be used in less-formal documents and online. There are also so-called "decorative" or "ornamental" fonts that can be serif or sans-serif. These font types are often used to draw attention to a specific design or theme.

AaBbCc Sans-serif font
AaBbCc Serif font
AaBbCc Serif font (red serifs)

Figure 11-2. Typeface Categories — Serif Fonts and Sans-Serif Fonts.

SELECTING A FONT FOR LEGIBILITY (SIZE AND STYLE)

Since content should be easy to read, selecting font size and font style are essential to legibility. Ornamental fonts and text in all capital letters, for example, are hard to read. And while the use of italics and bold text can be helpful when used correctly, they become a detraction when overused. Body text that is too small or too large can also be hard to read. High figure-ground contrast between text and background increases legibility. Dark text against a light background, for instance, is most legible.

- Limit the use of italics, boldface, and uppercase letters.

- Specify body text of at least 10-points (print) and 12-points (online).

- Specify point size of headings at least 2-points larger than the body text.

- Specify body text line-height (print) of at least 2-3 points greater than body text point size.

- Specify body text line-height (online) of at least 4-5 points greater than body text point size.

COMBINING FONTS

Most desktop publishing writers are aware of the many digital typefaces from which to choose. Some writers also have some amount of experience in selecting and choosing typefaces. There are writers, however, that are not aware of the visual noise of too many typefaces. Consider the following guidelines when using different typefaces in the same document:

- **Guideline 1: Limit the use of fonts to one typeface only**: A general rule is to use a single typeface throughout your content — that means for all text, including headings, body text, table content, and captions for images, charts, and tables. In such cases, you should choose a font that complements your presentation and is suited to your audience.

- **Guideline 2: Be consistent if you use multiple typefaces**: If you use more than one typeface, then no more than two typefaces are recommended. You might use one typeface for headings and another for body text. For image, chart, and table captions, you might want to consider the same typeface used for heading titles. For example, you might use Sego 14-point bold for headings, Sego 10-point regular for captions, and Minion Pro 10-point regular for body text.

- **Guideline 3: Limit use of boldface, italics, and ALL CAPS**: Overuse of any of these styles, which are all generally used for emphasis, can detract from your content.

> **NOTE:** 1) Consider limiting the use of italics to introducing new terms or terms you will later add to a glossary. You might also consider italics when citing a book or document title in the body text.
>
> **NOTE:** 2) It is critical to avoid the overuse of boldface. It is best to decide beforehand how you will use boldface. For example, if documenting a graphical user interface (GUI), you might apply bold to UI field labels and menu items mentioned in the body text.
>
> **NOTE:** 3) Use of all caps, especially, should be used very sparingly. Unless kept to very few words and short strings, all caps can be difficult to read and therefore should be avoided.

USING STRUCTURED CONTENT DESIGN ELEMENTS

The use of *structured content design elements* is a method of presenting similar content using a consistent design. In most content presentations, print or online, content has major divisions like book chapters, course modules, or website partitions, where each division has an informational purpose. Generally, each of these content divisions has a distinctive design that partitions the content. Each content division of a website, for example, may have its landing page, similar in design to the landing pages for the other divisions of the website. The idea is to create a recognizable format for each content element, such that similar divisions are presented in the same way.

In a book, a Chapter Title page is an apparent structural element repeated in each chapter. The same is true for a Module Title page in a course. If you have created a Summary topic for each major division, it should have the same appearance in each occurrence. The same is true for a Checklist topic or even an Exercise or Quiz topic. Structured content elements are typical in books or training courses but are also applicable to web content.

Finally, structural elements not only provide aesthetic appeal. Through repeated use, these elements enhance user accessibility by providing a consistent and predictable experience. Users can make mental pictures of what they have seen and also anticipate what to expect next. Some examples of content elements are described in Table 11-1. Depending on your content and audience, a particular content element may not have relevance or importance to your users. Consider each content element for its applicability and usefulness.

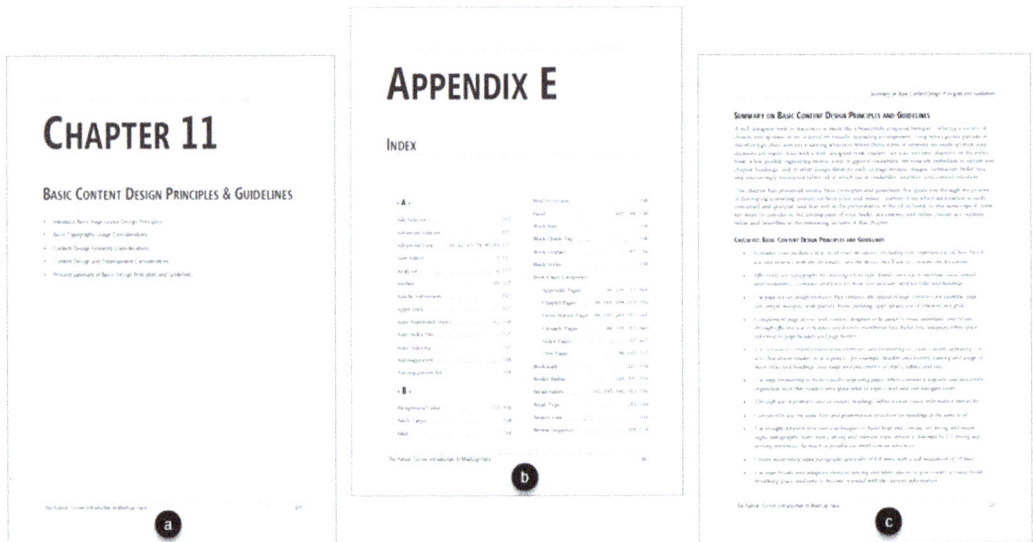

Figure 11-3. Content Elements a) Chapter Title Page, b) Appendix Title Page, and c) Summary Topic Page

CONTENT ELEMENTS

A well-planned set of structured content elements help ensure your content is coherent, consistent, and complete. Similar components in different sections — for example, each chapter should have the same design appearance. Some examples of structured content elements are described below:

Table 11-1. Examples of Structured Content Elements

Content Element	Description
Part Title & Summary	In a multi-part document, related chapters that together cover a subject are separated by this single-page element, containing a title and a 1-2 paragraph summary.
Chapter Title & Overview	In a multi-chapter document, each chapter starts with an identically styled chapter page that contains a title, a 1-2 paragraph overview, and perhaps a mini-TOC.
Mini-TOC (or Objectives)	This repeatable element places a list of topic headings from the current topic. The element is typically placed on the chapter first page or the landing page of online content).
About Topic	This topic, which might appear at the start of some chapters, is generally a 2-3 paragraph overarching summary for a complex technical or other in-depth content that is presented in several main or level-1 topics (with sub-topics). The heading of this topic represents the collective content.
Summary Topic	This repeatable element of 1-2 paragraphs summarizes what you, as an author, believe is the essence of the content. It is not a conclusion but a stepping-off point for the user.
Checklist Topic	This repeatable element is a carefully developed list at the end of each chapter, intended to bring to mind, for the reader, tasks to be performed or items to be considered.
Appendix Title Pages	This repeatable element (appendix start page) provides information supplemental to the formal chapters of a book, document, the or main body of online content.
Task Procedure Topics	This ordered list of procedural steps provides instructions to complete a task. This repeatable element should be presented in the same way for each procedure.
Exercise Topics	This repeatable element might be presented at the end of each chapter, course module, or similar content in the form of questions or problems that measure content retention.
Glossary Topic	A collection of essential terminology, generally in most print or online content — for example, in a book or a blog on some aspect of the stock market or economy. You can create a glossary topic by inserting a Glossary Proxy.
Index Topic	This element is a cross-referenced list of keywords and the page numbers where users can find the keyword in the content. You can create an Index manually by inserting markers or automatically using the Flare Index Proxy inserted in a topic.
Feedback Request	A simple and plainly structured format for making an informal request for feedback.

CONTENT DEVELOPMENT CONSIDERATIONS

Well-designed content must be presented in an ordered and visually appealing arrangement. Readers must be able to scan titles, Mini-TOCs, section headings, topic sentences, or an entire book while at the same time registering mental notes of readability, points of interest, and usefulness. These layered content elements gradually expose information about the yet unrevealed content.

TITLES

Whether for print or online content, a title must clearly and concisely capture the essence of the content that follows. The title must broadly but pointedly convey the main point of the content it represents. For online content, titles must also consider keyword usage for visibility in user searches.

The following are some guidelines for writing a solid title:

- Use a short-as-possible yet meaningful phrase.

- Consider keyword search visibility of the title.

- Broadly convey the primary purpose of the entire content.

SUMMARY

A summary is generally a brief paragraph containing a few sentences that capture the essence of the print or online content. As it presents a high-level overview, a summary provides an expanded description of the previous title. The title, in this case, might be the title of a document, book, a book section, or a menu or sub-menu item on a website. As an extension of the preceding title, a summary is a further elaboration of the title and main idea of the topic. The summary should confirm to the user whether the section warrants reading further.

HEADINGS

Like titles, headings are an essential part of the content landscape, acting like signposts on a road map. As readers scan the content, they are looking to gain a sense of organization. Primary (level-1) and secondary (level-2) headings provide a visual hierarchy and a meaningful connection between the chunks of information. By glancing at the headings, the main items of interest, readers or Web visitors gain an over-arching view of what to expect from the following body of information.

Even if a reader never reads the associated paragraphs, they should get the main idea from each heading. As you develop your content, determine what information represents a first-level heading (level-1), a second-level heading, or a third-level heading. More than three levels may tend to be confusing. Content headings of the same level should always use the same font and same grammatical phrasing.

The following are some guidelines for writing headings:

- The heading point size should be at least 2-points larger than the body text.

- Use at least a two-point size difference between heading-1 and heading-2.

- Headings should all have the same typeface and match the typeface of titles.

- Headings should all be grammatically parallel (all phrased consistently).

- Each higher-level heading should have at least two headings at the next-lower level.

- Never leave Headings at page bottom with less than 2-sentences (otherwise push to next page).

- Limit headings to 3-levels (Level-1=Section, Level-2=Major topic, Level-3=Minor topic).

TOPIC SENTENCES

A *topic sentence* must be a strong first sentence that tells readers the essence of the paragraph. As such, the topic sentence must be a clear statement that can be developed and supported by the remaining sentences in the paragraph. Strong paragraph development relies on a strong topic sentence that reflects adequate thought based on a clear understanding of the topic.

Like topic headings, which collectively pull together overarching points of interest and are quickly spotted by readers, topic sentences provide a similar function in pulling together the chief ideas in a paragraph. Furthermore, each topic sentence gradually reveals information contained in the topic heading.

PARAGRAPH DEVELOPMENT

Paragraph development should be straightforward and consistent within and among the paragraphs. Starting with a strong topic sentence, if well thought out, the paragraph should hold together tightly. The well-written paragraph consists of the topic sentence and at least 3-4 strong sentences. These are sentences that serve to clarify and explain using statements that support the topic sentence. A good paragraph should be complete in developing a single thought as stated in the topic sentence. Try to limit each paragraph to 4-5 sentences and from 8-10 lines.

ORDERED AND UNORDERED LISTS

Consider using ordered or unordered lists instead of enumerating or listing points separated by commas. Your points will always be straightforward and easier to understand when they stand alone in a list. Lists also provide visual clarity and hierarchy to your content. A note of caution is that while lists are a great tool, you must avoid overuse.

TABLES, CHARTS, AND IMAGES

Like ordered and unordered lists, tables, charts, and images serve to clearly capture and visually present the information you wish to convey. These elements all serve two primary functions in both your print and online content. First, each of these elements, if appropriately selected and presented, can quickly and visually convey complex information, more so than the textual content; and second, these elements add to the overall visual aesthetics of your content. Like white space, tables, charts, and images give readers a time and place to analyze the content.

A point worth noting is that readers will almost always continue reading well-presented and attractive content until determining whether the information is what they are looking for — even if they learn it is not exactly what they need. On the other hand, readers are less likely to continue reading or even start reading poorly-presented content — even if the content was what they needed.

PARALLEL TOPICS

The term *parallel topics*, also called *topic symmetry*, is a method of presenting one after the other two closely related issues. Examples of such topic pairs include *"input circuits and output circuits," "input memory and output memory,"* and finally, *"software configuration and hardware configuration."* Topics such as these, covered in conjunction and one after another, give readers a sense of symmetry while providing visual imagery that helps readers grasp and retain topics.

A parallel-topics presentation is quite suitable with topics that are related opposites. Readers can easily see similarities and differences and make their inferences and conclusions. With this parallel presentation, readers can get a clearer picture of certain concepts that would not have been as apparent if you had presented the topics separately. A final bi-product of topic symmetry is a predictable sequence for the reader, allowing them to anticipate what's next and time to become more engaged.

TEXT AND IMAGE MIRRORING

The concept of *text and image mirroring* is a method of presenting a brief topic and immediately following it with a single image that reflects the written text. This approach is not always required but very useful with some complex technical subjects. In such cases, an image can illuminate the text. Text and image mirroring are most effective when you condense each topic into a single chunk of information — typically 2-3 paragraphs.

Text and image mirroring combines imagery and text to echo and amplify a concept. This technique works well when combined with the use of parallel topics.

SUMMARY ON BASIC CONTENT DESIGN PRINCIPLES AND GUIDELINES

Well-designed content for print or online is much like a beautifully prepared banquet. Onlookers see a variety of options presented in an ordered and visually appealing arrangement. Before guests consume what is before them, their eyes scan the presentation. They identify items of interest with ease, and they determine preliminary choices. Also, with well-designed content, readers scan pages, sections, chapters, or even the entire book or site, while quickly registering mental notes of overall readability, usability, and content retention.

This chapter has presented some basic principles and guidelines to assist you in developing appealing content. Whether for print or online, information must be easily consumed and grasped, must aid in job performance, and give readers a way of quickly obtaining the desired information. Following are some guidelines for you to consider in developing your books, documents, and online content.

CHECKLIST: BASIC CONTENT DESIGN PRINCIPLES AND GUIDELINES

- *In all your decisions, consider your audience first — including role, experience level, how they'll use and interact with the content, and the devices they will use to consume content.*

- *Effectively use typography by choosing a font type, family, and size to increase visual appeal and readability — consider serif fonts for body text and sans serif for titles and headings.*

- *Consistently use the same font and grammatical structure for headings of the same level.*

- *Use design elements to enhance the appeal of your page layout and content — for example, page size, ample margins, wide gutters, frame padding, use of rules, columns, and grids.*

- *Complement page layout with informative headers and footers, ordered and unordered lists, all designed for easier reading, assimilation, and retention.*

- *Use page breaks and adequate element spacing and white spaces to give readers a visual break and breathing space and time to become oriented with the current information.*

- *Consider using structured content design elements that repeat throughout the content, giving users a visual road map of where they are and allowing them to anticipate what's next.*

- *Select content presentation elements and formatting to create content that draws readers in at a glance — for example, headers and footers, naming and usage of main titles and headings, and strategic use and placement of images, charts, tables, and lists.*

- *Use formatting that contributes to visually appealing pages — pages that are logically and intuitively organized, such that readers can navigate easily and anticipate what's next.*

- *Through the use of primary and secondary headings, define a clear visual information hierarchy.*

- *Use straightforward, structured techniques to build brief yet strong and meaningful paragraphs. Start each paragraph with a solid topic sentence, followed by 2-3 relevant supporting sentences.*

- *Create moderately-sized paragraphs generally of 6-8 lines, with a soft maximum of 10 lines.*

CHAPTER 12

BASIC GUIDELINES FOR MOVING TO ONLINE

PAGE LAYOUT CONSIDERATIONS FOR ONLINE

While print and online pages are different, the layout concepts and what attracts users are similar for both. Users will be viewing the online page in much the same way and scanning the layout and content while deciding whether to continue further or to leave. Your Home-Page appeal and choices for page layout and content presentation all will make an initial impact. Users expect each page to be visually appealing, logically organized, and easily navigated, just like print presentations.

The previous chapter covered some basic design guidelines and principles for developing page layouts and content that can produce attractive and engaging pages for both print and online. Visual design elements like headers and footers, vertical and horizontal grids, rules and borders, and structural content design elements are all applicable online. These elements, along with the others covered in this section, appropriately used, can add spark and appeal to your online layouts.

TOP-NAVIGATION SKIN OPTION

Top-navigation is a frameless HTML5 output that places menu navigation elements across the page top, similar to modern website designs. The top-navigation option is possible when you specify a top-navigation skin in your target. Like with other skin types, you can add a new the top-navigation skin to your project from the Project menu (**Project** > **New** > **Add Skin**), or from the **Project Organizer** > , **Skins** subfolder > right-click > **Add Skin**. Frameless output designs are much easier for web crawlers to find, thereby producing much better search engine results.

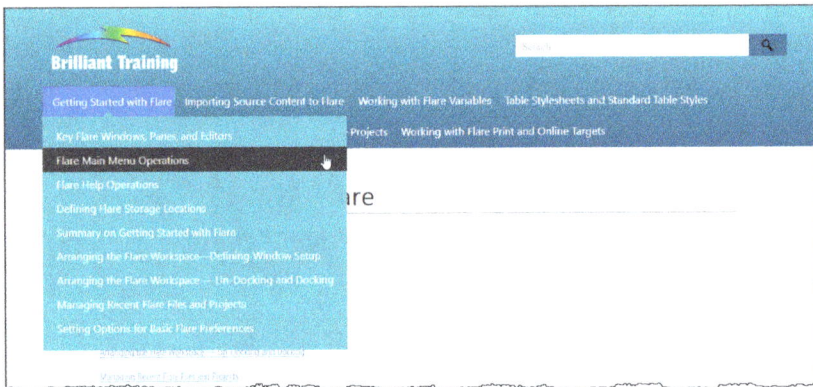

Figure 12-1. Top Navigation.

SIDE-NAVIGATION SKIN OPTION

Side-navigation is an HTML5 output with the option of placing the navigation element for menu operations to the left or right of the topic view window. The side-navigation option uses a flexible, frameless output but looks similar to the traditional and older Tripane format. This option is possible when you specify the side-navigation skin in your target. Like the top-navigation, this option is frameless and much more accessible for web crawlers to find — making search engine results much better.

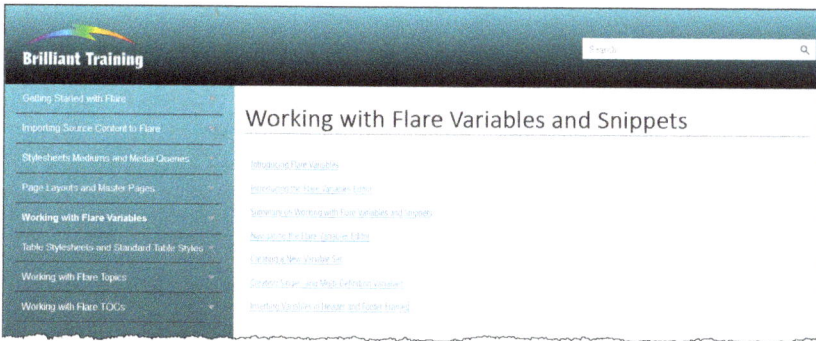

Figure 12-2. Side Navigation.

TRIPANE-NAVIGATION SKIN OPTION

Tripane-navigation is an HTML5 output option that produces the traditional format of three distinct frames — a navigation pane on the left, a toolbar and search bar on the top, and the main body or topic pages in the center. The tripane-navigation skin also supports the disablement of an online glossary, online index, and browse sequence.

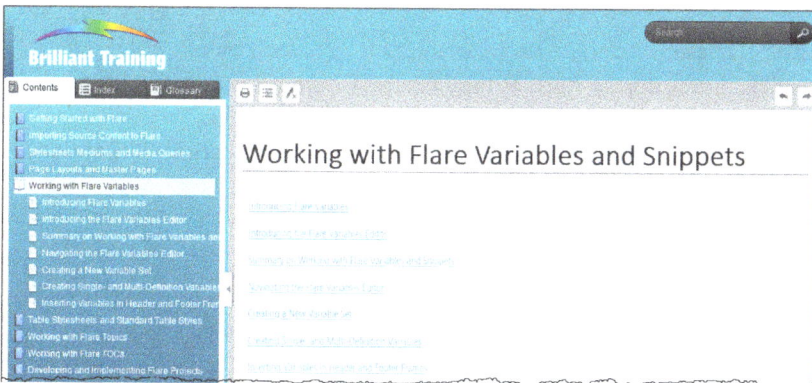

Figure 12-3. Tripane Navigation.

DEPLOYING NAVIGATION SKIN OPTIONS

To create the top, side, or tripane-navigation output, you will need to create and configure the appropriate skin in your project. You can create skins in the **Project Organizer > Project > Skins** folder using the **HTML5 Side-Navigation**, **Top-Navigation**, or **Tripane-Navigation** template.

Once created, you can configure the skin using the Flare **Skin Editor** to set the parameters for several **Setup** and **Styles** property groups. These property groups and the parameters will vary slightly, depending on the skin type you have chosen. Examples of the property groups include **Global**, **Header**, **Navigation**, and **Search Results**. A skin configuration is generally a fill-in-the-blanks approach simplified by drop-down selectors and other visual aids to specify a value for each parameter.

TEMPLATE PAGES

As described earlier in the discussion of Page Layout and Template Pages, you can use template pages to have specific content elements placed, and in some cases, repeated in specific topics of your online output. Elements like Breadcrumbs, Search Bars, Topic Toolbars, Menus, and Mini-TOCs can appear in one or multiple topics to which you apply the template page that contains these Flare proxies.

So, if you have three different groups of online topics, where each group would have common content elements inserted, you would create a template page for each topic group. For each topic group, you would apply the appropriate template page to all topics in the same group. If your homepage has a unique set of contents elements, you might create another template page for the home page only.

RESPONSIVE LAYOUTS

Responsive design formally referred to as *responsive web design (RWD)*, is a web design approach that makes web pages render appropriately on various devices and display sizes. This method uses styles and media queries to create layouts in which both the structure and content of online output can automatically adjust based on the size of the output display. On the other hand, *responsive layout*, is a layout technique used in Flare to achieve responsive designs for Web, Tablet, and Mobile devices. The Flare Responsive Layout window, opened from the **Home** ribbon, helps users quickly create layouts responsive to different devices and display sizes.

The HTML5 Side and Top-Navigation skins are always enabled for responsive output and are automatically adjusted depending on the display size. For the Tripane-Navigation output, you must enable the responsive output in the Skin Editor, which also has settings for Tablet and Mobile display widths. Responsive output adjustments can be made for all three of the HTML5 output types, using settings available on the **Skin** tab of the Target Editor.

USING FLARE ONLINE CONTENT ELEMENTS

In Flare, you can use many elements to make online content more accessible to users. Using one or more template pages, you can have certain content elements occur on multiple topics to which the template page is applied. Typical elements include breadcrumbs, search bars, search result panes, and toolbar menus, mini-TOCs, headers, and footers.

There are also linking and navigation elements like related topics and concept topics that give users access to other topics and files and links to external destinations like websites or other help systems. In addition to these, there are elements to support the gradual revealing of content — items like navigational menus, drop-down and expanding text, and togglers.

BREADCRUMBS

When included in a template page, the *breadcrumbs proxy* displays the relative path (breadcrumbs) that a user traverses when navigating through the TOC. The breadcrumbs are composed of the table of contents (TOC) entries (or path) displayed above the current topic. This element serves in a way similar to a page header in print output, as it helps users know their current location in the TOC.

BROWSE SEQUENCE

In Flare, a *browse sequence* is an ordered sequence to navigating some portion of the TOC in an online output. You might employ this method to provide users with a pre-defined series of topics, like with a process flow that sequentially presents the tasks to be performed.

You can create a browse sequence automatically or manually by adding books and links to topics, other browse sequences, and external files. While the Browse Sequence option is enabled, by default, in the HTML5 Tripane output skin, Flare does not support the browse sequence in the HTML5 Side Navigation, Top Navigation, or the skinless output. A browse sequence can also be associated with a menu proxy, supported in all HTML5 output formats.

CONCEPT TOPICS

In Flare, a *concept topic* is any one of a group of topics that you have designated as being directly related to one another (a single concept). This relationship is one in which each of the topics provide additional information that advances the complete concept. A *concept link* is a Help control that gives users access to all of the concept topics in the group. For example, the term (concept) "Import" links the related concept topics "Pre-Import Tasks," "Import Overview," "Using the Import Wizards," and "Post Import Tasks." To learn about importing, users can access all of the concept topics from the same link placed in the other topics in the group.

Whereas with related topic links, you associate particular topics (for one-to-one access), you associate a concept link with a group of topics (for one-to-many access) to provide access to each of the topics in the group. If you later want to add or remove topics from the concept group, you only need to do so in one place, and the changes are applied to all of the topics that contain the concept link.

> **NOTE:** Topics referenced in a Concept topic group are considered **"See also"** topics relevant to each other and comprise a list of topics representing a comprehensive article on the subject.

RELATED TOPICS

A *related topics link* is the traditional Help control method that allows users to insert a list of topic links to topics that you consider related information. Unlike concept topics, which are indeed a group of directly related topics, related topics are independent of one another. Instead, the list represents topics that you feel provide additional information or insight to the general context of the current topic. If you have used a related topic link in more than one topic and it is no longer needed, you must remove it wherever it is not required.

> **NOTE:** Topics referenced in a Related Topics list are topics that provide additional information relative to the context of the current topic in which they are listed.

TEXT POP-UP

A *text popup* is a Flare content display feature in which a short piece of content, for example, a definition, is presented in a small popup box when the user clicks the text popup link in the online output. The text popup link can be any text for which you have created and inserted as a hyperlink.

TOPIC POP-UP

In Flare, a *topic popup* is a content display feature whereby the user can open a topic within the same project, an external file, a website, or another HTML help file. The topic popup opens when the user clicks on a topic popup hyperlink. The topic popup link can be any text you have created and inserted as a hyperlink, designated as a **Topic Pop-up** link.

DROP-DOWN TEXT CONTENT

Drop-down text is a block of content that alternately hides and reveals content when a user clicks the drop-down link or hotspot. This technique is one of several content layering techniques, whereby users click a hotspot in the content to reveal additional information on demand. Drop-down text usually involves a heading or text just above a content block that alternates between hidden and revealed.

EXPANDING TEXT CONTENT

Using *expanded text*, you can insert a block of content that extends and retracts to the end of the same paragraph or another block element when a user clicks the associated hotspot. The hotspot, or expanding text link, immediately precedes the expanding text. A second click on the hotspot causes the expanded text to retract. Although like drop-down text, expanding text works with a single paragraph only.

TOGGLER CONTENT

A *toggler* is a link that lets you "toggle" between hiding and showing a tagged or named chunk of content — for example, a paragraph, image, table, or list. When a user clicks on the toggler link, the hidden content is revealed. The named content is called a *toggler target*. The toggler hotspot can be any non-contiguous content blocks in the topic. When a user clicks the link again, the content is hidden.

IMAGE THUMBNAILS

When you insert an image into Flare content, you can specify that it be displayed as a thumbnail in the output not to use as much real estate. When you use this feature, you can select ways to enlarge the image to see its full size or some percentage of full size. You may also specify toggle between showing the thumbnail or full size when the user clicks or hovers over the image.

ONLINE INDEX

In Flare, you can create an index for both online and print outputs. With an online index, users click on the index keyword or sub-keyword, and the content is opened where the keyword is found. If the keyword is in more than one topic, a list of the topics to select from is displayed. Like with an index for print outputs, you can also create online index keywords in several ways. You can insert index keyword markers in your topics or snippets; you can add keywords using the Index Window, where you can also associate them with topics; or you can create index keywords in the Auto-Index Editor. If you created an index for print output, you may have already created the AutoIndex file.

If your online output uses the HTML5 Tripane skin, you must enable the **Index** option on the skin and specify the tripane skin on the target file. When the target is built, and the output displayed, users can select the **Index** tab and click an index keyword to display the topic or list of topics where the keyword is found. For HTML5 Top-Navigation and Side-Navigation outputs, index terms are included in the search results unless they are excluded on the **Search** tab of the target file.

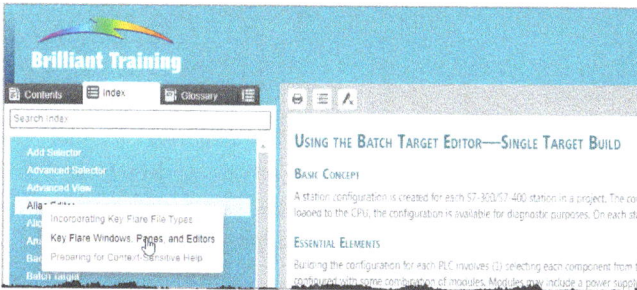

Figure 12-4. HTML5 Tripane Skin Output with Index Tab Selected.

ONLINE GLOSSARY

In Flare, a glossary can be developed for online and print outputs by first adding a glossary file. Using the Glossary Editor, you can directly enter a term and text definition or specify a separate topic containing the definition. If you enter both the term and definition in the Glossary editor, the definition opens immediately when the user clicks the term in the online output. If you pointed to a topic containing the definition, that topic opens when the user clicks the term.

If you've enabled the **Glossary** option in an HTML5 Tripane skin, then users can click on a term in the **Glossary** pane to display its definition. For HTML5 Top-Navigation and Side-Navigation outputs, users access glossary terms and definitions using the search results. This option is possible when the **Search Engine Type** is set for **MadCap Search** and the option to **Include Glossary in Results** is enabled. If you have created and inserted glossary term links directly in topics or snippets, users can display the glossary definition by hovering over or clicking the term where it is found in the content. Definitions can be displayed as popups, expanding text, or hyperlinks.

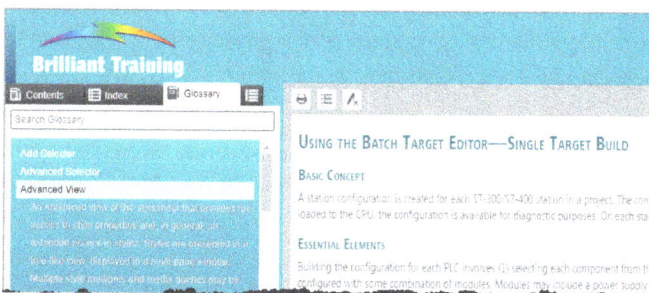

Figure 12-5. HTML5 Tripane Skin Output with Glossary Tab Selected.

PREPARING AND DEVELOPING CONTENT FOR ONLINE

Most contents developed today eventually finds its way to being present online. For the most part, this statement is undoubtedly true, with various documents and books developed for print. With that in mind, it makes sense to think about the eventual online presence for the books and documents that you develop for print or for being downloaded or viewed online.

> **NOTE:** In addition to the points covered here in this section, also return to the Flare Pre-Import Tasks covered in Chapter 2 — particularly the section "Shorten Chapter and Section Headings."

SELECT FROM EXISTING TOPICS TO MOVE ONLINE

Very often, an initial move to Flare will involve transitioning from an existing authoring and publishing tool. This move will generally involve importing several new and legacy documents to the Flare platform, which offers print and online publishing options. Although it is unlikely that all of this content will be suitable as online topics, some of it will need reviewing for suitability. The following are some ideas for selecting from print topics to move online:

- Consider Overview and About topics.

- Select topics that are independent and stand well alone.

- Select topics that will have broad appeal to your audience.

- Consider topics like New Features and Important Features.

- Consider User Guide content for how-to topics.

- Consider Reference Guide content for concept and information topics.

- Consider download elements, like Feature Articles, Success Stories, PDFs, and others.

REVIEW CONTENT FOR BREVITY, CONCISENESS, AND MODULARITY

Topic-based writing for online content, whether information-based or task-based, should be brief and concise, as well as modular and complete. Modular and complete topics convey a single idea, concept, or task and lend themselves to clarity, ease of understanding, and reuse. Such topics are also free of transitional sentences, designed to link paragraphs when moving from one paragraph to the next or from one section to the next. This method often used to guide the reader in print outputs, may not be as suitable for online content. In creating reusable topics, consider the following:

- Strive for brief, concise, and complete topics.

- Strive for topic independence and modularity.

- Avoid transitions between paragraphs and sections.

Preparing for Context-Sensitive Help

Context-sensitive help (CSH) is an online help method that creates a one-to-one link between a specific UI element of a desktop or Web-based application and a particular help topic. This link can also be to micro-content. The CSH topic or micro-content is displayed whenever the associated UI element is in focus. In many help systems, CSH is available in conjunction with standalone help, which traditionally consists of a collection of HTML topic files accessed from either a local or remote installation.

CSH development is typically a collaboration between a writing team and a software development team. In this joint effort, the writer and developer will have their own tasks, but collaborate on others. These tasks, in the end, accomplish the work of having specific topics appear when the associated UI element is displayed in the output. CSH implementation can be summarized as follows:

- Developed as a joint effort between Help System Developer and Software Developer.

- Determine topics to be associated with UI elements as CSH topics.

- Create header file with identifiers that maps CSH topics to the associated UI component.

- Software developer makes a call to unique CSH identifier when the UI component is in focus.

Determine Topic Association to Application UI Elements

This task involves someone identifying and creating a list of the topics associated with each UI component featured in the CSH. The job could be done by either the software developer, the help system developer, or in conjunction. Generally, the software developer will better know the UI elements that are identifiable in the code when the user has it in focus (suitable for CSH)— dialogs, tabs, buttons, or pages. The writer can now use the Flare Alias Editor to create and assign identifiers with the topic list.

The Flare CSH Header File

In a Flare CSH implementation, a *header file* is a simple text file that interfaces between a help system and a web-based or desktop application. This file contains information needed to link the application to help topics — information that consists of a series of definitions, each of which maps a specific UI component such as a web page, window, pane, tab, or dialog to its unique Help topic. Flare generates the header file from information the writer enters in the Flare Alias Editor, and stores in the Alias file.

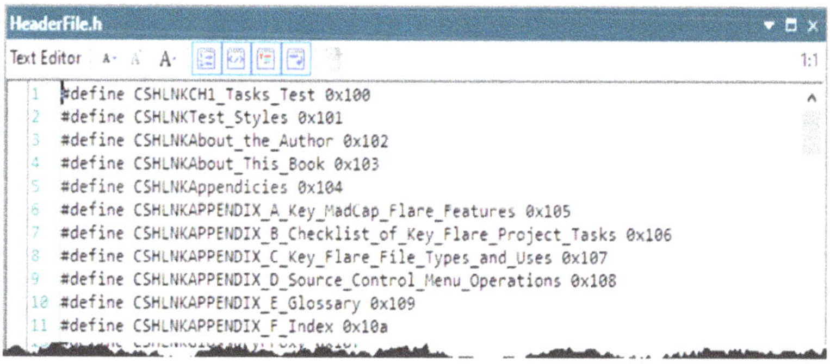

```
HeaderFile.h                                              ▾ ◻ ✕
Text Editor   A·  A  A·  [icons]                            1:1
1  #define CSHLNKCH1_Tasks_Test 0x100
2  #define CSHLNKTest_Styles 0x101
3  #define CSHLNKAbout_the_Author 0x102
4  #define CSHLNKAbout_This_Book 0x103
5  #define CSHLNKAppendicies 0x104
6  #define CSHLNKAPPENDIX_A_Key_MadCap_Flare_Features 0x105
7  #define CSHLNKAPPENDIX_B_Checklist_of_Key_Flare_Project_Tasks 0x106
8  #define CSHLNKAPPENDIX_C_Key_Flare_File_Types_and_Uses 0x107
9  #define CSHLNKAPPENDIX_D_Source_Control_Menu_Operations 0x108
10 #define CSHLNKAPPENDIX_E_Glossary 0x109
11 #define CSHLNKAPPENDIX_F_Index 0x10a
```

Figure 12-6. A Typical Header File.

TOPIC IDENTIFIERS

As part of preparing for CSH, each topic the output will open as a CSH topic must be given a unique identifier. These identifiers, which are alphanumeric strings, are created in the Flare Alias Editor and are stored in an Alias file. Each identifier is assigned a unique decimal or hexadecimal value.

The creation of topic identifiers may be done by the software developer or the assigned writer. If the writer develops the file, it must be shared with the developer, who uses the identifiers when triggering the calls to open a specific CSH topic. If the developer creates the identifiers, then the developer must share the file with the writer, who must then map the identifiers to the appropriate CSH topics.

THE FLARE CSH ALIAS FILE

Flare, uses the *alias file* to populate a header file with the information necessary for producing context sensitive Help (CSH). An Alias file is created using the user-friendly Alias File Editor, in which you can create and assign identifiers to each CSH topic. Each identifier is a one-to-one mapping of a numeric value and a specific help topic. These identifiers form links between each topic and a Context-Sensitive Help Call in the web-based or desktop application. In the code, a call is made to the identifier associated with a given UI element.

The Flare alias file has the extension <**.flali**> and is stored in the **Project Organizer**'s **Advanced** folder.

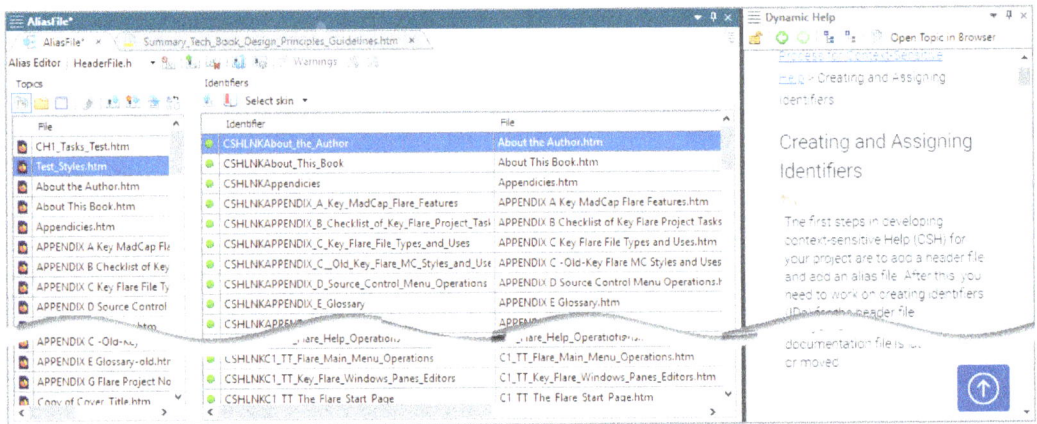

Figure 12-7. Alias File Editor and Assigning Topic Identifiers.

SUMMARY ON GUIDELINES FOR MOVING TO ONLINE

Like the well-designed book or document, the online content and presentation must draw visitors in and turn casual browsers into engaged consumers. A compelling home or landing page must first attract visitors and immediately summon their interest. They must then be able to readily scan and navigate menus or TOCs with clear, concise, meaningful, and relevant entries.

Starting with the Home page and upon landing on each page, visitors must scan headings and sub-headings, each of which should gradually expand upon what is indicated by topic titles. In other words, visitors should find precisely that for which they are looking. Information is step by step revealed through online methods like navigational menus, drop-down and expanding text, and related concepts. The less shown at a time on the page, the more a visitor can grasp.

This chapter has presented some basic principles and guidelines to offer a framework for moving online. As with books and documents, online content must be appealing and arresting from the first glance. The following checklist provides some tips and guidance to consider in moving content online. Also, following in the remainder of the chapter are some examples of tasks related to moving online.

CHECKLIST: GUIDELINES FOR MOVING TO ONLINE

- *Suppose you are moving to Flare and migrating content previously used in various print documents. In such cases, you will likely have a variety of material to edit and re-purpose for online.*

- *As with print outputs, consider your audience first in all your decisions — design choices, for example, font family, font size, line height, margins, and other elements, will all likely differ.*

- *Consider using Flare online design elements like drop-down text, expanding text, popup boxes, related topics, concept topics, and related topics. Think of ways to reveal the content gradually.*

- *Use Flare proxy elements like Breadcrumbs, Search Bar, Search Results, Topic Toolbar, Body Proxy, and Menu Proxy on Template Pages to be applied to associated topics.*

- *Consider using multiple Template Pages to apply to groups of topics where you want specific content to appear on every topic within the group (or to which the template page is applied).*

- *Create and configure settings for an HTML5 Top-Navigation skin, Side-Navigation skin, or the Tripane-Navigation Skin based on the desired online output you want to produce.*

- *Any **Responsive Output Settings** adjusted on the target Skin tab will override any settings made in the Tripane skin settings made on the Setup tab.*

- *When you have selected **MadCap Search Engine** on the HTML5 target, consider specifying the HTML5 target **Search Results**, including the **Advanced Search Options**, to enhance the results and minimize the impact of index terms, glossary terms, and micro-content on user searches.*

- *Consider implementing Context-Sensitive Help, starting with topics associated with UI elements, and then work with the development team to determine responsibilities. User Guides for desktop or Web-based applications are a good starting place for content development for CSH topics.*

SPECIFYING SIDE-NAVIGATION SKIN PARAMETERS

BASIC CONCEPT

Side-Navigation is one of the three full skin options you can use for your online output. Once you have created the file in your project, you can proceed with configuring the parameters that let you affect the appearance of the skin and elements you wish to include. Since the skin is based on a template, its basic form is already in place. Specifying the skin parameters requires using the available tabs and completing essential fields using the fill-in-the-blanks approach to add your design preferences.

ESSENTIAL ELEMENTS

Before you can specify the Side-Navigation Skin parameters, you must have created the skin file in your project. **Project Organizer > Skin** folder > right-click > **Add Skin** > **File Type** > **Skin** > **New From Template** > **HTML5 Side Navigation** > **Add**. Once you add the file, the main parameter segments you must configure to view some results include **Global, Header**, and **Side Navigation**.

APPLICATION TIPS

The Side-Navigation Skin has many settings on the Styles tab, all of which are not covered here. Only a selection of the parameters is covered to assist you in getting off to a good start. Also, the procedure does not cover adding the Side-Navigation skin to the project, which you must create before starting.

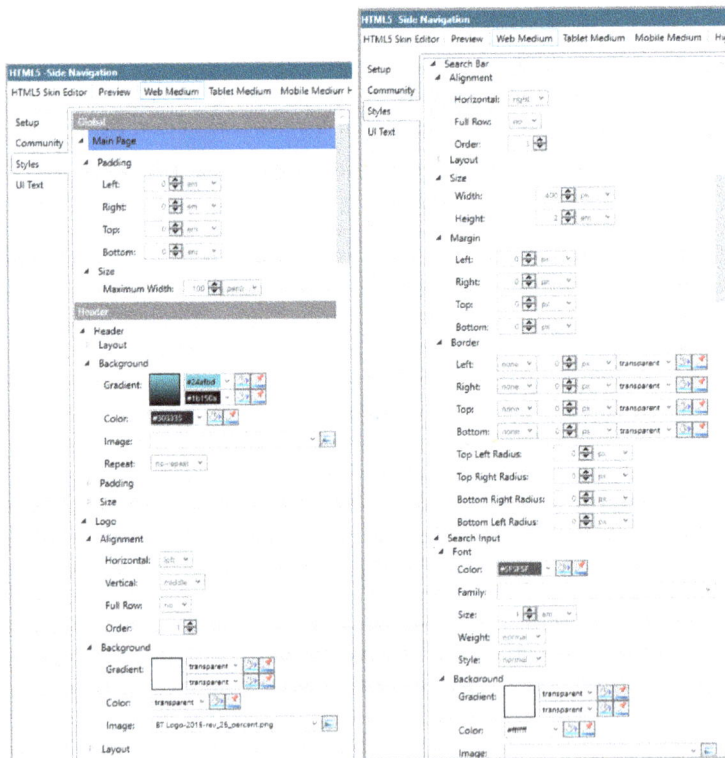

Figure 12-8. HTML5 Skin Editor — Side Navigation Tab

QUICK STEPS: SPECIFYING SIDE-NAVIGATION SKIN PARAMETERS

STEP	ACTION
1	In the **Project Organizer**, click the **Skins** folder and double-click on your Side Navigation skin file.
2	With the file open, select the **Setup** tab.
3	Use the **Navigation Pane** options to configure the following: a) **Main Menu Position:** specify for the **Left** (default) or **Right** for side navigation. b) **Pane Position:** specify to display to the **Left** or **Right** when the output is in tablet or mobile mode. c) **Slide-Out-Menu Style:** set for **Drilldown** or **Tree** in tablet or mobile mode, on hamburger icon click. d) **Fixed Header:** specify if header should be fixed when a user scrolls in **Web** display or for **All** displays. e) **Logo Url:** enter url to link to when the logo is clicked or use the default setting (startup topic on target).
4	Use **Skin ID** to enter a unique skin identifier, which is needed when multiple skins are used in an output.
5	Use **TOC Options** to enable option to **Automatically Synchronize TOC** and user's TOC navigation.
6	Select the **Styles** tab. On this tab, you can start with the **Global**, **Header** and **Side Navigation** settings.
7	Under **Global** > **Main Page** > **Padding**, use the appropriate fields to specify the padded distance of the main display page (topic area) from the **Left**, **Right**, **Top**, and **Bottom** window edges.
8	Under **Global** > **Main Page** > set **Maximum Width** of the main display — for example, 0-100 percent.
9	Under **Header** > **Header** > **Layout** > **Display**, choose **Default** or choose "**block**." **None** removes header.
10	Under **Header** > **Header** > **Background**, use the **Gradient** tools to specify a start and end color to create a top to bottom graded background; or use the **Color** tools to set an absolute header background color.
11	Under **Header** > **Background** > **Image**, click image drop-down or button to choose from a list of recently used images or browse and select an image. Choose image behavior as **Default**, **Repeat**, or **No Repeat**.
12	Under **Header** > **Header** > **Padding**, use the appropriate fields to specify the padded distance of header elements from the **Left**, **Right**, **Top**, and **Bottom** header edges.
13	Use **Header** > **Size** > **Maximum Width**, to specify the maximum width the header can occupy — for example, 0-100 percent.
14	Under **Header** > **Logo** > **Alignment** > **Horizontal**, specify the logo alignment as **Left**, **Right**, or **Middle**.
15	Under **Header** > **Logo** > **Alignment** > **Vertical**, specify the logo alignment as **Top**, **Middle**, or **Bottom**.
16	Under **Header** > **Logo** > **Alignment**, use **Full Row** drop-down to specify **Yes** or **No**, whether the logo should occupy a full row of its own.
17	Under **Header** > **Logo** > **Alignment**, use the **Order** field to enter a horizontal position, for example, 1-3, for placing the logo when other elements are positioned on the same row.
18	Under **Header** > **Logo** > **Background**, use the **Gradient** tools to specify a start and end color to create a graded logo background; or use the **Color** tools to set an absolute logo background color.
19	Under **Header** > **Logo** > **Background** > **Image**, click image drop-down or button to choose from list of images or browse and select a logo image. Choose image behavior as **Default**, **Repeat**, or **No Repeat**.
20	Under **Header** > **Logo** >**Layout** > **Display**, choose **Default** or choose "**block**." **None** removes the logo.
21	Continue with specifying side-navigation skin parameters for the **Search Bar** and **Search Input**.

SPECIFYING TRIPANE-NAVIGATION SKIN PARAMETERS

BASIC CONCEPT

Tripane-Navigation is one of the three full skin options you can use for your online output. Once you have created the file in your project, you can proceed with configuring the parameters that let you affect the appearance of the skin and elements you wish to include. Since the skin is based on a template, its basic form is already in place. Specifying the skin parameters requires using the available tabs and completing essential fields using the fill-in-the-blanks approach to add your design preferences.

ESSENTIAL ELEMENTS

Before you can specify the Tripane-Navigation Skin parameters, you must have created the skin file in your project. **Project Organizer** > **Skin** folder > right-click > **Add Skin** > **File Type** > **Skin** > **New From Template** > **HTML5 Tripane Navigation** > **Add**. Once you add the file, the main parameter segments you must configure to view some results include the **Global**, **Header**, **Navigation**, and **Topic**.

APPLICATION TIPS

The Tripane-Navigation Skin has many settings on the Styles tab, all of which are not covered here. Only a selection of the parameters is covered to assist you in getting off to a good start. Also, the procedure does not cover adding the Tripane skin to the project, which you must create before starting.

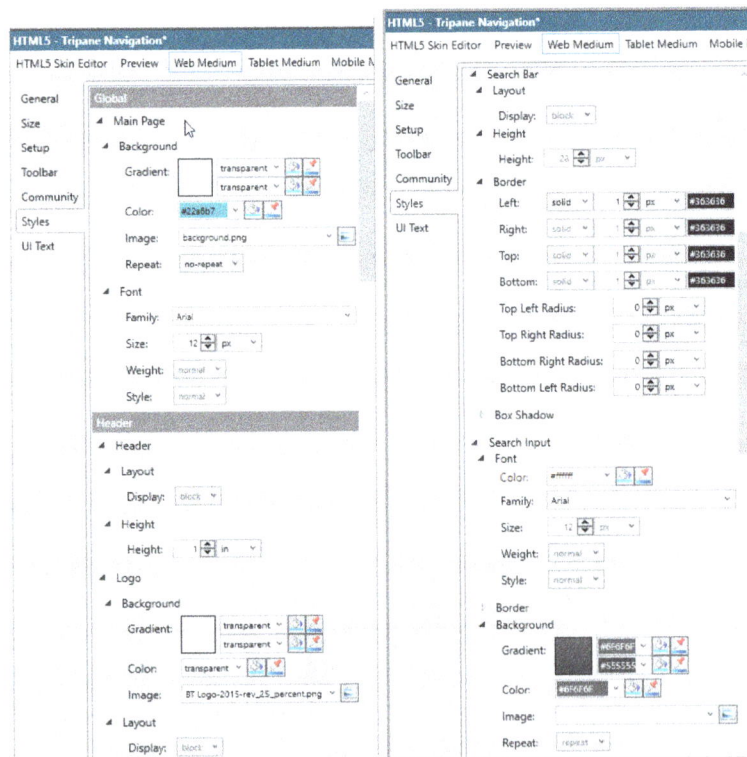

Figure 12-9. Skin Editor Tripane Skin a) Global and Header Settings, and b) Search Bar Settings.

QUICK STEPS: SPECIFYING TRIPANE NAVIGATION SKIN PARAMETERS

STEP	ACTION
1	In the **Project Organizer**, click the **Skins** folder and double-click on your Side Navigation skin file.
2	With the file open, select the **General** tab.
3	Use **Caption** to enter a title string to appear on a tabbed window of the output.
4	Use **Features** options t specify if **TOC**, **Index**, **Glossary**, or **Browse Sequence** panes should appear in skin.
5	Use **TOC Options** to enable option to **Automatically Synchronize TOC** and user's TOC navigation.
6	Use **Index Options** and **Glossary Options** to enable /disable **Partial Word Search**. Disabling these options can result in improved search results.
7	Select the **Setup** tab.
8	Specify individual **Browser Settings** or use the check box **Use Browser Default Settings**.
9	Use **Topic Settings** to specify whether a url hyperlink of each visited topic, should be placed at the topic top or bottom of the output.
10	Select **Enable Responsive Output** to modify the **Tablet-Max-Width** and **Mobile Max-Width** or use the given defaults. These settings are overridden by **Responsive Output Settings** set on the target **Skin** tab.
11	Use **Skin ID** to specify an identifier for this skin. An identifier is needed if the output uses multiple skins.
12	Select the **Styles** tab.
13	Under **Global** > **Main Page** > **Background**, use the **Gradient** tools to specify a start and end color for a top-to-bottom graded background; and use the **Color** tools to set a single absolute main background.
14	Under **Main Page** > **Background** > **Image**, click the drop-down or button to choose from recently used images, or browse and select an image. Choose the image behavior as **Default**, **Repeat**, or **No Repeat**.
15	Under **Main Page** > **Font**, set font settings for the main page, including header area and navigation area.
16	Under **Header** > **Header** > **Height**, specify the header height at the page top, for example 1 inch.
17	Under **Header** > **Header** > **Logo** > **Background**, use **Gradient** tools to specify a start and end color to create a graded logo background; or use the **Color** tools to set an absolute color (typically transparent).
18	Under **Header** > **Header** > **Logo** > **Image**, click **Select Image** button to browse and select a logo image.
19	Under **Search Bar** > **Height**, specify the header height in the desired unit of measure.
20	Use **Search Bar** > **Border** to specify the line type, thickness, and color for **Left**, **Right**, **Top**, and **Bottom**.
21	If desired, specify **Search Bar** rounded edges for **Top Left**, **Top Right**, **Bottom Left**, and **Bottom Right**.
22	Specify the **Search Input** field parameters for **Font** (Color, Family, Size, Weight, and Style).
23	Under **Search Input** > **Background**, use the **Gradient** tools to specify a start and end color to create a graded search input background; or use **Color** tools to set an absolute background for the search input.
24	Under **Search Filter Drop-Down** > **Background**, use **Gradient** tools to specify a start and end color to create a graded search filter background; or use **Color** tools to set an absolute color for the drop-down.
25	If desired, continue specifying tripane-navigation skin parameters for the **Navigation Panel**.
26	If desired, continue specifying tripane-navigation skin parameters for the **Topic**.

SPECIFYING TOP-NAVIGATION SKIN PARAMETERS

BASIC CONCEPT

Top-Navigation is one of the three full skin options you can use for your online output. Once you have created the file in your project, you can proceed with configuring the parameters that let you affect the appearance of the skin and elements you wish to include. Since the skin is based on a template, its basic form is already in place. Specifying the skin parameters requires using the available tabs and completing essential fields using the fill-in-the-blanks approach to add your design preferences.

ESSENTIAL ELEMENTS

Before you can specify the Top-Navigation Skin parameters, you must have created the skin file in your project. **Project Organizer > Skin** folder > **Right-Click > Add Skin > File Type > Skin > New From Template > HTML5 Top Navigation > Add**. Once you add the file, the main parameter segments you must configure to view some results include the **Global**, **Header**, and **Top Navigation**.

APPLICATION TIPS

The Top-Navigation Skin has many settings on the Styles tab, all of which are not covered here. Only a selection of the parameters is covered to assist you in getting off to a good start. Also, the procedure does not cover adding the Top-Navigation skin to the project, which you must create before starting.

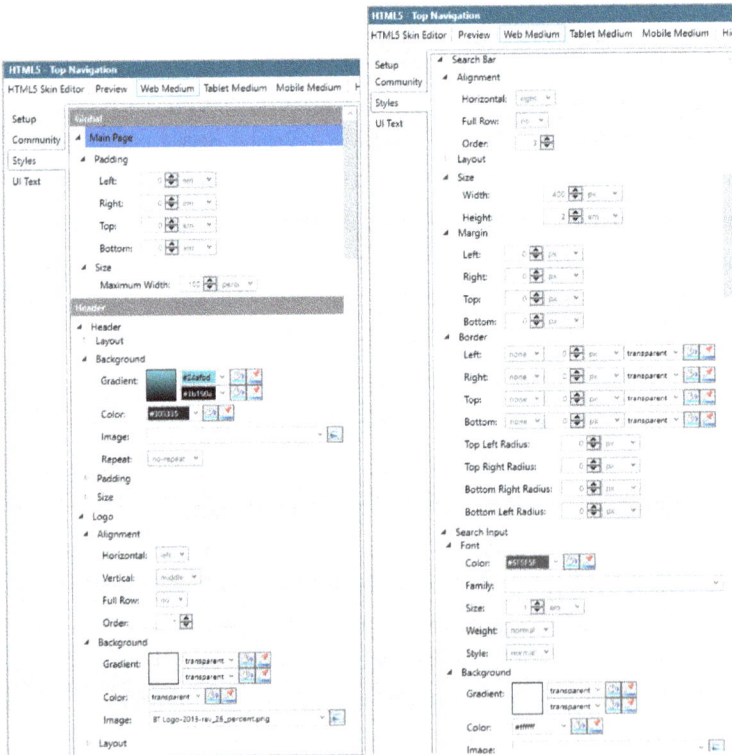

Figure 12-10. HTML5 Skin Editor — Top-Navigation Skin Styles Tab

QUICK STEPS: SPECIFYING TOP-NAVIGATION SKIN PARAMETERS

STEP	ACTION
1	In the **Project Organizer**, click the **Skins** folder and double-click on your Side Navigation skin file.
2	With the file open, select the **Setup** tab.
3	Use the **Navigation Pane** options to configure the following: a) **Main Menu Position:** set for the **Top** for top navigation. b) **Pane Position:** set to display to the **Left** or **Right** when the output is in tablet or mobile mode. c) **Slide-Out-Menu Style:** set for **Drilldown** or **Tree** in tablet or mobile mode, on hamburger icon click. d) **Fixed Header:** Specify if header should be fixed when user scrolls in **Web** display or for **All** displays. e) **Top Menu Levels to Show:** Specify the depth of TOC headings to show on the menu. f) **Logo Url:** enter url to link to when the logo is clicked or use the default setting (startup topic on target).
4	Use **Skin ID** to enter a unique skin identifier, which is needed when multiple skins are used in an output.
5	Use **TOC Options** to enable the option to **Automatically Synchronize TOC** and user's topic navigation.
6	Select the **Styles** tab. On this tab, you can start with the **Global**, **Header** and **Top Navigation** settings.
7	Under **Global** > **Main Page** > **Padding**, use the appropriate fields to specify the padded distance of the main display page (topic area) from the **Left**, **Right**, **Top**, and **Bottom** window edges.
8	Under **Global** > **Main Page** > set **Maximum Width** of the main display — for example, 0-100 percent.
9	Under **Header** > **Header > Layout** > **Display**, choose **Default** or choose "**block**." **None** removes header.
10	Under **Header** > **Header > Background**, use the **Gradient** tools to specify a start and end color to create a top to bottom graded background; or use the **Color** tools to set an absolute header background color.
11	Under **Header** > **Background** > **Image**, click the image drop-down or button to choose from recently used images or browse and select an image. Choose image behavior as **Default**, **Repeat**, or **No Repeat**.
12	Under **Header** > **Header > Padding**, use the appropriate fields to specify the padded distance of header elements from the **Left**, **Right**, **Top**, and **Bottom** header edges.
13	Use **Header** > **Size** > **Maximum Width** to specify the maximum width the header can occupy — for example, 0-100 percent.
14	Under **Header** > **Logo** > **Alignment** > **Horizontal**, specify the logo alignment as **Left**, **Right**, or **Middle**.
15	Under **Header** > **Logo** > **Alignment** > **Vertical**, specify the logo alignment as **Top**, **Middle**, or **Bottom**.
16	Under **Header** > **Logo** > **Alignment**, use **Full Row** drop-down to specify **Yes** or **No**, whether the logo should occupy a full row of its own.
17	Under **Header** > **Logo** > **Alignment**, use the **Order** field to enter a horizontal position, for example, 1-3, for placing the logo when other elements are positioned on the same row.
18	Under **Header** > **Logo** > **Background**, use the **Gradient** tools to specify a start and end color to create a graded logo background; or use the **Color** tools to set an absolute logo background color.
19	Under **Header** > **Logo** > **Background** > **Image**, click the image drop-down or button to choose from list of images or browse and select a logo image. Choose image behavior as **Default**, **Repeat**, or **No Repeat**.
20	Under **Header** > **Logo** >**Layout** > **Display**, choose **Default** or choose "**block**." **None** removes the logo.
21	Continue with specifying top-navigation skin parameters for the **Search Bar** and **Search Input**.

DEFINING AND LINKING RELATED TOPICS

BASIC CONCEPT

A *related topic* refers to any topic you identify as related to a particular topic and of possible interest to users — a topic that may offer additional information or insight. You may place a link to one or more related topics in any topic you choose. The links that give users access to these so-called related topics, and additional information, are typically placed at the bottom of the topic.

ESSENTIAL ELEMENTS

In this task, you must designate one or more topics related to the open topic and insert the **Related Topics Link** that provides user access. You can achieve both tasks using the **Insert Related Topics Control** dialog. With a topic open, the first step is to place the cursor where you want to insert the related topics link (typically at the bottom of the topic; you made to insert a new line). Then, from the **Insert** ribbon, select **Related Topics Control**, and choose one or more topics. You can re-arrange the order in which the topics are presented after choosing them, and you can choose an option of how the links are presented. Finally, choose the **Target Frame** to display the output of the destination file.

APPLICATION TIPS

Although similar to concept topics, related topics are independent topics whose links, if no longer needed, must be removed from wherever you inserted them.

Also, see the inherited MadCap styles for affecting the appearance of the elements of the related topics. You can view these styles in the CSS in the **Link Styles** category, for example, *MadCap|relatedTopics*.

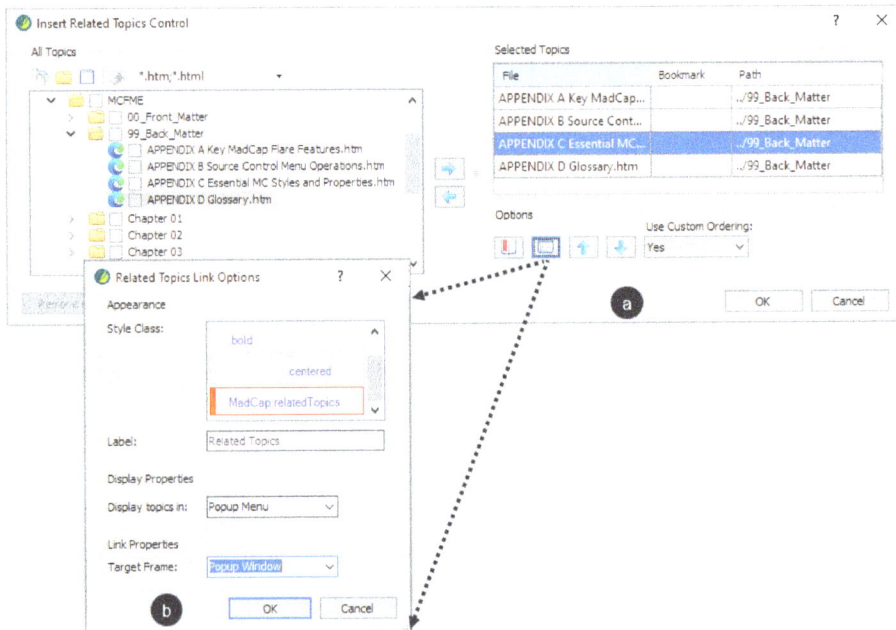

Figure 12-11. a) Insert Related Topics Control Dialog b) Related Topics Link Options Dialog.

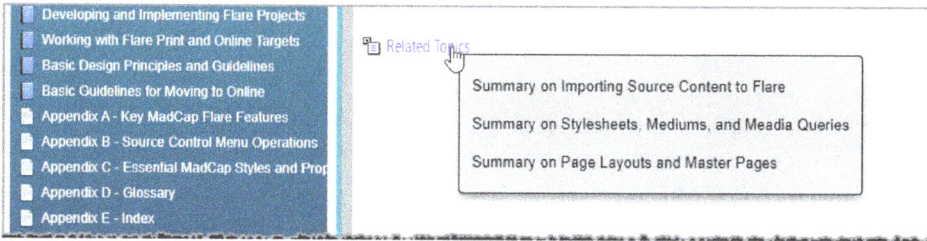

Figure 12-12. Related Topics Control Displayed in Popup Menu Format, in Online Output.

QUICK STEPS: DEFINING AND LINKING RELATED TOPICS

STEP	ACTION
1	Find and open a topic in which you want to insert a Related Topics control for one or more related topics.
2	With the topic open, click in the position where you want to insert the Related Topics control — typically at the bottom of the topic. You may need to insert a new line.
3	Click **Insert** > **Related Topics Control**. The **Insert Related Topics Control** dialog is opened.
4	From the **All Topics** pane, on the left, find and select one or more topics you wish to specify as related topics for the open topic.
5	With a topic selected, use the right directional arrow to push the topic to the **Selected Topics** pane.
6	If multiple topics are in the **Selected Topics** pane, you can set the **Use Custom Ordering** drop-down arrow to choose **Yes**, to adjust the sequential ordering of the listed topics, using the directional arrows.
7	Click on the Link **Options** button to specify parameter options for determining the link behavior.
8	Use the **Label** field if you want to modify the default **Related Topics** label.
9	Use the **Display Topics in** drop-down to choose whether to display the links in a **Popup Menu** or **List**.
10	Use the **Target Frame** drop-down to choose one of the following options for displaying the topic: a) **Page Default** to show the destination file in the same window as the output window. b) **Parent Frame** to show the destination file in the same as the current topic. The current topic is hidden. c) **New Window/Tab** to show the destination file opened in a new window. d) **Same Frame** to show the destination file opened in the same window frame as the current topic. e) **Top Frame** to output the topic in the same output window, and removes all other framesets. f) **Pop-up Window** to show the destination file opened in a popup box on top of the current topic.
11	Click **OK** , to save and insert the **Related Topics Control** button in the topic.
12	At any time, after inserting the Related Topics Control button, you can right-click on the button and select **Edit Related Topics Control**, to edit the control options.
13	Click the **Save** button to save your work.

Defining and Linking Concept Topics

Basic Concept

Concept topics refer to a group of topics you have designated as tightly related and work together to provide users with a complete set of information on a given subject. For example, a group of topics that include "Pre-Import Tasks," "Import Overview," "Using the Import Wizards," and "Post Import Tasks" form a concept topics group about importing to Flare. Each topic contains a concept marker that identifies it as part of the group and a control link that provides access to all the other topics.

Essential Elements

There are two main elements to defining and linking topics in a concept topic group. First, you must identify each topic by inserting an identifier label or a "concept." Once you insert the same concept marker in all of the topics, you must also insert, in each topic, the control link that gives users access to the topics (typically at the bottom of the topic; you may need to insert a new line). This link is considered a "**See Also**" link.

Application Tips

See the inherited MadCap styles for affecting the appearance of the concept link elements. You can view these styles in the CSS in the **Link Styles** category, for example, *MadCap|conceptLinkControlList*.

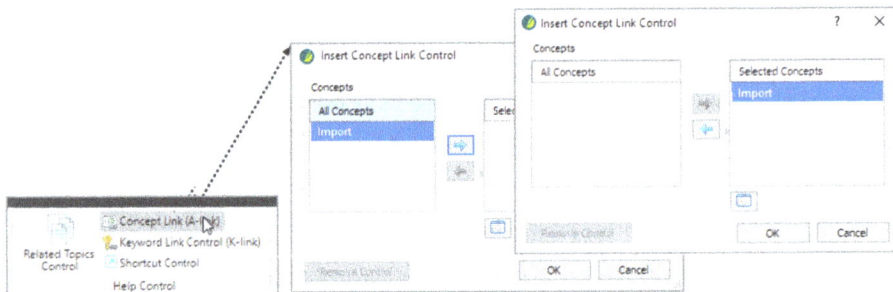

Figure 12-13. Insert Concept Link in Relevant Topics of Group.

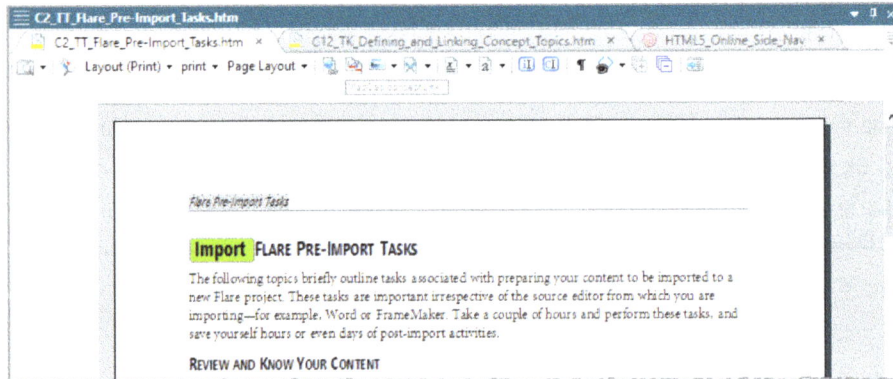

Figure 12-14. Concept Term Inserted in one of the Group Topics.

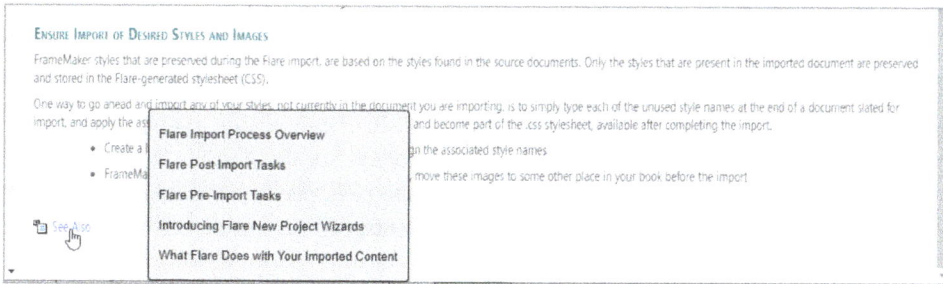

Figure 12-15. Concept Topics Displayed in Online Help.

QUICK STEPS: DEFINING AND LINKING CONCEPT TOPICS

STEP	ACTION
1	Find and open any one of the topics you want to include in the concept topics group. In this topic you will create and insert a concept, which is an identifier label you choose to identify the concept topics.
2	With the first topic open, click in the position where you wish to insert the concept — this is typically at the start of the topic, just before the topic title or first heading. This identifier is not shown in the output.
3	Click **View** > **Concept Window** (or **Shift + F9**), to open the **Concepts** window.
4	Click in the **Terms** field, and type in your concept term. In this example, "**Import**" is used. The concept term is inserted in the topic. See Figure 12-14.
5	If the concept term is not visible, click the **Show Tags** drop-down and select **Markers**.
6	Click the **Save** button to save the topic.
7	Continue first, by copying the concept term from the first topic, and pasting it in the remaining topics of the concept topics group. Paste the term inline and just before the topic title as done with the first topic.
8	Complete the following steps, to insert a concept link at the bottom of each topic. The concept link, is what users will click to view a list of links to the topics in the concept topics group.
9	Starting with the open topic, or any one of the topics from the concept topics group, and, at the end of the topic, insert a new paragraph after the last paragraph in the topic.
10	In the new paragraph position, click **Insert** > **Concept Link (A-link)**, to open the **Insert Concept Link Control** dialog.
	From the **Concepts** pane on the left, select the desired concept and use the directional arrow to push the concept to the right pane. The concept is inserted as a **See Also** link, that gives user's access to the group.
11	Complete the procedure by selecting and copying the inserted concept link, then opening and pasting it in a new paragraph at the bottom of each of the remaining topics in the concept topics group.
12	Click the **Save** button to save your work.

INSERTING A TEXT POPUP

BASIC CONCEPT

A *text popup* is a solution when you want to provide a small block of information to online users without having them leave the current topic. Although topic popups are also possible in Flare, text popups are more suitable when a small block of content needs to be displayed when users click on the popup link. The text popup link is the text you specify as the **Hotspot Text** when inserting the popup.

ESSENTIAL ELEMENTS

You can insert the text popup from the Flare **Insert** menu, after positioning your cursor where you want to insert the popup link or after selecting the text you want to use for the popup link. Insert the text popup using **Insert > Text Popup**. You would then use the **Hotspot Text** field to enter the link text and **The Popup Text** field to enter the text you want to be displayed when the user clicks the link. The text popup opens in a **Popup Box** when the user clicks the link in the online output.

APPLICATION TIPS

Flare places the text you entered as popup text as a footnote at the bottom of the topic. Consider the target file **Advanced** tab options to manage text popup and expanding text effects in print outputs. The choice includes **Convert to Footnotes**, **Expand Text Inline**, or **Remove the body**.

Also, see the inherited MadCap styles for affecting the appearance of the popup elements. You can view these styles under the stylesheet **Dynamic Effects** category, for example, *MadCap | popupBody*.

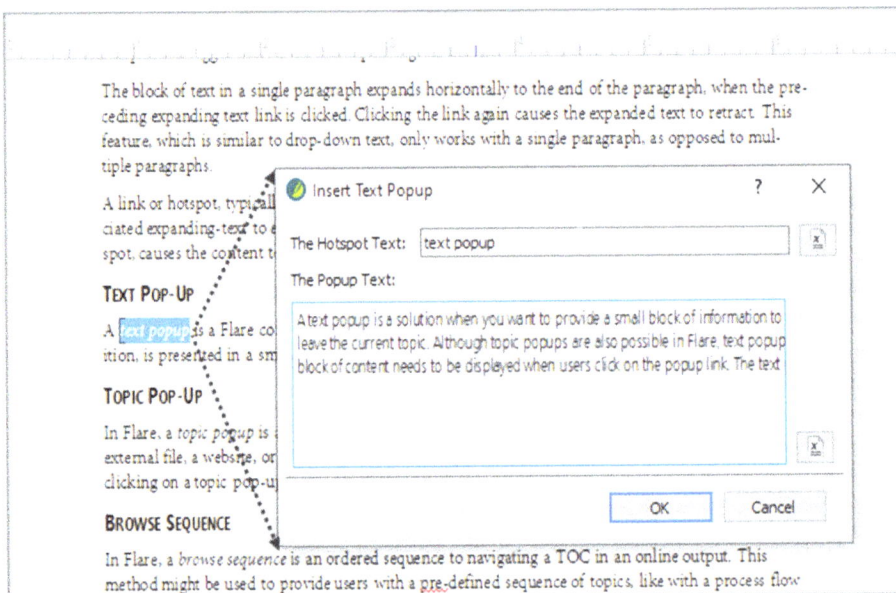

Figure 12-16. Insert Text Popup Dialog.

You are here: Basic Guidelines for Moving to Online > Inserting a Text Popup

INSERTING A TEXT POPUP

BASIC CONCEPT

A text popup is a solution when you want to provide a small block of information to online users without having them leave the current topic. Altho: popups are also possible in Flare, text popups are more suitable when a small block of content needs to be displayed when

Essential Elements You can insert   popup link is the text you specify as the Hotspot Text when inserting the popup.
the text popup from the Flare Insert
menu, or when you are positioned
at the insertion point, right-click and   Flare Insert menu, after positioning your cursor where you want to insert the or after selecting text you
select Insert > Hyperlink, you have   ert the text popup using Insert > Text Popup. When the topic is displayed in the online output, and user
the options of choosing a File in   spot Text, the content opens in a default Popup Box.

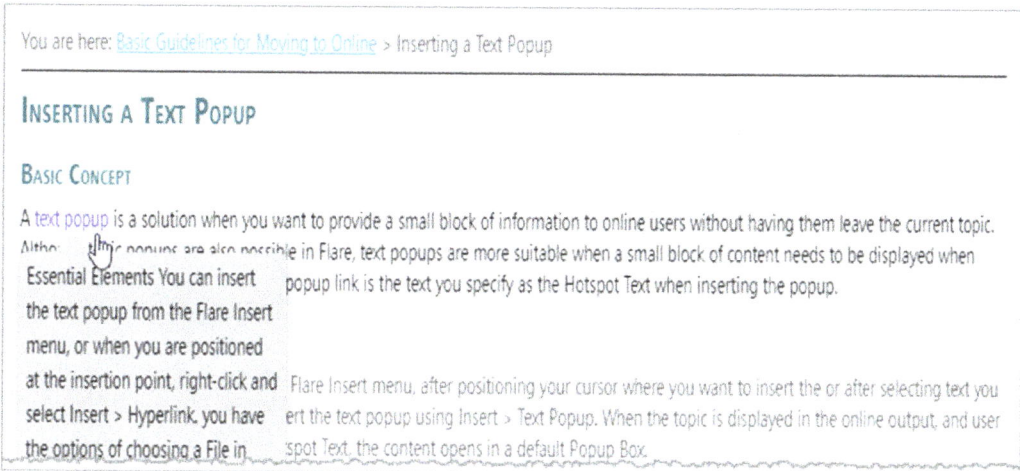

Figure 12-17. Text Popup Displayed in Online Output.

QUICK STEPS: INSERTING A TEXT POPUP

STEP	ACTION
1	Start by opening the topic or content file where you want to insert the text popup.
2	Consider copying or preparing the text you want to display in the popup box, before opening the dialog.
3	Select the text you want to use as the topic popup hotspot or control. If applicable, type in the hotspot text and then select it. In this example, the text "**text popup**" is used as the hotspot text.
4	From the **Insert** ribbon, select **Text Popup**.
5	Skip the next step if you had already entered or selected hotspot text. The text will appear in the dialog.
6	Use **The Hotspot Text** field to enter the text users will click to open the text popup. You may also insert a pre-defined variable into this field.
7	Use **The Popup Text** field to enter or paste the text you want to appear in the popup box. You may also insert a pre-defined variable into this field.
8	Click **OK** to save the text popup.
9	Click on the **Save** button to save your work.
10	Right-click on the popup link and select **Edit Popup** at any time , to modify the element.
11	Right-click on the popup link and select **Remove Popup** at any time , to remove the element.

INSERTING A TOPIC POPUP

BASIC CONCEPT

A *topic popup* is a solution for providing online users access to additional information — for example, an external file, a website, an HTML Help file (.chm), or a topic or bookmark in the same project. The topic popup is considered a hyperlink and opened by clicking on a popup link. A *topic popup link* is any text you designate as the link text when creating the element and that users will click to open the topic popup.

ESSENTIAL ELEMENTS

You can insert the topic popup from the Flare Insert menu or use the right-click at the point where you want to insert the element. When specifying the target content for the hyperlink, you have the option of choosing a **File in Project** (like a topic or PDF), a **Bookmark**, an **External Website**, or an **HTML Help System** (.CHM). When the user clicks the **Link Text**, the content opens in a default **Target Frame**, a **Popup Window**.

APPLICATION TIPS

Flare supports the topic popup feature in the HTML5 tripane-navigation and skinless outputs, but it is not supported in HTML5 side-navigation or top-navigation outputs.

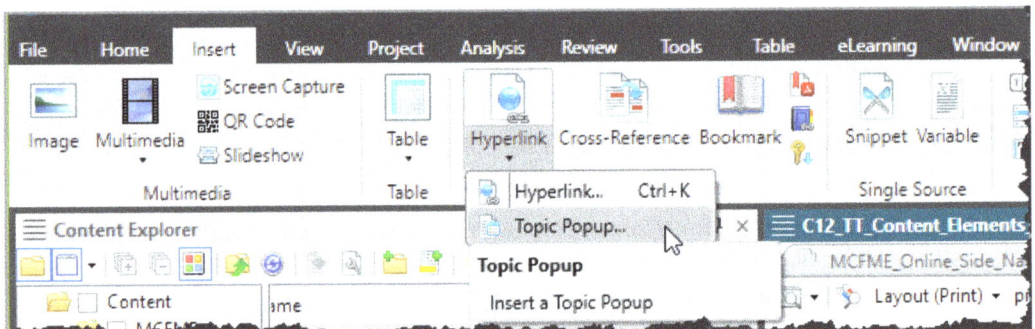

Figure 12-18. Insert Topic Popup Dialog.

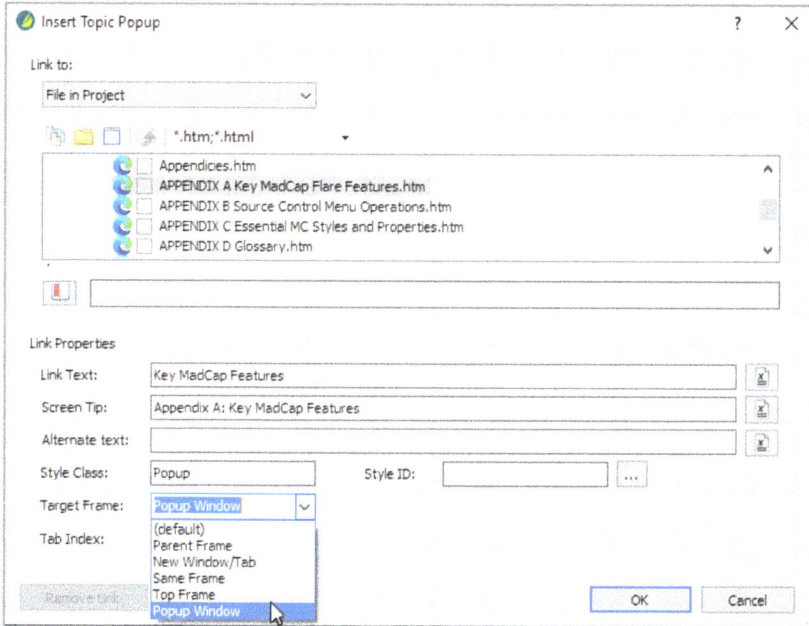

Figure 12-19. Insert Popup Dialog.

QUICK STEPS: INSERTING A TOPIC POPUP

STEP	ACTION
1	Start by opening the topic or content file where you want to insert the topic popup.
2	Select the text you want to use as the topic popup hotspot or link text. If applicable, type in the **Link Text** and then select it. In this example, the text "**Key MadCap Flare Features**" is used as the link text.
3	From the **Insert** ribbon, click the **Hyperlink** drop-down, and select **Topic Popup**. The **Insert Topic Popup** dialog opens, with a default list of HTML topics in the project. You can browse to find the topic.
4	Under the **Link Properties** group, enter the associated parameters as required.
5	The **Link Text** field will display any text you selected before opening the dialog. You can enter different text here, for the hotspot, if desired.
	Use the optional **Screen Tip** field to enter text that will appear when users hover over the hotspot text.
6	Use the optional **Style Class** and **Style ID** fields to choose a class, you have created, and ID to assign to the topic popup. If no style class is specified, Flare uses the parent style **a.Popup**.
7	Use the **Target Frame** drop-down to select **Pop-up Window** in which to output the topic.
8	Click **OK** to insert the element.
9	Click on the **Save** button to save your work.
10	Right-click on the popup link and select **Edit Hyperlink** at any time , to modify or remove the element.

INSERTING DROP-DOWN TEXT AND HOTSPOT

BASIC CONCEPT

Drop-down text is a block of content that alternately hides and reveals content when a user clicks the drop-down link or hotspot. This technique is one of several layering techniques whereby users click a hotspot to display additional information on demand. Drop-down text usually involves a heading or text just above a content block that is hidden or revealed. When a user clicks the drop-down link, the drop-down text expands just below the hotspot.

For additional examples of content layering techniques, see *"Inserting Expanding Text and Hotspot"* and *"Inserting Toggler Targets and Hotspot."*

ESSENTIAL ELEMENTS

This task will identify the drop-down text hotspot and the drop-down content by selecting them both. The drop-down hotspot is usually a text heading or title just above the drop-down content. When selecting drop-down content, it does not have to be text alone but can include images, tables, a list, or even an entire procedure. All of the hidden content is revealed in the online output when the user clicks the drop-down link.

After selecting both elements, from the **Insert** menu, click the drop-down arrow just to the right of the **Drop-Down Text** item, then choose **Drop-Down Text**. Flare inserts the drop-down icon just to the left of the drop-down link, and the drop-down text is the remainder of the content you selected.

APPLICATION TIPS

See the inherited MadCap styles for affecting the appearance of the drop-down elements. You can view these styles under the **Dynamic Effects** category, for example, *MadCap | dropDownBody*.

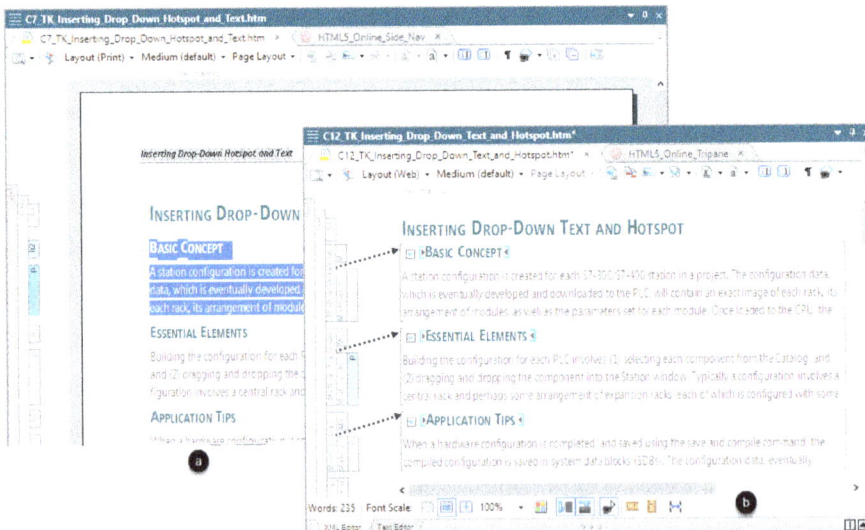

Figure 12-20. a) Selecting Drop-Down Hotspot and Text. b) Three separate drop-down text elements.

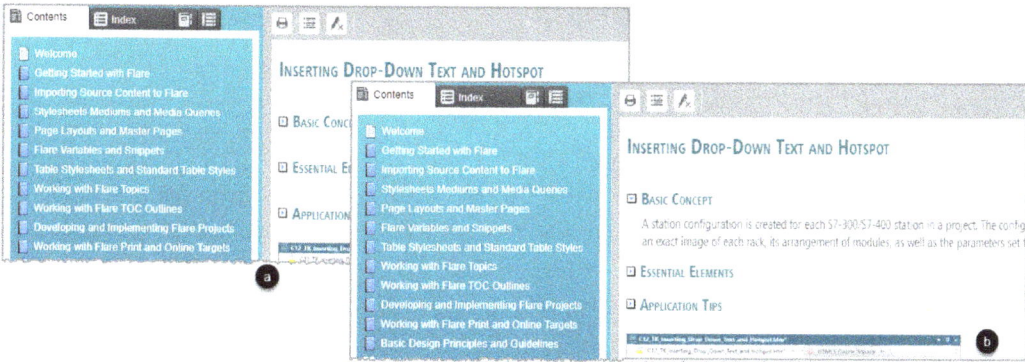

Figure 12-21. Selecting Drop-Down Hotspot and Text.

QUICK STEPS: INSERTING DROP-DOWN TEXT AND HOTSPOT

STEP	ACTION
1	Start by opening the topic or content file where you want to create the drop-down text.
2	Select both the text you want to create as drop-down content and the drop-down link. In this example, the heading **Basic Concept**, and the following paragraph were selected as the hotspot and content.
3	With the elements selected, on the **Insert** ribbon, click the **Drop-Down Text** arrow, and select **Drop-Down Text**. In the XML Editor, the drop-down icon is inserted just to the left of the drop-down hotspot. The remainder of the content that you selected is the drop-down text that will immediately follow the hotspot.
4	If you want to insert additional drop-down text in the same topic, it must be treated separately. In this example, the headings **Essential Elements**, and **Application Tips**, and the paragraph following each of these have been inserted as drop-down content. Each heading and paragraph was treated separately.
5	Save your work.

NOTE: You can view the drop-down link and text and its operation after building your online output.

INSERTING EXPANDING TEXT AND HOTSPOT

BASIC CONCEPT

Expanding text like other Flare layering methods, including the drop-down text and toggler, alternately hide and reveal a block of content when users click a hotspot. The feature involves a block of text that expands horizontally, in line with the hotspot, to the end of the paragraph when the user clicks the *expanding text link.* Clicking the link again causes the expanded text to retract. Similar to drop-down text, expanding text only supports a single paragraph instead of multiple paragraphs.

For additional examples of content layering techniques, see *"Inserting Drop-Down Text and Hotspot"* and *"Inserting Toggler Targets and Hotspot."*

ESSENTIAL ELEMENTS

Expanding text operates within a single paragraph, where you identify an associated hotspot, and in the same line, you define the expanding text content. You can insert the expanding text link and text from the Flare **Insert** menu after positioning your cursor to insert the hotspot or after selecting the text you want to use for the hotspot.

First, select the **Insert** menu, then click the **Expanding Text** drop-down and choose **Expanding Text**. Flare inserts two sets of facing blue brackets in line with the content. If you selected the hotspot before issuing the **Insert Expanding Text** command, Flare encloses the hotspot inside the first set of brackets; the second set of brackets is where you will insert the expanding text. If the text is already in the paragraph, you can cut it and paste it inside the brackets. Otherwise, you can type the expanding text inside the brackets.

APPLICATION TIPS

See the inherited MadCap styles for affecting the appearance of the expanding text elements. You can view these styles in the CSS **Dynamic Effects** category, for example, *MadCap | expandingBody.*

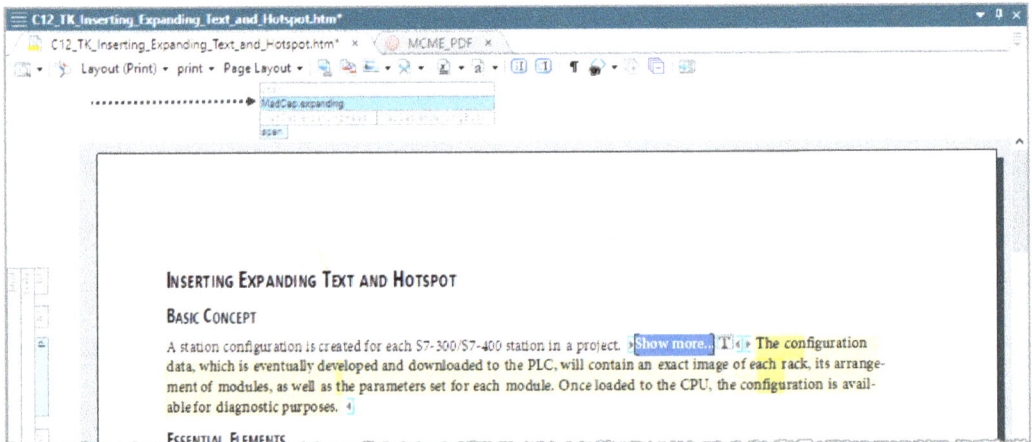

Figure 12-22. Inserting and Selecting Expanding Text Hotspot.

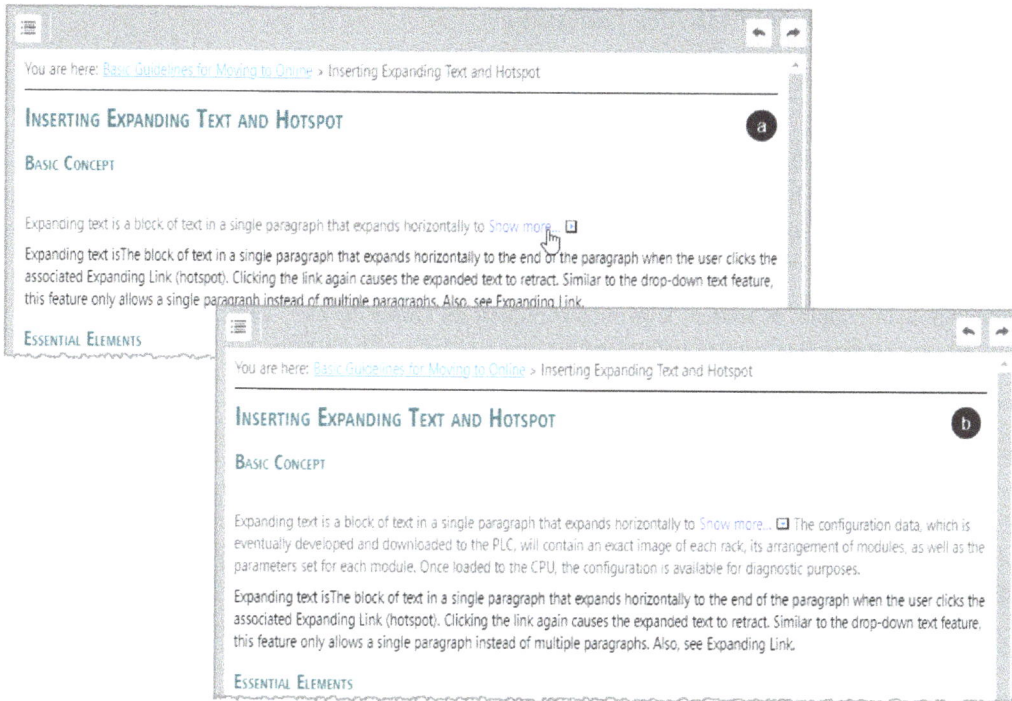

Figure 12-23. **a)** Expanded Text Retracted **b)** Expanded Text Extended.

QUICK STEPS: INSERTING EXPANDING TEXT AND HOTSPOT

STEP	ACTION
1	Start by opening the topic or content file where you want to insert the expanding text content.
2	First, select the hotspot text that will control the expanding text. In this example, **Show more...** is used; any text you choose following the hotspot, and up to the paragraph end, can be identified as expanding text.
3	From the **Insert** ribbon, click the **Expanding Text** drop-down arrow, and select **Expanding Text**. A set of blue brackets will appear around what you selected as the hotspot; and another set of empty brackets will immediately follow. If you do not see the brackets then the **Show Markers** option may not be enabled.
4	If you inserted the hotspot text inline before the text you want to have expanded and retracted, then you can copy that text, up to the paragraph end, and paste it inside of the empty brackets.
5	If the text you want to have expanded/retracted, was not already in your content, then you can type the text directly inside of the empty set of brackets. You now have identified both the expanding text and link.
6	Save your work.

> **NOTE:** Consider the target file **Advanced** tab options to manage text popup and expanding text effects in print outputs. The options include to **Convert to Footnotes**, **Expand Text Inline**, or **Remove the body**.

INSERTING TOGGLER TARGETS AND HOTSPOT

BASIC CONCEPT

A *toggler* is another method of alternately hiding and revealing content when a user clicks the associated hotspot. This technique, referred to as layering, allows the user to display additional information on demand. The hidden content associated with a toggler can be one or more non-contiguous chunks of the content located in different places on the topic page. All of the content is revealed when you click the hotspot. When you click the toggler hotspot again, the content is again hidden.

For additional examples of content layering techniques, see *"Inserting Drop-Down Text and Hotspot"* and *"Inserting Expanding Text and Hotspot."*

ESSENTIAL ELEMENTS

Defining a toggler involves identifying one or more chunks of hidden content that are revealed when the user clicks the hotspot. In this case, each piece of content must be "tagged" or "named." A chunk of content, for example, can be a paragraph, an image, a table, or a list. These content chunks are called toggler targets. The associated hotspot for a toggler, any text you choose, is also called a toggler link. All of the hidden content is revealed when the user clicks the toggler link.

APPLICATION TIPS

See the inherited MadCap styles for affecting the appearance of the toggler elements. You can view these styles in your stylesheet in the **Dynamic Effects** category, for example, *MadCap | toggler.*

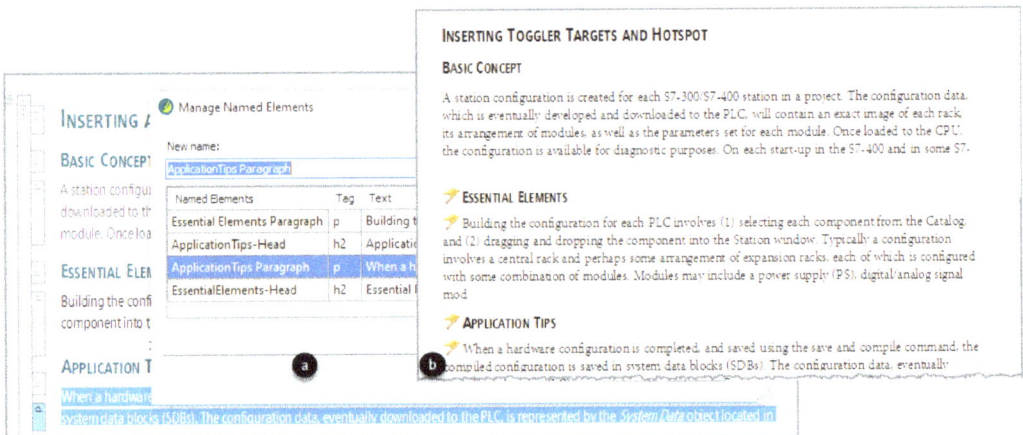

Figure 12-24. a) Create Named Elements and b) Named Elements shown Flagged in Topic, if Markers Enabled.

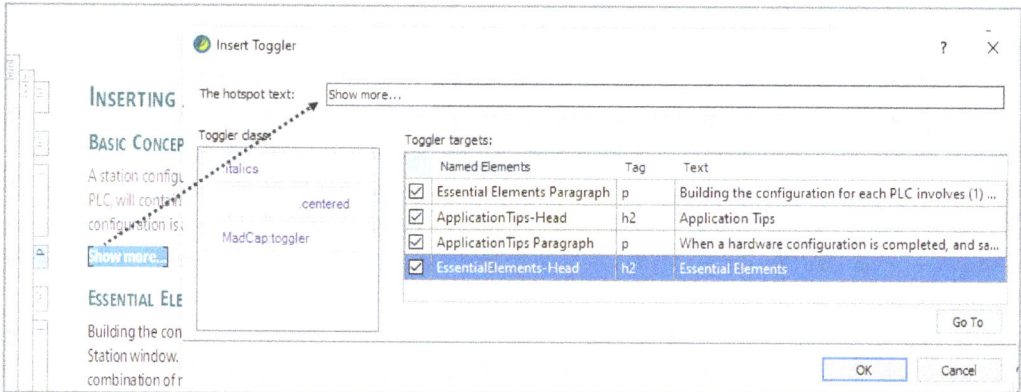

Figure 12-25. Insert Toggler Dialog, where Named Elements (Toggler Targets) are Selected.

QUICK STEPS: INSERTING TOGGLER TARGETS AND HOTSPOT

STEP	ACTION
1	Start by opening the topic or content file where you want to create the toggler targets and hotspot.
2	Click inside of any paragraph you wish to name as a toggler target (or named element) that is revealed when a user clicks the toggler hotspot.
3	Select **Home > Name**, and type a name you wish to give the toggler element.
4	Click **OK** to save the named element. A yellow flag will appear adjacent to the named element, if the show **Named Element** tag is enabled, and the **Show Markers** option is enabled.
5	Repeat the previous steps, from step 2, to create other named elements to be revealed by the toggler.
6	Select the text you want to use as the toggler hotspot. If applicable, type in the text and then select it. In this example, the text "**Show more...**" is used as the toggler hotspot.
7	From the **Insert** ribbon, select **Toggler**. The Insert Toggler dialog is opened, with a list of the named elements that can be selected as toggler targets.
8	Click to enable the check box adjacent to **Toggler targets** (named elements) you wish to select.
9	You are given the option to select from the list of style classes to assign to your toggler. This is not required, as you can later style the toggler from your stylesheet.
10	Click **OK**, to save the toggler hotspot. The toggler icon, is now displayed next to the hotspot in the XML Editor, but it is not displayed in the output.
11	Save your work.

ADDING A HEADER FILE

BASIC CONCEPT

As introduced earlier, the header file is a simple text file that provides the interface between the help system and a web-based or desktop application. The header file should be the first step in your CSH implementation. The file contains information needed to connect the application to the CSH topics. For each UI element, for example, a dialog, or page, a tab or a button, the header file has a unique definition or identifier that provides a one-to-one link or mapping between a UI element and a specific help topic.

ESSENTIAL ELEMENTS

In many CSH implementations, the software developer creates the header file. However, the software developer or you, the help system developer, can make the file. The responsibility for developing the header file must be agreed upon and shared, as both parties will use it. You can use the **Add File** dialog to create a new file or import an existing file the developer has previously created. Since the help developers owns the help files they are responsible for mapping each identifier to a specific help topic.

APPLICATION TIPS

Creating the header file is one of the first steps in the CSH implementation. Once created, you can then use the Flare **Alias Editor** to generate the header file contents. This editor provides a user-friendly interface to create and map the topic identifiers that Flare will eventually use to construct header file. Double-click on a header file to view its contents.

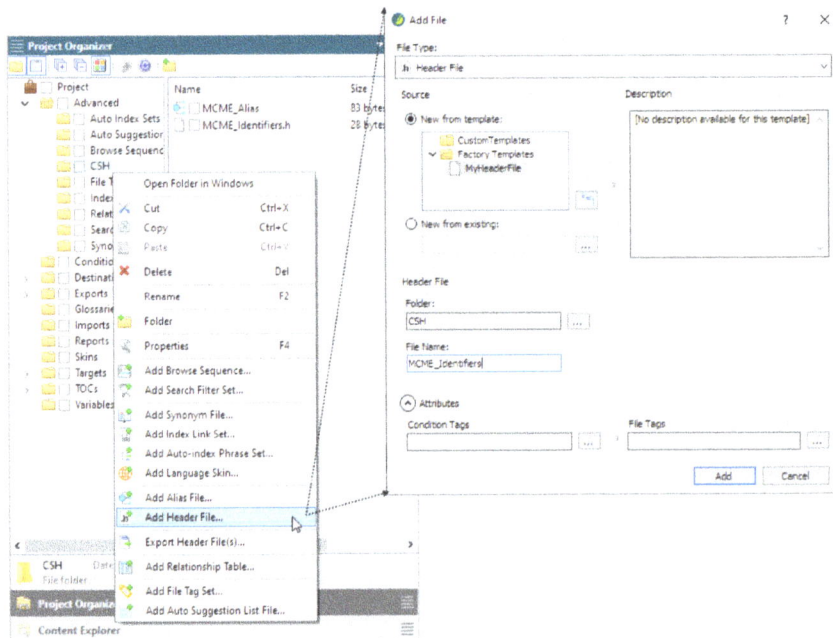

Figure 12-26. Add New Header File or Import Existing Header File.

QUICK STEPS: ADDING A HEADER FILE

STEP	ACTION
—	**To Create a Header File (if Help System Developer Writer Responsible)**
1	Open the **Project Organizer** and expand the **Advanced** folder.
2	Right-click on the **CSH** folder > select **Add Header File**. The **Add File** dialog opens.
3	Ensure that the **File Type** is set for **Header File**.
4	**To create the new header file use one of the following:**
	a) From Templates: Set the **Source** for **New From Template**, choose the **MyHeaderFile** template from the **Factory Templates** folder or choose a template from a user-defined **Custom Templates** folder.
	b) From Existing: Set the **Source** for **New From Existing**, and use the browse button ... to locate the existing Header file (**.h**). Your new header file will have the same contents or settings of the existing file.
5	Under **Header File**, use the **Folder** field and choose the default (**Project> Advanced > CSH**) folder, or browse and choose another folder in which to store the new header file.
6	Use the **File Name** field to specify a name for the new file. For example, **MyHeaderFile.h**.
7	Click the **Add** button to add the empty header file to your project.
—	**To Import a Header File (When Software Developer Responsible — See Note)**
1	Open the **Project Organizer** and expand the **Advanced** folder.
2	Right-click on the **CSH** folder > select **Add Header File**. The **Add File** dialog opens.
3	Ensure that the **File Type** is set for **Header File**.
4	Choose **New From Existing**, and use the browse button ... to locate an existing Header file to import.
5	Under **Header File**, use the **Folder** field and choose the default folder (**Project> Advanced > CSH**), or browse and choose another folder in which to store the new header file.
6	In the **File Name** field, use the existing file name already given or enter a new name for the header file.
7	Click the **Add** button to import the header file to your project.

NOTE: If the software developer is responsible for developing the header file, then identifiers for each UI element of the application will already have been created. In this case, you will need to import the existing header file and then use the Alias Editor to link each identifier to a CSH topic.

ADDING AN ALIAS FILE

BASIC CONCEPT

After you add the header file to your project, the next step is to add the alias file. As previously intro-duced, after you have added the alias file to the project, you can populate it using the Flare Alias Editor. This editor is a user-friendly way for you to establish the numeric topic identifiers and link them to the associated topics for the CSH. In implementing the CSH you should create the header file before creating the alias file.

ESSENTIAL ELEMENTS

As for creating a new alias file, as always in Flare, there are several ways: 1) from the **File** menu, select New and in the **Add File** dialog **File Type** > **Alias File**, 2) from the **Project** ribbon, click **New** > **Advanced** > **Add Alias File**, and from the **Project Organizer**, select the **Advanced** folder > right-click on **CSH** > **Add Alias File**. In each of these cases, you can choose to base the new file on a **Factory Template**, a user-defined **Custom Template**, or on an **Existing File**. A new alias file based on an exist-ing file will be identical to the existing file, but you can modify the file.

APPLICATION TIPS

Creating the alias file is a secondary step in the CSH implementation. Once you have added the file to your project, you can use the Flare **Alias Editor** to create and assign an identifier to each help topic that will eventually map to a specific UI component. Double-click on an alias file to open it in the editor. When you save the alias file, Flare generates the topic identifier definitions in the header file.

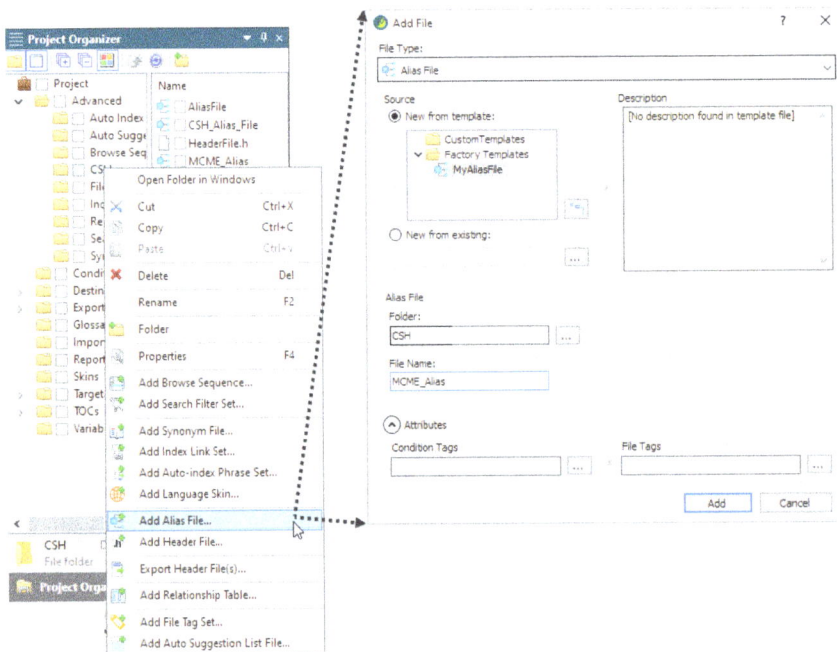

Figure 12-27. Add Alias File Option Selected — Add File Dialog with File Type set for Alias File.

QUICK STEPS: ADDING AN ALIAS FILE

STEP	ACTION
1	Open the **Project Organizer** and expand the **Advanced** folder.
2	Right-click on the **CSH** folder and choose **Add Alias File**. The **Add File** dialog opens.
3	Ensure that the **File Type** is set for **Alias File**.
4	**To create the new alias file use one of the following:**
	a) From Templates: Set the **Source** for **New From Template**, then select the **MyAliasFile** template from the **Factory Templates** folder or choose a template from a user-defined **Custom Templates** folder.
	b) From Existing: Set the **Source** for **New From Existing**, and use the browse button ⌐…⌐ to locate the existing alias file.
5	Under **Alias File**, use the **Folder** field and choose the default folder (**Project> Advanced > CSH**), or browse and choose another folder in which to store the new alias file.
6	Use the **File Name** field to specify a name for the new alias. For example, **MCME_Alias.flali**.
7	Click > **Add** to save the new alias file.

DEFINING THE ALIAS FILE IDENTIFIER OPTIONS

BASIC CONCEPT

After adding the Alias file to the project, consider defining the Alias File **Identifier Options** before creating and assigning identifiers in the **Alias Editor**. The task is to supply some optional information you want Flare to include in each new identifier you create.

ESSENTIAL ELEMENTS

In the **Identifier Options** dialog, you can specify a **Starting value**, a unique numeric value assigned to the identifier as a hook that the software developer can use to call for the specific CSH topic. Depending on software developer preference, you can supply the **Value Format** in **Decimal** or **Hexadecimal** for this value. Enable the **Use Prefix** parameter to specify a string you want to be placed at the start of each new identifier. You can also enable **Capitalize the new identifier** to use all caps in the identifier.

The identifier string can also **Include a file or phrase name**. By identifying a topic file name, you are thereby assigning the identifier as a CSH topic. Other options you can specify are a **Default Skin**, in which the CSH topic should appear, and a **Primary Header** file in which the identifier should be placed. Flare will create and assign each new topic identifier according to the options you specify in the **Identifier Options** dialog.

APPLICATION TIPS

You would specify the skin in the **Identifier Options** before creating and assigning as new identifiers if there are CSH topics you would like to appear in different skins. For HTML5 outputs, all of your skins must have the responsive output feature enabled or all disabled.

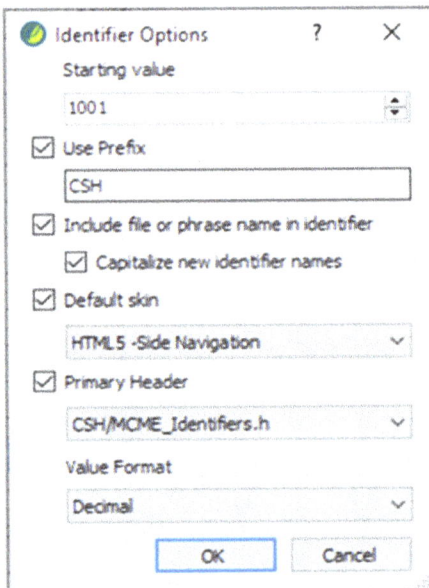

Figure 12-28. Alias File Identifier Options Dialog.

QUICK STEPS: DEFINING THE ALIAS FILE IDENTIFIER OPTIONS

STEP	ACTION
—	**To Specify Desired Identifier Options for the Alias File**
	The **Identifier Options** lets you choose from several options you can have appended to each identifier.
1	From the folder **Advanced** > **CSH** double-click on the alias file you wish to open in the Alias Editor.
2	Click the **Identifier Options** button to review or enter desired options. Do the following
	a) Use the **Starting value** field to enter a numeric value at which to begin the identifier numbering.
	b) Enable the **Use Prefix** option to enter a prefix you want added at the start of each new identifier.
	c) (Optional) Enable the **Include file or phrase name in identifier** option if you want the file name or a specific phrase included as part of the identifier. If this option is enabled, you can also indicate that you want to capitalize new identifier names. With manual entry you can enter the desired phrase.
	d) Enable **Default skin** option to choose a skin to display the CSH topic in, when their are several skins.
	e) Enable the **Primary Header** option to choose a header file, when their are several project header files.
	f) Use the **Value format** field to choose a number format (**Decimal** or **Hexadecimal**) for the identifier **Starting value**. Verify this selection with the software developer.
3	Click **OK** to save the selected options.

CREATING AND ASSIGNING TOPIC IDENTIFIERS

BASIC CONCEPT

After adding the Alias file to the project, you can open the file in the **Alias Editor**, a user-friendly editor for entering the information Flare eventually stores in the header file. The task is to create and assign an identifier to each context-sensitive help topic. This task would be the responsibility of the help developer if it were decided that the help developer has the responsibility of creating the header file. The alias file output of the Alias Editor is used by Flare to populate the header file.

ESSENTIAL ELEMENTS

You can manually create and assign a help topic identifier to each CSH topic. You can also use the button **Generate identifiers for this project** from the **Alias Editor** ribbon to cause Flare to automatically generate a list of the identifiers for all topics in the project. In either case, Flare will create and assign each topic identifier according to all of the specified options in the **Identifier Options** dialog.

When you are done creating and assigning topic identifiers, Flare constructs a definition line for each identifier. In its most basic form, the identifier will include the define instruction syntax (**#define**), an identifier or name (typically UI element name), and a unique numeric value (**hexadecimal** or **decimal**). The definition will also contain parameters specified in the **Identifier Options** dialog. When you save the Alias file, Flare generates the list of identifier definitions in the designated header file.

APPLICATION TIPS

Suppose you have multiple skins in your project and plan to display some CSH topics in different skins from others. In that case, you can specify the skin in the **Identifier Options** before assigning the topics. Also, for HTML5 outputs, all of your skins must have the responsive output feature enabled.

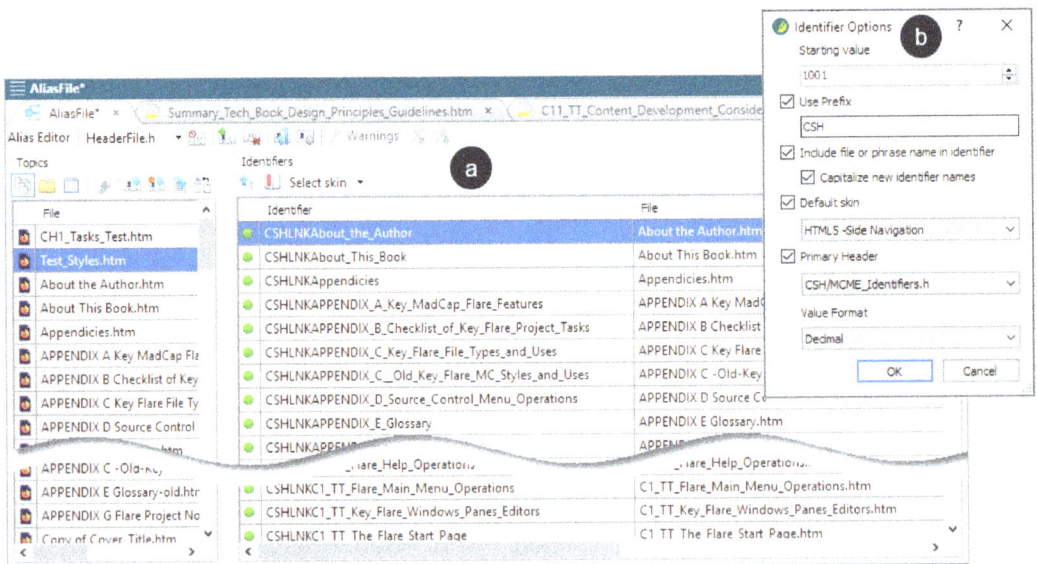

Figure 12-29. a) Creating and Assigning Identifiers b) Identifier Options Dialog.

QUICK STEPS: CREATING AND ASSIGNING TOPIC IDENTIFIERS

STEP	ACTION
—	**To Manually Enter Identifiers Help Topics**
	Use the following procedure to manually create and enter one or more identifiers (for each topic).
1	From the folder **Advanced** > **CSH** double-click on the alias file you want to open in the Alias Editor.
2	Click the **Identifier Options** button to confirm you want to have the currently set options applied.
3	Under the **Topics** pane, use the local buttons to determine how you want to view the list of topics.
4	With topics listed, select one or more topics for which you want to create and assign an identifier.
5	Click the **Create new identifier** button to generate and assign new identifiers for the selected topics; or you can right-click on a selected topic and choose **Assign to New Identifier**, to link the topic.
6	You can click slowly in the **Identifier** field and modify the label part of an identifier phrase as desired.
7	Click the **Save** button to save the alias file.
—	**To Automatically Generate Identifiers and Assign CSH Topics for the Entire Project.**
	Use the following procedure to generate identifiers and assign to all topics in the project.
1	From the folder **Advanced** > **CSH** double-click on the alias file you wish to open in the Alias Editor.
2	Click the **Generate identifiers** button to create identifiers for all of the topics in the project. The Generate Identifiers dialog opens.
3	Under **Header File**, enable **Choose Existing** and use the drop-down and select your existing header file.
4	Click the **Identifier Options** button to confirm you want to have the currently set options applied.
5	Use the **Skins** drop-down to select the desired skin in which to display the CSH topics.
6	Use the **Generate Identifiers** drop-down option to choose **All topics** as the option.
7	Use the **Existing Identifiers** drop-down and choose **Delete** to remove any existing identifiers.
8	Click **Create** to create and assign identifiers to all topics.
9	Click the **Save** button to save the alias file. You can view the identifiers in the header file.

> **NOTE:** In the list of generated **Identifiers**, a green bubble to the left of the identifier indicates that a CSH topic has been assigned to the identifier. A red bubble means no topic has been assigned to the identifier.

APPENDIX A

KEY MADCAP FLARE FEATURES

Flare offers several valuable features that support single-source authoring and publishing and content project management. Flare features facilitate an environment that supports multiple writers, projects, documents, and output formats. There are far more features than I could list here, but here I just wanted to list some of the features I've found to be quite helpful and that I think all Flare users should be aware of — even beginners!

Table A-1. A Small Selection of Key Flare Features.

Feature	Brief Description and Usage
Conditional Tags	You can create and apply conditional tags to many elements in your content. Then on each target, you can specify whether to include or exclude tagged content.
Context-Sensitive Right-Click	Commonly used commands, tools, and dialogs are available from the right-click, thereby simplifying many operations for the Flare element currently in focus. For example, editor, image, or table operations.
Customizable User Interface	You can arrange, save, and reload the Flare workspace however needed to best suit your working preference and convenience. This feature is handy if you have large or multiple screens. You can undock windows and panes, resize and relocate windows, and either leave them floating or docked. Windows can be placed in a fixed arrangement as **Standard Tabs** layered across the window top or bottom or as **Accordion Tabs** stacked at the window bottom.
Generic Classes	This is a useful style class in that it reduces the number of needed styles by allowing you to create generic styles that you can apply to any style class. Examples of generic styles include the following: **.center**, **.right**, **.italic**, **.bold**, **.red**, and **.blue**.
Global Project Linking	Allows the Content and Project Organizer files in one project to be automatically updated in other projects. In this way, you can maintain shared resources, like stylesheets, page layouts, table stylesheets in one project.
Import Selected Styles	Styles that you like in another project but prefer not to re-create can be imported to the current project.

Table A-1. A Small Selection of Key Flare Features. (cont).

Feature	Brief Description and Usage
Cross-Reference Support	Flare Cross-Reference support truly simplifies linking to a specific point in your project or topic. In addition to the ability to link to any topic, the dialog lets you select and link to specific paragraphs, ordered list items, drop-downs, expanding text, table components, and even content of particular styles.
Preview Window	Click the **Preview Window** button from the **View** menu or click **Preview** on the XML Editor ribbon, to open the current topic to see it as it will appear when output.
Send Files to Folder	You can send files like stylesheets, page layouts, and table stylesheets from one project to another. You have an option to synchronize the source and destination.
Snippets	Chunks of content, typically used repeatedly in different places, might be saved as a snippet. A snippet can then replace the repeated content throughout the project, and you can modify it in one place.
Snippet Variables	A snippet variable lets you insert standard variable text into a snippet wherever the snippet is in the content. With the snippet variable, you can slightly customize the snippet in each instance of the snippet.
Snippet Conditions	A snippet condition tag is a standard condition tag whose behavior you can specify at the snippet or at the topic level. In this fashion, you can determine whether tagged snippet content is included or excluded at the snippet or at the the topic
Source Control Integration	Flare supports several tightly integrated source control applications. In a source control environment, a copy of the project is stored on a remote server that supports file "check-in," "check-out," and synchronization between the server version of the project and the local changes made by different writers.
Table Stylesheets	Table Stylesheets allow you to create tables with consistent settings and appearance throughout your print and online outputs. Using the Table Stylesheet Editor, you have five dialogs that will enable you to quickly design very simple to very complex table stylesheets to create as many plain and patterned tables as needed.
Variables	Flare supports several variable types, including system variables and user variables that you can create. You can use variables throughout your project and in target outputs. You may also create unlimited variables using single definition variables, like company name, address, phone, and email, or multi-definition variables, such as a variable called Document Title, where several titles are defined.
Responsive Layout Window	An Flare tool that simplifies creation of responsive layouts that adjust your online content based on the device it is displayed — such as web, tablet, or phone.

APPENDIX B

KEY MADCAP STYLES AND PROPERTIES

You may have initially imported your stylesheet to Flare or developed it manually, using the stylesheet editor. In either case, consider using some of the many inherited MadCap styles (MadCap-prefix) and MadCap properties (mc-prefix) that are inserted automatically into your project's stylesheet. Here are a few MadCap style classes and style properties you may find helpful; however, there are many others!

Table B-1. Key Flare MC-Styles and MC-Style Properties

MC Style/MC Property	Brief Description/Usage
mc-thumbnail	Use this property to determine the manner in which the user can specify that an image switch from the thumbnail size to its full size.
mc-thumbnail-max-height	Use this property to set the maximum height for thumbnail images.
mc-thumbnail-max-width	Use this style property to set the maximum width for thumbnail images.
mc-auto-number-format	Use this property to apply alphanumeric numbering to parts of your content — for example, Figure Numbers, Table Numbers, or paragraph Headings.
mc-auto-number-offset	Use this property to place margin between the Auto-Number format position and the text content.
mc-auto-number-position	Use this property to specify the position of the Auto-Number format within the paragraph text. For example, float-left, float-right, inside-head, outside-head, or inside frame.
mc-conditions	Normally you apply a condition to content, a topic, a file, or a TOC entry. With this property you can set conditions on styles, which you can apply to content.
mc-caption-continuation	Use this property to specify a continuation text string for the caption, when a table continues to the next page. For example, you might specify mc-continuation to = "**(Continued)**".
mc-caption-repeat	Use to cause a table caption to repeat on the next page if the table continues to the next page. The mc-caption-repeat value must be set to "**true**" to repeat.

Table B-1. Key Flare MC-Styles and MC-Style Properties (cont).

MC Style/MC Property	Brief Description/Usage
mc-heading-level	Use this property to determine which level of indentation in the generated TOC each topic heading displayed. Each heading must be assigned an MC-heading level. If the mc-heading-level is "1," the heading is placed in the left-most position. If the mc-heading-level is "2," the heading is placed in the second position from the left. This property, which affects the indentation, will exclude a heading from the print TOC if the mc-heading level is '0'.
MadCap|glossaryProxy	Use this style to define the appearance of the Flare generated glossary container element for print output, for example, width, border, and background.
MadCap|glossaryTerm	Use this style to define the appearance of the glossary term links of the glossary proxy.
MadCap|indexProxy	Use this style to define the appearance of the Flare generated Index container element for a print output, for example, the width, border, and background.
MadCap|listOfProxy	Use this style to define the properties and appearance of the List-of-Proxy container element, for example, the width, border, padding, and background.
MadCap|miniTocProxy	Use this style to define the appearance of the generated Mini-TOC container element, for example, the width, border, padding, and background.
MadCap|TocProxy	Use this style to define the appearance of the Flare generated TOC container element, for example, the width, border, padding, and background.
MadCap|xref.TOCPageNumber	Use this style to define the appearance of Page Numbers only, of any of the Flare generated list — for example, TOC, List-Of-Figures, List-Of-Tables. Otherwise the page numbers in a generated list inherit their style from the list item just before the page number.
MadCap|breadcrumbsProxy	Use this style to modify the look of breadcrumbs in your online output — for example, font-family, font-size, margin (left, top, bottom, and right).
p.MiniTOC1 thru p.MiniTOC9 *	Use these styles to define the properties of the mini-TOC heading levels — properties like font family and size, indentation, and paragraph spacing.
p.TOC1 thru p.TOC9 *	Use these styles to define the properties of the TOC Proxy heading levels — properties like font family and size, indentation, and paragraph spacing.

NOTE: * p.MiniTOC1 thru **p.MiniTOC9** and **p.TOC1** thru **p.TOC9** are not MadCap styles, but are CSS styles that affect the appearance of the auto-generated TOC levels of the MiniTOC and TOC respectively.

APPENDIX C

GLOSSARY

- A -

Advanced Selector

A complex style selector may contain several style properties and precise criteria for affecting content appearance and behavior. As you complete the various fields of the New Selector dialog, the Advanced Selector field is populated accordingly.

Advanced View

An enhanced view of the stylesheet that provides full access to style properties and, in general, supports extended access to styles. Styles are presented in a tree-like view, displayed in a multi-pane window. You can display multiple mediums and media queries simultaneously in this view.

Alias Editor

A user-friendly editor you can use to create and assign topic identifiers in a header file. These identifiers form mapped links between each topic and a Context-Sensitive Help Call in the application code.

Alias File

This file is used to populate a header file with information necessary for producing context-sensitive Help (CSH). The Alias file contains a mapping of topics and identifiers. A Flare alias file has the <.flali> extension and is stored in the Advanced folder of the Project Organizer.

Anchor

A Flare method that locks page layout frames to the page margins so that if you later alter the page size, the frame is automatically re-sized.

Apache Subversion

An open source version control system. See Source Control.

Apply Style

To assign a defined style to some part of the project content to affect that content's appearance and behavior. See Style.

Attribute

See HTML Element Attribute.

Auto-Numbered Styles

A Flare category of CSS styles that supports style classes that can be numbered numerically or alphabetically. For example, Figure Number, Table Number, Chapter Number, and Appendix Number.

Auto Index File

A file where you enter search phrases and corresponding index keyword entries to support the Flare auto-indexing feature. When you generate the output, Flare scans the auto-index file, adds the words it finds to the generated index, and creates links to the associated topics.

Auto Indexing

A Flare feature that automatically adds words from a project to a generated index, rather than requiring the manual insertion of index markers. To do this, you can add phrases and corresponding index entries to an auto-index file. See Auto-Index File.

Autosuggestion

You can enable or disable this Flare feature from the Options dialog to offer suggestions as you work. As you start to type, based on previously used variables, snippets, words, or phrases, a popup containing suggested variables, words, or phrases is presented, from which you may select.

Autosuggestion Set

A file in which users can specify a list of words or phrases for inclusion to elements already presented in the autosuggestion popup. You can enable or disable list suggestions.

- B -

Background Color

A style property that you can apply to a frame or an entire page. In the Table Stylesheet Editor, the property can apply to a whole row, column, header, or footer cells. In the Stylesheet Editor, the background property can apply to a specific style - for example, paragraph, character, or table styles.

Batch Target

A Flare file that points to a set of targets and stores information such as whether to build or publish and scheduling commands. After creating a batch file, you can configure its settings for building or publishing in the Batch Target Editor. A batch target file is stored in the Project Organizer under the Targets folder and has the extension ".flbat."

Bind

In Flare, a method by which a connection is made between a project and a source control server application — for example, a project can be bound to a Git repository. The source control server is then aware of changes to the project. See unbind.

Bind Detection

You can enable a Flare option that automatically detects an existing source control binding to a source control application such as Git, Perforce, Microsoft Team Foundation Server, or Subversion.

Bleed

A page layout property specified on the Print Marks dialog defines the area beyond the edge of the page where printing occurs. This area, noted by printers, ensures that no unprinted edges occur in the final trimmed document.

Block-Level Styles

HTML elements that always have a line break after the closing tag. Typical block-level elements include <p>, <ol>, <ul>, and <li>. Block -level elements can also contain other elements. For example, an unordered list <ul> or an ordered list <ol> can contain list items <li>. Also called paragraph styles.

Block Bars

See Structure Bars.

Block Quote Tag

A Flare tag group style that is typically used to format text placed as a quotation within a topic. The blockquote tag usually has margin indentations to offset it from the content in which it is inserted but may also have a different font, color, or other emphases. See Tag Group.

Block Snippet

One of two Flare snippet types, this snippet is best suited for a block of content, like a bullet or numbered list, multiple paragraphs, or other large blocks of content. When inserted on a blank line in a topic, you cannot add other content to the content block. See Snippet; Text Snippet.

Body Frame

In a page layout, the primary frame type for arranging and flowing body text onto a page. One of five frame types you can use to create a page layout. You may place one or more body frames on a page layout. See header frame, footer frame, decoration frame, and image frame.

Body Proxy

A content placeholder that you place in a topic. Content manually entered above the Body proxy bar in the template page displays above the topic body as a header in the output. Content manually entered below the Body proxy bar on the template page, displays below the topic body as a footer in the output.

Bookmark

A defined marker that identifies a specific point within a topic and to which you can create a hyperlink. Typically section headings are defined as bookmarks. A link to a bookmark is generally in the same topic as the bookmark.

Border Radius

You can use this table style property to specify rounded borders be applied to a table's corners

Breadcrumbs Proxy

A proxy that, when is included in a template page, causes the output to display a "trail of breadcrumbs" composed of the table of contents (TOC) entries (or path) above the current topic in the TOC hierarchy. See Proxy.

Break Type

A parameter specified on the Flare TOC Printed Output tab. You can select a value of Chapter Break or Page Layout break to any TOC page or book. See Chapter Break; Page Layout Break.

Broken Link

A defined link that points to a file or destination that is no longer reachable — the topic, web page, bookmark, or other destination has been moved or no longer exists. In Flare, you can generate a broken links report.

Browse Sequence

An ordered sequence of topics users can navigate in online output. This method might be used, for example, to present users with a pre-defined series of topics to view, like with a process flow.

Build

See Target Build.

Build Window

A Flare UI window where you may initiate target builds, and check Build Status, Progress, Compile Status, and Warnings. When Flare completes a build, you may View Output, Open Build Log, Rebuild Target, or Open Output Folder.

- C -

Cascading Style Sheet (CSS)

A simple stylesheet language that is used to describe the presentation of a document written in HTML or XML. CSS describes how elements should be rendered on screen, on paper, in speech, or in other media. CSS enables the separation of presentation and content, including layout, colors, and fonts.

Cell Alignment

A table stylesheet property that specifies whether the cell content should align left, center, or right.

Cell Content Style

In a table stylesheet, you can specify that this tag style is applied to the text content of header cells, footer cells, row cells, or column cells.

Cell Padding

A table stylesheet property that defines a distance from the cell top, bottom, left, or right border to any text or image contained in the cell. See image padding; frame padding.

Cell Vertical Alignment

A table stylesheet property that specifies whether cell content will align with the starting content at the top, middle, or bottom of the cell.

Chapter Break

One of three "Break Type" options that can be specified when defining the properties of TOC outline entries to affect how the page layout is applied to printed output content, starting at a specific TOC entry. The Chapter Break option lets you identify a TOC outline entry as a new chapter breakpoint and apply the specified page layout file. The chapter break causes the chapter auto-number settings to be applied. See Break Type; Page Layout Break; None Break.

Chapter Pages

In page layout files, Chapter Pages represent the pages that comprise each chapter of a book—starting with the chapter title page and ending with the last page of the chapter. See Title Page, Front Matter Pages, Glossary Pages, and Appendix Pages.

ChapterA4

A Flare page layout template, designed to control the arrangement and flow of chapter pages of a document, and uses the international standard page size of 21 cm x 29.7 cm. See Chapter Pages.

ChapterLegal

A Flare page layout template, designed to control the arrangement and flow of chapter pages of a manual or document that uses the standard legal page size of 8.5 inches x 14 inches. See Chapter Pages.

ChapterLetter

A Flare page layout template, designed to control the arrangement and flow of chapter pages of a document that uses the standard letter page size of 8.5 inches x 11 inches. See Chapter Pages.

ChapterResizable

A Flare page layout template, designed to control the arrangement and flow of chapter pages of a book or manual, and in which the specified 8.5 inches x 11 inches page size can be resized without having to resize the page frames. See Chapter Pages; Anchor.

Character-Level Styles

A Flare Style Category. Contrasts with block-level styles. Also called span styles. See Span Styles.

Class

The most common child that you can create under a parent style like p, h1, and h2. For example, under the parent <p>, you might create the child classes p.body, p.footer, and p.header. When you first create a project, some child classes may already be available under certain parent styles.

Clean XHTML

A Flare output type that produces basic HTML files that do not contain MadCap-specific tags and are not dependent upon MadCap-generated files. The output does not include skins, search, navigation, or other features—it only has your single-sourced content. This type of output can be embedded in other applications.

Column-Break

A paragraph tag property can be specified to affect when a column break should occur for specific content—for example, a paragraph or heading. Selecting a column break in a paragraph is considered local formatting and only affects that one instance. Like always, it is preferable and more effective to apply the column break to a style.

Column-Break-After

A paragraph tag property that affects whether a column break occurs after the paragraph and the content flows to the next column. The options are: a) Always - which causes a column break to always occur after the paragraph b) Auto - which causes a column break to neither be forced nor prevented after the paragraph; c) Avoid - which avoids a column break after the paragraph; and d) Inherit - which uses the paren tag's column break setting.

Column-Break-Before

A paragraph tag property that can be specified to affect whether a column break occurs before the paragraph and the content flows to the next column. The options are a) Always - which causes a column break to always occur before the paragraph; b) Auto - which causes a column break to neither be forced nor prevented before the paragraph; c) Avoid - which causes a column break to not occur before the paragraph; and d) Inherit - which uses the parent tag's column break setting.

Column-Break-Inside

A paragraph tag property that can be specified to affect whether a column break occurs inside the paragraph and the content flows to the next column. The options are a) Auto - which causes a column break to neither be forced nor prevented inside the paragraph; and b) Avoid - which causes a column break to not occur inside a paragraph but to flow content to the next column.

Column Bar

In the XML Editor window, the graphical bars (one for each column) display just below a table bar. Table and column bars are shown whenever the cursor is positioned anywhere inside a table. An entire column is selected when you select a column bar. When the cursor is inside a column, the associated column bar is shaded. A left-click and hold on a column bar allows you to drag and reposition the column. See Table Bar.

Column Gap

A page layout frame property that you would use to specify the amount of space between columns.

Column Rule

The vertical line (rule) between columns of a table pattern entry, having a defined repeat of two or more columns. You can assign rule properties like line type, color, and width.

Column Separator

The vertical line separator between the final column in a column pattern, and the first column in the next pattern. You can assign separator properties like line type, color, and width.

Commit

A source control command that allows you to save to the local repository, modifications presented as Pending Changes. You have the option to commit one or more selected files or use Commit All to commit all files in pending changes.

Concept File

A Flare file that contains a list of "Concept Links" or "see also" links at the bottom of topics. An important characteristic of this file type is that if a concept link is later added or deleted, it is done in one place and is applied to every topic containing that concept link. See Concept Link.

Concept Link

A Help control feature lets users open topics assigned to a specific concept, each of which advances the complete concept information. Although a concept link is similar to a related topic link, you would generally use this feature when the associated topics are all assigned to the concept. Hence, you could place the concept link in several topics. If you later add or remove a concept link from the concept topics group, you would do this in one place. See Concept File.

Concept Proxy

A proxy that generates a list of all of the concepts in your project, with links to the corresponding content. See Concept File.

Concept Topics

Any one of a group of topics assigned to a specific concept. This relationship is one in which all of the topics assigned to a concept provide additional information that advances the concept information. When a concept topic is added or removed from the concept, the change is in one place and affects all of the associated topics. See Reference Topics, Task Topics, and Related Topics.

Condition Tag Indicators

A color like red, blue, or yellow is assigned to a condition tag when created. The indicator appears in different ways, depending on the Flare element. If you have turned Condition Tag Indicators on, Flare displays a box with the indicator color adjacent to tagged files and folders; and displays as a background color for tagged words, phrases, or paragraphs. If more than one condition has been applied to an element, then each indicator color is shown. See Condition Tags.

Condition Tag Set

A related set of condition tags. You may create as many condition tag sets as needed, and each set may have as many tags as needed.

Condition Tags

Flare condition tags, like "PrintOnly" and "ScreenOnly" and others that you can create in a project, may be applied to project content such as snippets, topics, files and folders, TOC entries, and other content elements like words, phrases, or paragraphs. Condition tags, when applied, can control whether a tagged element appears (is included) or does not appear (is excluded) in a given target output; or is only displayed when a particular device or screen size is used. By default, all content is included, regardless of tags, unless excluded by the tag expression defined in the target.

Container

See Element Container.

Content

The text, image, audio, video, multimedia, and other file types that are use in producing a print-based or online output. See Content Explorer.

Content Explorer

A Flare UI component that contains sub-folders containing various elements of the project content. These elements include topic files, snippets, micro-content files, image files, multimedia files, and various resource files such as Stylesheet, Page Layout, Tablestyles, and Template Page files used to produce online or print-based output targets. See Content Folders.

Content Folders

Flare folders that are presented in the Content Explorer and contain a project's content. Although you may add other folders, the Content Explorer, by default, includes the top-level Content folder and a Resources subfolder that usually contains Images, Stylesheets, Page Layouts, Table Stylesheets, and Template Pages folders. See Content Explorer.

Content Layering

A method of allowing the user to affect how content is gradually revealed, through techniques such as drop-down text, expanding text and togglers, whereby portions of the content are initially hidden, but can be revealed when users click on the associated hotspot.

Context-Sensitive Help (CSH)

An online help method involves a one-to-one correspondence between each UI element (window, pane, tab, or dialog) of a desktop or Web-based application and a specific online help topic. The CSH topic is displayed whenever the application element is in focus.

Contributor

See MadCap Contributor.

Controls/Forms Styles

A Flare category of CSS styles you can apply to content with controls such as buttons and forms.

Cross Reference

A cross-reference is a dynamic navigation link that allows the connection of one place within a topic to another within the same or a different topic. With cross-references, the source and destination files must be part of the same output within the same project.

CSS

See Cascading Style Sheet.

CSS Table Styles

See Table Styles.

CSS Variable

A stylesheet variable whose property may be color, Size, Font-Family, Iimage-URL, or Custom. You can define the variable as local, whereby the variable is set on a particular selector, or global, set on the :root selector.

- D -

Date-Time Variable

See System Variables.

Decoration Frame

One of five frame you can use to create a page layout. This frame is layout used to arrange and place aesthetic elements like images, decorative text, borders or other objects. Also, see body frame, footer frame, header frame, and image frame.

Default Medium

The default medium, which Flare uses unless another medium is specified. Any settings you specify in the default medium are inherited in all other style mediums. Explicitly modifying a style in a medium other than the default medium overrides the setting in the default medium. See Mediums.

Default Page Layout

A Flare created page layout file, used by default where a page layout is required, and no other file is specified. Generally, you will want to create one or more page layout files to control the content flow for each major section of a book or document.

Definition

See Variable Definition; Single-Definition Variable; Multi-Definition Variable.

Destination

See Publishing Destination.

Directional Synonym

A word that, when used in a search, operates in one direction only. For example, a search of the directional synonym "automobile" would find results that include the synonym "Honda. " A search for "Honda," on the other hand, would not find results for "automobile," since the synonym works in one direction only. See Synonym.

Div Tag

An HTML block style used to define logical divisions in a topic or to hold objects such as an image or text box that can be floated. Groupings can be named using the div tag, and you can define a set of styles to affect the different elements in the group — for example, a heading, a paragraph, and an ordered or unordered list. See Tag Groups.

Drop-down Link

A link or hotspot (typically a heading), that when clicked, causes the associated drop-down text to expand just below the drop-down link. Another click on the hotspot causes the content to collapse. Also, see Drop-down Text.

Drop-down Text

The block of text that is expanded and revealed when the user clicks the associated drop-down link. The text expands just below the drop-down link or hotspot. Also, see Drop-down Link.

Dynamic Effects Styles

A Flare category of CSS styles applied to content elements like menus, togglers, popups, and drop-down text and provides special Dynamic HTML effects. Several Dynamic Effects Styles are inherited in Flare, and you may add new selectors.

Dynamic Help

In the Flare Help System, this option is the equivalent of Context-Sensitive Help (CSH). Dynamic Help, enabled from the main toolbar, opens in an inline window alongside any open windows.

- E -

eBook

An "electronic book" (eBook). A book publication available in digital form, consisting of text, images, or both, and is readable on the flat-panel display of computers or other electronic devices. Users can read eBooks on dedicated e-reader devices and any computer device with a controllable viewing screen — including desktop computers, laptops, tablets, and smartphones.

Eclipse Help Output

A Flare output type that allows content developers to use Flare content as its source material to author an Eclipse Help plug-in.

Element Container

In Flare, a virtual element that is associated with or contains generated content like that produced by the Table of Contents, Mini TOC, List-of-Images, List-of-Figures, Glossary, and Index. You can define the appearance of each of these elements using specific MadCap styles and properties like border, background color, background, and image.

Empty Left

One of several page types you can specify in a page layout file. The Empty Left Page type is used to define the layout for how an empty left-hand page in a section will look. The Empty Left page type, for example, would be inserted when there is no content to flow onto the left-hand page and the following page is a First Right. See page types.

Empty Page

One of several page types you can specify in a page layout, to define an empty page flow in a section. The Empty page type, for example, may be used in a page layout when there is no left page and right page flow. See page types.

Empty Right

One of several page types you can specify in a page layout file. You would use the Empty Right Page to define how an empty right-hand page in a document section will look. The Empty Right page type, for example, would be inserted when there is no content to flow onto the right-hand page and the following page is a First Left. See page types.

EPUB

See EPUB Output.

EPUB Output

An online format for creating re-flowable digital books or ebooks. The structure is developed and maintained by the International Digital Publishing Forum (IDPF). The EPUB output is intended to be viewed electronically, somewhat like online outputs. Its structure, however, is much like a book or manual and is produced much like the print-based PDF output.

Expanding Text

The block of text in a single paragraph that expands horizontally to the end of the paragraph when the user clicks the associated Expanding Link. Clicking the link again causes the expanded text to retract. Similar to the drop-down text feature, this feature only allows a single paragraph instead of multiple paragraphs. Also, see Expanding Link.

Expanding Text Link

The hotspot that triggers or controls the associated expanding text, which immediately follows the hotspot. The text toggles between expanding and retracting. Also, see Expanding Text.

External Resources

A Flare feature that supports selection and mapping to a set of external files. External resources may consist of local or network files, which users can bring into the project using the External Resources window pane and kept synchronized with the source files through mappings. The external resources feature is ideal for shared files that are expected to change over time.

- F -

Favicon

An acronym for "favorite icons," which are supported in HTML5 outputs. Also known as a shortcut icon, website icon, tab icon, URL icon, or bookmark icon is a file containing one or more small icons. Browsers that typically provide favicon support display a page's favicon in the browser address bar and adjacent to the page name in a list of bookmarks.

Fieldset Tag

A Flare tag group style that is used to combine multiple tags into a group, and in the output, places a box around all of the content. A fieldset generally contains a set of data or information, for example, Customer Contact Information. See Tag Group.

File Tag Set

A Flare feature that supports creating and applying identifier tags to Flare project files. A tag set contains a grouping of associated tag values. A factory tag set is available in the Advanced folder of the Project Organizer, with pre-designed tag types of "Author" and "Status," however, you can create custom tag types for various purposes as needed.

First Left

One of several possible page types that you can specify in a page layout file. The First Left Page type defines how the first left page in a document section will look. For example, the first left page might be the first page that appears in each chapter of a book. See page types.

First Page

One of several possible page types you can specify in a page layout file. The First Page type defines the page flow for the first page in a document. The First Page type is typically used in page layouts not based on a left page and right page sequence, but instead where all pages are the same. The First Page type, in this layout, would typically be followed by normal pages. See page types.

First Right

One of several possible page types you can specify in a page layout file. The First Right Page type defines how every First Right page in a document section will look. For example, the first right page might be the first page that appears in each chapter of a book. See page types.

Footer Frame

In a page layout, the bottom-most frame element of a page layout you would use to arrange and flow text that appears at the bottom of every page. This frame is one of five frame types that users can use to create a page layout. See body frame, header frame, decoration frame, and image frame.

Footnote

A particular type of comment, generally associated with print-based outputs and is used to explain a specific area of text within a topic. When used, one or more footnotes are typically placed at the end of a page with an identifier number or symbol.

Footnote Styles

A category of CSS styles you can apply to footnotes. Several Footnote Styles are inherited in the stylesheet, and you can add new selectors.

Form Tag

A Flare block style used to create a form for user input in a topic. See Tag Group.

Frame-Break

A paragraph tag property that can be specified to affect when a frame break should occur for specific content, such as a paragraph or heading style. Selecting a frame break in a paragraph is considered local formatting and only affects that one instance. Like always, it is preferable and more effective to apply the frame break to a style.

Frame-Break-After

A paragraph tag property that can be specified to affect whether the frame break should occur after the paragraph and the content flow to the next frame. The options are a) Always - which causes a frame break to always occur after the element; b) Auto - which causes a frame break to neither be forced nor prevented after the paragraph; c) Avoid - which causes a frame break to not occur after the paragraph; and d) Inherit - which matches the frame break setting to that of the parent tag.

Frame-Break-Before

A paragraph tag property that can be specified to affect whether the frame break should occur before the paragraph and the content flow to the next frame. The options are a) Always - which causes a frame break to always occur before the paragraph; b) Auto - which causes a frame break to neither be forced nor prevented before the paragraph; c) Avoid - which causes a frame break to not occur before the paragraph; and d) Inherit - which matches the frame break setting to the parent tag.

Frame-Break-Inside

A paragraph tag property that can be specified to affect whether the frame break should occur inside the paragraph and the content flow to the next frame. The options are a) Auto - which causes a column break to neither be forced nor prevented inside the paragraph; and b) Avoid - which causes a frame break to not occur inside the paragraph and to flow content to the next frame.

Frame Anchors

Left, right, top, and bottom anchors allow a frame to be locked down to the page margins. If the page size changes, the frame is resized accordingly.

Frame Content Window

A Flare window pane used to add or edit text and other content in a page layout header, footer, or decoration frame. When a page is open in the Page Layout Editor, you can enable a selected frame for editing using the F2 key.

Frame Padding

A defined offset from the frame content to frame top, bottom, left, or right edge in a Page Layout file. This padding defines an offset from the frame edges to any text or images contained in the frame.

Frameless

An HTML5 output characteristic, whereby pages do not use <frameset> or <frame> tags, as with regular WebHelp outputs. In Flare, HTML5 Side and Top Navigation outputs are completely frameless, meaning they also do not contain iframes. The benefits of such designs are enhanced search engine optimization, better results with external searches and navigation, and improved scrolling and zooming in mobile devices.

FrameMaker Import Wizard

A Flare feature that uses a sequenced series of dialogs designed to guide users through importing Adobe FrameMaker files into a Flare project. The wizard allows the user to decide on topic breakpoints and other options.

FrameMaker Output

A Flare output type where the generated output is exported to FrameMaker in either .book, .fm, or .pdf format. You can create a PDF output directly without first developing the FrameMaker file.

Frames

See Page Layout Frames.

Front Matter Pages

In the context of creating page layout files, Front Matter Pages represent the pages that comprise the front section of a book or User document, like a User Guide, which might include page headings such as Preface, About the Author, About This Book, Acknowledgments, and Table of Contents. This section typically follows the Title/Cover Page and Copyright page and continues through to the beginning of the document or book.

FrontMatterResizable

A predefined Flare page layout template, designed to control the arrangement and flow of the front matter pages of a book or manual, and in which the specified 8.5 inches x 11 inches page size can be resized without having to resize the page frames. See Front Matter Pages; Anchor.

- G -

Generated Content Styles

A Flare category of CSS styles applied to Flare generated content, such as a generated TOC or generated glossary.

Generated TOC

A Flare generated table of contents based on the heading levels in your topics (h1 through h6). Topic level headings are still manually entered when with this method; however, Flare automatically creates TOC sub-entries for topic sub-headings. Users can enable the option on the Output section of the target's Advanced tab.

Generic Class

See Generic Style Class.

Generic Style Class

A style class that stands alone and is not associated with a specific HTML parent element but instead has a generic property—for example, "centered" or "right-justified." Users can apply a generic style to any style class, regardless of the parent. This feature eliminates creating several styles to achieve the same effect on styles with different HTML parents.

Git Source Control

See Source Control.

Global Project Linking

A Flare feature that allows content and project files contained in one project to be imported to another Flare project, thereby supporting project maintenance in one location but reuse in any other project. When importing, it is possible to include or exclude project content and resources as required.

Glossary

See Glossary File.

Glossary Editor

A Flare editor that allows glossary terms and definitions to be added to a glossary file (.flgo). A default glossary file is contained in the Project Organizer under the Glossary folder.

Glossary File

A Flare XML file to which users can add terms and definitions that can be used in online and print-based outputs, to aid users in understanding specific terms. Multiple authors can add to a glossary, which can be added to various targets or shared among projects. A glossary XML file has a .flglo extension stored in the Project Organizer under the Glossaries folder. You may create and use multiple glossary files in Flare.

Glossary Pages

In the context of page layout files, Glossary Pages are typically part of the Back Matter of some books, typically in technical books. Glossary page layouts may use single-column or double-column frames.

Glossary Proxy

A Flare proxy that users can employ to generate a glossary in your print-based output. The glossary proxy must be inserted into a topic and placed in the TOC where you want it to appear in the output. See Proxy.

Glossary Term

In a Flare Glossary, a word for which a definition is given.

Glossary Term Link

A word or phrase that links to a glossary term and can be inserted into your content - for example, topic or snippet.

GlossaryResizable

A Flare page layout template, designed to control the arrangement and flow of glossary pages of a book or manual, and in which the specified 8.5 inches x 11 inches page size can be resized without having to resize the page frames. See Glossary Pages; Anchor.

Group Synonyms

See Synonym Group.

- H -

Header File (.h file)

A text file containing essential information for connecting UI components like web pages, windows, panes, tabs, and dialogs to a specific Help topic in a Context-Sensitive Help System. The header file is generated from the information entered in the Alias Editor.

Header Frame

A page layout frame type you would use to arrange and flow text that appears at the top of every page where the frame is placed. This frame is one of five frame types you can use to create a page layout. See body frame, footer frame, decoration frame, and image frame.

Heading Styles

A Flare CSS style category that includes styles applied to the headings that are placed above other content — for example, to name a topic. Heading styles, for example, include H1, H2, and H3.

Heading Variables

A feature of Flare variables whereby the headings of your content can be automatically displayed in the headers of your page layouts. These variables are based on the mc-heading-level property that by default, is applied to the h1 through h6 heading styles of your project.

Hide Inherited

A Stylesheet Editor option that allows you to hide or not to display those styles that have been inherited in the stylesheet. See Inherited Styles.

HTML

An acronym for HyperText Markup Language.

HTML Element

Any one of several individual components that can make up an HTML page or document. Document components like Title, Headings, Body, Paragraphs, and Images. After the document root, each element is enclosed in an identifying Start and End Tag. For example, a paragraph has the start tage <p> and the end tag </p>.

HTML Element Attribute

A modifier that changes the default functionality of an HTML element, by providing additional information. Each attribute is generally declared in a name="value" pair that immediately follows the opening tag.

HTML Help Output

This HTML-based Help format runs on Windows 32-bit platforms and requires Internet Explorer on the end user system. This output type, which is used to create Help for Windows desktop applications, consists of a single .CHM file that is distributed to users.

HTML5 Output

In Flare, an output based on the latest evolution of the HTML standard. HTML5 has new elements, attributes, and behaviors and a more extensive set of technologies that support building more diverse and powerful Web sites and applications.

HTML5 Target

A Flare target file you would use to build and generate an HTML5 web-based output. Using the target file, you can specify various options, parameters, and variables that will affect the final content of the online output. See Target.

- I -

Identifier

In the CSH Alias file, a unique numerical value that you would assign to each of the context-sensitive-help topics as a topic ID.

Identifier Class

A unique style selector that you can only apply to a single element on an HTML page.

Image Frame

A page layout image frame you woulduse to arrange and place an image in a page layout. One of five frame types you can use to create a page layout. See body frame, footer frame, header frame, and decoration frame.

Image Hyperlink

A hyperlink applied to a picture or image as opposed to text, although it can behave similarly. After you insert an image, you can make it a hyperlink that can connect to another topic, an external file, or an email when clicked.

Image Padding

An Image Border and Margins property that allows a padded distance to be specified at the image top, bottom, left, or right.

Image Styles

A category of CSS styles applied to project images.

Import File

A file in which Flare saves the settings you specify when you import source content using a wizard. The Flare import file (filename.flimp), can be reused to reimport content as many times as needed while adjusting the import settings.

Import Styles Editor

A Flare feature that opens a style editor during an import process to allow you to change a style format during the import process.

Index Pages

In page layout files, Index Pages are typically part of the Back Matter of some books. These pages list keywords and the pages on which users can find each keyword in the body of the book.

Index Proxy

A Flare placeholder element that generates an index in your output. An index proxy topic is created by creating a topic specifically for inserting the index proxy. When you build the target, the index is generated in the target output, where you inserted the proxy topic in the TOC. See Proxy.

Index Sets

A Flare file that contains words identified as index keywords. Flare uses the keywords from this file when auto-generating an index in the print output.

IndexResizable

A Flare page layout template file, designed to control the arrangement and flow of index pages of a book or manual, and in which the specified 8.5 inches x 11 inches page size can be resized without having to resize the page frames. Also see Index Pages; Anchor.

Inherited Styles

Inheritance refers to styles or properties inherited in the stylesheet from elsewhere. Your stylesheet, for example, can inherit styles from stylesheets that were in the Flare application folder when you installed Flare. Inheritance also happens when one style is nested within another. In such cases, set properties are inherited from the parent or outer style until new values override them. Finally, styles and properties in your Print Medium inherit styles from the Default Medium. See Hide Inherited.

Inline Formatting or Inline Style

See Local Formatting.

Inside-Head

A property of the auto-number style, whereby the auto-number format is placed before the paragraph content and inside the content area. Text wrapped to the following line aligns under the auto-number format. See outside-head.

Internal Text Editor

A Flare editor in which you can view and modify the actual code for topics and files. Most files in your project can be opened and changed in the Internal Text Editor by right-clicking the file and selecting Open with > Internal Text Editor.

- L -

Layering

See Content Layering.

Layout Mode

Flare XML Editor rendering modes that support viewing the current topic based on the selected layout mode. See Web Layout, Web Layout (Tablet), Web Layout (Mobile), and Print Layout.

Left Page

A page type used in defining a page layout file. Using a Left Page type, you can arrange layout frames to define the layout for how every left-hand page in a document section will look. For example, the left page might have a header and footer that only appears on every left-hand page. See page layout page types.

Line Height

A paragraph property that defines the distance between the lines of a paragraph. A general rule, for example, is to set the line height to 2 points greater than the font size — a font size of 10 points might specify a line height of 12 points.

Link Styles

A CSS category of styles applied to content that represents links, like cross-reference or related topics links.

Links

An element that points and navigates to additional information from a specific area in the content. The link can locate and open information within the same topic, a different topic, or even a file outside of the project. Links may be used in print-based and online outputs.

List-Of Proxy

You can use this placeholder element to generate a list of any auto-numbered content from your projects, such as a list of tables or images. See Proxy.

List Styles

A Flare CSS style category that creates a formatted list, such as an ordered list as in a sequence of steps in a task, or an unordered bullet list.

Local Formatting

Formatting of content using the Flare toolbar formatting controls instead of applying a style from the stylesheet.

Local Repository

A local copy of the source control content that is generally a working copy of your Flare project. See Remote Repository.

Local Stylesheet

A stylesheet that has been applied directly (or locally), for example, at the topic level or target file

level, instead of the project level. A local stylesheet used at the topic level has precedence over a primary stylesheet applied at the target or project level. See Primary Stylesheet.

Locked Element

A project feature in which you can lock down areas within topics, such as paragraphs, to prevent editing. When content areas in a file have been locked, Flare grays the background of that area. You can switch off this feature. See Unlock Element.

- M -

MadCap Central

A cloud-based platform that supports planning, tracking, managing processes, content, and teams involved in developing, authoring, managing, and publishing an organization's content. Using Central integrated with Flare, you can manage storage/retrieval of projects to and from Central and locally in Flare.

MadCap Flare

A content authoring and single source publishing tool. Flare supports import from multiple source editors, like Word, HTML, FrameMaker, and Robohelp. The tool also supports print-based and web-based publishing options such as PDF, EPUB, HTML5, and other Web outputs suited to large screens, mobile devices, tablets, and smartphones.

MadCap Mimic

A MadCap movie-making and editing tool that can be tightly integrated with Flare. The tool can be used to insert movie links into topics, TOCs, and browse sequences.

Mapping Styles

See Style Mapping.

Margin Bottom

In a page layout, this is the specified distance, in a selected unit of measure, from the bottom of the body content to the bottom edge of the page — for example, 1 inch.

Margin Left

In a page layout, this is the specified distance, in a selected unit of measure, from the left edge of the body content to the left edge of the page — for example, 1 inch.

Margin Right

In a page layout, this is the specified distance, in a selected unit of measure, from the right edge of the body content to the right edge of the page — for example, 1 inch.

Margin Top

In a page layout, this is the specified distance, in a selected unit of measure, from the top of the body content to the top edge of the page — for example, 1 inch from the page-top edge.

MC-Heading-Level

A MadCap style property that, by default, is applied to the h1 through h6 heading styles that you use in your project. Setting the mc-heading-level to "0" causes a heading to not appear in the TOC. This parameter is a way of limiting the number of levels shown in the generated TOC.

Media Query

An alternative group of settings within a stylesheet that is automatically applied under certain conditions, like when the output is displayed on a given screen size or device type. As queries are defined with specific criteria, such as maximum screen width, screen orientation, or resolution, the appropriate media query is applied to the output when the specified criteria are met. By default, Flare provides a Tablet Media Query for devices like tablets; and a Mobile Media Query for use with smaller screens, like smartphones.

Medium

A group of style settings in a given stylesheet. A stylesheet can contain multiple mediums, each generally intended for a specific type of output. For example, one medium could be for online outputs and another for print-based outputs. Flare, by default, provides the Default Medium, intended for online outputs, and the Print Medium, intended for print-based outputs. You can create as many mediums as required to serve different purposes. The Default Medium is used for all outputs unless otherwise specified.

Menu Proxy

A Flare placeholder that you can use to create a menu based on a TOC file and allows users to navigate to other topics. The menu proxy is especially useful in an HTML5 Top Navigation or skinless output where you want a context-sensitive menu to display next to each topic. When the output is generated, Flare replaces the proxy with the generated menu. See Proxy.

Micro Content

A collection of brief phrases and associated responses, for example, questions and answers. These phrase/response combinations can be used in some of the different ways users interact with your output. Microcontent can also be used to create field-level context-sensitive Help, like tool-tips.

Mimic

See MadCap Mimic.

Mini TOC

A Flare element (Mini-TOC Proxy) that allows you to insert a portion of your table of contents (TOC) or topic headings at a particular location in the output. You can create mini-TOCs for both online and print-based outputs. You can insert a Mini-TOC proxy at the desired location in a template page or a topic for online outputs. For print-based output formats, you can insert a Mini-TOC proxy in any topic where you want a small TOC. For example, you might use a mini-TOC proxy to list the H1-level headings on the chapter page of each chapter.

Movie Link

A link to a movie created using a tool like MadCap Mimic or by inserting a Flash, Windows Media, or Quicktime movie file.

Multi-Definition Variable

A Flare variable with several defined values. Of the multiple definitions, only a single value can be specified for the variable at the target before the build.

Multimedia Content

Content files like video, audio, and 3D models, which can be inserted into topics or snippets.

- N -

Navigation Links

See Links.

New Topic Styles

During the Flare import process, this parameter lets you tell Flare, the styles it should use when breaking the source content into topics. For example, if New Topic Styles include BookTitle, ChapterTitle, Heading1 and Heading2, then as Flare reads the source files it creates a new topic each time one of these styles is encountered.

Normal Page

A page type that is used as part of a page layout file, to define a page flow in which the content flow is not based on a left-page/right-page sequence, but instead the flow is the same for all pages.

NormalResizable

A predefined 8.5 in x 11 in page layout template, designed to control the arrangement and flow of normal pages of a document. The page size can be resized without having to resize the page frames. See Normal Pages.

- O -

Online Help

The presentation of various forms of useful information to a user audience, via online methods, such as "Standalone Help" or "Context-Sensitive (CSH) Help. Online help is generally created using a help authoring tool. Most online help is designed to give assistance in the use of a software application, but can also be used to present information on a broad range of subjects as with a Knowledge base. When online help is interfaced to specific elements in an application, it is called Context-Sensitive Help.

Online Output

Represents Flare content output types that are generally intended for on-screen viewing. For example, HTML5, EPUB, Clean XHTML, and Eclipse Help.

Online Targets

Represents any one of several possible Flare output target types that are intended for on-screen viewing. For example, laptop, tablet, phone, or other device with an electronic display. A project may have multiple Online targets. See Output Types; Online Output; Print Targets.

Output File

The file, "Output File," associated with a built target in a project. Flare places the output file in the Output Folder where the project is located. The file-name given to the output, unless otherwise specified, is a default name for the main entry file to the output. A file name for the output can be specified directly or using a variable name, which is specified on the target settings on the General tab.

Output Folder

The folder designated on the General tab of the target file, as the location for saving a built target in a project. Flare places the output files in the main project folder, in the default Output subfolder, unless an alternate folder is otherwise specified.

Output Type

Any one of the several possible Flare print-based outputs, such as PDF, or WORD; or online outputs, such as HTML5, or XHTML. See HTML5, Clean XHTML, WebHelp, and EPUB.

Outside-Head

An autonumber property, whereby the autonumber format is placed before the paragraph content, but outside of the content area. Text wrapped to the next line aligns under the previous text and not under the autonumber. See inside-head.

- P -

Padding

A property that can be applied to certain elements, like images, text boxes, QR codes, page layout frames, or equations to affect the spacing around the element edge, thereby providing a free-space between the element edge and the nearest adjacent element edge. Edges, for example, can be the margin edge, content edge, border edge, or image edge. Padding, where applicable, can be added to the top, bottom, left, and right of an element.

Page-Break

A paragraph style property that can be specified to affect when a page break should occur with respect to specific content—for example, with respect to a paragraph or heading style. Specifying a page break break in a paragraph is considered local formatting and only affects that one instance. Where possible, it is preferable to apply the page break to a style.

Page-Break-After

A paragraph tag property that can be specified to affect whether the page break should occur after the paragraph and the content should flow to the next page. The options are a) always - which causes a page break to always occur after the paragraph; b) auto - which causes a page break to not be forced nor prevented after the paragraph; c) avoid - which causes a page break to not occur after the paragraph; and d) inherit - which causes the page break setting to match that of the parent tag.

Page-Break-Before

A paragraph tag property that can be specified to affect whether the page break should occur before the paragraph and the content to flow to the next page. The options are a) always - which causes a page break to always occur before the paragraph; b) auto - which causes a page break to not be forced nor prevented before the paragraph; c) avoid - which causes a page break to not occur before the paragraph; and d) inherit - which matches the page break setting of the parent tag.

Page-Break-Inside

A paragraph tag property that is specified to affect whether the page break should occur inside the paragraph and the content to flow to the next page. The options are a) auto - which causes a page break to neither be forced nor prevented inside the paragraph; and b) avoid - which causes a page break to not occur inside the paragraph and to flow content to the next page.

Page Layout

A file created in the Page Layout Editor to define specifications like page size, margins, registration marks, bleeds, and crop marks. The page layout also defines frame elements to control flow of content onto the page, based on the defined page type, and use of header, body, footer, and decoration frames. Page layouts are generally applied to print-based outputs.

Page Layout Break

One of three "Break Type" options you can specify when defining the properties of TOC file entries, to affect the usage of page layouts in your Printed Output. The Page Layout option lets you change the page layout starting at a specific TOC entry or breakpoint, but without creating a new chapter. You might use this option, for example, to switchover in mid-chapter, to use a layout that has a different page size or page orientation. See Break Type; Chapter Break; None Break.

Page Layout Editor

A Flare editor used to define page layouts, including individual pages and the frames within each. Page layouts are created to define how content is arranged and flows onto the pages of each of the sections of a document. See Page Layout.

Page Layout File

A Flare file that you can create book or document page layouts that define the arrangement and flow of text and image content onto the pages of the document. You can create multiple page layout files to accommodate the different parts of a book or document. See Page Layout.

Page Layout Frame

A page layout container-like element, used to arrange and flow the different types of content that appears on a page – for example header content, footer content and body content. A page can con-tain multiple frames. See body frame, header frame, footer frame, decorative frame, and image frame.

Page Margins

In the Page Layout Editor, when defining the layout for a page, the settings that define the margins for a page, which determine the amount of space to the left, right, top, and bottom of the body content.

Page Size

In the page layout editor, this property defines length and width dimensions of the page layout being specified. Although pages within a layout file are generally the same size, different sizes may be specified for the individual pages of a page layout. International standard sizes A3, A4, or A5 may also be selected or a custom dimension.

Page Types

In Flare, page type that can be defined in a page layout file. Page types include Title, Normal, First, Left, Right, First Left, First Right, Empty, Empty Left, and Empty Right. Page types represent one of the two main components of the Page Layout File, which allow you to control how content is arranged and flowed onto the pages of your document.

Paragraph Styles

A CSS style category of styles that are applied to an entire paragraph—for example, "p.body".

Parent Style

CSS primary styles that correspond to the HTML elements—for example, h1, h2, p, or img. These parent styles can have children that when created, inherit the basic properties of the parent. Whereas it is possible to create new child classes of a given parent style, you cannot create new parent styles.

Pattern

1) In table stylesheets, a property that allows alternating rows in which a specified number of rows with no background color is followed by some number of rows with a background color. A pattern may also be specified for columns. 2) With Flare image, text box, and QR code elements, You can add background settings which includes the ability to specify a color, or another image in the case of an image, and specify a repeating pattern for the background image.

PDF Target

A Flare target file created for use in building and generating a PDF output. Using the target file, you can specify a variety of options, parameters, and variables that will affect the building and final content of the PDF output. See Target.

Pending Changes

Source files listed in the Source Control Explorer, which have been added, modified or deleted in a project. From the explorer window, these files can be Committed, Reverted, Pushed to or Synchronized with the remote repository.

Perforce Source Control

See Source Control.

Precedence

In Flare, a characteristic that assigns a higher priority or preference to one condition or specification over another. For example, 1) As a general rule, a stylesheet assigned at the topic level has precedence over a primary stylesheet specified at the project level or at the target level; and 2) If a style color change is made to a style that also has a color gradient, the gradient has precedence over the solid color.

Preview Window Pane

A Flare XML Editor feature that allows a quick preview of how a topic, a snippet, or a template page will look in the final output, based on the setting of HTML5 or PDF. A similar preview feature is available in the Flare Skin Editor.

Primary Page Layout

A page layout file that is specified at the project level or target level, to be applied to all topics in the project or target, that does not have an associated page layout file. See Page Layout File.

Primary Stylesheet

A stylesheet file that is specified at the project level or target level, to be applied to all topics in the project or target where it is specified. A primary stylesheet can be used in conjunction with local stylesheets, although the local stylesheet has precedence. See Local Stylesheet.

Primary Target

Of the many targets you can have in a project, you can designate the one you work with most often as the primary target. From the Project ribbon menu, buttons are available to Build, View, or Publish the primary target.

Primary TOC

Whereas most Flare targets have a single associated TOC that is specified at the target level—for example Online TOC and Print TOC. In those cases where multiple TOCs are used in a project and can be linked or stitched together, one TOC can be designated as the Primary TOC. The Primary TOC is specified on the General tab of the Target file.

Print Layout

A Flare topic editor layout mode that when selected, renders topic pages as they will look with a page layout applied to it in a print-based output. This layout mode lets you view the actual page size and orientation, as well as the margins and any header or footer content. The print layout mode is generally tied to the print medium.

Print Medium

In Flare, a CSS stylesheet medium created to be associated specifically with a print target — for example, a PDF target. The Print Medium, like all mediums other than the Default Medium, are added to the project from the Stylesheet Editor using the Add New Medium" command, and are initially a replica of the Default Medium.

Print Output

Represents Flare content output types that are generally intended for printer output. For example, PDF, and WORD.

Print Targets

Represents any one of several possible instances of a Flare output type intended for print-based output. For example, PDF, WORD, FrameMaker. A project may have multiple print targets. See Output Types; Online Targets.

PrintOnly

One of two condition tags defined by default in the Flare Condition Tag Set Editor — the other is ScreenOnly. Content to which the PrintOnly tag is applied, can be excluded or included in the target build. See Condition Tag; ScreenOnly.

Project Folders

The folders that are automatically generated in the Project Organizer whenever you create a project. Additional folders may be added as deemed necessary. See Project Organizer.

Project Organizer

A Flare Explorer-like UI component that contains a set of folders that organize the various resource files that are associated with the entire project, and that assis in the production, control, management and maintenance of both online or print outputs. The Project Organizer includes items such as TOCs, Variable Sets, Output Targets, Reports, Conditional Text, and many other files.

Project Template

A template project that is based on a previously created project. The template project has a few elements that will be present in any new project created using the template. A project template might already contain, for instance, some standard topics, snippets, table stylesheets, variable sets, regular stylesheet, and predefined targets.

Property

A characteristic of an HTML element. Each element has many properties that allow it to be styled in a CSS rule. Text properties, for example, include font-family, font-size, font-variant, and weight.

Property Group

In the Advanced View of the Stylesheet Editor, for convenience during the assignment of property values, this is the logical grouping of the properties associated with a particular style.

Property Value

The exact setting defined for a property. Each property has valid values from which you may specify a value. The text properties, for example, font-family, font-size, font-variant, and font-weight, might have the values Segoe Condensed, 14 pts, small-caps, and bold respectively.

Proxy

A placeholder element for outputting auto-generated content or content that you have created elsewhere in a project. When the output containing a proxy is built, actual content is inserted in place of the proxy. Proxies may be added to topics and to template pages. A proxy added to a topic displays the associated content in the output only once, wherever the topic occurs; a proxy in a template page, displays the content in each topic to which the template page has been applied. See Breadcrumbs Proxy; Glossary Proxy; Index Proxy; List-Of-Proxy; Menu Proxy; Search Bar Proxy; TOC Proxy.

Pseudo Class

A special group of CSS style classes that specify how elements behave when they are in a specific state — for example, a font or link turns blue when it is clicked or turns purple when it is hovered over. In CSS, the pseudo-class takes the form of selector:pseudo_class { property: value; }, with a colon in between the selector name and pseudo name.

Pseudo Element

Whereas a pseudo class focuses on the state of an element, a pseudo element focuses on a specific part of an element — for example, the first letter, first line, or first bullet item of an element.

Publish Target

Once a target output has been built, it can then be published. To publish a target is to push the output files of the target to a predefined destination or location that can be accessed by others. Outputs, for example, may be published to a network, a website, or a remote server. Publishing can be accomplished manually, by copying the output files from the project folder to a desired location; or using FTP software to transfer to a remote server.

Publishing Destination

In Flare, a predefined location that designates where the output files of a project are placed for public access. You can manually copy the output files to the destination or you can specify one of several options that tells Flare where to automatically push your output files to, so they can be accessed by others. A destination, for example, may be a network drive, a website, or a remote server.

Pull

To retrieve your source controlled project from the remote repository and bring it to the local repository. See Push.

Push

To send the committed changes in your local repository to the remote repository of your source control application. See Pull.

- Q -

Quick Launch Bar

A Flare tool pane on the main menu ribbon, used to search for any Flare file or execute command (always located in upper-right corner of the interface). CTRL+Q places focus on the Quick Launch bar so you can begin typing. To search using the Quick Launch bar, type a few letters of a file name or command you want. Available results will appear in a drop-down list.

- R -

Reference Topics

Topics that provide detailed reference material on a subject. See Concept Topics; Task Topics.

Regular Stylesheet

The Flare stylesheet element (CSS), which is used to define and store styles for determining the look of the general content in a project.

Related Topic Link

In a given topic, links that you can insert to give users access to other topics that you have determined are related to the current topic. Related topic links are similar to concept topic links, but this feature is generally used when the linked topics are specifically related to the current topic and are not likely be accessed from other topics.

Related Topics

Refers to any topic you identify as related to a particular topic and of possible interest to the user — a topic that may offer additional information or insight. You may place, a link to one or more related topics in any topic you choose. Related topics, while similar to concept topics, are independent topics and whose links, if no longer needed must be removed from wherever they were inserted.

Relationship Table

An element that is similar to concept links and related topics links, and is used to link related topics together. Whereas a relationship table is a common DITA feature, use of DITA is not required in to use relationship tables in Flare.

Remote Repository

The remote copy of the source control content that is stored in a remote location, and to which users will push their local working copies of the project — typically a remote server. See Local Repository.

Repository

Refers to the logical container that holds the files of your Flare project. References can be made to the "remote repository," which resides on the source control server; or to the "local repository," which has been"pulled down" to your local or working directory. See Push; Pull.

Resizable Frames

A characteristic of page layout frames that are contained in "resizable pagelayout templates," and in which the frames are anchored to the page edges. Anchored frames maintain the same distance from the edges of the page, even if the page is resized. See Anchor.

Resources Folder

A subfolder of the Content Explorer, which generally contains non-topic files that are resources used by topic files. The folder, by default, contains subfolders forTemplatePages, PageLayouts, Stylesheets, and Tablestyles. Other resource folders, such as an Images folder can be added.

Responsive Design

Formally referred to as responsive web design (RWD), an approach to web design that makes web pages render well on a variety of devices and window or screen sizes. This method uses styles and media queries, to create a layout in which both the structure and content of the online output is able to automatically adjust based on the size of the screen.

Responsive Layout

A layout technique used in Flare to achieve responsive designs that automatically adjust and adapt to any device screen size. The Flare Responsive Layout window allows users to easily create responsive layouts.

Reusable Content Styles

A Flare CSS style category that includes styles that are applied to reusable project content like snippets, variables, page headers and page footers. Several Reusable Content Styles are inherited in Flare, and new selectors may be added.

Revert

Generally refers to a source control command option that allows you to discard modifications to source files that you do not wish to save or commit to source control, and to return it to its previously committed state. See Commit.

Right Page

A page type used in defining a page layout file. Using a Right page type, you can arrange layout frames to define the layout for how every right-hand page in a document section will look — for example, the right page might define a header and footer that only appears on the right-hand page. See page types.

Row Rule

A table stylesheet row property in which, line type, color and width can be set for the horizontal line (rule) between table rows of a pattern entry with a repeat of two or more rows.

Row Separator

A table stylesheet row property in which, line type, color, and width can be set for the row separator line between the final row in a row pattern and the first row in the next pattern.

Rule

See Column Rule; Row Rule.

Running Head Variables

A set of Flare variables that can be inserted into headers and footers in page layouts or template pages in order to display appropriate headings that are based on the mc-heading-level style property, which by default is applied to the h1 through h6 heading styles from your project. Running Head variables are useful when creating print-based output and it is desirable to place chapter or heading titles on each page.

- S -

ScreenOnly

One of two condition tags that have been pre-defined by default in the Flare Condition Tag Set Editor — the other is PrintOnly. Content to which the ScreenOnly tag has been applied, can be excluded or included in the target build. See Condition Tag; PrintOnly.

Search Bar Proxy

A Flare proxy that you can insert into the content to create a field that allows searches in the output. When the output is built, the proxy generates a search bar. See Proxy.

Search Filter File

A Flare element used to add search filter sets that lets users narrow their search based on concepts that you have inserted into topics.

Search Results Proxy

A Flare proxy that you can insert into the content to create a field in which the results returned from an end user search is displayed in the output. When the output is built, the proxy is replaced with the generated results. The Search Results proxy works with the Search Bar proxy. See Proxy.

Search Synonym File

A Flare file that supports the entry of specific words or phrases that can enhance the search results for searches that may otherwise not produce any results.

Selector

In CSS, a selector is defined and used to target specific HTML elements that you want to style. Often when we refer to a style in Flare, we are in fact referring to a selector. An example is H1.Heading1. In its simplest form, a selector is a basic style, however it can be used in a much more complex and targeted way to affect the styling or behavior of very specific parts of your content. See Advanced Selector.

Send to Folder

A useful Flare command, accessed using the right-click when focused on a folder, supports the copying of files from one folder to another, in the same or in different projects.

Separator

See Column Separator; Row Separator.

Side Navigation Output

A type of HTML5 output that places the navigation element for menu operations, either to the left or right of the topic view window. Similar to the top navigation design, the side navigation is a frameless output and does not contain iframes. The side-navigation is similiar to the traditional Tripane format.

Simplified View

A CSS stylesheet editor view in which styles are presented in a spreadsheet-like view in which a minimum set of style properties may be modified directly in a field, using the editor toolbar, or using a simple dialog opened by double-clicking on the style. See Advanced View.

Single-Definition Variable

A Flare variable that has only a single defined value. A single-definition variable named ReleaseDate, for example, would define a single date value as the release date.

Skin

A file that stores information that supports the behavior and appearance of an online output window. Appearance items for example, include size, position, menu and UI navigation controls, text appearance and user interface text; behavior elements include items such as buttons, search panes, and TOCs. See Skin Editor.

Skin Components

Smaller components of a skin, which work in conjunction with related Flare proxies to allow insertion of menus and toolbars into topic content.

Skin Editor

The Flare editor that displays when a skin file is opened from the Project Organizer, and is used to develop a skin for one or more online targets. The Skin Editor presents a user-friendly interface that consists of several tabs, each of which only displays

the settings relevant to the selected skin type and skin component. See Skins.

Snippet

A snippet, just as it sounds, is a small segment of content — as little as a phrase, a sentence, a single paragraph or even more. A snippet, much like a variable, can be inserted any number of times and places within the same or different topics. Content suitable for a snippet is generally the same in most places, but may be slightly different in some places. See block snippets; text snippets.

Snippet Condition

A snippet condition is a normal condition tag, created in the Condition Tag Editor, but is designed to be applied specifically to a part of a snippet, to determine whether that part of the snippet should be included or excluded in the output.

Snippet Variable

A snippet variable is a normal variable created in the Variables Editor but can also be modified at the snippet-level, where the snippet is inserted in a topic; or at the topic-level, in the Topic Properties. To modify the variable at the snippet-level means that the snippet is customized at each place the snippet is inserted in a topic or throughout the project; to modify the variable at the topic level, means that the variable snippet content, regardless of the number of times it is used in the topic will be identical in each place that it is used.

Source Control

A process in which a copy of the project is stored on a server that supports file "check-in" and "check out," and the synchronization between a server version of a project and local changes made by different writers. Source control provides a means for maintaining a constant backup of all project files. Flare supports several source control applications that integrate with the Flare application.

Source Control Explorer

A Flare tool in which source files that have been added, modified or deleted (Pending Changes), are listed and can be managed — for example, you can Commit, Revert, Push or Pull between the local and remote repositories.

Source Files

In the context of the Flare Import process, these are the files that contain your content and are imported from some external source editor, for example Microsoft Word or Adobe Framemaker. Also see Source Control.

Span

An HTML parent style that is used to affect the appearance of character-level content — for example, a single word or single sentence in a paragraph, as opposed to the entire paragraph.

Span Bars

In the Flare XML Editor window, the graphical bars that display just above the horizontal ruler at the page top. Span bars indicate character-level formatting within a paragraph by displaying as transparent boxes when the cursor is in the paragraph, and as shaded boxes when the cursor rests on the character-level formatting.

Span Styles

A Flare CSS style category that includes styles that can only be applied to a selected part of a paragraph as opposed to the entire paragraph — for example, "span.italics" or "span.bold".

Standalone Help

Often refers to an HTML help system that consists of a collection of folders (books) and files (topics or pages), and is accessed from a TOC or outline consisting of topic links. Contrasted to Context-Sensitive Help (CSH). See Context-Sensitive Help.

Structure Bars

An XML Editor element in the form of bars that display just above the horizontal ruler at the page top and to the left of the content area just outside the page edge. The bars provide a visual display of the topic style tags and structure, and information about the content without having to view the associated style tags within the text. There are two types of structure bar: tag bars (to page left) and span bars (across page top). Structure bars can be toggled on/off. See Tag Bar; Span Bar.

Style

A CSS element having specific attributes that affect the look and/or behavior of content to which it is applied. You can create your own styles, however, several styles will be inherited and already exist in stylesheets you create in your project. See Inherited Styles; Style Properties; Style Values.

Style Class

See Class.

Style Condition

In Flare, a condition tag that is set on a style. When that style is applied to any content, then the condition is applied to the content. An alternate method — and perhaps a more efficient way of applying conditions to content.

Style Identifier

Similar to a class, except that an ID is unique. An element in your stylesheet can have only one ID, whereas it can have multiple style classes. A limitation is that each page of your outputs can have only one element with a specific ID.

Style Mapping

A Flare import process step, whereby formatting styles that are contained in the source content (for example MS Word or FrameMaker) are each assigned (mapped) to a corresponding style that will exist in the CSS file after the import.

Style Property

The specific parameters or attributes of a particular style, which affect the look and behavior of the style, or more specifically the content to which it is applied. For example, properties of a paragraph style include Font, Font Size, Color, and Line Height. See Style; Style Values.

Style Window

The Flare Home toolbar window, from which styles are selected and applied to selected content.

Stylesheet

See Cascading Stylesheet.

Stylesheet Editor

The editor that displays when a stylesheet file is opened from the Content Explorer, and is used to modify styles contained in regular stylesheets.

Stylesheet Medium

See Medium.

Synchronize

A Flare source control command option that performs a pull to update the local database, with committed files from the remote repository, and then pushes any local commits to the remote repository. After issuing the synchronize command, the files of the local repository and the remote repository are in synch (the same).

Synchronized External Resources

A process whereby external resource files, after they have been mapped to Flare project files, can be synchronized to ensure that each file contains the same content. This process makes it possible to import content from the external files, export content from mapped files, in the project, or keep the most recently modified files.

Synonym

Terms that that have the same or very similar meaning — particularly in the context of search criteria. For example, the term "hat," may have as synonyms, fedora, sombrero, cap, and panama. In Flare, keywords can be entered into a synonym file to enhance a user's search result. See Synonym File.

Synonym File

A Flare file type that is created using the Synonym Editor and added to a project to enhance user search results. A synonym file contains a list of user defined synonyms or words that have the same or similar meaning. The synonyms feature supports use of single words only — use of phrases is not supported. See Synonyms; Synonym Group; Directional Synonym.

Synonym Group

A collection of words, any of which returns the same search results. This method is useful if you have several terms in your project that are similar and you want the same search results to be returned when users enter any of those terms. In the Synonyms Editor, a group of synonyms is entered with an equal sign between each term — for example, (bird=robin=sparrow=canary). A search on any of the terms, will result in a list of all topics in which any of those words are found.

System Variables

A Flare built-in variable set that includes: a) Chapter/Section/Volume Numbers, which supports the insertion and display of the associated variable in page layout header or footer frames in some outputs; b) Date/Time variables, which support insertion and display of various formats of date and time in variables; and c) Linked Title/Header/File system variables, which can be used in tables of contents (TOC) and browse sequences that are tied to information in linked topics. These variables ensure that TOC or browse sequence entries are always in sync with topic titles, headers, or file names.

- T -

Table Bar

In the XML Editor, the graphical bars that display just above the horizontal ruler at the page top, and above span bars if structure bars are enabled. The table bar is positioned just above one or more column bars. The entire table is selected when the table bar is selected. When the cursor is inside a column, the associated column bar is highlighted. Span bars, which also highlight table columns, can be used to drag and reposition columns.

Table Margins

In the TableStyles editor, these are property settings that define fixed distances between the table top, bottom, left, and right borders and any frame or other container edge or any text.

Table Styles

A Flare CSS style category that like other styles in your stylesheet, are discrete styles for affecting the appearance of the table components. Style tags, for example, for the table caption, header, rows, columns, and footer rows. Each of these CSS parent table styles, are inherited in your stylesheet, and as such, you can define child classes under each of these to suit your specific requirements for styling the individual table components.

Table Stylesheet

A Flare stylesheet type used specifically for controlling the look of tables to which the stylesheet is applied. A table stylesheet can be applied to multiple tables throughout a target output to ensure all tables have the same appearance.

Table Stylesheet Editor

A Flare editor used to define a set of styles that collectively control the appearance of tables and can be applied to new or existing tables.

Tag

In HTML, a tag is used to create an element. The name of the HTML element is the name used in angle brackets such as <p> for paragraph. Note that the end tag name is preceded by a slash character, </p>, and that in empty elements, the end tag is neither required nor is it syntactically valid.

Tag Bars

In the XML Editor, the graphical bars that display just left of the page edge, and that indicate the different tags and HTML structure for each block of content. When paragraphs are in view, tag bars are shown as transparent; when the cursor is in a paragraph, the tag bar is shaded. The bars are shown in an hierarchy from left to right starting with the the <html> root being the highest. A left-click on a shaded tag bar allows the content to be selected and dragged to a new position.

Tag Group

Any one of the four tag group types used, in Flare, to group selected content items in the XML Editor. The tag group types, which include the blockquote tag, div tag, fieldset tag, and form tag, each is used, for a different purpose, to create block-level content in a unique HTML "container". See Blockquote Tag; Div Tag; Fieldset Tag; and Form Tag.

Target Build

The process of compiling a target to produce a desired output — for example, a PDF. The target build and subsequent output, is based on the collection of project items that you speciy directly or indirectly by completing the target dialogs.

Target Editor

A graphical user interface, consisting of several tabs for manually specifying the various parameters associated with a particular target output type.

Target File

A Flare file type that contains the parameters you specify for building and generating a particular output — for example a PDF print output or an HTML5 online output. Using target files, you can produce any of several possible output types. A target file has the extension of .fltar. See Output.

Target Folder

See Output Folder.

Task Topics

Topics that provide step-by-step procedures for accomplishing a specific task. See Reference Topics; Concept Topics.

Template

A template is an existing file or element that can be used to create the same type of file or element. A template can be created for any Flare file type — for example, a project, topic, snippet, page layout file, or target file. Templates are stored in a template folder that you have previously created.

Template Page

A Flare element that is used to apply certain content to multiple topics — for example, in online outputs, the template page might contain breadcrumbs, menus, toolbars, search bars, mini-TOCs, or footer text. Although the template page is generally used in online outputs, it can also be used in print outpus such as for Word outputs.

Template Topics

Topics that you have created for a book or document, which can also be used in other documents. For this additional use, a template topic is not copied or created again, but simply referenced in a TOC where it is to be used.

Text Editor

In Flare, the Text Editor renders the HTML code view of the currently opened topic. See XML Editor; Internal Text Editor.

Text Hyperlink

A hyperlink that is applied to text. A basic form of navigation link that is created and inserted to open additional information at a destination that is internal or external to a topic. Hyperlinks are generally link to external destinations whereas cross-references generally link to internal destinations.

Text Popup

A Flare content display feature, whereby a short block of content, for example a definition, is presented in a small popup box when the associated text popup link is clicked in the online output.

Text Popup Link

A text hyperlink that online users click to open a popup box with a small block of text information.

Text Snippet

A text snippet that can be inserted on a line with other content, and is placed either before or after the existing content. A key difference between the block and text snippets, is that the text snippet can be placed on a line with other content. See Snippet; Block Snippet.

Title Page

One of several page types that can be specified in a page layout file. The Title Page type is used to define how a cover page or the first page in a document will look. See page types.

TOC Book

In the TOC topic hierarchy, represented by books and pages, a topic container. A book can contain subordinate books and pages (topics). Books generally represent a container that holds topics, although a topic can also be assigned to a book. When manually creating a TOC in Flare, books and topics can be inserted.

TOC Editor

The Flare editor used to manually create tables of contents (TOC). The TOC can be manually created in any desired structure by adding links to topics, movies, external files, other TOCs, browse sequences, or other entries.

TOC File

The TOC file in Flare is created manually or generated automatically based on the chapter and topic structure of an imported book or document. This structure is based on the chapters and topic files of each chapter, whereby the indent levels are based on their associated headings (for example, H1, H2, H3, and H4). In the Flare TOC, imported chapters become TOC books and converted topics are TOC pages. The TOC file, ultimately serves as the outline from which the sequential order of your print target is created; or the arrangement of books and pages of the tree structure in an online output with a side- or tripane-navigation.

TOC Page

A Flare TOC entry that represents a topic (and topic link).

TOC Proxy

A Flare placeholder for generating a TOC in the output. The TOC proxy is inserted into the topic, specifically for the purpose of generating a TOC. The topic with the TOC proxy is placed in the TOC outline at the point at which you wish the TOC to appear in the output. See Proxy.

TOC Styles

Flare Generated Content styles (TOC1, TOC2, TOC3, TOC4, and through TOC9) that are inherited in your stylesheet. You can modify these styles to determine the appearance of the Table of Contents (TOC) levels in your output.

Toggler Link

A link feature that lets you "toggle" between hiding and showing a tagged chunk of content—for example, a paragraph, image, table, or list. When a topic with the link is opened in the output, users can click on the toggler link or "toggler hotspot," to reveal hidden content. The toggler link can be any text in the topic. Also called toggler hotspot.

Toggler Target

A chunk of content that resides anywhere in the topic, and that is revealed when users click the associated toggler link. When users click the toggler link again, the content is hidden again.

Top Navigation Output

A method of frameless HTML5 output that places menu navigation elements across the page top, similar to modern website designs. This kind of output is possible when you specify the top-navigation skin type, and like the side-navigation website it is much easier for web crawlers to find, and thereby improves search engine results.

Topic

A chunk of information about a specific subject, has an identifiable purpose, and can stand alone. Topics are the most important part of a project.

Topic Identifier

The unique numerical value assigned to each of the context-sensitive-help topics as a topic ID. When building a context-sensitive Help (CSH) system, topic identifiers are assigned in the Flare Alias Editor. See Alias File; Header File.

Topic Popup

A content display feature, whereby online users can use a text hyperlink to access additional inform-ation, including a External File, a File or bookbark in the same project, an External Website, or an HTML Help System (.CHM). The topic popup is opened when users click on the associated topic popup hyperlink.

Topic Popup Link

A text hyperlink that opens a popup window that contains another topic.

Topic Styles

A Flare CSS style category that includes the HTML style and the classes that can be applied to affect the entire topic.

Topic Templates

Pre-defined topic elements from which you can cre-ate new topics. Flare provides several topic tem-plates and you can create your own templates.

Topic Title

In the Topic Properties dialog, the name given to a topic and that is displayed as the title in the TOC. The topic title assumes the first topic heading if the field is left blank.

Tripane Navigation Output

A a type of HTML5 output that produces the tra-ditional format with three distinct frames (a nav-igation pane on the left, a toolbar and search on the top, and the main body in the center). This output is possible with a Tripane skin type.

- U -

Unbind

In Flare, the disconnection of a project from the source control server application to which it was bound — for example, a project can be unbound

from Git. The source control server is thereafter not aware of changes to the project. See bind.

Unlock Element

In Flare, elements that have been locked to prevent editing, can later be unlocked in order to allow edit-ing. See Lock Element.

- V -

Variable

In Flare, a symbolic name associated with one or more small pieces of content referred to as a value, where each value is called a definition. Variables are typically used where a piece of content appears throughout a single document or across several doc-uments, and changes from time to time, like ver-sion numbers and dates. A variable can have a single definition, like today's date, or multiple defin-itions as with an array.

Variable Definition

The one or more text values that are assigned to a variable. A variable can have a single definition or multiple definitions.

Variable File

A Flare file <filename.flvar> that stores the defined variable set of a project, and is stored in the Vari-ables subfolder of the Project Organizer.

Variable Set

Each variable file is considered a variable set, and is typically a grouping of related variables that can include single and multi-definition variables. You may create as many Variable sets as needed.

Variable Set Editor

A Flare editor used in creating variable sets. See Variable Set.

- W -

W3C

World Wide Web Consortium (W3C) is an international community where member organizations, a full-time staff, and the public work together to develop open standards to ensure long term growth of the Web. The W3C was the primary developer of CSS styles and properties are used in Flare.

Web Layout

A Topic Editor layout mode that when selected, renders a topic as it will look online. Web layout mode generally uses the default medium.

Web Layout (Mobile)

A Topic Editor layout mode that when selected, renders a topic as it will look on a mobile device, for example a smartphone. The web layout mobile mode generally uses the default medium.

Web Layout (Tablet)

A Flare topic editor layout mode that when selected, renders the topic as it will look on a tablet device. The web layout tablet mode is generally tied to the default medium.

WebHelp Output

A Web-based Help that is used to create online documentation for the Internet or for desktop applications; and that can run on most browsers and platforms. The output consists of the main file that has an extension of .htm, and a collection of other files that must be distributed to users.

Word Import Wizard

A Flare feature that uses a sequenced series of dialogs, designed to guide users through the process of importing Word files. The wizard allows the user to decide on topic breakpoints, styles mapping, and other options.

Word Target

A Flare target file created for use in building and generating a Word output. Using the target file, you can specify a variety of options, parameters, and variables that will affect the building and final content of the Word output. See Target.

- X -

XML Editor

Flare standard tool for entering content like topics, snippets, and micro-content. The XML Editor presents a WYSIWYG view, and like with other such editors, you can type and format your content using standard paragraph editing tools.

APPENDIX D

INDEX

- V -

- W -

- X -

www.ingramcontent.com/pod-product-compliance
Lightning Source LLC
Chambersburg PA
CBHW080555030426
42336CB00019B/3197

* 9 7 8 1 8 8 9 1 0 1 1 0 1 *